Broadway Musicals

SHOW BY SHOW

FOURTH EDITION

Other Books By Stanley Green

The World of Musical Comedy

The Great Clowns of Broadway

Encyclopaedia of the Musical Theatre

Encyclopaedia of the Musical Film

Broadway Musicals of the 30s (Ring Bells! Sing Songs!)

Starring Fred Astaire

The Rodgers and Hammerstein Story

Rodgers and Hammerstein Fact Book (editor)

Hollywood Musicals Year by Year

Broadway Musicals

SHOW BY SHOW
FOURTH EDITION

by Stanley Green
REVISED AND UPDATED BY KAY GREEN

HAL•LEONARD™ CORPORATION

Published by HAL LEONARD PUBLISHING CORP.
P.O. Box 13819, 7777 W. Bluemound Road
Milwaukee, WI 53213 U.S.A.

First edition, 1985
Second edition, 1987
Third edition, 1990
Fourth edition, 1994

Library of Congress Cataloging-in-Publication Data

Green, Stanley.
    Broadway musicals, show by show / by Stanley Green, Kay Green — 4th ed.
    p.   cm.

Includes index.
ISBN 0-7935-3083-0 : $16.95
1. Musical revue, comedy, etc. — United States. I. Title.
ML1711.G735   1987
782.81'0973—dc19   90-17372

Contents

Show by Show

(For a complete alphabetical listing of the
shows included in this book, see page 297.)

Contents

Contents

Contents

Contents

Indexes

Preface

Broadway Musicals Show by Show is a combination history, guide, fact book, and photograph album of the most memorable productions presented both on and off Broadway from *The Black Crook* in 1866 right up to the present. There are over 300 entries, including 22 adaptations of foreign works and 16 revivals, comprising musical comedies, musical dramas, operettas (or comic operas), revues, two retrospective "catalogue" shows (*Ain't Misbehavin'* and *Sophisticated Ladies*), one all-dancing show (*Dancin'*), one gospel show (*Don't Bother Me, I Can't Cope*), and one celebration of a director's work (*Jerome Robbins' Broadway*). Among criteria for selection were length of run (all book musicals remaining over 500 performances are here), seminal importance, people involved, uniqueness of approach or subject matter, quality of the score, and general acceptance as a significant work in the field. Broadway revivals were included if they ran longer than the original productions, if they were notable in their own right, or if they were part of extended tours.

In the section devoted to a show's credits, I have included names in parentheses of writers, producers, directors, and choreographers who made major contributions to a production, but — for whatever reason — did not receive official credit. Cast listings contain the names of only principal actors (except when a future well-known performer had a bit part or was in the chorus). Song listings are usually only of the best-known musical numbers.

Reference books occasionally differ as to number of performances and, in general, I have followed the listings in *The Best Plays* yearbooks, currently edited by Otis Guernsey, Jr. and Jeffrey Sweet. Continuous runs have been credited to productions that went directly from off to on Broadway and those that may have been temporarily closed for vacations or other reasons. Return visits following a tour, however, have not been included under the original engagements. (The 1954 *Threepenny Opera,* which reopened 15 months after its initial Off-Broadway run, is a special case.)

Since shows today need to play much longer to succeed than in the past, I have cited the five longest running musicals of each decade to give a more accurate indication of their success.

Whenever a theatre is mentioned for the first time, I have noted its location, whether it is still in use, and, if so, whether it has changed its name. (Note that the Majestic Theatre that once stood on Columbus Circle is different from the one still in use, which is on West 44th Street.)

The symbols following most entries indicate if the show has been recorded, published in book form, or licensed for amateur and professional use. An original-cast recording is abbreviated by OC, a studio-cast recording by SC, and a subsequent original-cast recording contains the year that the new production was offered on Broadway. In most cases, the record company listed is the one under whose label the album is currently available. A musical whose text and lyrics (and occasionally songs) have been published as a trade book bears the name of the publisher and the year of publication. An asterisk indicates a softcover acting edition. In some cases, the musical's text is published in an anthology. Performing rights organizations that license musicals are represented by the following abbreviations: TW for Tams-Witmark (757 3rd Avenue, New York 10017); SF for Samuel French (25 West 45th Street, New York 10036); MTI for Music Theatre International (49 East 52nd Street, New York 10022); R&H for Rodgers & Hammerstein (598 Madison Avenue, New York, 10022); DPC for Dramatic Publishing Co. (4150 North Milwaukee Avenue, Chicago 60641); SO for Shubert Organization (234 West 44th Street, New York 10036); and TM for Theatre Maximus (1650 Broadway, New York 10019).

The following books were used to check facts: *Songs of the Theatre* by Richard Lewine and Alfred Simon (H. W. Wilson); *The City and the Theatre* by Mary C. Henderson (Preston); *The Collector's Guide to the American Musical Theatre* by David Hummel (Scarecrow); *At This Theatre* by Louis Botto (Dodd, Mead); *Musicals!* ("Directory of Musical Properties Available for Production") by Richard Chigley Lynch (American Library Assn.); *The American Musical Theatre* by Gerald Bordman (Oxford); *Show Music on Record* by Jack Raymond (Frederick Ungar); *American Song* ("The Complete Musical Theatre Companion") by Ken Bloom (Facts on File).

I am particularly grateful to my Hal Leonard associates — Keith Mardak (who first proposed that I write this book), Glenda Herro, and Mary Bultman — for their interest, cooperation, and support. My wife, Kay, as always, was indispensable in checking the manuscript, selecting photographs, and offering many helpful suggestions, and Susan Green and Rudy Green, as always, were available for welcome comments.

Stanley Green
Brooklyn, New York

November, 1989

When Stanley died in December of 1990, I never considered continuing any of his projects. However, after being prodded by Rick Walters, the editor at Hal Leonard, to come up with the name of a person who could, and after equal pressure from my friends to do it myself, I decided that I would update Stanley's book for this fourth edition. I have used the *Variety* listings for number of performances, and the daily newspapers for my sources of information. I generally conformed to the standards Stanley set for a show's inclusion in the book. For a number of reasons, the task has not been easy. I think I have produced a work he would have approved. I am grateful for the strength Susan Green, Rudy Green and Christie Mastrangeli have given me, and for the encouragement, guidance, and (a great deal of) direction from Rick Walters, all of whom knew all along that I could finish the project.

Kay Green
Brooklyn, New York

September, 1993

Foreword

With its glitter, its imagination, and its rhythmic beat, the Broadway musical has become a distinctive commodity, recognized and admired throughout the world, even though the form itself derived from many sources. The earliest example of musical comedy is generally cited as John Gay's *The Beggar's Opera,* first performed in London in 1728. Labeled a "ballad-opera," it used popular songs of the day as part of a story that satirized both corrupt political leaders and florid Italianate opera, best exemplified by the works of Handel. Later precursors include the English comic operas of Gilbert and Sullivan, the French *opéra bouffe* of Offenbach, and the Viennese operettas of Strauss, Lehar, Straus, and others. In fact, the first use of the term "musical comedy" dates back to the productions of George Edwardes at the Gaiety Theatre, London, at the end of the 19th Century.

America saw the first musical comedy in 1750 when a traveling company offered the premiere North American showing of *The Beggar's Opera* (whose most celebrated spinoff was Kurt Weill's *The Threepenny Opera*). Homegrown examples of the form were also on view during Colonial days, but it was not until 1866 when the first long-run musical smash, *The Black Crook,* was unveiled in New York to dazzle theatregoers with its spectacular scenic effects and its bevy of barelimbed coryphées. From then on, plays embellished with songs became a major attraction for seekers of theatrical entertainment along the Great White Way.

Possibly because their contributions distinguished this particular form of theatre and also because of the high quality of their work, composers were more noted than lyricists during the early years of the 20th Century. Victor Herbert, Rudolf Friml, Sigmund Romberg, Jerome Kern, George Gershwin, and Vincent Youmans were the most prominent figures during the first two decades, as well as George M. Cohan and Irving Berlin, who, because they wrote the words that went with their music, helped prepare the public for a greater awareness of the importance of lyrics. Due recognition was — eventually — given to the contributions of such practitioners as P. G. Wodehouse, Otto Harbach, Oscar Hammerstein II, Ira Gershwin, and B. G. DeSylva, but it was not until the emergence of Lorenz Hart (who shared equal billing with composer Richard Rodgers) and Cole Porter (who wrote his own music) that lyric-writing was elevated to the same level of public appreciation as that given to music-writing.

It took somewhat longer for the book or libretto (Italian for "little book") to be considered in the same league as music and lyrics, since up through the 1920s it was hardly more than a framework designed to provide opportunities to spotlight the singers, dancers, and comedians. That was also a factor in the popularity of the revue which did away with a story line completely in favor of short farcical or satirical sketches. Florenz Ziegfeld was easily the dominant figure of this kind of entertainment with his elaborate annual *Follies* which he guided through 21 editions. Rival showmen George White and Earl Carroll brought out their own annual *Scandals* and *Vanities,* and this form of musical theatre persisted in popularity through the Forties. Revues should not be confused with vaudeville or variety since they are assembled with a unity of style and can even have a unifying theme or concept. Early masters of the form were such directors as Hassard Short, John Murray Anderson, and Vincente Minnelli, and such writers as Howard Dietz and Arthur Schwartz, E. Y. Harburg, Harold Arlen, and Vernon Duke.

Through the influence of Kern and Hammerstein's *Show Boat,* Broadway's first serious attempt at a modern musical play, creators of musicals began showing greater concern for the stories and the way music and lyrics augmented and embellished them. Because of the country's dire economic condition in the Thirties and the increasing threat of war, musicals began to reflect a more adult and cynical attitude toward the world beyond the footlights, particularly to be seen in works involving George S. Kaufman, Moss Hart, Morrie Ryskind, Marc Blitzstein, and Harold Rome. Beginning in the Forties — largely because of the enormous success of Rodgers and Hammerstein's *Oklahoma!* — the emphasis was now on both the integration of songs, dances and story, and also on the adaptation of works of substance as suitable subject matter in the musical theatre. Plays and novels by Ferenc Molnar, Elmer Rice, Shakespeare, James Michener, Alan Paton, Marcel Pagnol, Bernard Shaw, Voltaire, Eugene O'Neill, Edmond Rostand, T. H. White, Thornton Wilder, Sholom Aleichem, Clifford Odets, Cervantes, Christopher Isherwood, and Nikos Kazantzakis — as well as the Bible — provided the bases for some of the most distinguished productions.

Once the library shelves were exhausted, the manner of telling a story through a particular staging device or personal viewpoint became of increasing concern. These so-called concept musicals developed through the emerging influence of such directors as Gower Champion, Harold Prince, Bob Fosse, Joe Layton, Michael Bennett, and Tommy Tune, and since these men — except for Prince — were all choreographers, their shows put a greater accent on dancing in communicating the deeper meanings of these frequently metaphorical musicals. Paradoxically, many have avoided the conventional linear story line — with its beginning, middle, and end — in favor of a freer, more episodic structure consisting of individual scenes interspersed with songs and dances. What they had created, of course, is a modern, stylized variation on the supposed outdated revue form.

It comes as no surprise that the amount of money involved in bringing a musical to Broadway has escalated appreciably in recent years. This is due not only to inflated production costs, but also to the increasing necessity of mounting large-scale advertising and promotion campaigns. Because of the enormous expenditure — and since movie sales are so infrequent — shows are rarely able to turn a profit withouth achieving a run of over 1,000 performances, sending out at least one touring company, and having presentations in foreign countries. That's part of the reason why ticket prices are scaled so high. In 1960, *Camelot* was capitalized at $670,000 and a orchestra seat cost $9.40. In 1971, *Follies* cost $700,000 and had a top weekend ticket price of $15.00. By 1981, *Dreamgirls* had production expenses totalling $3.6 million; two years later *My One and Only* was brought in for over $4 million, and *La Cage aux Folles* $5 million. *The Phantom of the Opera* and *Jerome Robbins' Broadway* both cost over $8.5 million. By 1991, *Miss Saigon* cost $10 million, and now in 1993 the standard top price for a musical on Broadway is $65.00.

The affluent and the expense-account set have always been able to afford not only top prices but scalper prices for tickets. Those of more modest means, however, are finding that the cheapest seats are proportionately more expensive than the high priced. During the 1958-1959 season, for example, it was possible to see such major attractions as *The Music Man* for $2.50 and *My Fair Lady* for $2.30. By 1993, even though some seats in the "rear mezzanine" (a politically correct term for the last row of the second balcony) were advertised for $15.00, prices ranged from $30.00 to $42.50 for seats in the second balcony. Two-fer tickets distributed to neighborhood stores, TKTS booths offering half-price seats, and the even lower priced mail-order tickets available to people in certain professions through TDF (Theatre Development Fund, which also operates the TKTS booths) help somewhat to ease the inflationary burden.

The matter of preserving Broadway musicals — other than on original-cast albums — has been of concern to a number of individuals and organizations. Though schools, community groups, and summer theatres may be relied on to revive the blockbuster hits of the past, other performing centers, such as Michael P. Price's Goodspeed Opera House in East Haddam, Connecticut, are dedicated to pumping new life into the long lost and barely remembered. Concert versions of vintage shows have also been cropping up throughout the country.

Another hopeful sign is the number of opera companies that have added musical-theatre works to their repertoires. Not only does this help break down artificial barriers, it also creates new audiences for such notable examples as the Kern-Hammerstein *Show Boat*, the Gershwin-Heyward *Porgy and Bess*, the Rodgers-Hammerstein *Carousel* and *South Pacific*, the Lerner and Loewe *Brigadoon*, the Weill-Hughes-Rice *Street Scene*, the Weill-Anderson *Lost in the Stars*, the Bernstein-Sondheim-Laurents *West Side Story*, the Bernstein-Wilbur *Candide*, the Sondheim-Wheeler *Sweeney Todd*, and *A Little Night Music*.

Show by Show

The Black Crook. Four alluring coryphées.

THE BLACK CROOK

Music & lyrics: Miscellaneous writers
Book: Charles M. Barras
Producers: William Wheatley & Henry Jarrett
Directors: William Wheatley & Leon Vincent
Choreographer: David Costa
Cast: Annie Kemp Bowler, Charles Morton, Marie Bonfanti, J.W. Blaisdell, E.B. Holmes, George Boniface
Songs: "You Naughty Naughty Men"; "March of the Amazons"; "Dare I Tell?"
New York run: Niblo's Garden, September 12, 1866; 475 p.

American plays embellished with songs were being offered in New York as early as Colonial days, but *The Black Crook* was the first long-running musical hit, with a record run that was not overtaken until *Adonis* established a new mark in the late 1880's. It also toured throughout the United States and was revived in New York at least fifteen times.

Although the musical score was partly made up of popular numbers of the day and the grafting of songs, dances and plot was crude, *The Black Crook* claims an important place in theatrical history by introducing such staples of the musical-comedy form as elaborate scenic effects, colorful costumes, and rows of barelimbed dancing girls. The production, however, was something of an accident. A Parisian ballet troupe was booked to appear at the Academy of Music in the fall of 1866, but the theatre burned down the previous May. William Wheatley, the manager of Niblo's Garden, a huge auditorium then at Broadway and Prince Street, had already scheduled a spectacular production of a new work, *The Black Crook*, as his fall attraction. With the ballet company now without a booking, he was persuaded that the play would benefit immeasurably from the addition of one hundred or so immodestly garbed female dancers, since it was obvious that Charles M. Barras's embarrassing script — a preposterous melodrama based on the *Faust* legend — could use all the help it could get. Thus, Henry Jarrett, the ballet company's sponsor, became the co-producer of *The Black Crook*, and the dancers crossed the Atlantic in August to join the production.

In the story, set in, around and even underneath the Harz Mountains of Germany, the year is 1600 and Hertzog, a crook-backed sorcerer (hence the play's title) makes a pact with the Arch Fiend, or Devil, that would allow him to live one extra year for every soul he delivers. The sorcerer's first intended victim is the virtuous Rudolphe, who has been imprisoned by the evil Count Wolfenstein. Rudolphe escapes, discovers a buried treasure, saves the life of Stalacta, the fairy queen, who then reciprocates by saving him from Hertzog's nefarious scheme. At the end, the Black Crook, having failed to deliver on his part of the arrangement, is himself carted off to Hell. (The theme of pact-making with the Devil has since shown up occasionally in the musical theatre, most notably in the 1955 success, *Damn Yankees*.)

But the main attraction was unquestionably the imported dancing girls — used primarily for sequences requiring demons, spirits and water sprites — who proved so alluring to post-Civil War audiences that at a ticket scale of 5¢ to $1.50 they kept flocking to view the spectacle. And it surely did not hurt the boxoffice — nor would it ever — when clergymen and editorial writers turned up their blue noses to denounce the sinful display of bare flesh.

In 1954, *The Girl in Pink Tights*, a Broadway musical with a score by Sigmund Romberg (his last) and Leo Robin, was loosely based on circumstances surrounding the production of *The Black Crook*. The cast was headed by Jeanmaire, Charles Goldner, Brenda Lewis, and David Atkinson, and the show ran for 115 performances.
Applause (1985).

EVANGELINE

Music: Edward E. Rice
Lyrics & book: J. Cheever Goodwin
Producer-director: Edward E. Rice
Cast: Ione Burke, James Dunn, W. H. Crane, J. W. Thoman, Connie Thompson
Songs: "Evangeline March"; "Spinning-Wheel Song"; "Thinking, Love, of Thee"; "Sweet Evangeline"
New York run: Niblo's Garden, July 27, 1874; 16 p.

Evangeline (or *The Belle of Acadia*) was among the first successful musicals to have a score specifically written by one song-writing team. It first opened in New York as an interim booking, then played Boston and toured extensively before returning to New York in 1877 at the Fifth Avenue Theatre (then at 24th Street) in a more elaborate production. After playing two months, it again went on tour, during which it was billed as *Rice's Beautiful Evangeline*. In all, it was revived periodically in New York for almost 30 years, with its most successful engagement being the 251-performance run in 1885 at the 14th Street Theatre.

The "American Opera-Bouffe Extravaganza" came about after its two authors had seen a performance in Boston of Lydia Thompson and her troupe of high-kicking British Blondes. Vowing that they could surely write a more tasteful entertainment that would also feature bare-legged dancers, they chose Longfellow's poem as general inspiration, and they enabled the female members of the cast to show their legs by putting them in tights and casting most of them in male roles. Two other attractions: a two-man dancing heifer and the character of the Lone Fisherman, who spent the evening sitting silently in a corner. In the story, our heroine has a number of comic adventures as she journeys from Acadia to Africa to Arizona in search of her beloved Gabriel.

THE MULLIGAN GUARD BALL

Music: David Braham
Lyrics & book: Edward Harrigan
Producers: Edward Harrigan & Tony Hart
Director: Edward Harrigan
Cast: Edward Harrigan, Tony Hart, Nellie Jones, Annie Yeamans, Annie Mack
Songs: "The Mulligan Guard"; "The Babies on Our Block"; "Pitcher of Beer"; "Skidmore Fancy Ball"
New York run: Theatre Comique, January 13, 1879; 153 p.

Edward "Ned" Harrigan and Tony Hart were the first team to offer plays with music populated by newly arrived immigrants living in the slums of New York. They began their series of shows about the Irish Mulligan Guard in 1878, and in all did seven productions featuring the drinking, brawling members of the social and military club. In this production, their most popular, they were concerned with the rivalry between the Mulligan Guard and a Negro group, the Skidmore Guard, who, through an error, both engage the Harp and Shamrock Ballroom for a social affair on the same night. A compromise of sorts is reached when the Skidmore group is given a room on the second floor right above the ballroom, but their dancing becomes so animated that they crash through the floor and land on top of the celebrating Mulligans. This was the first production to play the Theatre Comique, then located on lower Broadway, and the top ticket price was 75¢. Harrigan's use of working-class Americans as characters in his stories influenced the work of Charles H. Hoyt and George M. Cohan.

ROBIN HOOD

Music: Reginald DeKoven
Lyrics & book: Harry B. Smith
Producer: The Bostonians
Director: Harry Dixon
Cast: Tom Karl, Eugene Cowles, Caroline Hamilton, Jessie Bartlett Davis, W.H. MacDonald, Henry Clay Barnabee, George Frothingham
Songs: "Song of Brown October Ale"; "Oh, Promise Me!" (lyric: Clement Scott); "Tinkers' Chorus"; "Ah, I Do Love Thee"
New York run: Standard Theatre, September 28, 1891; 40 p.

The most celebrated American operetta of the 19th century, *Robin Hood* was produced by a touring company that first presented it in Chicago in June 1890. Though hastily put together at a total cost of $109.50, the musical caught on and was remounted in a more stylish production. It made an auspicious New York bow at the Standard Theatre (then on Broadway at 32nd Street), but its run was cut short because of a prior booking. Eight revivals were shown in the city, the last in 1944.

The story remains faithful to the familiar legend about Robin and his merry band of altruistic outlaws who dwell in Sherwood Forest and take from the have-lots and give to the have-nots. In addition to Robin's beloved Maid Marian, the well-known characters include Little John, Friar Tuck, Will Scarlet, and Alan-a-Dale (a traditionally female part originated by Jessie Bartlett Davis, who scored a hit singing the interpolated "Oh, Promise Me!"). This was the third musical created by the team of Reginald DeKoven and Harry B. Smith, who collaborated on a total of 17, including the unsuccessful sequel, *Maid Marian*.

A TRIP TO CHINATOWN

Music: Percy Gaunt
Lyrics: Percy Gaunt & Charles H. Hoyt
Book: Charles H. Hoyt
Producer: Charles H. Hoyt
Directors: Charles H. Hoyt & Julian Mitchell
Cast: Anna Boyd, Lloyd Wilson, George Beane Jr., Lillian Barr, Harry Conor
Songs: "Reuben and Cynthia"; "The Bowery"; "Push Dem Clouds Away"; "After the Ball" (Charles K. Harris)
New York run: Madison Square Theatre, November 9, 1891; 657 p.

In a large American city at the turn of the century, two young couples are encouraged by a coquettish widow to defy a rich merchant by having a merry night on the town at a fashionable restaurant. Complications arise when the merchant also shows up at the restaurant and is stuck with their bill — which he cannot pay because he doesn't have his wallet. If this outline reads like the plot of *Hello, Dolly!*, well it is. It is also the plot of *A Trip to Chinatown*, which came along 73 years earlier and which also set a long-running record for continuous performances. In fact, its tenure at the Madison Square Theatre (formerly the Fifth Avenue) was so extraordinary for its time that the show held the durability record for 28 years.

A Trip to Chinatown (though set in San Francisco, no one takes a trip anywhere near Chinatown) was the creation of Charles H. Hoyt, a prolific writer of American farces. It was also the first musical to boast no less than three song hits: "Reuben and Cynthia," "The Bowery," and the interpolated "After the Ball."
Indiana U. Press (1964)

THE FORTUNE TELLER

Music: Victor Herbert
Lyrics & book: Harry B. Smith
Producer: Frank L. Perley
Director: Julian Mitchell
Cast: Alice Nielsen, Eugene Cowles, Frank Rushworth, Marguerite Silva, Joseph Herbert, Joseph Cawthorn, May Boley
Songs: "Always Do as People Say You Should"; "Romany Life"; "Gypsy Love Song"; "Czardas"; "Only in the Play"
New York run: Wallack's Theatre, September 26, 1898; 40 p.

Like *Robin Hood, The Fortune Teller* was created for a touring company — in this case the Alice Nielsen Opera Company — which accounted for its brief stay at Wallack's Theatre (then located at Broadway and 30th Street). It was the third and most celebrated of the 13 shows written together by composer Victor Herbert and lyricist-librettist Harry B. Smith (whose total Broadway output was an incredible 123 productions). The musical, which did much to establish Herbert as America's preeminent composer of operetta, makes use of the popular theme of mistaken identity. Hungarian heiress Irma loves a dashing Hussar, but is promised in marriage to a wealthy count. To avoid this unwanted union, Irma gets gypsy fortune teller Musette (both roles being played by Alice Nielsen) to substitute for her. Eventually — somehow aided by a Hungarian military victory — Irma and Musette end up with their appropriate inamoratos. In 1946, a Broadway musical, *Gypsy Lady,* combined this score with that of another Herbert-Smith work, *The Serenade.* The plot, however, was relatively original.

FLORODORA

Music: Leslie Stuart
Lyrics: Leslie Stuart, Paul Rubens, Frank Clement
Book: Owen Hall
Producer: Tom Ryley & John Fisher
Directors: Lewis Hopper & Willie Edouin
Cast: Edna Wallace Hopper, Fannie Johnston, Willie Edouin, Sydney Deane, R.E. Graham, May Edouin
Songs: "The Shade of the Palm" (Stuart); "Tell Me, Pretty Maiden" (Stuart); "When I Leave Town" (Rubens); "I Want to Be a Military Man" (Clement)
New York run: Casino Theatre, November 12, 1900; 553 p.

Next to the Gilbert and Sullivan comic operas, *Florodora* was the most successful early British import staged in New York, even exceeding the original London run of 455 performances. The highlight of the show was the appearance of the dainty, parasol-twirling *Florodora* Sextette who, with six male partners, introduced the coquettish number, "Tell Me, Pretty Maiden." In the plotty plot, Florodora is both the name of an island in the Philippines and the locally manufactured perfume. The elderly manufacturer Cyrus Gilfain wants to marry Dolores, whose father had been cheated by Gilfain, but Dolores loves Gilfain's manager, whom Gilfain wants for his own daughter, even though she loves someone else. For some reason, everyone ends up in Wales where the complications get unknotted and the knots get properly tied. The Casino Theatre, which was torn down in 1930, stood at Broadway and 39th Street.

The last Broadway revival of *Florodora* occurred in 1920 and ran for 150 performances. Christie MacDonald, Eleanor Painter, Walter Woolf, and George Hassell were in the cast.
TW.

Florodora. Pictured on the sheet music cover are the ladies of the original Sextette: Daisy Greene, Marjorie Relyea, Vaughn Texsmith, Margaret Walker, Agnes Wayburn, and Marie L. Wilson.

THE WIZARD OF OZ

Music: Paul Tietjens, A. Baldwin Sloane
Lyrics & book: L. Frank Baum
Producer: Fred R. Hamlin
Director-choreographer: Julian Mitchell
Cast: David Montgomery, Fred Stone, Anna Laughlin, Arthur Hill, Bessie Wynn, Grace Kimball
Songs: "Alas for a Man Without Brains" (Tietjens); "When You Love Love Love" (Tietjens); "Sammy" (Edward Hutchinson - James O'Dea); "Hurrah for Baffin's Bay" (Theodore Morse - Vincent Bryan)
New York run: Majestic Theatre, January 20, 1903; 293 p.

The Wizard of Oz was the premiere attraction at the Majestic Theatre on the west side of Columbus Circle (demolished in 1954), and it also marked the legitimate theatre debut of two vaudeville clowns, Dave Montgomery and Fred Stone, as the Tin Woodman and the Scarecrow. In the spectacular production, which L. Frank Baum adapted from his own fairytale, The Wonderful Wizard of Oz, a cyclone blows Dorothy and her pet cow all the way from Kansas to the country of the Munchkins. After meeting the Scarecrow, the Tin Woodman, and the Cowardly Lion, Dorothy takes her three new friends on a number of adventures until they finally meet the Wizard in the Emerald City. The Victor Herbert-Glen MacDonough Babes in Toyland, a successor to The Wizard of Oz, followed it into the Majestic. In 1939, the classic screen version featured Judy Garland, Frank Morgan, Ray Bolger, Bert Lahr, and Jack Haley, and a new score by Harold Arlen and E.Y. Harburg. The Wiz, a contemporary black variation, opened on Broadway in 1975. (See page 241.)
TW (film score).

BABES IN TOYLAND

Music: Victor Herbert
Lyrics & book: Glen MacDonough
Producers: Fred R. Hamlin & Julian Mitchell
Director-choreographer: Julian Mitchell
Cast: William Norris, Mabel Barrison, George Denham, Bessie Wynn
Songs: "I Can't Do the Sum"; "Go to Sleep, Slumber Deep"; "Song of the Poet"; "March of the Toys"; "Toyland"; "Never Mind, Bo-Peep"
New York run: Majestic Theatre, October 13, 1903; 192 p.

Because of the popularity of The Wizard of Oz, producers Fred R. Hamlin and Julian Mitchell (who was Broadway's most prolific director of musicals with 78 shows to his credit) commissioned Victor Herbert and Glen MacDonough to come up with a successor, if not exactly a sequel, to follow their previous hit into the Majestic Theatre. Once again audiences were delighted with a fantasy about children that included a devastating storm, a frightening journey through the woods, and the eventual arrival at a mythical magical city, in this case substituting Toyland for the Emerald City. The book may have been no more that a serviceable variation, but the score — the second and most successful of the five collaborations between Herbert and MacDonough — was far superior to its predecessor's. Laurel and Hardy appeared in the 1934 screen version, and Ray Bolger and Ed Wynn were in the 1961 version.
MCA SC./Dramatic Publishing Co. (1978)*/DPC.

Babes in Toyland. William Norris and Mabel Barrison, as the two babes, lead Mother Hubbard's children in singing "I Can't Do the Sum." (Byron)

LITTLE JOHNNY JONES

Music, lyrics & book: George M. Cohan
Producer: Sam H. Harris
Director: George M. Cohan
Cast: George M. Cohan, Jerry Cohan, Helen Cohan, Donald Brian, Ethel Levey, Tom Lewis
Songs: "The Yankee Doodle Boy"; " Give My Regards to Broadway"; "Life's a Funny Proposition After All"
New York run: Liberty Theatre, November 7, 1904; 52 p.

George M. Cohan was cocky, straight-shooting, self-assured, quick-witted, fast-moving, naively patriotic — in short, the personification of the American spirit at the beginning of the 20th Century. He was also just about the most multi-talented man ever to hit Broadway, winning fame as an actor, composer, lyricist, librettist, playwright, director, and producer, with an output comprising 21 musicals and 20 plays.

Little Johnny Jones, Cohan's third musical and his first hit, had an initial run of less than two months at the Liberty Theatre (now a movie house on 42nd Street west of Times Square). After extensive revisions during the road tour, the show returned to New York twice in 1905 for a total run of 20 weeks. The musical was prompted by a newspaper article about Tod Sloan, an American jockey then in England. In Cohan's story, jockey Johnny Jones has gone to Britain to ride his horse Yankee Doodle in the Derby. Accused of throwing the race, Johnny discovers that he has been framed by an American gambler (played by the author's father, Jerry Cohan). With the help of a private detective, he clears his name and celebrates by singing and dancing "Give My Regards to Broadway" on a Southampton pier. In the third act, with the locale abruptly switched to San Francisco's Chinatown, Johnny discovers that his fiancée, Goldie Gates (played by Ethel Levey, Cohan's wife at the time) has been kidnapped. When the jockey and the private detective apprehend the abductor, he turns out to be the same villain who had framed our hero in England. In 1982, a revival of Little Johnny Jones with Donny Osmond tarried but one night on Broadway.

MLLE. MODISTE

Music: Victor Herbert
Lyrics & book: Henry Blossom
Producer: Charles Dillingham
Director: Fred Latham
Cast: Fritzi Scheff, Walter Percival, William Pruette, Claude Gillingwater, Josephine Bartlett
Songs: "Kiss Me Again"; "The Time, the Place and the Girl"; "I Want What I Want When I Want It"; "The Mascot of the Troop"
New York run: Knickerbocker Theatre, December 25, 1905; 202 p.

Mlle. Modiste inaugurated the partnership of composer Victor Herbert and librettist-lyricist Henry Blossom (they wrote eight scores together), and was their second in popularity to The Red Mill. The operetta was closely identified with prima donna Fritzi Scheff, who would be called upon to sing "Kiss Me Again" for the rest of her life (indeed, Miss Scheff returned to New York in Mlle. Modiste on five occasions, the last, when she was 50, in 1929). The musical, which opened at the Knickerbocker (then on Broadway and 38th Street), spins a Cinderella tale of a stagestruck Parisian named Fifi, who works in Mme. Cecile's hat shop on the Rue de la Paix. A wealthy American helps Fifi become a celebrated singer, which also helps smooth the way to her winning the approval of her sweetheart's aristocratic, crotchety uncle.
TW.

Mlle. Modiste. Fritzi Scheff in the final scene at the charity bazaar in the gardens of the Château de St. Mar. From the left are Walter Percival (in uniform), William Pruette, and Claude Gillingwater. (Byron)

Forty-five Minutes from Broadway. The dramatic will-tearing scene with Victor Moore and Fay Templeton. (Hall)

FORTY-FIVE MINUTES FROM BROADWAY
Music, lyrics & book: George M. Cohan
Producers: Marc Klaw & A. L. Erlanger
Director: George M. Cohan
Cast: Fay Templeton, Victor Moore, Donald Brian, Lois Ewell
Songs: "I Want to Be a Popular Millionaire"; "Mary's a Grand Old Name"; "So Long, Mary"; "Forty-five Minutes from Broadway"
New York run: New Amsterdam Theatre, January 1, 1906; 90 p.

More of a play with music than a musical comedy — there were only five songs in the score — *Forty-five Minutes from Broadway* was written as a vehicle for Fay Templeton, but it was Victor Moore, in his first leading role on Broadway, who stole everyone's attention. In the story, set in New Rochelle, New York — which is only 45 minutes from Broadway — a nasty millionaire has died leaving a will that no one can find. His nephew (Donald Brian), who has been assigned as his heir, visits his uncle's home with his secretary, Kid Burns (Mr. Moore), and his fiancée. Burns discovers the will — and the fact that everything has been left to housekeeper Mary Jane Jenkins (Miss Templeton). Since the Kid has fallen in love with Mary, his pride won't let him marry his beloved for her money. The only solution: Mary tears up the will. After only a modest run at the New Amsterdam (now a movie house on 42nd Street west of Times Square), the show became a hit on the road, then was revived in 1912 with Cohan himself taking over the Kid Burns part. Moore, however, again played the same character in Cohan's 1907 musical, *The Talk of New York*.
Dramatic Publishing Co. (1978)*/ DPC.

THE RED MILL
Music: Victor Herbert
Lyrics & book: Henry Blossom
Producer: Charles Dillingham
Director: Fred Latham
Cast: David Montgomery, Fred Stone, Augusta Greenleaf, Joseph Ratliff, Allene Crater, Edward Begley
Songs: "The Isle of Our Dreams"; "When You're Pretty and the World Is Fair"; "Moonbeams"; "Every Day Is Ladies Day With Me"; The Streets of New York"; "Because You're You"
New York run: Knickerbocker Theatre, September 24, 1906; 274 p.

The Red Mill was closer to being a musical farce than the kind of operetta usually associated with Victor Herbert. There was ample compensation, however, in the fact that it achieved the longest run of any of the composer's 41 book musicals produced during his lifetime. The show, which was typical of many of the period in depicting Americans as innocents abroad, is concerned with the adventures of Kid Conner and Con Kidder (Montgomery and Stone), two impoverished tourists stranded in Katwyk-aan-Zee, Holland. Their comic predicaments force them to don a number of disguises (including Sherlock Holmes and Dr. Watson), and they also manage to rescue a girl from a windmill by perching her precariously on one of the sails.
A 1945 production (see page 128) ran almost twice as long as the original, with Eddie Foy scoring a hit in the Dave Montgomery part. Also associated with the show were Stone's two daughters, co-producer Paula and featured actress Dorothy. The favorable reception that greeted this version sparked revivals of two other vintage shows as vehicles for major comedians: *Sweethearts* with Bobby Clark (1947) and *Sally* with Willie Howard (1948).
Capitol SC; Turnabout SC/ TW.

FOLLIES OF 1907

Music & lyrics: Miscellaneous writers
Sketches: Harry B. Smith
Producer: Florenz Ziegfeld
Director: Herbert Gresham
Choreographers: Julian Mitchell, Joe Smith, John O'Neil
Cast: Grace LaRue, Mlle. Dazie, Prince Tokio, Emma Carus, Harry Watson Jr., Marion Sunshine & Florence Tempest, George Bickel, Helen Broderick, Nora Bayes (added)
Songs: "Budweiser's a Friend of Mine" (Seymour Furth-Vincent Bryan); "I Think I Oughtn't Auto any More" (E. Ray Goetz-Bryan); " Handle Me With Care" (Jean Schwartz-William Jerome); "Miss Ginger from Jamaica" (Billy Gaston); "Bye Bye, Dear Old Broadway" (Gus Edwards - Will Cobb)
New York run: Jardin de Paris, July 8, 1907; 70 p.

With the *Follies of 1907*, showman Florenz Ziegfeld inaugurated the most celebrated and durable series of annual revues in the history of the Broadway theatre. From 1907 to 1931, there were 21 such entertainments designated as *Follies* (actually, there should have been 22, but the 1926 edition, due to a legal hassle, was initially called *No Foolin'*, then *Ziegfeld American Revue*). The title of the first edition came about through the suggestions of sketch writer Harry B. Smith, who had written a newspaper column called "Follies of the Day," and also because Ziegfeld, whose lucky number was 13, wanted the name to have 13 letters. It was not until 1911 that the impresario's ego triumphed over his superstition and thenceforth the series was known as the *Ziegfeld Follies*.

The idea for the series is credited to Ziegfeld's wife, Anna Held, who suggested that the producer put together a show based on the French revue style of entertainment that took satirical pot-shots at society, the theatre, and politics. The hallmark of the *Follies* was opulent production numbers, decoratively adorned showgirls, farcical and topical sketches, comic personalities, and a generous amount of songs. The first edition, presented on the roof garden of the New York Theatre (then at 45th Street on the east side of Broadway), used the theme of introducing Pocahontas and Capt. John Smith to modern life. Along the way they were enlightened by scenes involving the likes of John D. Rockefeller, Anthony Comstock, Oscar Hammerstein, Teddy Roosevelt, and Enrico Caruso, plus a "Dance of the Seven Veils" takeoff and 64 "Anna Held Girls" beating snare drums while marching up and down the aisles. The total production cost was $13,000, and the top ticket price was $2.50.

Known as "A National Institution Glorifying the American Girl," the *Ziegfeld Follies* was itself glorified through the years by the presence of such notable performers as Fanny Brice, Bert Williams, Ann Pennington, W.C. Fields, Will Rogers, Ray Dooley, Lillian Lorraine, Leon Errol, Eddie Cantor, Nora Bayes, Van and Schenck, John Steel, Ed Wynn, Ina Claire, Marilyn Miller, Ruth Etting, and Eddie Dowling. The *Follies* may not have been the first Broadway revue — that was *The Passing Show* in 1894 — but it was the one that established the model for this type of entertainment, and which spawned such diversified rivals as *George White's Scandals* (13 editions), the Messrs. Shubert's *Passing Shows* (12 editions), the *Earl Carroll Vanities* (11 editions), the *Greenwich Village Follies* (8 editions), and Irving Berlin's *Music Box Revues* (4 editions). There were also four productions of the *Ziegfeld Follies* — in 1934, 1936, 1943, and 1957 — that were presented on Broadway after Ziegfeld's death. For subsequent editions of the *Follies* see pages 20, 29, 31, 34, 38, 85, and 93.

THE MERRY WIDOW

Music: Franz Lehár
Lyrics: Adrian Ross
Book: (Basil Hood uncredited)
Producer: Henry W. Savage
Director: George Marion
Cast: Ethel Jackson, Donald Brian, Lois Ewell, R.E. Graham, William Weedon, Fred Frear
Songs: "A Dutiful Wife"; "In Marsovia"; "Oh, Come Away, Away!"; "Maxim's"; "Vilia"; "Silly, Silly Cavalier"; "I Love You So" ("The Merry Widow Waltz"); "The Girls at Maxim's"; "Love in My Heart"
New York run: New Amsterdam Theatre, October 21, 1907; 416 p.

The epitome of the lighthearted, melodious, romantic European operetta, Franz Lehár's *The Merry Widow* first swirled onto the stage in Vienna in 1905 under the title *Die Lustige Witwe*. The original text by Viktor Leon and Leo Stein was adapted for the highly successful London production by Basil Hood who refused program credit to spare the feelings of the original librettist whose work had been rejected. This version was also used in New York where the musical won such acclaim that it not only made celebrities of Ethel Jackson and Donald Brian, as the Widow and the Prince, it also prompted the introduction of Merry Widow hats, gowns, corsets, and cigarettes.

The first theatrical offshoot was a parody, *The Merry Widow Burlesque*, which opened less than three months after the operetta's première and continued for 156 performances. Producer Joe Weber (of Weber and Fields) even managed to get permission to use the Lehár music. A more lasting influence, however, was the rash of imported continental operettas that remained a major part of the Broadway scene until the outbreak of World War I. Among the most popular of these were Oscar Straus's *A Waltz Dream*, Leo Fall's *The Dollar Princess*, Straus's *The Chocolate Soldier*, Heinrich Reinhardt's *The Spring Maid*, Johann Strauss's *The Merry Countess (Die Fledermaus)*, Lehár's *The Count of Luxembourg*, Emmerich Kalman's *Sari*, and Edmund Eysler's *The Blue Paradise* (with interpolated songs by Sigmund Romberg).

Based on *L'Attaché d'Ambassade*, a French play by Henri Meilhac, *The Merry Widow* is set in Paris and concerns the efforts of Baron Popoff, the ambassador of the mythical kingdom of Marsovia, to induce his attaché, Prince Danilo, to marry wealthy widow Sonia Sadoya in order to aid the country's dwindling finances. Though the widow is wary of fortune-hunting suitors and the prince is chary of being taken for one, they find themselves falling in love to the seductive strains of "The Merry Widow Waltz." Danilo eventually proposes marriage — but only after Sonia has teasingly confessed that she has no money.

The Merry Widow has had five Broadway revivals, the last in 1943. That production, with a libretto coauthored by novelist Sidney Sheldon, had a successful run of 322 performances, then returned in October 1944 for an additional 32. The cast was headed by the husband-wife team of Jan Kiepura and Marta Eggerth. (See page 120.) In 1964, the operetta was mounted by the Music Theatre of Lincoln Center (with Patrice Munsel and Bob Wright), and in 1978 by the New York City Opera (with Beverly Sills and Alan Titus). There have been three Hollywood screen versions: a silent in 1925 directed by Erich Von Stroheim; the Ernst Lubitsch treatment in 1934 with lyrics by Lorenz Hart and starring Maurice Chevalier and Jeanette MacDonald; and a 1952 remake with Lana Turner and Fernando Lamas.
Columbia SC; RCA OC (1964); Angel OC (1978)/ TW.

THE CHOCOLATE SOLDIER

Music: Oscar Straus
Lyrics & book: Stanislaus Stange
Producer: Fred C. Whitney
Director: Stanislaus Stange
Choreographer: Al Holbrook
Cast: Ida Brooks Hunt, J. E. Gardner, Flavia Arcaro, William Pruette
Songs: "My Hero"; "Sympathy"; "Seek the Spy"; "That Would Be Lovely"; "Falling In Love"; "The Letter Song"; "Thank the Lord the War Is Over"
New York run: Lyric Theatre, September 13, 1909; 296 p.

Of all the European operettas imported by Broadway producers in the wake of the spectacular success of *The Merry Widow,* by far the most popular was *The Chocolate Soldier.* Originally presented in Vienna in 1908 as *Der Tapfere Soldat,* the musical was adapted from George Bernard Shaw's play, *Arms and the Man,* though the author always regretted having given his permission. (The next musical treatment of a Shaw play, *My Fair Lady,* came along 47 years later.)

Producer Fred Whitney secured the rights to the English-language version even before the operetta had had its première at the Theater an der Wien, and he opened it in New York at the Lyric Theatre (now a movie house on 42nd Street west of Times Square). The satire on heroes and heroism is set in 1885 during the Serbian invasion of Bulgaria. Lt. Bumerli, the chocolate-eating Swiss soldier serving in the Serb army, is more concerned about saving his neck than displaying valor on the battlefield. He hides in the home of Col. Popoff, a Bulgarian, and soon meets Popoff's daughter, Nadina. Though Nadina's hero is the swaggering Major Alexius Spiridoff, it is not long before she drops him for the peace-loving Bumerli. Other Broadway productions of *The Chocolate Soldier* were offered in 1921, 1930, 1931, 1934, and 1947 (the last in a revised version by Guy Bolton). The 1941 movie with Risë Stevens and Nelson Eddy used a different story. RCA SC.

MADAME SHERRY

Music: Karl Hoschna
Lyrics & book: Otto Harbach
Producers: A. H. Woods, H. H. Frazee, George Lederer
Director: George Lederer
Cast: Lina Abarbanell, Ralph Herz, Elizabeth Murray, Jack Gardner, Dorothy Jardon, Frances Demarest
Songs: "Every Little Movement"; "The Smile She Meant for Me"; "I Want to Play House With You"; "The Birth of Passion"; "Put Your Arms Around Me Honey" (Albert Von Tilzer - Junie McCree)
New York run: New Amsterdam Theatre, August 30, 1910; 231 p.

Madame Sherry remains the best remembered of the six productions written by Karl Hoschna and Otto Harbach (who spelled his name Hauerbach until World War I). It was adapted from an English musical of 1903, which had a different score, and which, in turn, had been based on a French musical. Among the reasons for its success were the insinuating number, "Every Little Movement" ("...has a meaning all its own") and the interpolated "Put Your Arms Around Me Honey." In this tangled tale of mistaken identity, Ed Sherry deceives his uncle, wealthy archeologist Theophilus Sherry, into accepting his Irish landlady as his wife and a dancing teacher's pupils as their children. At first Ed is smitten with Lulu, the dancing teacher, but then transfers his affections to Yvonne, his cousin (played by Metropolitan opera diva Lina Abarbanell). Audiences could enjoy matinee performances of *Madame Sherry* for a top ticket price of $1.50.

NAUGHTY MARIETTA

Music: Victor Herbert
Lyrics & book: Rida Johnson Young
Producer: Oscar Hammerstein
Director: Jacques Coini
Cast: Emma Trentini, Orville Harrold, Edward Martindel, Marie Duchene, Peggy Wood
Songs: "Tramp! Tramp! Tramp!"; "Naughty Marietta"; "'Neath the Southern Moon"; "Italian Street Song"; "Live for Today"; "I'm Falling in Love With Someone"; "Ah! Sweet Mystery of Life"
New York run: New York Theatre, November 7, 1910; 136 p.

Victor Herbert's crowning achievement came into being because mounting debts had forced opera impresario Oscar Hammerstein (grandfather of Oscar II) into the area of the more commercial musical theatre. Hammerstein had it staged with all the care of one of his Manhattan Opera productions, with two of his stars, Emma Trentini and Orville Harrold, in the leading roles of Marietta d'Altena and Capt. Dick Warrington.

Naughty Marietta takes place in New Orleans in 1780. Marietta is there to escape from an unwanted marriage in France and Capt. Dick is there to lead his Rangers against a pirate gang led by Bras Piqué ("Tattooed Arm"). Though Marietta is first attracted to Etienne Grandet, the son of the lieutenant governor, when he is revealed as the pirate leader she is happy to sing her romantic duets with Capt. Dick. She is, in fact, sure that he is the man for her because he is able to finish the "Dream Melody" ("Ah! Sweet Mystery of Life") that Marietta recalls from childhood. One historical error committed by the authors is that New Orleans is supposed to be a French posession, whereas in the year in which the story takes place the colony belonged to Spain. (This error was also made in *The New Moon* in 1928, which had the same locale and period.) The 1935 movie version co-starred Jeanette MacDonald and Nelson Eddy.
Smithsonian SC/ Weinberger, London (1959)*/ TW.

THE PINK LADY

Music: Ivan Caryll
Lyrics & book: C. M. S. McLellan
Producers: Marc Klaw & A. L. Erlanger
Director: Herbert Gresham
Choreographer: Julian Mitchell
Cast: Hazel Dawn, Alice Dovey, William Elliott, Frank Lalor, Jed Prouty
Songs: "On the Saskatchewan"; "My Beautiful Lady"; "Hide and Seek"; "Donny Did, Donny Didn't"
New York run: New Amsterdam Theatre, March 13, 1911; 312 p.

After winning success in London, composer Ivan Caryll indited the scores for 14 Broadway musicals. His most celebrated production was *The Pink Lady*, which contained the durable song "My Beautiful Lady" and gave Hazel Dawn a memorable role that allowed her to play the violin. The story, adapted from a French play, *Le Satyr*, takes place in one day, during which we visit a restaurant in the woods at Compiègne, a furniture shop on the Rue Honoré, and the Ball of the Nymphs and Satyrs. Before settling down to marriage with Angele, Lucien Garidel hopes to enjoy one last fling with Claudine (Miss Dawn), known as the Pink Lady because of her monochromatic wardrobe. When they accidentally meet Angele, Lucien covers his embarrassment by introducing Claudine as the wife of a friend. Following comic complications, the day ends with the involved couples properly sorted.
AEI SC.

THE FIREFLY

Music: Rudolf Friml
Lyrics & book: Otto Harbach
Producer: Arthur Hammerstein
Director: Fred Latham
Choreographer: Signor Albertieri, Sammy Lee
Cast: Emma Trentini, Craig Campbell, Roy Atwell, Sammy Lee, Audrey Maple, Melville Stewart
Songs: "Giannina Mia"; "When a Maid Comes Knocking at Your Heart"; "Love Is Like a Firefly"; "Sympathy"
New York run: Lyric Theatre, December 2, 1912; 120 p.

During a performance he was conducting of *Naughty Marietta*, Victor Herbert had a disagreement with the star, Emma Trentini, and stormed off the podium. He also refused to have anything to do with her next vehicle, *The Firefly*, for which he had been contracted. The composer's decision opened the way for Rudolf Friml, who had never written a Broadway score before, to become a leading creator of American operettas. It also began his partnership with librettist-lyricist Otto Harbach, with whom he would be associated on ten musicals. In the Cinderella tale, cut from a similar bolt of cloth as the one used for *Mlle. Modiste*, Nina Corelli, an Italian street singer in New York, disguises herself as a cabin boy to be near Jack Travers, a guest on a yacht sailing for Bermuda. After hearing her sing, a music teacher offers to give her lessons, and within three years she becomes both a renowned prima donna and Mrs. Jack Travers.
TW.

SWEETHEARTS

MUSIC: Victor Herbert
Lyrics: Robert B. Smith
Book: Harry B. Smith & Fred De Gresac
Producers: Louis Werba & Mark Luescher
Director: Fred Latham
Choreographer: Charles Morgan Jr.
Cast: Christie MacDonald, Thomas Conkey, Ethel Du Fre Houston, Edwin Wilson, Tom McNaughton
Songs: "Sweethearts"; "Angelus"; "Every Lover Must Meet His Fate"; "Pretty as a Picture"; "Jeannette and Her Little Wooden Shoes"
New York run: New Amsterdam Theatre, September 8, 1913; 136 p.

Though allegedly based on the real-life adventures of a 15th Century Neapolitan princess, *Sweethearts* was easily among Broadway's most farfetched musical romances, complete with a mythological country, an abducted princess, and a prince in disguise. To keep her from harm during a war, the infant Princess Sylvia of Zilania has been taken to Bruges where she is brought up believing she is the daughter of a laundress. While traveling incognito, Prince Franz falls in love with Sylvia even before they meet. After their true identities are revealed, they assume the throne as King and Queen of Zilania.

Prompted by the successful 1945 revival of Herbert's *The Red Mill* starring comic Eddie Foy Jr., Herbert's *Sweethearts* was resuscitated for comic Bobby Clark (see page 134). Here the secondary role of political operator Mikel Mikeloviz was retailored to Clark's specifications, and the resourceful clown turned the evening into a self-kidding, hilarious romp. The run was almost twice as long as the original. The 1938 Jeanette MacDonald-Nelson Eddy movie version had a different story.
MMG SC/ TW.

THE GIRL FROM UTAH

Music: Jerome Kern, etc.
Lyrics: Harry B. Smith, etc.
Book: James T. Tanner, Harry B. Smith
Producer: Charles Frohman
Director: J. A. E. Malone
Cast: Julia Sanderson, Donald Brian, Joseph Cawthorn, Queenie Vassar, Venita Fitzhugh
Songs: "Same Sort of Girl"; "They Didn't Believe Me" (lyric: Herbert Reynolds); "Gilbert the Filbert" (Herman Finck - Arthur Wimperis); "Why Don't They Dance the Polka?"; "The Land of Let's Pretend"
New York run: Knickerbocker Theatre, August 24, 1914; 120 p.

Based on a 1913 London musical with music by Paul Rubens and Sidney Jones and lyrics by Adrian Ross and Percy Greenbank, *The Girl from Utah* underwent a major sea change by the time it opened on Broadway, with no less than seven songs now credited to Jerome Kern (including his first hit, "They Didn't Believe Me"). Despite the somewhat misleading title, the story is set in London where Una Trance (Julia Sanderson) has fled to avoid marrying a bigamist Mormon. Though the Mormon pursues her, Una eventually finds true love in the arms of Sandy Blair (Donald Brian), a London song-and-dance man. The show was the first musical hit on Broadway following the outbreak of World War I. With its appealing Kern additions (it was the composer's sixth of 39 Broadway shows), the production was a transitional work leading to the soon-to-come American domination of the musical-comedy field.

WATCH YOUR STEP
Music & lyrics: Irving Berlin
Book: Harry B. Smith
Producer: Charles Dillingham
Director: R. H. Burnside
Cast: Vernon & Irene Castle, Frank Tinney, Charles King, Elizabeth Brice, Elizabeth Murray, Harry Kelly, Justine Johnstone
Songs: "Play a Simple Melody"; "They Always Follow Me Around"; "When I Discovered You"; "Settle Down in a One-Horse Town"; "The Syncopated Walk"
New York run: New Amsterdam Theatre, December 8, 1914; 175 p.

In 1911, at the age of 23, Irving Berlin had the entire country ragtime crazy with "Alexander's Ragtime Band." Three years later, he wrote his first Broadway score (out of a total of 21) which was the first to feature ragtime. It also introduced audiences to another Berlin skill in the contrapuntal "Play a Simple Melody." The songs accompanied a vehicle for dancers Vernon and Irene Castle (it would be the couple's last professional appearance together) that was so flimsy the program credit line read, "Plot, if any, by Harry B. Smith." That plot had to do with a will leaving $2 million to anyone who had never been in love, but by the second act the story was discarded and the evening was turned into a facsimile of a Fifth Avenue nightclub floor show. Also discarded was W.C. Fields. Then primarily a juggler, Fields had sailed from Australia to join the cast during the Syracuse tryout, only to be fired after one performance. The reason: producer Dillingham was fearful that Fields would be such a hit that audiences wouldn't pay attention to the Castles.

ZIEGFELD FOLLIES
Music: Louis A. Hirsch
Lyrics: Gene Buck
Sketches: Gene Buck, Rennold Wolf, Channing Pollock
Producer: Florenz Ziegfeld
Directors: Julian Mitchell, Leon Errol
Choreographer: Julian Mitchell
Cast: W.C. Fields, Ed Wynn, Ann Pennington, Mae Murray, Bernard Granville, George White, Bert Williams, Ina Claire, Justine Johnstone, Leon Errol, Carl Randall, Will West, Melville Stewart
Songs: "Hello, Frisco!"; "Hold Me in Your Loving Arms"; "I Can't Do Without Girls"; "A Girl For Each Month of the Year" (lyric: Wolf, Pollock)
New York run: New Amsterdam Theatre, June 21, 1915; 104 p.

To take the American public's mind off the grave news about World War I (the *Lusitania* had recently been torpedoed), Ziegfeld's ninth annual edition of his *Follies* was the most extravagant and spectacular to date. With its brilliant cast and the equally brilliant scenic designs created by Joseph Urban (his first of 12 *Follies*), this production ushered in an eight year period that is regarded as the pinnacle of the series. Among the show's pleasures: the opening underwater sequence ("The stage setting is the greatest Mr. Ziegfeld has ever presented," according to the program); the first-act finale called "America," with everyone and everything in red, white and blue and Justine Johnstone as the Spirit of Columbia; "The Silver Forest" scene with the girls parading about as months of the year; Ina Claire singing the hit song, "Hello, Frisco!"; the "Gates of Elysium" sequence with real elephants on the stage; and W.C. Fields's comic poolshooting routine (during the road tour Ed Wynn horned in on the act only to have Fields almost knock him unconscious with a cue).

THE BLUE PARADISE

Music: Sigmund Romberg, Edmund Eysler
Lyrics: Herbert Reynolds
Book: Edgar Smith
Producers: Messrs. Shubert
Director: J.H. Benrimo
Choreographer: Ed Hutchinson
Cast: Vivienne Segal, Cecil Lean, Cleo Mayfield, Ted Lorraine, Robert Pitkin, Frances Demarest, Teddy Webb
Songs: "Auf Wiedersehn" (Romberg); "One Step Into Love" (Romberg); "Vienna, Vienna" (Eysler); "A Toast to Woman's Eyes" (Romberg)
New York run: Casino Theatre, August 5, 1915; 356 p.

The fourth longest running book musical of the 1910's, *The Blue Paradise* gave Sigmund Romberg his first chance to compose the kind of sentimental, romantic songs with which he would become identified. (His total Broadway output — including shows for which he shared the writing assignment — was a record 57 productions.) Adapted from *Ein Tag im Paradies,* a Viennese operetta by Edmund Eysler, the musical also provided Vivienne Segal with her professional debut when she took over the female lead during the Washington tryout. In the story, Mizzi (Miss Segal), the flower seller at the Blue Paradise, a Viennese garden restaurant, must bid a tearful "Auf Wiedersehn" (Romberg's first song hit) to her sweetheart Rudolphe (Cecil Lean) as he leaves to make his fortune in America. With fortune made, Rudolphe returns many years later, only to discover that time had transformed sweet little Mizzi into a virago.

The Blue Paradise. Ted Lorraine and Vivienne Segal come to the aid of Teddy Webb, who has apparently bitten off more than he can swallow. (White)

21

VERY GOOD EDDIE

Music: Jerome Kern
Lyrics: Schuyler Greene
Book: Philip Bartholomae & Guy Bolton
Producers: Elisabeth Marbury & F. Ray Comstock
Director: (uncredited)
Choreographer: David Bennett
Cast: Ernest Truex, Alice Dovey, Oscar Shaw, Helen Raymond, John E. Hazzard, John Willard, Ada Lewis
Songs: "Some Sort of Somebody" (lyric: Elsie Janis); "Isn't It Great to Be Married?"; "On the Shore at Le Lei Wi" (music with Henry Kailimai; lyric: Herbert Reynolds); "Thirteen Collar"; "Babes in the Wood" (lyric with Kern); "Old Boy Neutral"; "Nodding Roses" (lyric with Reynolds)
New York Run: Princess Theatre, December 23, 1915; 341 p.

When, in 1914, producer F. Ray Comstock was having difficulty filling his 299-seat Princess Theatre (then on 39th Street near 6th Avenue), theatrical and literary agent Elisabeth Marbury suggested that they jointly sponsor a series of modern musical comedies, all with music written by Jerome Kern and librettos by Guy Bolton. The aim was to offer scaled-down shows with casts of no more that 30 (including chorus) and with the action taking place in only two different locations, thus allowing for one set in the first act and another in the second. The stories, all occurring in contemporary America, would have believable if bubbleheaded characters caught in comic situations that evolved naturally out of the action, and the songs would have more than a passing relevance to what was going on in the plot.

The first effort, *Nobody Home,* which opened in April 1915, was something of a compromise since it was based on an English musical, *Mr. Popple of Ippleton,* and it had interpolated numbers. The action, however, took place in New York City, and the story was filled with the same kind of romantic complications and misunderstandings that would be the concern of subsequent shows at the theatre. The second offering did, in fact, indicate greater assurance in fulfilling the goals that the Princess management had initially outlined. *Very Good Eddie* not only adhered to the general plan but also set the style and standard for three subsequent Kern musicals written with Bolton and P.G. Wodehouse — *Oh, Boy!, Leave It to Jane,* and *Oh, Lady! Lady!!* — that formed the seminal quartet known as the Princess Theatre Musicals.

Very Good Eddie — no comma in the title since it was an appraisal of character rather than an expression of approval — takes place at first aboard the Hudson River dayliner *Catskill,* which is carrying two honeymooning couples. Eddie Kettle (Ernest Truex) is short and timid and his wife Georgina (Helen Raymond) is tall and domineering, Percy Darling (John Willard) is tall and domineering and *his* wife Elsie (Alice Dovey) is short and timid. Georgina and Percy are accidentally left on shore before the boat sails, thereby resulting in embarrassing predicaments for Eddie and Elsie. Matters get straightened out in the second act at the Rip Van Winkle Inn where Eddie now asserts his authority over his suddenly subservient spouse.

In 1975, the Goodspeed Opera in East Haddam, Connecticut, revived the musical which then had a Broadway run almost as long as the original production. There were some changes in the score, and the final scene — in the renamed Honeymoon Inn — found both couples switching partners according to size and temperament after discovering that the minister who married them had no legal right to perform the ceremony.
DRG OC (1975)/ TW.

OH, BOY!

Music: Jerome Kern
Lyrics: P. G. Wodehouse
Book: Guy Bolton & P. G. Wodehouse
Producers: William Elliott & F. Ray Comstock
Directors: Edward Royce, Robert Milton
Choreographer: Edward Royce
Cast: Marie Carroll, Tom Powers, Anna Wheaton, Hal Forde, Edna May Oliver, Marion Davies, Justine Johnstone, Dorothy Dickson & Carl Hyson
Songs: "You Never Knew About Me"; "The Land Where the Good Songs Go"; "An Old-Fashioned Wife"; "A Pal Like You"; "Till the Clouds Roll By"; "Rolled into One"; "Nesting Time in Flatbush"
New York run: Princess Theatre, February 20, 1917; 463 p.

For *Oh, Boy!*, their third Princess Theatre Musical and the third longest running book musical of the 1910's, Jerome Kern and Guy Bolton were joined by British humorist P. G. Wodehouse, who helped give the characters the flavor of transplanted silly-ass Englishmen. Again the settings were modern and modest, the songs fitted the story, and the comic tale involved romantic and marital mixups. When George Budd (Tom Powers) arrives home to his Long Island apartment after eloping with Lou Ellen Carter (Marie Carroll), he finds his country club friends having a party in his digs. The newlyweds separate while Lou Ellen prepares her parents for the news of her marriage, and George becomes innocently involved with Jackie Sampson (Anna Wheaton), a madcap actress, who has climbed through his bedroom window to avoid the advances of a lecherous judge. After further complications, during which the judge turns out to be Lou Ellen's father and Jackie is alternately passed off as both George's wife and his Quaker aunt, the couple is reunited at the Meadowsides Country Club.

MAYTIME

Music: Sigmund Romberg
Lyrics & book: Rida Johnson Young
Producers: Messrs. Shubert
Director: Edward Temple
Choreographer: Allan K. Foster
Cast: Peggy Wood, Charles Purcell, Ralph Herbert, William Norris, Gertrude Vanderbilt
Songs: "The Road to Paradise"; "Will You Remember?"; "Jump Jim Crow"; "Dancing Will Keep You Young" (lyric: Cyrus Wood)
New York run: Shubert Theatre, August 16, 1917; 492 p.

Maytime established Sigmund Romberg as Victor Herbert's successor as the leading creator of sentimental operettas. The musical, with such pieces as "Will You Remember?" and "The Road to Paradise," became New York's most popular attraction during World War I, even though, ironically, it was based on a German operetta, *Wie Einst im Mai.* In Washington Square, New York, in 1840, wealthy Ottilie Van Zandt (Peggy Wood) and poor Richard Wayne (Charles Purcell) are unable to marry because Ottilie's father has other plans for her. Richard becomes rich and Ottilie, fallen upon hard times, must sell her house which is turned into a dress shop. Their grandchildren (played by the same actors) prove that love will find a way — even if it takes 60 years.

   The second longest running book musical of the decade, *Maytime* was seen in three New York theatres following its engagement at the Shubert (on 44th Street west of Broadway). During the run, Purcell was succeeded by future Metropolitan Opera tenor John Charles Thomas. The 1937 movie version, with Jeanette MacDonald and Nelson Eddy, changed the story and the score.

Maytime. Peggy Wood and Charles Purcell in the romantic climax of Act IV.

LEAVE IT TO JANE
Music: Jerome Kern
Lyrics: P. G. Wodehouse
Book: Guy Bolton & P. G. Wodehouse
Producers: William Elliot, F. Ray Comstock, Morris Gest
Director-Choreographer: Edward Royce
Cast: Edith Hallor, Robert Pitkin, Oscar Shaw, Georgia O'Ramey
Songs: "Wait Till Tomorrow"; "Just You Watch My Step"; "Leave It to Jane"; "The Crickets Are Calling"; "The Siren's Song"; "There It Is Again"; "Cleopatterer"; "The Sun Shines Brighter"; "I'm Going to Find a Girl"
New York run: Longacre Theatre, August 28, 1917; 167 p.

Except for the technicality that *Leave It to Jane* never played the Princess Theatre, in every other respect it qualifies as a Princess Theatre Musical. Its score was by Kern and Wodehouse, its book was by Bolton and Wodehouse, and it was presented by the Princess management. In fact, this version of George Ade's 1904 play, *The College Widow*, had been scheduled to follow *Oh, Boy!* into the Princess but that show was doing so well that *Jane* was shifted to a larger house (the Longacre is on 48th Street east of Broadway), with the top ticket price reduced from $3.50 to $2.50. *Leave It to Jane* takes place at good old Atwater College, where everyone is concerned about the Thanksgiving Day football game with rival Bingham. It is left to flirtatious Jane Witherspoon (Edith Hallor), the president's daughter, to induce All-American halfback Billy Bolton (Robert Pitkin), who is to play for Bingham, to switch colleges and play for Atwater under an assumed name. He does and wins both the game and Jane. Over 40 years later, the musical was successfully revived at a Greenwich Village theatre. DRG OC (1959)/ TW.

OH, LADY! LADY!!
Music: Jerome Kern
Lyrics: P. G. Wodehouse
Book: Guy Bolton & P. G. Wodehouse
Producers: William Elliott & F. Ray Comstock
Directors: Edward Royce, Robert Milton
Choreographer: Edward Royce
Cast: Vivienne Segal, Carl Randall, Harry C. Browne, Carroll McComas, Edward Abeles, Florence Shirley, Margaret Dale, Constance Binney
Songs: "Not Yet"; "Do Look at Him"; "I Found You and You Found Me"; "Moon Song"; "When the Ships Come Home"; "Before I Met You"; "Greenwich Village"
New York run: Princess Theatre, February 1, 1918; 219 p.

Using a minstrel-show catch line for a title, the last Kern-Wodehouse-Bolton Princess Theatre Musical was the exclamatory successor to *Oh, Boy!* In a plot that amounted to virtual self-plagiarism, the characters were again caught up in a series of amatory mixups and misunderstandings. Willoughby "Bill" Finch (Carl Randall) is about to marry Molly Farrington (Vivienne Segal) when May Barber (Carroll McComas), his former fiancee from East Giliad, Ohio, shows up at Molly's Long Island home. Though May is there only to deliver Molly's lingerie, her appearance — and that of a comic jewel thief — cause complications that result in the wedding being called off. In Act II the lovers are reunited at a party in Greenwich Village. Curiously, the best known song written for *Oh, Lady! Lady!!* was never used in the show. The heroine was originally to have sung "Bill," but the lyric did not accurately describe the show's Bill, and "Do Look at Him" was substituted. A slightly altered "Bill," of course, later turned up in *Show Boat.* TW.

26

Oh, Lady! Lady!! Vivienne Segal and Carl Randall. (White)

Sinbad. Showgirl Hazel Cox and Al Jolson. (White)

SINBAD

Music: Sigmund Romberg, etc.
Lyrics: Harold Atteridge, etc.
Book: Harold Atteridge
Producers: Messrs. Shubert
Director: J. C. Huffman
Choreographers: Jack Mason, Alexis Kosloff
Cast: Al Jolson, Kitty Doner, Mabel Withee, Forrest Huff, Grace Washburn, Alexis Kosloff
Songs: "Beauty and the Beast"; "Rock-a-Bye Your Baby With a Dixie Melody" (Jean Schwartz-Sam Lewis, Joe Young); "Why Do They All Take the Night Boat to Albany?" (Schwartz-Lewis, Young); " 'N Everything" (B. G. DeSylva-Gus Kahn)
New York run: Winter Garden, February 14, 1918; 388 p.

At a time when it was not uncommon for musicals to be built around the talents of one individual, no shows were more vehicular than those created to spotlight the exuberant personality of "Mammy" singer Al Jolson. Though they had large casts, such extravaganzas as *Robinson Crusoe, Jr.* (1916), *Sinbad*, *Bombo* (1921), and *Big Boy* (1925) were virtually one-man shows. All the Jolson entertainments were presented by the Messrs. Shubert, directed by J. C. Huffman, had easily ignored books by Harold Atteridge, were full of interpolated songs, and — except for *Bombo* — played the Winter Garden (on Broadway between 50th and 51st Streets).

In *Sinbad*, in which the star wore his customary black-face makeup, Jolson appeared in ancient Bagdad as a comical chap named Inbad who poses as Sinbad the Sailor. Between adventures, he literally stopped the show to introduce his own musical specialties, including "Avalon" (added after the opening) and George Gershwin's first hit, "Swanee" (added during the road tour).

ZIEGFELD FOLLIES

Music & lyrics: Miscellaneous writers
Sketches: Gene Buck, Rennold Wolf
Producer: Florenz Ziegfeld
Director-choreographer: Ned Wayburn
Cast: Marilyn Miller, Eddie Cantor, W. C. Fields, Will Rogers, Harry Kelly, Ann Pennington, Lillian Lorraine, Savoy & Brennan, Fairbanks Twins
Songs: "Syncopated Tune" (Louis A. Hirsch-Gene Buck); "Blue Devils of France" (Irving Berlin); "I'm Gonna Pin a Medal on the Girl I Left Behind" (Berlin); "Any Old Time at All" (Hirsch-Buck)
New York run: New Amsterdam Theatre, June 18, 1918; 151 p.

The star-filled 1918 *Follies* — the 12th annual edition — put the focus on World War I in most of its sketches, production numbers, and songs. These included a "Yankee Doodle" dance by Marilyn Miller (in her *Follies* debut); Will Rogers' topical monologues; a skit with Eddie Cantor playing a would-be aviator in a recruiting office; a stirring parade of showgirls representing the allied nations; a first-act finale of living statues created by Ben Ali Haggin titled "Forward, Allies"; and a sketch showing women on the home front performing jobs usually done by men (a reassuring note in the program contained the information that all members of the male chorus were rejected for military service). Popular pastimes of the day were covered in W. C. Fields' golf routine and a grand finale with everyone indulging in the current passion for jazz dancing. One of six *Follies* staged by the prolific Ned Wayburn, the revue also had the services of a 19-year-old rehearsal pianist named George Gershwin.

Ziegfeld Follies (1918). W.C. Fields, Will Rogers, Eddie Cantor, and Harry Kelly serenade Lillian Lorraine with "Any Old Time at All." (White)

Ziegfeld Follies (1919). Showgirls as ingredients in "The Follies Salad" — Spice, Oil, Paprika, Sugar, Lettuce, and Chicken. (White)

ZIEGFELD FOLLIES

Music & lyrics: Irving Berlin, etc.
Sketches: Gene Buck, Rennold Wolf
Producer: Florenz Ziegfeld
Director-choreographer: Ned Wayburn
Cast: Marilyn Miller, Eddie Cantor, Bert Williams, Eddie Dowling, Ray Dooley, Johnny Dooley, Delyle Alda, John Steel, Van & Schenck, Mary Hay
Songs: "My Baby's Arms" (Harry Tierney-Joseph McCarthy); "Tulip Time" (David Stamper-Gene Buck); "Mandy"; "A Pretty Girl Is Like a Melody"; "You'd Be Surprised"; "You Cannot Make Your Shimmy Shake on Tea" (Berlin-Rennold Wolf)
New York run: New Amsterdam Theatre, June 16, 1919; 171 p.

With more song hits than any previous *Follies*, the 13th edition even gave the entire series a theme song in Irving Berlin's "A Pretty Girl Is Like a Melody." Rivalling the 1918 production as the premier revue in the series, it offered showgirls clad as salad ingredients and classical music; Ben Ali Haggin's tableaux depicting the 13th Folly and a scene showing Lady Godiva astride a white horse; and a first-act finale offering a minstrel show with Eddie Cantor and Bert Williams as "Tambo" and "Bones," Marilyn Miller as George Primrose, and a tambourine-banging, high-strutting line of Mandys. The grand finale was a grand tribute to the Salvation Army's morale-boosting contributions to the war. The chief nonmilitary topic was the imminent arrival of Prohibition whose effects were shown in a nightclub scene with showgirls parading around as Coca-Cola, Sarsaparilla, Grape Juice, Lemonade, and Bevo. The production cost was now over $100,000, and the top ticket price was $3.50 at night, $2.00 for matinees. Smithsonian OC.

GREENWICH VILLAGE FOLLIES

Music & lyrics: Miscellaneous writers
Sketches: John Murray Anderson, Philip Bartholomae
Producer: The Bohemians Inc. (Al Jones & Morris Green)
Director: John Murray Anderson
Cast: Bessie McCoy Davis, Ted Lewis Orchestra, Cecil Cunningham, Harry K. Morton
Songs: "When My Baby Smiles at Me" (Billy Munro-Andrew Sterling); "I Want a Daddy who Will Rock Me to Sleep" (A. Baldwin Sloane-Arthur Swanstrom, John Murray Anderson); "(I'll See You in) C-U-B-A" (Irving Berlin)
New York run: Greenwich Village Theatre, July 15, 1919; 232 p.

A stylishly mounted, somewhat less elaborate variation on the *Ziegfeld Follies* format was the *Greenwich Village Follies* (Ziegfeld even threatened to sue over the use of the *Follies* name), which came along in 1919 and lasted through eight editions up to 1928. The guiding light was director John Murray Anderson, who made his professional debut with the first of the series and staged six in all. (Murray's total Broadway credits were 28 musicals.) Despite the title, all editions of the *Greenwich Village Follies* were moved uptown during their runs, with the 1919 production switched to the Nora Bayes Theatre (then on West 44th Street) soon after its Greenwich Village opening. The show, which called itself "A Revusical Comedy of New York's Latin Quarter," took satirical aim at the ballet, free love, Prohibition, and the arts in general. Among the distinguishing characteristics of the series were female impersonations and arty "ballet ballads" based on literary works. In 1925, Hassard Short took over as director (Anderson had replaced *him* at the *Music Box Revue*) and in 1928 it was J. C. Huffman.

IRENE

Music: Harry Tierney
Lyrics: Joseph McCarthy
Book: James Montgomery
Producers: Carle Carlton & Joseph McCarthy
Director-Choreographer: Edward Royce
Cast: Edith Day, Walter Regan, Bobbie Watson, Dorothy Walters, John Litel, Hobart Cavanaugh, Eva Puck
Songs: "Alice Blue Gown"; "Castle of Dreams"; "Irene"; "Skyrocket"; "The Last Part of Ev'ry Party"
New York run: Vanderbilt Theatre, November 18, 1919; 670 p.

By remaining at the Vanderbilt Theatre (then on 48th Street east of 7th Avenue), for one year eight months — and by running 11 performances longer than *A Trip to Chinatown* — *Irene* set a Broadway endurance record that it held onto for 18 years. What made it such a hit for its day (at one time it claimed 17 road companies) resulted from what critics hailed as its intelligent book, diverting comedy, brisk pacing, melodious songs that fitted logically into the story, and talented performers. The show, in fact, won not only critical applause but also gratitude for relieving what Alexander Woollcott termed "Broadway's desperate plight with only 17 or 18 musical comedies in view." Actually, the plot was little more than another version of the Cinderella tale, which has served as the basis for many other musicals including *Mlle. Modiste, The Firefly, Sally, Sunny, Annie Get Your Gun, My Fair Lady, Annie,* and *42nd Street.*

In this variation, a chatty upholsterer's assistant, Irene O'Dare (Edith Day), is sent to a Long Island mansion to mend some cushions. There she meets the instantly smitten Donald Marshall (Walter Regan), who persuades his friend, a male couturier known as Madame Lucy (Bobbie Watson), to hire Irene to pose as a socialite and show off his latest creations. Even though her humble origin is revealed, Irene makes a hit at an elegant party wearing and singing about her Alice blue gown, and ends in Donald's arms.

The show was designed as a star vehicle for Edith Day (who left the cast after only five months to head the London company) and it was the first — of seven — Broadway musicals with songs by Harry Tierney and Joseph McCarthy. During the New York run, Irene Dunne became the fourth actress to play Irene, and Jeanette MacDonald joined the cast as a Long Island belle. Busby Berkeley played Madame Lucy on the road. As for Miss Day, though she appeared on Broadway in two subsequent musicals, her career flourished mostly in London where she was known as the Queen of Drury Lane.

Prompted by the successful revival of *No, No, Nanette* in 1971, *Irene* was brought back two years later by the same producer, Harry Rigby, who had first thought of bringing back *Nanette.* (See page 238.) The new production was also plagued at the outset by the same kind of problems that had affected the previous show, including the replacement of a major cast member (George S. Irving for Billy DeWolfe as Madame Lucy) and the director (Gower Champion for Sir John Gielgud). Though greeted by mixed reviews in New York, the musical remained a year and a half at the newly built Minskoff Theatre, located on the west side of Broadway between 44th and 45th Streets. Debbie Reynolds, who was succeeded during the run by Jane Powell, made her Broadway debut as Irene. Her occupation, however, was changed to that of a piano tuner so that the title song might be used for a male chorus tapping away on top of four uprights as they sing of the charms of Irene. Only five numbers were retained from the original score, with others either pop tunes of the period (though all had lyrics by Joseph McCarthy) or new songs. A screen version was filmed in 1940 with Anna Neagle and Ray Milland.

M-E London OC (1920); Columbia OC (1973)/ TW.

SALLY

Music: Jerome Kern
Lyrics: Clifford Grey, etc.
Book: Guy Bolton
Producer: Florenz Ziegfeld
Director-choreographer: Edward Royce
Cast: Marilyn Miller, Leon Errol, Walter Catlett, Irving Fisher, Mary Hay, Stanley Ridges, Dolores
Songs: "Look for the Silver Lining" (lyric: B.G. DeSylva); "Sally"; "Wild Rose"; "Whip-Poor-Will"; "The Lorelei" (lyric: Anne Caldwell); "The Church 'Round the Corner" (lyric: P.G. Wodehouse)
New York run: New Amsterdam Theatre, December 21, 1920; 570 p.

Just as *Irene* was a Cinderella tale created to show off the talents of singer Edith Day, so *Sally* was a Cinderella tale created to show off the talents of dancer Marilyn Miller (then spelling her first name "Marilynn") in her first starring role. Producer Florenz Ziegfeld commmissioned the Princess Theatre triad of Kern, Bolton and Wodehouse to come up with a suitable vehicle and the team settled on an unproduced musical they had written called *The Little Thing.* Early in the preparations, Wodehouse withdrew from the project, and in the altered script, initially known as *Sally of the Alley,* Sally Green first appears as a dishwashing drudge at the Alley Inn in Greenwich Village dreaming of fame and singing "Look for the Silver Lining." Invited by one of the waiters, really the exiled Duke of Czechogovinia (Leon Errol), Sally goes to an elegant ball in the guise of Mme. Nookerova, a celebrated ballerina. In *Irene* fashion, her true identity is discovered, but here the heroine not only wins the affluent young tenor she is also signed for the *Ziegfeld Follies* and dances a Butterfly Ballet by Victor Herbert. *Sally* was the third longest running Broadway musical of the Twenties. An unsuccessful revival was presented in 1948 with Bambi Linn as Sally and Willie Howard as the duke. Miss Miller was also in the 1929 movie version.
M-E London OC (1921)/ TW.

Sally. Marilyn Miller as a Russian ballerina. (White)

SHUFFLE ALONG

Music: Eubie Blake
Lyrics: Noble Sissle
Book: Flournoy Miller & Aubrey Lyles
Producer: Nikko Producing Co. (Al Mayer)
Director: Walter Brooks
Choreographer: Lawrence Deas
Cast: Flournoy Miller, Aubrey Lyles, Noble Sissle, Gertrude Saunders, Roger Matthews, Lottie Gee, Lawrence Deas, Eubie Blake
Songs: "I'm Just Wild About Harry"; "Love Will Find a Way"; "Bandana Days"; "If You've Never Been Vamped by a Brownskin"
New York run: 63rd St. Music Hall, May 23, 1921; 504 p.

Developed from a vaudeville sketch, *Shuffle Along* became the first successful musical written, directed, and acted by black people. Little money was spent on costumes or scenery, but white audiences were happy to travel a bit north of the theatre district to enjoy the show's earthy humor, fast pacing, spirited dancing, and infectious rhythms. The plot is concerned with the race for mayor of Jimtown, in Dixieland, between the venal Steve Jenkins (Flournoy Miller) and the virtuous Harry Walton (Roger Matthews), about whom, we are repeatedly advised, everyone is just wild. Though Steve wins, Harry eventually has him and his equally corrupt police chief, Sam Peck (Aubrey Lyles), thrown out of office. During the run, Paul Robeson joined the cast briefly as a member of a vocal quartet, and Josephine Baker was added to the touring company as a chorus girl. There were three titular successors to *Shuffle Along: Keep Shufflin'* (1928), *Shuffle Along of 1933* (1932), and another *Shuffle Along* (1952). All of them availeth not. New World OC.

ZIEGFELD FOLLIES

Music, lyrics & sketches: Miscellaneous writers
Producer: Florenz Ziegfeld
Directors: Edward Royce, George Marion
Choreographer: Edward Royce
Cast: Fanny Brice, W. C. Fields, Raymond Hitchcock, Ray Dooley, Mary Milburn, Van & Schenck, Florence O'Denishawn, Vera Michelena, Mary Eaton, Channing Pollock, Mary Lewis
Songs: "Strut, Miss Lizzie" (Henry Creamer-Turner Layton); "Second Hand Rose" (James Hanley-Grant Clarke); "Sally, Won't You Come Back?" (David Stamper-Gene Buck); "My Man" (Maurice Yvain-Channing Pollock)
New York run: Globe Theatre, June 21, 1921; 119 p.

The 15th annual *Ziegfeld Follies* was among the Great Glorifier's most elaborate revues, with another star-filled cast and a number of memorable scenes and songs. It was also the first of two editions to play the Globe Theatre (now the Lunt-Fontanne on 46th Street just west of Broadway), since *Sally* was still packing them in at the New Amsterdam, the *Follies'* customary home. The show got off to an unexpected display of social consciousness with a scene celebrating the arrival of immigrants from all over the world. More accustomed forms of spectacle and spoofing then took over, with an array of chorus girls depicting various types of roses; a takeoff on both the Barrymore clan and *Camille* with Fanny Brice, W. C. Fields, and Raymond Hitchcock; and a W. C. Fields sketch about the frustrations of subway travel. Two of the show's highlights involved Miss Brice alone, first her comic lament "Second Hand Rose," then her masochistic wail, "My Man," which, though a French song, became a personal expression about the singer's recently convicted gangster husband.

Shuffle Along. Flournoy Miller and Aubrey Lyles. (White)

Music Box Revue (1921). Irving Berlin with "The Eight Little Notes," including Miriam Hopkins at the upper right. (White)

Music Box Revue (1924). Oscar Shaw and Grace Moore singing "All Alone." (White)

Music Box Revue (1924). Bobby Clark and Fanny Brice as Adam and Eve. (White)

MUSIC BOX REVUE

Music & lyrics: Irving Berlin
Sketches: Miscellaneous writers
Producer: Sam H. Harris
Directors: Hassard Short, William Collier
Choreographers: Bert French, I. Tarasoff
Cast: William Collier, Wilda Bennett, Paul Frawley, Sam Bernard, Ivy Sawyer, Joseph Santley, Florence Moore, Brox Sisters, Chester Hale, Irving Berlin, Miriam Hopkins
Songs: "In a Cozy Kitchenette Apartment"; "My Little Book of Poetry"; "Say It With Music"; "Everybody Step"; "The Schoolhouse Blues"; "They Call It Dancing"; "The Legend of the Pearls"
New York run: Music Box, September 22, 1921; 440 p.

The *Music Box Revues* were the only annual revue series to be created with the express purpose of providing a showcase for the songs of just one composer. The project stemmed from Irving Berlin's suggestion to producer Sam H. Harris that the Music Box would be an ideal name for a theatre designed specifically for musicals. Harris and Berlin built the theatre (located on 45th Street west of Broadway) and opened it with the appropriately titled *Music Box Revue.* The initial edition — there would be three more — was an elaborate and colorful show that greatly benefited from the ingenious staging of Hassard Short (whose credits would total 40 Broadway musicals) and a collection of appealing Berlin ballads (including "Say It With Music," sung by Wilda Bennett and Paul Frawley, which was used as a theme for the entire series). Among the visual pleasures were scenes showing chorus girls parading as a pageant of fans, displaying themselves as courses in a restaurant meal, and succumbing to the craze for syncopation in "Everybody Step." Berlin himself appeared in a scene with an octet dubbed "The Eight Little Notes" (the eighth was future film star Miriam Hopkins). As Alexander Woollcott wrote in *The Times*, the show's creators "crowded the stage with such a sumptuous and bespangled revue as cannot possibly earn them anything more substantial than the heart-warming satisfaction of having produced it at all."

None of the subsequent *Music Box Revues* ran as long as the first, yet all were well received. The 1922 edition featured the buffoonery of Bobby Clark and Paul McCullough and the antics of long-legged Charlotte Greenwood, as well as the singing of John Steel ("Lady of the Evening" was his most popular number) and Grace LaRue (who recalled the charms of "Crinoline Days"). The McCarthy Sisters were also on hand to stir things up with "Pack Up Your Sins and Go to the Devil" and "Bring on the Pepper." In 1923, Grace Moore sang "Tell Me a Bedtime Story," "The Waltz of Long Ago," "An Orange Grove in California," and — added during the run — "What'll I Do?" (the last two as duets with John Steel). It was also in this revue that Robert Benchley delivered his classic "Treasurer's Report." For the final edition, in 1924, John Murray Anderson took over as director, with Hassard Short replacing him at the *Greenwich Village Follies.* Clark and McCullough were back, with Clark doing an Adam and Eve sketch with Fanny Brice. On her own Miss Brice was an immigrant pleading "Don't Send Me Back to Petrograd" and a flat-footed gazelle proclaiming "I Want to Be a Ballet Dancer." Grace Moore returned to sing "Tell Her in the Springtime," "Rockabye Baby," and, in a duet with Oscar Shaw, the interpolated "All Alone."

Sam Harris, who produced 32 musicals on Broadway, was also associated with Irving Berlin on *The Cocoanuts, Face the Music,* and *As Thousands Cheer.* Ironically, because of its relatively small size, (1,010 seats), the Music Box is no longer considered economically feasible as a showplace for large-scale musical productions.

BLOSSOM TIME
Music: Sigmund Romberg, based on Franz Schubert
Lyrics & book: Dorothy Donnelly
Producers: Messrs. Shubert
Director: J. C. Huffman
Choreographer: F. M. Gillespie
Cast: Bertram Peacock, Olga Cook, Howard Marsh, Roy Cropper
Songs: "Serenade"; "Three Little Maids"; " Song of Love"; "Tell Me Daisy"
New York run: Ambassador Theatre, September 29, 1921; 516 p.

For the first Broadway musical with songs based on themes from classical compositions, Sigmund Romberg was assigned by the producing Shuberts to adapt melodies by the composing Schubert. The fanciful biographical libretto — a variation on a Viennese operetta, *Das Dreimaederlhaus* — deals with the composer's supposed unrequited love for one Mitzi Kranz. When, at Schubert's request, his friend Baron Schober sings the composer's "Song of Love" to Mitzi, she becomes enamored of the baron, and poor Schubert, no longer inspired, is unable to complete his "Unfinished Symphony." Four road companies of *Blossom Time* were sent out soon after the opening at the Ambassador Theatre (on 49th Street west of Broadway), and the operetta had five revivals in New York, the most recent in 1943.

Broadway has also offered musicals with scores derived from works by such composers as Offenbach in *The Love Song* (1925) and *The Happiest Girl in the World* (1961); Tschaikowsky in *Nadja* (1925) and *Music in My Heart* (1947); Chopin in *White Lilacs* (1928) and *Polonaise* (1945); Grieg in *Song of Norway* (1944); Fritz Kreisler in *Rhapsody* (1944); Villa Lobos in *Magdalena* (1948); Borodin in *Kismet* (1953); and Rachmaninoff in *Anya* (1965).
SO.

ZIEGFELD FOLLIES
Music: Louis A. Hirsch, David Stamper
Lyrics: Gene Buck
Sketches: Miscellaneous writers
Producer: Florenz Ziegfeld
Director: Ned Wayburn
Choreographers: Ned Wayburn, Michel Fokine
Cast: Will Rogers, Gilda Gray, Gallagher & Shean, Evelyn Law, Andrew Tombes, Florence O'Denishawn, Lulu McConnell, Mary Eaton, Nervo & Knox, Mary Lewis, Alexander Gray, Jack Whiting
Songs: "My Rambler Rose"; "Mr. Gallagher and Mr. Shean" (Ed Gallagher-Al Shean, Ernest Ball); " 'Neath the South Sea Moon"; "Oh! Gee, Oh! Gosh, Oh! Golly, I'm in Love" (Ole Olsen-Chic Johnson, Ernest Brewer)
New York run: New Amsterdam Theatre, June 5, 1922; 541 p.

Because of a Summer Edition that began June 25, 1923, and followed without a break, the 1922 *Follies* had the longest run of any revue in the series produced during Ziegfeld's lifetime. Now proclaiming itself "A National Institution Glorifying the American Girl," the 16th annual edition ended the eight-year period generally annointed The Great *Follies*. Humorist Will Rogers made his fourth *Follies* appearance in the show, and hits were also scored by shimmy dancer Gilda Gray and the team of Gallagher and Shean. Among the lavish scenes were "Lace Land," with girls parading in lace before lace costumes in front of lace draperies, and a dance featuring Greek statues coming to life in an art museum. Eddie Cantor, Ann Pennington, and Ilse Marvenga joined the Summer Edition cast.

GEORGE WHITE'S SCANDALS

Music: George Gershwin
Lyrics: B. G. DeSylva
Sketches: George White, Andy Rice
Producer-director-choreographer: George White
Cast: W. C. Fields, Winnie Lightner, Paul Whiteman Orchestra, Lester Allen, George White, Jack McGowan, Pearl Regay, Dolores Costello
Songs: "Cinderelatives"; "I Found a Four-Leaf Clover"; "I'll Build a Stairway to Paradise" (lyric: DeSylva, Ira Gershwin); "Argentina"; "Blue Monday Blues"
New York run: Globe Theatre, August 28, 1922; 88 p.

Of all the revues that enjoyed more than one annual edition, the *George White's Scandals* series was the nearest to the *Ziegfeld Follies* in fame and longevity. Beginning in 1919, George White, who had danced in two *Follies*, turned out 13 editions in 21 years. His series was faster paced, more youthful, less ornately mounted than their model, with a greater emphasis on dancing and new dance steps. They also differed from the *Follies* in having one songwriter or team of songwriters responsible for an entire score, e.g. George Gershwin who, with various lyricists, composed the music for five editions between 1920 and 1924. The 1922 *Scandals* introduced Gershwin's first Broadway hit, "I'll Build a Stairway to Paradise," performed as the first-act finale, and "Blue Monday," an "Opera ala Afro-American." Though it was not well received and was removed after opening night, the work was a forerunner of the composer's later full-length opera, *Porgy and Bess*. For subsequent editions of the *George White's Scandals* see pages 52 and 76.

POPPY

Music: Stephen Jones, Arthur Samuels
Lyrics: Dorothy Donnelly, etc.
Book: Dorothy Donnelly (Howard Dietz, W. C. Fields uncredited)
Producer: Philip Goodman
Director: Dorothy Donnelly
Choreographer: Julian Alfred
Cast: Madge Kennedy, W. C. Fields, Robert Woolsey, Alan Edwards, Luella Gear
Songs: "Two Make a Home"; "Alibi Baby" (music: Samuels; lyric: Howard Dietz); "On Our Honeymoon"; "What Do You Do Sunday, Mary?" (music: Jones; lyric: Irving Caesar)
New York run: Apollo Theatre, September 3, 1923; 346 p.

Poppy was a tour-de-force for W. C. Fields, though initially he received featured billing while Madge Kennedy, who played the eponymous heroine, was solo starred. Fields, however, won stardom when Miss Kennedy's understudy took over her role, and he was co-starred with Miss Kennedy for the tour. In the part of Professor Eustace McGargle, the bulbous-nosed comedian established the character of the bogusly elegant, ornately speaking conman by which he was identified in his later career. Set in 1874 in a Connecticut town, *Poppy* presented Fields as a carnival grifter, juggler, card shark, and shell-game artist who attempts to pass off his foster daughter, Poppy, as a long-lost heiress — only to discover that she really is an heiress. The Apollo Theatre, where *Poppy* was shown, still stands on 42nd Street west of Broadway. Fields appeared in two film versions of the musical: in 1925 (renamed *Sally of the Sawdust*), a silent directed by D. W. Griffith, and in 1936.

Poppy. W. C. Fields demonstrates his latest musical creation, the kadoola-kadoola. (White)

ANDRE CHARLOT'S REVUE OF 1924

Music, lyrics & sketches: Miscellaneous writers
Producer: Arch Selwyn
Director: Andre Charlot
Choreographer: David Bennett
Cast: Beatrice Lillie, Gertrude Lawrence, Jack Buchanan, Douglas Furber, Herbert Mundin, Jessie Matthews, Constance Carpenter
Songs: "Parisian Pierrot" (Noël Coward); "You Were Meant for Me" (Eubie Blake-Noble Sissle); "Limehouse Blues" (Philip Braham-Douglas Furber); "March With Me!" (Ivor Novello-Furber); "There's Life in the Old Girl Yet" (Coward)
New York run: Times Square Theatre, January 9, 1924; 298 p.

London impresario Andre Charlot entered New York's crowded revue field with a sly, sophisticated, witty, intimate show made up of songs, dances, and sketches from his West End revues. He also introduced New York audiences to three performers — Beatrice Lillie, Gertrude Lawrence, and Jack Buchanan — whose careers would flourish on both sides of the Atlantic. The show, which played the Times Square Theatre (now a movie house on 42nd Street west of Times Square), offered such highlights as Miss Lillie as a dignified but disoriented Britannia in "March With Me!," Miss Lawrence crooning "Parisian Pierrot" and "Limehouse Blues," and Jack Buchanan's version of the tired businessman trying to get some peace and quiet at home.

The success of his first endeavor on Broadway prompted Charlot to follow it up with *The Charlot Revue of 1926*, which opened November 10, 1925, at the Selwyn Theatre (right next to the Times Square). The triad of Lillie, Lawrence and Buchanan was again on hand, with Miss Lillie as Wanda Allova in a ballet takeoff, Lillie and Lawrence in a sketch as two precocious babies in their prams, Miss Lawrence singing Noël Coward's moralistic "Poor Little Rich Girl," and Lawrence and Buchanan in a duet of "A Cup of Coffee, a Sandwich and You." A third *Andre Charlot Revue* opened in January 1927 as featured attraction of the "International Edition" of the *Earl Carroll Vanities*. Jessie Matthews and Herbert Mundin headed the cast.

ROSE-MARIE

Music: Rudolf Friml*, Herbert Stothart#
Lyrics & book: Otto Harbach & Oscar Hammerstein II
Producer: Arthur Hammerstein
Director: Paul Dickey
Choreographer: David Bennett
Cast: Mary Ellis, Dennis King, William Kent, Dorothy Mackaye, Eduardo Ciannelli, Pearl Regay, Arthur Deagon
Songs: "Rose-Marie"*; "The Mounties"*#; "Indian Love Call"*; "Why Shouldn't We?"#; "Totem Tom-Tom"*#; "The Door of Her Dreams"*
New York run: Imperial Theatre, September 2, 1924; 557 p.

With such settings as Saskatchewan, the Kootenay Pass in the Canadian Rockies, and the Chateau Frontenac in Quebec, *Rose-Marie* offered audiences at the Imperial Theatre (on 44th Street west of Broadway) an entirely new locale for an opulent, romantic musical. It was, in fact, the idea of doing the first musical with a Canadian setting that prompted producer Arthur Hammerstein to send nephew Oscar Hammerstein II and his lyricist-librettist partner, Otto Harbach, to research a rumored annual ice carnival in Quebec that he felt would make a spectacular stage background. Though the writers were unable to locate the carnival, they did devise an original tale that would take advantage of Canadian locales: singer Rose-Marie La Flamme (Mary Ellis) and fur trapper Jim Kenyon (Dennis King) are in love, but a jealous suitor tries to pin a false murder rap on Jim. True to tradition, the Mounties get their man — who turns out to be a woman — and Rose-Marie and Jim go off into the sunset. The fact that the story deals with a murder was considered something of a novelty for a musical as was the conscientious effort, though it was not entirely successful, to integrate the musical pieces into the story (the program listed only the above five songs that "stand out independent of their dramatic association").

Rose-Marie was composer Rudolf Friml's biggest hit and the fourth longest running musical of the Twenties. In 1936, Jeanette MacDonald and Nelson Eddy were seen in a popular — though completely altered — screen version. The second one, with Howard Keel and Ann Blyth, came out in 1954. RCA SC/ TW.

LADY, BE GOOD!

Music: George Gershwin
Lyrics: Ira Gershwin
Book: Guy Bolton & Fred Thompson
Producers: Alex A. Aarons & Vinton Freedley
Director: Felix Edwardes
Choreographer: Sammy Lee
Cast: Fred & Adele Astaire, Walter Catlett, Cliff Edwards, Alan Edwards, Kathlene Martyn
Songs: "Hang on to Me"; "Fascinating Rhythm"; "So Am I"; "Oh, Lady Be Good!"; "The Half of It Dearie Blues"; "Little Jazz Bird"; "Swiss Miss" (lyric with Arthur Jackson)
New York run: Liberty Theatre, December 1, 1924; 330 p.

With their first of 14 Broadway musicals written as a team, George and Ira Gershwin established the jazzy, pulsating sound of the Broadway musicals of the Twenties. The show also made Fred and Adele Astaire Broadway's leading song-and-dance team. Originally titled *Black Eyed Susan*, *Lady, Be Good!* had a simple-minded story about Dick and Suzie Trevor, a carefree vaudeville team who are dispossessed but continue their dancing and singing at the homes of wealthy friends. Along the way Suzie poses as a Spanish heiress to collect a large inheritance but the ruse is found out. Somehow, she and Dick come into money anyway and somehow she saves Dick from a disastrous marriage. As Stark Young wrote in the *Times,* it is "a drama of outcasts, rents, social shining, loving resolutions, and well-ending marital fortunes." Though the score had enough hits — especially "Fascinating Rhythm" and "Oh, Lady Be Good!" — one eventual hit, "The Man I Love," was dropped from the show during the pre-Broadway tryout.
M-E OC; Smithsonian OC/ TW.

Lady, Be Good! Fred Astaire surrounded by a dozen ostrich-plumed lovelies. (White)

THE STUDENT PRINCE IN HEIDELBERG

Music: Sigmund Romberg
Lyrics & book: Dorothy Donnelly
Producers: Messrs. Shubert
Director: J. C. Huffman
Choreographer: Max Scheck
Cast: Howard Marsh, Ilse Marvenga, Greek Evans, George Hassell, Roberta Beatty
Songs: "Golden Days"; "To the Inn We're Marching"; "Come Boys, Let's All Be Gay, Boys" ("Students March Song"); "Drinking Song"; "Deep in My Heart, Dear"; "Serenade"; "Just We Two"
New York run: Jolson's 59th Street Theatre, December 2, 1924; 608 p.

Bucking the popularity of fast-moving, up-to-date musical comedy and the plotless revue, *The Student Prince in Heidelberg* (the complete title was used throughout the New York run) set the record as the longest running musical of the decade. That fact is all the more impressive since the theatre in which it played, on 59th Street and 7th Avenue, was some distance from the theatre district (the playhouse, later renamed the New Century, was demolished in 1962).

Based on *Old Heidelberg*, a popular turn-of-the-century play which had been adapted from the German *Alt Heidelberg*, the sentimental operetta is set in 1860 in the German university town where Prince Karl Franz (Howard Marsh) has gone with his tutor, Dr. Engel (Greek Evans), to complete his education. There he meets Kathie (Ilse Marvenga), a waitress at the Inn of the Three Golden Apples, and it isn't long before they are professing their love through the melting strains of, "Deep in my heart, dear, I have a dream of you. . ." The prince, however, is soon called away to assume the throne. Two years later, King Karl Franz returns to Heidelberg in a vain effort to recapture the golden days of his youth. *The Student Prince* toured the United States between 1925 and 1933, was revived on Broadway in 1931 and 1943, and joined the repertory of the New York City Opera in 1980. A silent film verson, with Ramon Novarro and Norma Shearer, was made in 1927; a Technicolor version, with Edmund Purdom (using Mario Lanza's singing voice) and Ann Blyth, was made in 1954. A previous Broadway musical, *The Prince of Pilsen* of 1903, also had a Heidelberg student prince as a leading romantic character.
M-E London OC (1926); Odyssey SC/ TW.

The Student Prince in Heidelberg. Howard Marsh and Ilse Marvenga. (White)

THE GARRICK GAIETIES

Music: Richard Rodgers
Lyrics: Lorenz Hart
Sketches: Miscellaneous writers
Producer: Theatre Guild
Director: Philip Loeb
Choreographer: Herbert Fields
Cast: Sterling Holloway, Romney Brent, Betty Starbuck, Libby Holman, June Cochrane, Edith Meiser, Philip Loeb, Sanford Meisner, Lee Strasberg
Songs: "April Fool"; "Manhattan"; "Do You Love Me?"; "Sentimental Me"; "On with the Dance", "Old Fashioned Girl" (lyric: Edith Meiser)
New York run: Garrick Theatre, June 8, 1925; 211 p.

The Garrick Gaieties was an impudent, high-spirited modestly mounted revue created by and featuring young members of the Theatre Guild company to help raise money for tapestries at the Guild's new Guild Theatre on West 52nd Street. The entertainment, however, served equally as a showcase for the talents of the songwriting team of Richard Rodgers and Lorenz Hart, whose score included their first hit, "Manhattan." This was not their first professional show — that was *Poor Little Ritz Girl* in 1919 — but it did provide the stimulus for a partnership that lasted through 26 Broadway musicals until 1943.

Though originally scheduled for only two performances at the Garrick Theatre (then on 35th Street east of Broadway), the revue caught on and had a successful commercial run. Besides the songs, highlights were satirical jibes at the theatre in general and the Theatre Guild in particular whose usually pretentious offerings provided ready targets. A second edition of the *Gaieties* opened the following year with almost the same cast, and a Rodgers and Hart score that included "Mountain Greenery" and an operetta burlesque called "The Rose of Arizona." A third edition, in 1930, was shown at the Guild Theatre (currently named the Virginia). The cast included Sterling Holloway, Edith Meiser, and Philip Loeb, plus newcomers Imogene Coca and Ray Heatherton. A brief return engagement the same year gave Rosalind Russell her first Broadway assignment.

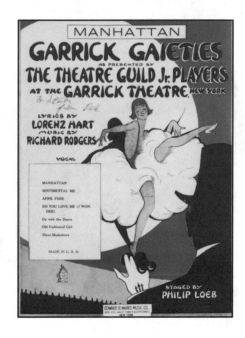

NO, NO, NANETTE

Music: Vincent Youmans
Lyrics: Irving Caesar
Book: Otto Harbach & Frank Mandel
Producer-director: H. H. Frazee
Choreographer: Sammy Lee
Cast: Louise Groody, Charles Winninger, Josephine Whittell, Wellington Cross, Eleanor Dawn, Georgia O'Ramey, Mary Lawlor, John Barker
Songs: "Call of the Sea"; "Too Many Rings Around Rosie"; "I Want to Be Happy"; "No, No, Nanette" (lyric: Otto Harbach); "Tea for Two"; " 'Where Has My Hubby Gone?' Blues"; "You Can Dance With Any Girl at All"
New York run: Globe Theatre, September 16, 1925; 321 p.

Thanks to its worldwide reception, *No, No, Nanette* was probably the most popular musical of the Twenties. It was also the quintessential example of the kind of song-and-dance show of that period that was affectionately satirized in Sandy Wilson's spoof, *The Boy Friend*. In the story, based on a 1919 play, *My Lady Friends*, Jimmy Smith (Charles Winninger), a married bible publisher and guardian of the play's doubly admonished heroine (Louise Groody), has been giving financial support to three comely young ladies living in three different cities. When the Smiths and their friends, including Lucille and Billy Early (Josephine Whittell and Wellington Cross) — plus the three recipients of Jimmy's largesse and a sassy housemaid named Pauline (Georgia O'Ramey) — all turn up at the Smiths' Chickadee Cottage in Atlantic City, no end of comical embarrassments ensue.

The musical's initial production underwent a difficult break-in period on the road. When it first opened in Detroit in April 1924, the reviews were encouraging but the attendance wasn't. Producer H.H. Frazee then took drastic steps. He ordered composer Vincent Youmans and lyricist Irving Caesar (who had replaced Otto Harbach for most of the songs) to come up with two hits — and they obliged with "Tea for Two" and "I Want to Be Happy." He also took over the direction himself and replaced most of the principals in the cast. The result was that the show clicked so well in Chicago that it remained for a year. By the time *No, No, Nanette* arrived in New York a second road company had been touring since January 1925 (with Cleo Mayfield, Cecil Lean, Donald Brian, and Ona Munson), and a London facsimile had been running for six months. Three years later, an affirmative successor yclept *Yes, Yes, Yvette*, did not fare so well, despite the contributions by *Nanette* veterans H.H. Frazee, Irving Caesar, Charles Winninger, and choreographer Sammy Lee.

In 1971, a new production of *No, No, Nanette* opened in New York after experiencing an equally difficult tryout tour (see page 231). Harry Rigby, who conceived the idea of the revival, was bought out by his co-producer Cyma Rubin, Burt Shevelove replaced Busby Berkeley as director, and Jack Gilford and Susan Watson took over the roles of Jimmy and Nanette. Once more, however, the production was whipped into proper shape, and — helped by a sudden nostalgia craze — it went on to a lengthy and profitable run. One of the major attractions of this version was the appearance of Ruby Keeler, who returned to Broadway after an absence of over 41 years to play the part of Sue Smith, Jimmy's wife. During the New York engagement, leading roles were assumed by Penny Singleton (Sue), Benny Baker (Jimmy), and Martha Raye (Pauline). The first road company was headed by June Allyson, Dennis Day, and Judy Canova; the second by Evelyn Keyes, Don Ameche, and Ruth Donnelly.

Movie versions of *No, No, Nanette* were made in 1930 and 1940. Bernice Claire and Alexander Grey were in the first, Anna Neagle and Victor Mature were in the second.

Stanyan London OC (1925); Columbia OC (1971)/ TW.

DEAREST ENEMY

Music: Richard Rodgers
Lyrics: Lorenz Hart
Book: Herbert Fields
Producer: George Ford
Directors: John Murray Anderson, Charles Sinclair, Harry Ford
Choreographer: Carl Hemmer
Cast: Helen Ford, Charles Purcell, Flavia Arcaro, Detmar Poppen
Songs: "Here in My Arms"; "I Beg Your Pardon"; "Cheerio"; "I'd Like To Hide It";
"Bye and Bye"; "Sweet Peter"; "Old Enough to Love"; "Here's a Kiss"
New York run: Knickerbocker Theatre, September 18, 1925; 286 p.

Dearest Enemy, the first of eight book musicals written together by songwriters Rodgers and Hart and librettist Herbert Fields, found the trio going back to the unlikely subject of the American Revolution for inspiration. Set in 1776 in the mansion of Mrs. Robert Murray — of the Murray Hill Murrays — the saga tells how the wily patriot and her lady friends manage to divert Gen. Howe's British troops long enough for Gen. Putnam's men to link up with the forces under the command of Gen. Washington. The attraction between Irish-American lass Betsy Burke (Helen Ford) and British Captain Sir John Copeland (Charles Purcell) provides a romantic alliance — cemented by their duet, "Here in My Arms" — that is resumed after the war.

The only previous Broadway musical dealing with the American Revolution was *A Daughter of the Revolution* in 1895. Later works concerned with the conflict were *Virginia* (1937), *Arms and the Girl* (1950), *Ben Franklin in Paris* (1964), and the most successful of all, *1776* (1969).
R&H.

THE VAGABOND KING

Music: Rudolf Friml
Lyrics: Brian Hooker
Book: Brian Hooker, Russell Janney, W. H. Post
Producer: Russell Janney
Director: Max Figman
Choreographer: Julian Alfred
Cast: Dennis King, Carolyn Thomson, Max Figman, Herbert Corthell
Songs: "Song of the Vagabonds"; "Some Day"; "Only a Rose"; "Huguette Waltz"; "Love Me Tonight"; "Love for Sale"; "Nocturne"
New York run: Casino Theatre, September 21, 1925; 511 p.

Originally, producer Russell Janney planned this operetta to have a score by the youthful team of Richard Rodgers and Lorenz Hart who had already transformed the venerable novel and play, *If I Were King*, into an amateur musical. When he was unable to get financial backing, however, Janney turned to the more experienced team of Rudolf Friml and Brian Hooker. *The Vagabond King* is concerned with the amours and adventures of the 15th Century outlaw Francois Villon (Dennis King) during the reign of King Louis XI. In this attractively mounted, picaresque tale, the poet-vagabond is appointed King of France for a day (it was a week in the original story) in order to save both his neck and Paris by leading his rabble of low degree against the Duke of Burgundy's forces. As a fitting capper to his successful endeavors, Villon even wins the hand of the aristocratic Katherine de Vaucelles (Carolyn Thomson). There were two screen versions: King and Jeanette MacDonald were co-starred in 1930; Oreste and Kathryn Grayson in 1956.
RCA SC/ Samuel French (1929)*/ SF.

Dearest Enemy. Discovered swimming in the nude, Helen Ford keeps Charles Purcell at bay with an umbrella as he tries to return her shoe. (White)

The Vagabond King. Dennis King leads his followers in the "Song of the Vaga-bonds." (White)

Sunny. Esther Howard, Joseph Cawthorn, Dorothy Francis, Clifton Webb, Marilyn Miller, Paul Frawley, Mary Hay, and Jack Donahue. (White)

SUNNY

Music: Jerome Kern
Lyrics & book: Otto Harbach & Oscar Hammerstein II
Producer: Charles Dillingham
Director: Hassard Short
Choreographers: Julian Mitchell, David Bennett, Alexis Kosloff, John Tiller, Fred Astaire
Cast: Marilyn Miller, Jack Donahue, Clifton Webb, Mary Hay, Joseph Cawthorn, Paul Frawley, Cliff Edwards, Pert Kelton, Moss & Fontana, Esther Howard, Dorothy Francis, George Olsen Orchestra
Songs: "Sunny"; "Who?"; "Let's Say Good Night Till It's Morning"; "D'Ye Love Me?"; "Two Little Bluebirds"; "I Might Grow Fond of You"
New York run: New Amsterdam Theatre, September 22, 1925; 517 p.

In another variation on the Cinderella story, *Sunny* tells the saga of Sunny Peters (Marilyn Miller), a spirited bareback rider appearing with a circus in Southampton, England, whose heart has been stolen away by Tom Warren (Paul Frawley), an American tourist. In pursuit of this glittering prize, Sunny stows aboard the ocean liner taking him back to the United States. In order to be allowed to land, Sunny weds Tom's friend, Jim Deming (Jack Donahue), but once the agreed-to divorce has been granted Sunny and Tom are happily reunited at a fashionable Southern resort. (In the London version, in which Jim was played by popular star Jack Buchanan, Sunny decided that he was really the man for her. This denouement has also been used in American revivals.)

    Sunny was the alliterative successor to *Sally*, a musical that also had Marilyn Miller singing and dancing to Jerome Kern melodies. Here, however, the composer was collaborating for the first time with Otto Harbach and Oscar Hammerstein II. Miss Miller repeated her role in the first movie version in 1930; Anna Neagle followed 10 years later.

Stanyan London OC (1926)/ Chappell, London (1926)*/ TW.

The Cocoanuts. Groucho Marx auctioning off Florida land assisted by brothers Chico, Zeppo, and Harpo. (White)

THE COCOANUTS

Music & lyrics: Irving Berlin
Book: George S. Kaufman (Morrie Ryskind uncredited)
Producer: Sam H. Harris
Director: Oscar Eagle
Choreographer: Sammy Lee
Cast: The Marx Brothers, Margaret Dumont, John Barker, Mabel Withee, Frances Williams, Brox Sisters, Basil Ruysdael, George Hale
Songs: "Lucky Boy"; "Why Am I a Hit With the Ladies?"; "A Little Bungalow"; "Florida by the Sea"; "The Monkey Doodle-Doo"
New York run: Lyric Theatre, December 8, 1925; 276 p.

The Cocoanuts was the second of three musicals that the Marx Brothers starred in on Broadway, the others being *I'll Say She Is* and *Animal Crackers*. As might be expected, it offered a gag-filled, loosely constructed spree in which the madcap team was allowed enough room to improvise and add new routines, such as the now classic Groucho-Chico exchange based on the misunderstanding of the word "viaduct" for "Why a duck?" The story is set in Cocoanut Beach, Florida, where Groucho, as Henry W. Schlemmer, runs a hotel and is also a shady real-estate developer trying to cash in on the Florida land boom. Complications arise when jewel thieves posing as hotel guests steal the gems from rich dowager Margaret Dumont, and try to pin the blame on the fiancé of the dowager's daughter. Adding to the mayhem were Chico and Harpo, as hotel guests and Zeppo as a desk clerk. The 1929 screen version of *The Cocoanuts* was the Marx Brothers' first feature-length movie.

The Marx Brothers were leading characters in two later Broadway musicals: the biographical *Minnie's Boys* (1970) and the second half of the "Musical Double Feature," *A Day in Hollywood/A Night in the Ukraine* (1980). St. Martin's Press (1979).

TIP-TOES

Music: George Gershwin
Lyrics: Ira Gershwin
Book: Guy Bolton & Fred Thompson
Producers: Alex A. Aarons & Vinton Freedley
Director: John Harwood
Choreographer: Sammy Lee
Cast: Queenie Smith, Allen Kearns, Andrew Tombes, Harry Watson Jr., Jeanette MacDonald, Robert Halliday, Gertrude McDonald
Songs: "Looking for a Boy"; "When Do We Dance?"; "These Charming People"; "That Certain Feeling"; "Sweet and Low-Down"; "Nice Baby"; "Nightie Night"
New York run: Liberty Theatre, December 28, 1925; 194 p.

Tip-Toes was something of a creative successor to *Lady, Be Good!*, since it shared the same songwriting team (whose new hit was "That Certain Feeling"), librettists, producers, and choreographer, and it even played the same theatre. There was also a thematic similarity in that the new story was again concerned with down-on-their-luck vaudevillians who become involved with high society. Tip-Toes Kaye (Queenie Smith) and her uncles Al and Harry (Andrew Tombes and Harry Watson Jr.) are stranded in Palm Beach where the uncles try to pass off Tip-Toes as a blueblood to win a rich husband. She falls for glue king Steve Burton (Allen Kearns) and sticks with him even after — as a test, of course — he admits to being penniless. A 1928 screen variation, made in England, featured Dorothy Gish and Will Rogers.
M-E London OC (1926)/ TW.

GEORGE WHITE'S SCANDALS

Music: Ray Henderson
Lyrics: B. G. DeSylva & Lew Brown
Sketches: George White, William K. Wells
Producer-director-choreographer: George White
Cast: Willie & Eugene Howard, Frances Williams, Harry Richman, Tom Patricola, Ann Pennington, McCarthy Sisters, Fairbanks Twins, Buster West, Portland Hoffa
Songs: "Lucky Day"; "Black Bottom"; "Birth of the Blues"; "St. Louis Blues" (W.C. Handy); "Rhapsody in Blue" (music: George Gershwin); "The Girl Is You and the Boy Is Me"
New York run: Apollo Theatre, June 14, 1926; 424 p.

Possibly the foremost edition in the series, the 1926 *Scandals* — the eighth of that title — had by far the longest run. Its attributes included a strong score by DeSylva, Brown and Henderson (the second *Scandals* for the trio), plus a sure-fire combination of mirth (mostly resting on the capable if stooped shoulders of Willie Howard) and production numbers (George White's new dance sensation was the successor to the "Charleston" called the "Black Bottom"). The first-act finale offered a musical debate between the blues and the classics, with such examples of the former as "Birth of the Blues" (sung by Harry Richman), "St. Louis Blues," and the "Rhapsody in Blue" (with lyrics!). The producer was so confident of the show's success that he charged $55.00 per ticket for the first eight rows on opening night (the top price reverted to $5.50 after that).

COUNTESS MARITZA

Music: Emmerich Kalman
Lyrics & book: Harry B. Smith
Producer: Messrs. Shubert
Director: J. C. Huffman
Choreographers: Carl Randall, Jack Mason
Cast: Yvonne D'Arle, Walter Woolf, Odette Myrtil, Carl Randall, Harry K. Morton, Vivian Hart, George Hassell
Songs: "Play, Gypsies — Dance, Gypsies"; "I'll Keep on Dreaming"; "The One I'm Looking For"; "The Call of Love"
New York run: Shubert Theatre, September 18, 1926; 321 p.

One of the few transplanted mid-Twenties operettas to retain its original European score, *Countess Maritza* was the last successful show written by Harry B. Smith. It was also his 115th Broadway production! Originally presented as *Grafin Mariza* two and a half years earlier in Vienna, the work has a certain kinship with *The Merry Widow* in that it offers a heroine constantly on her guard against fortune hunters and a hero who is afraid of being considered one. Set in Hungary, the plot finds the impecunious Count Tassilo (Walter Woolf) working under an assumed name as the overseer on the estate of his beloved countess (Yvonne D'Arle), and leading the merry peasants in the stirring strains of "Play, Gypsies — Dance, Gypsies." After he is dismissed when Maritza erroneously pegs him for a gold digger, the countess — too proud to admit her mistake verbally — proposes to Tassilo via a letter.

OH, KAY!

Music: George Gershwin
Lyrics: Ira Gershwin
Book: Guy Bolton & P. G. Wodehouse
Producers: Alex A. Aarons & Vinton Freedley
Director: John Harwood
Choreographer: Sammy Lee
Cast: Gertrude Lawrence, Oscar Shaw, Victor Moore, Harland Dixon, Fairbanks Twins, Gerald Oliver Smith, Betty Compton, Constance Carpenter
Songs: "Dear Little Girl"; "Maybe"; "Clap Yo' Hands"; "Do Do Do"; "Someone to Watch Over Me"; "Fidgety Feet"; "Heaven on Earth" (lyric with Howard Dietz); "Oh, Kay!" (lyric with Dietz)
New York run: Imperial Theatre, November 8, 1926; 256 p.

Following her Broadway appearances in the *Charlot Revues*, Gertrude Lawrence was besieged with offers to star in an American musical comedy. By accepting the leading role in *Oh, Kay!*, Miss Lawrence became the first British actress to originate a part on Broadway before repeating it in London. The production reunited the Princess Theatre librettists, Guy Bolton and P.G. Wodehouse, whose book for *Oh, Kay!* retained something of the Anglo-American flavor of their previous *Oh, Boy!* and *Oh, Lady! Lady!!* The action takes place at the home of Jimmy Winter (Oscar Shaw) in the imaginary town of Beachampton, Long Island. Jimmy is about to wed when he discovers that he has fallen in love with Kay Denham, who is posing as a cook in his house to be near the hooch that her brother, a titled English bootlegger, has stashed in Jimmy's cellar. Though Kay and Jimmy make their feelings clear in the duet "Maybe," and Kay plaintively pleads for someone to watch over her, the couple must survive obstacles, both legal and matrimonial, before settling down to a life of musical-comedy bliss. A revival of *Oh, Kay!*, somewhat revised, was produced Off Broadway in 1960. Smithsonian part OC; Columbia SC; DRG OC (1960)/ TW.

THE DESERT SONG
Music: Sigmund Romberg
Lyrics: Otto Harbach & Oscar Hammerstein II
Book: Otto Harbach, Oscar Hammerstein II & Frank Mandel
Producers: Laurence Schwab & Frank Mandel
Director: Arthur Hurley
Choreographer: Bobby Connolly
Cast: Vivienne Segal, Robert Halliday, Eddie Buzzell, Pearl Regay, William O'Neal
Songs: "The Riff Song"; "Romance"; "French Military Marching Song"; "I Want a Kiss"; " 'It' "; "The Desert Song"; "Let Love Go"; "One Flower Grows Alone in Your Garden"; "One Alone"
New York run: Casino Theatre, November 30, 1926; 471 p.

Possibly the decade's most enduring operetta, *The Desert Song* marked Sigmund Romberg's first association with librettists-lyricists Otto Harbach and Oscar Hammerstein II (Romberg and Hammerstein would do four other musicals together). Though a swashbuckling romance created along familiar lines, the work was equally inspired by such recent events as the Riff uprising in French Morocco, the accomplishments of Lawrence of Arabia, and the sizzling Rudolph Valentino films *The Sheik* and *The Son of the Sheik*. The operetta is primarily concerned with Margot Bonvalet (Vivienne Segal), a French woman who is abducted into the Sahara — to the emotional strains of "The Desert Song" — by the mysterious Red Shadow (Robert Halliday), the masked leader of the rebellious Riffs. To the surprise of all, he turns out to be Pierre Birabeau, the simpering son of the Governor of Morocco (thus providing a variation on the *Naughty Marietta* story). During the out-of-town tryout, when the show was called *Lady Fair,* Miss Segal was rushed in to replace another actress in the leading female role. *The Desert Song* had an unsuccessful New York revival in 1973. Film versions were released in 1929, 1943, and 1953.
M-E London OC (1927); Columbia SC/ SF.

PEGGY-ANN
Music: Richard Rodgers
Lyrics: Lorenz Hart
Book: Herbert Fields
Producers: Lew Fields & Lyle D. Andrews
Director: Robert Milton
Choreographer: Seymour Felix
Cast: Helen Ford, Lester Cole, Lulu McConnell, Betty Starbuck, Edith Meiser
Songs: "A Tree in the Park"; "A Little Birdie Told Me So"; "Where's That Rainbow?"; "Maybe It's Me"
New York run: Vanderbilt Theatre, December 27, 1926; 333 p.

A daring work for its day, *Peggy-Ann* was loosely adapted from a 1910 Marie Dressler vehicle, *Tillie's Nightmare*. Most of the show was set in a Freudian dreamworld in which Peggy-Ann of Glens Falls, New York, travels to New York City's Fifth Avenue, takes a trip on a yacht, gets married in her step-ins, is thrown overboard by a mutinous crew, and attends the horse races in Havana. At the end, she awakes happily in the arms of her Glens Falls boyfriend. Among the staging innovations: no songs were sung within the first fifteen minutes, the scenery and costumes were changed in full view of the audience, and the first and last scenes were played in almost total darkness. The show was the fourth of five Rodgers and Hart musicals that were presented on Broadway during 1926; the fifth, *Betsy,* opened just one night after *Peggy-Ann.*

RIO RITA

Music: Harry Tierney
Lyrics: Joseph McCarthy
Book: Guy Bolton & Fred Thompson
Producer: Florenz Ziegfeld
Director: John Harwood
Choreographers: Sammy Lee, Albertina Rasch
Cast: Ethelind Terry, J. Harold Murray, Bert Wheeler, Robert Woolsey, Ada May, Vincent Serrano
Songs: "Rio Rita"; "The Rangers' Song"; "The Kinkajou"; "If You're in Love You'll Waltz"; "Following the Sun Around"
New York run: Ziegfeld Theatre, February 2, 1927; 494 p.

Rio Rita was Florenz Ziegfeld's premiere attraction at his Ziegfeld Theatre, then located on the northwest corner of 6th Avenue and 54th Street. In the spectacular production, Capt. James Stewart (J. Harold Murray) leads his Texas Rangers in the stirring "Rangers' Song" as they chase a bank robber known as the Kinkajou. The pursuit takes Capt. Jim across the Rio Grande into the town of Santa Luca where he falls in love with tempestuous Rita Ferguson (Ethelind Terry), whose name is fluvially linked only in the show's title and in song. Their romance hits a snag when Capt. Jim suspects Rita's brother to be the Kinkajou, but he eventually turns out to be a Mexican general (Vincent Serrano) who also has eyes for Rita. (This was still another variation on the outlaw-in-disguise theme of such previous offerings as *Naughty Marietta* and *The Desert Song*.) The 1929 film version, with Bebe Daniels and John Boles, was the first successful screen adaptation of a Broadway musical.
M-E London OC/ TW.

Rio Rita. Ethelind Terry, Vincent Serrano, and J. Harold Murray. (White)

HIT THE DECK!

Music: Vincent Youmans
Lyrics: Clifford Grey & Leo Robin
Book: Herbert Fields
Producers: Lew Fields & Vincent Youmans
Director: Alexander Leftwich
Choreographer: Seymour Felix
Cast: Louise Groody, Charles King, Stella Mayhew, Madeline Cameron, Brian Donlevy, Jack McCauley
Songs: "Join the Navy"; "Harbor of My Heart"; "Lucky Bird"; "Looloo"; "Why, Oh Why?''; ''Sometimes I'm Happy'' (lyric: Irving Caesar); "Hallelujah"
New York run: Belasco Theatre, April 25, 1927; 352 p.

Vincent Youmans' *Hit the Deck!* was second only to *No, No, Nanette* as the most popular of the composer's 12 Broadway musicals. Based on the 1922 play *Shore Leave*, the show was about a Newport, Rhode Island, coffee-shop owner known as Looloo (Louise Groody, the previous Nanette), who is so totally smitten with sailor Bilge Smith (Charles King) that she follows him all the way to China and even spends her inheritance to salvage a scow for him after his Navy hitch is over. The production, one of the few musicals to play the Belasco Theatre (on 44th Street east of Broadway), introduced audiences to two enduring songs: "Sometimes I'm Happy" and "Hallelujah." The second of three movie versions, retitled *Follow the Fleet*, and released in 1936, featured Fred Astaire and Ginger Rogers and new songs by Irving Berlin. TW.

GOOD NEWS!

Music: Ray Henderson
Lyrics: B. G. DeSylva & Lew Brown
Book: Laurence Schwab & B. G. DeSylva
Producers: Laurence Schwab & Frank Mandel
Director: Edgar MacGregor
Choreographer: Bobby Connolly
Cast: Mary Lawlor, John Price Jones, Gus Shy, Inez Courtney, Zelma O'Neal, George Olsen Orchestra
Songs: "Just Imagine"; "He's a Ladies Man"; "The Best Things in Life Are Free"; "The Varsity Drag"; "Lucky in Love"; "Good News"
New York run: 46th Street Theatre, September 6, 1927; 551 p.

The fifth longest running musical of the Twenties, *Good News!* was the first of a quartet of breezy, youthful DeSylva, Brown and Henderson musical comedies that capitalized on popular sports, fads, occupations, and innovations. (The others: *Hold Everything!, Flying High,* and *Follow Thru.*) In this caper about America's flaming youth, the setting is Tait College, where students spend their time dancing "The Varsity Drag," where the burning issue is whether football hero Tom Marlowe will be allowed to lead the team despite his failing grade in astronomy, and where hero can console heroine Connie Laine by assuring her "The Best Things in Life Are Free." Helping to establish the collegiate atmosphere of the entertainment were the members of George Olsen's Orchestra who, before playing the overture, marched down the theatre aisles sporting diamond-pattern sweaters and barking football cheers. In the fall of 1974, Alice Faye and Gene Nelson opened on Broadway in a revival that lasted two weeks. June Allyson and Peter Lawford were in the 1947 screen version.
Samuel French (1932)*/ SF.

Hit the Deck! Charles King and Louise Groody. (White)

A CONNECTICUT YANKEE

Music: Richard Rodgers
Lyrics: Lorenz Hart
Book: Herbert Fields
Producers: Lew Fields & Lyle D. Andrews
Director: Alexander Leftwich
Choreographer: Busby Berkeley
Cast: William Gaxton, Constance Carpenter, Nana Bryant, June Cochrane, William Norris, Jack Thompson
Songs: "My Heart Stood Still"; "Thou Swell"; "I Feel at Home With You"; "On a Desert Island With Thee"
New York run: Vanderbilt Theatre, November 3, 1927; 418 p.

Long before winning notice with their songs for *The Garrick Gaieties*, Rodgers and Hart — along with librettist Herbert Fields — had tried unsuccessfully to interest producers in their version of Mark Twain's *A Connecticut Yankee in King Arthur's Court*. By 1927, however, they had little trouble getting Lew Fields to present it at the Vanderbilt Theatre following the run of the trio's first dream fantasy, *Peggy-Ann*, and it became their biggest hit of the 1920s.

The curtain rises on a hotel room in modern-day Hartford, where Martin (William Gaxton), about to be married, gets bopped on the head by his intended spouse. He dreams of being a stranger at the court of King Arthur, where he sings "Thou Swell" and "My Heart Stood Still" with Dame Alisande (Constance Carpenter), and becomes a confidant of the king by industrializing the realm. Upon awakening Martin realizes that he is marrying the wrong girl and turns to Alisande's modern-day double, Alice Carter. (A more serious approach to the Arthurian legend was Lerner and Loewe's *Camelot* in 1960.)

A Connecticut Yankee was revived in 1943 with Dick Foran, Vivienne Segal, Julie Warren, and Vera Ellen. Five of the original songs were retained and six new ones were added, including Miss Segal's showstopper, "To Keep My Love Alive." For the present-day scenes all the characters appeared in military uniforms. This production, which ran 135 performances, opened just five days before Lorenz Hart's death.
AEI OC (1943)/ TW.

A Connecticut Yankee. Yankee William Gaxton is frightened by one of King Arthur's knights.

FUNNY FACE

Music: George Gershwin
Lyrics: Ira Gershwin
Book: Paul Gerard Smith & Fred Thompson
Producers: Alex A. Aarons & Vinton Freedley
Director: Edgar MacGregor
Choreographer: Bobby Connolly
Cast: Fred & Adele Astaire, Victor Moore, William Kent, Allen Kearns, Betty Compton, Dorothy Jordan
Songs: "Funny Face"; "High Hat"; "He Loves and She Loves"; " 'S Wonderful"; "Let's Kiss and Make Up"; "My One and Only"; "The Babbitt and the Bromide"
New York run: Alvin Theatre, November 22, 1927; 244 p.

The second musical the Gershwin brothers wrote for Fred and Adele Astaire, *Funny Face* was another popular lighter-than-air concoction that —like *Lady, Be Good!*—gave the dancing siblings plenty of room for their specialties. In the plot, Frankie Wynne (Adele), the ward of Jimmie Reeve (Fred), persuades aviator Peter Thurston (Allen Kearns), to steal her incriminating diary from Jimmie's wall safe. By mistake, Peter steals a bracelet, which sets off a mad chase that takes the dramatis personae — including two comic burglars — to Lake Wapatog, New Jersey, then on to the Paymore Hotel and the Two-Million Dollar Pier in Atlantic City.

When tried out under the title of *Smarty*, with Robert Benchley as coauthor, the musical was greeted with such disfavor that drastic alterations were quickly made. The name was changed, Benchley was replaced by librettist Paul Gerard Smith, Victor Moore was added as one of the burglars, Allen Kearns took over the male romantic lead, and seven songs were dropped in favor of five new ones (including "He Loves and She Loves," which replaced "How Long Has This Been Going On?"). *Funny Face* became both a hit and the first attraction at the newly built Alvin Theatre (named for the show's producers), which, renamed the Neil Simon, is on 52nd Street west of Broadway.

In 1983, six songs from *Funny Face* were used in the score of *My One and Only,* which had a different book. The 1957 film, *Funny Face,* starring Fred Astaire and Audrey Hepburn, kept four of the original songs but also changed the story.

M-E OC; Smithsonian OC.

Funny Face. Fred Astaire leading the boys in the "High Hat" number. (White)

SHOW BOAT

Music: Jerome Kern
Lyrics & book: Oscar Hammerstein II
Producer: Florenz Ziegfeld
Director: Zeke Colvan (Oscar Hammerstein II uncredited)
Choreographer: Sammy Lee
Cast: Charles Winninger, Norma Terris, Howard Marsh, Helen Morgan, Jules Bledsoe, Edna May Oliver, Eva Puck, Sammy White, Tess Gardella, Charles Ellis, Francis X. Mahoney
Songs: "Make Believe"; "Ol' Man River"; "Can't Help Lovin' Dat Man"; "Life Upon the Wicked Stage"; "You Are Love"; "Why Do I Love You?"; "Bill" (lyric with P. G. Wodehouse); "After the Ball" (Charles K. Harris)
New York run: Ziegfeld Theatre, December 27, 1927; 572 p.

Both Jerome Kern and Oscar Hammerstein II had felt for some time that the Broadway musical theatre was suffering from too much sameness and tameness. After reading Edna Ferber's sprawling novel of life on the Mississippi, they became convinced that it was the story best suited to help them make the kinds of changes they felt were needed. Their efforts resulted in a recognized landmark in the history of the theatre, one that broke ground in steering a course away from lightweight musical comedy and overweight operetta. Their characters were more three-dimensional, the music was more skillfully integrated into the libretto, and their plot dared to deal with such unaccustomed subjects as unhappy marriages, miscegenation, and the hard life of black stevedores (as expressed through "Ol' Man River").

The saga covers the period from the mid 1880s to the then current 1927, and is primarily concerned with the fortunes of impressionable Magnolia Hawks (Norma Terris) — whose father Cap'n Andy Hawks (Charles Winninger) runs the showboat *Cotton Blossom* — and ne'er-do-well riverboat gambler Gaylord Ravenal (Howard Marsh). Meeting on the Natchez levee, the couple fall in love at first sight (singing "Make Believe"), then become actors on the showboat, marry, and move to Chicago (revealing their devotion in "Why Do I Love You?"). After they separate when Ravenal loses his money gambling, Magnolia has a tearful meeting with her father while singing at the Trocadero on New Year's Eve. She goes on to become a musical-comedy star, as does her daughter Kim, and years later she and Ravenal are reunited aboard the *Cotton Blossom*. A secondary plot involves Magnolia's mulatto friend, the tragic Julie La Verne (Helen Morgan), and her devotion to *her* man, Steve Baker (though the song she sings about him is called "Bill"). *Show Boat* was the second longest running musical of the 1920's. For the 10-month tour, Irene Dunne replaced Norma Terris.

In 1932, Ziegfeld brought the musical back with basically the original cast, except that Howard Marsh was succeeded by Dennis King and Jules Bledsoe by Paul Robeson (for whom the part of the stevedore Joe had originally been intended). The 1946 *Show Boat* was the most successful revival, running 418 performances. The major change was the addition of "Nobody Else but Me" (the last song Kern wrote) in the final scene. (See page 128.) Twenty years later, the musical was remounted by the Music Theatre of Lincoln Center, with Barbara Cook, Stephen Douglass, David Wayne, Constance Towers, and William Warfield. The fourth revival, in 1983, was by the Houston Grand Opera with Donald O'Connor, Sheryl Woods, Ron Raines, Lonette McKee, and Bruce Hubbard.

Three movie versions were filmed: a part-talkie in 1929 with Laura LaPlante and Joseph Schildkraut; the 1936 reproduction with Irene Dunne, Allan Jones, Helen Morgan, Charles Winninger, and Paul Robeson; and the 1951 reconstruction with Kathryn Grayson, Howard Keel, Ava Gardner, Joe E. Brown, and William Warfield.

CSP part OC (1932); Columbia OC (1946); RCA OC (1966); EMI SC/ Chappell, London (1934)*/ R&H.

Show Boat. A dramatic scene with Helen Morgan surrounded by Francis X. Mahoney, Charles Ellis, Eva Puck, Norma Terris, Charles Winninger, and Edna May Oliver. (White)

Show Boat. Edna May Oliver (right) is unable to stop the wedding of Howard Marsh and Norma Terris. Others in foreground are Charles Winninger, Sammy White, and Eva Puck. (White)

Rosalie. Marilyn Miller and ladies of the ensemble. (White)

ROSALIE

Music: George Gershwin, Sigmund Romberg
Lyrics: Ira Gershwin, P. G. Wodehouse
Book: William Anthony McGuire & Guy Bolton
Producer: Florenz Ziegfeld
Director: William Anthony McGuire
Choreographers: Seymour Felix, Michel Fokine
Cast: Marilyn Miller, Jack Donahue, Frank Morgan, Margaret Dale, Bobbe Arnst, Oliver McLennan
Songs: "Say So!" (music: Gershwin); "West Point Song" (Romberg - Wodehouse); "Oh Gee! Oh Joy!" (music: Gershwin); "How Long Has This Been Going On?" (Gershwin - Gershwin); "Ev'rybody Knows I Love Somebody" (Gershwin - Gershwin).
New York run: New Amsterdam Theatre, January 10, 1928; 335 p.

Although Florenz Ziegfeld is said to have agreed to produce the musical only because it was named after his mother and the score did not represent either Gershwin or Romberg at his best, *Rosalie* became one of the hits of the season — thanks chiefly to twinkling star Marilyn Miller, dancing comedian Jack Donahue, and a stylishly mounted production. The story was "inspired" by two recent events: Lindbergh's solo flight to Paris and the visit of Rumania's Queen Marie and her daughter to the United States. After West Point ace Richard Fay has flown to the mythical kingdom of Romanza to be near the princess he loves, the royal family goes on a state visit to America. Luckily for Richard, he has been appointed leader of the guard of honor; luckily for Richard and Rosalie, the king abdicates so that his daughter might be free to marry a commoner.

The reason the two composers shared the assignment is that Romberg could not undertake it alone because he was then also creating the music for *The New Moon.* Though he was occupied with *Funny Face* at the time, Gershwin agreed to join the project to help relieve the work load. The 1936 movie version, with Eleanor Powell and Nelson Eddy, scrapped all their songs and came up with a new score by Cole Porter.
TW.

THE THREE MUSKETEERS

Music: Rudolf Friml
Lryics: Clifford Grey
Book: William Anthony McGuire
Producer: Florenz Ziegfeld
Directors: William Anthony McGuire, Richard Boleslawsky
Choreographer: Albertina Rasch
Cast: Dennis King, Vivienne Segal, Lester Allen, Vivienne Osborne, Yvonne D'Arle, Reginald Owen, Joseph Macaulay, Harriet Hoctor, Douglass Dumbrille, Detmar Poppen, Clarence Derwent
Songs: "March of the Musketeers" (lyric with P.G. Wodehouse); "Ma Belle"; "Your Eyes" (lyric: Wodehouse); "One Kiss"; "My Sword and I"; "Queen of My Heart"
New York run: Lyric Theatre, March 13, 1928; 318 p.

Just as *The Vagabond King* had offered Dennis King as the dashing Francois Villon singing Rudolf Friml songs in a tale of adventure and intrigue in the days of Louis XI, so *The Three Musketeers* offered King as the dashing d'Artagnan singing Friml songs in a tale of adventure and intrigue in the days of Louis XIII. In this operetta version of the popular Alexandre Dumas novel, the story covers d'Artagnan's first meeting with Musketeers Athos, Porthos, and Aramis (Douglass Dumbrille, Detmar Poppen, and Joseph Macaulay), his romance with Constance Bonacieux (Vivienne Segal), and his noble efforts to save the honor of Queen Anne (Yvonne D'Arle), whom the wily Cardinal Richelieu (Reginald Owen) tries to blackmail. A revised version of the musical had a brief stay on Broadway in 1984.
M-E London OC (1930)/ Chappell, London (1937)*/ TW.

BLACKBIRDS OF 1928

Music: Jimmy McHugh
Lyrics: Dorothy Fields
Sketches: (uncredited)
Producer-director: Lew Leslie
Cast: Adelaide Hall, Bill Robinson, Aida Ward, Tim Moore, Elizabeth Welch, Mantan Moreland, Cecil Mack, Hall Johnson Choir
Songs: "Diga Diga Doo"; "I Can't Give You Anything but Love"; "Porgy"; "Doin' the New Low-Down"; "I Must Have That Man"
New York run: Liberty Theatre, May 9, 1928; 518 p.

Proclaiming itself "A Distinctive and Unique Entertainment with an All-Star Cast of 100 Colored Artists," *Blackbirds of 1928* was the brainchild of impresario Lew Leslie who had first exhibited a *Blackbirds* revue in London in 1926. Florence Mills scored such a hit in that production that Leslie planned to build a show around her in New York, but she died before rehearsals began. Leslie then secured Adelaide Hall and Bill Robinson (who joined the cast during tryout and had only one number, "Doin' the New Low-Down"), and assigned Jimmy HcHugh and Dorothy Fields to write the songs. Among the musical offerings were their first hit, "I Can't Give You Anything but Love," a spirited jungle number, "Diga Diga Doo," and a capsule version of the play, *Porgy,* thus preceding the Gershwin opera by six years. Leslie sponsored *Blackbirds* revues on Broadway in 1930 (with Ethel Waters and Buck and Bubbles), in 1933 (with Bill Robinson), and in 1939 (with Lena Horne), but none flew very high.
Columbia part OC.

THE NEW MOON

Music: Sigmund Romberg
Lyrics: Oscar Hammerstein II
Book: Oscar Hammerstein II, Frank Mandel, Laurence Schwab
Producers: Laurence Schwab & Frank Mandel
Director: (Edgar MacGregor uncredited)
Choreographer: Bobby Connolly
Cast: Evelyn Herbert, Robert Halliday, Gus Shy, Max Figman, William O'Neal
Songs: "Marianne"; "Softly, as in a Morning Sunrise"; "Stouthearted Men";
    "One Kiss"; "Wanting You"; "Lover, Come Back to Me"
New York run: Imperial Theatre, September 19, 1928, 509 p.

The New Moon had to endure a tryout so disastrous that it was shut down completely while extensive alterations were made to the story, the score, and the cast. (Part of the problem was that both Sigmund Romberg and Oscar Hammerstein had to devote much of their time to other shows then in preparation: Romberg had *Rosalie* and Hammerstein had *Show Boat*.) After eight months the new *New Moon* reopened on the road with such musical pleasures as "Softly, as in a Morning Sunrise" and "Lover, Come Back to Me," and went on to win acclaim in New York.

What kept audiences happy was, in fact, deliberately designed as the successor to the same writers' *Desert Song,* with a similar improbably heroic tale loosely based on fact accompanied by a lush, pulse-pounding score. The story takes place in New Orleans in 1788, where Robert Misson (Robert Halliday), a French nobleman wanted for murder, serves as a bondsman and recruits stouthearted men in the cause of liberty. After his arrest, Robert is sent back to France on *The New Moon*, a vessel also carrying his beloved Marianne Beaunoir (Evelyn Herbert). Misson's followers, disguised as pirates, rescue their leader, who takes Marianne with him to establish a colony of free men on the Isle of Pines. *The New Moon* has something of a kinship with *Naughty Marietta* since they both dealt with a person of noble birth in disguise, and they were both set in New Orleans at roughly the same time. (They also shared the same historical error of making New Orleans a French colony when at the time it belonged to Spain.) Jeanette MacDonald and Nelson Eddy were in the 1940 movie version.
M-E London OC (1929); Capitol SC/ Chappell, London (1937)*/ TW.

Hold Everything! Frank Allworth, Bert Lahr, Victor Moore, Buddy Harak, and Harry Locke. (White)

HOLD EVERYTHING!
Music: Ray Henderson
Lyrics: B. G. DeSylva & Lew Brown
Book: B. G. DeSylva & John McGowan
Producers: Alex A. Aarons & Vinton Freedley
Director: (uncredited)
Choreographers: Sam Rose, Jack Haskell
Cast: Jack Whiting, Ona Munson, Bert Lahr, Betty Compton, Victor Moore, Nina Olivette, Frank Allworth, Gus Schilling
Songs: "Don't Hold Everything"; "You're the Cream in My Coffee"; "Too Good to Be True"; "To Know You Is to Love You"
New York run: Broadhurst Theatre, October 10, 1928; 413 p.

Bearing a title more applicable to a tale about wrestling, *Hold Everything!* was a saga of the manly art of boxing. In it, we are concerned with the ambitions of Sonny Jim Brooks (Jack Whiting), a welterweight challenger, and his girl, Sue Burke (Ona Munson), who is the cream in his coffee. Sonny Jim becomes temporarily distracted by socialite Norine Lloyd (Betty Compton) and for a while even considers her advice to try using boxing skills rather than slug it out with the champion. But when our hero finds out that the champ has insulted Sue, his killer instincts are aroused and he wins both the crown and his lady. The major attraction of the show turned out to be the uninhibited buffoon, Bert Lahr, as a punch-drunk pug. (When asked in one scene what book he was reading, Bert replied, "Da Woiks, by William Shakespeare.") During the run at the Broadhurst Theatre (on 44th Street west of Broadway), Whiting was succeeded by George Murphy. The film version was released in 1930 with Joe E. Brown and Winnie Lightner.

WHOOPEE

Music: Walter Donaldson
Lyrics: Gus Kahn
Book: William Anthony McGuire
Producer: Florenz Ziegfeld
Director: William Anthony McGuire
Choreographers: Seymour Felix, Tamara Geva
Cast: Eddie Cantor, Ruth Etting, Ethel Shutta, Paul Gregory, Frances Upton, Tamara Geva, Albert Hackett, George Olsen Orchestra, Buddy Ebsen
Songs: "I'm Bringing a Red Red Rose"; "Makin' Whoopee"; "Until You Get Somebody Else"; "Love Me or Leave Me"
New York run: New Amsterdam Theatre, December 4, 1928; 379 p.

Eddie Cantor was an eye-popping, bouncing comedian who had appeared in five *Ziegfeld Follies* before starring in this lavish Ziegfeld book musical. In the story, adapted from the 1923 play *The Nervous Wreck,* hypochondriac Henry Williams, in California for his health, becomes unwittingly involved with the daughter of a ranch owner whom he helps escape from marrying the local sheriff. After comic adventures that involve hiding out on an Indian reservation and Henry (in black-face) posing as a singing waiter, the girl is reunited with her true love, an Indian halfbreed who turns out to be white. The score, written by pop songwriters Walter Donaldson and Gus Kahn, produced two hits, "Love Me or Leave Me" and the Cantor specialty, "Makin' Whoopee." During the show's run, Paul Whiteman's Orchestra replaced George Olsen's for two months. A Broadway revival in 1979, originally presented at the Goodspeed Opera House in Connecticut, ran 204 performances. Eddie Cantor also starred in the 1930 film version. Smithsonian OC.

Whoopee. Eddie Cantor as Henry Williams.

FOLLOW THRU

Music: Ray Henderson
Lyrics: B. G. DeSylva & Lew Brown
Book: Laurence Schwab & B. G. DeSylva
Producers: Laurence Schwab & Frank Mandel
Director: Edgar MacGregor
Choreographer: Bobby Connolly
Cast: Jack Haley, Zelma O'Neal, Irene Delroy, Eleanor Powell, Madeline Cameron, John Barker
Songs: "My Lucky Star"; "Button Up Your Overcoat"; "You Wouldn't Fool Me, Would You?"; "I Want to Be Bad"
New York run: 46th Street Theatre, January 9, 1929; 403 p.

After collaborating on musical comedies about football *(Good News!)* and boxing *(Hold Everything!)*, DeSylva, Brown and Henderson followed up with *Follow Thru*, which was about golf. Subtitled "A Musical Slice of Country Club Life," the show was an appropriately fleet-footed successor to the previous sporty musicals, with another catchy score (including "Button Up Your Overcoat"), some comic situations for Jack Haley (in his first major Broadway role), and a negligible plot about female rivalry for both the club championship and the golf pro. Most important, however, was the show's contagious high spirits. As Gilbert Gabriel reported in the *American,* "Wild-faced, free-legged kids shouted catch lines across the footlights that fairly roped and yanked the audience onto the stage." Jack Haley repeated his role in the 1930 movie version, which also featured Nancy Carroll and Buddy Rogers.
TW.

THE LITTLE SHOW

Music: Arthur Schwartz etc.
Lyrics: Howard Dietz, etc.
Sketches: Howard Dietz, George S. Kaufman, etc.
Producers: William A. Brady Jr. & Dwight Deere Wiman
Directors: Dwight Deere Wiman, Alexander Leftwich
Choreographer: Danny Dare
Cast: Clifton Webb, Fred Allen, Libby Holman, Romney Brent, Portland Hoffa, Bettina Hall, Jack McCauley, Peggy Conklin, Constance Cummings
Songs: "I've Made a Habit of You"; "Can't We Be Friends?" (Kay Swift-Paul James); "Hammacher-Schlemmer, I Love You"; "A Little Hut in Hoboken" (Herman Hupfeld); "I Guess I'll Have to Change My Plan"; "Moanin' Low" (music: Ralph Rainger)
New York run: Music Box, April 30, 1929; 321 p.

The Little Show was the first of 11 Broadway musicals to feature songs by the team of Arthur Schwartz and Howard Dietz. In its smartness, style, and intimacy (in 1929 a show with 29 in the cast qualified as little), the revue was something of an American counterpart to the British *Charlot Revues* and *This Year of Grace.* The most dramatic scene was the torrid dance Clifton Webb and Libby Holman performed after Miss Holman moaned "Moanin' Low" in a squalid Harlem tenement. The funniest sketch was George S. Kaufman's "The Still Alarm," about some nonchalant hotel guests, including Webb and Fred Allen, totally impervious to their being in the midst of a blazing fire. There were two subsequent *Little Shows,* neither one a success, though *The Third Little Show,* in 1931, co-starred Beatrice Lillie and Ernest Truex. Miss Lillie introduced Noël Coward's "Mad Dogs and Englishmen" in that one.

SWEET ADELINE

Music: Jerome Kern
Lyrics & book: Oscar Hammerstein II
Producer: Arthur Hammerstein
Director: Reginald Hammerstein
Choreographer: Danny Dare
Cast: Helen Morgan, Charles Butterworth, Irene Franklin, Robert Chisholm, Violet Carlson, Max Hoffman Jr.
Songs: " 'Twas Not So Long Ago"; "Here Am I"; "Why Was I Born?"; "The Sun About to Rise"; "Some Girl Is on Your Mind"; "Don't Ever Leave Me"
New York run: Hammerstein's Theatre, September 3, 1929; 234 p.

Because of their admiration for Helen Morgan's performance in *Show Boat,* Jerome Kern and Oscar Hammerstein collaborated on a nostalgic musical designed as a vehicle to show off the singer's talents. Set in and around New York in 1898, the story concerns Addie Schmidt, the daughter of a Hoboken beergarden owner, and her three loves. After Tom Martin has gone to fight in the Spanish-American War, Addie — now known as Adeline Belmont — becomes a Broadway star and falls for wealthy socialite James Day. But his family disapproves and she happily ends up in the arms of composer Sid Barnett. Full of period charm, *Sweet Adeline* was something of a Hammerstein family affair, since it was produced by Oscar's uncle Arthur, directed by his brother Reginald, and played in Arthur's theatre (now a CBS television playhouse on Broadway between 53rd and 54th Streets). Irene Dunne starred in the 1935 movie. TW.

BITTER SWEET

Music, lyrics & book: Noël Coward
Producers: Florenz Ziegfeld & Arch Selwyn
Director: Noël Coward
Choreographer: Tilly Losch
Cast: Evelyn Laye, Gerald Nodin, Max Kirby, Mireille, John Evelyn
Songs: "The Call of Life"; "If You Could Come With Me"; "I'll See You Again"; "Ladies of the Town"; "Dear Little Café"; "If Love Were All"; "Tokay"; "Ziguener"
New York run: Ziegfeld Theatre, November 5, 1929; 159 p.

Though celebrated for the brittle wit of his revue songs and sketches, as well as his plays, the multitalented Noël Coward was equally at home in the world of operetta. Indeed, no less than six of his eight book musicals were awash in old-fashioned sentiment, elegant period decor, and melodious, emotional ballads. The first of these, *Bitter Sweet,* was written simply because Coward felt that the time was right for a romantic renaissance in the theatre. After Gertrude Lawrence's vocal limitations ruled out her taking the leading role, the part went to the American actress, Peggy Wood, who starred in the London production, and the English actress, Evelyn Laye, who then starred in New York.

Living in Grosvenor Square, the widowed Marchioness of Shayne aids her niece in deciding whether to marry for love or position by recalling that day in 1875 when, as Sarah Millick, she joined music teacher Carl Linden in singing "I'll See You Again" — and promptly eloped with him to Vienna. Five years later, they were poor but happy café entertainers until Carl was killed in a duel. Sarah went on to become the renowned prima donna, Madame Sari Linden, then the wife of the wealthy Marquis of Shayne. Jeanette MacDonald and Nelson Eddy were in the second screen version, released in 1941.
Angel SC/ Heinemann, London (1934)/ TW.

Fifty Million Frenchmen. Helen Broderick and William Gaxton. (White)

FIFTY MILLION FRENCHMEN
Music & lyrics: Cole Porter
Book: Herbert Fields
Producer: E. Ray Goetz
Director: Monty Woolley
Choreographer: Larry Ceballos
Cast: William Gaxton, Genevieve Tobin, Helen Broderick, Betty Compton, Evelyn Hoey, Jack Thompson, Thurston Hall
Songs: "You Do Something to Me"; "You've Got That Thing"; "Find Me a Primitive Man"; "The Tale of an Oyster"; "Paree, What Did You Do to Me?"; "You Don't Know Paree"
New York run: Lyric Theatre, November 27, 1929; 254 p.

Noted for his throbbing, minor-key melodies and his wordly, highly polished lyrics, Cole Porter was responsible for the scores of 23 Broadway musicals. His first hit — dubbed "A Musical Comedy Tour of Paris" — was a carefree tale concerning wealthy Peter Forbes (William Gaxton) who has a wager with a friend that he and Looloo Carroll (Genevieve Tobin) will be betrothed within a month. This gives Peter the excuse to become an impoverished tour guide so that, in pursuit of his beloved, he can determine if Looloo really loves him — and also so that they might enjoy such landmarks of the city as the Ritz Hotel Bar (where they mutually confess "You Do Something to Me"), the Café de la Paix, the Longchamps Racetrack, the Hotel Claridge, and Les Halles. The 1931 screen version retained the services of William Gaxton and Helen Broderick, but eliminated the songs. TW.

STRIKE UP THE BAND

Music: George Gershwin
Lyrics: Ira Gershwin
Book: Morrie Ryskind
Producer: Edgar Selwyn
Director: Alexander Leftwich
Choreographer: George Hale
Cast: Bobby Clark & Paul McCullough, Blanche Ring, Jerry Goff, Doris Carson, Dudley Clements, Red Nichols Orchestra
Songs: "I Mean to Say"; "Soon"; "Strike Up the Band"; "Mademoiselle in New Rochelle"; "I've Got a Crush on You"
New York run: Times Square Theatre, January 14, 1930; 191 p.

Strike Up the Band was first scheduled for a Broadway opening in 1927, but the original George S. Kaufman book was so uncompromisingly grim in its antiwar sentiment that the show closed on the road. Morrie Ryskind then rewrote the story, putting most of the action in a dream, and the leading roles were given to the zany team of Clark and McCullough. The revised script dealt with a war between the United States and Switzerland over the issue of tariffs on imported Swiss chocolate, with plenty of room for barbs aimed at jingoists, politicians, and White House advisers. Musical-comedy conventions, however, helped make it palatable to 1930 audiences. This was the first of a number of book shows and revues of the Thirties that, influenced by the Depression and the growing threat of another World War, were emboldened to make satirical observations on the problems then besetting the country and the world. Of interest to jazz buffs is that Red Nichols' pit band included such future luminaries as Benny Goodman, Gene Krupa, Glenn Miller, Jimmy Dorsey, and Jack Teagarden.

Flying High. Bert Lahr and Kate Smith. (Vandamm)

FLYING HIGH

Music: Ray Henderson
Lyrics: B. G. DeSylva & Lew Brown
Book: John McGowan, B. G. DeSylva & Lew Brown
Producer: George White
Directors: George White, Edward Clark Lilley
Choreographer: Bobby Connolly
Cast: Bert Lahr, Oscar Shaw, Kate Smith, Grace Brinkley, Russ Brown, Pearl Osgood
Songs: "I'll Know Him"; "Thank Your Father"; "Good for You — Bad for Me"; "Red Hot Chicago"; "Without Love"
New York run: Apollo Theatre, March 3, 1930; 357 p.

With athletic inspiration apparently exhausted, DeSylva, Brown and Henderson followed their musicals about football, boxing, and golf with one dealing with another current obsession, air travel. *Flying High*, however, was still something of a successor to *Hold Everything!* since it again put Bert Lahr in a role that enabled him to play a terrified cluck who must endure torturous preparations before he can triumph in a hazardous occupation. In this show, Lahr appeared as Rusty Krause, an airplane mechanic whose preparations for flight include a hilarious examining-room scene, and whose achievement is setting a record for the number of hours he is able to keep an airplane aloft—because he doesn't have the slightest idea how to get it down. Kate Smith played the comic role of Bert's mail-order fiancée. Lahr repeated his part in the 1931 film version, which also featured Pat O'Brien and Charlotte Greenwood.

71

FINE AND DANDY
Music: Kay Swift
Lyrics: Paul James
Book: Donald Ogden Stewart (Joe Cook uncredited)
Producers: Morris Green & Lewis Gensler
Directors: Morris Green, Frank McCoy
Choreographers: David Gould, Tom Nip
Cast: Joe Cook, Nell O'Day, Dave Chasen, Eleanor Powell, Alice Boulden, Joe Wagstaff
Songs: "Fine and Dandy"; "Can This Be Love?"; "Let's Go Eat Worms in the Garden"; "The Jig Hop"
New York run: Erlanger's Theatre, September 23, 1930; 255 p.

Comic Joe Cook was an innocent looking clown with a wide smile whose specialties were non sequitur stories (including his trademark routine about why he would not imitate four Hawaiians), Rube Goldberg-type inventions, and acrobatic and juggling skills. *Fine and Dandy*, a follow-up to his popular vehicle, *Rain or Shine*, not only included the Cook specialties but also featured a superior score (including the durable title song), the tapping of Eleanor Powell, and a tale that found Cook as Joe Squibb, the general manager of the Fordyce Drop Forge and Tool Factory, who ineptly copes with problems of labor and management. Erlanger's Theatre, now the St. James, stands on 44th Street west of Broadway.

GIRL CRAZY
Music: George Gershwin
Lyrics: Ira Gershwin
Book: Guy Bolton & John McGowan
Producers: Alex A. Aarons & Vinton Freedley
Director: Alexander Leftwich
Choreographer: George Hale
Cast: Willie Howard, Allen Kearns, Ginger Rogers, William Kent, Ethel Merman, Antonio & Renee DeMarco, Lew Parker, Roger Edens, Red Nichols Orchestra
Songs: "Bidin' My Time"; "Could You Use Me?"; "Embraceable You"; "I Got Rhythm"; "But Not for Me"; "Sam and Delilah"; "Treat Me Rough"
New York run: Alvin Theatre, October 14, 1930; 272 p.

Temporarily turning from the satiric world of their recent *Strike Up the Band*, the Gershwin brothers joined their former colleagues, librettist Guy Bolton and producers Aarons and Freedley, to escape to the more innocent world of conventional musical comedy. For *Girl Crazy*, however, they abandoned the East Coast haunts of high society that had been their customary locales in favor of the wide open spaces of Custerville, Arizona. There playboy Danny Churchill (Allen Kearns) has been sent by his wealthy father to manage a ranch in order to keep out of the clutches of predatory females. Arriving by taxi from New York, Danny soon turns the place into a dude ranch where Kate Fothergill (Ethel Merman in her first Broadway role) entertains guests with the undeniable assertion, "I Got Rhythm." Later our hero gets to croon "Embraceable You" with Molly Gray (Ginger Rogers in her second Broadway role), and helps taxi driver-turned-sheriff Gieber Goldfarb (Willie Howard in a part intended for Bert Lahr) apprehend the outlaw who has been threatening his life. Red Nichols' band included the same impressive personnel as in *Strike Up the Band*. Three film adaptations were made of *Girl Crazy*, with Judy Garland and Mickey Rooney co-starred in the 1943 version.
Columbia SC/ TW.

Three's a Crowd. Libby Holman singing "Something to Remember You By" as she bids farewell to matelot Fred MacMurray. (Apeda)

THREE'S A CROWD

Music: Arthur Schwartz, etc.
Lyrics: Howard Dietz, etc.
Sketches: Miscellaneous writers
Producer: Max Gordon
Director: Hassard Short
Choreographer: Albertina Rasch
Cast: Clifton Webb, Fred Allen, Libby Holman, Tamara Geva, Portland Hoffa, Earl Oxford, Fred MacMurray
Songs: "Something to Remember You By"; "Body and Soul" (Johnny Green-Edward Heyman, Robert Sour); "The Moment I Saw You"; "Forget All Your Books" (music: Burton Lane); "Right at the Start of It"
New York run: Selwyn Theatre, October 15, 1930; 272 p.

Once the sponsors of *The Second Little Show* decided that the stars of the first *Little Show* — Clifton Webb, Fred Allen, and Libby Holman — would not be in their new revue, fledgling producer Max Gordon persuaded the trio to appear in his own revue. He further assured that *Three's a Crowd* would be accepted in fact if not in name as the sequel to *The Little Show* by bringing along composer Arthur Schwartz and lyricist Howard Dietz (with Dietz additionally credited with having "conceived and compiled" the new show). The musical standouts of the evening were Miss Holman's masochistic "Body and Soul" and her "Something to Remember You By," a tearful ballad of farewell she sang to a matelot played by Fred MacMurray. Fred Allen won his biggest laughs as explorer Admiral Byrd, who has just returned from the Antarctic to announce his discovery of 500,000 square miles of brand new snow.

THE NEW YORKERS
Music & lyrics: Cole Porter
Book: Herbert Fields
Producer: E. Ray Goetz
Director: Monty Woolley
Choreographer: George Hale
Cast: Frances Williams, Charles King, Hope Williams, Ann Pennington, Richard Carle, Marie Cahill, Fred Waring Orchestra, Clayton, Jackson and Durante, Kathryn Crawford, Oscar Ragland
Songs: "Where Have You Been?"; "Love for Sale"; "Take Me Back to Manhattan"; "Let's Fly Away"; "I Happen to Like New York"
New York run: Broadway Theatre, December 8, 1930; 168 p.

The first stage production at the Broadway Theatre (on 53rd Street), *The New Yorkers* was something of a forerunner of *Pal Joey* in its amoral characters, cynical outlook, and flashy nightclub atmosphere. Just as Cole Porter and Herbert Fields' previous *Fifty Million Frenchmen* had offered a musical tour of Paris, so the new outing (with the same producer and director) offered a musical tour of high and low life in Manhattan, stopping off at a Park Avenue apartment, a speakeasy, a bootleg distillery, the Cotton Club in Harlem, and Reuben's Restaurant on Madison Avenue. The surrealistic satire concerns a socialite (Hope Williams) in love with a bootlegger (Charles King) because she is impressed with the way he bumps people off. Other characters include the lady's philandering parents and an irrepressible gangster henchman (Jimmy Durante), who brings the first act to a riotous close with his description of the varied products made from wood. Soon after the show's opening, Elisabeth Welch replaced Kathryn Crawford to sing the torchy invitation of a streetwalker, "Love for Sale."

THE BAND WAGON
Music: Arthur Schwartz
Lyrics: Howard Dietz
Sketches: George S. Kaufman, Howard Dietz
Producer: Max Gordon
Director: Hassard Short
Choreographer: Albertina Rasch
Cast: Fred & Adele Astaire, Frank Morgan, Helen Broderick, Tilly Losch, Philip Loeb, John Barker
Songs: "Sweet Music"; "High and Low"; "Hoops"; "Confession"; "New Sun in the Sky"; "I Love Louisa"; "Dancing in the Dark"; "White Heat"
New York run: New Amsterdam Theatre, June 3, 1931; 260 p.

Put together by the same creative team that had been responsible for *Three's a Crowd, The Band Wagon* may well have been the most sophisticated, imaginative, and musically distinguished revue ever mounted on Broadway. To assure that the production would have the same homogeneity of style as a book musical, there were no interpolations in the score and only two writers were credited for the sketches. Among the evening's pleasures: Fred and Adele Astaire (in their tenth and last Broadway appearance together) as two French children cavorting to "Hoops"; the principals riding on a Bavarian merry-go-round while singing "I Love Louisa"; Tilly Losch dancing to "Dancing in the Dark" on a slanted, mirrored stage; "The Pride of the Claghornes" sketch spoofing the Southern aristocracy's honor-of-the-family code. *The Band Wagon* was also the first New York production to use a double revolving stage for both its musical numbers and sketches. The 1953 Fred Astaire-Cyd Charisse film retained five songs, added others, and threw in a story line.
RCA OC.; Smithsonian part OC.

Cover designed by John Held, Jr.

The Band Wagon. Adele and Fred Astaire singing "Hoops." (Vandamm)

The Band Wagon. "The Pride of the Claghornes" sketch with Helen Broderick, Adele Astaire, Frank Morgan, and Fred Astaire. (Vandamm)

EARL CARROLL VANITIES

Music: Burton Lane, etc.
Lyrics: Harold Adamson, etc.
Sketches: Ralph Spence, Eddie Welch
Producer-director: Earl Carroll
Choreographers: George Hale, Gluck Sandor
Cast: Will Mahoney, Lillian Roth, William Demarest, Mitchell & Durant, Milton Watson
Songs: "Have a Heart"; "Heigh Ho, the Gang's All Here"; "Good Night, Sweetheart" (Ray Noble-Jimmy Campbell, Reg Connelly); "Tonight or Never" (Vincent Rose-Ray Klages, Jack Meskill)
New York run: Earl Carroll Theatre, August 27, 1931; 278 p.

A major rival to the *Ziegfeld Follies* and the *George White's Scandals* series was the *Earl Carroll Vanities,* which Carroll introduced in 1923. He staged 11 editions of a revue featuring girls even less modestly garbed and production numbers even more overblown than found in similar entertainments then being offered to keep the tired businessman awake. The 1931 edition was the first attraction at the newly built Earl Carroll Theatre at 50th Street and 7th Avenue, situated on the site of the previous theatre of the same name. No longer in existence, the playhouse was as much attraction as the show. Because of its 3,000-seat size, it enabled Carroll to sell orchestra seats at a top price of $3.30, for which theatregoers could enjoy such gaudy delights as a massive "Bolero" ballet accompanied by tom-toms and a "living curtain" of undraped showgirls posing as allegorical figures.

GEORGE WHITE'S SCANDALS

Music: Ray Henderson
Lyrics: Lew Brown
Sketches: Lew Brown, George White, Irving Caesar
Producer-director-choreographer: George White
Cast: Rudy Vallee, Ethel Merman, Willie & Eugene Howard, Everett Marshall, Ray Bolger, Ethel Barrymore Colt, Alice Faye
Songs: "Life Is Just a Bowl of Cherries"; "The Thrill Is Gone"; "This Is the Missus"; "Ladies and Gentlemen, That's Love"; "That's Why Darkies Were Born"; "My Song"
New York run: Apollo Theatre, September 14, 1931; 202 p.

The only challenger to the 1926 *Scandals* (see page 52) as the best of the series was the 11th Edition, which came along in 1931. Ray Henderson and Lew Brown (but minus B. G. DeSylva) were on hand for their fourth and last *Scandals* together with an impressive array of song hits introduced by pop crooner Rudy Vallee, powerhouse belter Ethel Merman (who had joined the cast during the tryout), and robust baritone Everett Marshall. Among the attractions were a celebration of the opening of the Empire State Building with Ray Bolger as a dancing Al Smith (with decor by former Ziegfeld designer Joseph Urban); a chins-up Depression anthem, "Life Is Just a Bowl of Cherries," trumpeted by Miss Merman; Willie and Eugene Howard in their classic comedy sketch "Pay the Two Dollars"; and a bold first-act finale, "That's Why Darkies Were Born," that took a compassionate view of Negro fortitude in the face of injustice.

The Cat and the Fiddle. Georges Metaxa, George Meader, and Bettina Hall. (White)

THE CAT AND THE FIDDLE

Music: Jerome Kern
Lyrics & book: Otto Harbach
Producer: Max Gordon
Director: José Ruben
Choreographer: Albertina Rasch
Cast: Georges Metaxa, Bettina Hall, Odette Myrtil, Eddie Foy Jr., José Ruben, Lawrence Grossmith, Doris Carson, George Meader
Songs: "The Night Was Made for Love"; "I Watch the Love Parade"; "Try to Forget"; "Poor Pierrot"; "She Didn't Say 'Yes' "; "A New Love Is Old"; "One Moment Alone"
New York run: Globe Theatre, October 15, 1931; 395 p.

The Cat and the Fiddle was a generally successful attempt to put the florid operetta form into a contemporary, intimate setting. In creating the work, Jerome Kern and Otto Harbach did without choruses, spectacles, and dragged-in comedy routines to keep the focus on the main story of what they called "A Musical Romance." Set in modern Brussels, it tells of the attraction between Victor Florescu (Georges Metaxa), a serious-minded Rumanian composer, and Shirley Sheridan (Bettina Hall), a vivacious American composer with a penchant for jazz. Though Victor is furious when a producer tries to lighten his rather heavy operetta, *The Passionate Pilgrim*, with some of Shirley's bright, uptempo numbers, true love eventually has hero and heroine singing in harmony. The true hero of the evening, however, was Jerome Kern whose score was an almost continuous flow of melodic pleasures, with songs well integrated into the story and with a highly advanced use of musical underscoring. In 1934, a film version was released starring Jeanette MacDonald and Ramon Novarro.
Epic (SC)/ TW.

OF THEE I SING

Music: George Gershwin
Lyrics: Ira Gershwin
Book: George S. Kaufman & Morrie Ryskind
Producer: Sam H. Harris
Director: George S. Kaufman
Choreographer: George Hale
Cast: William Gaxton, Victor Moore, Lois Moran, Grace Brinkley, June O'Dea, George Murphy, Dudley Clements, Edward H. Robins, Florenz Ames, Ralph Riggs, George E. Mack
Songs: "Wintergreen for President"; "Because, Because"; "Love Is Sweeping the Country"; "Of Thee I Sing, Baby"; "Here's a Kiss for Cinderella"; "Who Cares?"; "Hello, Good Morning"; "The Illegitimate Daughter"
New York run: Music Box, December 26, 1931; 441 p.

Constructed more in the style of a Gilbert and Sullivan comic opera than of a Broadway musical comedy, *Of Thee I Sing* was an extension of the satirical approach of the same writers' previous *Strike Up the Band*. Here, however, the technique was surer and the compromises to popular taste less apparent, with songs and story complementing each other and expressing a uniform point of view. Sharply and deftly skewered were such institutions as political conventions and campaigns, beauty pageants, marriage, the Vice Presidency, the Supreme Court, foreign affairs, and motherhood.

The fanciful tale covers the fortunes of the Presidential ticket of John P. Wintergreen and his running mate, Alexander Throttlebottom — abetted by Wintergreen's bride, Mary Turner (Lois Moran) — which, with its campaign song "Of Thee I Sing, Baby," sweeps the country on a platform of Love. Once in office, however, the President is threatened with impeachment because he jilted Diana Devereaux (Grace Brinkley), the Miss America contest winner he had promised to marry. She, it seems, is "the illegitimate daughter of the illegitimate son of an illegitimate nephew of Napoleon," and France is insulted because of this slight. After the First Lady somehow saves the day by giving birth to twins, France's honor is assuaged when Throttlebottom agrees to wed Diana because, according to the Constitution, "When the President of the United States is unable to fulfil his duties, his obligations are assumed by the Vice President."

Of Thee I Sing, the third longest running musical of the Thirties, became the first musical ever awarded the Pulitzer Prize for drama (though ironically George Gershwin was not included in the citation since his was a musical contribution and therefore not considered eligible for a literary award). It also established brash, sharp-featured William Gaxton and bumbling, dumpling-shaped Victor Moore, who played Wintergreen and Throttlebottom, as Broadway's leading musical-comedy team. After touring, the show returned to New York for a month-long engagement in May 1933. It then resumed its tour with a cast headed by Oscar Shaw, Donald Meek, and Ann Sothern.

In October 1933, a sequel, *Let 'Em Eat Cake,* written by the same writers and featuring the original leading players, opened on Broadway. Supposedly a satire on dictatorship, the show proved too acerbic and thematically confusing, and it remained only three months. The song "Mine," which was in this production, was added to *Of Thee I Sing* when the musical was revived in 1952. Jack Carson and Victor Moore were signed to play Wintergreen and Throttlebottom, but Moore decided against repeating his original role and the part went to Paul Hartman. George S. Kaufman again directed. In 1987, a concert version was performed with *Let 'Em Eat Cake* at the Brooklyn Academy of Music.
Capitol OC (1952); CBS OC (1987)/ Knopf (1932); Samuel French (1935)*; Chilton (1973)/ SF.

Of Thee I Sing. Victor Moore and William Gaxton, surrounded by political advisers, getting ready for the campaign. (Vandamm)

FACE THE MUSIC
Music & lyrics: Irving Berlin
Book: Moss Hart
Producer: Sam H. Harris
Directors: Hassard Short, George S. Kaufman
Choreographer: Albertina Rasch
Cast: Mary Boland, J. Harold Murray, Andrew Tombes, Hugh O'Connell, Katherine Carrington, David Burns
Songs: "Let's Have Another Cup o' Coffee"; "On a Roof in Manhattan"; "Soft Lights and Sweet Music"; "I Say It's Spinach"
New York run: New Amsterdam Theatre, February 17, 1932; 165 p.

The mood of cynicism created by the Depression continued to spawn a number of sharply satirical Broadway musicals. The Gershwin brothers, George S. Kaufman, and Morrie Ryskind had led the way with *Strike Up the Band* and *Of Thee I Sing,* and now it was the turn of Irving Berlin and Moss Hart (with Kaufman joining the project as director). In *Face the Music* the concern was with New York politicians and policemen with little tin boxes, the reduced financial circumstances of the city's elite (former wealthy socialites sing "Let's Have Another Cup o' Coffee" in the Automat), and the insane world of the theatre. In the leading role, Mary Boland played Mrs. Martin Van Buren Meshbesher, the wife of a police sergeant "lousy with money," who tries to lose some of it by backing a tasteless Broadway show, *The Rhinestone Girl,* that surprisingly becomes a hit. Despite the Seabury investigation into police corruption (which also figured in the 1959 musical, *Fiorello!*), the boys in blue manage to beat the rap when Mrs. Meshbesher contributes the profits from the show to the city's depleted treasury. Early in 1933 *Face the Music* returned to Broadway for a month-long run.

FLYING COLORS

Music: Arthur Schwartz
Lyrics & sketches: Howard Dietz
Producer: Max Gordon
Director: Howard Dietz
Choreographer: Albertina Rasch
Cast: Clifton Webb, Charles Butterworth, Tamara Geva, Patsy Kelly, Philip
Loeb, Vilma & Buddy Ebsen, Larry Adler, Imogene Coca, Monette Moore
Songs: "Two-Faced Woman"; "A Rainy Day"; "A Shine on Your Shoes"; "Alone
Together"; "Louisiana Hayride"; "Smokin' Reefers"
New York run: Imperial Theatre, September 15, 1932, 188 p.

Flying Colors flew in a direct line from *The Little Show, Three's a Crowd,* and *The Band Wagon.* Like all three, it had music by Arthur Schwartz and lyrics by Howard Dietz (though this time Dietz also received credit as sole sketch writer and director). Like the most recent two revues, it was produced by Max Gordon and was choreographed by Albertina Rasch, and it also featured two veterans of the series, Clifton Webb and Tamara Geva. Though too closely patterned after its illustrious predecessors (Brooks Atkinson headed his Sunday *Times* piece, "Flying the Band Wagon Colors"), the show was witty and attractive, and had its share of standout numbers: "A Shine on Your Shoes" presented Vilma and Buddy Ebsen dancing around a shoeshine stand accompanied by Larry Adler's harmonica; "Alone Together" offered Webb and Geva in a dramatic, sinuous dance; and "Louisiana Hayride" brought the first act to a jubilant close. Then there was Charles Butterworth's hilarious soapbox speech, "Harvey Woofter's Five Point Plan," on how to end the Depression. Times were tough for the show, too. After opening it at a $4.40 top, Gordon was soon forced to lower the ticket price to $2.20.

Flying Colors. Buddy Ebsen, Monette Moore, Vilma Ebsen, and Larry Adler performing "A Shine on Your Shoes." (White)

MUSIC IN THE AIR

Music: Jerome Kern
Lyrics & book: Oscar Hammerstein II
Producer: Peggy Fears (A. C. Blumenthal uncredited)
Directors: Jerome Kern & Oscar Hammerstein II
Cast: Reinald Werrenrath, Natalie Hall, Tullio Carminati, Katherine Carrington, Al Shean, Walter Slezak, Nicholas Joy, Marjorie Main
Songs: "I've Told Ev'ry Little Star"; "There's a Hill Beyond a Hill"; "And Love Was Born"; "I'm Alone"; "I Am So Eager"; "One More Dance"; "When the Spring Is in the Air"; "In Egern on the Tegern See"; "The Song Is You"; "We Belong Together"
New York run: Alvin Theatre, November 8, 1932; 342 p.

Hailed by Alexander Woollcott in *The New Yorker* as "that endearing refuge, that gracious shelter from a troubled world," the Jerome Kern-Oscar Hammerstein *Music in the Air* continued along the same path as the Jerome Kern-Otto Harbach *Cat and the Fiddle.* The setting was again modern Europe, the story again had to do with the preparations for an operetta, and the songs — among Kern's most memorable — and the underscoring again enhanced the characters and the situations. The plot of this "Musical Adventure" concerns Sieglinde and Karl (Katherine Carrington and Walter Slezak), two Bavarian naifs, who hike from Edendorf to Munich to help Sieglinde's father, Dr. Walther Lessing (Al Shean), interest a music publisher in his new composition, "I've Told Ev'ry Little Star." Soon they become involved with glamorous star Frieda Hatzfeld (Natalie Hall) and her lover, librettist Bruno Mahler (Tullio Carminati), during the rehearsals of Bruno's new work, *Tingle-Tangle.* When the temperamental diva walks out on the production, Sieglinde is given her big chance. Contrary to show-business legend, however, she proves totally inept, and when Frieda comes back Sieglinde sadly returns to her mountain village.

Hammerstein brought *Music in the Air* back to Broadway in 1951, with a cast headed by Jane Pickens (Frieda), Dennis King (Bruno), and Charles Winninger (Lessing). Because of possible anti-German sentiment following World War II, he changed the locale from Munich to Zurich and made everybody Swiss. The show remained less than two months. The 1934 Hollywood version starred Gloria Swanson, John Boles, and Al Shean.
Capitol SC/ Chappell, London (1934)*/ TW.

Music in the Air. Katherine Carrington, Al Shean and Walter Slezak. (Vandamm)

TAKE A CHANCE

Music: Richard A. Whiting, Nacio Herb Brown, Vincent Youmans
Lyrics: B. G. DeSylva
Book: B. G. DeSylva, Laurence Schwab, Sid Silvers
Producers: Laurence Schwab & B. G. DeSylva
Director: Edgar MacGregor
Choreographer: Bobby Connolly
Cast: Jack Haley, Ethel Merman, Jack Whiting, Sid Silvers, June Knight, Mitzi Mayfair, Oscar Ragland, Robert Gleckler
Songs: "Should I Be Sweet?" (Youmans); "Turn Out the Lights" (Whiting, Brown); "Rise 'n' Shine" (Youmans); "You're an Old Smoothie" (Whiting, Brown); "Eadie Was a Lady" (Whiting; lyric with Roger Edens)
New York run: Apollo Theatre, November 26, 1932; 243 p.

In September 1932, a musical titled *Humpty Dumpty* began its tryout tour in Pittsburgh. It involved Lou Holtz, Ethel Merman, and Eddie Foy Jr. in what was basically a revue with songs and sketches dealing with incidents in American history. It was so poorly received that the show closed in five days. Within three weeks, however, the production was totally revised, partly recast (Holtz and Foy were replaced by Jack Whiting and Jack Haley), and had five new songs by Vincent Youmans. Retitled *Take a Chance* — to indicate something of the risks involved — the show was now an old-fashioned book musical concerned with a romance between the leading man and leading lady (Whiting and June Knight) who are appearing in a revue about American history called *Humpty Dumpty*. What turned it into a hit, though, were the comedy and specialty numbers, with Miss Merman given two show stoppers — "Rise 'n' Shine" and "Eadie Was a Lady" — that let her blast her way clear up to the second balcony. During the Broadway run, Haley and Sid Silvers were succeeded by the vaudeville team of Olsen and Johnson. The film version, released in 1933, featured June Knight and Lillian Roth.

GAY DIVORCE

Music & lyrics: Cole Porter
Book: Dwight Taylor
Producers: Dwight Deere Wiman & Tom Weatherly
Director: Howard Lindsay
Choreographers: Carl Randall, Barbara Newberry
Cast: Fred Astaire, Claire Luce, Luella Gear, Betty Starbuck, Erik Rhodes, Eric Blore, G. P. Huntley Jr.
Songs: "After You, Who?"; "Night and Day"; "How's Your Romance?"; "I've Got You on My Mind"; "Mister and Missus Fitch"
New York run: Ethel Barrymore Theatre, November 29, 1932; 248 p.

The first musical to play the Ethel Barrymore Theatre (on 47th Street west of Broadway), *Gay Divorce* was the only stage production in which Fred Astaire performed without sister Adele. In the story, adapted from an unproduced play, Astaire was seen as Guy Holden, a British novelist, who goes to a seaside resort to woo would-be divorcée Mimi Pratt (Claire Luce), primarily by convincing her — through song and dance — that night and day she is the one. Complications arise when Guy is mistaken for a professional corespondent (Erik Rhodes) who has been hired to ease Mimi's divorce. Though Astaire proved that he could carry both a weak plot and a new dancing partner, *Gay Divorce* (without the definite article, please) marked his final appearance on Broadway. The 1934 film version, retitled *The Gay Divorcee,* co-starred Fred with Ginger Rogers.

AS THOUSANDS CHEER

Music & lyrics: Irving Berlin
Sketches: Moss Hart
Producer: Sam H. Harris
Director: Hassard Short
Choreographer: Charles Weidman
Cast: Marilyn Miller, Clifton Webb, Helen Broderick, Ethel Waters, Hal Forde, Jerome Cowan, Harry Stockwell, José Limon, Letitia Ide, Thomas Hamilton, Leslie Adams
Songs: "How's Chances?"; "Heat Wave"; "Lonely Heart"; "Easter Parade"; "Supper Time"; "Harlem on My Mind"; "Not for All the Rice in China"
New York run: Music Box, September 30, 1933; 400 p.

Though it was a revue, the Irving Berlin-Moss Hart *As Thousands Cheer* was considered a successor to the Berlin-Hart book musical, *Face the Music,* since it also dealt satirically with topics of current interest. In fact, it was so concerned with topicality that the entire show was structured in the form of a newspaper, with various stories and features — each one preceded by a blowup of a headline — depicted in songs, dances and sketches. In addition to general news, there were sections devoted to comics, rotogravure (an opportunity to show the Easter Parade of half a century earlier), society, theatre, the weather report ("Heat Wave"), and advice to the lovelorn ("Lonely Heart"). As might be expected in a lighthearted entertainment, serious topics were avoided except for Ethel Waters' purposely jarring "Supper Time," introduced by the headline "UNKNOWN NEGRO LYNCHED BY FRENZIED MOB." Newsworthy individuals impersonated in the noteworthy show were Barbara Hutton and Joan Crawford (by Marilyn Miller in her 12th and final Broadway appearance); Douglas Fairbanks Jr., John D. Rockefeller, and Mahatma Gandhi (by Clifton Webb); Louise Hoover, Aimee Semple MacPherson, Queen Mary, and the Statue of Liberty (by Helen Broderick); and Josephine Baker (by Miss Waters).

As Thousands Cheer. King George V (Leslie Adams) and Queen Mary (Helen Broderick) are upset to read of the latest romantic escapade involving the Prince of Wales (Thomas Hamilton). (Vandamm)

ROBERTA

Music: Jerome Kern
Lyrics & book: Otto Harbach
Producer: Max Gordon
Director: (Hassard Short uncredited)
Choreographer: José Limon (John Lonergan uncredited)
Cast: Lyda Roberti, Bob Hope, Fay Templeton, Tamara, George Murphy, Sydney Greenstreet, Ray Middleton, Fred MacMurray
Songs: "Let's Begin"; "You're Devastating"; "Yesterdays"; "The Touch of Your Hand"; "I'll Be Hard to Handle" (lyric: Bernard Dougall); "Smoke Gets in Your Eyes"; "Something Had to Happen"
New York run: New Amsterdam Theatre, November 18, 1933; 295 p.

Based on Alice Duer Miller's popular novel, *Gowns by Roberta* (the original title was still used during the tryout), the production was expected to follow *The Cat and the Fiddle* and *Music in the Air* as another of Jerome Kern's well-integrated modern operettas set in present-day Europe. The work, however, turned out to be more of a formula musical comedy dependent upon sumptuously mounted production numbers (one was a fashion show), some comic interpolations, and a superior collection of songs — including "Smoke Gets in Your Eyes" and "Yesterdays" — that bore little relevance to the plot. Said plot had to do with a former All-American fullback, John Kent (Ray Middleton), who inherits a Paris dress salon owned by his Aunt Minnie (Fay Templeton). John also ends with Minnie's assistant, Russian Princess Stephanie (Tamara), as both business and marital partner. Bob Hope, in his first major Broadway role, played John's bandleader chum, Huckleberry Haines. Though *Roberta* was initially directed by Kern himself, the composer was replaced by the more experienced Hassard Short who refused program credit. In 1935, the first of two screen versions co-starred Irene Dunne, Fred Astaire, and Ginger Rogers.
Columbia SC/ TW.

Roberta. Bob Hope catches Lyda Roberti and Ray Middleton in an embarrassing situation. (Vandamm)

Ziegfeld Follies. Willie Howard and Fanny Brice in the sketch based on *Sailor, Beware!*

ZIEGFELD FOLLIES

Music: Vernon Duke, etc.
Lyrics: E. Y. Harburg, etc.
Sketches: Miscellaneous writers
Producer: Billie Burke Ziegfeld (Messrs. Shubert uncredited)
Directors: Bobby Connolly, Edward Clark Lilley, John Murray Anderson
Choreographers: Bobby Connolly, Robert Alton
Cast: Fanny Brice, Willie & Eugene Howard, Everett Marshall, Jane Froman, Vilma & Buddy Ebsen, Patricia Bowman, Cherry & June Preisser, Eve Arden, Robert Cummings, Ina Ray Hutton
Songs: "I Like the Likes of You"; "Suddenly"; "What Is There to Say?"; "The Last Round-Up" (Billy Hill); "Wagon Wheels" (Peter DeRose-Hill)
New York run: Winter Garden, January 4, 1934; 182 p.

In the mid-Thirties the Shubert brothers offered five revues at the Winter Garden that won general approval for their high level of comedy, inventive staging, attractive decor, and musical quality. The first of these, the 1934 *Ziegfeld Follies,* had begun its tryout tour so unpromisingly, however, that director John Murray Anderson and choreographer Robert Alton were rushed in to replace Bobby Connolly. They just barely whipped things into shape in time for the Broadway opening. To add authenticity to the show, the nominal sponsor was Ziegfeld's widow, Billie Burke, and the leading comic attracton was *Follies* veteran Fanny Brice. Miss Brice did takeoffs on evangelist Aimee Semple MacPherson and strip-tease dancers, impersonated a bratty child known as Baby Snooks, and appeared with another great clown, Willie Howard, in a frantic burlesque of the play *Sailor, Beware!* The durable "I Like the Likes of You" was sung in the show by Robert Cummings and danced to by Vilma and Buddy Ebsen.

NEW FACES

Music, lyrics & sketches: Miscellaneous writers
Producer: Charles Dillingham (Leonard Sillman uncredited)
Director-choreographer: Leonard Sillman
Cast: Leonard Sillman, Imogene Coca, Nancy Hamilton, Charles Walters, Henry Fonda, Teddy Lynch, James Shelton, Billie Heywood
Songs: "Lamplight" (James Shelton); "My Last Affair" (Haven Johnson); "The Gutter Song" (Shelton); "You're My Relaxation" (Charles Schwab-Robert Sour)
New York run: Fulton Theatre, March 15, 1934; 149 p.

Originally presented in Pasadena as *Low and Behold,* Leonard Sillman's *New Faces* had to give 137 auditions before the needed $15,000 was raised to open at the Fulton Theatre (then on 46th Street west of Broadway). Under the "supervision" of Elsie Janis, Sillman's dewy-eyed, intimate revue served much the same function as *The Garrick Gaieties* by providing a showcase for hitherto undiscovered talent — such as Henry Fonda, future film director Charles Walters, and chief comedienne Imogene Coca (though she had been around since 1925). Audiences particularly enjoyed Miss Coca's impish fan dance while bundled in an oversized polo coat, Nancy Hamilton's sketch in which "The Three Little Pigs" was presented in the manner of three recent dramas, and the song, "Lamplight," sung by its composer James Shelton. *New Faces* marked the 62nd and final Broadway musical credited to producer Charles Dillingham, who had merely lent the prestige of his name to the entertainment and who died five months after the opening. Sillman staged six subsequent editions of the tyro talent show, with the most successful offered in 1952 (see page 154.)

New Faces. Imogene Coca in her polo coat.

LIFE BEGINS AT 8:40

Music: Harold Arlen
Lyrics: Ira Gershwin & E. Y. Harburg
Sketches: Miscellaneous writers
Producers: Messrs. Shubert
Directors: John Murray Anderson, Philip Loeb
Choreographers: Robert Alton, Charles Weidman
Cast: Bert Lahr, Ray Bolger, Luella Gear, Frances Williams, Brian Donlevy, Dixie Dunbar, Earl Oxford
Songs: "You're a Builder-Upper"; "Fun to Be Fooled"; "What Can You Say in a Love Song?"; "Let's Take a Walk Around the Block"; "Things"
New York run: Winter Garden, August 27, 1934; 237 p.

The second of the Shubert-sponsored Winter Garden revues in the mid-Thirties, *Life Begins at 8:40* had something of the style of *The Band Wagon* and the topicality of *As Thousands Cheer*. With John Murray Anderson in overall charge, it was also the successor to the Anderson-directed *Ziegfeld Follies* that had opened the same year. (The show's title, which recalled Walter Pitkin's bestseller, *Life Begins at Forty*, referred to the time the curtain went up.) Again the accent was on comedy, with Bert Lahr winning praise for his newly acquired satirical skill, as revealed in his characterizations of a suicidally bent Frenchman, a stiff-upper-lip Englishman, and a pompous concert baritone sputtering about "the utter utter utter loveliness of things." Also well received were Ray Bolger's dance interpretation of the recent Max Baer-Primo Carnera championship fight and Luella Gear's takeoff on the peripatetic Eleanor Roosevelt breathlessly enumerating her day's activities.

THE GREAT WALTZ

Music: Johann Strauss Jr.
Lyrics: Desmond Carter
Book: Moss Hart
Producer: Max Gordon
Director: Hassard Short
Choreographer: Albertina Rasch
Cast: Marion Claire, Marie Burke, Guy Robertson, H. Reeves-Smith, Ernest Cossart, Alexandra Danilova
Songs: "You Are My Song"; "Love Will Find You"; "Like a Star in the Sky"; "With All My Heart"; "While You Love Me"; "Danube So Blue"
New York run: Center Theatre, September 22, 1934; 298 p.

One of the truly mammoth undertakings of the mid-Thirties, *The Great Waltz* opened at the 3,822-seat Center Theatre (then in Rockefeller Center one block south of the Radio City Music Hall) with 23 actors, 77 singers, 33 ballet dancers, 53 musicians, 90 backstage workers, and a wardrobe of over 500 costumes. The production cost, among the highest of any show to date, was $246,000. Based on an English version of a Viennese musical called *Waltzes from Vienna*, the operetta deals with the rivalry between Johann Strauss Sr. and Johann Strauss Jr., played by H. Reeves-Smith and Guy Robertson. After jealously thwarting his son's advancement, the old Waltz King — in the show's spectacular climax at Dommayer's Gardens — reluctantly abdicates his title when the younger man takes over the baton to conduct "The Blue Danube" (here titled "Danube So Blue"). Though critics were divided, *The Great Waltz* had a respectable run (at a $3.30 top), and reopened for an additional 49 performances in August 1935. AEI SC/ Capitol Los Angeles OC (1965)/ TW.

ANYTHING GOES

Music & lyrics: Cole Porter
Book: Guy Bolton & P. G. Wodehouse, Howard Lindsay & Russel Crouse
Producer: Vinton Freedley
Director: Howard Lindsay
Choreographer: Robert Alton
Cast: William Gaxton, Ethel Merman, Victor Moore, Bettina Hall, Vera Dunn, Leslie Barrie, Vivian Vance, Helen Raymond, George E. Mack, Houston Richards
Songs: "I Get a Kick Out of You"; "There'll Always Be a Lady Fair"; "All Through the Night"; "You're the Top"; "Anything Goes"; "Blow, Gabriel, Blow"; "Be Like the Bluebird"; "The Gypsy in Me"
New York run: Alvin Theatre, November 21, 1934; 420 p.

Following the debacle of a musical comedy called *Pardon My English* early in 1933, producer Vinton Freedley had to flee the country to avoid creditors. To help clear his mind and regain his health, Freedley spent most of his time in a fishing boat off the Pearl Island in the Gulf of Panama. While fishing he envisaged the perfect musical comedy with which he would launch his comeback: William Gaxton, Victor Moore, and Ethel Merman would play the leading roles, the score would be written by Cole Porter, and the libretto would be by the veteran team of Guy Bolton and P. G. Wodehouse who would tie everything together in a fun-filled story about a group of oddball characters on an ocean liner that is facing a bomb threat.

Once he returned to New York and paid off his debts, the producer rounded up his people for what was originally called *Bon Voyage,* then *Hard to Get.* With rehearsals about to begin, disaster struck when the *S.S. Morro Castle* went down in flames off the New Jersey coast with a loss of over 125 lives. Obviously, the script had to be changed. Since Bolton and Wodehouse were then in Europe, Freedley, in desperation, turned to his director, Howard Lindsay, who agreed to undertake the rewriting with a press agent and part-time librettist named Russel Crouse (Thereby launching the celebrated team that would be responsible for a total of seven musical-comedy librettos and eight plays).

Though still taking place on shipboard, the new story eliminated the bomb scare but retained the leading characters of the original plot: nightclub singer Reno Sweeney (Merman), her chum Billy Crocker (Gaxton) who stows away to be near Hope Harcourt (Bettina Hall), the debutante he loves, and Moon-Face Mooney (Moore). Public Enemy No. 13, who masquerades as a clergyman to avoid the long arm of the FBI. It may have been created out of tragedy, but *Anything Goes* (the title was chosen to indicate the desperation with which the show was put together) turned out to be the fourth longest running musical of the Thirties as well as one of the decade's most durable attractions. Porter's score, considered his best to date, included three Merman trademarks — "I Get a Kick Out of You," "You're the Top" (a duet with Gaxton), and "Blow, Gabriel, Blow." During the Broadway run, Miss Merman was succeeded by Benay Venuta.

Anything Goes was revived Off Broadway in 1962 with Hal Linden, Eileen Rodgers, and Mickey Deems, and a number of Porter interpolations. It ran 239 performances. In 1987, it was given a new production at Lincoln Center's Vivian Beaumount Theatre, which had the longest run of all. During the engagement, Patti LuPone was succeeded by Leslie Uggams, Howard McGillin by Gregg Edelman. (See page 277.) The 1936 film version offered Ethel Merman plus Bing Crosby and Charlie Ruggles; the 1956 film of the same name, also with Crosby, had nothing in common with the original except for 5 songs.
Smithsonian part OC; Epic OC (1962), RCA (1987)/TW.

Anything Goes. Ethel Merman leading the chorus in "Blow, Gabriel, Blow." (Vandamm)

AT HOME ABROAD
Music: Arthur Schwartz
Lyrics: Howard Dietz
Sketches: Miscellaneous writers
Producers: Messrs. Shubert
Directors: Vincente Minnelli, Thomas Mitchell
Choreographers: Gene Snyder, Harry Losee
Cast: Beatrice Lillie, Ethel Waters, Herb Williams, Eleanor Powell, Paul Haakon, Reginald Gardiner, Eddie Foy Jr., Vera Allen, John Payne
Songs: "Hottentot Potentate"; "Paree"; "Thief in the Night"; "Love Is a Dancing Thing"; "Loadin' Time"; "What a Wonderful World"; "Get Yourself a Geisha"; "Got a Bran' New Suit"
New York run: Winter Garden, September 19, 1935; 198 p.

Structured in the form of an around-the-world cruise — though carefully avoiding such countries as Germany, Italy, and Russia — *At Home Abroad* provided theatregoers with the chance to be abroad at home as they savored the pleasures of a variety of comic and colorful locales. These included a London department store for Beatrice Lillie's classic tongue-twisting sketch about ordering two dozen double damask dinner napkins; an African jungle where Ethel Waters proclaims herself the "Hottentot Potentate"; the Moulin Rouge in Paris to offer Miss Lillie's paean to the wonders of the city; a Balkan country where Eleanor Powell taps out spy messages; a West Indies dockside for Miss Waters' throbbing description "Loadin' Time"; and a Japanese garden where Miss Lillie joins a bevy of Nipponese maidens in extolling the advantages of getting one's self a geisha. The third Shubert-sponsored Winter Garden revue of the mid-Thirties, *At Home Abroad* marked the first complete stage production directed by Vincente Minnelli. In 1948, Arthur Schwartz and Howard Dietz conducted a more limited revue tour, *Inside U.S.A.*, which also starred Beatrice Lillie. Smithsonian OC.

Porgy and Bess. Ruby Elzy and J. Rosamond Johnson in the saucer burial scene. Anne Brown and Todd Duncan are to their left. (Vandamm)

Porgy and Bess. The setting of Catfish Row, designed by Sergei Soudeikine. (Vandamm)

PORGY AND BESS

Music: George Gershwin
Lyrics: DuBose Heyward, Ira Gershwin
Book: DuBose Heyward
Producer: Theatre Guild
Director: Rouben Mamoulian
Cast: Todd Duncan, Anne Brown, Warren Coleman, John W. Bubbles, Abbie Mitchell, Ruby Elzy, Georgette Harvey, Edward Matthews, Helen Dowdy, J. Rosamond Johnson
Songs: "Summertime" (Heyward); "A Woman Is a Sometime Thing" (Heyward); "My Man's Gone Now" (Heyward); "I Got Plenty o' Nuttin'" (Heyward, Gershwin); "Bess, You Is My Woman Now" (Heyward, Gershwin); "It Ain't Necessarily So" (Gershwin); "I Loves You, Porgy" (Heyward, Gershwin); "There's a Boat Dat's Leavin' Soon for New York" (Gershwin); "I'm on My Way" (Heyward)
New York run: Alvin Theatre, October 10, 1935; 124 p.

Universally accepted as the most popular opera written by an American composer, *Porgy and Bess* began life in 1925 as the novel *Porgy* by DuBose Heyward. Heyward's setting of Catfish Row in Charleston, South Carolina, and his dramatic story of the crippled beggar Porgy, the seductive Bess, the menacing Crown, and the slinky cocaine dealer Sportin' Life fired George Gershwin's imagination even before Heyward and his wife, Dorothy, adapted the book into a play two years later. After a number of delays, Gershwin began writing the opera late in 1933 with Heyward as librettist-lyricist and brother Ira Gershwin as co-lyricist. The composer's last Broadway score, the work was completed — including Gershwin's own orchestrations — in 20 months.

The initial production, with Todd Duncan and Anne Brown in the leads, was treated as such a major event that the larger dailies dispatched both their drama and music critics to cover the opening. It was not, however, a commercial success, though many of the solos and duets — "Summertime," "Bess, You Is My Woman Now," "I Got Plenty o' Nuttin'," "It Ain't Necessarily So" — soon caught on. Four revivals of *Porgy and Bess* have had extended Broadway runs. In 1942, again with Todd Duncan and Anne Brown but with Avon Long replacing John W. Bubbles as Sportin' Life, the musical ran successfully for 286 performances (at a $2.75 top ticket price) in a somewhat streamlined version with a smaller orchestra and no recitative. It was produced by Cheryl Crawford and directed by Robert Ross. The production then toured for 17 months, including a two-month return visit to New York. Ten years later, one of the most ambitious projects in theatre history was inaugurated with a four-year international tour directed by co-producer Robert Breen. Still more musical drama than opera, *Porgy and Bess* was performed in 23 cities in the United States and Canada, and — under the auspices of the State Department — in 28 countries throughout Europe (including well-publicized engagements in Leningrad and Moscow), the Middle East and Latin America. This company's 1953 stay in New York had the longest run the work has had to date. (See page 156.)

A mounting in 1976 by the Houston Grand Opera was staged at the Uris (now the Gershwin) Theatre on 51st Street west of Broadway. With an acclaimed performance by Clamma Dale as Bess and all the original musical portions restored, the production came closest to the composer's concept of the work as an opera. It was also the basis for the 1983 revival, the first adult, full-scale dramatic work ever staged at the 6,000-seat Radio City Music Hall. Two years later, on its 50th anniversary, *Porgy and Bess* entered the repertory of the Metropolitan Opera. In 1959, a screen adaptation was released with Sidney Poitier, Dorothy Dandridge, and Sammy Davis Jr.

MCA OC (1942); Columbia SC; RCA OC (1953); RCA OC (1976)/ Chilton (1973)/ TW.

JUBILEE

Music & lyrics: Cole Porter
Book: Moss Hart
Producers: Sam H. Harris & Max Gordon
Directors: Hassard Short, Monty Woolley
Choreographer: Albertina Rasch
Cast: Mary Boland, June Knight, Melville Cooper, Charles Walters, Derek Williams, Mark Plant, Montgomery Clift, May Boley, Margaret Adams
Songs: "Why Shouldn't I?"; "Begin the Beguine"; "A Picture of Me Without You"; "Me and Marie"; "Just One of Those Things"
New York run: Imperial Theatre, October 12, 1935; 169 p.

Seeking suitable inspiration for an elegant song-and-dance entertainment, Cole Porter and Moss Hart took off on a four-and-a-half month, 34,000-mile cruise around the world. Their hegira resulted in an airy concoction sparked by the recent Silver Jubilee of Britain's King George V and Queen Mary. The tale concerns itself with what might happen if members of a mythical royal family — thanks to a supposed uprising — were given the chance to do what they wanted while gadding about town incognito. King Melville Cooper spends his time perfecting sleight-of-hand tricks, Queen Mary Boland is thrilled to meet Mowgli the movie ape man, Prince Charles Walters learns how to begin the beguine from dancer June Knight, and Princess Margaret Adams answers her own question in "Why Shouldn't I?" by having just one of those crazy flings with a Noel Coward-type playwright. Then it's back to the pomp and circumstance of the royal jubilee. Though beloved by her theatre-going subjects, Miss Boland had to return to Hollywood after only four months; her successor Laura Hope Crews couldn't keep the celebration going a month.

Jubilee. Mary Boland and Melville Cooper singing "Me and Marie." (Vandamm)

JUMBO

Music: Richard Rodgers
Lyrics: Lorenz Hart
Book: Ben Hecht & Charles MacArthur
Producer: Billy Rose
Directors: John Murray Anderson, George Abbott
Choreographer: Allan K. Foster
Cast: Jimmy Durante, Paul Whiteman Orchestra, Donald Novis, Gloria Grafton, A. P. Kaye, A. Robins, Poodles Hanneford, Big Rosie, Tilda Getze
Songs: "Over and Over Again"; "The Circus Is on Parade"; "The Most Beautiful Girl in the World"; "My Romance"; "Little Girl Blue"
New York run: Hippodrome, November 16, 1935; 233 p.

The Hippodrome, once located on 43rd Street and 6th Avenue, was a huge barn of a theatre that had not been in use for five years when showman Billy Rose decided that it would be just the place to house the spectacular circus musical he named *Jumbo.* Designer Albert Johnson completely rebuilt the auditorium to make it resemble an actual circus, with a grandstand sloping up from a single circular revolving stage. The show marked the first of 34 musicals directed by George Abbott as well as the return to Broadway of Rodgers and Hart after almost three years in Hollywood. Plotted by Ben Hecht and Charles MacArthur to give plenty of opportunity for the specialty acts recruited from all over the world, the book had to do with a debt-ridden circus and what the well-meaning but inept publicity man Claudius B. Bowers (Jimmy Durante) does to help save the day. *Jumbo* cost an unprecedented $340,000 to open; it closed after rehearsing for six months and playing for five. The evening's highlight: the blue-tinted first-act finale, "Little Girl Blue," in which heroine Gloria Grafton (who had replaced Ella Logan before the premiere) dreams she is a child again being entertained by her favorite circus performers. Durante was also in the 1962 screen version, along with Doris Day and Martha Raye.

ZIEGFELD FOLLIES

Music: Vernon Duke
Lyrics: Ira Gershwin
Sketches: David Freedman
Producer: Billie Burke Ziegfeld (Messrs. Shubert uncredited)
Directors: John Murray Anderson, Edward Clark Lilley
Choreographers: Robert Alton, George Balanchine
Cast: Fanny Brice, Bob Hope, Gertrude Niesen, Josephine Baker, Hugh O'Connell, Harriet Hoctor, Eve Arden, Judy Canova, Cherry & June Preisser, Nicholas Brothers, John Hoysradt, Stan Kavanaugh
Songs: "Island in the West Indies"; "Words Without Music"; "That Moment of Moments"; "I Can't Get Started"
New York run: Winter Garden, January 30, 1936; 115 p.

Fanny Brice returned for her second Shubert-sponsored *Ziegfeld Follies* (it was her 15th and final Broadway show), along with a number of holdovers from the 1934 edition. They were joined by ballet choreographer George Balanchine making his Broadway debut. The revue was deemed superior to its predecessor, with Miss Brice up to her old shtick kidding modern dancing and playing Baby Snooks, and Bob Hope getting the chance to butter up Eve Arden in the classic "I Can't Get Started." Another highlight was the first-act finale spoofing the latest Hollywood extravaganza, "The Broadway Gold Melody Diggers of 42nd Street." The *Follies* reopened in the fall for 112 additional performances with Jane Pickens, Gypsy Rose Lee, and Cass Daley joining the cast.

ON YOUR TOES

Music: Richard Rodgers
Lyrics: Lorenz Hart
Book: Richard Rodgers, Lorenz Hart & George Abbott
Producer: Dwight Deere Wiman
Director: Worthington Miner (George Abbott uncredited)
Choreographer: George Balanchine
Cast: Ray Bolger, Luella Gear, Tamara Geva, Monty Woolley, Doris Carson, David Morris, Demetrios Vilan, George Church
Songs: "The Three B's"; "It's Got to Be Love"; "Too Good for the Average Man"; "There's a Small Hotel"; "The Heart Is Quicker Than the Eye"; "Quiet Night"; "Glad to Be Unhappy"; "On Your Toes"; "Slaughter on Tenth Avenue" (ballet)
New York run: Imperial Theatre, April 11, 1936; 315 p.

On Your Toes made a star of rubberlegged dancer Ray Bolger, and it also gave George Balanchine his first opportunity to create dances for a book musical. Most important, it signaled a major breakthrough in form by utilizing ballet as an integral part of the story. Junior Dolan (Bolger), an ex-vaudevillian now teaching music at Knickerbocker University, a WPA extension in New York, enlists the help of patroness Peggy Porterfield (Luella Gear) to persuade Sergei Alexandrovich (Monty Woolley), the director of the Russian Ballet, to stage a friend's jazzy "Slaughter on Tenth Avenue" ballet. While he may dream of sharing the pleasures of a small hotel with girlfriend Frankie Frayne (Doris Carson), Junior becomes involved with the company's prima ballerina, Vera Barnova (Tamara Geva), and even takes over the male lead in "Slaughter." This so enrages Vera's lover and regular dancing partner that he hires two thugs to kill Junior while he is performing on stage. To avoid being a target Junior keeps dancing even after the ballet is over, then — once the gunmen have been arrested — falls exhausted to the floor.

Richard Rodgers and Lorenz Hart had originally written the musical as a movie vehicle for Fred Astaire, but the dancer turned it down because he was afraid his public would not accept him without his trademark attire of top hat, white tie and tails. The team then rewrote the script as a stage musical and Lee Shubert took an option on it with Ray Bolger set for the male lead. When Shubert lost interest, the rights were picked up by Dwight Deere Wiman (it was the first of five Rodgers and Hart shows he would produce), with George Abbott joining the project as co-author and director. Production delays, however, prompted Abbott to withdraw as director, though he did return to restage the musical after its poorly-received Boston opening. Originally, Marilyn Miller and Gregory Ratoff were sought for the roles that went to Miss Geva and Mr. Woolley.

There have been two revivals of *On Your Toes* on Broadway. In 1954, Abbott and Balanchine put together a production starring Bobby Van, Vera Zorina (she had appeared in the role of the ballerina in London and in the movie version), and Elaine Stritch (who played Peggy and sang the interpolated "You Took Advantage of Me"). The general verdict was that the musical was hopelessly dated and it remained only two months. Twenty-nine years later, however, again staged by Abbott, it succeeded so well that it bested the original Broadway run. Natalia Makarova of the American Ballet Theatre made an impressive Main Stem debut in the show. She was replaced during the engagement by ballerinas Galina Panova and Valentina Kozlova, and Dina Merrill was replaced by Kitty Carlisle. (See page 264.) The 1939 movie, with Eddie Albert as Junior, used music only as background and for the ballets.

Columbia SC; MCA OC (1954); Polydor OC (1983)/ R&H.

On Your Toes. Luella Gear, Monty Woolley, Ray Bolger, and Demetrios Vilan. (White)

On Your Toes. Ray Bolger, George Church, and Tamara Geva in a dramatic moment from "Slaughter on Tenth Avenue." (White)

Red, Hot and Blue! Ethel Merman and Bob Hope. (Vandamm)

RED, HOT AND BLUE!

Music & lyrics: Cole Porter
Book: Howard Lindsay & Russel Crouse
Producer: Vinton Freedley
Director: Howard Lindsay
Choreographer: George Hale
Cast: Jimmy Durante, Ethel Merman, Bob Hope, Polly Walters, Paul & Grace Hartman, Vivian Vance, Lew Parker
Songs: "Ours"; "Down in the Depths (on the Ninetieth Floor)"; "You've Got Something"; "It's De-Lovely"; "Ridin' High"; "Red, Hot and Blue"
New York run: Alvin Theatre, October 29, 1936; 183 p.

Anxious to repeat the success of *Anything Goes,* producer Vinton Freedley signed its three stars and its three writers for his next musical, *Red, Hot and Blue!* But after overhearing Freedley promise Ethel Merman that hers would be the most prominent role, William Gaxton and Victor Moore bowed out and were replaced by Bob Hope and Jimmy Durante. The show, which seemed to be aiming for *Of Thee I Sing*-type political satire, offered Miss Merman as Nails O'Reilly Duquesne, a manicurist-turned-wealthy widow, Hope as Bob Hale, her lawyer and love interest, and Durante as Policy Pinkle, the captain of the polo team at Larks Nest Prison. Pinkle is released to help win a Congressional committee's approval for Nails and Bob's national lottery in which the first prize goes to the ticket holder who finds a girl who had sat on a hot waffle iron when she was four. The Supreme Court, however, declares the lottery unconstitutional on the grounds that it might benefit the American people. Though no red hot smash, the musical served to introduce three certifiable Cole Porter standards: "It's De-Lovely," "Down in the Depths," and "Ridin' High." It is also remembered for the battle of the billing, which was resolved by crossing the names of Jimmy Durante and Ethel Merman above the show's title.
AEI OC.

Note that Vincente Minnelli's name is misspelled twice.

THE SHOW IS ON

Music & lyrics: Miscellaneous writers
Sketches: David Freedman, Moss Hart
Producers: Messrs. Shubert
Directors: Vincente Minnelli, Edward Clark Lilley
Choreographer: Robert Alton, Harry Losee
Cast: Beatrice Lillie, Bert Lahr, Reginald Gardiner, Mitzi Mayfair, Paul Haakon, Gracie Barrie, Charles Walters, Vera Allen, Jack McCauley
Songs: "Now" (Vernon Duke-Ted Fetter); "Rhythm" (Richard Rodgers- Lorenz Hart); "Song of the Woodman" (Harold Arlen-E. Y. Harburg); "Long as You've Got Your Health" (Will Irwin-Harburg, Norman Zeno); "By Strauss" (George Gershwin-Ira Gershwin); "Little Old Lady" (Hoagy Carmichael-Stanley Adams)
New York run: Winter Garden, December 25, 1936; 237 p.

The fifth and final mid-Thirties revue presented by the Shuberts at the Winter Garden was one of the brightest, merriest, and most elegant of the decade's stage attractions. Featuring two superior clowns, Beatrice Lillie and Bert Lahr, *The Show Is On* was something of a successor to *At Home Abroad,* only this time the theme was around the world of show business. In songs, sketches, and production numbers, it looked in on a variety of phenomena and events — from excessively rhythmic pop singers to raffish burlesque shows, from John Gielgud's production of *Hamlet* (which is ruined by the outbursts of Miss Lillie's boorish socialite) to coquettish music-hall entertainers (Miss Lillie perched on a migratory half moon dispensing garters to favored gentlemen), and from he-man concert baritones (Lahr's classic "Song of the Woodman") to an old-fashioned tent show production of *Uncle Tom's Cabin. The Show Is On* returned briefly in the fall of 1937 with Rose King and Willie Howard.

BABES IN ARMS

Music: Richard Rodgers
Lyrics: Lorenz Hart
Book: Richard Rodgers & Lorenz Hart
Producer: Dwight Deere Wiman
Director: Robert Sinclair
Choreographer: George Balanchine
Cast: Mitzi Green, Wynn Murray, Ray Heatherton, Duke McHale, Alfred Drake, Ray McDonald, Grace McDonald, Nicholas Brothers, Dan Dailey
Songs: "Where or When"; "Babes in Arms"; "I Wish I Were in Love Again"; "My Funny Valentine"; "Johnny One Note"; "Imagine"; "All at Once"; "The Lady Is a Tramp"; "You Are So Fair"
New York run: Shubert Theatre, April 14, 1937; 289 p.

With such songs as "I Wish I Were in Love Again," "Johnny One Note," "The Lady Is a Tramp," "My Funny Valentine," and "Where or When," *Babes in Arms* could claim more hits than any other Rodgers and Hart musical. In the high-spirited, youthful show, a group of teenagers, whose parents are out-of-work vaudevillians, stage a revue to keep from being sent to a work farm. Unfortunately, the show is a bomb. Later, when a transatlantic French flyer lands nearby, they are able to attract enough publicity to put on a successful show and build their own youth center. Because the sets were modest and the cast boasted no stellar names, producer Dwight Deere Wiman priced his tickets at a $3.85 top. Among the show's Broadway debuts were those of Alfred Drake (he sang the title song) and Dan Dailey. The 1939 movie version featured Judy Garland and Mickey Rooney.
Columbia SC/ R&H.

I'D RATHER BE RIGHT

Music: Richard Rodgers
Lyrics: Lorenz Hart
Book: George S. Kaufman & Moss Hart
Producer: Sam H. Harris
Director: George S. Kaufman
Choreographers: Charles Weidman, Ned McGurn
Cast: George M. Cohan, Taylor Holmes, Joy Hodges, Austin Marshall, Marion Green, Mary Jane Walsh
Songs: "Have You Met Miss Jones?"; "Sweet Sixty-Five"; "We're Going to Balance the Budget"; "I'd Rather Be Right"; "Off the Record"
New York run: Alvin Theatre, November 2, 1937; 290 p.

I'd Rather Be Right was the most anxiously awaited theatrical event of the decade for two reasons: the central character was President Franklin D. Roosevelt and the part was being played by the legendary George M. Cohan, who was returning to the musical stage for the first time in ten years in the only song-and-dance show he ever appeared in that he did not write himself. The work, however, was considered not quite up to the satirical standards set by *Of Thee I Sing*, with which it was most frequently compared. The locale is New York's Central Park on the 4th of July. Peggy and Phil (Joy Hodges and Austin Marshall) hope to get married but Phil's boss won't give him a raise until Roosevelt balances the budget. Phil falls asleep and dreams that they meet FDR strolling through the park. After Phil explains the couple's dilemma, Roosevelt promises to help — which is only an excuse for some genial ribbing at the expense of Cabinet members, the Supreme Court, the PWA, fireside chats, Alf Landon, press conferences, and the President's decision to seek a third term.
Random House (1937)/ R&H.

I'd Rather Be Right. George M. Cohan as President Franklin D. Roosevelt giving a 4th of July speech. (Vandamm)

PINS AND NEEDLES
Music & lyrics: Harold Rome
Sketches: Miscellaneous writers
Producer: ILGWU
Director: Charles Friedman
Choreographer: Gluck Sandor
Cast: ILGWU members
Songs: "Sing Me a Song With Social Significance"; "Sunday in the Park"; "Nobody Makes a Pass at Me"; "Chain Store Daisy"; "One Big Union for Two"; "Four Little Angels of Peace"; "Doin' the Reactionary"
New York run: Labor Stage, November 27, 1937; 1,108 p.

Pins and Needles was initially presented for a limited engagement at the tiny Labor Stage (formerly the Princess Theatre) by and for members of the International Ladies Garment Workers Union, but it soon attracted audiences in such droves that it kept on running until it overtook *Irene* as the long-run record holder for musicals. Though reflecting a basically liberal, pro-union slant, the attitude was generally good-humored as it took aim at warmongers, bigots, reactionaries, Nazis, Fascists, Communists, and the DAR — and it even managed a few digs at the labor movement itself. Retitled *New Pins and Needles* in 1939, the show moved to the Windsor Theatre, then on 48th Street east of 7th Avenue, at a top ticket price of $1.65. Among those associated with the revue, songwriter Harold Rome, making his professional debut, was the one most responsible for its special flavor and appeal. In September 1938, Rome joined George S. Kaufman and Moss Hart in creating *Sing Out the News,* a more polished variation on *Pins and Needles,* which proved less successful.
Columbia SC.

HOORAY FOR WHAT!
Music: Harold Arlen
Lyrics: E. Y. Harburg
Book: Howard Lindsay & Russel Crouse
Producers: Messrs. Shubert
Directors: Vincente Minnelli, Howard Lindsay
Choreographers: Robert Alton, Agnes de Mille
Cast: Ed Wynn, Jack Whiting, Paul Haakon, June Clyde, Vivian Vance, Ruthanna Boris, Hugh Martin, Ralph Blane, Meg Mundy
Songs: "God's Country"; "I've Gone Romantic on You"; "Moanin' in the Mornin' "; "Down With Love"; "In the Shade of the New Apple Tree"
New York run: Winter Garden, December 1, 1937; 200 p.

Although it starred the clownish Ed Wynn, and even made room for his vaudeville specialties, *Hooray for What!* was primarily concerned with such weighty and timely matters as poison gas, munitions, diplomatic duplicity, espionage, and actual warfare. In the outlandish, satirical plot, Chuckles, a horticulturist, invents a gas to kill worms but then discovers that it can also kill humans. The invention sets off an arms race among the European powers who meet at a so-called Peace Conference in Geneva, where spies try to steal the formula from Chuckles' room at the Hotel de l'Espionage. When, using a mirror, a seductive spy copies the formula backwards, the gas turns out to be harmless and war is miraculously averted. *Hooray for What!* marked Agnes de Mille's first efforts as a Broadway choreographer, though most of her work was cut by the time the show reached New York.

THE CRADLE WILL ROCK

Music, lyrics & book: Marc Blitzstein
Producer: Sam H. Grisman
Director: Orson Welles
Cast: Howard DaSilva, Will Geer, Hiram Sherman, Olive Stanton, John
      Hoysradt, Marc Blitzstein
Songs: "The Freedom of the Press"; "Honolulu"; "Art for Art's Sake"; "Nickel
      Under the Foot"; "The Cradle Will Rock"; "Joe Worker"
New York run: Windsor Theatre, January 3, 1938; 108 p.

One of the most controversial stage productions of the decade, Marc Blitzstein's *The Cradle Will Rock* was initially a project of the WPA's Federal Theatre, with John Houseman as producer and Orson Welles as director. A grim parable dealing with the struggle for union recognition in a steel town, the work was scheduled to open June 16, 1937, at the Maxine Elliott Theatre, with a ticket scale of 25¢, 40¢, and 55¢. Because of political pressure, the Federal Theatre cancelled the production at the last minute, but Welles was determined to put on the show anywhere and anyway he could. That same night, he managed to secure the Venice Theatre (once known as Jolson's 59th Street Theatre), where the actors — who were forbidden from appearing on any stage by their own union — performed from their seats in various parts of the theatre, while Blitzstein provided piano accompaniment. The musical gave 19 performances in this fashion.

When producer Sam Grisman offered *The Cradle Will Rock* at his Windsor Theatre, the cast did perform on stage, though there was no scenery and the music was still played by the composer at the piano. The story of this "Play in Music" is little more than an animated left-wing political cartoon. In Steeltown, USA, the noble union organizer Larry Foreman (Howard DaSilva) does battle against the powerful and corrupt Mr. Mister (Will Geer), who owns everything and everyone in town, and eventually leads the workers to victory. In addition to the labor-management struggle, Blitzstein also turned his attention to the issue of prostitution, contrasting the character of a wistful street walker with the venality of journalists, artists, educators, religious leaders, and doctors. *The Cradle Will Rock* had brief revivals in 1947 with Alfred Drake as Larry Foreman, in 1964 with Jerry Orbach, and in 1983 (in a John Houseman production) with Randle Mell. American Legacy OC; Composer OC (1964)/ Random House (1938)/ TW.

The Cradle Will Rock. Marc Blitzstein at the piano.

I Married an Angel. Vera Zorina and Dennis King.

I MARRIED AN ANGEL

Music: Richard Rodgers
Lyrics: Lorenz Hart
Book: Richard Rodgers & Lorenz Hart
Producer: Dwight Deere Wiman
Director: Joshua Logan
Choreographer: George Balanchine
Cast: Dennis King, Vera Zorina, Vivienne Segal, Walter Slezak, Audrey Christie, Charles Walters
Songs: "Did You Ever Get Stung?"; "I Married an Angel"; "I'll Tell the Man in the Street"; "How to Win Friends and Influence People"; "Spring Is Here"; "A Twinkle in Your Eye"; "At the Roxy Music Hall"
New York run: Shubert Theatre, May 11, 1938; 338 p.

"Musical comedy has met its masters, and they have reared back and passed a 44th Street miracle," wrote Brooks Atkinson in the *Times* following the opening of *I Married an Angel.* That miracle had to do not only with the pleasures of the entertainment but also with the audience's total acceptance that the disillusioned hero's vow to marry only an angel actually comes true. The setting of this fantasy is Budapest where banker Willy Palaffi (Dennis King) finds that his celestial bride (Vera Zorina) causes all kinds of embarrassing problems with her heavenly honesty. Willy's sharp-tongued sister Peggy (Vivienne Segal) manages to save the marriage by dispensing such worldly advice to the angel as the proper use of a twinkle in her eye. The show's show stopper, unrelated to the proceedings or the locale, was the witty travesty of a typical Radio City Music Hall presentation. *I Married an Angel* was adapted by Rodgers and Hart from a Hungarian play on which they had previously based an unused movie script. The musical, the first of 14 staged by Joshua Logan, also marked the occasion of Zorina's Broadway debut. Jeanette MacDonald and Nelson Eddy were in the 1942 film. AEI part OC/ R&H.

HELLZAPOPPIN

Music: Sammy Fain, etc.
Lyrics: Charles Tobias, etc.
Sketches: Ole Olsen & Chic Johnson
Producers: Ole Olsen & Chic Johnson (Messrs. Shubert uncredited)
Director: Edward Duryea Dowling
Cast: Ole Olsen & Chic Johnson, Barto & Mann, Radio Rogues, Hal Sherman, Ray Kinney
Songs: "Fuddle Dee Duddle"; "Abe Lincoln" (Earl Robinson-Alfred Hayes); "It's Time to Say Aloha"; "Boomps-a-Daisy" (Annette Mills)
New York run: 46th Street Theatre, September 22, 1938; 1,404 p.

It was more of a raucous vaudeville show than a revue, it featured no performers whose names could attract Broadway theatregoers, and it received generally unfavorable notices. Yet when this legendary freak success closed up shop it had bested the long-run record for musicals recently established by *Pins and Needles. Hellzapoppin* was basically the same rowdy act that Olsen and Johnson had been performing all over the country for 14 years. But customers were attracted to its lowbrow high jinks, especially such audience-participation gimmicks as dancing in the aisles, and such running gags as the one of the little man walking through the audience with a plant for Mrs. Jones that grows and grows and grows. Within two months after its opening the show was transferred to the Winter Garden where it remained for the rest of its engagement. Olsen and Johnson, along with Martha Raye, were in the 1941 screen version.

Hellzapoppin. Behind Ole Olsen and Chic Johnson are the Radio Rogues (Sidney Chatton, Jimmy Hollywood, Eddie Bartel). The girls are Sally Bond and Margie Young. (DeMirjian)

Knickerbocker Holiday. Walter Huston, Jeanne Madden, and ladies of New Amsterdam. (Lucas)

KNICKERBOCKER HOLIDAY

Music: Kurt Weill
Lyrics & book: Maxwell Anderson
Producer: Playwrights' Company
Director: Joshua Logan
Choreographers: Carl Randall, Edwin Denby
Cast: Walter Huston, Ray Middleton, Jeanne Madden, Richard Kollmar, Robert Rounseville, Howard Freeman, Clarence Nordstrom
Songs: "There's Nowhere to Go but Up"; "It Never Was You"; "How Can You Tell an American?"; "September Song"; "The Scars"
New York run: Ethel Barrymore Theatre, October 19, 1938; 168 p.

A victim of Hitler's Germany, Kurt Weill settled in New York to become one of the Broadway theatre's most admired and influential composers. For *Knickerbocker Holiday*, the second of his eight American works, he was joined by playwright Maxwell Anderson to create what was probably the first musical to use an historical subject as the means through which views on contemporary matters could be expressed. Here the theme was totalitarianism versus democracy, as personified by Pieter Stuyvesant (Walter Huston), the autocratic governor of New Amsterdam in 1647, and Brom Broeck (Richard Kollmar), the freedom-loving "first American" who is opposed to any kind of government interference. The point became somewhat muddied when it appeared that Anderson's target was President Roosevelt rather than any of the peace-menacing dictators then in power. There was confusion of a more dramatic kind since Walter Huston, in his only Broadway musical, made Stuyvesant such a likable chap — especially when he sang of the anxieties of growing old in "September Song" — that audience sympathies tended to be with the wrong man. The 1944 screen version featured Nelson Eddy and Charles Coburn.
AEI OC/ Anderson House (1938)/ R&H.

Leave It to Me! Mary Martin.
(Vandamm)

LEAVE IT TO ME!

Music & lyrics: Cole Porter
Book: Bella & Samuel Spewack
Producer: Vinton Freedley
Director: Samuel Spewack
Choreographer: Robert Alton
Cast: William Gaxton, Victor Moore, Sophie Tucker, Tamara, Mary Martin, Edward H. Robins, Alexander Asro, George Tobias, Gene Kelly
Songs: "Get Out of Town"; "From Now On"; "Most Gentlemen Don't Like Love"; "My Heart Belongs to Daddy"; "I Want to Go Home"
New York run: Imperial Theatre, November 9, 1938; 291 p.

With a book distantly related to their own play, *Clear All Wires,* Bella and Samuel Spewack came up with a spoof of Communism and U.S. diplomacy that offered comedian Victor Moore one of his meatiest roles as mild-mannered Alonzo P. "Stinky" Goodhue. Goodhue is unwillingly named Ambassador to the Soviet Union because his ambitious wife (Sophie Tucker) has contributed generously to President Roosevelt's re-election campaign. Aided by foreign correspondent Buckley Joyce Thomas (William Gaxton), the Ambassador does everything he can to be recalled, but each blunder only succeeds in making him a bigger hero. Finally, he introduces a plan to ensure world peace — which, of course, no one wants — and Stinky is soon happily on his way back to Kansas. Mary Martin made a notable Broadway debut in *Leave It to Me!,* singing and coyly stripping to "My Heart Belongs to Daddy" while being stranded on a Siberian railroad station with a male quartet that included Gene Kelly. Two months after the musical closed it paid a two-week return visit to New York.
Chilton (1976)/ TW.

The Boys from Syracuse. Marcy Wescott, Wynn Murray, and Muriel Angelus singing "Sing for Your Supper." (Vandamm)

The Boys from Syracuse. Betty Bruce, Teddy Hart, and Eddie Albert. (Vandamm)

THE BOYS FROM SYRACUSE

Music: Richard Rodgers
Lyrics: Lorenz Hart
Book: George Abbott
Producer-director: George Abbott
Choreographer: George Balanchine
Cast: Jimmy Savo, Teddy Hart, Eddie Albert, Wynn Murray, Ronald Graham, Muriel Angelus, Marcy Wescott, Betty Bruce, Burl Ives
Songs: "Falling in Love With Love"; "The Shortest Day of the Year"; "This Can't Be Love"; "He and She"; "You Have Cast Your Shadow on the Sea"; "Sing for Your Supper"; "What Can You Do With a Man?"
New York run: Alvin Theatre, November 23, 1938; 235 p.

The genesis of *The Boys from Syracuse* began when Rodgers and Hart, while working on another show, were discussing the fact that no one had yet written a Broadway musical based on a play by Shakespeare. Their obvious choice was *The Comedy of Errors* (whose plot Shakespeare had borrowed from Plautus' *Menaechmi*), partly because Hart's brother, Teddy Hart, was always being confused with another comic actor, Jimmy Savo. The action takes place in Ephesus in ancient Asia Minor, and the mildly ribald tale concerns the efforts of two boys from Syracuse, Antipholus and his servant Dromio (Eddie Albert and Jimmy Savo), to find their long-lost twins who — for reasons of plot confusion — are also named Antipholus and Dromio (Ronald Graham and Teddy Hart). Complications arise when the wives of the Ephesians, Adriana (Muriel Angelus) and her servant Luce (Wynn Murray), mistake the two strangers for their husbands, though the couples eventually get sorted out after Adriana's sister Luciana (Marcy Wescott) and the Syracuse Antipholus admit their love while protesting "This Can't Be Love." In 1963, an Off-Broadway revival had a longer run than the original. Allan Jones, Joe Penner, and Martha Raye were in the 1940 film.

In 1981, *Oh, Brother!*, a second musical adaptation of the same basic tale, had a brief stay on Broadway. Other musicals inspired by Shakespeare have been *Swingin' the Dream* (1939) and *Babes in the Wood* (1964), both from *A Midsummer Night's Dream*; *Kiss Me, Kate* (1948), from *The Taming of the Shrew*; *West Side Story* (1957) and *Sensations* (1970), both from *Romeo and Juliet*; *Love and Let Love* (1968), *Your Own Thing* (1968), and *Music Is* (1976), all from *Twelfth Night*; *Two Gentlemen of Verona* (1971); and *Rockabye Hamlet* (1976). Columbia SC; Capitol OC (1963)/ R&H.

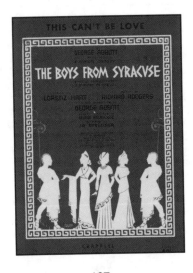

Too Many Girls. Eddie Bracken and Hal LeRoy help and inebriated Desi Arnaz confront Marcy Wescott. (Vandamm)

TOO MANY GIRLS

Music: Richard Rodgers
Lyrics: Lorenz Hart
Book: George Marion Jr.
Producer-director: George Abbott
Choreographer: Robert Alton
Cast: Marcy Wescott, Desi Arnaz, Hal LeRoy, Mary Jane Walsh, Diosa Costello, Richard Kollmar, Eddie Bracken, Leila Ernst, Van Johnson
Songs: "Love Never Went to College"; "Spic and Spanish"; "I Like to Recognize the Tune"; "I Didn't Know What Time It Was"; "She Could Shake the Maracas"; "Give It Back to the Indians"
New York run: Imperial Theatre, October 18, 1939; 249 p.

By 1939 — after such shows as *Leave It to Jane* and *Good News!* — a rah-rah college musical about football may not have been the most original idea along the Main Stem, but blessed with spirited songs by Rodgers and Hart, a youthful, talented cast, and fast-paced direction by George Abbott, *Too Many Girls* won high marks with both critics and public. Set in Pottawatomie College, Stop Gap, New Mexico (described as "one of those colleges that play football on Friday"), the musical featured an All-American backfield composed of Desi Arnaz, Hal LeRoy, Richard Kollmar (succeeded by Van Johnson for the tour), and Eddie Bracken, who also, unknown to her, act as bodyguards for wealthy coed Marcy Wescott. Soon boy students are pairing off with girl students, and Kollmar and Wescott get the chance to voice such sentiments as "Love Never Went to College" and "I Didn't Know What Time It Was." The 1940 movie version with Lucille Ball and Ann Miller also included members of the original cast.
Painted Smiles SC/ R&H.

DUBARRY WAS A LADY

Music & lyrics: Cole Porter
Book: Herbert Fields & B. G. DeSylva
Producer: B. G. DeSylva
Director: Edgar MacGregor
Choreographer: Robert Alton
Cast: Bert Lahr, Ethel Merman, Betty Grable, Benny Baker, Ronald Graham, Charles Walters, Kay Sutton
Songs: "When Love Beckoned (in Fifty-Second Street)"; "Well, Did You Evah?"; "But in the Morning, No"; "Do I Love You?"; "It Was Written in the Stars"; "Give Him the Oo-la-la"; "Katie Went to Haiti"; "Friendship"
New York run: 46th Street Theatre, December 6, 1939; 408 p.

Broadway's fifth longest-running musical of the Thirties, *DuBarry Was a Lady* was the first of three smash hits offered in succession by producer B.G. DeSylva. The show evolved through the merging of two ideas: Herbert Fields wanted to write a musical with Mae West as DuBarry and DeSylva wanted to write one about a washroom attendant in a swanky New York nightclub who is smitten by a Brenda Frazier-type debutante. Both concepts were combined by having the attendant, named Louis Blore, switch his affections to May Daly, the club's flashy singing star, and by having Louis — after taking a mickey finn — dream that he is King Louis XV and the singer his unaccommodating concubine. Ethel Merman and Bert Lahr, who stopped the show nightly with their raucous avowal of eternal friendship, were hailed as Broadway's royal couple, and Betty Grable won such favorable notice that she was soon whisked off to Hollywood stardom. During the Broadway run, Miss Merman was succeeded by Gypsy Rose Lee and Frances Williams. The show's movie version, in 1943, featured Lucille Ball, Gene Kelly, and Red Skelton.
TW.

DuBarry Was a Lady. Bert Lahr and Ethel Merman.

Louisiana Purchase. William Gaxton, Vera Zorina, Victor Moore, and Irene Bordoni at the Mardi Gras. (Lucas & Monroe)

LOUISIANA PURCHASE
Music & lyrics: Irving Berlin
Book: Morrie Ryskind & B. G. DeSylva
Producer: B. G. DeSylva (Irving Berlin uncredited)
Director: Edgar MacGregor
Choreographer: George Balanchine
Cast: William Gaxton, Vera Zorina, Victor Moore, Irene Bordoni, Carol Bruce, Nick Long Jr., Hugh Martin, Ralph Blane, Edward H. Robins
Songs: "Louisiana Purchase"; "It's a Lovely Day Tomorrow"; "Outside of That I Love You"; "You're Lonely and I'm Lonely"; "Latins Know How"; "What Chance Have I?"; "The Lord Done Fixed Up My Soul"; "Fools Fall in Love"; "You Can't Brush Me Off"
New York run: Imperial Theatre, May 28, 1940; 444 p.

After playing a Vice President in *Of Thee I Sing* and *Let 'Em Eat Cake* and an Ambassador in *Leave It to Me!,* Victor Moore endeared himself to audiences again by impersonating a United States Senator in *Louisiana Purchase.* In the libretto, prompted by recent revelations of corruption involving the late political leader Huey Long, the seemingly innocent Senator Oliver P. Loganberry goes to New Orleans to investigate the shady operations of the Louisiana Purchasing Company. Jim Taylor (William Gaxton), the company's president, tries to block the probe by involving the incorruptible Senator first with Marina Van Linden (Vera Zorina), a Viennese refugee, then with Mme. Yvonne Bordelaise (Irene Bordoni), a local restaurateuse. Loganberry manages to get out of the trap by marrying Yvonne, but he is ultimately defeated when, being a politician, he is unwilling to cross the picket line in front of the building in which his hearings are to take place. The second of producer B. G. DeSylva's three hits in a row, *Louisiana Purchase* marked Irving Berlin's return to Broadway after an absence of almost seven years. Moore, Zorina, and Bordoni were joined by Bob Hope for the 1941 movie.

CABIN IN THE SKY

Music: Vernon Duke
Lyrics: John Latouche
Book: Lynn Root
Producers: Albert Lewis & Vinton Freedley
Directors: George Balanchine, Albert Lewis
Choreographer: George Balanchine
Cast: Ethel Waters, Todd Duncan, Dooley Wilson, Katherine Dunham, Rex Ingram, J. Rosamond Johnson
Songs: "Taking a Chance on Love" (lyric with Ted Fetter); "Cabin in the Sky"; "Love Turned the Light Out"; "Honey in the Honeycomb"; "My Old Virginia Home (on the River Nile)"; "Do What You Wanna Do"
New York run: Martin Beck Theatre, October 25, 1940; 156 p.

The first major musical to play the Martin Beck Theatre (on 45th Street west of 8th Avenue), *Cabin in the Sky* was a parable of Southern Negro life with echoes of Ferenc Molnar's *Liliom* (which would be turned into the musical *Carousel*) and Marc Connelly's *The Green Pastures*. The fantasy deals with the struggle between the Lawd's General (Todd Duncan) and Lucifer Jr. (Rex Ingram) for the soul of shiftless Little Joe Jackson (Dooley Wilson), who has been fatally wounded in a street brawl. Because of the fervent prayers of Joe's devoted wife, Petunia (Ethel Waters), Joe is granted six months to make amends to allow him to get into Heaven. Lucifer Jr. offers temptation in the form of Georgia Brown (Katherine Dunham), but with Petunia's help Joe eventually manages to squeeze through the Pearly Gates. Miss Waters won resounding acclaim in this her only book musical, in which she sang the showstopper, "Taking a Chance on Love." In 1964, Rosetta LeNoire appeared in an adaptation which ran briefly Off Broadway. The 1943 film version gave Miss Waters the chance to repeat her role. Capitol OC (1964).

PANAMA HATTIE

Music & lyrics: Cole Porter
Book: Herbert Fields & B. G. DeSylva
Producer: B. G. DeSylva
Director: Edgar MacGregor
Choreographer: Robert Alton
Cast: Ethel Merman, Arthur Treacher, James Dunn, Rags Ragland, Pat Harrington, Frank Hyers, Phyllis Brooks, Betty Hutton, Joan Carroll, June Allyson, Lucille Bremer, Vera Ellen, Betsy Blair
Songs: "My Mother Would Love You"; "I've Still Got My Health"; "Fresh as a Daisy"; "Let's Be Buddies"; "Make It Another Old-Fashioned, Please"; "I'm Throwing a Ball Tonight"
New York run: 46th Street Theatre, October 30, 1940; 501 p.

According to Ethel Merman, Hattie Maloney in *Panama Hattie* was an expansion of the Katie who went to Haiti in *DuBarry Was a Lady*. The show was the first in which Miss Merman received solo star billing and it had the longest run of the five musicals in which she was spotlighted singing the songs of Cole Porter. Ethel's Hattie is a brassy, gold-hearted nightclub owner in Panama City who becomes engaged to divorcé Nick Bullitt (James Dunn), a Philadelphia Main Liner. In order for the couple to marry, however, Hattie must first win the approval of Nick's snotty eight-year-old daughter (Joan Carroll), which she accomplishes through the conciliatory "Let's Be Buddies." *Panama Hattie* was the last of the three-in-a-row hits produced by B. G. DeSylva. In 1942, a movie version co-starred Ann Sothern and Red Skelton. TW.

PAL JOEY

Music: Richard Rodgers
Lyrics: Lorenz Hart
Book: John O'Hara (George Abbott uncredited)
Producer-director: George Abbott
Choreographer: Robert Alton
Cast: Vivienne Segal, Gene Kelly, June Havoc, Jack Durant, Leila Ernst, Jean Casto, Van Johnson, Stanley Donen, Tilda Getze
Songs: "You Mustn't Kick It Around"; "I Could Write a Book"; "That Terrific Rainbow"; "Happy Hunting Horn"; "Bewitched"; "The Flower Garden of My Heart"; "Zip"; "Den of Iniquity"; "Take Him"
New York run: Ethel Barrymore Theatre, December 25, 1940; 374 p.

With its heel for a hero, its smoky nightclub ambiance, and its true-to-life, untrue-to-anyone characters, *Pal Joey* was a major breakthrough in bringing about a more adult form of musical theatre. The idea originated with author John O'Hara who suggested to Rodgers and Hart that they collaborate on a musical treatment of O'Hara's series of *New Yorker* short stories about Joey Evans, a small-time Chicago entertainer. In the libretto (written with an uncredited assist from producer-director George Abbott), Joey gets a job at Mike's Club where he is attracted to Linda English (Leila Ernst) but drops her in favor of the rich, bewitched dowager, Vera Simpson (Vivienne Segal). Vera builds a glittering nightclub, the Chez Joey, for her paramour, but she soon tires of him, and at the end — after an encounter with blackmailers Ludlow Lowell (Jack Durant) and Gladys Bumps (June Havoc) — Joey is off in search of other conquests. *Pal Joey* marked the only Broadway musical in which Gene Kelly played a major role.

Though it was well received, the musical had to wait until a 1952 revival to be fully appreciated. Miss Segal repeated her original role and Harold Lang played Joey. During the run Helen Gallagher was succeeded by Nancy Walker as Gladys. (See page 153). In 1976, *Pal Joey* returned to Broadway for two months with Joan Copeland and Christopher Chadman. The 1957 screen version featured Frank Sinatra, Rita Hayworth, and Kim Novak.

CSP part OC (1952); Capitol part OC (1952)/ Random House (1952)/ R&H.

Pal Joey. Gene Kelly, June Havoc, and Jack Durant. (Fred Fehl)

LADY IN THE DARK

Music: Kurt Weill
Lyrics: Ira Gershwin
Book: Moss Hart
Producer: Sam H. Harris
Directors: Hassard Short, Moss Hart
Choreographer: Albertina Rasch
Cast: Gertrude Lawrence, Victor Mature, Danny Kaye, Macdonald Carey, Bert Lytell, Evelyn Wyckoff, Margaret Dale, Ron Field
Songs: "One Life to Live"; "Girl of the Moment"; "This Is New"; "The Princess of Pure Delight"; "My Ship"; "Jenny"; "Tschaikowsky"
New York run: Alvin Theatre, January 23, 1941; 467 p.

Though he originally conceived it as a vehicle for Katharine Cornell, Moss Hart turned *Lady in the Dark* into a vehicle for Gertrude Lawrence by enlisting the services of Kurt Weill and Ira Gershwin and changing it from a play to a musical. The work is concerned with *Allure* magazine editor Liza Elliott, whose inability to make up her mind has led her to seek psychiatric help. This feeling of insecurity contributes to her doubts about marrying her lover, publisher Kendall Nesbitt (Bert Lytell), and makes her think she is falling in love with movie star Randy Curtis (Victor Mature). In the end, however, she realizes that the man who can cure her neuroses is really Charley Johnson (Macdonald Carey), the magazine's cynical advertising manager. How does she know? Charley can complete the song "My Ship," which Liza had learned as a child but is now unable to finish. ("Ah! Sweet Mystery of Life" had served a similar function in *Naughty Marietta*.) All other musical pieces in *Lady in the Dark* — including the tongue-twisting "Tschaikowsky" for Danny Kaye and the raucous showstopper "Jenny" for Miss Lawrence, both part of the colorful circus scene — are performed within the dreams that Liza reveals to her doctor.

Lady in the Dark closed for vacation in June 1941, then reopened in September with Lytell replaced by Paul McGrath, Mature by Willard Parker, Carey by Walter Coy, and Kaye by Eric Brotherson. Following a tour, the musical returned to Broadway in February 1943 and remained for 83 performances. Ginger Rogers and Ray Milland were in the 1944 movie version.

RCA OC; AEI OC; Columbia SC/ Random House (1941)/ R&H.

Lady in the Dark. Margaret Dale, Danny Kaye, and Gertrude Lawrence. (Vandamm)

BEST FOOT FORWARD

Music & lyrics: Hugh Martin & Ralph Blane
Book: John Cecil Holm
Producer: George Abbott (Richard Rodgers uncredited)
Director: George Abbott
Choreographer: Gene Kelly
Cast: Rosemary Lane, Marty May, Gil Stratton Jr., Maureen Cannon, Nancy Walker, June Allyson, Kenny Bowers, Victoria Schools, Tommy Dix, Danny Daniels
Songs: "The Three B's"; "Buckle Down, Winsocki"; "Just a Little Joint With a Jukebox"; "What Do You Think I Am?"; "Ev'ry Time"; "Shady Lady Bird"
New York run: Ethel Barrymore Theatre, October 1, 1941; 326 p.

Taking place at Winsocki, a Pennsylvania prep school, *Best Foot Forward* is all about the complications that result from the arrival of Hollywood glamour girl Gale Joy (Rosemary Lane) who, as a publicity stunt, has accepted the invitation of Bud Hooper (Gil Stratton Jr.) to be his date at the annual prom. Not only does this provoke hurt feelings on the part of Bud's steady girl, Helen Schlessinger (Maureen Cannon), it also results in a near-riot when souvenir hungry promtrotters strip the movie star down to her essentials. (John Cecil Holm's libretto was based on his own experience when, as a student at the Perkiomen School near Philadelphia, he had invited movie star Betty Compson to be his prom date. The story he wrote was his idea of what might have happened had she shown up.) The rousing "Buckle Down, Winsocki" became the best-known song in the show, which was the first to present Nancy Walker and June Allyson in major roles. In 1963, an Off-Broadway revival performed a similar function for 17-year-old Liza Minnelli and Christopher (then Ronald) Walken. The 1943 screen version featured Lucille Ball, and Misses Walker and Allyson.
Cadence OC (1963)/ TW.

Best Foot Forward. June Allyson, Victoria Schools, and Nancy Walker singing "The Three B's." (Vandamm)

Let's Face It! An awkward situation involving Houston Richards, Benny Baker, Mary Jane Walsh, Danny Kaye, and Jack Williams. (Vandamm)

LET'S FACE IT!

Music & lyrics: Cole Porter
Book: Herbert & Dorothy Fields
Producer: Vinton Freedley
Director: Edgar MacGregor
Choreographer: Charles Walters
Cast: Danny Kaye, Eve Arden, Benny Baker, Mary Jane Walsh, Edith Meiser, Vivian Vance, Nanette Fabray, Mary Parker & Billy Daniel, Jack Williams, Houston Richards
Songs: "Farming"; "Ev'rything I Love"; "Ace in the Hole"; "Let's Not Talk About Love"; "A Little Rumba Numba"; "I Hate You, Darling"; "Melody in 4-F" (Sylvia Fine - Max Liebman)
New York run: Imperial Theatre, October 29, 1941; 547 p.

Producer Vinton Freedley got the idea for *Let's Face It!* while reading a newspaper account about a number of patriotic women who were so anxious to help the morale of World War II soldiers that they wrote to army camps requesting permission to entertain servicemen in their homes. Using a 1925 Broadway hit, *The Cradle Snatchers,* as foundation, the script by Herbert and Dorothy Fields was about three Southampton matrons who, having grown suspicious of their husbands' frequent hunting trips, have enlisted the service of three rookies from a nearby army camp for an evening of fun and games. The inevitable embarrassments occur when the husbands and their girl friends — as well as the soldiers' girl friends — show up at the party. Danny Kaye (in his first starring role) scored a hit particularly with special material coauthored by his wife, Sylvia Fine. Kaye was succeeded during the Broadway run by José Ferrer. Bob Hope and Betty Hutton were in the 1943 movie version.
Smithsonian OC.

By Jupiter. Ray Bolger and Bertha Belmore singing "Life With Father." (Vandamm)

BY JUPITER

Music: Richard Rodgers
Lyrics: Lorenz Hart
Book: Richard Rodgers & Lorenz Hart
Producers: Dwight Deere Wiman & Richard Rodgers
Director: Joshua Logan
Choreographer: Robert Alton
Cast: Ray Bolger, Constance Moore, Benay Venuta, Ronald Graham, Bertha Belmore, Ralph Dumke, Vera Ellen, Margaret Bannerman
Songs: "Jupiter Forbid"; "Life With Father"; "Nobody's Heart"; "Ev'rything I've Got"; "Careless Rhapsody"; "Wait Till You See Her"
New York run: Shubert Theatre, June 3, 1942; 427 p.

Because of its ancient Greek characters and its Asia Minor setting, *By Jupiter* was something of a successor to the previous Rodgers and Hart hit, *The Boys from Syracuse.* The new work, which tried out in Boston under the title *All's Fair,* was based on the 1932 play, *The Warrior's Husband,* in which Katharine Hepburn had first attracted notice. The musical deals with the conflict between the Greeks and the legendary female warriors called Amazons, who live in a gynarchic land ruled by Queen Hippolyta (Benay Venuta). As one of his 12 labors, Hercules (Ralph Dumke) arrives with a Greek army led by Theseus (Ronald Graham) to steal the queen's magical girdle of Diana, the source of her strength. But when Hippolyta's sister Antiope (Constance Moore) takes one look at Theseus, she soon lays down her spear for love, a gesture her sister warriors only too willingly emulate. During the run, Miss Moore was succeeded by Nanette Fabray.

By Jupiter, which remained the longest on Broadway of any Rodgers and Hart musical during the team's partnership, was the last original show they wrote together. It could have stayed longer had not Ray Bolger (in his first starring role as Sapiens, the queen's husband) quit the cast to entertain American troops in the Far East. One curious aspect of the show's score is that "Wait Till You See Her," its best-known song, was dropped a month after the Broadway opening. In 1967, an Off-Broadway revival of *By Jupiter* ran for 118 performances. RCA OC (1967)/ R&H.

This Is the Army. Ezra Stone, Julie Oshins, and Philip Truex singing "The Army's Made a Man Out of Me." (Vandamm)

THIS IS THE ARMY

Music & lyrics: Irving Berlin
Sketches: (uncredited)
Producer: Uncle Sam
Directors: Ezra Stone, Joshua Logan
Choreographers: Robert Sidney, Nelson Barclift
Cast: Ezra Stone, Burl Ives, Gary Merrill, Julie Oshins, Robert Sidney, Alan Manson, Earl Oxford, Nelson Barclift, Stuart Churchill, Philip Truex, Irving Berlin
Songs: "This Is the Army, Mr. Jones"; "The Army's Made a Man Out of Me"; "I Left My Heart at the Stage Door Canteen"; "Mandy"; "I'm Getting Tired So I Can Sleep"; "Oh, How I Hate to Get Up in the Morning"; "American Eagles"; "This Time"
New York run: Broadway Theatre, July 4, 1942; 113 p.

Having already written songs for the all-soldier show, *Yip Yip Yaphank*, during World War I, Irving Berlin followed up with songs for the all-soldier show, *This Is the Army,* during World War II. The revue, put together as a benefit for the Army Emergency Relief Fund, both kidded and extolled the military life in a song-and-dance mixture of horseplay, nostalgia, and patriotism. Though most of the show reflected a draftee's view of the Army, there was also room for tributes to the Navy and the Air Force. Highlights included the opening "Military Minstrel Show"; the scene at the Stage Door Canteen with soldiers impersonating celebrities who worked and performed there; Berlin himself leading his World War I buddies in singing, "Oh, How I Hate to Get Up in the Morning"; and the finale with the cast members in full battle dress booming their determination to make certain that this time would be the last. *This Is the Army* played a limited 12-week engagement in New York, was filmed in 1943 with Ronald Reagan, then toured overseas until October 1945. In 1946, the Broadway revue *Call Me Mister* dealt with the adjustment of World War II servicemen to civilian life.
CSP OC.

Oklahoma! Joan Roberts singing "Many a New Day."

Oklahoma! Celeste Holm and Lee Dixon.

Oklahoma! Howard Da Silva and Alfred Drake singing "Pore Jud." (Vandamm)

OKLAHOMA!

Music: Richard Rodgers
Lyrics & book: Oscar Hammerstein II
Producer: Theatre Guild
Director: Rouben Mamoulian
Choreographer: Agnes de Mille
Cast: Betty Garde, Alfred Drake, Joan Roberts, Joseph Buloff, Celeste Holm, Howard Da Silva, Lee Dixon, Joan McCracken, Bambi Linn, George S. Irving, George Church, Ralph Riggs, Marc Platt, Katharine Sergava
Songs: "Oh, What a Beautiful Mornin'"; "The Surrey With the Fringe on Top"; "Kansas City"; "I Cain't Say No"; "Many a New Day"; "People Will Say We're in Love"; "Pore Jud"; "Out of My Dreams"; "The Farmer and the Cowman"; "All er Nothin' "; "Oklahoma"
New York run: St. James Theatre, March 31, 1943; 2,212 p.

A recognized landmark in the evolution of the American musical theatre, *Oklahoma!* was the initial collaboration between Richard Rodgers and Oscar Hammerstein II (in all, they wrote nine Broadway shows together). Under the direction of Rouben Mamoulian and with choreography by Agnes de Mille (her first of 15 book musicals), the production not only fused story, songs, and dances, but introduced the dream ballet to reveal hidden fears and desires of the principal characters. In addition, the musical continued in the paths of *Show Boat* (written by Hammerstein) and *Porgy and Bess* (directed by Mamoulian) by further expanding Broadway's horizons in its depiction of the pioneering men and woman who had once tilled the land and tended the cattle of the American Southwest.

Based on Lynn Riggs' 1931 play *Green Grow the Lilacs*, *Oklahoma!* is set in Indian Territory soon after the turn of the century. The simple tale is mostly concerned with whether the decent Curly McLain (Alfred Drake) or the menacing Jud Fry (Howard Da Silva) will take Laurey Williams (Joan Roberts) to the box social. Though in a fit of pique, Laurey chooses Jud, she really loves Curly and they soon make plans to marry. At their wedding, there is a joyous celebration of Oklahoma's impending statehood, Jud is accidently killed in a fight with Curly, and the newlyweds prepare to ride off in their surrey with the fringe on top. A comic secondary plot has to do with a romantic triangle involving man-crazy Ado Annie Carnes (Celeste Holm), cowboy Will Parker (Lee Dixon), and peddler Ali Hakim (Joseph Buloff).

After trying out under the title *Away We Go!*, the show was renamed *Oklahoma!* for its Broadway engagement at the St. James Theatre (formerly Erlanger's). It remained there five years nine months, thereby setting a long-run record for musicals that it held until overtaken by *My Fair Lady* 15 years later. Among actors who replaced original-cast members were Howard Keel (Curly), Mary Hatcher (Laurey), and Shelley Winters (Ado Annie). A National Company toured for over a decade, including a return visit to New York that lasted 100 performances. The first road company was headed by Harry Stockwell (Curly), Evelyn Wyckoff (Laurey), Pamela Britton (Ado Annie), and David Burns (Ali Hakim). Those who subsequently toured included John Raitt (Curly), Florence Henderson (Laurey), and Barbara Cook (Ado Annie).

In 1969, the Music Theatre of Lincoln Center mounted a revival with Bruce Yarnell (Curly), Leigh Beery (Laurey), April Shawhan (Ado Annie), Margaret Hamilton (Aunt Eller), and Lee Roy Reams (Will). Ten years later, a new production directed by William Hammerstein (Oscar's son) returned to New York for eight months as part of a two-and-a-half year tour. (See page 255.) The 1955 movie version, the first film in Todd-AO, featured Gordon MacRae and Shirley Jones in the leading roles.

MCA OC; CSP part tour OC; RCA OC (1979)/ Random House (1943)/ R&H.

THE MERRY WIDOW

Music: Franz Lehár
Lyrics: Adrian Ross, Robert Gilbert
Book: Sidney Sheldon & Ben Roberts
Producer: Yolanda Mero-Irion for the New Opera Co.
Director: Felix Brentano
Choreographer: George Balanchine
Cast: Jan Kiepura, Marta Eggerth, Melville Cooper, Ruth Matteson, Robert Rounseville, David Wayne, Ralph Dumke, Gene Barry, Lubov Roudenko, Milada Mladova
Songs: Same as original production
New York run: Majestic Theatre, August 4, 1943; 322 p.

(See page 15.)

ONE TOUCH OF VENUS

Music: Kurt Weill
Lyrics: Ogden Nash
Book: S. J. Perelman & Ogden Nash
Producer: Cheryl Crawford
Director: Elia Kazan
Choreographer: Agnes de Mille
Cast: Mary Martin, Kenny Baker, John Boles, Paula Laurence, Teddy Hart, Ruth Bond, Sono Osato, Harry Clark, Allyn Ann McLerie, Helen Raymond, Lou Wills Jr., Pearl Lang
Songs: "One Touch of Venus"; "How Much I Love You"; "I'm a Stranger Here Myself"; "West Wind"; "Foolish Heart"; "The Trouble With Women"; "Speak Low"; "That's Him"; "Wooden Wedding"
New York run: Imperial Theatre, October 7, 1943; 567 p.

One Touch of Venus combined the music of composer Kurt Weill (it was his most lighthearted score) with the libretto of two celebrated humorists, poet Ogden Nash and short-story writer S.J. Perelman (it was their only Broadway book musical). In her first starring role, Mary Martin played a statue of Venus recently unveiled in a New York museum, the Whitelaw Savory Foundation of Modern Art, that comes to life after barber Rodney Hatch (Kenny Baker) places a ring on the statue's finger. There is much comic confusion when Savory (John Boles) falls in love with Venus and Venus falls in love with Rodney, but after dreaming of her humdrum life as a barber's wife in Ozone Heights, the goddess happily turns back to marble. Fortunately, Rodney meets a girl who looks just like the statue (Miss Martin, of course) who just loves living in Ozone Heights.

Though *One Touch of Venus* (whose hit song was the torchy "Speak Low") was a fantasy in the modern sophisticated vein of Rodgers and Hart's *I Married an Angel,* its origin was a short novel, *The Tinted Venus,* written in 1885 by the English author F. Anstey (né Thomas Anstey Guthrie) who had based his story on the Pygmalion myth. The musical's first draft, by Bella Spewack, suggested Marlene Dietrich for the role of Venus, but when the actress turned down the part the concept was changed from worldly exotic to youthfully innocent after Perelman and Nash replaced Spewack and Mary Martin replaced Dietrich. The movie version, released in 1948, starred Ava Gardner, Robert Walker, and Dick Haymes.
AEI OC/ Little, Brown (1943); Chilton (1973)/ TW.

One Touch of Venus. Barber Kenny Baker slipping the ring on statue Mary Martin's finger. (Vandamm)

CARMEN JONES

Music: Georges Bizet
Lyrics & book: Oscar Hammerstein II
Producer: Billy Rose
Directors: Hassard Short, Charles Friedman
Choreographer: Eugene Loring
Cast: Muriel Smith (or Inez Matthews), Luther Saxon, Carlotta Franzell, Glenn Bryant, June Hawkins, Cosy Cole
Songs: "Dat's Love"; "You Talk Just Like My Maw"; "Dere's a Café on de Corner"; "Beat Out dat Rhythm on a Drum"; "Stan' Up and Fight"; "Whizzin' Away Along de Track"; "Dis Flower"; "My Joe"
New York run: Broadway Theatre, December 2, 1943; 502 p.

Adapting his libretto from Meilhac and Halevy's for the 1875 premiere production of *Carmen,* and adhering as closely as possible to the original form, Oscar Hammerstein II set his idiomatic lyrics to Georges Bizet's music and updated the story to World War II. Now Carmen is a worker in a parachute factory in the South (rather than a cigarette factory in Seville), Joe (Don José) is an army corporal who falls in love with the temptress, Cindy Lou (Micaela) is the country girl who loves Joe, and Husky Miller is the boxer (replacing Escamillo the bull fighter) who wins Carmen away from Joe. As did the original, the work ends in tragedy as Joe stabs Carmen to death outside a sports stadium while the crowd can be heard cheering Husky. In addition to the staging, Hassard Short was also responsible for the striking color schemes used throughout the production. *Carmen Jones* returned twice to New York during its year-and-a-half nationwide tour. The 1954 film adaptation featured Dorothy Dandridge, Harry Belafonte, and Diahann Carroll. MCA OC/ Knopf (1945)/ R&H.

MEXICAN HAYRIDE

Music & lyrics: Cole Porter
Book: Herbert & Dorothy Fields
Producer: Michael Todd
Directors: Hassard Short, John Kennedy
Choreographer: Paul Haakon
Cast: Bobby Clark, June Havoc, George Givot, Wilbur Evans, Luba Malina, Corinna Mura, Paul Haakon, Edith Meiser, Bill Callahan, Candy Jones
Songs: "Sing to Me, Guitar"; "I Love You"; "There Must Be Someone for Me"; "Abracadabra"; "Carlotta"; "Girls"; "Count Your Blessings"
New York run: Winter Garden, January 28, 1944; 481 p.

One of Broadway's most lavish wartime attractions (it had a cast of 89), *Mexican Hayride* owed its success largely to its appealing Latin-flavored score by Cole Porter (including the hit ballad "I Love You"), its eye-dazzling decor, its rows of long-stemmed show girls, and — most of all — the buffooneries of prankish, leering Bobby Clark. Clark was seen as Joe Bascom, alias Humphrey Fish, a numbers racketeer on the lam in Mexico where, at a bull fight, he is mistakenly selected as the "Amigo Americano," or good-will ambassador. Alternately hailed by the populace and trailed by the police, Bascom bounds from Mexico City to Chepultepec, Xochimilco, and Taxco, assuming a number of disguises including that of a mariachi flute player and a tortilla-vending, cigar-chomping Indian squaw with a baby strapped to her back. Because of the sumptuousness of the production, the top ticket price was $5.50. Abbott and Costello (but no Porter songs) were in the 1948 Hollywood version. CSP OC.

Mexican Hayride. Bobby Clark (in his squaw disguise) and June Havoc cutting up during the "Count Your Blessings" number.

FOLLOW THE GIRLS

Music: Phil Charig
Lyrics: Dan Shaprio & Milton Pascal
Book: Guy Bolton, Eddie Davis & Fred Thompson
Producers: Dave Wolper & Albert Borde
Directors: Harry Delmar, Fred Thompson
Choreographer: Catherine Littlefield
Cast: Gertrude Niesen, Jackie Gleason, Buster West, Tim Herbert, Irina Baronova, Frank Parker, William Tabbert
Songs: "You're Perf"; "Twelve O'Clock and All Is Well"; "Follow the Girls"; "I Wanna Get Married"; "I'm Gonna Hang My Hat"
New York run: New Century Theatre, April 8, 1944; 882 p.

Though it was one of Broadway's most popular wartime attractions, *Follow the Girls* is all but forgotten today. The raucous and lively show did, however, make a star of Gertrude Niesen in her only book musical, and her rendition of "I Wanna Get Married" was an authentic musical-comedy showstopper. The disposable plot had something to do with a burlesque queen, Bubbles LaMarr, who becomes a favorite of sailors at the Spotlight Canteen in Great Neck, Long Island. The show, however, served to throw the spotlight not only on Miss Niesen as Bubbles, but also on the antics of Jackie Gleason as Goofy Gale and on the dancing of ballerina Irina Baronova. *Follow the Girls* was the first attraction to play the reopened and refurbished Jolson's 59th Street Theatre, renamed the New Century.

SONG OF NORWAY

Music & lyrics: Robert Wright & George Forrest based on Edvard Grieg
Book: Milton Lazarus
Producer: Edwin Lester
Directors: Edwin Lester, Charles K. Freeman
Choreographer: George Balanchine
Cast: Irra Petina, Lawrence Brooks, Robert Shafer, Helena Bliss, Sig Arno, Alexandra Danilova, Maria Tallchief, Ruthanna Boris
Songs: "The Legend"; "Hill of Dreams"; "Freddy and His Fiddle"; "Now!"; "Strange Music"; "Midsummer's Eve"; "Three Loves"; "I Love You"; "Piano Concerto in A Minor" (instrumental)
New York run: Imperial Theatre, August 21, 1944; 860 p.

Song of Norway had its premiere a continent away from Broadway in July 1944, when it was presented by Edwin Lester's Los Angeles and San Francisco Civic Light Opera Association. Following in the tradition of *Blossom Time,* it offered a score based on themes by a classical composer combined with a biographical plot unencumbered by too much fidelity to historical accuracy. Here we have a romanticized tale of the early years of Edvard Grieg (Lawrence Brooks) who, with his friend, poet Rikard Nordraak (Robert Shafer), is anxious to bring new artistic glory to their beloved Norway. Though temporarily distracted from this noble aim by a dalliance in Rome with a flirtatious (and fictitious) Italian prima donna (Irra Petina), Grieg is so affected by the news of Nordraak's death that he returns home to his indulgent wife (Helena Bliss). Suitably inspired after singing a reprise of their love duet, "Strange Music," the composer creates the A-Minor Piano Concerto. *Song of Norway* which was presented by the New York City Opera in 1981, was filmed in 1970 with Tauralv Maurstad and Florence Henderson. For other musicals with scores based on classical themes, see *Blossom Time,* page 38.
MCA OC; Columbia OC (1958)/ TW.

BLOOMER GIRL

Music: Harold Arlen
Lyrics: E. Y. Harburg
Book: Sig Herzig & Fred Saidy
Producers: John C. Wilson & Nat Goldstone
Directors: E. Y. Harburg, William Schorr
Choreographer: Agnes de Mille
Cast: Celeste Holm, David Brooks, Dooley Wilson, Joan McCracken, Richard Huey, Margaret Douglass, Mabel Taliaferro, Matt Briggs, Herbert Ross
Songs: "When the Boys Come Home"; "Evelina"; "It Was Good Enough for Grandma"; "The Eagle and Me"; "Right as the Rain"; "T'morra, T'morra"; "Sunday in Cicero Falls"; "I Got a Song"
New York run: Shubert Theatre, October 5, 1944; 654 p.

Continuing the Americana spirit of *Oklahoma!, Bloomer Girl* was not only concerned with the introduction of bloomers during the Civil War, it also covered various aspects of the women's reform movement and the struggle for civil rights. The action occurs in Cicero Falls, New York, in 1861, and covers the rebellion of Evelina Applegate (Celeste Holm) against her tyrannical father, a manufacturer of hoopskirts, who wants her to marry one of his salesmen. Evelina is so provoked that she joins her aunt, Amelia "Dolly" Bloomer (Margaret Douglass), in both her crusade for more practical clothing for women and in her abolitionist activities. Evelina's convictions, however, do not prevent her from singing the romantic duet, "Right as the Rain," with Jefferson Calhoun (David Brooks), a visiting Southern slaveholder, who is eventually won over to her cause. *Bloomer Girl* made a star of Celeste Holm (who was succeeded in her role by Nanette Fabray), and it was also noted for Agnes de Mille's "Civil War Ballet," depicting the anguish felt by women who must remain at home while their men are off fighting. The musical returned to New York for six weeks early in 1947.

Broadway has also seen the following Civil War musicals: *The Girl from Dixie* (1903), *Caroline* (1923), *My Maryland* (1927), *My Darlin' Aida* (1952), *Maggie Flynn* (1968), and *Shenandoah* (1975).
MCA OC/ TW.

Bloomer Girl. Joan McCracken showing off her bloomers to Margaret Douglass and Celeste Holm. (Vandamm)

ON THE TOWN

Music: Leonard Bernstein
Lyrics & book: Betty Comden & Adolph Green
Producers: Oliver Smith & Paul Feigay
Director: George Abbott
Choreographer: Jerome Robbins
Cast: Sono Osato, Nancy Walker, Betty Comden, Adolph Green, John Battles, Cris Alexander, Alice Pearce, Allyn Ann McLerie
Songs: "New York, New York"; "Come Up to My Place"; "I Get Carried Away"; "Lonely Town"; "Lucky to Be Me"; "Ya Got Me"; "Some Other Time"
New York run: Adelphi Theatre, December 28, 1944; 463 p.

On the Town heralded the Broadway arrival of four major talents — composer Leonard Bernstein, writing partners Betty Comden and Adolph Green, and choreographer Jerome Robbins. Based on the Robbins-Bernstein ballet, *Fancy Free,* the musical expanded the work into a carefree tour of New York City, where three sailors — played by John Battles, Adolph Green, and Cris Alexander — become involved with three girls — Sono Osato, Betty Comden, and Nancy Walker — on a 24-hour shore leave. One of the sailors (Battles) becomes so smitten by the current winner of the subway's "Miss Turnstiles" competition (Miss Osato) that he and his buddies pursue her through the Museum of Natural History, Central Park, Times Square, and Coney Island. The Adelphi Theatre was once located on 54th Street east of 7th Avenue.

There have been two New York revivals of *On the Town.* Joe Layton staged an Off-Broadway version in 1959, with Harold Lang, Wisa D'Orso, and Pat Carroll, and Ron Field staged a Broadway version in 1971 with Ron Husmann, Donna McKechnie, Bernadette Peters, and Phyllis Newman. The movie adaptation, released in 1949, co-starred Gene Kelly, Vera-Ellen, Frank Sinatra, and Betty Garrett. MCA part OC; Columbia OC/ TW.

UP IN CENTRAL PARK

Music: Sigmund Romberg
Lyrics: Dorothy Fields
Book: Herbert & Dorothy Fields
Producer: Michael Todd
Director: John Kennedy
Choreographer: Helen Tamiris
Cast: Wilbur Evans, Maureen Cannon, Betty Bruce, Noah Beery, Maurice Burke, Charles Irwin, Robert Rounseville
Songs: "Carousel in the Park"; "When You Walk in the Room"; "Close as Pages in a Book"; "The Big Back Yard"; "April Snow"
New York run: New Century Theatre, January 27, 1945; 504 p.

Celebrated for his lush scores for operettas in exotic locales (*The Desert Song, The New Moon*), Sigmund Romberg joined with lyricist Dorothy Fields to recapture the vintage Currier and Ives charms found up in New York's Central Park in the 1870s. The story, a combination of fact and fiction, deals with the efforts of John Matthews (Wilbur Evans), a *New York Times* reporter, to expose Tammany boss William Marcy Tweed (Noah Beery) and the other grafters who are lining their pockets with funds designated for the building of the park. Romance is supplied when John and Rosie Moore (Maureen Cannon), the daughter of a Tweed crony, vow love everlasting in their ardent duet, "Close as Pages in a Book." Deanna Durbin and Dick Haymes were in the 1948 movie version. MCA SC.

Carousel. The opening scene with John Raitt and Jan Clayton. (Vandamm)

CAROUSEL

Music: Richard Rodgers
Lyrics & book: Oscar Hammerstein II
Producer: Theatre Guild
Director: Rouben Mamoulian
Choreographer: Ágnes de Mille
Cast: John Raitt, Jan Clayton, Murvyn Vye, Jean Darling, Christine Johnson, Eric Mattson, Bambi Linn, Peter Birch, Pearl Lang
Songs: "Carousel Waltz" (instrumental); "You're a Queer One, Julie Jordan"; "Mr. Snow"; "If I Loved You"; "Blow High, Blow Low"; "June Is Bustin' Out All Over"; "When the Children Are Asleep"; "Soliloquy"; "What's the Use of Wond'rin'?"; "You'll Never Walk Alone"; "The Highest Judge of All"
New York run: Majestic Theatre, April 19, 1945; 890 p.

With *Carousel*, Rodgers and Hammerstein solidified their position as the dominant creators of musical theatre in the Forties. Reunited for the production with their *Oklahoma!* colleagues, the partners transported Ferenc Molnar's 1921 fantasy *Liliom* from Budapest to a New England fishing village between 1873 and 1888. Billy Bigelow (John Raitt), a swaggering carnival barker, meets Julie Jordan (Jan Clayton), a local factory worker, and — in the soaring duet, "If I Loved You" — they are soon admitting their feelings for each other. After their marriage, Billy learns of his impending fatherhood — with his ambivalent emotions expressed in the "Soliloquy" — and, desperate for money, is killed in an attempted robbery. He is, however, allowed to return to earth to do one good deed. This is accomplished when, unseen by his daughter Louise (Bambi Linn), he shows up at her high school graduation to encourage the lonely girl to have confidence in herself by heeding the words to "You'll Never Walk Alone." For almost two years, *Carousel* at the Majestic Theatre (on 44th Street west of Broadway) played across the street from *Oklahoma!* at the St. James. During the Broadway run (the fifth longest of the decade), Raitt was replaced for a time by Howard Keel. The National Company traveled for one year nine months, ending its tour with a Broadway stand lasting 48 performances. Twenty years after the opening, John Raitt again played Billy Bigelow in a revival presented by the Music Theatre of Lincoln Center. The 1956 film version starred Gordon MacRae and Shirley Jones.
MCA OC; RCA OC (1965); MCA SC (1987)/ Random House (1945)/ R&H.

THE RED MILL

Music: Victor Herbert
Lyrics: Henry Blossom, Forman Brown
Book: (uncredited)
Producers: Paula Stone & Hunt Stromberg Jr.
Director: Billy Gilbert
Choreographer: Aida Broadbent
Cast: Eddie Foy Jr., Michael O'Shea, Odette Myrtil, Dorothy Stone, Charles Collins, Ann Andre, Lorna Byron
Songs: Same as original production
New York run: Ziegfeld Theatre, October 16, 1945; 531 p.

(See page 13.)

SHOW BOAT

Music: Jerome Kern
Lyrics & book: Oscar Hammerstein II
Producers: Jerome Kern & Oscar Hammerstein II
Directors: Hassard Short, Oscar Hammerstein II
Choreographer: Helen Tamiris
Cast: Jan Clayton, Ralph Dumke, Carol Bruce, Charles Fredericks, Buddy Ebsen, Colette Lyons, Kenneth Spencer, Pearl Primus, Talley Beatty
Songs: Same as original production plus "Nobody Else but Me"
New York run: Ziegfeld Theatre, January 5, 1946; 418 p.

(See page 60.)

Show Boat. Buddy Ebsen and Colette Lyons strutting through "Goodbye, My Lady Love." (Eileen Darby)

ST. LOUIS WOMAN

Music: Harold Arlen
Lyrics: Johnny Mercer
Book: Arna Bontemps & Countee Cullen
Producer: Edward Gross
Director: Rouben Mamoulian
Choreographer: Charles Walters
Cast: Harold Nicholas, Fayard Nicholas, Pearl Bailey, Ruby Hill, Rex Ingram, June Hawkins, Juanita Hall, Lorenzo Fuller
Songs: "Cakewalk Your Lady"; "Come Rain or Come Shine"; "I Had Myself a True Love"; "Legalize My Name"; "Any Place I Hang My Hat Is Home"; "A Woman's Prerogative"; "Ridin' on the Moon"
New York run: Martin Beck Theatre, March 30, 1946; 113 p.

Though based on Arna Bontemps' novel, *God Sends Sunday, St. Louis Woman* seems also to have been a close relative of *Porgy and Bess.* Set in St. Louis in 1898, the musical tells of fickle Della Green (Ruby Hill in a part intended for Lena Horne), who is the woman of tough saloon owner Biglow Brown (Rex Ingram), but who falls for Li'l Augie (Harold Nicholas), a jockey with an incredible winning streak. Before Brown is killed by a discarded girlfriend, he puts a curse on Li'l Augie which ends both the winning streak and Della's affection. The two, however, are reunited for the final reprise of their ardent "Come Rain or Come Shine." In 1959, a revised version of *St. Louis Woman*, with other Harold Arlen songs added and now set in New Orleans, was performed in Amsterdam and Paris under the title *Free and Easy.*
Capitol OC/ N.A.L. (1973).

CALL ME MISTER

Music & lyrics: Harold Rome
Sketches: Arnold Auerbach, Arnold B. Horwitt
Producers: Melvyn Douglas & Herman Levin
Director: Robert H. Gordon
Choreographer: John Wray
Cast: Betty Garrett, Jules Munshin, Bill Callahan, Lawrence Winters, Paula Bane, Maria Karnilova, George S. Irving
Songs: "Goin' Home Train"; "Along With Me"; "The Red Ball Express"; "Military Life"; "The Face on the Dime"; "South America, Take It Away"; "Call Me Mister"
New York run: National Theatre, April 18, 1946; 734 p.

With its theme dealing with servicemen readjusting to civilian life, *Call Me Mister* was something of a follow-up to *This Is the Army.* The show's cast consisted of ex-GIs and ex-USO entertainers, and it took a somewhat satirical, yet basically good-humored and optimistic attitude toward military life and demobilization. Its most popular number was "South America, Take It Away," performed by Betty Garrett as a rumba-hating canteen hostess. Its funniest sketch found the Air Corps getting its lumps as the flyers were shown enjoying the glamorous life while periodically offering toasts "To the Blue Lady of the Clouds." In a serious moment, the revue faced up to post-war racial discrimination when Lawrence Winters, as a former driver with the supplies-carrying "Red Ball Express," is unable to get a job as a truck driver. *Call Me Mister* played the National Theatre (now the Nederlander) on 41st Street west of 7th Avenue. The 1951 movie version (with plot) co-starred Betty Grable and Dan Dailey.
CSP OC.

ANNIE GET YOUR GUN

Music & lyrics: Irving Berlin
Book: Herbert & Dorothy Fields
Producers: Richard Rodgers & Oscar Hammerstein II
Director: Joshua Logan
Choreographer: Helen Tamiris
Cast: Ethel Merman, Ray Middleton, Marty May, Kenny Bowers, Lea Penman, Betty Anne Nyman, William O'Neal, Lubov Roudenko, Daniel Nagrin, Harry Belaver, Ellen Hanley
Songs: "Doin' What Comes Natur'lly"; "The Girl That I Marry"; "You Can't Get a Man With a Gun"; "There's No Business Like Show Business"; "They Say It's Wonderful"; "Moonshine Lullaby"; "My Defenses Are Down"; "I'm an Indian Too"; "I Got Lost in His Arms"; "I Got the Sun in the Morning"; "Anything You Can Do"
New York run: Imperial Theatre, May 16, 1946; 1,147 p.

Annie Get Your Gun was the first of two shows Irving Berlin wrote for Ethel Merman (the other was *Call Me Madam*). The third longest running musical of the Forties, it was also the biggest Broadway hit of their respective careers. Originally, however, composer Jerome Kern was to have written the songs with lyricist Dorothy Fields (also the co-librettist), but Kern's death as he was about to begin the assignment brought Berlin into the project for both music and lyrics. The idea for the show, the only Rodgers and Hammerstein musical production without a Rodgers and Hammerstein score, is credited to Miss Fields who felt that Ethel Merman as Annie Oakley would be surefire casting.

Though unspecified, the period of the story is the mid-1880s. Annie Oakley, an illiterate hillbilly living near Cincinnati, demonstrates her remarkable marksmanship, and is persuaded — through the convincing claim "There's No Business Like Show Business" — to join Col. Buffalo Bill's travelling Wild West Show. Annie, who needs only one look to fall hopelessly in love with Frank Butler (Ray Middleton), the show's featured shooting ace, soon eclipses Butler as the main attraction, which doesn't help the cause of romance. She exhibits her skills at such locales as the Minneapolis Fair Grounds (where she hits the targets while riding on a motorcycle) and at Governor's Island, New York, where, in a shooting contest with Frank, she realizes that the only way to win the man is to let him win the match. The National Company's tour, which began in October 1947, lasted for one year seven months with Mary Martin heading the original touring cast. In 1966, Miss Merman recreated the role of Annie Oakley for a production sponsored by the Music Theatre of Lincoln Center. This revival, which also had Bruce Yarnell and Jerry Orbach in the cast, included a new Berlin song, "An Old-Fashioned Wedding." After a brief tour, the show played two months at the Broadway Theatre. Betty Hutton and Howard Keel were in the 1950 screen adaptation.

Following *Annie Get Your Gun,* other show business musical biographies have been written about Gypsy Rose Lee (Sandra Church in *Gypsy,* 1959); Edmund Kean (Alfred Drake in *Kean,* 1961); Sophie Tucker (Libi Staiger in *Sophie,* 1963); Laurette Taylor (Mary Martin in *Jennie,* 1963); Fanny Brice (Barbra Streisand in *Funny Girl,* 1964); George M. Cohan (Joel Grey in *George M!,* 1968); the Marx Brothers (Lewis J. Stadlen, Daniel Fortus, Irwin Pearl, and Alvin Kupperman in *Minnie's Boys,* 1970); Mack Sennett and Mabel Normand (Robert Preston and Bernadette Peters in *Mack & Mabel,* 1974); Phineas T. Barnum (Jim Dale in *Barnum,* 1980); Federico Fellini (Raul Julia in *Nine,* 1982); Tallulah Bankhead (Helen Gallagher in *Tallulah,* 1983); Marilyn Monroe (Alyson Reed in *Marilyn,* 1983); Ned Harrigan and Tony Hart (Harry Groener and Mark Hamill in *Harrigan 'n Hart,* 1985); and Ellie Greenfield (Dinah Manoff in *Leader of the Pack,* 1985).
MCA OC; RCA OC (1966)/ R&H.

Cover designed by Lucinda Ballard.

Annie Get Your Gun. "There's No Business Like Show Business" sing William O'Neal, Marty May, Ethel Merman, and Ray Middleton. (Vandamm)

131

STREET SCENE

Music: Kurt Weill
Lyrics: Langston Hughes
Book: Elmer Rice
Producers: Dwight Deere Wiman & The Playwrights' Co.
Director: Charles Friedman
Choreographer: Anna Sokolow
Cast: Norman Cordon, Anne Jeffreys, Polyna Stoska, Brian Sullivan, Hope Emerson, Sheila Bond, Danny Daniels, Don Saxon, Juanita Hall
Songs: "Somehow I Never Could Believe"; "Ice Cream"; "Wrapped in a Ribbon and Tied in a Bow"; "Wouldn't You Like to Be on Broadway?"; "What Good Would the Moon Be?"; "Moon-Faced, Starry-Eyed"; "Remember That I Care"; "We'll Go Away Together"
New York run: Adelphi Theatre, January 9, 1947; 148 p.

Adapted by Elmer Rice from his 1929 play, *Street Scene* was the most operatic of all the Broadway productions with music by Kurt Weill. Something of a white Northern counterpart to *Porgy and Bess,* the work takes a melodramatic look at the inhabitants of a New York City tenement during an oppressively hot summer day. Among those inhabitants are the members of the Maurrant family — Anna (Polyna Stoska) whose loveless marriage (as revealed through the impassioned aria "Somehow I Never Could Believe") drives her to an affair that ends in tragedy; Anna's bullying, drunken husband Frank (Norman Cordon); and their frustrated daughter Rose (Anne Jeffreys) who cannot give herself either to the smooth-talking sharpie Harry Easter (Don Saxon) or to the earnest neighbor Sam Kaplan (Brian Sullivan). In 1959, *Street Scene* entered the repertory of the New York City Opera.
Columbia OC/ R&H.

Street Scene. Anne Jeffreys and Don Saxon.
(Vandamm)

Finian's Rainbow. Albert Sharpe, David Wayne, and Anita Alvarez in a tense moment.

FINIAN'S RAINBOW

Music: Burton Lane
Lyrics: E. Y. Harburg
Book: E. Y. Harburg & Fred Saidy
Producers: Lee Sabinson & William Katzell
Director: Bretaigne Windust
Choreographer: Michael Kidd
Cast: Ella Logan, Albert Sharpe, Donald Richards, David Wayne, Anita Alvarez, Robert Pitkin
Songs: "How Are Things in Glocca Morra?"; "If This Isn't Love"; "Look to the Rainbow"; "Old Devil Moon"; "Something Sort of Grandish"; "Necessity"; "When the Idle Poor Become the Idle Rich"; "When I'm Not Near the Girl I Love"; "That Great Come-and-Get-It Day"
New York run: 46th Street Theatre, January 10, 1947; 725 p.

E. Y. Harburg got the idea for *Finian's Rainbow* because he wanted to satirize an economic system that requires gold reserves to be buried at Fort Knox. He then began thinking of leprechauns and their legendary crock of gold that could grant three wishes. In the story that Harburg and Fred Saidy devised, Finian McLonergan (Albert Sharpe), an Irish immigrant, is in Rainbow Valley, Missitucky, to bury a crock of gold which, he is sure, will grow and make him rich. Also part of the fantasy are Og (David Wayne), the leprechaun whose crock has been stolen, Finian's daughter Sharon (Ella Logan), who dreams wistfully of Glocca Morra, Woody Mahoney (Donald Richards), a labor organizer who blames "That Old Devil Moon" for the way he feels about Sharon, and a bigoted Southern Senator, Billboard Rawkins (Robert Pitkin), who — as one of the three wishes — turns black. At the end, everyone comes to understand that riches are found not in gold but in people trusting one another. A 1960 revival had a brief Broadway run. The 1968 movie version starred Fred Astaire, Petula Clark, and Tommy Steele.
Columbia OC; RCA OC (1960)/ Berkley Books (1968)/ TW.

SWEETHEARTS

Music: Victor Herbert
Lyrics: Robert B. Smith
Book: John Cecil Holm
Producers: Paula Stone & Michael Sloane
Director: John Kennedy
Choreographers: Catherine Littlefield, Theodore Adolphus
Cast: Bobby Clark, Marjorie Gateson, Gloria Story, Mark Dawson, Robert Shackleton, June Knight, Cornell MacNeil
Songs: 6 cut from original production; "To the Land of My Own Romance" (lyric: Harry B. Smith) and "I Might Be Your Once-in-a-While" added.
New York run: Shubert Theatre, January 21, 1947; 288 p.

(See page 19.)

BRIGADOON

Music: Frederick Loewe
Lyrics & book: Alan Jay Lerner
Producer: Cheryl Crawford
Director: Robert Lewis
Choreographer: Agnes de Mille
Cast: David Brooks, Marion Bell, Pamela Britton, Lee Sullivan, George Keane, James Mitchell, William Hansen, Elliott Sullivan, Helen Gallagher, Hayes Gordon, Lidija Franklin
Songs: "Brigadoon"; "Down on MacConnachy Square"; "Waiting for My Dearie"; "I'll Go Home With Bonnie Jean"; "The Heather on the Hill"; "Come to Me, Bend to Me"; "Almost Like Being in Love"; "There but for You Go I"; "My Mother's Wedding Day"; "From This Day On"
New York run: Ziegfeld Theatre, March 13, 1947; 581 p.

By dealing with themes of substance, by their adherence to the concept of the integrated musical, and by their ability to make the past come vividly alive to modern audiences, Lerner and Loewe established their special niche in the musical theatre while still laying claim to being the stylistic heirs of Rodgers and Hammerstein. *Brigadoon,* their third Broadway musical and first hit, was motivated partly by Lerner's fondness for the works of James M. Barrie and partly by a German story, *Germelshausen,* by Friedrich Gerstäcker.

The fantasy is about two American tourists, Tommy Albright and Jeff Douglas (David Brooks and George Keane), who stumble upon a mist-clouded Scottish town that, they eventually discover, reawakens only one day every hundred years. Tommy, who enjoys wandering through the heather on the hill with a local lass, Fiona MacLaren (Marion Bell), returns to New York after learning of the curse that has caused the town's excessively somnolent condition. True love, however, pulls him back to the highlands. The tale was made believable not only through its evocative score but also through Agnes de Mille's ballets, especially the emotion-charged "Sword Dance" performed by James Mitchell during a wedding ceremony and the anguished "Funeral Dance" performed by Lidija Franklin.

A Broadway revival of *Brigadoon* in 1980 did not remain awake very long, but a 1986 production by the New York City Opera was well received. Hollywood's 1954 version co-starred Gene Kelly, Cyd Charisse, and Van Johnson. RCA OC/ Coward-McCann (1947); Chilton (1973)/ TW.

Brigadoon. George Keane, David Brooks, and William Hansen. (Vandamm)

HIGH BUTTON SHOES

Music: Jule Styne
Lyrics: Sammy Cahn
Book: Stephen Longstreet (George Abbott, Phil Silvers uncredited)
Producers: Monte Proser & Joseph Kipness
Director: George Abbott
Choreographer: Jerome Robbins
Cast: Phil Silvers, Nanette Fabray, Jack McCauley, Mark Dawson, Joey Faye, Lois Lee, Sondra Lee, Helen Gallagher, Nathaniel Frey, Johnny Stewart, Paul Godkin
Songs: "Can't You Just See Yourself?"; "You're My Girl"; "Papa, Won't You Dance With Me?"; "On a Sunday by the Sea"; "I Still Get Jealous"
New York run: New Century Theatre, October 9, 1947; 727 p.

High Button Shoes, Jule Styne's initial Broadway assignment, offered Phil Silvers his first starring opportunity in the typical role of a brash, bumbling con artist. Though Stephen Longstreet was credited with adapting the story from his own semi-autobiographical novel, *The Sisters Liked Them Handsome,* the musical was completely rewritten by director George Abbott, with an assist from Silvers. In the plot, set in New Brunswick, New Jersey, in 1913, Harrison Floy (Silvers) hoodwinks the Longstreet family into letting him sell some of the valueless property they own. After running off with the profits to Atlantic City (where Jerome Robbins' classic "Keystone Kops" ballet is staged), Floy loses and recovers the money — then loses it forever by betting on the wrong college football team. The musical's showstopper was an old-fashioned song-and-dance polka, "Papa, Won't You Dance With Me?," performed by Nanette Fabray and Jack McCauley.
RCA OC/ TW.

ALLEGRO

Music: Richard Rodgers
Lyrics & book: Oscar Hammerstein II
Producer: Theatre Guild
Director: Agnes de Mille (Oscar Hammerstein II uncredited)
Choreographer: Agnes de Mille
Cast: John Battles, Annamary Dickey, William Ching, John Conte, Muriel O'Malley, Lisa Kirk, Roberta Jonay
Songs: "A Fellow Needs a Girl"; "You Are Never Away"; "So Far"; "Money Isn't Ev'rything"; "The Gentleman Is a Dope"; "Allegro"
New York run: Majestic Theatre, October 10, 1947; 315 p.

The third Rodgers and Hammerstein Broadway musical, *Allegro* was their first with a story that had not been based on a previous source. It was a particularly ambitious undertaking, with a theme dealing with the corrupting effect of big institutions on the young and idealistic. The saga is told through the life of a doctor, Joseph Taylor Jr. (John Battles), from his birth in a small midwest American town to his 35th year. We follow Joe's progress as he grows up, goes to school, marries a local belle (Roberta Jonay), joins the staff of a large Chicago hospital that panders to wealthy hypochondriacs, discovers that his wife is unfaithful, and, in the end, returns to his home town with his adoring nurse (Lisa Kirk) to rededicate his life to healing the sick and helping the needy. The show's innovations included a Greek chorus to comment on the action both to the actors and the audience, and the use of multi-level performing areas with nonrepresentational sets.
RCA OC/ Random House (1947)/ R&H.

MAKE MINE MANHATTAN

Music: Richard Lewine
Lyrics & sketches: Arnold B. Horwitt
Producer: Joseph Hyman
Directors: Hassard Short, Max Liebman
Choreographer: Lee Sherman
Cast: Sid Caesar, David Burns, Sheila Bond, Joshua Shelley, Kyle McDonnell, Danny Daniels, Nelle Fisher, Ray Harrison, Jack Kilty, Larry Carr
Songs: "Phil the Fiddler"; "Saturday Night in Central Park"; "I Fell in Love With You"; "My Brudder and Me"; "Gentleman Friend"
New York run: Broadhurst Theatre, January 15, 1948; 429 p.

Partly because of the increasing importance of books in book musicals and partly because of the increasing influence of television, 1948 was the last year in which traditional revues found large and receptive audiences. Adhering to its titular request, *Make Mine Manhattan* took a mostly satirical but always light-hearted look at the city's most prominent borough as it covered such matters as the forthcoming establishment of the United Nations' permanent home, the pretentions of Rodgers and Hammerstein's *Allegro*, the distinctive menu at the Schrafft's restaurant chain, the continuous cacophony of street noises, and — recognizing the existence of two other boroughs — the problems of a Bronx boy who must use an intricate series of subway trains to travel to see his girl at the far end of Brooklyn. Sid Caesar, who did imitations, including one of a penny gum machine, was succeeded for the tour by Bert Lahr.
Painted Smiles SC.

INSIDE U.S.A.

Music: Arthur Schwartz
Lyrics: Howard Dietz
Sketches: Arnold Auerbach, Arnold B. Horwitt, Moss Hart
Producer: Arthur Schwartz
Director: Robert H. Gordon
Choreographer: Helen Tamiris
Cast: Beatrice Lillie, Jack Haley, John Tyers, Herb Shriner, Valerie Bettis, Lewis Nye, Carl Reiner, Thelma Carpenter, Estelle Loring, Eric Victor, Talley Beatty, Jack Cassidy
Songs: "Inside U.S.A."; "Blue Grass"; "Rhode Island Is Famous for You"; "Haunted Heart"; "At the Mardi Gras"; "My Gal Is Mine Once More"; "First Prize at the Fair"
New York run: New Century Theatre, April 30, 1948; 399 p.

Expanding the geographical area of the recently opened *Make Mine Manhattan*, and contracting it from their 1935 revue *At Home Abroad*, Arthur Schwartz and Howard Dietz put together an All-American revue, *Inside U.S.A.*, which borrowed nothing more than the title from John Gunther's sociological survey. With Beatrice Lillie and Jack Haley as comical cicerones, the itinerary included visits to Pittsburgh (where a choral society takes on industrial pollution), the Kentucky Derby (for a lament of one whose lover has been lost betting the ponies), a San Francisco waterfront (the scene of the ballad "Haunted Heart"), the Wisconsin State Fair, the New Orleans Mardi Gras (Bea Lillie is queen), a Wyoming rodeo, and Alberquerque (where two Indians, Miss Lillie and Haley, resolutely refuse to take the country back). *Inside U.S.A.* was the last of seven revues written by Schwartz and Dietz.

LOVE LIFE

Music: Kurt Weill
Lyrics & book: Alan Jay Lerner
Producer: Cheryl Crawford
Director: Elia Kazan
Choreographer: Michael Kidd
Cast: Nanette Fabray, Ray Middleton, Johnny Stewart, Cheryl Archer, Jay Marshall
Songs: "Here I'll Stay"; "Progress"; "I Remember It Well"; "Green-Up Time"; "Economics"; "Mr. Right"
New York run: 46th Street Theatre, October 7, 1948; 252 p.

The only collaboration between Kurt Weill and Alan Jay Lerner, *Love Life* was a highly unconventional work. Billed as "A Vaudeville," it related the story of a non-aging couple (Nanette Fabray and Ray Middleton) and their two children from 1791 to the present, with the theme being the gradual changes in the relationship between people as life in America becomes more complex. The musical pieces were incorporated into the show mostly as commentaries on the characters and situations, in much the same way that Weill had used songs in his early German works. As for the musical's structure, there was no linear plot — with beginning, middle and end — but rather a series of separate but connecting scenes interspersed with vaudeville acts through which the authors conveyed their views. Not quite the format for a long-running smash, perhaps, but the show's innovations did turn up in later productions such as *Company* and *A Chorus Line* (nonlinear stories), *Hallelujah, Baby!* (characters did not age over a long period of time), and *Chicago* (conceived as "A Musical Vaudeville").

WHERE'S CHARLEY?

Music & lyrics: Frank Loesser
Book: George Abbott
Producers: Cy Feuer & Ernest Martin
Director: George Abbott
Choreographer: George Balanchine
Cast: Ray Bolger, Allyn Ann McLerie, Byron Palmer, Doretta Morrow, Horace Cooper, Jane Lawrence, Paul England, Cornell MacNeil
Songs: "The New Ashmoleon Marching Society and Students' Conservatory Band"; "My Darling, My Darling"; "Make a Miracle"; "Lovelier Than Ever"; "Once in Love With Amy"; "At the Red Rose Cotillion"
New York run: St. James Theatre, October 11, 1948; 792 p.

Where's Charley? was based on Brandon Thomas's durable 1892 London farce, *Charley's Aunt.* The first Broadway book musical with a score by Frank Loesser (he wrote five shows in all), the musical is concerned with the madcap doings that result when Oxford undergraduates Charley Wykeham (Ray Bolger) and Jack Chesney (Byron Palmer) entertain their proper lady friends, Amy Spettigue (Allyn Ann McLerie) and Kitty Verdun (Doretta Morrow), in their rooms. To do so, Charley must also play chaperon by disguising himself as his own rich aunt "from Brazil where the nuts come from." Transvestite misunderstanding results in complications when the "aunt" must flee the amorous advances of the girls' money-hungry guardian, and when the real aunt makes an unexpected appearance. The show gave Ray Bolger his biggest hit, plus the nightly opportunity to lead the audience in joining him in singing "Once in Love With Amy." Bolger brought the touring company back to Broadway in 1951 for 48 performances, and repeated his part in the 1952 movie version.
M-E London OC (1958)/ MTI.

AS THE GIRLS GO

Music: Jimmy McHugh
Lyrics: Harold Adamson
Book: William Roos
Producer: Michael Todd
Director: Howard Bay
Choreographer: Hermes Pan
Cast: Bobby Clark, Irene Rich, Bill Callahan, Kathryn Lee, Betty Jane Watson, Hobart Cavanaugh, Betty Lou Barto, Dick Dana, Gregg Sherwood, Jo Sullivan, Buddy Schwab
Songs: "As the Girls Go"; "You Say the Nicest Things, Baby"; "There's No Getting Away from You"; "Lucky in the Rain"; "Father's Day"
New York run: Winter Garden, November 13, 1948; 420 p.

A throwback to the days when a great personality could carry a musical to success without any help from the book, *As the Girls Go* was a gaudy, rowdy, fast-paced song-and-dance show totally dependent on the antics of one of the theatre's outstanding clowns, Bobby Clark, here making his final Broadway appearance. Clark played Waldo Wellington, the husband of the first woman President of the United States (Irene Rich), and initially the production was planned as a political satire in the tradition of *Of Thee I Sing*. After a disastrous tryout in Boston, however, the plot was largely discarded as Clark leered, pranced, chased Amazonian show girls, blew soap bubbles out of a trumpet, masqueraded as a female barber, and, without looking, tossed his hat clear across the stage and onto a hatrack. During the run, Fran Warren replaced Betty Jane Watson in the romantic lead. *As the Girls Go* was the first Broadway attraction to charge $7.20 for orchestra seats.

LEND AN EAR

Music, lyrics & sketches: Charles Gaynor
Producers: William Katzell, Franklin Gilbert, William Eythe
Directors: Gower Champion, Hal Gerson
Choreographer: Gower Champion
Cast: William Eythe, Carol Channing, Yvonne Adair, Gene Nelson, Jennie Lou Law, Gloria Hamilton, Bob Scheerer
Songs: "Give Your Heart a Chance to Sing"; "Doin' the Old Yahoo Step"; "Molly O'Reilly"; "Who Hit Me?"
New York run: National Theatre, December 16, 1948; 460 p.

Billed as "An Intimate Musical Revue" (there were 21 in the cast), *Lend an Ear* was the first of 14 musicals to be directed and choreographed by Gower Champion. It also revealed the triple talents of writer Charles Gaynor, and it marked the Broadway debut of a squeaky-voiced, saucer-eyed blonde named Carol Channing. Initially presented seven years earlier in Pittsburgh, the youthful show came to New York after a successful engagement in Los Angeles. Among its satirical topics: psychoanalysts; the influence of gossip columnists; a tourist-eye view of Santo Domingo; a third-rate opera company that must speak its lines because it cannot afford orchestral accompaniment; queens of the silent screen; and "The Gladiola Girl," an encapsulated typical musical comedy of the mid-Twenties about flappers and lounge lizards on a Long Island estate where everyone dances "The Old Yahoo Step."
Samuel French (1971)*/ SF.

Kiss Me, Kate. Alfred Drake taming his shrew Patricia Morison. (Eileen Darby)

KISS ME, KATE

Music & lyrics: Cole Porter
Book: Samuel & Bella Spewack
Producers: Saint Subber & Lemuel Ayers
Director: John C. Wilson
Choreographer: Hanya Holm
Cast: Alfred Drake, Patricia Morison, Harold Lang, Lisa Kirk, Harry Clark, Jack Diamond, Annabelle Hill, Lorenzo Fuller, Marc Breaux
Songs: "Another Op'nin', Another Show"; "Why Can't You Behave?"; "Wunderbar"; "So in Love"; "We Open in Venice"; "Tom, Dick or Harry"; "I've Come to Wive It Wealthily in Padua"; "I Hate Men"; "Were Thine That Special Face"; "Too Darn Hot"; "Where Is the Life That Late I Led?"; "Always True to You in My Fashion"; "Bianca"; "Brush Up Your Shakespeare"; "I Am Ashamed That Women Are So Simple" (lyric: Shakespeare)
New York run: New Century Theatre, December 30, 1948; 1,070 p.

After having collaborated ten years earlier on *Leave It to Me!*, Cole Porter and the husband-wife team of Samuel and Bella Spewack were reunited for *Kiss Me, Kate,* the composer's biggest hit and the fourth longest running musical of the Forties. The idea for the show began germinating in 1935 when producer Saint Subber, then a stagehand for the Theatre Guild's production of *The Taming of the Shrew*, became aware that its stars, Alfred Lunt and Lynn Fontanne, quarrelled in private almost as much as did the charaters they were portraying in the play. *Kiss Me, Kate* takes place backstage and onstage at Ford's Theatre in Baltimore, from five p.m. to midnight during one day of a tryout of a musical version of *The Taming of the Shrew*. In the plot, egotistical actor-producer Fred Graham (Alfred Drake) and his temperamental co-star and ex-wife, Lili Vanessi (Patricia Morison) fight and make up and eventually demonstrate their enduring affection for each other — just like Shakespeare's Petruchio and Kate. A subplot involves actress Lois Lane (Lisa Kirk) whose romance with actor Bill Calhoun (Harold Lang) is complicated by Bill's weakness for gambling.

Because of the musical's construction, it is possible to follow the story of *The Taming of the Shrew* even though the play-within-the-play is offered only in excerpts. For his lyrics in the musical numbers sung during *The Shrew's* performance, Porter made use of such Shakespearean lines as "I come to wive it wealthily in Padua," "Were thine that special face," "Where is the life that late I led?," and Kate's finale speech beginning "I am ashamed that women are so simple." The more modern sentiments — "Why Can't You Behave?," "So in Love," "Too Darn Hot," and "Always True to You in My Fashion" — were restricted to the theatre's backstage area.

Kiss Me, Kate (the title is from Petruchio's last command in *The Taming of the Shrew)* marked Alfred Drake's first starring part on Broadway and the only major musical in which Patricia Morison originated a leading role. (She won it after it had been rejected by Jarmila Novotna, Mary Martin, Lily Pons, and Jeanette MacDonald.) During the run, Drake was succeeded by Keith Andes and Ted Scott, Miss Morison by Anne Jeffreys, Lisa Kirk by Betty Ann Grove, and Harold Lang by Danny Daniels. The National Company, which toured for one year 11 months, started out with a cast headed by Andes, Jeffreys, Julie Wilson, and Marc Platt, with the first three eventually succeeded by Bob Wright, Frances McCann, and Betty George. In 1953, the Hollywood version put Howard Keel, Kathryn Grayson, Ann Miller, and Tommy Rall in the leads. For other musicals based on Shakespeare, see *The Boys from Syracuse,* page 107.
Columbia OC; Capitol OC/ Knopf (1953); Chilton (1973)/ TW.

South Pacific. Mary Martin and Ezio Pinza.

South Pacific. William Tabbert singing "Younger Than Springtime" to Betta St. John.

SOUTH PACIFIC

Music: Richard Rodgers
Lyrics: Oscar Hammerstein II
Book: Oscar Hammerstein II & Joshua Logan
Producers: Richard Rodgers & Oscar Hammerstein II, Leland Hayward & Joshua Logan
Director: Joshua Logan
Cast: Mary Martin, Ezio Pinza, Myron McCormick, Juanita Hall, William Tabbert, Betta St. John, Martin Wolfson, Harvey Stephens, Richard Eastham, Henry Slate, Fred Sadoff, Archie Savage
Songs: "A Cockeyed Optimist"; "Some Enchanted Evening"; "Bloody Mary"; "There Is Nothin' Like a Dame"; "Bali Ha'i"; "I'm Gonna Wash That Man Right Outa My Hair"; "A Wonderful Guy"; "Younger Than Springtime"; "Happy Talk"; "Honey Bun"; "You've Got to Be Carefully Taught"; "This Nearly Was Mine"
New York run: Majestic Theatre, April 7, 1949; 1,925 p.

The catalyst for the musical was director Joshua Logan who, early in 1948, strongly urged Rodgers and Hammerstein to adapt a short story in James Michener's wartime collection *Tales of the South Pacific* as their next Broadway production. "Fo' Dolla," the story Logan recommended, was about Lt. Joe Cable's tender and tragic romance with a Polynesian girl, but it struck the partners as too close to *Madama Butterfly* to sustain interest throughout an entire evening. Their solution was to make this a secondary plot while using another Michener tale, "Our Heroine," as the main story. That one had to do with the unlikely attraction between Nellie Forbush, a naive Navy nurse from Little Rock, and Emile de Becque, a worldly French planter living on a Pacific island, who fall in love on an enchanted evening. Both stories were combined by having Cable and de Becque go on a dangerous mission together behind Japanese lines, from which only de Becque returns. One of the musical's major themes — expressed through the song "You've Got to Be Carefully Taught" — is the folly of the racial prejudice, an issue that comes up when Emile tells Nellie that he had lived with a native woman who bore him two children.

South Pacific was the first of two musicals (the other was *The Sound of Music*) in which Mary Martin, who played Nellie, was seen as a Rodgers and Hammerstein heroine, and it marked the Broadway debut of Metropolitan Opera basso Ezio Pinza, who played de Becque. It was the second longest running musical of the decade as well as the second musical to be awarded the Pulitzer Prize for drama. Among actors who appeared in the production during its Broadway tenure were Martha Wright and Cloris Leachman (both played Nellie), Ray Middleton (de Becque), Shirley Jones (one of the nurses), Gene Saks (Professor), and Jack Weston (Stewpot).

The touring company, which was seen in 118 cities over a period of five years, had a cast originally headed by Janet Blair (Nellie), Richard Eastham (de Becque), Diosa Costello (Bloody Mary), Ray Walston (Luther), Julia Migenes (de Becque's daughter), and Alan Baxter (Comdr. Harbison). Cast replacements on the road included Connie Russell (Nellie), Irene Bordoni (Bloody Mary), and David Burns and Benny Baker (Luther). In 1967, *South Pacific* was revived by the Music Theatre of Lincoln Center with Florence Henderson and Giorgio Tozzi in the leads; 20 years later it was staged by the New York City Opera. The 1958 screen version co-starred Mitzi Gaynor and Rosanno Brazzi (with Tozzi's voice). Columbia OC; Columbia OC (1967); CBS SC (1986)/ Random House (1949)/ R&H.

MISS LIBERTY

Music & lyrics: Irving Berlin
Book: Robert E. Sherwood
Producers: Irving Berlin, Robert E. Sherwood & Moss Hart
Director: Moss Hart
Choreographer: Jerome Robbins
Cast: Eddie Albert, Allyn Ann McLerie, Mary McCarty, Charles Dingle, Philip Bourneuf, Ethel Griffies, Herbert Berghof, Tommy Rall, Janice Rule, Maria Karnilova, Dody Goodman
Songs: "Little Fish in a Big Pond"; "Let's Take an Old-Fashioned Walk"; "Homework"; "Paris Wakes Up and Smiles"; "Only for Americans"; "Just One Way to Say I Love You"; "You Can Have Him"; "Give Me Your Tired, Your Poor" (poem: Emma Lazarus)
New York run: Imperial Theatre, July 15, 1949; 308 p.

Miss Liberty boasted impressive credentials: songs by Irving Berlin, book by Robert E. Sherwood (his only musical), and direction by Moss Hart. If the results fell somewhat short of expectations, the show was still very much in the Americana mold of *Oklahoma!* and *Bloomer Girl* that offered a comforting view of the past to make audiences feel confident about the future. Here the story — set in New York and Paris in 1885 — deals with the rivalry between two newspapers, the *Herald* and the *World*, and the search for the model who posed for the Statue of Liberty. When the wrong model is brought to New York amid much hoopla, there is the inevitable consternation when the error is discovered. A happy ending is devised, however, just in time for the statue's dedication when all join in singing "Give Me Your Tired, Your Poor."
Columbia OC/ Samuel French (1986)*/ SF.

LOST IN THE STARS

Music: Kurt Weill
Lyrics & book: Maxwell Anderson
Producer: Playwrights' Company
Director: Rouben Mamoulian
Cast: Todd Duncan, Leslie Banks, Warren Coleman, Inez Matthews, Julian Mayfield, Frank Roane, Sheila Guyse, Herbert Coleman
Songs: "The Hills of Ixipo"; "Thousands of Miles"; "Train to Johannesburg"; "The Little Grey House"; "Trouble Man"; "Lost in the Stars"; "Stay Well"; "Cry, the Beloved Country"; "Big Mole"; "A Bird of Passage"
New York run: Music Box, October 30, 1949; 273 p.

Regarding the musical adaptation of Alan Paton's novel of South Africa, *Cry, the Beloved Country,* Kurt Weill once explained, "We wanted to treat the race problem as part of the human problem. The tragedy through which we are living is the tragedy of all men, white or black, rich or poor, young or old." After Absalom Kumalo (Julian Mayfield), the son of black minister Stephen Kumalo (Todd Duncan), accidentally kills a white man in an attempted robbery in Johannesburg, he is courageous enough to admit his guilt and face hanging, even though his companions, protesting their innocence, go free. As Absalom is about to die, Stephen is visited by the father of the slain man. Though James Jarvis (Leslie Banks) is a firm believer in apartheid, he admires the minister for his courage and honesty, and the play ends with each man saying, "I have a friend." *Lost in the Stars* was Kurt Weill's last Broadway production. In 1958, the work became part of the repertory of the New York City Opera, and in 1972 it was presented on Broadway with Brock Peters as Stephen Kumalo. Peters and Melba Moore were in the 1974 film version.
MCA OC/ Chilton (1976)/ R&H.

Miss Liberty. Allyn Ann McLerie, Eddie Albert, Mary McCarty, Charles Dingle, Maria Karnilova, and Tommy Rall lead the cast in singing "Give Me Your Tired, Your Poor."

Lost in the Stars. Warren Coleman, Todd Duncan, and Herbert Coleman. (Karger-Pix)

GENTLEMEN PREFER BLONDES

Music: Jule Styne
Lyrics: Leo Robin
Book: Joseph Stein & Anita Loos
Producers: Herman Levin & Oliver Smith
Director: John C. Wilson
Choreographer: Agnes de Mille
Cast: Carol Channing, Yvonne Adair, Jack McCauley, Eric Brotherson, Alice Pearce, Rex Evans, Anita Alvarez, George S. Irving, Mort Marshall, Howard Morris, Charles "Honi" Coles, Cholly Atkins
Songs: "Bye, Bye, Baby"; "A Little Girl from Little Rock"; "Just a Kiss Apart"; "It's Delightful Down in Chile"; "Diamonds Are a Girl's Best Friend"
New York run: Ziegfeld Theatre, December 8, 1949; 740 p.

Based on Anita Loos' popular 1926 novel and play of the same name, *Gentlemen Prefer Blondes* took a satirical look at the wild and wacky Twenties, though there was no attempt at parodying the songs and styles as in the manner of Sandy Wilson's *The Boy Friend.* Carol Channing, in her first major role, scored such a success as the gold-digging little girl from Little Rock that she was elevated to stardom during the show's run. The scenes occur mostly aboard the *Ile de France,* which is taking Lorelei Lee and her chum Dorothy Shaw (Yvonne Adair) to Paris, courtesy of Lorelei's generous friend, button tycoon Gus Esmond (Jack McCauley). En route, the girls meet a number of accommodating gentlemen, including Sir Francis Beekman (Rex Evans) who loses a diamond tiara to Lorelei (who thereby wins a best friend) and Henry Spofford (Eric Brotherson), a Philadelphia Main Liner who loses his heart to Dorothy. The 1953 movie version offered Marilyn Monroe and Jane Russell, plus a hybrid score.

In 1973, a new stage version, called *Lorelei,* retained ten songs from the original score and added five new ones by Jule Styne, Betty Comden and Adolph Green. Carol Channing again headed the cast which included Tamara Long (Dorothy), Peter Palmer (Gus), Lee Roy Reams (Henry), and Jack Fletcher (Sir Francis). The book, now credited to Kenny Solms and Gail Parent, retained the same basic story, except for a modern-day prologue and epilogue that found Lorelei reminiscing about the past. After touring 11 months, *Lorelei* opened on Broadway in January 1974, and gave 320 performances.
Columbia OC; MGM OC (1973, 1974).

Gentlemen Prefer Blondes. Carol Channing singing "Diamonds Are a Girl's Best Friend." (Fred Fehl)

Call Me Madam. Ethel Merman as Sally Adams. (Vandamm)

CALL ME MADAM
Music & lyrics: Irving Berlin
Book: Howard Lindsay & Russel Crouse
Producer: Leland Hayward
Director: George Abbott
Choreographer: Jerome Robbins
Cast: Ethel Merman, Paul Lukas, Russell Nype, Galina Talva, Pat Harrington, Alan Hewitt, Tommy Rall, Nathaniel Frey
Songs: "The Hostess With the Mostes' on the Ball"; "Can You Use Any Money Today?"; "Marrying for Love"; "It's a Lovely Day Today"; "They Like Ike"; "The Best Thing for You"; "You're Just in Love"
New York run: Imperial Theatre, October 12, 1950; 644 p.

Once President Harry S. Truman named Washington party-giver Perle Mesta Ambassador to Luxembourg, the foundation was laid for a musical-comedy satire that would kid politics, foreign affairs, and the familiar sight of the comically gauche American abroad. Once Ethel Merman and Irving Berlin joined Howard Lindsay and Russel Crouse in the enterprise, the foundation was laid for a solid Broadway hit. The story, according to the program, takes place "in two mythical countries, one is Lichtenburg, the other the United States of America." When Sally Adams, the hostess with the mostes' on the ball, becomes Ambassador to the tiny duchy, she surprises and charms the local gentry, especially Foreign Minister Cosmo Constantine (Paul Lukas), with her no-nonsense, undiplomatic manner. In a subplot, Sally's young aide Kenneth Gibson (Russell Nype) finds himself falling for Lichtenburg's Princess Marie (Galina Talva), a condition that prompts the ambassador to itemize the symptoms in the classic contrapuntal duet, "You're Just in Love." In a running gag, Sally periodically chats with President Truman on the telephone, thereby justifying the nightly gimmick of Truman look-alike Irving Fisher taking a bow during the curtain calls. The film version, also starring Ethel Merman, was released in 1953. Three years later, Miss Merman appeared in *Happy Hunting,* another Lindsay-Crouse stage musical contrasting American brashness with European courtliness that was also sparked by a topical event, the wedding of Grace Kelly and Prince Rainier of Monaco. RCA OC (minus Merman); MCA OC (only Merman)/ Irving Berlin Ltd., London (1956)*/ MTI.

GUYS AND DOLLS

Music & lyrics: Frank Loesser
Book: Abe Burrows
Producers: Cy Feuer & Ernest Martin
Director: George S. Kaufman
Choreographer: Michael Kidd
Cast: Robert Alda, Vivian Blaine, Sam Levene, Isabel Bigley, Pat Rooney Sr., B. S. Pully, Stubby Kaye, Tom Pedi, Johnny Silver, Peter Gennaro, Onna White, Buddy Schwab
Songs: "Fugue for Tinhorns"; "Follow the Fold"; "The Oldest Established"; "I'll Know"; "A Bushel and a Peck"; "Adelaide's Lament"; "Guys and Dolls"; "If I Were a Bell"; "My Time of Day"; "I've Never Been in Love Before"; "Take Back Your Mink"; "More I Cannot Wish You"; "Luck Be a Lady"; "Sue Me"; "Sit Down, You're Rockin' the Boat"; "Marry the Man Today"
New York run: 46th Street Theatre, November 24, 1950; 1,200 p.

Though it turned out to be one of Broadway's most hilarious musical comedies — as well as an acknowledged classic in the field — *Guys and Dolls* was originally planned as a serious romantic story. Much impressed by the success of *South Pacific,* producers Cy Feuer and Ernest Martin felt that if such a compelling musical play could be written about the unlikely romance between naive Nellie Forbush and sophisticated Emile de Becque, an equally affecting story could be created out of the unlikely romance between a pure-at-heart Salvation Army-type reformer and a slick Broadway gambler, the two leading characters in Damon Runyon's short story "The Idyll of Miss Sarah Brown." For the score, the producers enlisted Frank Loesser (with whom they had been associated on *Where's Charley?*), then tried some 11 librettists though none came up with an acceptable script. The last of these writers, Jo Swerling, had a contract giving him primary credit as author no matter how many subsequent changes might be made, which is the reason his name always appears on programs as co-librettist. After so many script rejections, Feuer and Martin changed their minds and now decided that *Guys and Dolls* could only work if it were played for laughs. This led them to Abe Burrows, a radio and television comedy writer without theatrical experience, who wrote an entirely new book that he fitted to Loesser's already existing score.

In this so-called "Musical Fable of Broadway," the high-minded lowlifes and spunky do-gooders of Damon Runyon's world come colorfully alive in such characters as Sky Masterson (Robert Alda), the bet-on-anything gambler; Nathan Detroit (Sam Levene), the perpetually harried organizer of the oldest established permanent floating crap game in New York, who bets Sky that he can't make the next girl he sees fall in love with him; Miss Sarah Brown (Isabel Bigley) of the Save-a-Soul Mission on Times Square, who *is* the next girl Sky sees and who does succumb; and Miss Adelaide (Vivian Blaine), the main attraction at the Hot Box nightclub, whose psychosomatic perpetual cold stems from her being engaged to Nathan for 14 years. One of the show's memorable scenes occurs in the mission where Nicely-Nicely Johnson (Stubby Kaye) confesses his sins in the rousing "Sit Down, You're Rockin' the Boat." *Guys and Dolls* was the fifth longest-running Broadway musical of the Fifties. Its touring company traveled for two years four months with a cast originally headed by Allan Jones (Sky), Pamela Britton (Adelaide), Julie Oshins (Nathan), and Jan Clayton (Sarah).

A Broadway revival of *Guys and Dolls* with an all-black cast was mounted in 1976. In it were James Randolph (Sky), Norma Donaldson (Adelaide), Robert Guillaume (Nathan), Ernestine Jackson (Sarah), and Ken Page (Nicely-Nicely). The run lasted 239 performances. The film version, released in 1955, starred Marlon Brando, Vivian Blaine, Frank Sinatra, and Jean Simmons. MCA OC; Motown OC (1976)/ Doubleday Anchor (1956)/ MTI.

Guys and Dolls. Sam Levene and Vivian Blaine singing "Sue Me." (Eileen Darby)

Guys and Dolls. Robert Alda throws the dice as Stubby Kaye, B. S. Pully, Johnny Silver, and Sam Levene watch. (Eileen Darby)

The King and I. Anna and son (Gertrude Lawrence and Sandy Kennedy) arrive in Bangkok. (Vandamm)

The King and I. ''Shall We Dance?'' Anna (Gertrude Lawrence) asks the King (Yul Brynner). (Vandamm)

THE KING AND I

Music: Richard Rodgers
Lyrics & book: Oscar Hammerstein II
Producers: Richard Rodgers & Oscar Hammerstein II
Director: John van Druten
Choreographer: Jerome Robbins
Cast: Gertrude Lawrence, Yul Brynner, Dorothy Sarnoff, Doretta Morrow, Larry Douglas, Johnny Stewart, Sandy Kennedy, Lee Becker Theodore, Gemze de Lappe, Yuriko, Baayork Lee
Songs: "I Whistle a Happy Tune"; "My Lord and Master"; "Hello, Young Lovers"; "March of the Siamese Children" (instrumental); "A Puzzlement"; "Getting to Know You"; "We Kiss in a Shadow"; "Shall I Tell You What I Think of You?"; "Something Wonderful"; "I Have Dreamed"; "Shall We Dance?"
New York run: St. James Theatre, March 29, 1951; 1,246 p.

Upon reading Margaret Landon's novel, *Anna and the King of Siam,* and seeing the film version, Gertrude Lawrence became convinced that this would be the ideal vehicle for her return to the musical stage. She first sounded out Cole Porter about the project, then turned to Rodgers and Hammerstein who, though aware of her vocal limitations, readily agreed to write and produce it. Based on the diaries of an adventurous Englishwoman, Anna Leonowens, the story of *The King and I* (a title Miss Lawrence never liked) is set in Bangkok in the early 1860s. Anna, the new governess and teacher to King Mongkut's many children, has frequent clashes with the autocratic, semi-barbaric ruler, but eventually — and discretely — comes to love him. She exerts great influence in helping to democratize the country, and after the King's death remains as adviser to his successor, Crown Prince Chulalongkorn (Johnny Stewart). A tragic secondary plot concerns the furtive romance between Tuptim (Doretta Morrow), one of Mongkut's wives, and her lover Lun Tha (Larry Douglas). Of dramatic importance in the plot was Jerome Robbins' narrative ballet, "The Small House of Uncle Thomas," based on *Uncle Tom's Cabin.*

Cast as the King was Yul Brynner, a virtually unknown actor who won the role after attempts had been made to interest Rex Harrison, Noël Coward, and Alfred Drake (Drake did replace Brynner briefly during the run). Following Miss Lawrence's death in September 1952, Anna was played successively by Constance Carpenter, Annamary Dickey, and Patricia Morison. *The King and I's* Broadway run was the fourth longest of the decade, and the musical toured for over a year and a half with Miss Morison and Brynner.

Though in 1964 Darren McGavin played the Siamese monarch opposite Risë Stevens' Anna in the premiere production of the Music Theatre of Lincoln Center, and others have played it throughout the country, the role of King Mongkut became the virtual personal property of Yul Brynner. By the sheer force of his personality and without any change in the script, he managed to switch the dramatic spotlight from Anna to the King. In 1956, Brynner co-starred in the film version with Deborah Kerr. Twenty years later, now solo starred, he began touring in a new stage production (with Constance Towers as Anna) that played New York in 1977 (see page 248), and London 1979. Brynner resumed touring in 1981 and returned to New York in December 1984, with Mary Beth Peil as Anna. By the end of this engagement, King Yul had had a reign lasting 4,625 performances.

MCA OC; RCA OC (1964); RCA OC (1977)/ Random House (1951)/ R&H.

A TREE GROWS IN BROOKLYN

Music: Arthur Schwartz
Lyrics: Dorothy Fields
Book: George Abbott & Betty Smith
Producers: George Abbott & Robert Fryer
Director: George Abbott
Choreographer: Herbert Ross
Cast: Shirley Booth, Johnny Johnston, Marcia Van Dyke, Nomi Mitty, Nathaniel Frey, Harland Dixon, Lou Wills Jr.
Songs: "Make the Man Love Me"; "I'm Like a New Broom"; "Look Who's Dancing"; "Love Is the Reason"; "I'll Buy You a Star"; "He Had Refinement"; "Growing Pains"
New York run: Alvin Theatre, April 19, 1951; 270 p.

Far removed from the sophisticated revues and book musicals Arthur Schwartz and Dorothy Fields were usually associated with was this sentimental, nostalgic view of a Brooklyn working-class family at the turn of the century. Betty Smith, who had originally written her autobiographical novel as a play, shared adaptation credit with director-producer George Abbott for a work that was initially supposed to have a score by Irving Berlin. The story relates the saga of the Nolan clan: the charming but weak Johnny (Johnny Johnston), who finds relief in the bottle; his hard-working, devoted wife Katie (Marcia Van Dyke); their daughter Francie (Nomi Mitty), who idolizes her father; and Katie's sister, the amiable, available Cissy (Shirley Booth), whose affairs with a string of unwed husbands help lighten the basically tragic story. Miss Booth, who scored an impressive hit, was seen two years later in *By the Beautiful Sea,* another Arthur Schwartz-Dorothy Fields musical that was also set in turn-of-the-century Brooklyn. Columbia OC/ Harper (1951).

PAINT YOUR WAGON

Music: Frederick Loewe
Lyrics & book: Alan Jay Lerner
Producer: Cheryl Crawford
Director: Daniel Mann
Choreographer: Agnes de Mille
Cast: James Barton, Olga San Juan, Tony Bavaar, James Mitchell, Kay Medford, Gemze de Lappe, Marijane Maricle
Songs: "I Talk to the Trees"; "What's Goin' on Here?"; "They Call the Wind Maria"; "I Still See Elisa"; "Another Autumn"; "Wand'rin' Star"
New York run: Shubert Theatre, November 12, 1951; 289 p.

Filling their musical play with authentic incidents and backgrounds, Lerner and Loewe struck it rich both musically and dramatically with a work that captured the flavor of the roistering, robust California gold fields of 1853. James Barton, returning to the musical stage for the first time in 20 years, took the part of Ben Rumson, a grizzled prospector whose daughter Jennifer (Olga San Juan) discovers gold near their camp. Word of the strike quickly spreads and before long there are over 4,000 inhabitants of the new town of Rumson. Jennifer, who has fallen in love with Julio (Tony Bavaar), a Mexican prospector, goes East to school but returns to Julio when the gold strike peters out. Rumson is now virtually a ghost town, and Ben is left with nothing but his hopes and dreams. During the Broadway run, Barton was succeeded by Burl Ives and Eddie Dowling. The 1969 film version, with Clint Eastwood, Lee Marvin and Jean Seberg told a different story.
RCA OC/ Coward-McCann (1952)/ TW.

PAL JOEY

Music: Richard Rodgers
Lyrics: Lorenz Hart
Book: John O'Hara (George Abbott uncredited)
Producers: Jule Styne & Leonard Key
Directors: Robert Alton, David Alexander
Choreographer: Robert Alton
Cast: Vivienne Segal, Harold Lang, Helen Gallagher, Lionel Stander, Patricia Northrop, Elaine Stritch, Helen Wood, Barbara Nichols, Jack Waldron, Robert Fortier
Songs: Same as original production
New York run: Broadhurst Theatre, January 3, 1952; 540 p.

(See page 112.)

Pal Joey. Harold Lang (as Joey) is distracted by Patricia Northrop much to the irritation of patroness Vivienne Segal. (Eileen Darby)

NEW FACES OF 1952
Music, lyrics & sketches: Miscellaneous writers
Producer: Leonard Sillman
Directors: John Murray Anderson, John Beal
Choreographer: Richard Barstow
Cast: Ronny Graham, Eartha Kitt, Robert Clary, June Carroll, Virginia de Luce, Alice Ghostley, Carol Lawrence, Paul Lynde
Songs: "Lucky Pierre" (Ronny Graham); "Guess Who I Saw Today" (Murray Grand-Elisse Boyd); "Love Is a Simple Thing" (Arthur Siegel-June Carroll); "Boston Beguine" (Sheldon Harnick); "Lizzie Bordon" (Michael Brown); "I'm in Love with Miss Logan" (Graham); "Penny Candy" (Siegel-Carroll); "Monotonous" (Siegel-Carroll)
New York run: Royale Theatre, May 16, 1952; 365 p.

Of the seven *New Faces* revues assembled by Leonard Sillman, the 1952 edition was the most admired, both for the talent of the performers and the cleverness of the writing. Among the numbers were "Boston Beguine," Alice Ghostley's revelation of improper behavior in a proper surrounding; "Lizzie Borden," a sprightly hoedown celebrating an unsightly deed; "Guess Who I Saw Today," a rueful ballad of infidelity sung by June Carroll; "Monotonous," in which Eartha Kitt purred about her boring life; Ronny Graham's sendup of Truman Capote called "Oedipus Goes South"; Mel Brooks' burlesque of *Death of a Salesman,* in which a pickpocket feels betrayed by a son who shuns the family business; and Paul Lynde's speech, while swathed in bandages, about his misadventures on an African safari. The Royale Theatre is on 45th Street west of Broadway. In 1954, the film version was released with the original performers. RCA OC.

WISH YOU WERE HERE
Music & lyrics: Harold Rome
Book: Arthur Kober & Joshua Logan
Producers: Leland Hayward & Joshua Logan
Director: Joshua Logan
Choreographer: Joshua Logan (Jerome Robbins uncredited)
Cast: Sheila Bond, Jack Cassidy, Patricia Marand, Sidney Armus, Paul Valentine, Harry Clark, Florence Henderson, Tom Tryon, Larry Blyden, Phyllis Newman, Reid Shelton
Songs: "Social Director"; "Goodbye Love"; "Could Be"; "Tripping the Light Fantastic"; "Where Did the Night Go?"; "Summer Afternoon"; "Don José of Far Rockaway"; "Wish You Were Here"; "Flattery"
New York run: Imperial Theatre, June 25, 1952; 598 p.

It was known as the musical with the swimming pool, but *Wish You Were Here* had other things going for it, including a cast of ingratiating actors, a warm and witty score by Harold Rome, and a director, Joshua Logan, who wouldn't stop making improvements even after the Broadway opening (among them were new dances choreographed by Jerome Robbins). The musical, which Arthur Kober and Logan adapted from Kober's 1937 play, *Having Wonderful Time,* is set in Camp Karefree, an adult summer camp "where friendships are formed to last a whole lifetime through," and is concerned with middle-class New Yorkers trying to make the most of a two-week vacation in the Catskills. Mainly it's about Teddy Stern (Patricia Marand), a secretary from Brooklyn, who finds true love — after a series of misunderstandings — with Chick Miller (Jack Cassidy), a law student working as a waiter by day and a dancing partner by night. RCA OC/ MTI.

WONDERFUL TOWN

Music: Leonard Bernstein
Lyrics: Betty Comden & Adolph Green
Book: Joseph Fields & Jerome Chodorov
Producer: Robert Fryer
Director: George Abbott (Jerome Robbins uncredited)
Choreographer: Donald Saddler
Cast: Rosalind Russell, George Gaynes, Edie Adams, Henry Lascoe, Dort Clark, Dody Goodman, Nathaniel Frey, Joe Layton
Songs: "Christopher Street", "Ohio"; "One Hundred Easy Ways"; "What a Waste"; "A Little Bit in Love"; "A Quiet Girl"; "Conga!"; "Swing!"; "It's Love"; "Wrong Note Rag"
New York run: Winter Garden, February 25, 1953; 559 p.

Because it again showed New York as just about the liveliest, friendliest place on earth, and because it again had a score by Leonard Bernstein, Betty Comden and Adolph Green and direction by George Abbott, *Wonderful Town* is generally accepted as the successor to *On The Town*. The songwriters, in fact, became involved in the project only five weeks before rehearsals when they took over the assignment from Leroy Anderson and Arnold Horwitt, who had bowed out over a disagreement with librettists Joseph Fields (brother of Herbert and Dorothy) and Jerome Chodorov. The musical was based on Ruth McKinney's *New Yorker* short stories — which Fields and Chodorov had already turned into the 1940 Broadway hit *My Sister Eileen* — and concerns the adventures of Miss McKinney and her sister in Greenwich Village after arriving from Ohio seeking careers. Ruth has problems getting her stories accepted by *The Manhatter* magazine and Eileen (Edie Adams) has problems warding off admirers. On a freelance newspaper assignment, Ruth gets to interview seven over-amorous, Conga-dancing Brazilian naval cadets, who cause a near-riot. Though this lands Ruth in jail, she also manages to land a handsome magazine editor (George Gaynes). Rosalind Russell, as Ruth, scored resoundingly in her only major musical-comedy role, and was succeeded during the run by Carol Channing.
MCA OC/ Random House (1953); Chilton (1976)/ TW.

Wonderful Town. Edie Adams and Rosalind Russell singing "Ohio." (Vandamm)

PORGY AND BESS

Music: George Gershwin
Lyrics: DuBose Heyward, Ira Gershwin
Book: DuBose Heyward
Producers: Blevins Davis & Robert Breen
Director: Robert Breen
Cast: LeVern Hutcherson (or Leslie Scott, Irving Barnes), Leontyne Price (or Urylee Leonardos), Cab Calloway, John McCurry, Helen Colbert, Helen Thigpen, Georgia Burke, Helen Dowdy
Songs: Same as original production
New York run: Ziegfeld Theatre, March 10, 1953; 305 p.

(See page 91.)

CAN-CAN

Music & lyrics: Cole Porter
Book: Abe Burrows
Producers: Cy Feuer & Ernest Martin
Director: Abe Burrows
Choreographer: Michael Kidd
Cast: Lilo, Peter Cookson, Hans Conried, Gwen Verdon, Erik Rhodes, Dania Krupska, Phil Leeds, DeeDee Wood
Songs: "Never Give Anything Away"; "C'est Magnifique"; "Come Along With Me"; "Live and Let Live"; "I Am in Love"; "Montmart' "; "Allez-vous-en"; "Never Never Be an Artist"; "It's All Right With Me"; "I Love Paris"; "Can-Can"
New York run: Shubert Theatre, May 7, 1953; 892 p.

To make sure that his script for *Can-Can* would be historically authentic, Abe Burrows traveled to Paris where he researched the records of the courts, the police, and the Chamber of Deputies. To his surprise, Burrows discovered that there were then a number of blue-nose organizations devoted to the suppression of such immoral exhibitions as the high-kicking, derriere-baring dance. This gave him the outline for his plot. Set in 1893, it tells of La Mome Pistache who is so distressed about the investigation of her Bal du Paradis — where the chief attraction is the Can-Can — that she tries to vamp the highly moral investigating judge, Aristide Forestier. Eventually, the two fall in love and when the case comes to trial, Forestier himself takes over the defense and wins acquittal. Though originally intended for Carol Channing, the role of Pistache went to the French actress Lilo (who introduced "I Love Paris"), but most of the kudos were for Gwen Verdon (who stopped the show with an Apache dance and the sexy "Garden of Eden" ballet) in her first major Broadway role.

In 1981, *Can-Can* again kicked up its heels — albeit briefly — in a revival starring Zizi Jeanmaire and Ron Husmann that was directed by Burrows. The altered Hollywood version, released in 1960, featured Frank Sinatra, Shirley MacLaine, and Maurice Chevalier.
Capitol OC/ TW.

Me and Juliet. Isabel Bigley singing "I'm Your Girl" to Bill Hayes. (Eileen Darby)

ME AND JULIET

Music: Richard Rodgers
Lyrics & book: Oscar Hammerstein II
Producers: Richard Rodgers & Oscar Hammerstein II
Director: George Abbott
Choreographer: Robert Alton
Cast: Isabel Bigley, Bill Hayes, Joan McCracken, Ray Walston, Mark Dawson, George S. Irving, Barbara Carroll, Shirley MacLaine
Songs: "A Very Special Day"; "Marriage-Type Love"; "Keep It Gay"; "The Big Black Giant"; "No Other Love"; "It's Me"; "I'm Your Girl"
New York run: Majestic Theatre, May 28, 1953; 358 p.

Writing in the lighter form of musical comedy rather than in their more accustomed "serious" form of musical play, Rodgers and Hammerstein created *Me and Juliet* as their Valentine to show business. The action — in *Kiss Me, Kate* fashion — takes place both backstage and onstage of a theatre during the performance of a play. Here the tale concerns a romance between a singer in the chorus (Isabel Bigley) and the assistant stage manager (Bill Hayes) whose newfound bliss is temporarily threatened by the jealous, heavy-drinking electrician (Mark Dawson). The melody of the show's best-known song, "No Other Love," had been previously used as background for the "Beneath the Southern Cross" episode in the NBC-TV series, *Victory at Sea. Me and Juliet* was the 29th and penultimate Broadway musical choreographed by Robert Alton.
RCA OC/ Random House (1953)/ R&H.

KISMET

Music & lyrics: Robert Wright & George Forrest based on Alexander Borodin
Book: Charles Lederer & Luther Davis
Producers: Charles Lederer, Edwin Lester
Director: Albert Marre
Choreographer: Jack Cole
Cast: Alfred Drake, Doretta Morrow, Joan Diener, Henry Calvin, Richard Kiley, Steve Reeves, Beatrice Kraft
Songs: "Sands of Time"; "Rhymes Have I"; "Not Since Nineveh"; "Baubles, Bangles and Beads"; "Stranger in Paradise"; "Night of My Nights"; "And This Is My Beloved"; "The Olive Tree"
New York run: Ziegfeld Theatre, December 3, 1953; 583 p.

The story of *Kismet* was adapted from a 1911 play by Edward Knoblock that was closely identified with Otis Skinner. The music of *Kismet* was adapted from themes Alexander Borodin composed for such works as the "Polovtsian Dances" ("Stranger in Paradise") and the D-Major String Quartet ("And This Is My Beloved," "Baubles, Bangles and Beads"). In this "Musical Arabian Night," the action occurs within a 24-hour period from dawn to dawn in ancient Baghdad, where a roguish public poet (Alfred Drake) assumes the identity of Hajj the beggar and has a series of unlikely adventures. By the time they have ended, he has drowned the wicked Wazir (Henry Calvin), has seen his daughter Marsinah (Doretta Morrow) wedded to the handsome Caliph (Richard Kiley), has been appointed Emir of Baghdad, and has gone off into the desert with the Wazir's luscious wife Lalume (Joan Diener). Before coming to New York, *Kismet* had first been presented in the summer of 1953 by Edwin Lester's Los Angeles and San Francisco Civic Light Opera Association. The film version, with Howard Keel and Ann Blyth, was released in 1955.

In 1965 the musical was revived by the Music Theatre of Lincoln Center with Alfred Drake again giving a bravura performance, and in 1985 it was added to the repertory of the New York City Opera. An all-black variation, *Timbuktu,* arrived on Broadway in 1978 and remained for 221 performances. It kept the music but switched the locale to the ancient African kingdom of Mali, and its cast was headed by Eartha Kitt, Ira Hawkins, Melba Moore, and Gilbert Price. For other musicals with scores based on classical themes, see *Blossom Time* page 38. Columbia OC; RCA OC (1965)/ Random House (1954)/ MTI.

The Threepenny Opera. Lotte Lenya as Jenny.

THE THREEPENNY OPERA

Music: Kurt Weill
Lyrics & book: Marc Blitzstein
Producers: Carmen Capalbo & Stanley Chase
Director: Carmen Capalbo
Cast: Lotte Lenya, Scott Merrill, Leon Lishner, Jo Sullivan, Charlotte Rae, Beatrice Arthur, Gerald Price, John Astin, Joseph Beruh, Gerrianne Raphael
Songs: "The Ballad of Mack the Knife"; "Army Song"; "Love Song"; "Pirate Jenny"; "Tango-Ballad"; "Ballad of the Easy Life"; "Barbara Song"; "Useless Song"; "Solomon Song"
New York run: Theatre de Lys, March 10, 1954; 95 p. Reopened: September 20, 1955; 2,611 p.

The reason for the two engagements noted above is that the initial showing of Marc Blitzstein's English-language version of the Kurt Weill-Bertold Brecht *Die Dreigroschenoper* at the Theatre de Lys (now the Lucille Lortel) had to be terminated because of a prior booking. Led by critic Brooks Atkinson, public demand brought it back 15 months after the closing, with cast replacements including Frederic Downs for Leon Lishner, Jane Connell for Charlotte Rae, Tige Andrews for Gerald Price, Eddie Lawrence for Joseph Beruh, and Chris Chase for Gerrianne Raphael. At this writing, the return engagement is the second longest running production ever mounted Off Broadway. In its original form, the work was presented in Berlin in 1928 on the 200th anniverasy of *The Beggar's Opera* — credited as the first ballad opera, or musical comedy — on which it was based. The play's bitter, raffish view of contemporary morality, combined with its jingly, beer-hall tunes, quickly made it a favorite throughout Europe, and in 1933 the first American adaptation had a brief run on Broadway.

Set in Victorian London, *The Threepenny Opera* spins the tale of Macheath (Scott Merrill), an outlaw known as Mack the Knife. Mack marries Polly Peachum (Jo Sullivan), the daughter of the leader of Soho's underworld, but he is betrayed by his in-laws and is sent to Newgate Prison. After being freed by Lucy Brown (Beatrice Arthur), the police chief's daughter, Mack is again betrayed — this time by Jenny the whore (Lotte Lenya, Weill's widow, who had originated the role in Berlin). Sentenced to be hanged, Mack receives a last-minute reprieve from the queen, thus providing the play with a mock-heroic ending. Among the more than 200 actors who played the 22 parts during the show's run were Carole Cook, Valerie Bettis, and Dolly Haas (Jenny); James Mitchell and Jerry Orbach (Mack); Pert Kelton and Nancy Andrews (Mrs. Peachum); Georgia Brown (Lucy); Edward Asner (Peachum); and Estelle Parsons (Mrs. Coaxer). The 1964 film version featured Hildegarde Neff and Kurt Jurgens.

In 1976, Joseph Papp's New York Shakespeare Festival at Lincoln Center offered an even more abrasive version of *The Threepenny Opera* in an adaptation by Ralph Manheim and John Willett. With a cast headed by Raul Julia (Mack) and Ellen Greene (Jenny), the show also played Broadway for a total run of 307 performances.

The Beggar's Opera, the 18th Century English musical that had inspired the German version, was first presented in America in 1750. Its most recent production was in 1972 when the Chelsea Theatre of Brooklyn staged a revival that was also shown at an Off Broadway theatre in Manhattan. It ran 253 performances. Another variation, *Beggar's Holiday,* updating the scene to modern America, opened on Broadway in 1946. The music was by Duke Ellington, the lyrics and libretto by John Latouche, and the cast included Alfred Drake, Zero Mostel, and Bernice Parks.

Polydor OC; Columbia OC (1976)/ R&H.

The Golden Apple. Salesman Jonathan Lucas displays his wares for Kaye Ballard, Priscilla Gillette, and Stephen Douglass. (Vandamm)

THE GOLDEN APPLE

Music: Jerome Moross
Lyrics & book: John Latouche
Producers: T. Edward Hambleton & Norris Houghton
Director: Norman Lloyd
Choreographer: Hanya Holm
Cast: Priscilla Gillette, Stephen Douglass, Kaye Ballard, Jack Whiting, Bibi Osterwald, Jonathan Lucas, Portia Nelson, Jerry Stiller, Dean Michener, Shannon Bolin
Songs: "My Love Is on the Way"; "It's the Going Home Together"; "Helen Is Always Willing"; "Lazy Afternoon"; "Windflowers"
New York run: Phoenix Theatre, March 11, 1954; 173 p.

Using Homer's *Odyssey* and *Iliad* as models, Jerome Moross and John Latouche updated the epics to the period between 1900 and 1910 and relocated the action in the state of Washington. With spoken dialogue cut to a minimum, the story is told through a steady stream of musical numbers (including the popular hit, "Lazy Afternoon") and relates the consternation caused in the town of Angel's Roost (near Mt. Olympus) when a salesman named Paris (Jonathan Lucas) flies in in a balloon and abducts old Menelaus' always-willing wife, Helen (Kaye Ballard). The stalwart Ulysses (Stephen Douglass), who has just returned from the Spanish-American War, feels so duty-bound to retrieve the errant Helen that he leaves his wife Penelope (Priscilla Gillette) to go in search of the pair. Ulysses stays away ten years, during which time he resists various temptations, whips Paris in a bareknuckles fight, and is finally reunited with his incredibly patient spouse. Following its well-received opening at the downtown Phoenix Theatre, *The Golden Apple* moved uptown to the Alvin where it had a disappointingly short run.
Elektra OC/ Random House (1954)/ TW.

THE PAJAMA GAME

Music & lyrics: Richard Adler & Jerry Ross
Book: George Abbott & Richard Bissell
Producers: Frederick Brisson, Robert Griffith & Harold Prince
Directors: George Abbott & Jerome Robbins
Choreographer: Bob Fosse
Cast: John Raitt, Janis Paige, Eddie Foy Jr., Carol Haney, Reta Shaw, Ralph Dunn, Stanley Prager, Peter Gennaro, Shirley MacLaine
Songs: "I'm Not at All in Love"; "I'll Never Be Jealous Again"; "Hey, There"; "Once a Year Day"; "Small Talk"; "There Once Was a Man"; "Steam Heat"; "Hernando's Hideaway"
New York run: St. James Theatre, May 13, 1954; 1,063 p.

When Frank Loesser was approached to write the score for the musical adaptation of Richard Bissell's novel, *7½ Cents,* he had to turn it down, but he did recommend a young team, Richard Adler and Jerry Ross, who had never before written songs for a book musical. Their work — including such hits as "Hey, There" and "Hernando's Hideaway" — was impressive and so was the show, which Bissell, another Broadway newcomer, adapted in collaboration with veteran director George Abbott. (Other neophytes involved were co-director Jerome Robbins, choreographer Bob Fosse, and the trio of producers.)

The Pajama Game is concerned with the activities at the Sleep-Tite Pajama Factory in Cedar Rapids, Iowa, where Sid Sorokin (John Raitt), the new plant superintendent, has taken a shine to Babe Williams (Janis Paige), a union activist. Their romance suffers a setback when the workers go on strike for a seven-and-a-half cents hourly raise, but eventually management and labor are again singing in tune. During the run, chorus dancer Shirley MacLaine attracted notice when she substituted for Carol Haney in the "Steam Heat" number and was soon off to Hollywood. The musical toured for two years with Larry Douglas and Fran Warren. In 1973, the show was revived briefly on Broadway with a cast headed by Hal Linden, Barbara McNair, and Cab Calloway. John Raitt and Eddie Foy, Jr. repeated their original roles in the 1957 movie, which also starred Doris Day.

In 1958, Richard Bissell's novel, *Say, Darling,* which the author had based on his experience with *The Pajama Game,* was itself turned into a musical by Bissell, his wife Marian, and Abe Burrows. Burrows also directed, and Jule Styne, Betty Comden and Adolph Green supplied nine songs. The show ran 10 months. Columbia OC/ Random House (1954)/ MTI.

The Pajama Game. The picnic scene with Shirley MacLaine, John Raitt, and Janis Paige. (Talbot)

THE BOY FRIEND

Music, lyrics & book: Sandy Wilson
Producers: Cy Feuer & Ernest Martin
Director: Vida Hope (Cy Feuer uncredited)
Choreographer: John Heawood
Cast: Julie Andrews, John Hewer, Eric Berry, Ruth Altman, Bob Scheerer, Ann Wakefield, Millicent Martin, Dilys Lay, Stella Claire, Buddy Schwab
Songs: "The Boy Friend"; "Won't You Charleston With Me?"; "I Could Be Happy With You"; "Sur La Plage"; "A Room in Bloomsbury"; "The Riviera"; "It's Never Too Late to Fall in Love"; "Poor Little Pierrette"
New York run: Royale Theatre, September 30 ,1954; 485 p.

Though he was the first British writer of musicals since Noël Coward to win success in New York, composer-lyricist-librettist Sandy Wilson has, to date, seen only one of his works performed on Broadway. *The Boy Friend,* which had opened in London (where it would achieve a run of 2,048 performances), was in the tradition of Charles Gaynor's "Gladiola Girl" in *Lend an Ear* in that it offered an affectionate sendup of musical comedies of the Twenties, with the songs not only recalling the styles of that era but also establishing their own musical individuality. The tale is set in 1926 on the Riviera where Polly Browne, an English heiress attending Mme. Dubonnet's finishing school, meets Tony who, though of noble lineage, is posing as a delivery boy. They fall in love to such sweet sentiments as "I Could Be Happy With You" ("If you could be happy with me"), and though they have the expected misunderstanding, are happily reunited when, costumed as Pierrette and Pierrot, they both show up at the Carnival Ball. The musical also served to introduce Broadway to the charms of Julie Andrews who played Polly.

 The Boy Friend enjoyed an even longer run in a 1958 Off Broadway production that lasted 763 performances. Ellen McCown played Polly, Gerrianne Raphael her friend Maisie, and Bill Mullikin was Tony. The musical was again revived, this time on Broadway, in 1970, with Judy Carne (Polly), Sandy Duncan (Maisie), and Ronald Young (Tony). This version remained for four months. The cast of the 1972 film treatment included Twiggy and Tommy Tune.
RCA OC; MCA OC (1970)/ Dutton (1955)/ MTI.

The Boy Friend. Julie Andrews with Millicent Martin, Dilys Lay, Ann Wakefield, and Stella Claire. (Eileen Darby)

Peter Pan. "I'm Flying" sings Mary Martin as Peter Pan. (John Engstead)

PETER PAN

Music: Mark Charlap*; Jule Styne**
Lyrics: Carolyn Leigh*; Betty Comden & Adolph Green**
Play: James M. Barrie
Producers: Richard Halliday, Edwin Lester
Director-choreographer: Jerome Robbins
Cast: Mary Martin, Cyril Ritchard, Kathy Nolan, Margalo Gillmore, Joe E. Marks, Sondra Lee, Joseph Stafford, Robert Harrington
Songs: "Tender Shepherd"*; "I've Got to Crow"*; "Neverland"**; "I'm Flying"*; "Wendy"**; "I Won't Grow Up"*; "Mysterious Lady"**; "Captain Hook's Waltz"**
New York run: Winter Garden, October 20, 1954; 152 p.

When Jerome Robbins decided that the time was ripe to stage a new version of *Peter Pan,* with Mary Martin as the boy who wouldn't grow up and Cyril Ritchard as Captain Hook, he initially planned to use only a few incidental songs by newcomers Mark Charlap and Carolyn Leigh. After the play began evolving into a full-fledged musical, however, he went to the more experienced team of Jule Styne, Betty Comden and Adolph Green for the additional numbers. Following its unveiling as part of Edwin Lester's Los Angeles and San Francisco Civic Light Opera series, the show came to New York offering such pleasures as Miss Martin singing and flying at the same time and Ritchard playing the villainous Hook as a giggling, mincing Restoration dandy.

Peter Pan was first presented in New York in 1905 with Maude Adams as Peter, a role she virtually made her own for eight years. It was revived in 1924 with Marilyn Miller singing two songs by Jerome Kern, and in 1950 with Jean Arthur, Boris Karloff plus five songs by Leonard Bernstein. That version lasted nine months. A 1979 revival, starring Sandy Duncan in a production based on the 1954 musical, turned out to be the longest running — or flying — *Peter Pan* ever performed in New York. (See page 254.)
RCA OC/ SF.

Fanny. Ezio Pinza and Walter Slezak.
(Zinn Arthur)

FANNY

Music & lyrics: Harold Rome
Book: S. N. Behrman & Joshua Logan
Producers: David Merrick & Joshua Logan
Director: Joshua Logan
Choreographer: Helen Tamiris
Cast: Ezio Pinza, Walter Slezak, Florence Henderson, William Tabbert, Nejla
Ates, Gerald Price, Alan Carney
Songs: "Restless Heart"; "Never Too Late for Love"; "Why Be Afraid to
Dance?"; "Welcome Home"; "I Like You"; "Fanny"; "To My Wife";
"Love Is a Very Light Thing"; "Be Kind to Your Parents"
New York run: Majestic Theatre, November 4, 1954; 888 p.

Fanny takes us to the colorful, bustling port of Marseilles "not so long ago" for
a musical version of Marcel Pagnol's French film trilogy, *Marius, Fanny,* and
César. Compressed into one story, the heavily plotted tale — with its intensely
emotional score — concerns Marius (William Tabbert), who yearns to go to sea;
his father, César (Ezio Pinza), the local café owner; Panisse (Walter Slezak), a
well-to-do middle-aged sail maker; and Fanny Cabanis (Florence Henderson),
the girl beloved by both Marius and Panisse. Though Fanny conceives a child
with Marius just before he ships off, Panisse marries her and brings up the boy
as his own. When Marius returns demanding both Fanny and their son, César
convinces him that Panisse has the more rightful claim. Years later, however, the
dying Panisse dictates a letter to Marius offering him Fanny's hand in marriage.

Although Rodgers and Hammerstein had been sought to write it, *Fanny* became a collaboration between Harold Rome and Joshua Logan, who had worked
together on *Wish You Were Here,* plus playwright S.N. Behrman. It also marked
the first of 27 Broadway musicals produced by David Merrick. During the Broadway run, Pinza was succeeded by another former Metropolitan Opera star, Lawrence Tibbett, and Slezak by Billy Gilbert. No songs were retained for the 1960
movie version with Leslie Caron, Maurice Chevalier, and Charles Boyer.
RCA OC/ Random House (1955)/ TW.

House of Flowers. Pearl Bailey as Mme.
Fleur. (Zinn Arthur)

HOUSE OF FLOWERS
Music: Harold Arlen
Lyrics: Truman Capote & Harold Arlen
Book: Truman Capote
Producer: Saint Subber
Director: Peter Brook
Choreographer: Herbert Ross
Cast: Pearl Bailey, Diahann Carroll, Juanita Hall, Ray Walston, Dino DiLuca,
Geoffrey Holder, Rawn Spearman, Frederick O'Neal, Carmen De
Lavallade, Alvin Ailey, Arthur Mitchell
Songs: "A Sleepin' Bee"; "Smellin' of Vanilla"; "House of Flowers"; "Two La-
dies in de Shade of de Banana Tree"; "I'm Gonna Leave Off Wearin' My
Shoes"; "I Never Has Seen Snow"
New York run: Alvin Theatre, December 30, 1954; 165 p.

The genesis of *House of Flowers* occurred in 1948 when Truman Capote was
visiting Port-au-Prince, Haiti, where he enjoyed frequenting the lively local bor-
dellos. He first wrote a short story about one such establishment, then turned it
into the libretto for a Broadway musical. Producer Saint Subber brought in Harold Arlen who also shared lyric-writing chores with Capote. In the plot, Madame
Fleur (Pearl Bailey) is the protective, domineering horticulturist of the House of
Flowers, which is in competition with a similar enterprise run by Madame Tango
(Juanita Hall). Fleur is delighted to discover a new floral attraction named Ottilie
(Diahann Carroll), but the innocent girl gives up all possibilities of professional
advancement in favor of keeping herself for the equally innocent Royal (Rawn
Spearman). *House of Flowers,* the first musical directed by Peter Brook, is partic-
ularly remembered for its colorful Oliver Messel sets and its atmospheric Harold
Arlen music. In 1968, a somewhat revised version was offered Off Broadway
with Josephine Premice as Madame Fleur.
Columbia OC; UA OC (1968)/ Random House (1968).

PLAIN AND FANCY

Music: Albert Hague
Lyrics: Arnold B. Horwitt
Book: Joseph Stein & Will Glickman
Producers: Richard Kollmar & James Gardiner
Director: Morton Da Costa
Choreographer: Helen Tamiris
Cast: Richard Derr, Barbara Cook, David Daniels, Shirl Conway, Stefan Schnabel, Gloria Marlowe, Nancy Andrews
Songs: "It Wonders Me"; "Plenty of Pennsylvania"; "Young and Foolish"; "This Is All Very New to Me"; "Follow Your Heart"; "I'll Show Him"
New York run: Mark Hellinger Theatre, January 27, 1955; 461 p.

Like *Brigadoon, Plain and Fancy* used the visit of two sophisticated New Yorkers to a strange rural community so that audiences might become acquainted with its special customs and traditions. Here visitors Don King and Ruth Winters (Richard Derr and Shirl Conway) have come to Bird-in-Hand, Pennsylvania, to sell a farm Don owns to Amish farmer Jacob Yoder (Stefan Schnabel), a member of a fundamentalist religious sect that gets along without telephones, automobiles, indoor plumbing, or even buttons. Yoder has arranged an unwanted marriage for his daughter, Katie (Gloria Marlowe), though her young and foolish heart still belongs to her childhood sweetheart Peter Reber (David Daniels). When Yoder's barn is struck by lightning and burns down, Peter is blamed for putting a hex on it and he is shunned by members of the community. By rescuing his brother from a carnival brawl, however, he proves himself worthy of their — and Katie's — esteem. The Mark Hellinger Theatre, originally a movie house named the Hollywood, stands at 51st Street and Broadway.
Capitol OC/ Random House (1955)/ SF.

SILK STOCKINGS

Music & lyrics: Cole Porter
Book: George S. Kaufman, Leueen McGrath & Abe Burrows
Producers: Cy Feuer & Ernest Martin
Director: Cy Feuer
Choreographer: Eugene Loring
Cast: Hildegarde Neff, Don Ameche, Gretchen Wyler, George Tobias, Leon Belasco, Henry Lascoe, David Opatoshu, Julie Newmar, Onna White
Songs: "Paris Loves Lovers"; "It's a Chemical Reaction, That's All"; "All of You"; "Too Bad"; "Satin and Silk"; "Without Love"; "Silk Stockings"; "The Red Blues"
New York run: Imperial Theatre, February 24, 1955; 478 p.

Cole Porter's last Broadway musical — and his sixth with a French setting — was based on the popular 1939 film, *Ninotchka,* in which Greta Garbo was seen as a dour Russian official who succumbs to the charms of both Paris and a French count played by Melvyn Douglas. In the musical, Ninotchka (Hildegarde Neff) is again doubly seduced, though this time the man is the fast-talking American talent agent Steve Canfield (Don Ameche), involved in convincing a Soviet composer to write the score for a gaudy movie version of *War and Peace.* During the Philadelphia tryout, prospects for the show looked so bleak that co-producer Cy Feuer took over as director from George S. Kaufman, and Abe Burrows was summoned to take over as librettist from Kaufman and Leueen McGrath (then Mrs. Kaufman). The movie version was released in 1957 with Fred Astaire and Cyd Charisse in the leads.
RCA OC/ TW.

DAMN YANKEES

Music & lyrics: Richard Adler & Jerry Ross
Book: George Abbott & Douglass Wallop (Richard Bissell uncredited)
Producers: Frederick Brisson, Robert Griffith & Harold Prince
Director: George Abbott
Choreographer: Bob Fosse
Cast: Gwen Verdon, Stephen Douglass, Ray Walston, Russ Brown, Shannon Bolin, Rae Allen, Jean Stapleton, Nathaniel Frey, Robert Shafer
Songs: "Heart"; "Shoeless Joe from Hannibal, Mo."; "A Little Brains — a Little Talent"; "Whatever Lola Wants"; "Near to You"; "Two Lost Souls"
New York run: 46th Street Theatre, May 5, 1955; 1,019 p.

Damn Yankees was something of a stylistic follow-up to *The Pajama Game* since it was put together by the same songwriters, librettist-director, choreographer, producers, music director (Harold Hastings), and orchestrator (Don Walker). With the author as collaborator, they adapted the work from Douglass Wallop's novel, *The Year the Yankees Lost the Pennant,* and managed to turn it into such a clean hit that it broke the longheld jinx against shows dealing with baseball. In this variation on the *Faust* legend (which had been used in musical theatre as far back as *The Black Crook* in 1866), a middle-aged Washington Senators fan (Robert Shafer) is so devoted that he sells his soul to the devil (Ray Walston as "Mr. Applegate") just for a chance to play on his favorite team. Suddenly transformed into a young man, now named Joe Hardy (Stephen Douglass), the fan not only joins the team but becomes its ace pitcher and hitter. Fortunately for him, there is a contractural escape clause, and Applegate — even aided by the seductive Lola (Gwen Verdon) who usually gets what she wants — cannot prevent Joe from returning home to his wife at the end of a year. (Miss Verdon, who also appeared in the 1958 screen version, was elevated to stardom during the show's run.) The touring company, led by Sherry O'Neil and Bobby Clark (in his last stage role as Applegate), traveled for one year four months.
RCA OC/ Random House (1956)/ MTI.

Damn Yankees. Gwen Verdon and Ray Walston. (Talbot)

MY FAIR LADY

Music: Frederick Loewe
Lyrics & book: Alan Jay Lerner
Producer: Herman Levin
Director: Moss Hart
Choreographer: Hanya Holm
Cast: Rex Harrison, Julie Andrews, Stanley Holloway, Cathleen Nesbitt, Robert Coote, John Michael King, Christopher Hewett, Reid Shelton
Songs: "Why Can't the English?"; "Wouldn't It Be Loverly?"; "With a Little Bit of Luck"; "I'm an Ordinary Man"; "The Rain in Spain"; "I Could Have Danced All Night"; "On the Street Where You Live"; "Show Me"; "Get Me to the Church on Time"; "A Hymn to Him"; "Without You"; "I've Grown Accustomed to Her Face"
New York run: Mark Hellinger Theatre, March 15, 1956; 2,717 p.

The most influential musical of the Fifties and one of the most distinguished productions of all time came about as a result of the efforts of Hungarian film producer Gabriel Pascal, who devoted the last two years of his life to a quest for writers to adapt George Bernard Shaw's 1914 play *Pygmalion* into a stage musical. After being rejected by the likes of Rodgers and Hammerstein and Noël Coward, Pascal won the committment of Alan Jay Lerner and Frederick Loewe once they decided to use most of Shaw's original dialogue and to expand the action to include scenes at Tottenham Court Road, the Ascot races, and the Embassy Ball. They were also scrupulous to maintain the Shavian flavor in the songs, most apparent in such pieces as "Why Can't the English?," "Show Me," "Get Me to the Church on Time," and "Without You."

Shaw's concern with class distinction and his belief that barriers would fall if all Englishmen would learn to speak their language properly was conveyed through a story about Eliza Doolittle, a scruffy cockney flower seller in Covent Garden, who takes lessons from phonetician Henry Higgins to help her qualify for a job in a florist shop. Eliza succeeds so well that she outgrows her social station and, in a development added by librettist Lerner, even gets the misogynous speech professor to fall in love with her — or at least grow accustomed to her face. Rex Harrison (who played Higgins), Julie Andrews (who won the part of Eliza after Mary Martin had turned it down), and Stanley Holloway (as Eliza's roistering father, Alfred P. Doolittle) all became forever identified with their roles in *My Fair Lady* which, for over nine years, was the longest running musical in Broadway history. The touring company, originally headed by Brian Aherne and Anne Rogers, traveled for six years nine months.

Two major revivals were staged in New York. In 1976, the musical ran for 377 performances with Ian Richardson, Christine Andreas, and George Rose. In 1981, it lasted 119 with Rex Harrison, Nancy Ringham, and Milo O'Shea. Harrison and Holloway repeated their roles in the 1964 movie version, also starring Audrey Hepburn.

A previous musical based on a Shaw play was the 1909 *Chocolate Soldier* (from *Arms and the Man*); a subsequent musical was the 1968 *Her First Roman* (from *Caesar and Cleopatra*). The notable success of *My Fair Lady* prompted a number of adaptations — offered on Broadway and off — of classics of British literature: Jane Austen's *Pride and Prejudice* (*First Impressions,* 1959); William Wycherley's *The Country Wife* (*She Shall Have Music,* 1959); Oscar Wilde's *The Importance of Being Earnest* (*Ernest in Love,* 1960); Sheridan's *The Rivals* (*All in Love,* 1961); Goldsmith's *She Stoops to Conquer* (*O, Marry Me!,* 1961); Dickens' *Oliver Twist* (*Oliver!,* 1963); H.G. Wells' *Kipps* (*Half a Sixpence,* 1965); Dickens' *Pickwick Papers* (*Pickwick,* 1965); and Arnold Bennett's *Buried Alive* (*Darling of the Day,* 1968).

Columbia OC; Columbia OC (1976); London SC (1987)/ Coward-McCann (1956)/ TW.

My Fair Lady. Stanley Holloway, with cronies Gordon Dilworth and Rod McLennon, singing "With A Little Bit of Luck." (Friedman-Abeles)

My Fair Lady. Robert Coote, Julie Andrews, and Rex Harrison in "The Rain in Spain" number. (Friedman-Abeles)

THE MOST HAPPY FELLA

Music, lyrics & book: Frank Loesser
Producers: Kermit Bloomgarden & Lynn Loesser
Director: Joseph Anthony
Choreographer: Dania Krupska
Cast: Robert Weede, Jo Sullivan, Art Lund, Susan Johnson, Shorty Long, Mona Paulee
Songs: "Somebody Somewhere"; "The Most Happy Fella"; "Standing on the Corner"; "Joey, Joey, Joey"; "Rosabella"; "Abbondanza"; "Sposalizio"; "Happy to Make Your Acquaintance"; "Big 'D' "; "My Heart Is So Full of You"; "Warm All Over"
New York run: Imperial Theatre, May 3, 1956; 676 p.

Serving as his own librettist, composer-lyricist Frank Loesser adapted Sidney Howard's 1924 play, *They Knew What They Wanted,* into a cohesive, ambitious work, with more than 30 separate musical numbers including arias, duets, trios, quartets, and choral pieces, plus recitatives. Robust, emotional expressions ("Joey, Joey, Joey," "My Heart Is So Full of You") were interspersed with more traditional Broadway specialties ("Big 'D'," "Standing on the Corner"), though in the manner of an opera the program credits did not list individual selections.

Set in California's Napa Valley, *The Most Happy Fella* is about Tony Esposito (Robert Weede), an aging Italian vineyard owner, who proposed by mail to Rosabella (Jo Sullivan), a San Francisco waitress, and she accepts, partly because Tony has sent her a photograph of Joe (Art Lund), his handsome ranch foreman. Rosabella is so upset at finding Tony physically unattractive that on her wedding night she gives herself to Joe. Tony is distraught over his wife's pregnancy, but there is a reconciliation, and the vintner (somewhat similar to the situation in *Fanny*) offers to raise the child as his own. In 1979, *The Most Happy Fella* was revived on Broadway with Giorgio Tozzi as Tony.
Columbia OC/ MTI.

The Most Happy Fella. Robert Weede and neighbors singing the title song. (Arthur Cantor)

LI'L ABNER

Music: Gene de Paul
Lyrics: Johnny Mercer
Book: Norman Panama & Melvin Frank
Producers: Norman Panama, Melvin Frank & Michael Kidd
Director-choreographer: Michael Kidd
Cast: Edie Adams, Peter Palmer, Howard St. John, Stubby Kaye, Charlotte Rae, Tina Louise, Joe E. Marks, Julie Newmar, Grover Dale
Songs: "If I Had My Druthers"; "Jubilation T. Cornpone"; "Namely You"; "The Country's in the Very Best of Hands"; "Oh, Happy Day"
New York run: St. James Theatre, November 15, 1956; 693 p.

Following the lead of *Finian's Rainbow, Li'l Abner* was a musical fantasy set in a rural Southern community that aimed satirical darts at existing social conditions. Here the main targets are the government's propensity for bull-dozing areas for atom-bomb tests, right-wing militarists, inefficient politicians, and conformity. Based on the comic strip by Al Capp (who, ironically, would later adopt some of the views the show derided), *Li'l Abner* takes place in Dogpatch, U.S.A., where mini-skirted Daisy Mae (Edie Adams) is forever trying to get dimwitted Abner Yokum (Peter Palmer) to marry her, where Marryin' Sam (Stubby Kaye) exuberantly leads the townspeople in singing the praises of the South's most incompetent general, Jubilation T. Cornpone, and where the annual big event (as well as the musical's big production number) is the frenetic man-chasing race on Sadie Hawkins' Day. The 1959 movie again featured Peter Palmer as Abner.

Comic strips also supplied the bases for such other Broadway musicals as *Buster Brown* (1905), *Little Nemo* (1908), *Bringing Up Father* (1925), *It's a Bird It's a Plane It's Superman* (1966), *You're a Good Man, Charlie Brown* (1967), *Annie* (1977), *Snoopy* (1982), and *Doonesbury* (1983). Columbia OC/ TW.

BELLS ARE RINGING

Music: Jule Styne
Lyrics & book: Betty Comden & Adolph Green
Producer: Theatre Guild
Director: Jerome Robbins
Choreographers: Jerome Robbins, Bob Fosse
Cast: Judy Holliday, Sydney Chaplin, Jean Stapleton, Eddie Lawrence, Dort Clark, George S. Irving, Peter Gennaro, Bernie West
Songs: "It's a Perfect Relationship"; "Hello, Hello There!"; "Is It a Crime?"; "I Met a Girl"; "Long Before I Knew You"; "Just in Time"; "Drop That Name"; "The Party's Over"; "I'm Going Back"
New York run: Shubert Theatre, November 29, 1956; 924 p.

Ever since appearing with Judy Holliday in a nightclub revue, Betty Comden and Adolph Green had wanted to write a musical for her. The story they eventually hit upon was one in which Miss Holliday played Ella Peterson, a chatty telephone operator at the Susanswerphone service (run by Jean Stapleton) who gets so involved with one client, playwright Jeff Moss (Sydney Chaplin), that — without revealing her identity — she arranges to meet him and help him overcome his writer's block. They also sing and dance in the subway, entertain fellow New Yorkers in Central Park, and fall in love. With Miss Holliday's winning performance and a score containing three enduring songs ("Long Before I Knew You," "Just in Time," and "The Party's Over"), *Bells Are Ringing* had the longest run of the eight musicals written together by Styne, Comden and Green. Miss Holliday repeated her role in the 1960 movie version, which also starred Dean Martin. Columbia OC/ Random House (1957)/ TW.

Candide. Max Adrian, Louis Edmonds, Barbara Cook, and Robert Rounseville. (Friedman-Abeles)

CANDIDE

Music: Leonard Bernstein
Lyrics: Richard Wilbur, etc.
Book: Lillian Hellman
Producer: Ethel Linder Reiner
Director: Tyrone Guthrie
Cast: Max Adrian, Robert Rounseville, Barbara Cook, Irra Petina, William Olvis, Louis Edmonds, Conrad Bain
Songs: "The Best of All Possible Worlds"; "Oh, Happy We"; "It Must Be So"; "Glitter and Be Gay"; "I Am Easily Assimilated" (lyric: Bernstein); "Eldorado" (lyric: Hellman); "Bon Voyage"; "What's the Use?"; "Make Our Garden Grow"
New York run: Martin Beck Theatre, December 1, 1956; 73 p.

Based on Voltaire's classic satire on mindless optimism, *Candide* covers the travels and travails of the eponymous hero (Robert Rounseville) who journeys from his home in Westphalia searching for his beloved Cunegonde (Barbara Cook) in Lisbon (during the Spanish Inquisition), Paris, Buenos Aires, Venice, and back to Westphalia. Throughout the tale the gullible young man remains firm in his belief — as espoused by his philosophy professor, Dr. Pangloss (Max Adrian) — that "this is the best of all possible worlds." In the end, at last reunited with Cunegonde, Candide (like the hero of the later musical, *Pippin*) comes to realize that perfection can never be attained and that one must accept life's realities and try to do one's best. Despite the musical's highly praised score (Leonard Bernstein's original lyricist, John Latouche, had died early in the preparation) and attractive production, the show's initial run lasted less than three months.

In 1973, a revised version was staged by the Chelsea Theatre Center of Brooklyn. Hugh Wheeler contributed a new libretto, Stephen Sondheim some new lyrics, and Harold Prince a total-theatre concept. Following its limited run, the musical was successfully remounted at the Broadway Theatre. The auditorium was completely remodeled, with musicians playing from various parts of the house, and the audience seated on stools surrounded by ten different acting areas linked by ramps, bridges, platforms, and trap doors. (See page 239.) In 1982, *Candide* was added to the repertory of the New York City Opera.

Columbia OC; Columbia OC (1973); New World OC (1982)/ Random House (1957)/ MTI.

NEW GIRL IN TOWN

Music & lyrics: Bob Merrill
Book: George Abbott
Producers: Frederick Brisson, Robert Griffith & Harold Prince
Director: George Abbott
Choreographer: Bob Fosse
Cast: Gwen Verdon, Thelma Ritter, George Wallace, Cameron Prud'homme, Mark Dawson
Songs: "Sunshine Girl"; "Flings"; "It's Good to Be Alive"; "Look at 'Er"; "At the Check Apron Ball"; "If That Was Love"
New York run: 46th Street Theatre, May 14, 1957; 431 p.

Composer-lyricist Bob Merrill had first conceived of the idea of a musical version of Eugene O'Neill's 1921 play *Anna Christie* as a movie under the title of *A Saint She Ain't*. When that was abandoned he found director George Abbott highly receptive to its possibilities as a stage musical, particularly as a vehicle for Gwen Verdon. In the story, set near New York's waterfront at the turn of the century, barge captain Chris Christopherson (Cameron Prud'homme) is excited at the news that his daughter Anna will be returning from St. Paul. When she does appear, she is quickly sized up by Chris' slattern friend Marthy (Thelma Ritter) as a street walker. After Anna joins her father on his barge, she meets sailor Matt Burke (George Wallace), and they fall in love. When she tells her story to the two men they get smashed, but fortunately there is a reconciliation. In 1959, Merrill wrote the songs for *Take Me Along,* based on another O'Neill play *Ah, Wilderness!*
RCA OC/ Random House (1958)/ MTI.

New Girl in Town. Harvey Hohnecker, Gwen Verdon, and Harvey Jung dancing "At the Check Apron Ball." (Friedman-Abeles)

Carol Lawrence and Larry Kert.

West Side Story. The Jets performing the "Gee, Officer Krupke" number. (Eileen Darby)

WEST SIDE STORY

Music: Leonard Bernstein
Lyrics: Stephen Sondheim
Conception: Jerome Robbins
Book: Arthur Laurents
Producers: Robert Griffith & Harold Prince
Director: Jerome Robbins
Choreographers: Jerome Robbins & Peter Gennaro
Cast: Carol Lawrence, Larry Kert, Chita Rivera, Art Smith, Mickey Calin, Ken LeRoy, Lee Becker Theodore, David Winter, Tony Mordente, Eddie Roll, Martin Charnin
Songs: "Something's Coming"; "Maria"; "Tonight"; "America"; "Cool"; "One Hand, One Heart"; "I Feel Pretty"; "Somewhere"; "Gee, Officer Krupke"; "A Boy Like That"; "I Have a Love"
New York run: Winter Garden, September 26, 1957; 732 p.

In 1949, Jerome Robbins brought together composer Leonard Bernstein and playwright Arthur Laurents (his first experience as a librettist) to work on a modern musical version of *Romeo and Juliet*. Called *East Side Story*, it was about a Jewish boy's star-crossed romance with an Italian Catholic girl set against the clashing street gangs on New York's lower East Side. Heavy schedules, however, forced the trio to suspend the project for six years and by the time they got together again the conflict seemed dated. Far more timely, they now felt, would be the love story of a native-born boy of Polish descent and a newly arrived Puerto Rican girl set against the clashing street gangs on the city's West Side. At this time Bernstein decided against writing his own lyrics and he turned the task over to Stephen Sondheim, a 27-year-old Broadway neophyte.

In *West Side Story*, Tony (Larry Kert), once the leader of the Jets street gang, now tries to keep his distance from his former group and the rival Puerto Rican Sharks. He becomes particularly committed to peaceful coexistence once he meets a girl named Maria (Carol Lawrence) at a high school dance, and — with Maria's fire escape as a balcony — they express their mutual devotion to the soaring sentiments of "Tonight." But after Tony kills Maria's brother Bernardo (Ken LeRoy) while trying to break up a rumble, warfare erupts anew, and even Maria's best friend, Anita (Chita Rivera), urges her to stay away from Tony. In the end, Tony is killed by one of the Sharks and Maria is left grieving over his body.

With its galvanic choreography, compelling music and lyrics, and unflinching look at contemporary street life, *West Side Story* was a jolting work, not alone for its theme but for its advanced use of dance within the framework of a musical play. After cutting short its initial Broadway run to go on tour, the company returned to New York ten weeks later for an additional 249 performances.

Since then there have been two major revivals. In 1968, the Music Theatre of Lincoln Center sponsored a production that ran for 89 performances. Tony was played by Kurt Peterson, Maria by Victoria Mallory, and Anita by Barbara Luna. In 1980, the musical was mounted at the Minskoff Theatre under Robbins' direction, and had a 333-performance run. The cast was headed by Ken Marshall, Jossie de Guzman, and Debbie Allen. The film version, with Richard Beymer, Natalie Wood, George Chakiris, and Rita Moreno, was released in 1961. For other Broadway musicals based on Shakespeare, see *The Boys from Syracuse,* page 107.

Columbia OC; DGG SC (1985)/ Random House (1958); Chilton (1973)/ MTI.

JAMAICA

Music: Harold Arlen
Lyrics: E.Y. Harburg
Book: E.Y. Harburg & Fred Saidy (Joseph Stein uncredited)
Producer: David Merrick
Driector: Robert Lewis
Choreographer: Jack Cole
Cast: Lena Horne, Ricardo Montalban, Josephine Premice, Adelaide Hall, Ossie Davis, Erik Rhodes, Joe Adams, Alvin Ailey, Billy Wilson
Songs: "Pretty to Walk With"; "Push the Button"; "Little Biscuit"; "Cocoanut Sweet"; "Pity the Sunset"; "Take It Slow, Joe"; "Ain't It the Truth?"; "I Don't Think I'll End It All Today"
New York run: Imperial Theatre, October 31, 1957; 558 p.

Aided by evocative music, provocative lyrics, lush decor, and the sparkling presence of Lena Horne, *Jamaica* overcame a weak book to become one of the hits of the season. Something of a Caribbean companion to Harold Arlen's most recent musical *House of Flowers,* the new work dealt with a fisherman named Koli (Ricardo Montalban), who enjoys the simple life on mythical Pigeon Island near Jamaica, and Savannah (Miss Horne) , his inamorata who yearns for the glittering, mechanized life on another mythical island called Manhattan. After being tempted by a slick pearl dealer, Savannah — to no one's surprise — is content to remain with Koli in their tropical paradise. Originally, Harry Belafonte was to have been starred in the show but illness forced his replacement by the equally stellar Lena Horne, thereby altering the story's emphasis.
RCA OC/ TW.

Jamaica. Ricardo Montalban and Lena Horne. (Friedman-Abeles)

THE MUSIC MAN

Music, lyrics & book: Meredith Willson
Producer: Kermit Bloomgarden
Director: Morton Da Costa
Choreographer: Onna White
Cast: Robert Preston, Barbara Cook, David Burns, Pert Kelton, Iggie Wolfington, The Buffalo Bills, Eddie Hodges, Helen Raymond
Songs: "Rock Island"; "Trouble"; "Goodnight My Someone"; "Seventy-Six Trombones"; "Sincere"; "The Sadder-but-Wiser Girl"; "Marian the Librarian"; "My White Knight"; "Wells Fargo Wagon"; "Shipoopi"; "Lida Rose"; "Gary, Indiana"; "Till There Was You"
New York run: Majestic Theatre, December 19, 1957; 1,375 p.

It took eight years to write — including over 30 drafts and 40 songs — but by the time it was produced on Broadway, *The Music Man* had clearly established newcomer Meredith Willson among the most impressive talents of the musical theatre. The idea for the show had first been suggested by Willson's friend, Frank Loesser, who enjoyed listening to the composer's tales of growing up in a small Iowa town. Though the plot was credited in part to Frank Lacey, the musical emerged as a very personal expression through which Willson captured all the innocent charm of a bygone America. The story begins on the Fourth of July, 1912, in River City, Iowa. Enter "Professor" Harold Hill, who has arrived to hornswoggle the citizens into believing he can teach the local youngsters how to play in a marching band that would rival the once-mammoth parade featuring "Seventy-Six Trombones." But instead of skipping town before the instruments arrive, Hill is persuaded to remain by the town's librarian, Marian Paroo (Barbara Cook). The musical ends with the children being hailed by their parents, even though they can barely produce any recognizable sound from their instruments.

The role of Professor Harold Hill was rejected by a number of actors, including Danny Kaye, Dan Dailey, Phil Harris, and Gene Kelly, before it went to Robert Preston who gave a memorably dynamic performance in his first appearance on the musical stage. Preston also repeated the part in the 1962 movie version. During the show's Broadway run, the third longest of the decade's musicals, Preston was succeeded by Eddie Albert and Bert Parks. For the road tour, which lasted three years seven months, Forrest Tucker played the professor and Joan Weldon was Marian. *The Music Man* returned briefly to New York in 1980, with a cast headed by Dick Van Dyke and Meg Bussert.
Capitol OC/ Putnam (1958)/ MTI.

The Music Man. Barbara Cook and Robert Preston singing "Till There Was You." (Friedman-Abeles)

Flower Drum Song. Miyoshi Umeki singing "A Hundred Million Miracles," accompanied by Juanita Hall and Keye Luke. (Friedman-Abeles)

FLOWER DRUM SONG

Music: Richard Rodgers
Lyrics: Oscar Hammerstein II
Book: Oscar Hammerstein II & Joseph Fields
Producers: Richard Rodgers, Oscar Hammerstein II & Joseph Fields
Director: Gene Kelly
Choreographer: Carol Haney
Cast: Miyoshi Umeki, Larry Blyden, Pat Suzuki, Juanita Hall, Ed Kenney, Keye Luke, Arabella Hong, Jack Soo, Anita Ellis
Songs: "You Are Beautiful"; "A Hundred Million Miracles"; "I Enjoy Being a Girl"; "I Am Going to Like It Here"; "Don't Marry Me"; "Grant Avenue"; "Love, Look Away"; "Sunday"
New York run: St. James Theatre, December 1, 1958; 600 p.

Upon reading Chin Y. Lee's novel, *The Flower Drum Song,* librettist Joseph Fields bought the dramatic rights and then took the idea to Rodgers and Hammerstein. The resulting production — the only Broadway musical ever directed by Gene Kelly — dealt in a lighthearted way with the conflict between San Francisco's traditionalist older Chinese-Americans and their Americanized children who are anxious to break away. Mei Li (Miyoshi Umeki), a timid "picture bride" from China, has arrived to fulfill her contract to marry Sammy Fong (Larry Blyden), a local nightclub owner, but Sammy prefers Linda Low (Pat Suzuki), who quite obviously enjoys being a girl. The problem is resolved when Sammy's friend Wang Ta (Ed Kenney) conveniently falls in love with Mei Li. Miyoshi Umeki appeared in the 1961 film version, along with Nancy Kwan and James Shigeta. Columbia OC/ Farrar, Straus (1959)/ R&H.

REDHEAD

Music: Albert Hague
Lyrics: Dorothy Fields
Book: Herbert & Dorothy Fields, Sidney Sheldon, David Shaw
Producers: Robert Fryer & Lawrence Carr
Director-choreographer: Bob Fosse
Cast: Gwen Verdon, Richard Kiley, Leonard Stone, Doris Rich, Cynthia Latham
Songs: "The Right Finger of My Left Hand"; "Just for Once"; "Merely Marvelous"; "The Uncle Sam Rag"; "Erbie Fitch's Twitch"; "My Girl Is Just Enough Woman for Me"; "Look Who's In Love"
New York run: 46th Street Theatre, February 5, 1959; 452 p.

One of the theatre's rare musical whodunits, *Redhead* had been in the works — it was first called *The Works* — ever since 1950 when Herbert and Dorothy Fields began writing it with Beatrice Lillie in mind for the starring role. Six years later, with Sidney Sheldon joining them, they rewrote it for Gewn Verdon, but there were further complications caused by Miss Verdon's contract with Robert Fryer and Lawrence Carr to star in a musical being written by David Shaw. The problem was solved when the producers decided to switch their activities to *Redhead* and Shaw was added to the roster of writers. The show, which was the first to charge $9.20 for orchestra seats, also marked Bob Fosse's initial effort as a director as well as choreographer. The story takes place in London in the early 1900s. At the Simpson Sisters' Waxworks, where all the wax images are made by Essie Whimple, a model of a recently murdered young woman offends her brother, Tom Baxter (Richard Kiley). Essie and Tom join forces to solve the murder which, after Essie gets the chance to perform "Erbie Fitch's Twitch" at the Odeon Music Hall, they do.
RCA OC/ MTI.

Redhead. Richard Kiley and Gwen Verdon in a tense situation. (Friedman-Abeles)

DESTRY RIDES AGAIN

Music & lyrics: Harold Rome
Book: Leonard Gershe
Producer: David Merrick
Director-choreographer: Michael Kidd
Cast: Andy Griffith, Dolores Gray, Scott Brady, Jack Prince, Swen Swenson, Marc Breaux, George Reeder
Songs: "Ballad of the Gun"; "I Know Your Kind"; "Anyone Would Love You"; "Once Knew a Fella"; "That Ring on the Finger"; "I Say Hello"
New York run: Imperial Theatre, April 23, 1959; 473 p.

Hollywood's classic Western had been filmed three times before David Merrick decided to turn the durable sagebrush saga into a Broadway musical. A whoopin', shootin', hollerin' show, it starred Andy Griffith (in his only musical) as Thomas Jefferson Destry Jr., the violence-hating sheriff, and Dolores Gray as the peppery saloon entertainer known as Frenchy. The story, set in the brawling frontier town of Bottleneck just before the turn of the century, involves the traditional confrontation between good guys and bad guys in scenes set in such equally traditional locales as the Last Chance Saloon and Rose Lovejoy's establishment in Paradise Alley. Contrary to the movie industry's morals code that never permitted a happy ending for a woman of easy virtue, Frenchy is not killed protecting Destry but ends up in his arms. The show's choreographic highlight: the crackling, whipcracking dance performed by outlaws Swen Swenson, Marc Breaux, and George Reeder.
MCA OC/ TW.

Destry Rides Again. An embarrassing moment when Destry accidentally tears off part of Frenchy's dress. Andy Griffith, Scott Brady, and Dolores Gray. (Friedman-Abeles)

Once Upon a Mattress. Carol Burnett explaining that she's really so "Shy." (Friedman-Abeles)

ONCE UPON A MATTRESS

Music: Mary Rodgers
Lyrics: Marshall Barer
Book: Jay Thompson, Dean Fuller & Marshall Barer
Producers: T. Edward Hambleton, Norris Houghton, William & Jean Eckart
Director: George Abbott
Choreographer: Joe Layton
Cast: Joseph Bova, Carol Burnett, Allen Case, Jack Gilford, Anne Jones, Matt Mattox, Harry Snow, Jane White
Songs: "Many Moons Ago"; "In a Little While"; "Shy"; "Sensitivity"; "Happily Ever After"; "Very Soft Shoes"
New York run: Phoenix Theater, May 11, 1959; 460 p.

Once Upon a Mattress was first created as a one-act musical by Mary Rodgers (daughter of Richard Rodgers) and Marshall Barer at an adult summer camp. With Jay Thompson and Dean Fuller, they expanded the work, based on the fairy tale *The Princess and the Pea,* into a full evening's entertainment. Carol Burnett made a notable stage debut in the show as Princess Winnifred who arrives dripping wet in the throne room of an ancient kingdom because, as she explains, "I swam the moat." She is there as a contender for the hand of Prince Dauntless the Drab (Joseph Bova), whose domineering mother, Queen Agravain (Jane White), has decreed that he will wed only a true princess of royal blood. Winnifred passes the test being unable to sleep on a pile of mattresses with a pea on the bottom — though, as the finale reveals — her sleeplessness was really caused by a helpful Minstrel (Harry Snow) who had filled her bed with all sorts of uncomfortable objects. After opening at the downtown Phoenix Theatre, *Once Upon A Mattress* then played the Alvin, the Winter Garden, the Cort, and the St. James. MCA OC/ R&H.

GYPSY

Music: Jule Styne
Lyrics: Stephen Sondheim
Book: Arthur Laurents
Producers: David Merrick & Leland Hayward
Director-choreographer: Jerome Robbins
Cast: Ethel Merman, Jack Klugman, Sandra Church, Lane Bradbury, Maria Karnilova, Paul Wallace, Jacqueline Mayro, Karen Moore, Joe Silver
Songs: "Let Me Entertain You"; "Some People"; "Small World"; "Little Lamb"; "You'll Never Get Away from Me"; "If Momma Was Married"; "All I Need Is the Girl"; "Everything's Coming Up Roses"; "Together"; "You Gotta Have a Gimmick"; "Rose's Turn"
New York run: Broadway Theatre, May 21, 1959; 702 p.

With Ethel Merman giving the performance of her life a Gypsy Rose Lee's ruthless mother and with an exceptionally strong score and story, *Gypsy* was one of the musical theatre's most distinguished achievements. The germination of the show began with producer David Merrick, who needed to read but one chapter of Miss Lee's autobiography to convince him of its stage potential. Stephen Sondheim, joining *West Side Story* colleagues Arthur Laurents and Jerome Robbins, was originally to have supplied the music as well as the lyrics, but Miss Merman wanted a more experienced composer and Jule Styne was brought is. The Styne-Sondheim team created such overwhelming expressions of raw ambition as "Some People" and "Everything's Coming Up Roses" that they seen took their place among Miss Merman's most closely identified songs.

In the story, Mama Rose is determined to escape from a life of playing bingo and paying rent by pushing the vaudeville career of her younger daughter Jun (Lane Bradbury); after June elopes with a hoofer, she focuses all her attention on her older, less talented daughter, Louise (Sandra Church). Eventually, Louise becomes burlesque stripper Gypsy Rose Lee, and Rose suffers a breakdown — expressed through the shattering "Rose's Turn" — when she realizes that she is no longer needed in her daughter's career. Mama Rose was the last stage role Ethel Merman created and the first in which she toured. In 1974, a new production of *Gypsy* opened in New York after playing in London. Angela Lansbury starred, Arthur Laurents directed, and it ran 120 performances. The film version, in 1962, starred Rosalind Russell and Natalie Wood. A celebrated revival of the musical opened on Broadway in 1989, starring Tyne Daley. For other show-business musical biographies, see *Annie Get Your Gun,* page 130. Columbia OC; RCA OC (1974)/Random House (1960); Chilton (1973)/TW.

Gypsy. Sandra Church, Ethel Merman, and Jack Klugman. (Friedman-Abeles)

Gypsy. Ethel Merman doing her climactic "Rose's Turn." (Friedman-Abeles)

TAKE ME ALONG
Music & lyrics: Bob Merrill
Book: Joseph Stein & Robert Russell
Producer: David Merrick
Director: Peter Glenville
Choreographer: Onna White
Cast: Jackie Gleason, Walter Pidgeon, Eileen Herlie, Robert Morse, Una Merkel, Peter Conlow, Susan Luckey, Valerie Harper
Songs: "I Would Die"; "Sid Ol' Kid"; "Staying Young"; "I Get Embarrassed"; "We're Home"; "Take Me Along"; "Promise Me a Rose"; "Nine O'Clock"; "But Yours"
New York run: Shubert Theatre, October 22, 1959; 448 p.

Having written a score for a musical version of Eugene O'Neill's somber *Anna Christie,* Bob Merrill followed it up with a score for a musical version of O'Neill's 1933 sentimental comedy, *Ah, Wilderness!* Though casting the exuberant Jackie Gleason as the bibulous Sid Davis tended to divert the focus from the main story, *Take Me Along* was a faithful rendering of the playwright's view of an adolescent's growing pains.

The action takes place in the cozy environs of Centerville, Connecticut, during July 1910. Young Richard Miller (Robert Morse), the son of newspaper publisher Nat Miller (Walter Pidgeon), ardently woos Muriel Macomber (Susan Luckey) by quoting literary morsels that her father finds so objectionable he withdraws his advertisements from Nat's paper. With Muriel forbidden to see him, Richard goes on a binge; once they are reconciled he gets ready to go to Yale. A secondary plot concerns Sid's repeated efforts to quit drinking, get a steady job, and marry Nat's spinster sister Lily (Eileen Herlie). During the Broadway run, Pidgeon was succeeded by Sidney Blackmer and Gleason by William Bendix. The musical's Broadway revival in 1985 gave only one performance.
RCA OC/ TW.

THE SOUND OF MUSIC

Music: Richard Rodgers
Lyrics: Oscar Hammerstein II
Book: Howard Lindsay & Russel Crouse
Producers: Leland Hayward, Richard Halliday, Richard Rodgers & Oscar Hammerstein II
Director: Vincent J. Donehue
Choreographer: Joe Layton
Cast: Mary Martin,Theodore Bikel, Patricia Neway, Kurt Kasznar, Marion Marlowe, Lauri Peters, Brian Davies, John Randolph, Nan McFarland, Joey Heatherton
Songs: "The Sound of Music"; "Maria"; "My Favorite Things"; "Do-Re-Mi"; "Sixteen Going on Seventeen"; "The Lonely Goatherd"; "How Can Love Survive?"; "So Long, Farewell"; "Climb Ev'ry Mountain"; "An Ordinary Couple"; "Edelweiss"
New York run: Lunt-Fontanne Theatre, November 16, 1959; 1,443 p.

The second longest running Broadway musical of the Fifties, *The Sound of Music* also marked the 35th and final work of Oscar Hammerstein II, who died nine months after the opening (his last lyric was for "Edelweiss"). Primarily at the urging of director Vincent J. Donehue, the story was adapted as a star vehicle for Mary Martin from Maria Von Trapp's autobiography *The Trapp Family Singers* and also the German film version. Miss Martin's husband, Richard Halliday, and Leland Hayward became partners in sponsoring the project and Howard Lindsay and Russel Crouse were engaged to write the book. Initially, they planned to use only authentic music sung by the Trapps in their concerts plus an additional song to be supplied by Rodgers and Hammerstein. When the songwriters balked at this arrangement, they were asked to contribute the entire score and they also joined Halliday and Hayward as producers.

The musical, set in 1938, takes place in Salzburg in the Austrian Tyrol. Maria Rainer, a free-spirited postulant at Nonnberg Abbey, has been giving her superiors concern because of her fondness for taking off to the mountains listening to the sound of music. At the request of the Mother Abbess (Patricia Neway), — and as something of a variation on *The King and I* — Maria is hired as governess to the seven children of the wealthy, autocratic Capt. Georg Von Trapp (Theodore Bikel). Maria soon wins the affection of her charges — in part by teaching them such songs as "Do-Re-Mi," "The Lonely Goatherd," and "So Long, Farewell." Though Von Trapp is engaged to the socially prominent Elsa Schraeder (Marion Marlowe), he and Maria fall in love and marry. Their happiness, however, is almost immediately shattered by the German invasion of Austria. The Von Trapp family, which has become celebrated for its amateur concerts, gives a final performance before heeding the message of "Climb Ev'ry Mountain" and fleeing over the Alps to the safety of Switzerland. A subplot in *The Sound of Music* concerns the teenage romance between Von Trapp's daughter Liesl (Lauri Peters) and Rolf Gruber, an incipient Nazi (Brian Davies).

During the Broadway run (the Lunt-Fontanne Theatre, where the show opened, was once the Globe), Miss Martin was succeeded by Martha Wright, Jeannie Carson, and Nancy Dussault. In 1961, Jon Voight took over the part of Rolf. Florence Henderson and John Myhers originally headed the touring company which traveled two years nine months. The popular movie version, which came out in 1965, co-starred Julie Andrews and Christopher Plummer. Columbia OC/ Random House (1960)/ R&H.

The Sound of Music. Theodore Bikel, Marion Marlowe, and Kurt Kasznar. (Friedman-Abeles)

The Sound of Music. Brian Davies and Lauri Peters. (Toni Frissell)

The Sound of Music. Mary Martin and Theodore Bikel lead the Trapp Family in "Edelweiss." (Friedman-Abeles)

LITTLE MARY SUNSHINE

Music, lyrics & book: Rick Besoyan
Producers: Howard Barker, Cynthia Baer, Robert Chambers
Directors: Ray Harrison, Rick Besoyan
Choreographer: Ray Harrison
Cast: Eileen Brennan, William Graham, John McMartin, Elmarie Wendel
Songs: "Look for a Sky of Blue"; "Tell a Handsome Stranger"; "Once in a Blue Moon"; "Colorado Love Call"; "Every Little Nothing"; "Do You Ever Dream of Vienna?"; "Naughty, Naughty Nancy"
New York run: Orpheum Theatre, November 18, 1959; 1,143 p.

Little Mary Sunshine was a witty, melodious takeoff on the *Rose-Marie* school of robust heroics and excessively ardent love songs. Its engagement at the Orpheum Theatre on lower 2nd Avenue is currently the seventh longest of any Off-Broadway musical. Set in the Colorado Rockies early in the century, the tale is primarily concerned with Mary Potts (Eileen Brennan), proprietress of the Colorado Inn, and valorous Capt. "Big Jim" Warrington of the Forest Rangers (William Graham), who gets to rescue his beloved from the clutches of the lecherous Indian Yellow Feather just in time for their echoing "Colorado Love Call" duet. The production marked the impressive New York theatre debuts of both Eileen Brennan and composer-lyricist-librettist Rick Besoyan. Besoyan (who died in 1970 at the age of 45) followed up in 1963 with *The Student Gypsy,* a less successful spoof of European mythical-kingdom operettas, which also featured Miss Brennan. The earliest operetta burlesque on Broadway was Rodgers and Hart's "Rose of Arizona" in the 1926 *Garrick Gaieties.*
Capitol OC/Samuel French, London(1960)*/ SF

FIORELLO!

Music: Jerry Bock
Lyrics: Sheldon Harnick
Book: Jerome Weidman & George Abbott
Producers: Robert Griffith & Harold Prince
Director: George Abbott
Choreographer: Peter Gennaro
Cast: Tom Bosley, Patricia Wilson, Ellen Hanley, Howard Da Silva, Mark Dawson, Nathaniel Frey, Pat Stanley, Eileen Rodgers, Ron Husmann
Songs: "Politics and Poker"; "The Name's LaGuardia"; "I Love a Cop"; "Till Tomorrow"; "When Did I Fall in Love?"; "Little Tin Box"
New York run: Broadhurst Theatre, November 23, 1959; 795 p.

New York's favorite mayor, Fiorello LaGuardia, was a peppery, pugnacious reformer whose exuberant personality readily lent itself to depiction on the musical stage. With Tom Bosley making an auspicious Broadway bow in the title role, *Fiorello!* encompassed the ten-year period in LaGuardia's life before he became mayor. Beginning with his surprise election to Congress prior to World War I, it includes such events as his enlistment in the Air Force, his first race for mayor against the unbeatable James J. Walker (who was himself the subject of a 1969 musical *Jimmy,* with Frank Gorshin in the title part), the death of LaGuardia's first wife, the revelation of Walker's cronies with their hands caught in little tin boxes, and the preparations for the victorious LaGuardia campaign of 1933 which he won as a Fusion candidate. *Fiorello!* had the distinction of being the third musical to be awarded the Pulitzer Prize for drama. A year after the show's opening, its composer, lyricist, librettists, director, producers, music director (Harold Hastings), and orchestrator (Irwin Kostal) were reunited for *Tenderloin,* which was about another New York reformer just before the turn of the century.
Capitol OC/ Random House (1960); Chilton (1976)/ TW.

Fiorello! Tom Bosley, Patricia Wilson, Nathaniel Frey, and Ellen Hanley singing "Till Tomorrow." (Eileen Darby)

GREENWILLOW

Music & lyrics: Frank Loesser
Book: Lesser Samuels & Frank Loesser
Producer: Robert Willey
Director: George Roy Hill
Choreographer: Joe Layton
Cast: Anthony Perkins, Cecil Kelloway, Pert Kelton, Ellen McCown, William Chapman, Grover Dale
Songs: "A Day Borrowed from Heaven"; "The Music of Home"; "Gideon Briggs, I Love You"; "Summertime Love"; "Walking Away Whistling"; "Never Will I Marry"; "Faraway Boy"
New York run: Alvin Theatre, March 8, 1960; 95 p.

B.J. Chute's novel was turned into a homespun fantasy that had to do with quaint superstitions and folklore of a mythical village located on the Meander River — or somewhere down the road from Brigadoon and Glocca Morra. The whimsical tale takes up the conflict of young Gideon Briggs (Anthony Perkins) who would like nothing better than to remain at home and marry his summertime love, Dorrie (Ellen McCown), but who fears that the curse of his family's "call to wander solitary" will someday make him run off to sail distant seas. Though tarrying on Broadway only three months, *Greenwillow* has long been admired for the airy, otherworldly charms of Frank Loesser's atypical score. The production also marked Anthony Perkins' first — and so far only — Broadway musical. Columbia OC.

BYE BYE BIRDIE

Music: Charles Strouse
Lyrics: Lee Adams
Book: Michael Stewart
Producer: Edward Padula
Director-choreographer: Gower Champion
Cast: Chita Rivera, Dick Van Dyke, Kay Medford, Paul Lynde, Dick Gautier, Michael J. Pollard, Susan Watson, Charles Nelson Reilly
Songs: "An English Teacher"; "The Telephone Hour"; "How Lovely to Be a Woman"; "Put on a Happy Face"; "One Boy"; "One Last Kiss"; "A Lot of Livin' to Do"; "Kids"; "Baby, Talk to Me"; "Rosie"
New York run: Martin Beck Theatre, April 14, 1960; 607 p.

Bye Bye Birdie provided the launching pad for the Broadway careers of songwriters Charles Strouse and Lee Adams, librettist Michael Stewart, and director-choreographer Gower Champion (his first of nine book musicals). It was also the earliest musical about the rock and roll phenomenon and the effect of its idols on impressionable teenagers. The attitude, however, was generally sympathetic toward adolescent emotions, offering something of a fresh-air antidote to the picture of modern youth conveyed by *West Side Story.* The singing idol in this case is Conrad Birdie (suggesting Elvis Presley), and the young people he is shown affecting are the clean-cut kids of Sweet Apple, Ohio. Birdie is managed by Albert Peterson (Dick Van Dyke) who, with his secretary Rose Grant (Chita Rivera), contrives a publicity stunt involving Kim McAfee (Susan Watson) kissing Birdie on Ed Sullivan's television show just before he is drafted into the Army. Complications involve Kim's jealous boyfriend (Michael J. Pollard) and her exasperated father (Paul Lynde), as well as Albert's querulous mother (Kay Medford) and his relationship with Rose, who wants him to get out of the music business and become an English teacher. During the run, Dick Van Dyke was succeeded by Gene Rayburn, Chita Rivera by Gretchen Wyler. Van Dyke repeated his role in the 1963 film version (also starring Ann-Margret), and Miss Rivera repeated her role in the short-lived 1981 sequel, *Bring Back Birdie* (also with Donald O'Connor). Columbia OC/ DBS Publications (1962)/ TW.

The Fantasticks. Jerry Orbach, Rita Gardner, and Kenneth Nelson. (Friedman-Abeles))

THE FANTASTICKS

Music: Harvey Schmidt
Lyrics & book: Tom Jones
Producer: Lore Noto
Director: Word Baker
Cast: Jerry Orbach, Rita Gardner, Kenneth Nelson, William Larson, Hugh Thomas, Tom Jones, George Curley, Richard Stauffer
Songs: "Try to Remember"; "Much More"; "It Depends on What You Pay"; "Soon It's Gonna Rain"; "I Can See It"; "Plant a Radish"; "Round and Round"; "They Were You"
New York run: Sullivan Street Playhouse, May 3, 1960; (still running 10/1/93)

The statistics alone are, well, fantastic. No other New York stage production has ever played so many performances, and there is still no end in sight. Moreover, by the time of the show's 33rd year at the 150-seat Greenwich Village Theatre, there had been over 10,000 productions throughout the World, of which some 500 were performed in more than 66 foreign countries. There have also been 15 national touring companies. As for profits, the original backers have so far received a return of over 10,000% on their initial investment of $16,500. Curiously, the original critical reception was not encouraging and producer Lore Noto seriously considered closing the show after its first week. But an Off-Broadway award, the popularity of the song "Try to Remember," and, most important, word of mouth, all helped turn the musical's fortunes around.

The whimsical fantasy is concerned with the theme of seasonal rebirth — or the paradox of "why Spring is born out of Winter's laboring pains." The tale, freely adapted from Edmond Rostand's 1894 play, *Les Romanesques*, is told with a cast of eight and performed on a platform with a minimum of props. The neighboring fathers (Hugh Thomas and William Larsen) of Luisa and Matt (Rita Gardner and Kenneth Nelson), though good friends, feel they must appear as enemies to make sure that their progenies fall in love. Having thought up this bit of logic they next find a way to reverse themselves by hiring El Gallo (Jerry Orbach), aided by The Old Actor (Tom Jones) and The Indian (George Curley), to perform a mock rape by moonlight so that Matt might prove his valor, thus paving the way for a reconciliation. But daylight reveals the parental deception, the lovers quarrel, and the young man goes off to see the world. After a number a degrading experiences, he returns home to Luisa's waiting arms firm in the knowledge that "without a hurt the heart is hollow."

To date, the New York company has had over 34 El Gallos (including Bert Convy, David Cryer, and Keith Charles), over 32 Luisas (including Eileen Fulton, Betsy Joslyn, Kathryn Morath, and Judy Blazer), and over 26 Matts (including Craig Carnelia and Bruce Cryer). F. Murray Abraham played The Old Actor in 1967, and producer Lore Noto played the Boy's Father from 1970 to 1986.

Harvey Schmidt and Tom Jones had originally written the musical under the title *Joy Comes to Dead Horse*, in which the characters were Mexican and Anglo families living on adjoining ranches in the American Southwest. Dissatisfied with the overblown concept, they cut the story down to one act, reduced the number of characters, and retitled the show *The Fantasticks*. It was staged in this fashion at Barnard College in the summer of 1959. Lore Noto saw it there, and at his urging Schmidt and Jones rewrote it once again, this time as an intimate two-act musical.

Ploydor OC/Drama Book Publishers (1964)/MTI.

IRMA LA DOUCE

Music: Marguerite Monnot
Lyrics & book: Julian More, David Heneker & Monty Norman
Producer: David Merrick
Director: Peter Brook
Choreographer: Onna White
Cast: Elizabeth Seal, Keith Michell, Clive Revill, George S. Irving, Stuart Damon, Fred Gwynne, Elliott Gould
Songs: "The Bridge of Caulaincourt"; "Our Language of Love"; "Dis-Donc"; "Irma la Douce"; "There Is Only One Paris for That"
New York run: Plymouth Theatre, September 29, 1960; 524 p.

Broadway's first hit with music by a French composer, *Irma la Douce* originated in Paris in 1956 with book and lyrics by Alexandre Breffort and ran for four years. The English-language adaptation opened two years later in London and gave 1,512 performances. With Elizabeth Seal, Keith Michell, and Clive Revill recreating their roles in New York — Miss Seal was the only female member of the cast — the production at the Plymouth Theatre (on 45th Street west of Broadway) was a virtual carbon of the West End original. In the story, Irma is a pure-at-heart Parisian prostitute and Nestor (Mr. Michell) is a poor student who is anxious to have Irma all for his own. The student gets the idea to disguise himself as an aged benefactor named Oscar who supposedly has enough money to be the lady's only patron. Nestor, however, grows jealous of Irma's affection for Oscar and "kills" him. He is sent to Devil's Island, but manages to escape, prove his innocence, and return to his beloved. All the songs — including the chief ballad, "Our Language of Love" — were cut from the 1963 film version starring Shirley MacLaine and Jack Lemmon.
Columbia OC/ TW.

Irma la Douce. The main performers in the scene are Keith Michell, Elizabeth Seal, and Clive Revill. (Friedman-Abeles)

THE UNSINKABLE MOLLY BROWN

Music & lyrics: Meredith Willson
Book: Richard Morris
Producers: Theatre Guild & Dore Schary
Director: Dore Schary
Choreographer: Peter Gennaro
Cast: Tammy Grimes, Harve Presnell, Cameron Prud'homme, Mony Dalmes, Edith Meiser, Mitchell Gregg, Christopher Hewett
Songs: "I Ain't Down Yet"; "Belly Up to the Bar, Boys"; "Colorado, My Home"; "I'll Never Say No to You"; "My Own Brass Bed"; "Are You Sure?"; "Dolce Far Niente"
New York run: Winter Garden, November 3, 1960; 532 p.

Providing Tammy Grimes with her most rewarding role in a musical, *The Unsinkable Molly Brown* retold the saga of a near-legendary figure of the Colorado silver mines who rose from a poverty-stricken background in Hannibal, Missouri, through her spunky determination to be "up where the people are," and by having the good fortune to marry a lucky prospector, "Leadville Johnny" Brown (Harve Presnell). After failing to crash Denver society, Molly drags Johnny off to Europe where despite her gaucheries, or because of them, she becomes a social leader in Monte Carlo. Molly almost loses Johnny, but following her heroism displayed during the sinking of the *Titanic,* she wins back her husband and wins over the elite of Denver. The score Meredith Willson turned out was much in the same Americana vein as *The Music Man,* complete with breezy marches, rugged male choruses, back country dance numbers, and revivalistic exhortations. The movie version came out in 1964 with Debbie Reynolds as Molly and Presnell again as Johnny.
Capitol OC/ Putnam (1961)/ MTI.

The Unsinkable Molly Brown. Tammy Grimes and Harve Presnell. (Friedman-Abeles)

Camelot. Julie Andrews and Richard Burton.
(Friedman-Abeles)

Camelot. Julie Andrews leading the courtiers in "The Lusty Month of May." (Friedman-Abeles)

CAMELOT

Music: Frederick Loewe
Lyrics & book: Alan Jay Lerner
Producers: Alan Jay Lerner, Frederick Loewe & Moss Hart
Director: Moss Hart (Alan Jay Lerner uncredited)
Choreographer: Hanya Holm
Cast: Richard Burton, Julie Andrews, Roddy McDowall, Robert Coote, Robert Goulet, M'el Dowd, John Cullum, Bruce Yarnell, David Hurst, Michael Kermoyan
Songs: "I Wonder What the King Is Doing Tonight"; "The Simple Joys of Maidenhood"; "Camelot"; "Follow Me"; "C'est Moi"; "The Lusty Month of May"; "Then You May Take Me to the Fair"; "How to Handle a Woman"; "Before I Gaze at You Again"; "If Ever I Would Leave You"; "What Do the Simple Folk Do?"; "Fie on Goodness!"; "I Loved You Once in Silence"; "Guenevere"
New York run: Majestic Theatre, December 3, 1960; 873 p.

Lerner and Loewe's first Broadway undertaking following their spectacular success, *My Fair Lady,* was based on T.H. White's retelling of the Arthurian legend, *The Once and Future King.* Originally titled *Jenny Kissed Me, Camelot* reunited the composer and lyricist with director Moss Hart (who joined Lerner and Loewe as co-producer), fair lady Julie Andrews, Col. Blimpish actor Robert Coote, choreographer Hanya Holm, scene designer Oliver Smith, music director Franz Allers, and orchestrators Robert Russell Bennett and Philip J. Lang. During the tryout, Moss Hart (who died a year later) was hospitalized with a heart attack and Lerner temporarily took over as director. The show had the biggest advance sale in Broadway history up to that time.

The opulently mounted production was a somewhat somber affair that dealt with the chivalrous Knights of the Round Table and the tragic romantic triangle involving noble King Arthur (Richard Burton), his errant Queen Guenevere (Julie Andrews), and Arthur's trusted Sir Lancelot du Lac (Robert Goulet). At the end, with his kingdom in ruins and his wife with another man, the King can still urge a young boy to tell everyone the story "that once there was a fleeting wisp of glory call Camelot." The touring company, which traveled for a year and a half, had a cast headed by William Squire (Arthur), Kathryn Grayson (Guenevere), Robert Peterson (Lancelot), Jan Moody (Morgan Le Fay), and Arthur Treacher (King Pellinore).

In 1980, Richard Burton recreated his original role in a touring revival that played a limited New York engagement in July. Christine Ebersole played Guenevere and Richard Muenz was Lancelot. Because of ill health, Burton was succeeded on the road by Richard Harris who also came back briefly to New York — in November 1981 — with Meg Bussert now playing the queen. In all, this company toured for almost three years. Harris had previously played King Arthur in the 1967 film version, which also starred Vanessa Redgrave (Guenevere) and Franco Nero (Lancelot).

A previous — and far more lighthearted — view of King Arthur's court was found in Rodgers and Hart's 1927 hit, *A Connecticut Yankee.*
Columbia OC/ Random House (1961); Chilton (1976)/ TW.

DO RE MI

Music: Jule Styne
Lyrics: Betty Comden & Adolph Green
Book: Garson Kanin
Producer: David Merrick
Director: Garson Kanin
Choreographers: Marc Breaux & DeeDee Wood
Cast: Phil Silvers, Nancy Walker, John Reardon, David Burns, George Mathews, George Givot, Nancy Dussault
Songs: "It's Legitimate"; "I Know About Love"; "Cry Like the Wind"; "Fireworks"; "What's New at the Zoo?"; "The Late Late Show"; "Adventure"; "Make Someone Happy"
New York run: St. James Theatre, December 26, 1960; 400 p.

A raucous satire on the music business — with special emphasis on the jukebox industry — *Do Re Mi* was full of characters reminiscent of the raffish denizens of *Guys and Dolls*. It was particularly blessed by offering two outstanding clowns in Phil Silvers as the pushiest of patsies and Nancy Walker as his long-suffering spouse. The story, which Garson Kanin adapted from his own novel, concerns Hubie Cram, a would-be bigshot, who induces three retired slot-machine mobsters (David Burns, George Mathews, and George Givot) to muscle in on the jukebox racket. Though this does not make him the fawned-upon tycoon he has always dreamed of becoming, Hubie does succeed in turning a waitress (Nancy Dussault) into a singing star. He also shows his musical knowledge by instructing a group of studio musicians on how each one is to play his instrument. His modest comment: "You hang around, you learn."
RCA OC/ TW.

Do Re Mi. "It's Legitimate" sing Phil Silvers, George Mathews, George Givot, and David Burns. (Friedman-Abeles)

CARNIVAL
Music & lyrics: Bob Merrill
Book: Michael Stewart
Producer: David Merrick
Director-choreographer: Gower Champion
Cast: Anna Maria Alberghetti, James Mitchell, Kaye Ballard, Pierre Olaf, Jerry Orbach, Henry Lascoe, Anita Gillette
Songs: "Direct from Vienna"; "Mira"; "Yes, My Heart"; "Love Makes the World Go Round"; "Beautiful Candy"; "Grand Imperial Cirque de Paris"; "Always Always You"; "She's My Love"
New York run: Imperial Theatre, April 13, 1961; 719 p.

Though the 1953 movie *Lili* had but one song, it did have two extended dance sequences which qualified it as the first screen musical to be adapted as a stage musical. Since the single song was "Hi Lili, Hi Lo," it presented a challenge for Bob Merrill to come up with a "theme" for *Carnival* with the same flavor but sufficiently distinctive on its own. He met the challenge with "Love Makes the World Go Round," whose melody from a wheezing concertina opens the show on a bare, pre-dawn setting as the weary members of a seedy French carnival set up the tents. With this strikingly effective opening (there is no overture), director Gower Champion reaffirmed his reputation for imaginative stagecraft, which was later bolstered by a joyously self-deluding dance number as the company proudly imagines itself as the "Grand Imperial Cirque de Paris." In the story, Anna Maria Alberghetti appeared as the waif who comes from the town of Mira to join the carnival where she falls for the egotistical magician Marco the Magnificent (James Mitchell), befriends the show's puppets, and ends in the arms of the disillusioned crippled puppeteer (Jerry Orbach). During the Broadway run, Miss Alberghetti was succeeded by Susan Watson and sister Carla Alberghetti. Polydor OC/ DBS Publications (1968)/ TW.

MILK AND HONEY
Music & lyrics: Jerry Herman
Book: Don Appell
Producer: Gerald Oestreicher
Director: Albert Marre
Choreographer: Donald Saddler
Cast: Robert Weede, Mimi Benzell, Molly Picon, Tommy Rall, Lanna Saunders, Juki Arkin
Songs: "Shalom"; "Milk and Honey"; "There's No Reason in the World"; "That Was Yesterday"; "Let's Not Waste A Moment"; "Like A Young Man"; "As Simple As That"
New York run: Martin Beck Theatre, October 10, 1961, 543 p.

For his initial Broadway assignment, composer-lyricist Jerry Herman joined playwright Don Appell to create the first musical with an Israeli setting. After spending some weeks in Israel, the writers agreed on a story concerning American tourists so that the score would not have to be written entirely in a minor key. *Milk and Honey* (originally titled *Shalom*) was primarily about a romance that blooms in a desert *moshav* between a middle-aged man separated from his wife (Robert Weede) and an almost middle-aged widow (Mimi Benzell). Though Phil would like Ruth to remain with him, she is unhappy about an extended non-matrimonial relationship, and — when last seen — Phil is on his way to make one final appeal for a divorce. Comic relief was provided by Molly Picon (a star of the Yiddish theatre in her only Broadway musical) as a husband-hunting widow. RCA OC/ TW.

How to Succeed in Business Without Really Trying. Robert Morse and Bonnie Scott. (Friedman-Abeles)

HOW TO SUCCEED IN BUSINESS WITHOUT REALLY TRYING

Music & lyrics: Frank Loesser
Book: Abe Burrows
Producers: Cy Feuer & Ernest Martin
Director: Abe Burrows
Choreographers: Bob Fosse, Hugh Lambert
Cast: Robert Morse, Rudy Vallee, Bonnie Scott, Virginia Martin, Charles Nelson Reilly, Ruth Kobart, Sammy Smith, Donna McKechnie
Songs: "Coffee Break"; "The Company Way"; "A Secretary Is Not a Toy"; "Grand Old Ivy"; "Paris Original"; "Rosemary"; "I Believe in You"; "Brotherhood of Man"
New York run: 46th Street Theatre, October 14, 1961; 1,417 p.

The program credit for *How to Succeed in Business Without Really Trying* indicates that the musical was based on Shepherd Mead's tongue-in-cheek manual, but since the book had no plot Abe Burrows' script was actually based on an unproduced play by Jack Weinstock and Willie Gilbert (whose program credit, also incorrect, indicates that they were co-librettists). That play had been sent to producers Cy Feuer and Ernest Martin who then enlisted Burrows and Frank Loesser, their *Guys and Dolls* team, to turn it into a musical comedy. Bob Fosse was brought in during rehearsals to take charge of the musical staging.

In the sassy sendup of the Horatio Alger myth, our disarmingly boyish hero J. Pierpont Finch (Robert Morse) owes his advancement — from window washer to Chairman of the Board of the World Wide Wicket Company — not to hard work but to his ability to make others work hard for him. As it traces Finch's step-by-step back-stabbing way up the corporate ladder, the show skewers such aspects of Big Business as nepotism, old-school ties, the coffee break, the office party, the sycophantic yes-men, the executive washroom (where Finch serenades his image in the mirror with the worshipful "I Believe in You"), and the boardroom presentation. The musical became the fourth to win the Pulitzer Prize for drama. Robert Morse and Rudy Vallee, who played J.B. Biggley, the stuffy president of the company, were also in the 1967 movie.
RCA OC/ Frank Music, London (1963)*/ MTI.

NO STRINGS

Music & lyrics: Richard Rodgers
Book: Samuel Taylor
Producer: Richard Rodgers
Director-choreographer: Joe Layton
Cast: Richard Kiley, Diahann Carroll, Polly Rowles, Noelle Adam, Bernice Massi, Don Chastain, Alvin Epstein, Mitchell Gregg
Songs: "The Sweetest Sounds"; "Loads of Love"; "La La La"; "Nobody Told Me"; "Look No Further"; "Maine"; "No Strings"
New York run: 54th Street Theatre, March 15, 1962; 580 p.

One appearance on the Jack Paar television show was all it took for Diahann Carroll to convince Richard Rodgers that she should be starred on Broadway in a Richard Rodgers musical. *No Strings,* the musical that resulted, was Rodgers' first production after the death of his partner, Oscar Hammerstein II, and the only one for which the composer also supplied his own lyrics. The work proved to be highly innovative in a number of ways: it placed the orchestra backstage, it put musicians onstage to accompany singers, it had the principals and chorus move scenery and props in full view of the audience, and — conforming to the show's title — it removed the string section from the orchestra. In addition, it was concerned with an interracial love affair, though the matter of race was never discussed. The leading characters were Barbara Woodruff (Miss Carroll), a high fashion model living in Paris, and David Jordan (Richard Kiley), a former Pulitzer Prize-winning novelist now a sponging "Europe bum." After meeting they enjoy hearing the sweetest sounds in such romantic surroundings as Monte Carlo, Honfleur, Deauville, and St. Tropez. The story ends, with no strings attached, as the writer returns home alone to Maine to try to resume his career. During the run, Kiley and Miss Carroll were succeeded by Howard Keel and Barbara McNair, who then toured. The 54th Street Theatre, formerly the Adelphi, was renamed the George Abbott before it was demolished.
Capitol OC/ Random House (1962)/ R&H.

No Strings. Diahann Carroll and Richard Kiley.
(Friedman-Abeles)

A FUNNY THING HAPPENED ON THE WAY TO THE FORUM

Music & lyrics: Stephen Sondheim
Book: Burt Shevelove & Larry Gelbart
Producer: Harold Prince
Director: George Abbott (Jerome Robbins uncredited)
Choreographer: Jack Cole
Cast: Zero Mostel, John Carradine, Raymond Walburn, Jack Gilford, David Burns, Ruth Kobart, Brian Davies, Preshy Marker, Ronald Holgate, Eddie Phillips
Songs: "Comedy Tonight"; "Love I Hear"; "Free"; "Lovely"; "Pretty Little Picture"; "Everybody Ought to Have a Maid"; "I'm Calm"; "Impossible"; "Bring Me My Bride"; "That'll Show Him"
New York run: Alvin Theatre, May 8, 1962; 964 p.

Having already written a musical at Yale inspired by the farcical plays of Titus Maccius Plautus (254 BC-184 BC), Burt Shevelove got together with Larry Gelbart and Stephen Sondheim to give Broadway a taste of what once convulsed Roman audiences. To come up with a suitable script — which would also adhere to the classic unities of time, place and action — the writers researched all 21 of the playwright's surviving comedies, then put together an original story incorporating such typical, laugh-catching Plautus characters as the conniving slave, the callow hero (named Hero), the doddering old man, the seductive courtesan, the lustful husband and his shrewish wife, and the macho warrior. One situation in the musical — regarding the doddering old man who is kept from entering his house because he thinks it is haunted — was discovered in a play with the curiously prophetic title of *Mostellaria.*

Originally intended as a vehicle for Phil Silvers, then for Milton Berle, *A Funny Thing Happened on the Way to the Forum* opened with Zero Mostel as Pseudolus, a slave who is forced to go through a series of outlandish adventures before being allowed his freedom. Though Broadway audiences immediately took to George Abbott's frantically paced show, the outlook had not looked promising during the pre-New York tryout and director Jerome Robbins was called in. His most important change: beginning the musical with the song "Comedy Tonight," which set just the right mood for the madcap doings that followed. In addition to being Harold Prince's first solo producing effort, the show was the first Broadway offering with music as well as lyrics by Stephen Sondheim. During the run, Mostel was succeeded by Dick Shawn, David Burns by Frank McHugh (as Senex, a lascivious slave owner), Jack Gilford by Lee Goodman (as Hysterium, a nervous slave) and John Carradine by Erik Rhodes (as Marcus Lycus, a dealer in courtesans). The touring cast included Jerry Lester (Pseudolus), Paul Hartman (Senex), Arnold Stang (Hysterium), Erik Rhodes (Marcus Lycus), Edward Everett Horton (Erronius, the doddering old man), and Donna McKechnie (Philia, a slave).

In 1972, Phil Silvers got his chance to play Pseudolus in a well-received revival whose run was cut short by the star's illness. Larry Blyden, who was also co-producer, appeared as Hysterium, and others in the cast were Mort Marshall (Senex), Carl Ballantine (Lycus), and Reginald Owen (Erronius). Burt Shevelove was the director. Both Mostel (as Pseudolus) and Silvers (as Lycus) were in the 1966 screen version along with Jack Gilford.
Capitol OC/ Dodd, Mead (1963)/ MTI.

A Funny Thing Happened on the Way to the Forum. John Carradine and Zero Mostel. (Friedman-Abeles)

STOP THE WORLD — I WANT TO GET OFF

Music, lyrics & book: Leslie Bricusse & Anthony Newley
Producer: David Merrick
Director: Anthony Newley
Choreographers: Virginia Mason, John Broome
Cast: Anthony Newley, Anna Quayle, Jennifer Baker, Susan Baker
Songs: "Typically English"; "Gonna Build a Mountain"; "Once in a Lifetime"; "Someone Nice Like You"; "What Kind Of Fool Am I?"
New York run: Shubert Theatre, October 3, 1962; 555 p.

A hit in London a year before it was presented in New York, *Stop the World — I Want to Get Off* unveiled the multiple talents of the British team of Leslie Bricusse and Anthony Newley. Newley starred in the musical, in which he played Littlechap, and the allegorical tale had much to say about man's drive for fame and power and the disillusionment that sets in once these goals are attained. (Rodgers and Hammerstein had previously dealt with the same general theme in *Allegro*.) In a setting designed by Sean Kenny to resemble a circus tent, Littlechap — wearing white-face clown makeup — rises in the world of business and politics after marrying the boss's daughter (Anna Quayle). Not above a little philandering with Russian, German, and American girls (all played by Miss Quayle), Littlechap ends his days ruminating — in "What Kind of Fool Am I?" — about his misspent life. Newley was succeeded during the run by Joel Grey, and his part in the 1966 movie was played by Tony Tanner. A revised adaptation came back to Broadway in 1978 with Sammy Davis Jr. Davis also did a film version of this verison under the modest rubric *Sammy Stops the World.* Polydor OC/ TW.

LITTLE ME

Music: Cy Coleman
Lyrics: Carolyn Leigh
Book: Neil Simon
Producers: Cy Feuer & Ernest Martin
Directors: Cy Feuer & Bob Fosse
Choreographer: Bob Fosse
Cast: Sid Caesar, Virginia Martin, Nancy Andrews, Mort Marshall, Joey Faye,
Swen Swenson, Peter Turgeon, Mickey Deems, Gretchen Cryer
Songs: "The Other Side of the Tracks"; "I Love You"; "Be a Performer";
"Boom-Boom"; "I've Got Your Number"; "Real Live Girl"; "Poor Little
Hollywood Star"; "Here's to Us"
New York run: Lunt-Fontanne Theatre, November 17, 1962; 257 p.

Although Neil Simon's wickedly funny, outlandishly plotted libretto for *Little Me*
was based on Patrick Dennis' novel about the rise of a voluptuous beauty from
Drifters' Row, Venezuela, Illinois, to a Southampton estate, it was written primarily to show off the protean comic gifts of Sid Caesar playing all seven of the men
who figured prominently in our heroine's life. Chief among the Caesar characterizations was Noble Eggleston, the over-achieving snob who loves poor Belle
Schlumpfert as much as he is able ("considering you're riffraff and I am
well-to-do"), studies medicine and law at Harvard and Yale, becomes a flying ace
in World War I, wins election as governor of both North and South Dakota, and,
eventually, is the man with whom Belle literally walks into the sunset. The actor
was also seen as Amos Pinchley, an 88-year-old miserly banker; Val du Val, a
flashy French entertainer; Fred Poitrine, the hick soldier who marries Belle and
quickly expires; Otto Schnitzler, a dictatorial Hollywood director; Prince
Cherney, the lachrymose impoverished ruler of the duchy of Rosenzweig; and
Noble Jr., an over-achieving chip who studies both at Juilliard and Georgia Tech
to become a musical engineer. Highlights of the score were the wistful "Real Live
Girl," sung by World War I doughboys, and the sassy, seductive "I've Got Your
Number," sung and danced by Swen Swenson, as Belle's faithful admirer.

In 1982, a revised version of *Little Me* — with James Coco, Victor Garber
and Mary Gordon Murray — had a disappointingly short run on Broadway.
RCA OC/ Random House (1977)/ TW.

Little Me. Sid Caesar (as Amos
Pinchley) and Virginia Martin.
(Friedman-Abeles)

OLIVER!

Music, lyrics & book: Lionel Bart
Producers: David Merrick & Donald Albery
Director: Peter Cole
Cast: Clive Revill, Georgia Brown, Bruce Prochnik, Willoughby Goddard, Hope Jackman, Danny Sewell, David Jones, Geoffrey Lumb
Songs: "Food Glorious Food"; "Where Is Love?"; "Consider Yourself"; "You've Got to Pick a Pocket or Two"; "It's a Fine Life"; "Oom-Pah-Pah"; "I'd Do Anything"; "As Long as He Needs Me"; "Who Will Buy?"; "Reviewing the Situation"
New York run: Imperial Theatre, January 6, 1963; 774 p.

Lionel Bart's *Oliver!*, which opened in London in 1960, held the West End long-run record for a musical until overtaken by *Jesus Christ Superstar,* and its Broadway facsimile—also directed by Peter Cole and designed by Sean Kenny—was the longest running musical import until overtaken by *Evita.* Adapted from Charles Dickens' *Oliver Twist,* the stage version offered a somewhat jollied up view of the ordeal of an orphan (played by Bruce Prochnik) who dares to ask for more food at the workhouse, is sent out into the cruel world, fall in with a band of juvenile pickpockets under the benign control of Fagin (Clive Revill), and is eventually rescued from a life of fraternal crime by kindly, wealthy Mr. Brownlow (Geoffrey Lumb), who turns out to be Oliver's grandfather. Kenny's ingenious, atmospheric settings were much admired as were the tuneful. rousing score. The work, however, did not last long in a 1984 revival with Ron Moody (the London and 1968 film version Fagin) and Patti LuPone.

Five other Dickens novels were seen on Broadway in musical adaptations: *Barnaby Rudge* (*Dolly Varden,* 1902); *The Posthumous Papers of the Pickwick Club* (*Mr Pickwick,* 1903; *Pickwick,* 1965); *A Christmas Carol* (*Comin' Uptown,* 1979); *David Copperfield* (*Copperfield,* 1981); *The Mystery of Edwin Drood* 1985). For other musicals based on British literary classics, see *My Fair Lady,* page 168.
RCA OC.TW.

Oliver! Georgia Brown, David Jones, Bruce Prochnik, and Clive Revill in the "I'd Do Anything" number. (Friedman-Abeles)

She Loves Me. Daniel Massey and Barbara Cook. (Eileen Darby)

SHE LOVES ME

Music: Jerry Bock
Lyrics: Sheldon Harnick
Book: Joe Masteroff
Producer-director: Harold Prince
Choreographer: Carol Haney
Cast: Barbara Cook, Daniel Massey, Barbara Baxley, Jack Cassidy, Ludwig Donath, Nathaniel Frey, Ralph Williams
Songs: "Days Gone By"; "Tonight at Eight"; "Will He Like Me?"; "Dear Friend"; "Ice Cream"; "She Loves Me"; "A Trip to the Library"; "Grand Knowing You"; "Twelve Days to Christmas"
New York run: Eugene O'Neill Theatre, April 23, 1963; 301 p.

With its beguiling European setting, attractive characters, tender love story, and, most important, closely integrated, melody drenched score, *She Loves Me* recalled the atmosphere and charm of the Kern-Harbach *The Cat and the Fiddle* and the Kern-Hammerstein *Music in the Air*. The new musical, the first to be directed as well as produced by Harold Prince, was based on a Hungarian play, *Parfumerie,* by Miklos Laszlo, that had already been used as the basis for two films, *The Shop Around the Corner* and *In the Good Old Summertime.* Set in the 1930s in "A City in Europe" — which could only be Budapest — the tale is concerned with the people who work in Maraczek's Parfumerie, principally the constantly squabbling sales clerk Amalia Balash (Barbara Cook) and the manager Georg Nowack (Daniel Massey). It is soon revealed that they are anonymous pen pals who agree to meet one night at the Café Imperiale, though neither knows the other's identity. Georg realizes who Amalia is when he sees her waiting for him in the restaurant, but he doesn't let on and the unhappy Amalia pours out her heart in a longing plea to her unknown "Dear Friend." After she calls in sick, their relationship blossoms into love when Georg brings her ice cream; eventually, he is emboldened to reveal his identity by quoting from one of Amalia's letters.

She Loves Me would have starred Julie Andrews had she not been tied up with a film. A successful revival of the musical opened on Broadway in June of 1993.

Polydor OC/Dodd, Mead (1963)/TW.

110 IN THE SHADE

Music: Harvey Schmidt
Lyrics: Tom Jones
Book: N. Richard Nash
Producer: David Merrick
Director: Joseph Anthony
Choreographer: Agnes de Mille
Cast: Robert Horton, Inga Swenson, Stephen Douglass, Will Geer, Steve Roland, Anthony Teague, Lesley Ann Warren, Gretchen Cryer
Songs: "Love, Don't Turn Away"; "Rain Song"; "You're Not Foolin' Me"; "Old Maid"; "Everything Beautiful Happens at Night"; "Melisande"; "Simple Little Things"; "Little Red Hat"; "Is It Really Me?"
New York run: Broadhurst Theatre, October 24, 1963; 330 p.

Harvey Schmidt and Tom Jones followed their runaway Off-Broadway hit, *The Fantasticks,* with an equally wistful and appealing score for *110 in the Shade,* which N. Richard Nash adapted from his own 1954 play, *The Rainmaker.* The action of the story takes place in a drought-stricken Western town on a hot summer day from dawn to midnight. The sudden appearance of a brash rainmaker, Bill Starbuck (Robert Horton in a part first announced for Hal Holbrook), lifts the spirits of all but plain Lizzie Curry (Inga Swenson) who calls him a fake. Lizzie, whose life is as parched as the weather, is attracted to the flamboyant con man and they make love while the town is enjoying its annual picnic. Starbuck wants Lizzie to run away with him, but since her dreams are really only of simple little things, she is happy to remain with the more dependable suitor, Sheriff File (Stephen Douglass). Then darned if a miracle doesn't happen and the rains come. RCA OC/ TW.

110 in the Shade. Robert Horton and Inga Swenson. (Friedman-Abeles)

HELLO, DOLLY!

Music & lyrics: Jerry Herman
Book: Michael Stewart
Producer: David Merrick
Director-choreographer: Gower Champion
Cast: Carol Channing, David Burns, Eileen Brennan, Sondra Lee, Charles Nelson Reilly, Jerry Dodge, Gordon Connell, Igors Gavon, Alice Playten, David Hartman
Songs: "It Takes a Woman"; "Put on Your Sunday Clothes"; "Ribbons Down My Back"; "Dancing"; "Before the Parade Passes By"; "Hello, Dolly!"; "It Only Takes a Moment"; "So Long, Dearie"
New York run: St. James Theatre, January 16, 1964; 2,844 p.

For over ten months — until it was overtaken by *Fiddler on the Roof* — *Hello, Dolly!* held the record as Broadway's longest running musical. Its tryout tour, however, was hardly a harbinger of even a moderate success. New writers had to be called in, three songs were dropped and three added (including the first-act finale, "Before the Parade Passes By"), and Jerry Dodge replaced one of the two leading juveniles. But director Gower Champion made it all work and the musical won a rousing Broadway reception.

The turn-of-the-century tale centers around Dolly Gallagher Levi, a New York matchmaker engaged to help a pompous Yonkers merchant, Horace Vandergelder (David Burns), in his pursuit of a mate. But the matchmaker sets her cap for Vandergelder herself, and eventually he acknowledges that it fits. Along the way, the exuberant Dolly helps two of Vandergelder's clerks, Barnaby Tucker and Cornelius Hackl (Jerry Dodge and Charles Nelson Reilly) enjoy a night at the Harmonia Gardens restaurant with dressmaker Irene Malloy and her assistant Minnie Fay (Eileen Brennan and Sondra Lee). After her grand entrance into the restaurant, Dolly sets off a rousing, high-kicking reception by the waiters welcoming her back to a once favored haunt.

Hello, Dolly! had an unusually lengthy history. Its first version, in 1835, was a London play, *A Day Well Spent,* by John Oxenford. Seven years later, *Einen Jux Will er Sich Machen (He Wants to Have a Lark),* a Viennese variation by Johann Nestroy, was produced. In 1938, Thornton Wilder turned the Nestroy play into *The Merchant of Yonkers,* and 17 years after that he rewrote it as *The Matchmaker.* Both Wilder plays had Broadway runs. Another forerunner of *Hello, Dolly!* was the 1891 musical, *A Trip to Chinatown.*

Once Ethel Merman had turned down the chance to be the first song-and-dance Dolly, Carol Channing seized the opportunity to make it one of her two most closely identified roles. During the Broadway run she was succeeded by Ginger Rogers, Martha Raye, Betty Grable, Bibi Osterwald, Pearl Bailey (who starred in an all-black company and was frequently spelled by Thelma Carpenter), Phyllis Diller, and — at last — Ethel Merman. David Burns was replaced by Max Showalter, and Cab Calloway had the Vandergelder part opposite Miss Bailey. During Miss Merman's tenure, Russell Nype played Cornelius. The show returned to New York in 1974 with Miss Bailey and Billy Daniels leading an all-black cast, and in 1978 it came back with Miss Channing and Eddie Bracken as part of a year-and-a-half tour. In 1965, Mary Martin and Loring Smith headed the first touring company, which played the Far East (primarily for U.S. troops) and London. A second company toured two years nine months originally with Miss Channing (succeeded by Eve Arden and Dorothy Lamour) and Horace MacMahon. A third company, starring Miss Grable (then Miss Rogers and Miss Lamour) traveled for two years four months. The show's film version, released in 1969, co-starred Barbra Streisand and Walter Matthau.

RCA OC (Channing); RCA OC (Bailey); RCA OC (Martin)/ DBS (1966)/ TW.

Carol Channing

Ginger Rogers

Martha Raye

Betty Grable

Pearl Bailey

WHAT MAKES SAMMY RUN?

Music & lyrics: Ervin Drake
Book: Budd & Stuart Schulberg
Producer: Joseph Cates
Director: Abe Burrows
Choreographer: Matt Mattox
Cast: Steve Lawrence, Sally Ann Howes, Robert Alda, Bernice Massi, Barry Newman, Walter Klavun
Songs: "A Tender Spot"; "My Home Town"; "A Room Without Windows"; "Something to Live For"; "The Friendliest Thing"
New York run: 54th Street Theatre, February 27, 1964; 540 p.

Unscrupulous Sammy Glick was first immortalized in Budd Schulberg's novel about the double dealing world of Hollywood. In the musical version, adapted by Schulberg and his brother Stuart, he was something of a relative to *How to Succeed's* J. Pierpont Finch, as the story covers Sammy's rise from his days as a newspaper copy boy, through his job as a script writer at World Wide Pictures and his affair with fellow-writer Kit Sargent (Sally Ann Howes), to his elevation as studio chief and his marriage to his boss's nymphomaniac daughter (Bernice Massi). At the play's end, left without friends and with an unfaithful wife, Sammy is still running. Playing the role of Sammy was nightclub and recording star Steve Lawrence, who helped turn a vision of romantic isolation, "A Room Without Windows," into a popular song hit.
Columbia OC/ Random House (1965)/ TW.

Funny Girl. Barbra Streisand singing "I'm the Greatest Star" as Danny Meehan watches. (Henry Grossman)

FUNNY GIRL

Music: Jule Styne
Lyrics: Bob Merrill
Book: Isobel Lennart
Producer: Ray Stark
Directors: Jerome Robbins, Garson Kanin
Choreographer: Carol Haney
Cast: Barbra Streisand, Sydney Chaplin, Kay Medford, Danny Meehan, Jean Stapleton, Roger DeKoven, Joseph Macaulay, Lainie Kazan, Buzz Miller, George Reeder, Larry Fuller
Songs: "I'm the Greatest Star"; "Cornet Man"; I Want to Be Seen With You Tonight"; "People"; "You Are Woman"; "Don't Rain on My Parade"; "Sadie, Sadie"; "Who Are You Now?"; "The Music That Makes Me Dance"
New York run: Winter Garden, March 26, 1964; 1,348 p.

The funny girl of the title refers to Fanny Brice, and the story, told mostly in flashback, covers the major events in the life of the celebrated comedienne — her discovery by impresario Florenz Ziegfeld, her triumphs in the *Ziegfeld Follies,* her infatuation with and stormy marriage to smooth-talking con man Nick Arnstein, and the breakup of that marriage after Nick has served time for masterminding the theft of Wall Street securities. Film producer Ray Stark, Miss Brice's son-in-law, had long wanted to make a movie based on the Fanny Brice story, but he became convinced that it should first be done on the stage. Mary Martin, Anne Bancroft, and Carol Burnett had all turned down the leading part before it was won by Barbra Streisand, whose only other Broadway experience had been in a supporting role in *I Can Get It for You Wholesale.* Miss Streisand succeeded so well — her recording of "People" was a hit before *Funny Girl* opened — that she became even more renowned than the woman she portrayed.

At first there was hope that the *Gypsy* team of Jule Styne and Stephen Sondheim would be reunited to write the score, but Sondheim wasn't interested and Styne contacted Bob Merrill. Some of their songs, however, virtually replaced those used in comparable situations in *Gypsy* — "I'm the Greatest Star" for "Some People," "Don't Rain on My Parade" for "Everything's Coming Up Roses," and "The Music That Makes Me Dance" (which suggested Fanny Brice's closely identified theme song, "My Man") for "Rose's Turn." When Jerome Robbins, the original director, walked out in a dispute with the author, he was succeeded by Bob Fosse, who didn't stay long, then by Garson Kanin, who quit after Robbins was lured back.

The musical was variously announced under such titles as *A Very Special Person, My Man,* and *The Luckiest People* before David Merrick (who was to have been the show's co-producer) suggested *Funny Girl.* Numerous script alterations — including 40 rewrites of the final scene alone — and five opening-night postponements were required before the show was considered ready for its official premiere. During the Broadway run, Miss Streisand was followed by Mimi Hines, and Sydney Chaplin, who played Nick Arnstein, by Johnny Desmond. The road company, which toured for 13 months was headed by Marilyn Michaels (Fanny), Anthony George (Nick), and Lillian Roth (Fanny's mother). Miss Streisand also starred in the 1968 film version and its 1975 sequel, *Funny Lady.* For other show-business musical biographies, see *Annie Get Your Gun,* page 130.
Capitol OC/ Random House (1964)/ TW.

HIGH SPIRITS

Music, lyrics & book: Hugh Martin & Timothy Gray
Producers: Lester Osterman, Robert Fletcher & Richard Horner
Director: Noël Coward (Gower Champion uncredited)
Choreographer: Danny Daniels
Cast: Beatrice Lillie, Tammy Grimes, Edward Woodward, Louise Troy
Songs: "Was She Prettier Than I?"; "The Bicycle Song"; "Forever and a Day"; "I Know Your Heart"; "Faster Than Sound"; "If I Gave You"; "Home Sweet Heaven"; "Something Is Coming to Tea"
New York run: Alvin Theatre, April 7, 1964; 375 p.

Hugh Martin and Timothy Gray had wanted to adapt Noël Coward's 1941 play *Blithe Spirit* as early as 1953, but permission was not granted until seven years later. In their musical version — initially titled *Faster Than Sound* — Beatrice Lillie (in her 13th and final Broadway appearance) portrayed the antic spiritualist Mme. Arcati who disrupts the second marriage of writer Charles Condomine (Edward Woodward) by bringing the shade of his first wife, Elvira (Tammy Grimes), back from the dead. In an attempt to take her former husband with her to the spirit world, Elvira accidentally causes the death of Ruth (Louise Troy), the second wife, who takes revenge by playing some ghostly tricks of her own. As director, Noël Coward made sure that *High Spirits* was in the proper blithe spirit of his play, but friction during the Philadelphia tryout between him and Miss Lillie prompted Mr. Coward's replacement by Gower Champion.
ABC Paramount OC/ TW.

Fiddler on the Roof. Tevye (Zero Mostel) is none too happy that daughter Tzeitel (Joanna Merlin) is marrying a poor tailor (Austin Pendleton). (Friedman-Abeles)

FIDDLER ON THE ROOF

Music; Jerry Bock
Lyrics: Sheldon Harnick
Book: Joseph Stein
Producer: Harold Prince
Director-choreographer: Jerome Robbins
Cast: Zero Mostel, Maria Karnilova, Beatrice Arthur, Joanna Merlin, Austin Pendleton, Bert Convy, Julia Migenes, Michael Granger, Tanya Everett, Leonard Frey, Maurice Edwards
Songs: "Tradition"; "Matchmaker, Matchmaker"; "If I Were a Rich Man"; "Sabbath Prayer"; "To Life"; "Miracle of Miracles"; "Sunrise, Sunset"; "Now I Have Everything"; "Do You Love Me?"; "Far from the Home I Love"; "Anatevka"
New York run: Imperial Theatre, September 22, 1964; 3,242 p.

One of Broadway's classic musicals, *Fiddler on the Roof* defied the accepted rules of commercial success by dealing with persecution, poverty, and the problems of holding on to traditions in the midst of a hostile world. But despite a story and setting that many thought had limited appeal, the theme struck such a universal response that the fiddler was perched precariously on his roof for seven years nine months, thus becoming the longest running production — musical or nonmusical — in Broadway history. (The record, however, was broken by *Grease* in December 1979.)

The plot is set in the Jewish village of Anatevka, Russia, in 1905, and deals mainly with the efforts of Tevye (Zero Mostel), a dairyman, his wife Golde (Maria Karnilova), and their five daughters to cope with their harsh existence. Tzeitel (Joanna Merlin), the oldest daughter, marries a poor tailor (Austin Pendleton), after Tevye had promised her to a well-to-do middle-aged butcher (Michael Granger). Hodel (Julia Migenes), the second daughter, marries a revolutionary (Bert Convy) and follows him to Siberia. Chava (Tanya Everett), the third daughter, marries out of her religion. When, at the end, the Czar's Cossacks destroy Anatevka, Tevye, still holding on to his faith and his traditions, bravely prepares to take what's left of his family to America. Though Zero Mostel became closely identified with the role of Tevye he proved not to be indispensable, since the musical had no trouble continuing with his successors Luther Adler, Herschel Bernardi, Harry Goz, Jerry Jarrett, Paul Lipson, and Jan Peerce. Six actresses replaced Maria Karnilova as Golde, including Martha Schlamme, Dolores Wilson, and Peg Murray. During the Broadway engagement, Pia Zadora took over as Bielke, the youngest daughter, and Bette Midler was seen for a time as Tzeitel. In 1976, *Fiddler on the Roof* came back to New York with Mostel and Thelma Lee in the leading roles; in 1981, it returned — at Lincoln Center's New York State Theatre — with Herschel Bernardi and Maria Karnilova. The national tour, originally featuring Luther Adler and Dolores Wilson, was on the road for two years three months. Topol, who played Tevye in London, was seen in the 1971 screen version which also featured Norma Crane and Molly Picon.

The idea for *Fiddler on the Roof* was planted when Jerry Bock, Sheldon Harnick, and Joseph Stein decided to make a musical out of Sholom Aleichem's short story, "Tevye and His Daughters." They took the first draft to producer Harold Prince who advised them that no other director but Jerome Robbins could possibly give the material the universal quality that it required. The first choice for Tevye was Danny Kaye; among others considered at various times were Howard Da Silva, Tom Bosley, and Danny Thomas.
RCA OC/ Crown (1964); Chilton (1973)/ MTI.

GOLDEN BOY

Music: Charles Strouse
Lyrics: Lee Adams
Book: Clifford Odets, William Gibson
Producer: Hillard Elkins
Director: Arthur Penn
Choreographer: Donald McKayle
Cast: Sammy Davis Jr., Billy Daniels, Paula Wayne, Kenneth Tobey, Ted Beniades, Louis Gossett, Jaime Rogers, Lola Falana
Songs: "Night Song"; "Don't Forget 127th Street"; "Lorna's Here"; "This Is the Life"; "While the City Sleeps"; "I Want to Be With You"
New York run: Majestic Theatre, October 20, 1964; 569 p.

For his first offering as a Broadway producer, Hillard Elkins hit upon the idea that by changing the leading character in Clifford Odets' 1937 drama *Golden Boy* from an Italian-American boxer named Joe Bonaparte to a Negro American boxer named Joe Wellington, the result would be a musical play of substance and significance. Odets himself agreed to write the libretto but his death during the show's early stages created major problems that remained unsolved until playwright William Gibson took over the adaptation and Arthur Penn replaced the original director during the tryout. With Sammy Davis Jr. giving a sensitive performance as the young man who breaks out of his Harlem surroundings by becoming a professional fighter, and with such effectively choreographed scenes as the opening gym workout and the climactic prizefight, *Golden Boy* won a favorable Broadway decision and remained almost a year and a half.
Capitol OC/ Atheneum (1965)/ SF.

DO I HEAR A WALTZ?

Music: Richard Rodgers
Lyrics: Stephen Sondheim
Book: Arthur Laurents
Producer: Richard Rodgers
Director: John Dexter
Choreographer: Herbert Ross
Cast: Elizabeth Allen, Sergio Franchi, Carol Bruce, Madeline Sherwood, Julienne Marie, Stuart Damon, Fleury D'Antonakis, Jack Manning
Songs: "Someone Woke Up"; "This Week Americans"; "What Do We Do? We Fly!"; "Someone Like You"; "Here We Are Again"; "Take the Moment!"; "Moon in My Window"; "We're Gonna Be All Right"; "Do I Hear a Waltz?"; "Stay"; "Thank You So Much"
New York run: 46th Street Theatre, March 18, 1965; 220 p.

Since Stephen Sondheim was something of a protégé of Oscar Hammerstein II, it was almost inevitable that Richard Rodgers would team up with him after Hammerstein's death. Their single joint effort resulted in *Do I Hear a Waltz?*, which Arthur Laurents adapted from his own play, *The Time of the Cuckoo*, first produced in 1952. Taking place in Venice, the tale concerns Leona Samish (Elizabeth Allen), who has an intense but foredoomed affair with Renato Di Rossi (Sergio Franchi), a married shopkeeper. Though initially, there was to have been no dancing in the musical, the authors felt during the Boston tryout that the rueful story needed more movement and choreographer Herbert Ross was called in. His contribution was most apparent in the scene in which Leona — who has always been sure she will know true love if she hears an imaginary waltz — hears it, sings about it, and dances to it.
Columbia OC/ Random House (1966)/ R&H.

HALF A SIXPENCE

Music & lyrics: David Heneker
Book: Beverly Cross
Producers: Allen-Hodgdon, Stevens Productions, Harold Fielding
Director: Gene Saks
Choreographer: Onna White
Cast: Tommy Steele, Ann Shoemaker, James Grout, Carrie Nye, Polly James, Grover Dale, Will Mackenzie, John Cleese
Songs: "Half a Sixpence"; "Money to Burn"; "She's Too Far Above Me"; "If the Rain's Got to Fall"; "Long Ago"; "Flash Bang Wallop"
New York run: Broadhurst Theatre, April 25, 1965; 512 p.

H.G. Wells' novel, *Kipps,* supplied the basis for this period musical in which Tommy Steele (for whom it was written) starred in London in 1963, in New York in 1965, and on film in 1967. *Half a Sixpence* is about Arthur Kipps, an orphan who becomes a draper's apprentice in Folkestone, England, at the turn of the century. Arthur inherits a fortune, becomes engaged to highborn Helen Walsingham (Carrie Nye), breaks off the engagement to marry Ann Pornick (Polly James), a working class girl, loses his money to Helen's brother (John Cleese) in a phony business scheme, and ends up contentedly as the owner of a book shop. There were some changes in the score for the New York engagement, which was enlivened by Onna White's rousing dances, especially the high-kicking, banjo-plucking "Money to Burn." During the run, Steele was succeeded by Tony Tanner, Joel Grey, and Dick Kalman. For other Broadway musicals based on British literary classics, see *My Fair Lady,* page 168.
RCA OC/ Dramatic Publ. Co. (1967)*/ DPC.

Half a Sixpence. Tommy Steele playing the banjo for his pub cronies in the "Money to Burn" number. (Friedman-Abeles)

The Roar of the Greasepaint — The Smell of the Crowd. Cyril Ritchard and Anthony Newley. (Henry Grossman)

THE ROAR OF THE GREASEPAINT — THE SMELL OF THE CROWD

Music, lyrics & book: Leslie Bricusse & Anthony Newley
Producer: David Merrick
Director: Anthony Newley
Choreographer: Gillian Lynne
Cast: Anthony Newley, Cyril Ritchard, Sally Smith, Gilbert Price, Joyce Jillson
Songs: "A Wonderful Day Like Today"; "Where Would You Be Without Me?"; "My First Love Song"; "Look at That Face"; "The Joker"; "Who Can I Turn To?"; "Feeling Good"; "Nothing Can Stop Me Now!"; "My Way"; "Sweet Beginning"
New York run: Shubert Theatre, May 16, 1965; 232 p.

The Roar of the Greasepaint — The Smell of the Crowd was another allegorical musical in the same style as the previous Anthony Newley-Leslie Bricusse *Stop the World — I Want to Get Off.* Again Newley starred and directed, Sean Kenny designed the symbolic set (this one resembling a huge gaming table), and David Merrick was the producer. Here the writers are concerned with the weighty theme of Playing the Game, which covers such universal topics as religion (the supplicating ballad, "Who Can I Turn To?," is addressed to God), hunger, work, love, success, death, and rebellion. Leading the cast were Cyril Ritchard as Sir, representing ruling class authority, and Anthony Newley as Cocky, representing the masses who submissively play the game according to the existing rules — no matter how unfair they are. In the end, emboldened by a character called The Negro (Gilbert Price), Cocky challenges Sir's dominance, and they both realize that power must be shared between them. Though the musical folded in England without opening in London, Merrick secured the American rights and sent the production on a 13½-week tryout tour, thus allowing the infectious music-hall type songs to win favor before the show reached Broadway.
RCA OC/ TW.

ON A CLEAR DAY YOU CAN SEE FOREVER

Music: Burton Lane
Lyrics & book: Alan Jay Lerner
Producer: Alan Jay Lerner
Director: Robert Lewis
Choreographer: Herbert Ross
Cast: Barbara Harris, John Cullum, Titos Vandis, William Daniels, Clifford David, Rae Allen
Songs: "Hurry! It's Lovely Up Here"; "On a Clear Day"; "On the S.S. Bernard Cohn"; "She Wasn't You"; "Melinda"; "What Did I Have That I Don't Have?"; "Wait Till We're Sixty-Five"; "Come Back to Me"
New York run: Mark Hellinger Theatre, October 17, 1965; 280 p.

Alan Jay Lerner's fascination with the phenomenon of extrasensory perception (ESP) led to his teaming with composer Richard Rodgers in 1962 to write a musical called *I Picked a Daisy*. When that partnership failed to work out, Lerner turned to Burton Lane, and the show was retitled *On a Clear Day You Can See Forever*. Though Barbara Harris was the only actress ever considered for the female lead, at least six actors were announced for the male lead until it went to Louis Jordan — and *he* was replaced by John Cullum during the Boston tryout. The musical (the first with a top ticket price of $11.90) is concerned with Daisy Gamble who can predict the future and, when hypnotized by Dr. Mark Bruckner, can also recall her life as Melinda Wells in 18th Century London. When Mark's infatuation with Melinda makes her something of a rival to the real-life alter ego, Daisy runs away. In the end, however, his stirring plea "Come Back to Me" is so persuasive that the couple is reunited. The 1970 film version starred Barbra Streisand and Yves Montand.
RCA OC/ Random House (1966)/ TW.

On a Clear Day You Can See Forever. John Cullum and Barbara Harris. (Bert Andrews)

Man of La Mancha. Richard Kiley as Don Quixote. (Bob Golby)

MAN OF LA MANCHA

Music: Mitch Leigh
Lyrics: Joe Darion
Book: Dale Wasserman
Producers: Albert Selden & Hal James
Director: Albert Marre
Choreographer: Jack Cole
Cast: Richard Kiley, Joan Diener, Irving Jacobson, Ray Middleton, Robert Rounseville, Jon Cypher, Gerrianne Raphael
Songs: "Man of La Mancha"; "Dulcinea"; "I Really Like Him"; "Little Bird, Little Bird"; "To Each His Dulcinea"; "The Impossible Dream"; "Knight of the Woeful Countenance"
New York run: ANTA Washington Square Theater, November 22, 1965; 2,328 p.

When, in *Man of La Mancha*, the dauntless, demented Don Quixote proclaims his quest to dream the impossible dream, the words not only expressed the theme of the musical but they could also have applied to the production itself. Though it won acclaim off Broadway (the theatre in which it opened, on West 4th Street, is no longer standing) and on Broadway (when it was transferred to the Martin Beck in March 1968), the idea of a windmill-tilting old gaffer as hero of a musical hardly seemed a formula for a successful run. Nor was there any encouraging track record for the show's composer, lyricist, or librettist. In fact, after the musical first tried out at the Goodspeed Opera House in Connecticut, it was considered so special that it was deliberately unveiled in New York far from the theatre district. Yet after its run of five years seven months, *Man of La Mancha* went into the record books as the third longest running musical of the Sixties.

The idea of transforming Dale Wasserman's television play, *I, Don Quixote*, into a musical first occurred to director Albert Marre. Originally, the score was to have been a collaboration between composer Mitch Leigh and co-lyricists W.H. Auden and Chester Kallman, and Michael Redgrave was announced for the role of the Don. The plot of *Man of La Mancha* unfolds as a story that novelist Miguel de Cervantes y Saavedra, imprisoned for debts during the Spanish Inquisition, tells to his fellow prisoners. In addition to Don Quixote, the major characters are the Don's faithful servant Sancho (Irving Jacobson) and the serving wench Aldonza (Joan Diener), whom the Don worships as the virginal Dulcinea and for whom he does battle to be worthy of knighthood. Though she scorns him for his foolishness, Aldonza is eventually won over — as the Don lays dying — to believing in his dream.

Richard Kiley gave his most celebrated performance as the Man of La Mancha, a role he relinquished during the run to José Ferrer, John Cullum, David Atkinson, Hal Holbrook, Bob Wright, Claudio Brook (from Mexico), Keith Michell (from England), Somegoro Ichikawa (from Japan), Charles West (from Australia), and Gideon Singer (from Israel). James Coco took over the small part of the Barber in 1966, and Joey Faye replaced Irving Jacobson as Sancho in 1968. The National Company toured for three years six months, with José Ferrer playing the original lead. In 1972, Kiley, Diener, and Jacobson were reunited when *Man of La Mancha* gave 140 performances at Lincoln Center's Vivian Beaumont Theatre. Kiley also played the Don in New York in 1977, heading a cast that included Emily Yancy and Tony Martinez, and remained for 124 performances. The 1972 screen version starred Peter O'Toole, Sophia Loren, and James Coco (as Sancho). Historic note: In 1889, Reginald De Koven and Harry B. Smith collaborated on an operetta based on the same story. Called *Don Quixote*, it was tried out in Chicago but never reached New York.
MCA OC/ Random House (1966); Chilton (1976)/ TW.

Sweet Charity. Gwen Verdon singing "If My Friends Could See Me Now." (Friedman-Abeles)

SWEET CHARITY

Music: Cy Coleman
Lyrics: Dorothy Fields
Book: Neil Simon
Producers: Robert Fryer, Lawrence Carr, Sylvia & Joseph Harris
Director-choreographer: Bob Fosse
Cast: Gwen Verdon, John McMartin, Helen Gallagher, Thelma Oliver, James Luisi, Ruth Buzzi, Barbara Sharma
Songs: "Big Spender"; "If My Friends Could See Me Now"; "There's Gotta Be Something Better Than This"; "The Rhythm of Life"; "Baby Dream Your Dreams"; "Sweet Charity"; "Where Am I Going?"; "I'm a Brass Band"
New York run: Palace Theatre, January 29, 1966; 608 p.

Charity Hope Valentine — with her heart not only on her sleeve but tattooed on her arm — is a New York taxi dancer who knows there's gotta be something better to do than work at the Fan-Dango Ballroom. She gets innocently involved with an Italian movie star (James Luisi), then seriously involved with straight-laced Oscar Lindquist (John McMartin) after they meet in a stuck elevator at the 92nd Street "Y." Though Oscar eventually asks Charity to be his wife, the revelation of her employment makes the union impossible, and when last seen Charity is still a girl who lives "hopefully ever after."

The play's heroine was brought touchingly to life by Gwen Verdon after Bob Fosse, her husband at the time, decided to adapt as well as direct a musical treatment of Federico Fellini's film *Nights of Cabiria*. Originally intended as the first half of a double bill of one-act musicals, *Sweet Charity* was fleshed out to two acts when Neil Simon took over the writing. The musical was also the first legitimate show to play the Palace, the legendary vaudeville mecca on Broadway at 47th Street. A revival was mounted in 1986 (see page 272), with Debbie Allen (succeeded by Ann Reinking) as Charity, and a 1969 screen version starred Shirley MacLaine. The 1973 musical *Seesaw*, also with songs by Coleman and Fields and a book (though uncredited) by Neil Simon, was another New York tale of an ill-matched too-trusting kook and a too-square guy.

Columbia OC; EMI OC (1986)/ Random House (1966)/ TW.

MAME

Music & lyrics: Jerry Herman
Book: Jerome Lawrence & Robert E. Lee
Producers: Robert Fryer, Lawrence Carr, Sylvia & Joseph Harris
Director: Gene Saks
Choreographer: Onna White
Cast: Angela Lansbury, Beatrice Arthur, Jane Connell, Willard Waterman, Frankie Michaels, Charles Braswell, Jerry Lanning
Songs: "It's Today"; "Open a New Window"; "My Best Girl"; "We Need a Little Christmas"; "Mame"; "Bosom Buddies"; "That's How Young I Feel"; "If He Walked Into My Life"
New York run: Winter Garden, May 24, 1966; 1,508 p.

Once Mary Martin had turned down the title role in *Mame,* some 40 other actresses had to be eliminated before the part went to Angela Lansbury — who quickly established herself as one of the reigning queens of Broadway. Her vehicle, the fifth longest running musical of the Sixties, was an adaptation of Patrick Dennis' novel, *Auntie Mame,* which had also been the basis of the 1954 play. The show's musical-comedy lineage, however, could be traced to *Hello, Dolly!,* since it again spotlighted an antic, middle-aged matchmaking widow, and it again had a bubbling score by Jerry Herman including another strutting title song.

Set mostly in and around Mame's home at 3 Beekman Place, New York, the tale covers the period from 1928 to 1946. Firmly dedicated to the credo that "Life is a banquet and most poor sons-of-bitches are starving to death," Mame Dennis brings up her orphaned nephew Patrick (Frankie Michaels) in an aggressively permissive atmosphere as she urges him to live life to the fullest by opening a new window every day. After being wiped out by the stock market crash, Mame lands a part in — and manages to ruin — a musical comedy starring her bosom buddy Vera Charles (Beatrice Arthur), then recoups her fortunes by marrying Southern aristocrat Beauregard Jackson Pickett Burnside (Charles Braswell). Even Beau's death climbing an Alp cannot deter the indomitable Mame, whose final triumph is steering Patrick out of the clutches of a birdbrained snob and into the arms of a more appropriate mate. During the Broadway run, Miss Lansbury was followed by Celeste Holm, Janis Paige, Jane Morgan, and Ann Miller. Heading the four road companies were, respectively, Miss Holm, Miss Lansbury, Susan Hayward, and Janet Blair. Miss Lansbury also starred in a 1983 Broadway revival which had a brief run. The 1974 Hollywood version found Miss Arthur repeating her original role in a cast headed by Lucille Ball and Robert Preston. Columbia OC/ Random House (1967)/ TW.

Mame. Bosom buddies Angela Lansbury and Beatrice Arthur. (Friedman-Abeles)

THE APPLE TREE

Music: Jerry Bock
Lyrics: Sheldon Harnick
Book: Jerry Bock & Sheldon Harnick, with Jerome Coopersmith
Producer: Stuart Ostrow
Director: Mike Nichols
Choreographers: Herbert Ross, Lee Theodore
Cast: Barbara Harris, Larry Blyden, Alan Alda, Carmen Alvarez, Robert Klein
Songs: "Here in Eden"; "Eve"; "Beautiful, Beautiful World"; "Go to Sleep, Whatever You Are"; "It's a Fish"; "What Makes Me Love Him"; "Oh, to Be a Movie Star"; "Gorgeous"
New York run: Shubert Theatre, October 18, 1966; 463 p.

While they were initially to have been linked by the unifying theme of man, woman, and the devil, the three one-act musicals that comprised *The Apple Tree* had nothing in common except for some subtle interrelated musical themes and a whimsical reference to the color brown. In Broadway's first — and so far only — musical triple bill, Act I was based on Mark Twain's "The Diary of Adam and Eve" and dealt with the dawn of humanity and innocence; Act II was based on Frank R. Stockton's short story "The Lady or the Tiger?," in which a warrior's fate, unresolved in the plot, was determined by the choice of door he enters; and Act III was based on Jules Feiffer's fantasy, "Passionella," about a poor chimney sweep who yearned to become — and did become — a mooooooooooovie star. Though originally to have been directed by Gower Champion, *The Apple Tree* marked Mike Nichols' first association with a musical. Historic note: A full-length musical version of "The Lady or the Tiger?" was presented on Broadway in 1888 with DeWolf Hopper in the lead.
Columbia OC/ Random House (1967)/ MTI.

Cabaret. Lotte Lenya and Jack Gilford singing "It Couldn't Please Me More." (Friedman-Abeles)

Cabaret. "Willkommen, bienvenue, welcome," sings Joel Grey. (Friedman-Abeles)

CABARET

Music: John Kander
Lyrics: Fred Ebb
Book: Joe Masteroff
Producer-director: Harold Prince
Choreographer: Ron Field
Cast: Jill Haworth, Jack Gilford, Bert Convy, Lotte Lenya, Joel Grey, Peg Murray, Edward Winter
Songs: "Willkommen"; "Don't Tell Mama"; "Perfectly Marvelous"; "Two Ladies"; "It Couldn't Please Me More"; "Tomorrow Belongs to Me"; "The Money Song"; "Married"; "If You Could See Her"; "Cabaret"
New York run: Broadhurst Theatre, November 20, 1966; 1,165 p.

Claiming derivation from both Christopher Isherwood's *Berlin Stories* and John van Druten's 1951 dramatization, *I Am a Camera, Cabaret* turned a sleazy Berlin nightclub into a metaphor for the decadent world of pre-Hitler Germany, with the floorshow numbers used as commentaries on situations in the plot. At the Kit Kat Klub, where the epicene Master of Ceremonies (Joel Grey) bids one and all "Willkommen, bienvenue, welcome," the star attraction is the hedonistic British expatriate Sally Bowles (Jill Haworth), who also beckons customers with her own siren song to "Come to the cabaret, old chum." The main stories revolve around Sally's brief liaison with Clifford Bradshaw (Bert Convy), an American writer, and the more tragic romance between Fraulein Schneider (Lotte Lenya), a pragmatic landlady, and her Jewish suitor Herr Schultz (Jack Gilford). Helping to recreate the mood of a world in decay was the fluid direction of Harold Prince (it was his idea to add the Master of Ceremonies as a unifying symbol), a John Kander-Fred Ebb score that purposely evoked Kurt Weill, and the settings of Boris Aronson that recalled the paintings of George Grosz.

During the Broadway run, Miss Haworth was succeeded by Anita Gillette, Melissa Hart, and Tandy Cronyn. For the tour, which lasted one year seven months, the leads were taken by Miss Hart, Leo Fuchs (Schultz), Gene Rupert (Clifford), Signe Hasso (Fraulein), and Robert Salvio (MC). The 1972 film version retained Joel Grey (who also starred in the 1987 Broadway revival), but added Liza Minnelli, Michael York, Marisa Berenson, and a new story line.
Columbia OC/ Random House (1967); Chilton (1976)/ TW.

I Do! I Do! Robert Preston and Mary Martin.
(Friedman-Abeles)

I DO! I DO!

Music: Harvey Schmidt
Lyrics & book: Tom Jones
Producer: David Merrick
Director: Gower Champion
Cast: Mary Martin, Robert Preston
Songs: "I Love My Wife"; "My Cup Runneth Over"; "Love Isn't Everything";
"Nobody's Perfect"; "The Honeymoon Is Over"; "Where Are the
Snows?"; "When the Kids Get Married"; "Someone Needs Me"; "Roll
Up the Ribbons"
New York run: 46th Street Theatre, December 5, 1966; 560 p.

I Do! I Do! may have been the first Broadway musical ever to have a cast consisting entirely of two people, but since those people were Mary Martin and Robert Preston, no one could possibly have felt the need for anyone else on stage. In all other ways, however, the musical —which was adapted from Jan de Hartog's 1951 play, *The Fourposter* — was an ambitious undertaking, covering 50 years in the life of a married couple, Agnes and Michael, from their wedding day to the day they move out of their house. In between, they bring up a family, quarrel, threaten to break up, have a reconciliation, plan for a life without children in the house, and reveal in song exactly what they mean to each other. Apart from its stars, who were followed on Broadway by Carol Lawrence and Gordon MacRae, the production was especially noted for Gower Champion's inventive direction. A later musical with only two characters — but each with three alter egos — was the 1979 hit, *They're Playing Our Song.*
RCA OC/ MTI.

YOU'RE A GOOD MAN, CHARLIE BROWN

Music, lyrics & book: Clark Gesner
Producers: Arthur Whitelaw & Gene Persson
Director: Joseph Hardy
Choreographer: Patricia Birch
Cast: Bill Hinnant, Reva Rose, Karen Johnson, Bob Balaban, Skip Hinnant, Gary Burghoff
Songs: "You're a Good Man, Charlie Brown"; "My Blanket and Me"; "The Kite"; "Book Report"; "T.E.A.M. (The Baseball Game)"; "Little Known Facts"; "Suppertime"; "Happiness"
New York run: Theatre 80 St. Marks, March 7, 1967; 1,597 p.

With Charles Schultz's appealing comic strip "Peanuts" as general inspiration, Clark Gesner created a musical out of events in "a day made up of little moments picked from all the days of Charlie Brown, from Valentine's Day to the baseball season, from wild optimism to utter despair, all mixed with the lives of his friends (both human and non-human) and strung together on the string of a single day, from bright uncertain morning to hopeful starlit evening." The human characters, none supposedly older than six, include crabby, authoritarian Lucy (Reva Rose), music-loving Schroeder (Skip Hinnant), sweet and innocent Patty (Karen Johnson), blanket-hugging Linus (Bob Balaban), and perplexed, uncertain and eternally put-upon Charlie Brown himself (Gary Burghoff). The non-human character, of course, is Charlie Brown's highly imaginative pet dog Snoopy (Bill Hinnant), who likes to pretend that he's a World War I flying ace forever in search of the infamous Red Baron.

Gesner at first had no plans for his "Peanuts" songs other than as a recording, and initially MGM issued the album as part of its kiddie line. Producer Arthur Whitelaw, however, persuaded the writer to put together a theatrical concept, and he presented it at a tiny East Village theatre where it remained four years. Between 1967 and 1971, six road companies were performing throughout the United States. A second musical based on the "Peanuts" characters was *Snoopy*, written by Larry Grossman and Hal Hackaday. It opened Off Broadway in 1982 and ran for 152 performances. For other musicals taken from American comic strips, see *Li'l Abner*, page 171.
Polydor OC/ Random House (1967)/ TW.

You're a Good Man, Charlie Brown. Karen Johnson, Bob Balaban, Skip Hinnant, Reva Rose, Bill Hinnant, and Gary Burghoff. (Lawrence Belling)

YOUR OWN THING

Music & lyrics: Hal Hester & Danny Apolinar
Book: Donald Driver
Producers: Zev Bufman & Dorothy Love
Director: Donald Driver
Cast: Leland Palmer, Marian Mercer, Rusty Thacker, Tom Ligon, Danny Apolinar, Michael Valenti, John Kuhner
Songs: "The Flowers"; "I'm Me!"; "Come Away Death" (lyric: Shakespeare); "I'm on My Way to the Top"; "The Now Generation"; "The Middle Years"
New York run: Orpheum Theatre, January 13, 1968; 933 p.

An Off-Broadway musical of the Now, Me-Too and Let-It-All-Hang-Out Generation, *Your Own Thing* retold in contemporary style (accompanied by film and slide projections) the story of Shakespeare's *Twelfth Night* as it might apply to a twin brother and sister singing team (Tom Ligon and Leland Palmer) who are shipwrecked on Manhattan Island. Once the siblings split up, much confusion is caused when sister Viola disguises herself in male attire to join The Four Apocalypse, a rock group at a discotheque owned by Olivia (Marian Mercer). Thinking Viola a man, Olivia is attracted to her, but matters eventually get sorted out — Olivia happily settles for twin brother Sebastian and Viola wins Orson (Rusty Thacker), the group's manager. Coincidentally, shortly before *Your Own Thing* opened, another musical based on *Twelfth Night,* called *Love and Let Love,* began a brief Off-Broadway run. After it closed, Marcia Rodd, who played Olivia, took over the same part in *Your Own Thing.* Additional cast replacements were Raul Julia (Orson) and Sandy Duncan (Viola). For other musicals based on Shakespeare, see *The Boys from Syracuse,* page 107.
RCA OC/ Dell (1970)/ TW.

THE HAPPY TIME

Music: John Kander
Lyrics: Fred Ebb
Book: N. Richard Nash
Producer: David Merrick
Director-choreographer: Gower Champion
Cast: Robert Goulet, David Wayne, Mike Rupert, Julie Gregg, George S. Irving, Charles Durning
Songs: "The Happy Time"; "Tomorrow Morning"; "Please Stay"; "I Don't Remember You"; "The Life of the Party"; "Seeing Things"; "A Certain Girl"
New York run: Broadway Theatre, January 18, 1968; 286 p.

A gentle, nostalgic look at a French-Canadian family, *The Happy Time* was adapted from the novel by Robert Fontaine and the play by Samuel Taylor. The story is primarily concerned with the coming of age of Bibi Bonnard (Mike Rupert) and his desire to see the world with his Uncle Jacques (Robert Goulet), a footloose magazine photographer who has returned to his family for a brief visit. But Bibi's plans to run off with Jacques are opposed by the usually permissive Grandpère Bonnard (David Wayne) who manages — with Jacques' help — to convince Bibi to remain at home. The use of blow-up photographs to establish the mood for the various scenes was one of director Gower Champion's most effective touches. *The Happy Time* bore a certain resemblance to *110 in the Shade,* a previous musical by N. Richard Nash that had also been presented by David Merrick. That one also offered a smooth-talking visitor to a small town who excites the people's imagination, and leaves them with renewed appreciation of their own values.
RCA OC/ Dramatic Publ. Co. (1969)*/ DPC.

GEORGE M!

Music & lyrics: George M. Cohan
Book: Michael Stewart, John & Fran Pascal
Producers: David Black, Konrad Matthaei, Lorin Price
Director-choreographer: Joe Layton
Cast: Joel Grey, Betty Ann Grove, Jerry Dodge, Jill O'Hara, Bernadette Peters, Jamie Donnelly, Jacqueline Alloway, Loni Ackerman
Songs: "Musical Comedy Man"; "All Aboard for Broadway"; "My Town"; "Billie"; "Ring to the Name of Rose"; "Give My Regards to Broadway"; "Forty-Five Minutes from Broadway"; "So Long, Mary"; "Mary's a Grand Old Name"; "Yankee Doodle Dandy"; "Nellie Kelly, I Love You"; "Harrigan"; "Over There"; "You're a Grand Old Flag"
New York run: Palace Theatre, April 10, 1968; 427 p.

In this biographical musical celebrating the achievements of composer-lyricist-librettist-playwright-director-producer-actor-singer-dancer George M. Cohan, the story takes us from his birth in Providence, Rhode Island, in 1878, through his successes and failures and ends with his final Broadway triumph in 1937 playing President Roosevelt in *I'd Rather Be Right,* the only musical in which he appeared that he did not write himself. With Joel Grey as the pushy, not entirely sympathetic flag-waving hero, the show devoted its first-act finale to the reconstruction of the scene — familiar to anyone who has seen James Cagney in the movie *Yankee Doodle Dandy* — in which Cohan introduced "Give My Regards to Broadway" on the Southampton pier in *Little Johnny Jones.* For other show-business biographies see *Annie Get Your Gun*, page 130.
Columbia OC/ TW.

George M! Joel Grey strutting through "Give My Regards to Broadway." (Friedman-Abeles)

HAIR

Music: Galt MacDermot
Lyrics & book: Gerome Ragni & James Rado
Producer: Michael Butler
Director: Tom O'Horgan
Choreographer: Julie Arenal
Cast: Steve Curry, Ronald Dyson, Sally Eaton, Leata Galloway, Paul Jabara, Diane Keaton, Lynn Kellogg, Melba Moore, Shelley Plimpton, James Rado, Gerome Ragni, Lamont Washington
Songs: "Aquarius"; "Manchester England"; "Ain't Got No"; "I Got Life"; "Hair"; "Frank Mills"; "Hare Krishna"; "Where Do I Go?"; "Easy to Be Hard"; "Good Morning Starshine"; "Let the Sunshine In"
New York run: Biltmore Theatre, April 29, 1968; 1,750 p.

As much a product of its time as *Pins and Needles* and *This Is the Army* were of theirs, *Hair* grew out of the emotional turmoil of the Vietnam War years with its concomitant anti-establishment movement that produced a generation of drug-influenced, sex-obsessed social dropouts. With barely a discernable story line, this loosely structured musical celebrated the untethered lifestyle of hippies and flower children who welcomed the dawning of the Age of Aquarius by opposing the draft, the work ethic, and accepted standards of behavior and dress.

The "American Tribal Love-Rock Musical" (as it was billed) was first presented on October 29, 1967 under the direction of Gerald Freedman at Joseph Papp's New York Shakespeare Festival Public Theatre near Astor Place. At a $2.50 ticket price, it remained for about a month and a half, then moved to a Broadway nightclub called Cheetah. At that point, Michael Butler, a fledgling producer, took over the show for a Broadway run at the Biltmore Theatre (on 47th Street west of Broadway). Butler had it restaged by Tom O'Horgan, rechoreographed, redesigned, recostumed, relighted, and reorchestrated, and there were cast changes such as Lynn Kellogg for Jill O'Hara, Melba Moore for Jonelle Allen, and coauthor James Rado for Walker Daniels in the role of a draftee who spends his last civilian hours with a tribe of hippies. During its run — the fourth longest of a musical during the Sixties — *Hair* achieved something of a Broadway breakthrough by ending the first act in semi-darkness with the entire cast totally starkers. At one time, seven road companies were touring the United States. In 1977, Butler revived the musical but this time it ran only a month. The 1979 film version had a cast headed by John Savage, Treat Williams, and Beverly D'Angelo.

RCA OC (1967); RCA OC (1968)/ Pocket Books (1969); Stein & Day (1979)/ TW.

Hair. James Rado and Gerome Ragni. (Dagmar)

Zorba. Maria Karnilova and Herschel Bernardi in the "Y'assou" number. (Friedman-Abeles)

ZORBA

Music: John Kander
Lyrics: Fred Ebb
Book: Joseph Stein
Producer-director: Harold Prince
Choreographer: Ron Field
Cast: Herschel Bernardi, Maria Karnilova, John Cunningham, Carmen Alvarez, Lorraine Serabian, James Luisi
Songs: "Life Is"; "The First Time"; "The Top of the Hill"; "No Boom Boom"; "The Butterfly"; "Only Love"; "Y'assou"; "Happy Birthday"; "I Am Free"
New York run: Imperial Theatre, November 17, 1968; 305 p.

Although it reunited the *Cabaret* team of composer John Kander, lyricist Fred Ebb, and producer-director Harold Prince, *Zorba* was more of an Aegean counterpart to *Fiddler on the Roof,* with its larger-than-life aging hero and its stageful of earthy, ethnic types. It also had the same producer, librettist, set designer (Boris Aronson), and costume designer (Patricia Zipprodt), and its leading roles were played by two *Fiddler* alumni, Herschel Bernardi and Maria Karnilova. The story, however, was far grimmer, and the people of Crete a colder, more menacing lot than the colorful villagers of Anatevka. The tale involves the ebulient Zorba (Bernardi) with a studious young man named Nikos (John Cunningham) who has inherited an abandoned mine on the island of Crete. This sets off a series of tragic events, including the suicide of a Cretan youth out of unrequited love for a young Widow (Carmen Alvarez), the vengeful murder of the Widow by the youth's family, the discovery that the mine is inoperable, and the death of Hortense (Maria Karnilova), a coquettish French cocotte in love with Zorba. Nothing, however, can dampen Zorba's lust for life and his determination to live it to the fullest.

The production, the first to charge $15 for Saturday night orchestra seats, was based on Nikos Kazantzakis's novel *Zorba the Greek,* which became a 1964 movie with Anthony Quinn and Lila Kedrova, directed by Michael Cacoyannis. Cacoyannis also directed Quinn and Kedrova in a new production of the musical in 1983. It began its cross-country tour early in the year, had a longer Broadway run than the original, then toured again through July 1986. (See page 268.) Capitol OC; RCA OC (1983)/ Random House (1969)/ SF.

PROMISES, PROMISES

Music: Burt Bacharach
Lyrics: Hal David
Book: Neil Simon
Producer: David Merrick
Director: Robert Moore
Choreographer: Michael Bennett
Cast: Jerry Orbach, Jill O'Hara, Edward Winter, Norman Shelly, A. Larry Haines, Marian Mercer, Ken Howard, Donna McKechnie
Songs: "You'll Think of Someone"; "She Likes Basketball"; "Knowing When to Leave"; "Wanting Things"; "Whoever You Are"; "A Young Pretty Girl Like You"; "I'll Never Fall in Love Again"; "Promises, Promises"
New York run: Shubert Theatre, December 1, 1968; 1,281 p.

Two of the most successful pop song writers of the mid-Sixties, Burt Bacharach and Hal David, made a worthy — and so far only — contribution to the Broadway theatre with their score for *Promises, Promises.* Adapted from the 1960 movie, *The Apartment,* the musical followed such other recent offerings as *How to Succeed in Business Without Really Trying, I Can Get It for You Wholesale,* and *What Makes Sammy Run?* by revealing yet another method of getting ahead in the business world. Chuck Baxter (Jerry Orbach), the faceless hero of *Promises, Promises,* does it simply by lending his apartment to various executives of Consolidated Life for their extramarital dalliances. Among them is J.D. Sheldrake (Edward Winter) whose paramour, Fran Kubelik (Jill O'Hara), just happens to be the girl beloved by Chuck. Fran eventually reciprocates his feeling when he rescues her from a suicide attempt after J.D. decides to go back to his wife.

During the Broadway run, Orbach was succeeded by Tony Roberts, Miss O'Hara by Jenny O'Hara (her sister) and Lorna Luft. Roberts and Melissa Hart headed the road company which toured for 14 months.
United Artists OC/ Random House (1969)/ TW.

DAMES AT SEA

Music: Jim Wise
Lyrics & book: George Haimsohn & Robin Miller
Producers: Jordan Hott & Jack Millstein
Director-choreographer: Neal Kenyon
Cast: Bernadette Peters, David Christmas, Steve Elmore, Tamara Long
Songs: "It's You"; "That Mister Man of Mine"; "Choo-Choo Honeymoon"; "The Sailor of My Dreams"; "Good Times Are Here to Stay"; "Dames at Sea"; "Raining in My Heart"; "Singapore Sue"; "Star Tar"
New York run: Bouwerie Lane Theatre, December 20, 1968; 575 p.

Dames at Sea, an affectionate spoof of early Hollywood musicals, was inspired in part by the same 1933 backstage movie on which the more elaborate *42nd Street* was later based. In this imaginative six-character show, Ruby (Bernadette Peters), a sweet young thing fresh from Centerville, Utah, lands a job in the chorus of a Broadway-bound musical, *Dames at Sea,* meets sailor-songwriter Dick (David Christmas), and . . . well, you know what happens. One switch, though, is that because the musical in preparation loses its theatre and must be performed on the deck of a battleship, Ruby gets her big break when the star (Tamara Long) can't go on because she's seasick. During the run, Miss Peters was succeeded by Pia Zadora, Bonnie Franklin, Barbara Sharma, and Loni Ackerman. The musical, which returned for an additional 170 performances at the Plaza 9 Music Hall in the Plaza Hotel, was revived Off Broadway in 1985.
Columbia OC/ Samuel French (1969)*/ SF.

1776

Music & lyrics: Sherman Edwards
Book: Peter Stone
Producer: Stuart Ostrow
Director: Peter Hunt
Choreographer: Onna White
Cast: William Daniels, Howard Da Silva, Paul Hecht, Clifford David, Ken Howard, Virginia Vestoff, Ronald Holgate, Betty Buckley
Songs: "Sit Down, John"; "The Lees of Old Virginia"; "But Mr. Adams"; "He Plays the Violin"; "Cool, Cool, Considerate Men"; "Momma Look Sharp"; "The Egg"; "Molasses to Rum"; "Is Anybody There?"
New York run: 46th Street Theatre, March 16, 1969; 1,217 p.

After researching the project for seven years, Sherman Edwards took two-and-a-half years to write the songs and the libretto for a musical history lesson about the signing of the Declaration of Independence. During preparations, however, the more experienced librettist Peter Stone was brought in. Sticking to the actual events with as much fidelity as possible, Edwards and Stone concentrated their musical on the debates, intrigues, and compromises involving the delegates to the second Continental Congress that met for three stifling summer months in Philadelphia to produce the historic document. Major figures in the production were such advocates of independence as John Adams of Massachusetts (William Daniels), Benjamin Franklin of Pennsylvania (Howard Da Silva), Thomas Jefferson (Ken Howard) and Richard Henry Lee (Ronald Holgate) both of Virginia, and such opponents as John Dickinson of Pennsylvania (Paul Hecht) and Edward Rutledge of South Carolina (Clifford David). Although the writers based their work on historical fact, they did take such liberties as having the debate on the wording of the Declaration occur before, not after, the actual vote for independence. Also altered was the signing of the document, which actually took many months to complete but which — for dramatic effectiveness — was made to take place on the 4th of July, the day the Declaration was proclaimed.

 1776 was the only musical by Sherman Edwards, who died in 1981. During the Broadway engagement, Daniels was succeeded by John Cunningham, Da Silva by Jay Garner, and David by John Cullum. The touring company, which traveled for two years two months, included Patrick Bedford (Adams), Rex Everhart (Franklin), George Hearn (Dickinson), and Jon Cypher (Jefferson). Daniels, Da Silva, Howard, and Holgate were also in the 1972 screen version. For other musicals about the American Revolution, see *Dearest Enemy,* page 48.
Columbia OC/ Viking (1969); Chilton (1973)/ MTI.

1776. William Daniels, Howard Da Silva, Betty Buckley, and Ken Howard. (Martha Swope)

PURLIE

Music: Gary Geld
Lyrics: Peter Udell
Book: Ossie Davis, Philip Rose, Peter Udell
Producer-director: Philip Rose
Choreographer: Louis Johnson
Cast: Cleavon Little, Melba Moore, John Heffernan, Sherman Hemsley, Novella Nelson, George Faison
Songs: "Walk Him Up the Stairs"; "New Fangled Preacher Man'"; "Purlie'"; "Skinnin' a Cat"; "I Got Love"; "First Thing Monday Mornin' "
New York run: Broadway Theatre, March 15, 1970: 688 p.

With little ballyhoo, *Purlie* opened on Broadway to generally favorable notices and enthusiastic audiences, and became the sleeper hit of the season. The musical was adapted from the 1961 play *Purlie Victorious,* a folkish satire on racial stereotypes written by co-librettist Ossie Davis, and is concerned with the efforts of a self-styled new-fangled preacher man (Cleavon Little) to buy the Big Bethel Church in a rural Georgia town. This puts Purlie in confrontation with the bigoted plantation owner, Cap'n Cotchipee (John Heffernan), who also wants the church. Eventually, of course, the Cap'n is outsmarted and Purlie emerges victorious with both his church and his new wife Lutiebelle (Melba Moore). Robert Guillaume, who succeeded Cleavon Little during the Broadway run, toured in the musical which returned briefly to New York at the end of 1972.
Ampex OC/ Samuel French (1971)*/ SF.

APPLAUSE

Music: Charles Strouse
Lyrics: Lee Adams
Book: Betty Comden & Adolph Green
Producers: Joseph Kipness & Lawrence Kasha
Director-choreographer: Ron Field
Cast: Lauren Bacall, Len Cariou, Robert Mandan, Ann Williams, Brandon Maggart, Penny Fuller, Lee Roy Reams, Bonnie Franklin
Songs: "Think How It's Gonna Be"; "But Alive"; "Who's That Girl?"; "Applause"; "Fasten Your Seat Belts"; "Welcome to the Theatre"; "One of a Kind"; "Something Greater"
New York run: Palace Theatre, March 30, 1970; 896 p.

It took only one Broadway musical for Lauren Bacall to join the roster of powerhouse female stars who have won distinction in the theatre. And she did it by appearing as another powerhouse female star, Margo Channing, in a musical version of the 1950 movie, *All About Eve.* The genesis of *Applause* took place in 1966 when Charles Strouse and Lee Adams were signed to create the score. Miss Bacall agreed to be in the show two years later, but it was not until early 1969 that the original librettist was replaced by Betty Comden and Adolph Green. The ambitions, tensions, insecurities, loyalties, and disloyalties of the theatre were exposed in a somewhat farfetched tale in which theatre doyenne Margo Channing befriends an adoring fan, Eve Harrington (Penny Fuller), who promptly schemes to take over her part, her man, and anything else needed to help Eve's career. Though Margo is not a musical-comedy star, thereby eliminating show-within-a-show numbers, Ron Field found opportunities for dance routines in such hangouts as a Greenwich Village gay bar and Joe Allen's restaurant. During the Broadway run, the leading role was assumed by Anne Baxter (Eve in the movie) and Arlene Dahl.
MCA OC/ Random House (1971); Chilton (1976)/ TW.

COMPANY

Music & lyrics: Stephen Sondheim
Book: George Furth
Producer-director: Harold Prince
Choreographer: Michael Bennett
Cast: Dean Jones, Elaine Stritch, Barbara Barrie, John Cunningham, Charles Kimbrough, Donna McKechnie, Charles Braswell, Susan Browning, Steve Elmore, Beth Howland, Pamela Myers, Merle Louise
Songs: "Company"; "The Little Things You Do Together"; "Sorry-Grateful"; "You Could Drive a Person Crazy"; "Someone Is Waiting"; "Another Hundred People"; "Getting Married Today"; "What Would We Do Without You?"; "Barcelona"; "The Ladies who Lunch"; "Being Alive"
New York run: Alvin Theatre, April 26, 1970: 706 p.

Company was the first of six Broadway musicals created by the most influential and daring team of the Seventies, composer-lyricist Stephen Sondheim and director Harold Prince. In putting this work together they avoided the conventional dramatic structure of the linear story by using five separate stories dealing with marriage that were held together by a single character who influences and is influenced by his "good and crazy" married friends. Moreover, it was a bold example of the concept musical — in which the style of telling is as important as what is being told — with songs used as commentaries on the situations and characters, and the actors performing in a cage-like skeletal setting (by Boris Aronson) that made use of stairways, an elevator, and projections.

Initially, *Company* was a collection of 11 one-act plays by George Furth. Prince, however, saw it as a musical reflecting how life in a big city influences various couples, and Furth then revised three of the plays and added two others. The character of the bachelor Robert was brought in to connect the episodes, with the occasion of his 35th birthday party used as a framework. While the couples are less than idyllically happy — they fight, make plans to divorce, smoke pot, drink too much — the general philosophy, summed up in Robert's closing solo "Being Alive," is that it's better to be married than single.

Because of illness, Dean Jones, the original Robert, was replaced by Larry Kert within a month after the Broadway opening. During the run, Elaine Stritch, as a middle-aged guzzler who has the sardonic show-stopper "The Ladies who Lunch," was succeeded by Jane Russell and Vivian Blaine. The show's year-long tour had a cast headed by George Chakiris and Miss Stritch.
Columbia OC/ Random House (1970); Chilton (1973)/ MTI.

Company. Susan Browning, Donna McKechnie, and Pamela Myers. (Martha Swope)

The Rothschilds. Hal Linden as Mayer Rothschild. (Martha Swope)

THE ROTHSCHILDS

Music: Jerry Bock
Lyrics: Sheldon Harnick
Book: Sherman Yellen
Producers: Lester Osterman & Hillard Elkins
Director-choreographer: Michael Kidd
Cast: Hal Linden, Paul Hecht, Leila Martin, Keene Curtis, Jill Clayburgh, Chris Sarandon
Songs: "One Room"; "He Tossed a Coin"; "Sons"; "Rothschild and Sons"; "I'm in Love! I'm in Love!"; "In My Own Lifetime"
New York run: Lunt-Fontanne Theatre, October 19, 1970; 507 p.

Adapted from Frederic Morton's best-selling account of the rise of the international banking family, *The Rothschilds* had several points of similarity with *Fiddler on the Roof.* Its songs were written by the same team, Jerry Bock and Sheldon Harnick (it was their seventh and last work together), the subject matter also concerned the struggle of European Jews to live in an oppressive world, and it even substituted a family of five sons for a family of five daughters. But unlike their poor Anatevka relatives, the Rothschilds did manage to escape the bonds of the Frankfort ghetto and, led by Mayer Rothschild (Hal Linden), work their way up to a position of wealth and affluence all over Europe. Actually, Bock and Harnick had been offered the story while they were still working on *Fiddler,* and it wasn't until some time later, when the musical had a new libretto by Sherman Yellen, that they felt it was sufficiently strong enough to withstand inevitable comparisons.
Columbia OC/ SF.

NO, NO, NANETTE

Music: Vincent Youmans
Lyrics: Irving Caesar
Book: Burt Shevelove
Producer: Pyxidium Ltd. (Cyma Rubin)
Director: Burt Shevelove
Choreographer: Donald Saddler
Cast: Ruby Keeler, Jack Gilford, Bobby Van, Helen Gallagher, Patsy Kelly,
Susan Watson, Roger Rathburn, Loni Ackerman
Songs: Same as original production, plus "I've Confessed to the Breeze" (lyric:
Otto Harbach); "Take a Little One-Step" (lyric: Zelda Sears)
New York run: 46th Street Theatre, January 19, 1971; 861 p.

No, No, Nanette. Helen Gallagher and Bobby Van dancing to "You Can Dance With Any Girl at All."
(Friedman-Abeles)

Follies. Alexis Smith singing "Could I Leave You?" (Martha Swope)

FOLLIES

Music & lyrics: Stephen Sondheim
Book: James Goldman
Producer: Harold Prince
Directors: Harold Prince & Michael Bennett
Choreographer: Michael Bennett
Cast: Alexis Smith, Gene Nelson, Dorothy Collins, John McMartin, Yvonne DeCarlo, Fifi D'Orsay, Mary McCarty, Ethel Shutta, Arnold Moss, Ethel Barrymore Colt, Michael Bartlett, Sheila Smith, Justine Johnston, Virginia Sandifur, Kurt Peterson, Victoria Mallory, Marti Rolph
Songs: "Waiting for the Girls Upstairs"; "Ah, Paris!"; "Broadway Baby"; "The Road You Didn't Take"; "In Buddy's Eyes"; "Who's That Woman?"; "I'm Still Here"; "Too Many Mornings"; "The Right Girl"; "Could I Leave You?"; "Losing My Mind"; "The Story of Lucy and Jessie"
New York run: Winter Garden, April 4, 1971; 522 p.

Taking place at a reunion of performers who had appeared in various editions of the *Weismann Follies* (a fictitious counterpart of the Ziegfeld revue), the musical dealt with the reality of life as contrasted with the unreality of the theatre, a theme it explored principally through the lives of two couples, the upper-class, unhappy Phyllis and Ben Stone (Alexis Smith and John McMartin) and the middle-class, unhappy Sally and Buddy Plummer (Dorothy Collins and Gene Nelson). The second of the Stephen Sondheim-Harold Prince musicals, *Follies* also depicted these couples as they were in their youth, a flashback device that prompted the composer to come up with songs purposely reminiscent of the styles of some of the theatre's great songwriters of the past. In 1985, a highly acclaimed all-star concert version was staged at Avery Fisher Hall. The musical bore a certain kinship with *Company,* which also was about jaded, ambivalent characters, took a disenchanted view of marriage, and used the structural device of a party to bring a group of people together.
Capitol OC; RCA OC (1985)/Random House (1971)/ MTI.

GODSPELL

Music & lyrics: Stephen Schwartz
Book: John-Michael Tebelak
Producers: Edgar Lansbury, Stuart Duncan, Joseph Beruh
Director: John-Michael Tebelak
Cast: Lamar Alford, David Haskell, Johanne Jonas, Robin Lamont, Sonia Manzano, Jeffrey Mylett, Stephen Nathan
Songs: "Prepare Ye the Way of the Lord"; "Save the People"; "Day by Day"; "All for the Best"; "All Good Gifts"; "Light of the World"; "Turn Back, O Man"; "We Beseech Thee"; "On the Willows"
New York run: Cherry Lane Theatre, May 17, 1971; 2,651 p.

The Seventies brought the Bible to the New York musical stage. Genesis supplied the source of both *Two by Two* (Noah and the Ark) in 1970 and *Joseph and the Amazing Technicolor Dreamcoat* in 1976 (performed at the Brooklyn Academy of Music); the Gospel According to St. Matthew was the origin of *Godspell* in 1971, *Jesus Christ Superstar* also in 1971, and *Your Arms Too Short to Box With God* in 1976. *Godspell* was a whimsical retelling of the last seven days of Christ, with Jesus in clownlike makeup sporting a superman "S" on his shirt; his disciples dressed like flower children; and the parables enacted in a frolicsome, contemporary manner. The work was first shown in nonmusical form as a workshop production at Café La Mama. When it was decided to turn *Godspell* into a musical, songs were then added by Stephen Schwartz. The show was presented in a Greenwich Village theatre for three months, then moved to the Promenade (on Broadway and 76th Street) for a total run of 2,124 performances, making it currently the fourth longest running Off-Broadway musical. The show's official "on" Broadway opening took place June 22, 1976, at the Broadhurst, where it ran for 527 performances. At one time there were seven road companies touring the United States. *Godspell* was revived in 1988 and gave 248 Off-Broadway performances. The film version, released in 1973, featured Victor Garber and David Haskell.
Arista OC/ TM.

JESUS CHRIST SUPERSTAR

Music: Andrew Lloyd Webber
Lyrics: Tim Rice
Conception: Tom O'Horgan
Producer: Robert Stigwood
Director: Tom O'Horgan
Cast: Jeff Fenholt, Yvonne Elliman, Ben Vereen, Barry Dennen, Anita Morris
Songs: "Heaven on Their Minds"; "What's the Buzz?"; "Everything's Alright"; "I Don't Know How to Love Him"; "King Herod's Song"; "Could We Start Again, Please?"; "Superstar"
New York run: Mark Hellinger Theatre, October 12, 1971; 720 p.

Even though conceived as a theatre work, *Jesus Christ Superstar* appeared as a record before being presented on the stage because composer Andrew Lloyd Webber and lyricist Tim Rice were unable to find a producer willing to take a chance on so daring a production. Once it became a Gold Record album, however, the path was smoothed for its Broadway premiere. The self-described "rock opera" retold the last seven days of Christ in such a flamboyant, campy, and mind-blowing fashion that despite a mixed press and the opposition from various religious groups the show became a media hype and a boxoffice hit. The movie version was released in 1973 with Ted Neeley and Carl Anderson.
MCA OC/ Stein & Day (1979)/ MTI.

TWO GENTLEMEN OF VERONA

Music: Galt MacDermot
Lyrics: John Guare
Book: John Guare & Mel Shapiro
Producer: Joseph Papp for the New York Shakespeare Festival
Director: Mel Shapiro
Choreographer: Jean Erdman
Cast: Jonelle Allen, Diana Davila, Clifton Davis, Raul Julia, Norman Matlock, Alix Elias, John Bottoms, Stockard Channing
Songs: "Follow the Rainbow"; "Bring All the Boys Back Home"; "Night Letter"; "Who Is Silvia?" (lyric: Shakespeare); "Calla Lily Lady"
New York run: St. James Theatre, December 1, 1971; 627 p.

Two Gentlemen of Verona was originally scheduled to be presented without songs as part of the New York Shakespeare Festival's series of free productions in Central Park. At the recommendation of director Mel Shapiro, a rock score was added to help give the modern adaptation of the play the proper contemporary flavor. The show proved so popular in its open-air presentation in the Summer of 1971 that it was transferred to Broadway, where its blend of anachronistic colloquialisms, ethnic references, and the Bard's own words (the song "Who Is Silvia?" uses the original text) won a receptive audience. The story spins the tale of two Veronese friends, the noble Valentine (Clifton Davis) and the ignoble Proteus (Raul Julia), whose adventures in Milan are complicated by Julia (Diana Davila), who loves Proteus, and Silvia (Jonelle Allen), who Loves Valentine. For other musicals based on Shakespeare, see *The Boys from Syracuse,* page 107. ABC OC/ Holt, Rinehart (1971); Stein & Day (1979)/ TW.

GREASE

Music, lyrics & book: Jim Jacobs & Warren Casey
Producers: Kenneth Waissman & Maxine Fox
Director: Tom Moore
Choreographer: Patricia Birch
Cast: Adrienne Barbeau, Barry Bostwick, Carole Demas, Timothy Meyers
Songs: "Summer Nights"; "Freddy, My Love"; "Greased Lightnin' "; "Mooning"; "Look at Me, I'm Sandra Dee"; "We Go Together"; "It's Raining on Prom Night"; "Beauty School Dropout"; "Alone at a Drive-In Movie"; "There Are Worse Things I Could Do"
New York run: Eden Theatre, February 14, 1972; 3,388 p.

A surprise runaway hit, *Grease* opened at the Off-Broadway Eden Theatre (formerly the Phoenix), then moved on Broadway to the Broadhurst and then the Royale. And there it remained until April 13, 1980, for a record run that was not overtaken until *A Chorus Line* danced past the mark. The show, which began life as a five-hour amateur production in a Chicago trolley barn, took a satirically on-target view of the dress, manners, morals, and music of teenagers at the beginning of the rock and roll era. Set in the fictitious Rydell High School in Chicago, it is chiefly concerned with the attraction between greaser Danny Zuko (Barry Bostwick) and prim and proper Sandy Dumbrowski (Carole Demas), who eventually learns that there is little virtue in virtue. Mocking individuality and championing conformity, the musical hit a responsive chord in youthful audiences that could identify with teenagers having little on their minds except hanging out and making out. On Broadway, Danny was played by nine actors including Treat Williams. John Travolta, who was Danny in the 1978 movie opposite Olivia Newton-John, played Doody in the first of three touring companies.
Polydor OC/ Pocket Books (1972); Stein & Day (1979)/ SF.

SUGAR

Music: Jule Styne
Lyrics: Bob Merrill
Book: Peter Stone
Producer: David Merrick
Director-choreographer: Gower Champion
Cast: Robert Morse, Tony Roberts, Cyril Ritchard, Elaine Joyce, Sheila Smith, Steve Condos, Pamela Blair
Songs: "Sun on My Face"; "Sugar"; "What Do You Give to a Man Who's Had Everything?"; "When You Meet a Man in Chicago"
New York run: Majestic Theatre, April 9, 1972; 505 p.

Given the creative talents involved and the fact that it was based on the popular 1959 movie *Some Like It Hot, Sugar* might have been expected to be a more distinguised offering than it was. But there was so much dissention during the show's preparations (at one point the composer, lyricist and librettist were all threatened with replacement) that it was something of a miracle that the musical did turn out to be both entertaining and profitable. In the farcical story, set in 1931, Robert Morse and Tony Roberts played two dance-band musicians who witness the St. Valentine's Day gangland massacre in Chicago. They manage to escape from Spats Palazzo's thugs by disguising themselves as members of an all-girl orchestra, Sweet Sue and Her Society Syncopaters, which takes them to Miami for a series of romantic complications resulting when boys are mistaken for girls. Elaine Joyce appeared as Sugar Kane, the part immortalized on the screen by Marilyn Monroe.
United Artists OC/ TW.

DON'T BOTHER ME, I CAN'T COPE

Music & lyrics: Micki Grant
Conception: Vinnette Carroll
Producers: Edward Padula & Arch Lustberg
Director: Vinnette Carroll
Choreographer: George Faison
Cast: Alex Bradford, Hope Clarke, Micki Grant, Bobby Hill, Arnold Wilkerson
Songs: "Don't Bother Me, I Can't Cope"; "Fighting for Pharaoh"; "Good Vibrations"; "It Takes a Whole Lot of Human Feeling"; "Thank Heaven for You"
New York run: Playhouse Theatre, April 19, 1972; 1,065 p.

A generally good-humored look at the social problems faced by black people today, *Don't Bother Me, I Can't Cope* was essentially a procession of musical numbers, both sung and danced, based on gospel, rock, calypso, and folk music. The show originated as a workshop project of Vinnette Carroll's Urban Arts Corps Theatre, after which it made appearances in Washington, Philadelphia, and Detroit before opening in New York at the Playhouse Theatre (on 48th Street east of 7th Avenue). Though stressing black pride and dignity, this "Musical Entertainment" still found room for some tongue-in-cheek self kidding which helped give it a broad enough appeal to keep it running on Broadway for two and one-half years.
Polydor OC/ Samuel French (1972)*/ SF.

Pippin. Ben Vereen, flanked by Ann Reinking and Candy Brown, in the "Magic to Do" number. (Martha Swope)

PIPPIN

Music & lyrics: Stephen Schwartz
Book: Roger O. Hirson (Bob Fosse uncredited)
Producer: Stuart Ostrow
Director-choreographer: Bob Fosse
Cast: Eric Berry, Jill Clayburgh, Leland Palmer, Irene Ryan, Ben Vereen, John Rubinstein, Ann Reinking
Songs: "Magic to Do"; "Corner of the Sky"; "Simple Joys"; "No Time at All"; "Morning Glow"; "On the Right Track"; "Kind of Woman"; "Extraordinary"; "Love Song"
New York run: Imperial Theatre, October 23, 1972; 1,944 p.

Stephen Schwartz collaborated on the original version of *Pippin* — called *Pippin Pippin* — when he was still a student at Carnegie Tech, but it was not until the success of *Godspell* that a producer was willing to take a chance on him or his work. As insurance, however, Stuart Ostrow brought in playwright Roger O. Hirson to rewrite the book and, most signifcantly, Bob Fosse to serve as director-choreographer. Fosse, also the uncredited co-librettist, put his conceptual stamp on the musical by expanding it into a razzle-dazzle magic show within the framework of a *commedia dell'arte* performance. Helping to give the production a unifying concept was another Fosse touch, the half-God half-Devil Leading Player (Ben Vereen), a character developed from the Master of Ceremonies in *Cabaret.*

In the tale, Pippin (John Rubinstein), the son of Charlemagne (Eric Berry), is a Candide-like figure seeking glory first in war, then as a lover, and finally as a leader of social causes. After failing at all three, he is happy to compromise by settling down to middle-class domesticity with a widow named Catherine (Jill Clayburgh). During the Broadway run — the fourth longest of the decade — Betty Buckley succeeded Miss Clayburgh, and Dorothy Stickney took over as the fifth actress to play Berthe, Pippin's grandmother, whose showstopper was the vaudeville sing-along, "No Time at All." Two road companies toured in *Pippin,* the second of which traveled a full year.
Motown OC/ Drama Book Specialists (1975)/ MTI.

A LITTLE NIGHT MUSIC

Music & lyrics: Stephen Sondheim
Book: Hugh Wheeler
Producer-director: Harold Prince
Choreographer: Patricia Birch
Cast: Glynis Johns, Len Cariou, Hermione Gingold, Victoria Mallory, Laurence Guittard, Patricia Elliott, Mark Lambert, D. Jamin-Bartlett, George Lee Andrews
Songs: "Night Waltz"; "The Glamorous Life"; "Remember?"; "You Must Meet My Wife"; "Liaisons"; "In Praise of Women"; "Every Day a Little Death"; "A Weekend in the Country"; "It Would Have Been Wonderful"; "Send in the Clowns"; "The Miller's Son"
New York run: Shubert Theatre, February 25, 1973; 600 p.

Not Mozart's K. 525 but Ingmar Bergmen's 1955 film *Sommarnattens Leende (Smiles of a Summer Night)* was the inspiration for *A Little Night Music,* which offered a wry, witty view of a group of men and women from the standpoints of age and social position. The work claimed two musical innovations: the entire Stephen Sondheim score was composed in 3/4 time (or multiples thereof) and it had an overture sung by a quintet (whose members reappeared throughout the evening in the manner of a Greek chorus). Is also contained, in "Send in the Clowns," the best known song the composer has written to date.

Taking place in Sweden at the turn of the century, the story deals with the complicated romantic world of a middle-aged lawyer, Fredrik Egerman (Len Cariou); his virginal child-bride Anne (Victoria Mallory); his con Henrik (Mark Lambert), who is in love with Anne; his former mistress,.the actress Desirée Armfeldt (Glynis Johns); Desirée's current lover, the vain, aristocratic Count Carl-Magnus Malcolm (Laurence Guittard); and the count's suicidal wife, Charlotte (Patricia Elliott). The proper partners are paired off at a weekend at the country house of Desirée's mother (Hermoine Gingoid), a former concubine of assorted members of the nobility. The musical toured for a year with Jean Simmons, Margaret Hamilton, and George Lee Andrews. It was added to the repertory of the New York City Opera in 1990. A film version, released in 1978, co-starred Elizabeth Taylor, Len Cariou, Diana Rigg, and Hermione Gingold.
Columbia OC/Dodd, Mead (1973); Chilton (1976)/MTI.

A Little Night Music. Len Cariou and Glynis Johns. (Martha Swope)

Irene. Debbie Reynolds and Patsy Kelly singing "Mother, Angel, Darling." (Friedman-Abeles)

IRENE

Music: Harry Tierney, etc.
Lyrics: Joseph McCarthy, etc.
Book: Joseph Stein, Hugh Wheeler, Harry Rigby
Producers: Harry Rigby, Albert Selden, Jerome Minskoff
Director: Gower Champion
Choreographer: Peter Gennaro
Cast: Debbie Reynolds, Patsy Kelly, George S. Irving, Monte Markham, Ruth Warrick, Janie Sell, Carmen Alvarez
Songs: "Alice Blue Gown"; "They Go Wild, Simply Wild Over Me" (music: Fred Fisher); "Mother, Angel, Darling" (Charles Gaynor); "The Last Part of Ev'ry Party"; "Irene"; "You Made Me Love You" (music: James Monaco); "I'm Always Chasing Rainbows"(music: Harry Carroll) (added)
New York run: Minskoff Theatre, March 13, 1973; 604 p.

(See page 32.)

RAISIN

Music: Judd Woldin
Lyrics: Robert Brittan
Book: Robert Nemiroff & Charlotte Zaltzberg (Joseph Stein uncredited)
Producer: Robert Nemiroff
Director-choreographer: Donald McKayle
Cast: Virginia Capers, Joe Morton, Ernestine Jackson, Ralph Carter, Debbie Allen, Robert Jackson, Ted Ross
Songs: "Whose Little Angry Man"; "A Whole Lotta Sunlight"; "Sweet Time"; "You Done Right"; "He Come Down This Morning"; "Sidewalk Tree"; "Not Anymore"; "Measure the Valleys"
New York run: 46th Street Theatre, October 18, 1973; 847 p.

Faithfully adapted from Lorraine Hansberry's 1959 play, *A Raisin in the Sun*, *Raisin* offered a warm, touching picture of a black family living in Chicago's Southside ghetto in the 1950s. Matriarch Lena Younger (Virginia Capers) wants to use her late husband's insurance money to buy a house in the white neighborhood of Clybourne Park, while her son, Walter Lee (Joe Morton), wants to use it to buy a liquor store. Lena gives Walter Lee part of the money for the store, but one of his partners absconds with it, and Walter Lee is faced with the temptation of buckling under and selling the house back to the Clybourne Park Association. At the end, with pride intact, the Youngers prepare to move into their new home. Miss Capers, who won high praise for her performance, headed the touring company for a year and a half. The play's title was taken from a poem by Langston Hughes — "What happens to a dream deferred?/ Does it dry up/ Like a raisin in the sun?"
Columbia OC/ Samuel French (1978)*/ SF.

CANDIDE

Music: Leonard Bernstein
Lyrics: Richard Wilbur, etc.
Book: Hugh Wheeler
Producer: Chelsea Theatre Center of Brooklyn
Director: Harold Prince
Choreographer: Patricia Birch
Cast: Lewis J. Stadlen, Mark Baker, Maureen Brennan, Sam Freed, June Gable, Deborah St. Darr
Songs: "Life Is Happiness Indeed" (lyric: Stephen Sondheim); "The Best of All Possible Worlds"; "Oh, Happy We"; "It Must Be So"; "Glitter and Be Gay"; "Auto Da Fé" ("What a Day") (lyric: Sondheim); "This World" (lyric: Sondheim); "I Am Easily Assimilated" (lyric: Bernstein); "Bon Voyage"; "Make Our Garden Grow"
New York run: Broadway Theatre, March 10, 1974; 740 p.

(See page 172.)

THE MAGIC SHOW

Music & lyrics: Stephen Schwartz
Book: Bob Randall
Producers: Edgar Lansbury, Joseph Beruh, Ivan Reitman
Director-choreographer: Grover Dale
Cast: Doug Henning, Dale Soules, David Ogden Stiers, Anita Morris
Songs: "Up to His Old Tricks"; "Lion Tamer"; "Style"; "The Goldfarb Variations"; "West End Avenue"
New York run: Cort Theatre, May 28, 1974; 1,920 p.

The fact that the program credit, "MAGIC BY DOUG HENNING," was on the same line and in the same size letters as that of the songwriter and the librettist indicates the importance of Henning's contribution. For *The Magic Show* was little more than a sleight-of-hand show accompanied by a slight-of-substance plot — something about an ambitious young magician at a seedy Passaic, New Jersey, nightclub who triumphs over a jealous old-timer — plus a collection of ten songs. While Henning won praise as an illusionist, his bag of tricks was not his exclusive property since Joe Adalbo took over the part during half the show's run at the Cort Theatre (on 48th Street east of 7th Avenue). The fifth longest running Broadway musical of the 1970s, *The Magic Show* was Stephen Schwartz's third in a row — the others were *Godspell* and *Pippin* — to play over 1,900 performances.
Bell OC.

The Magic Show. Doug Henning manages to separate Anita Morris. (Kenn Duncan)

The Wiz. Andre De Shields and Tiger Haynes. (Martha Swope)

THE WIZ

Music & Lyrics: Charlie Smalls
Book: William F. Brown
Producer: Ken Harper
Director: Geoffrey Holder (Gilbert Moses uncredited)
Choreographer: George Faison
Cast: Tiger Haynes, Ted Ross, Hinton Battle, Stephanie Mills, Clarice Taylor, Mabel King, Andre De Shields, Tasha Thomas, DeeDee Bridgewater
Songs: "He's the Wizard"; "Ease on Down the Road"; "Slide Some Oil to Me"; "Be a Lion"; "Don't Nobody Bring Me No Bad News"; "If You Believe"
New York run: Majestic Theatre, January 5, 1975; 1,672 p.

Though following such illustrious *Wizard of Oz* predecessors as the stage version of 1903 and the screen version of 1939, *The Wiz* was an original concept with an all-black cast, a new rock score, and dialogue that made the fairytale relevant to modern audiences. It still, however, told the same basic story about Dorothy (Stephanie Mills), the little girl from Kansas who is blown by a tornado into Munchkinland in the Land of Oz, meets the Scarecrow (Hinton Battle), the Tinman (Tiger Haynes), and the Lion (Ted Ross) on the Yellow Brick Road, defeats the evil witch (Mabel King), and has an audience with the supposedly all-powerful Wizard (Andre De Shields). Though the Wiz is a phony, he does convince Dorothy that she can do anything she wants if she just believes in herself.

The idea for *The Wiz* originated with producer Ken Harper who had to surmount myriad problems in guiding the show to Broadway. After almost shutting down the musical in Baltimore, he replaced director Gilbert Moses with Geoffrey Holder (also the costume designer) in Detroit, and posted the closing notice on opening night in New York. But a concerted publicity and advertising campaign —plus favorable audience reaction — helped produce a real miracle, and *The Wiz* went on to a four-year run. It also spawned two touring companies that traveled for three years. The 1978 movie version featured Diana Ross, Michael Jackson, Nipsey Russell, Ted Ross, Lena Horne, and Richard Pryor. Atlantic OC/ Stein & Day (1979)/ SF.

SHENANDOAH

Music: Gary Geld
Lyrics: Peter Udell
Book: James Lee Barrett, with Philip Rose, Peter Udell
Producers: Philip Rose, Gloria & Louis Sher
Director: Philip Rose
Choreographer: Robert Tucker
Cast: John Cullum, Donna Theodore, Penelope Milford, Joel Higgins, Ted
 Agress, Gordon Halliday, Chip Ford
Songs: "I've Heard It All Before"; "Next to Lovin' I Like Fightin' "; "The Pickers
 Are Comin' "; "Meditation"; "We Make a Beautiful Pair"; "Violets and
 Silverbells"; "Freedom"; "The Only Home I Know"
New York run: Alvin Theatre, January 7, 1975; 1,050 p.

Of all the movies that have been turned into Broadway musicals, the 1965 release, *Shenandoah,* would seem to have been the most unsuitable. A strongly anti-war polemic, the story is set in the Shenandoah Valley of Virginia during the Civil War. Charlie Anderson (John Cullum), the widowed patriarch of a family of farmers, is determined that the only cause in which any of his six sons will take up arms is in defense of their land. When his youngest son is kidnapped by Northern soldiers, however, Charlie and most of his family go off to find him. While they are away, the eldest son, his wife and baby are all killed, and there is further suffering before what is left of the Anderson family have an emotional reunion in church. First tried out at the Goodspeed Opera House in Connecticut, *Shenandoah* had an appealing Rodgers and Hammerstein flavor and it enjoyed an unexpected long run. It was revived briefly in 1989 with John Cullum. For other musicals about the Civil War, see *Bloomer Girl,* page 125.
RCA OC/ Samuel French (1975)*/ SF.

A Chorus Line. Donna McKechnie performing "The Music and the Mirror."
(© Martha Swope)

A CHORUS LINE

Music: Marvin Hamlisch
Lyrics: Edward Kleban
Conception: Michael Bennett
Book: James Kirkwood & Nicholas Dante
Producer: Joseph Papp for the New York Shakespeare Festival
Director: Michael Bennett
Choreographers: Michael Bennett & Bob Avian
Cast: Kelly Bishop, Pamela Blair, Wayne Cilento, Kay Cole, Patricia Garland, Baayork Lee, Priscilla Lopez, Robert LuPone, Donna McKechnie, Michel Stuart, Thommie Walsh, Sammy Williams
Songs: "I Hope I Get It"; "At the Ballet"; "Nothing"; "The Music and the Mirror"; "One"; "What I Did for Love"
New York run: Public Theatre, April 15, 1975; 6,137 p.

Although it dealt with the hopes, fears, frustrations, and insecurities of a specific group of dancers auditioning for a chorus line, the musical skillfully conveyed the universal experience of anyone who has ever stood in line in an effort to present his or her qualifications for a job. Since that means just about all of us. *A Chorus Line* managed to create such a strong empathetical bond with its audiences that it became far and away the longest running production — musical or dramatic — ever staged on Broadway.

Director-choreographer Michael Bennett — who also receives program credit for having "conceived" the show — had long wanted to stage a work that would be a celebration of chorus dancers, known as "gypsies," who contribute so much and receive so little glory. Early in 1974, Bennett rented a studio where he invited 24 dancers to talk about themselves and their careers. Out of these rap sessions came some 30 hours of taped revelations, which gave the director the idea of creating his musical in the form of an audition. After he and Nicholas Dante, one of his dancers, had edited the tapes, producer Joseph Papp offered to sponsor the project as a workshop production at his Hew York Shakespeare Festival Public Theatre. Marvin Hamlisch and Edward Klaban were engaged to write the score, and playwright James Kirkwood was brought in to work with Dante on the book. The show opened at the Newman Theatre (part of the Public Theatre's complex) in mid April 1975, at a $10 top ticket price. Word of mouth made it a hit even before the critics were invited to view it on May 21, and it remained at the downtown playhouse for 101 performances. On July 25, 1975, *A Chorus Line* moved to the Shubert Theatre. It won the Pulitzer Prize for drama for the 1975-76 season.

Avoiding a linear plot structure, the musical is basically a series of vignettes as 18 applicants vie for places in an eight-member chorus line. Goaded by a largely unseen — and rather sadistic — director named Zach (Robert LuPone), each applicant in turn reveals truths that, supposedly, will help the director make his final choices. Among those auditioning are Cassie (Donna McKechnie), a former featured dancer now down on her luck who was once romantically involved with Zach; the street-smart but vulnerable Sheila (Kelly Bishop) who recalls how she had been attracted to dancing because "everything was beautiful at the ballet"; the still-hopeful Diana (Priscilla Lopez), who had once failed a method acting class; the voluptuous Val (Pamela Blair) who uses silicone to enlarge her talent; and the pathetic Paul (Sammy Williams) who relates his humiliating experience as a drag queen.

There have been two touring companies of *A Chorus Line,* the first traveling for seven years, the second for five years eight months. The film version was released in 1985.
Columbia OC/TW.

Chicago. Lawyer Jerry Orbach coaches murderess Gwen Verdon how to appear demure in the courtroom. (Martha Swope)

CHICAGO

Music: John Kander
Lyrics: Fred Ebb
Book: Fred Ebb & Bob Fosse
Producers: Robert Fryer & James Cresson
Director-choreographer: Bob Fosse
Cast: Gwen Verdon, Chita Rivera, Jerry Orbach, Barney Martin, Mary McCarty, M. O'Haughey, Graciela Daniele
Songs: "All That Jazz"; "All I Care About"; "Roxie"; "My Own Best Friend"; "Mr. Cellophane"; "Razzle Dazzle"; "Class"; "Nowadays"
New York run: 46th Street Theatre, June 3, 1975; 898 p.

Bob Fosse first planned a musical production of Maurine Dallas Watkins' 1926 play as early as the mid-Fifties, with Gwen Verdon as the star and Robert Fryer as the producer. It took some 13 years, however, for him to clear the rights to the story of Roxie Hart, a married chorus girl who kills her faithless lover, avoids prison through the histrionic efforts of razzle-dazzle lawyer Billy Flynn (Jerry Orbach), and ends up as a vaudeville headliner with another "scintillating sinner," Velma Kelly (Chita Rivera). Though the show was a scathing indictment of American huckstering, vulgarity, and decadence, its atmosphere strongly recalled the Berlin of *Cabaret,* which also had songs by John Kander and Fred Ebb and whose film version was directed by Bob Fosse.

In Fosse's conceptual treatment, which had much in common with his *commedia dell'arte* approach in *Pippin, Chicago* was created as "A Musical Vaudeville" with a Master of Ceremonies introducing each number as if it were a variety act. (A previous effort to combine vaudeville within a musical play was the Kurt Weill-Alan Jay Lerner *Love Life.*) Soon after *Chicago's* Broadway opening, Miss Verdon was temporarily replaced by Liza Minnelli because of illness; during the run she was succeeded by Ann Reinking.
Arista OC/ Samuel French (1976)*/ SF.

PACIFIC OVERTURES

Music & lyrics: Stephen Sondheim
Book: John Weidman
Producer-director: Harold Prince
Choreographer: Patricia Birch
Cast: Mako, Soon-Teck Oh, Yuki Shimoda, Sab Shimono, Isao Sato
Songs: "There Is No Other Way"; "Four Black Dragons"; "Chrysanthemum
Tea"; "Welcome to Kanagawa"; "Someone in a Tree"; "Please Hello";
"A Bowler Hat"; "Pretty Lady"; "Next"
New York run: Winter Garden, January 11, 1976; 193 p.

Few Broadway musicals have ever dared so much on so many levels as *Pacific Overtures*. In recounting the history of the emergence of Japan from a serenely isolated country to its present position in the forefront of international commerce, the musical covers a 120-year period, beginning with Comm. Matthew Perry's threateningly persuasive visit to the Floating Kingdom in 1853, and taking us through changes in social order, customs and dress that were the price Japan paid for its present-day affluence. To present such an ambitiously didactic work, the musical's creators chose to relate the saga not only from the Japanese point of view but also through an approximation of the ancient form of Japanese theatre known as Kabuki. Moreover, Stephen Sondheim's score, while accessible to Occidental ears, was a far more faithful recreation of Oriental music and poetic expression than had ever before been attempted on Broadway. Also adding to the show's dramatic impact were director Harold Prince's lavish conceptual approach and the stunning visual effects created by designer Boris Aronson. In 1984, a revival of *Pacific Overtures* was offered in a scaled-down, Off-Broadway production.
RCA OC/ Dodd, Mead (1977)/ MTI.

I LOVE MY WIFE

Music: Cy Coleman
Lyrics & book: Michael Stewart
Producers: Terry Allen Kramer & Harry Rigby
Director: Gene Saks
Choreographer: Onna White
Cast: Ilene Graff, Lenny Baker, Joanna Gleason, James Naughton
Songs: "Love Revolution"; "Someone Wonderful I Missed"; "Sexually Free";
"Hey There, Good Times"; "Lovers on Christmas Eve"; "Everybody
Today Is Turning On"; "I Love My Wife"
New York run: Ethel Barrymore Theatre, April 17, 1977; 872 p.

The sexual revolution of the 1960s hit Broadway a bit late with a musical about mate-swapping in the sinful citadel of Trenton, New Jersey. At the urging of the husbands, two happily married, well-adjusted couples agree to catch up with the amoral freedom they've been hearing and reading about by having themselves a *ménage à quatre*. Of course, since they are such basically decent, clean-living people, they abandon the idea at the last minute because — as the men agree in song — "I love my wife." The idea for the musical began when Michael Stewart saw a French farce in which songs were introduced by lip-synching actors without any attempt to fit them into the story line. *I Love My Wife* followed this general concept by using the musical numbers — sung by both the four actors and an instrumental quartet that turns up throughout the show — to make observations on the morals and mores of the time. During the run, Tom and Dick Smothers were among those who succeeded Lenny Baker and James Naughton.
Atlantic OC/ Samuel French (1980)*/ SF.

Annie. Annie (Andrea McArdle), Daddy Warbucks (Reid Shelton), and Sandy. (Martha Swope)

Annie. Orphans Diana Barrows, Robyn Finn, Donna Graham, Danielle Brisebois, Shelley Bruce, and Janine Ruane singing "You're Never Fully Dressed Without a Smile." (Martha Swope)

ANNIE

Music: Charles Strouse
Lyrics: Martin Charnin
Book: Thomas Meehan
Producer: Mike Nichols
Director: Martin Charnin
Choreographer: Peter Gennaro
Cast: Andrea McArdle, Reid Shelton, Dorothy Loudon, Sandy Faison, Robert Fitch, Barbara Erwin, Raymond Thorne, Laurie Beechman, Danielle Brisebois, Shelley Bruce
Songs: "Maybe"; "It's the Hard-Knock Life"; "Tomorrow"; "Little Girls"; "I Think I'm Gonna Like It Here"; "N.Y.C."; "Easy Street"; "You're Never Fully Dressed Without a Smile"; "Something Was Missing"; "I Don't Need Anything but You"; "Annie"; "A New Deal for Christmas"
New York run: Alvin Theatre, April 21, 1977; 2,377 p.

The idea of turning Harold Gray's "Little Orphan Annie" comic strip into a musical was the inspiration of lyricist-director Martin Charnin, who then contacted playwright Thomas Meehan and composer Charles Strouse to join him in the project. Though their initial reaction was an unqualified "Ughhh," Meehan and Strouse were soon won over by Charnin's approach, which was to use only the three continuing characters in the strip — Annie, Daddy Warbucks, and Annie's mutt Sandy — and fit them into an original story. Because Meehan saw Annie as "a metaphorical figure standing for innate decency, courage and optimism in the face of hard times, pessimism and despair," he decided to set his fable in New York City in the midst of the Depression. Annie (Andrea McArdle), an 11-year-old foundling at the Municipal Orphanage, yearns for her parents to rescue her from the clutches of mean-spirited, bibulous Agatha Hannigan (Dorothy Loudon), the orphanage's matron. Presently, a miraculous parent-figure does show up in the person of billionaire Oliver Warbucks (Reid Shelton) whose secretary, Grace Farrell (Sandy Faison), has invited Annie to spend Christmas with him. Warbucks, in fact, becomes so fond of the child that he plans to adopt her, a situation that is temporarily blocked by the machinations of Miss Hannigan. But the industrialist enlists the aid of his friend President Roosevelt (Raymond Thorne), and everyone — at least everyone who believes that tomorrow is only a day away — looks forward to having a New Deal for Christmas. (It should be noted that Lionel Bart's musical *Oliver!* is also about a young orphan who escapes a life of deprivation by being adopted by a wealthy gentleman.)

When tried out at the Goodspeed Opera House in Connecticut (where Miss McArdle replaced another girl shortly before the opening and Miss Loudon was not yet in the cast), *Annie* won the approval of Mike Nichols who offered to produce it on Broadway. The show was quickly adopted by theatregoers who made it the third longest running musical of the 1970s. During the run, Warbucks was also played by Keene Curtis, John Schuck, Harve Presnell, and Rhodes Reason; Annie by Shelley Bruce, Sarah Jessica Parker, Allison Smith, and Alyson Kirk; and Miss Hannigan by Alice Ghostley, Dolores Wilson, Betty Hutton, Marcia Lewis, Ruth Kobart, and June Havoc. There were four road companies of *Annie,* with the first traveling three and a half years. In 1982, the movie version was released with Albert Finney, Aileen Quinn, Ann Reinking, and Carol Burnett.

For other musicals taken from comic strips, see *Li'l Abner,* page 171.
Columbia OC/ MTI.

THE KING AND I

Music: Richard Rodgers
Lyrics & book: Oscar Hammerstein II
Producers: Lee Guber & Shelly Gross
Director: Yuriko
Choreographer: Jerome Robbins (dances recreated by Yuriko)
Cast: Yul Brynner, Constance Towers, Michael Kermoyan, Hye-Young Choi, Martin Vidnovic, June Angela, Susan Kikuchi, John Michael King, Gene Profanato, Marianne Tatum
Songs: Same as original production
New York run: Uris Theatre, May 2, 1977; 696 p.

See page 151.

The King and I. King Yul Brynner giving a royal command to governess Constance Towers. (Ernst Haas)

On the Twentieth Century.
Kevin Kline, John Cullum, and
Judy Kaye. (Martha Swope)

ON THE TWENTIETH CENTURY

Music: Cy Coleman
Lyrics & book: Betty Comden & Adolph Green
Producers: Robert Fryer, Mary Lea Johnson, James Cresson, etc.
Director: Harold Prince
Choreographer: Larry Fuller
Cast: John Cullum, Madeline Kahn, Imogene Coca, George Coe, Dean Dittman, Kevin Kline, Judy Kaye, George Lee Andrews
Songs: "On the Twentieth Century"; "I Rise Again"; "Veronique"; "Never"; "Our Private World"; "Repent"; "We've Got It All"
New York run: St. James Theatre, February 19, 1978; 449 p.

Ben Hecht and Charles MacArthur's 1932 show-business farce, *Twentieth Century* (which they had based on a play by Bruce Millholland) was turned into a musical that was not so much backstage as on track, since most of the action takes place aboard the Twentieth Century Limited (in a stunning art-deco set by Robin Wagner) as it speeds from Chicago to New York. Producer-director Oscar Jaffee (John Cullum), the flamboyant High Priest of Broadway now in desperate straights, makes a last-ditch effort to rise again by signing tempestuous movie star Lily Garland (Madeline Kahn), to act in his next epic, *The Passion of Mary Magdalene*. Oscar, who had once been Lily's mentor and lover — and had changed her name from Mildred Plotka — must now also contend with Lily's latest love, actor Bruce Granit (Kevin Kline), and a rival producer, Max Jacobs (George Lee Andrews). But we know that the two are meant for each other when Lily, tricked into signing Oscar's contract, affixes the name Peter Rabbit.

Though the character of Oscar Jaffee had been originally modeled after David Belasco and Jed Harris, Cullum played him as John Barrymore, with the love-hate relationship of Oscar and Lily also recalling Fred and Lili in *Kiss Me, Kate*. Two months after the opening, Miss Kahn was replaced by Judy Kaye. Columbia OC/ Drama Book Specialists (1981)/ SF.

DANCIN'

Music & lyrics: Miscellaneous writers
Producers: Jules Fisher, Shubert Organization, Columbia Pictures
Director-choreographer: Bob Fosse
Cast: Sandahl Bergman, Rene Ceballos, Christopher Chadman, Wayne Cilento, Vicki Frederick, Edward Love, Ann Reinking, Charles Ward
Songs: 23 musical pieces from Bach to Jerry Jeff Walker
New York run: Broadhurst Theatre, March 27, 1978; 1,774 p.

An extension of Bob Fosse's previous work in *Pippin* and *Chicago* — plus Michael Bennett's in *A Chorus Line* — *Dancin'* represented the final triumph of the Broadway choreographer by doing away with practically everything else but. In essence, it was Fosse's attempt to create a popular-dance version of a ballet program performed on Broadway for a commercial run, and it succeeded so well in attracting an audience — especially foreign visitors who might have difficulty in following a book musical — that it remained in New York for four years three months, and toured for over a year. The precision, grace and sheer vitality of the dancers (particularly Ann Reinking) merited high praise in such numbers as the easy-going, high-strutting "I Wanna Be a Dancin' Man," performed by the entire company; the dithyrambic recreation of Benny Goodman's "Sing, Sing, Sing"; and the finale, "America," a collage of ten routines by turn comic, ironic, and rousing.

THE BEST LITTLE WHOREHOUSE IN TEXAS

Music & lyrics: Carol Hall
Book: Larry L. King & Peter Masterson
Producer: Universal Pictures (Stevie Phillips)
Directors: Peter Masterson & Tommy Tune
Choreographer: Tommy Tune
Cast: Carlin Glynn, Henderson Forsythe, Delores Hall, Pamela Blair, Jay Garner, Clint Allmon
Songs: "A Li'l Ole Bitty Pissant Country Place"; "Girl, You're a Woman"; "Twenty-Four Hours of Lovin' "; "Texas Has a Whorehouse in It"; "Bus from Amarillo"; "Good Old Girl"; "Hard Candy Christmas"
New York run: Entermedia Theatre, April 17, 1978; 1,703 p.

The legendary Texas brothel known as the Chicken Ranch (so-called because in the Depression customers were allowed to pay with poultry) was in existence from the 1840s to 1973, when it was shut down through the efforts of a crusading, oilier-than-thou Houston radio commentator and his vigilante Watch Dogs. The story of the brothel and its last days became the subject of a raunchy, romping musical that was tried out at the Actor's Studio, opened at the Off-Broadway Entermedia Theatre (formerly the Eden), where it played 64 performances, then moved to the 46th Street Theatre on June 19. The show was put together entirely by four transplanted Texans who wanted to collaborate on a musical about the Lone Star State that would be, in the words of songwriter Carol Hall, "funny and nostalgic and tender." Carlin Glynn played Miss Mona Stangley, the whorehouse proprietor, and Henderson Forsythe the blunt-talking local sheriff, Ed Earl Dodd, who had once been Mona's lover. Alexis Smith was seen as Miss Mona in the second of three road companies that toured for three and a half years. The film version, released in 1982, co-starred Dolly Parton and Burt Reynolds.
MCA OC/ Samuel French (1983)*/ SF.

AIN'T MISBEHAVIN'

Music: Fats Waller
Lyrics: Miscellaneous writers
Conception: Murray Horwitz & Richard Maltby Jr.
Producers: Emanuel Azenberg, Dasha Epstein, Shubert Organization, Jane Gaynor, Ron Dante
Director: Richard Maltby Jr.
Choreographer: Arthur Faria
Cast: Nell Carter, Andre De Shields, Armelia McQueen, Ken Page, Charlaine Woodard
Songs: 30 written or recorded by Fats Waller
New York run: Longacre Theatre, May 9, 1978; 1,604 p.

While it was not the first entertainment presented on or off Broadway to feature the songs of a particular composer or lyricist, *Ain't Misbehavin'*, "The New Fats Waller Musical Show," was such a popular attraction that it opened the way for two subsequent "catalogue" musicals, *Eubie!*, spotlighting the work of Eubie Blake, and *Sophisticated Ladies*, which did the same for Duke Ellington. *Ain't Misbehavin'* began as a limited-run cabaret entertainment at the Manhattan Theatre Club on February 8, 1978. Its enthusiastic reception prompted its transfer to Broadway at the Longacre Theatre, where Charlaine Woodard replaced Irene Cara. Among the numbers performed were 18 written by Waller either as songs or instrumental pieces (some with new lyrics by Richard Maltby Jr. and Murray Horwitz) and 12 others that Waller recorded. Through costuming, decor, and arrangements, the show evoked the flavor of a Harlem nightclub in the Thirties, with the playful spirit of Waller himself coming through in the performances and the staging. During the Broadway run, Miss Woodard was succeeded by Debbie Allen. The musical's touring company traveled for two years seven months. In 1988 the show had a brief Broadway revival.
RCA OC/ MTI.

Ain't Misbehavin'. Armelia McQueen, Ken Page, Charlaine Woodard, Andre De Shields, and Nell Carter. (Martha Swope)

I'M GETTING MY ACT TOGETHER AND TAKING IT ON THE ROAD

Music: Nancy Ford
Lyrics & book: Gretchen Cryer
Producer: Joseph Papp for the New York Shakespeare Festival
Director: Word Baker
Cast: Gretchen Cryer, Joel Fabiani, Betty Aberlin, Don Scardino
Songs: "Natural High"; "Miss America"; "Dear Tom"; "Old Friend"; "Strong Woman Number"; "Happy Birthday"
New York run: Public Theatre, June 14, 1978; 1,165 p.

In all their works to date, composer Nancy Ford and lyricist-librettist Gretchen Cryer have been preeminently identified as feminist writers. *I'm Getting My Act Together and Taking It on the Road,* by far their most personal expression, even had the central role, that of a divorced 39-year-old pop singer attempting a comeback, played by Miss Cryer herself. The story finds her auditioning a new act for her dubious manager (Joel Fabiani), in which she presents herself as honestly as she can, without makeup or fancy gowns or any kind of audience-pandering. Through her songs, the singer gradually becomes the embodiment of the outspoken, totally liberated woman who knows exactly who she is and where she is going. After six months at the New York Shakespeare Festival Public Theatre, the musical was transferred to the Circle in the Square in Greenwich Village. During the run, Miss Cryer was succeeded by Virginia Vestoff, Betty Aberlin, Carol Hall, Betty Buckley, Anne Kaye, Nancy Ford, and Phyllis Newman. CSP OC/ Samuel French (1980)*/ SF.

THEY'RE PLAYING OUR SONG

Music: Marvin Hamlisch
Lyrics: Carole Bayer Sager
Book: Neil Simon
Producer: Emanuel Azenberg
Director: Robert Moore
Choreographer: Patricia Birch
Cast: Lucie Arnaz, Robert Klein
Songs: "Fallin' "; "If He Really Knew Me"; "They're Playing Our Song"; "Just for Tonight"; "When You're in My Arms"; "Right"
New York run: Imperial Theatre, February 11, 1979; 1,082 p.

They're Playing Our Song was based in part on composer Marvin Hamlisch's own frequently stormy affair with his then lyricist-in-residence, Carole Bayer Sager. In this musical *drame à clef,* Vernon Gersch, a wise-cracking, neurotic songwriter who likes to spend his time telling his troubles to a tape recorder, and Sonia Walsk, a wise-cracking, neurotic lyric writer whose wardrobe is made up of used theatre costumes, try to have both a professional and a personal relationship despite constant interruptions caused by telephone calls from Sonia's former lover for whom she still feels great affection. To tell their story, the authors hit upon the notion — as in *I Do! I Do!* — of using only two characters, though in this case each one has three singing alter egos. Four actors succeeded Robert Klein during the Broadway run (including Tony Roberts and Victor Garber), and five succeeded Lucie Arnaz (including Stockard Channing and Anita Gillette). The show's first road company (with Garber and Ellen Greene) toured for two years; the second (with John Hammil and Lorna Luft) for one year three months. Casablanca OC/ Random House (1980)/ SF.

Sweeney Todd. Angela Lansbury and Len Cariou.
(Martha Swope)

SWEENEY TODD

Music & lyrics: Stephen Sondheim
Book: Hugh Wheeler
Producers: Richard Barr, Charles Woodward, Robert Fryer, etc.
Director: Harold Prince
Choreographer: Larry Fuller
Cast: Angela Lansbury, Len Cariou, Vistor Garber, Ken Jennings, Merle
Louise, Edmund Lyndeck, Sarah Rice, Cris Groenendaal
Songs: "The Ballad of Sweeney Todd"; "The Worst Pies in London";
"Johanna"; "Pretty Women"; "Epiphany"; "A Little Priest"; "By the
Sea"; "Not While I'm Around"
New York run: Uris Theatre, March 1, 1979; 557 p.

Easily the most grisly musical ever presented for a commercial Broadway run,
the near-operatic *Sweeney Todd* was a bold, even audience-intimidating attack
on the cannibalizing effects of the Industrial Revolution on a Brechtian, vermin-
infested London. The indictment was conveyed through the tale of a half-mad
barber (Len Cariou) who returns home after escaping from an unjust imprison-
ment to take vengeance on the judge who sentenced him, then ravished his wife,
and now plans to marry his daughter. But Sweeney doesn't limit himself to one
victim; he turns his indiscriminate rage against everyone in London by systematically slitting the throats of his customers, whose corpses are then made into
meat pies by Todd's enterprising accomplice, Mrs. Lovett (Angela Lansbury). At
the end, of course, all the bad ones are properly and gruesomely punished.

First shown on the London stage in 1847 as *A String of Pearls, or The Fiend
of Fleet Street,* by George Dibdin Pitt, the Grand Guignol story has been presented in many versions since then, most recently Christopher Bond's 1973 London play, *Sweeney Todd,* on which Hugh Wheeler based his libretto. The fifth and
most uncompromising collaboration between composer-lyricist Stephen
Sondheim and director Harold Prince, the production was also noted for its tow-
ering setting (by Eugene and Franne Lee) made from an iron foundry. During the
run at the Uris Theatre (now the Gershwin, on 51st west of Broadway), Miss
Lansbury was succeeded by Dorothy Loudon, Mr. Cariou by George Hearn. In
1984, the musical entered the repertory of the New York City Opera; in 1989, it
was revived Off-Broadway with Bob Gunton and Beth Fowler.
RCA OC/ Dodd, Mead (1979)/ MTI.

PETER PAN

Music: Mark Charlap; Jule Styne
Lyrics: Carolyn Leigh; Betty Comden & Adolph Green
Play: James M. Barrie
Producers: Zev Bufman & James Nederlander
Director-choreographer: Rob Iscove (Ron Field, uncredited)
Cast: Sandy Duncan, George Rose, Beth Fowler, Arnold Soboloff, Marsha Kramer
Songs: Same as original production
New York run: Lunt-Fontanne Theatre, September 6, 1979; 551 p.

(See page 163.)

EVITA

Music: Andrew Lloyd Webber
Lyrics: Tim Rice
Producer: Robert Stigwood
Director: Harold Prince
Choreographer: Larry Fuller
Cast: Patti LuPone, Mandy Patinkin, Bob Gunton, Mark Syers, Jane Ohringer
Songs: "On This Night of a Thousand Stars"; "Buenos Aires"; "I'd Be Surprisingly Good for You"; "Another Suitcase in Another Hall"; "A New Argentina"; "Don't Cry for Me, Argentina"; "High Flying Adored"; "Rainbow Tour"; "The Actress Hasn't Learned"; "And the Money Kept Rolling In"; "Dice Are Rolling"
New York run: Broadway Theatre, September 25, 1979; 1,567 p.

Because of its huge success in London (where it opened in 1978 and ran 2,900 performances), *Evita* was such a pre-sold hit in New York that it was able to surmount a mixed critical reception and remain on Broadway for three years nine months. Based on events in the life of Argentina's notorious Eva Peron, the musical —with Patti LuPone as Eva — begins in 1934 when Eva Duarte is 15, takes her from her hometown to Buenos Aires where she becomes a model, film actress, and the wife of Gen. Juan Peron (Bob Gunton). When Peron is elected president, Eva becomes the most powerful woman in South America, and though she does little to improve the conditions of her people, is regarded as a saint when she dies of cancer at the age of 33. Another character in the musical, the slightly misplaced Che Guevera (Mandy Patinkin), serves as narrator, observer, and conscience.

Though the plot is told entirely through song and dance (there is no credit for librettist) and the work had originated as a record project, the highly theatrical concept devised by authors Andrew Lloyd Webber and Tim Rice and director Harold Prince — as well as the popularity of "Don't Cry for Me, Argentina" — helped turn *Evita* into an internationally acclaimed musical. During the Broadway run, six actresses took over the title role from Miss LuPone: Terri Klausner, Nancy Opel, and Pamela Blake (matinees), and Derin Altay, Loni Ackerman, and Florence Lacey (evenings). The show's three touring companies traveled a total of three and one-half years.
MCA OC/ MTI.

SUGAR BABIES
Music: Jimmy McHugh, etc.
Lyrics: Dorothy Fields, etc.
Conception: Ralph G. Allen & Harry Rigby
Sketches: Ralph G. Allen
Producers: Terry Allen Kramer & Harry Rigby
Directors: Ernest Flatt, Rudy Tronto
Choreographer: Ernest Flatt
Cast: Mickey Rooney, Ann Miller, Sid Stone, Jack Fletcher, Ann Jillian, Bob Williams, Scot Stewart
Songs: "A Good Old Burlesque Show" (lyric: Arthur Malvin); "I Feel a Song Comin' On"; "Don't Blame Me"; "Mr. Banjo Man" (music & lyric: Malvin); "I'm Keeping Myself Available for You" (lyric: Malvin); "Warm and Willing" (lyric: Jay Livingston & Ray Evans); "Exactly Like You"; "I Can't Give You Anything but Love"; "I'm Shooting High" (lyric: Ted Koehler); "On the Sunny Side of the Street"; "You Can't Blame Your Uncle Sammy" (lyric: Al Dubin & Irwin Dash).
New York run: Mark Hellinger Theatre, October 8, 1979; 1,208 p.

Like *Star and Garter, Wine, Women and Song,* and *Michael Todd's Peep Show* of an earlier era, *Sugar Babies* was an idealized version of a burlesque show. According to sketch writer Ralph G. Allen, who conceived the entertainment with co-producer Harry Rigby, the show was a celebration of American variety entertainment from 1905 to 1930 and the aim was to recreate as authentically as possible some of the classic low-comedy sketches and routines of that period. Making his Broadway debut top banana Mickey Rooney appeared in such traditional roles as the lascivious judge in a manic courtroom scene, as the naughty little boy in "The Little Red Schoolhouse," and as Countess Francine, complete with cotton-candy wig and exaggerated bosoms, leading her troupe of female minstrels. Also memorable, if hardly authentic, was the session at the grand piano with Mickey and Ann Miller going through Jimmy McHugh standards. Rooney was followed on Broadway by Joey Bishop, Rip Taylor, and Eddie Bracken, then headed the touring company with the leg-flashing Miss Miller. The show was on the road for almost three and a half years.
B'way Entertainment OC/ Samuel French (1983)*/ SF.

OKLAHOMA!
Music: Richard Rodgers
Lyrics & book: Oscar Hammerstein II
Producers: Zev Bufman & James Nederlander
Director: William Hammerstein
Choreographer: Agnes de Mille (dances recreated by Gemze de Lappe)
Cast: Laurence Guittard, Christine Andreas, Mary Wickes, Christine Ebersole, Martin Vidnovic, Harry Groener, Bruce Adler
Songs: Same as original production
New York run: Palace Theatre, December 13, 1979; 293 p.

(See page 119.)

BARNUM

Music: Cy Coleman
Lyrics: Michael Stewart
Book: Mark Bramble
Producers: Judy Gordon, Cy Coleman, Maurice & Lois Rosenfield
Director-choreographer: Joe Layton
Cast: Jim Dale, Glenn Close, Marianne Tatum, Terri White, Leonard John Crofoot, William C. Witter
Songs: "There Is a Sucker Born Ev'ry Minute"; "The Colors of My Life"; "One Brick at a Time"; "Bigger Isn't Better"; "Come Follow the Band"; "Black and White"; "The Prince of Humbug"; "Join the Circus"
New York run: St. James Theatre, April 30, 1980; 854 p.

The story of America's "Prince of Humbug," Phineas Taylor Barnum, had long attracted producers and writers as a fitting subject for a musical, but it was not until Cy Coleman, Michael Stewart, and Mark Bramble got together with director-choreographer Joe Layton that a way was found to depict the colorful impresario's life on stage. Their solution: don't bother too much with character-ization or biographical detail, simply offer the show as a total circus concept with the entire cast constantly in motion tumbling, clowning, marching, twirling, and flying through the air. Best of all, give the title role to Jim Dale, an actor who can dance, juggle, leap off a trampoline, and sing and walk a tightrope at the same time.

The musical offers a guided tour of the highlights of Barnum's career from 1835 to 1880, when the showman joins James A. Bailey (William C. Witter) in cre-ating "The Greatest Show on Earth." Along the way, we are treated to such leg-endary sucker-bait attractions as Joice Heth (Terri White), George Washington's alleged 160-year-old nurse, the midget Tom Thumb (Leonard John Crofoot), Jumbo the elephant, the Swedish Nightingale Jenny Lind (Marianne Tatum), and — finally — the three-ring circus. What conflict there is is supplied by the unful-filled desire of Barnum's wife Chairy (Glenn Close) to settle down to a more pro-saic life. During the run, Dale was succeeded by Tony Orlando and Mike Burstyn. For other show-business biographies, see *Annie Get Your Gun,* page 130. Columbia OC/ Doubleday (1980)/ TW.

Barnum. Jim Dale and Glenn Close. (Martha Swope)

42nd Street. Jerry Orbach and
Wanda Richert. (Martha Swope)

42nd STREET
Music: Harry Warren
Lyrics: Al Dubin
Book: Michael Stewart & Mark Bramble
Producer: David Merrick
Director-choreographer: Gower Champion
Cast: Jerry Orbach, Tammy Grimes, Wanda Richert, Lee Roy Reams, Joseph Bova, Carole Cook
Songs: "Young and Healthy"; "Shadow Waltz"; "Go Into Your Dance"; "You're Getting to Be a Habit With Me"; "Dames"; "We're in the Money"; "Lullaby of Broadway"; "About a Quarter to Nine"; "Shuffle Off to Buffalo"; "Forty-Second Street"
New York run: Winter Garden, August 25, 1980; 3,486 p.

Re-creating the classic 1933 backstage movie musical of the same name, *42nd Street* followed its cliché-riddled model with a minimum of camp but with a maximum of high-powered, ingenious choreography devised by Gower Champion (who died the day the musical opened on Broadway). Once again the simple-minded saga relates the tale of stage-struck chorus girl Peggy Sawyer (Wanda Richert) from Allentown, Pennsylvania, who gets her big chance when Dorothy Brock (Tammy Grimes), the star of *Pretty Lady,* breaks her ankle during the show's tryout, and Peggy goes on to triumph on "naughty, bawdy, gaudy, sporty 42nd Street." Among changes from the movie: the ending now indicated a possible romance between Peggy and the hard driving director Julian Marsh (Jerry Orbach) rather than juvenile lead Billy Lawlor (Lee Roy Reams), and nine more Harry Worred songs (seven of which also written with Al Dubin) were added to the four Warren-Dublin numbers that were retained.

The musical, which opened with a new top ticket price of $30, had two Broadway antecedents. A sketch in the *Ziegfeld Follies of 1939* offered Fanny Brice and Bob Hope in a takeoff on the film, which was also spoofed in the 1968 Off-Broadway hit *Dames at Sea.* During the run, the part of Dorothy was also played by Millicent Martin, Elizabeth Allen, Anne Rodgers, and Dolores Gray; Julian by Barry Nelson and Jamie Ross. The first touring company was originally headed by Nelson and Miss Gray, the second by Jon Cypher and Miss Martin. RCA OC/ TW.

The Pirates of Penzance. Kevin Kline, Rex Smith, and pirates (© Martha Swope)

THE PIRATES OF PENZANCE

Music: Arthur Sullivan
Lyrics & book: William S. Gilbert
Producer: Joseph Papp for the New York Shakespeare Festival
Director: Wilford Leach
Choreographer: Graciela Daniele
Cast: Kevin Kline, Estelle Parsons, Linda Ronstadt, George Rose, Rex Smith, Tony Azito
Songs: "Oh, Better Far to Live and Die"; "Oh, Is There Not One Maiden Breast?"; "Poor Wandering One"; "I Am the Very Model of a Modern Major-General"; "When the Foeman Bares His Steel"; "When a Felon's Not Engaged in His Employment"; "With Cat-Like Tread"
New York run: Uris Theatre, January 8, 1981; 772 p.

When, on December 31, 1879, *The Pirates of Penzance* opened in New York at the 5th Avenue Theatre, it marked the only occasion that a Gilbert and Sullivan comic opera had its première in a city other than London. When, 101 years later, it opened in New York at the Uris Theatre, it marked the only occasion — so far — that a Gilbert and Sullivan comic opera had a commercial Broadway run. With its modern orchestrations, bravura performances, and slightly campy approach, this version had been acclaimed when it was presented the previous summer in Central Park, where it played 42 free performances as part of Joseph Papp's New York Shakespeare Festival. (When moved to Broadway, the only major cast change was Estelle Parsons for Patricia Routledge as Ruth.) The operetta's ardent arias and duets and sprightly patter songs are mated to a charmingly inane tale of poor Frederic (Rex Smith), who after accidentally being apprenticed to a pirate (Kevin Kline), falls in love with Mabel (Linda Ronstadt), one of the eight daughters of a very model of a modern Major- General (George Rose).

Among those who appeared in the Broadway production after the original cast were Treat Williams (Pirate King); Kaye Ballard (Ruth); Maureen McGovern, Kathryn Morath, and Pam Dawber (Mabel); George S. Irving (Major-General); and Robby Benson, Patrick Cassidy, and Peter Noone (Frederic). The road company was initially headed by Barry Bostwick, Jo Anne Worley, Pam Dawber, Clive Revill, and Andy Gibb. The original Broadway cast — except for the substitution of Angela Lansbury for Miss Parsons — appeared in the 1983 film version. Elektra OC/ MTI.

Sophisticated Ladies. The "Caravan" number led by Gregg Burge. (Kenn Duncan)

SOPHISTICATED LADIES

Music: Duke Ellington
Lyrics: Miscellaneous writers
Conception: Donald McKayle
Producers: Roger Berlind, Manheim Fox, Sondra Gilman, Burton Litwin, Louise Westergaard
Director: Michael Smuin
Choreographers: Donald McKayle, Michael Smuin, Henry LeTang
Cast: Gregory Hines, Judith Jamison, Phyllis Hyman, P. J. Benjamin, Hinton Battle, Terri Klausner, Gregg Burge, Mercedes Ellington, Priscilla Baskerville
Songs: 36 from the Duke Ellington catalogue
New York run: Lunt-Fontanne Theatre, March 1, 1981; 767 p.

Though different in concept, *Sophisticated Ladies* followed the lead of *Ain't Misbehavin'* and *Eubie!* by being an entertainment built around the catalogue of a single composer. Here the celebration of the music of Duke Ellington was far more of an elaborate, brassy nightclub floor show than its predecessors, with a 21-piece on-stage orchestra (led by Ellington's son Mercer Ellington) and a castful of such highpowered steppers as Gregory Hines, Judith Jamison, Hinton Battle, and Gregg Burge. The show's Broadway success was totally unexpected. Its opening-night tryout in Washington had gone so badly that director Donald McKayle, who had conceived the production, was replaced by ballet choreographer Michael Smuin. Despite his inexperience in the world of Broadway, Smuin turned things around by adding nine songs, rearranging the sequence of the 36 numbers, introducing new dance routines, and dropping all existing dialogue.

During the Broadway run, Gregory Hines was succeeded by his brother, Maurice Hines, and P. J. Benjamin by Don Correia. The first of two road companies was headed by Harold Nicholas, Paula Kelly, and Freda Payne.
RCA OC/ R&H.

WOMAN OF THE YEAR

Music: John Kander
Lyrics: Fred Ebb
Book: Peter Stone
Producers: Lawrence Kasha, David Landay, James Nederlander, etc.
Director: Robert Moore
Choreographer: Tony Charmoli
Cast: Lauren Bacall, Harry Guardino, Roderick Cook, Marilyn Cooper, Eivind
        Harum, Grace Keagy, Rex Everhart, Jamie Ross
Songs: "Woman of the Year"; "One of the Boys"; "The Grass Is Always Green-
        er"; "We're Gonna Work It Out"
New York run: Palace Theatre, March 29, 1981; 770 p.

Updating the 1942 movie, *Woman of the Year* told a battle-of-the-sexes story with Lauren Bacall as Tess Harding, a Barbara Walters-type television personali-ty, and Harry Guardino as Sam Craig, a satirical cartoonish suggesting Garry Trudeau. Angered by some television comments made by Tess about "funnies," Sam retaliates by putting her in his strip as a character named "Tessie Cat." The two meet, explode, marry, continue to explode, and eventually decide to try to work things out. *Woman of the Year* had certain points of similarity with Miss Bacall's previous musical, *Applause*. Both shows were told in flashback, and both involved a strong-willed public personality trying to solve the problem of jug-gling a career and marriage. During the musical's run, Miss Bacall was succeed-ed by Raquel Welch, Debbie Reynolds, and Louise Troy.
Arista OC/ Samuel French (1984)*/ SF.

JOSEPH AND THE AMAZING TECHNICOLOR DREAMCOAT

Music: Andrew Lloyd Webber
Lyrics: Tim Rice
Producers: Zev Bufman & Susan Rose
Director-choreographer: Tony Tanner
Cast: Bill Hutton, Laurie Beechman, David Ardeo, Tom Carder
Songs: "Joseph's Coat"; "One More Angel in Heaven"; "Go, Go, Go Joseph";
        "Pharaoh's Story"; "Those Canaan Days"; "Benjamin Calypso"; "Any
        Dream Will Do"
New York run: Entermedia Theatre, November 18, 1981; 824 p.

Joseph and the Amazing Technicolor Dreamcoat, the first collaboration of An-drew Lloyd Webber and Tim Rice, lasted all of 15 minutes when it was initially presented in a London school in 1968. Five years later, by now expanded to 40 minutes, the work was offered on the West End and then expanded again to al-most 90 minutes. In 1976, *Joseph* had its first New York showing at the Brooklyn Academy of Music. The 1981 production, which ran 77 performances in an East Village theatre, moved to the Royale on January 27, 1982, where it remained for 747 performances. Told entirely in song, this biblical cantata — actually an eclec-tic grabbag of rock, country, vaudeville song-and-dance, French ballad, and ca-lypso — relates the Old Testament tale of Joseph (Bill Hutton), Jacob's favorite of 12 sons, to whom papa gives a resplendent coat of many colors. Joseph's jealous brothers thereupon sell him into slavery and he is taken to Egypt where he interprets the dream of an Elvis Presley-type Pharaoh (Tom Carder). His wise prophecy so impresses the Pharaoh that he becomes Egypt's Number Two man and saves the country from famine. During the Broadway run, Andy Gibb and David Cassidy were two of the four actors who succeeded Bill Hutton.
Chrysalis OC/ Holt, Rinehart (1982)/ MTI.

DREAMGIRLS

Music: Henry Krieger
Lyrics & book: Tom Eyen
Producers: Michael Bennett, Bob Avian, Geffen Records
Director: Michael Bennett
Choreographers: Michael Bennett, Michael Peters
Cast: Obba Babatunde, Cleavant Derricks, Loretta Devine, Ben Harney, Jennifer Holliday, Sheryl Lee Ralph, Deborah Burrell
Songs: "Fake Your Way to the Top"; "Cadillac Car"; "Steppin' to the Bad Side"; "Dreamgirls"; "And I Am Telling You I'm Not Going"; "I Am Changing"; "When I First Saw You"; "Hard to Say Goodbye, My Love"
New York run: Imperial Theatre, December 20, 1981; 1,522 p.

With *Dreamgirls,* Michael Bennett returned to the heartbreak world of show business that he had explored in *A Chorus Line* to create another high-voltage concept musical. Tom Eyen's tough-tender book about the corruption of innocence was primarily based on the story of the Supremes. The success of the black vocal trio of the 1960s was maneuvered by Motown Records chief Berry Gordy at the price of dropping lead singer Florence Ballard in favor of Diana Ross because Ballard didn't present the right image (she drifted into obscurity and died at the age of 32). In the musical, it is Effie Melody White (Jennifer Holliday), the heavyset lead singer of a rhythm and blues trio (the other two: Sheryl Lee Ralph and Loretta Devine), who is sacrificed because a slick manager (Ben Harney) feels that the singers — whom he names the Dreams — must offer a more glamorous appearance to enable them to cross over to the more lucrative pop mainstream. Unlike Florence Ballard, however Effie surmounts a difficult period and goes on to win fame on her own.

To keep his glitzy, glittery show in constant fluid motion through some 20 scenes — beginning in 1962 on the stage of the Harlem Apollo and ending ten years later in Hollywood — Bennett was aided by set designer Robin Wagner, costume designer Theoni V. Aldredge, and lighting designer Tharon Musser (all of whom had worked on *A Chorus Line*). Also contributing to the production's close weave was Henry Krieger's Motown-influenced score with over 30 musical numbers used both for specialties and as dramatic dialogue. Impressive newcomer Jennifer Holliday repeated her role in the touring company. A new touring production of *Dreamgirls* returned to Broadway in 1987.
Geffen OC.

Dreamgirls. Loretta Devine, Jennifer Holliday, Sheryl Lee Ralph, and Cleavant Derricks. (Martha Swope)

NINE

Music & lyrics: Maury Yeston
Book: Arthur Kopit, Mario Fratti
Producers: Michel Stuart, Harvey Klaris, Roger Berlind, etc.
Director: Tommy Tune
Choreographers: Tommy Tune, Thommie Walsh
Cast: Raul Julia, Karen Akers, Shelly Burch, Taina Elg, Lilianne Montevecchi, Anita Morris, Kathi Moss
Songs: "My Husband Makes Movies"; "A Call from the Vatican"; "Only With You"; "Folies Bergères"; "Nine"; "Be Italian"; "Unusual Way"; "The Grand Canal"; "Simple"; "Be on Your Own"
New York run: 46th Street Theatre, May 9, 1982; 732 p.

The influence of the director-choreographer was emphasized again with Tommy Tune's highly stylized, visually striking production of *Nine*. The musical evolved from composer-lyricist Maury Yeston's fascination with Federico Fellini's semi-autobiographical 1963 film *8½,* and — appropriately — it took nine years for it to make it to Broadway. During the show's creation, disagreements arose over the libretto by Mario Fratti, prompting his replacement by Arthur Kopit, and Tune's decision to have a cast of 21 women and only one adult male. The story spotlights Guido Contini (Raul Julia), a celebrated but tormented director who has come to a Venetian spa for a rest, and his relationships with his wife (Karen Akers), his mistress (Anita Morris), his protégé (Shelly Burch), his producer (Lilianne Montevecchi), and his mother (Taina Elg). The production, which flashes back to Guido's youth and also takes place in his imagination, offers such inventive touches as an "overture" in which Guido conducts his women as if they were instruments, and an impressionistic version of the Folies Bergères. During the Broadway run, Julia was succeeded by Bert Convy and Sergio Franchi. CBS OC/ Doubleday (1983)/ SF.

LITTLE SHOP OF HORRORS

Music: Alan Menken
Lyrics & book: Howard Ashman
Producers: WPA Theatre, David Geffen, Cameron Mackintosh
Director: Howard Ashman
Choreographer: Edie Cowan
Cast: Ellen Greene, Lee Wilkof, Hy Anzell, Franc Luz, Leilani Jones
Songs: "Little Shop of Horrors"; "Skid Row"; "Grow for Me"; "Somewhere That's Green"; "Suddenly Seymour"
New York run: Orpheum Theatre, July 27, 1982; 2,209 p.

A campy musical about a man-eating Venus's-flytrap with all the principals dead by the end of the show would seem far riskier than the usual theatrical enterprise, but *Little Shop of Horrors* won over a majority of the critics to its offbeat humor, and remained for over 2,000 performances at its Lower East Side theatre. Based on the low-budget 1960 Roger Corman movie, the musical is set in a flower shop inconveniently located on Skid Row where meek Seymour Krelbourn (Lee Wilkof) breeds a tiny plant that he names Audrey II out of love for salesgirl Audrey (Ellen Greene). Since the mysterious plant needs blood to live, Seymour, in a Faustian pact, agrees to feed it in return for a guarantee that it will attract publicity to make him rich and famous. Soon this unlikely Sweeney Todd has found a way to do in anyone he wants, and when last seen the monstrous mutant is about to devour the audience. A film version was released in 1986. Geffen OC/ Doubleday (1982)/ SF.

CATS

Music: Andrew Lloyd Webber
Lyrics: Based on T.S. Eliot
Producers: Cameron Mackintosh, Really Useful Co., Ltd., David Geffen
Directors: Trevor Nunn, Gillian Lynne
Choreographer: Gillian Lynne
Cast: Betty Buckley, Rene Clemente, Harry Groener, Stephen Hanan, Reed
Jones, Christine Langner, Terrence V. Mann, Anna McNeely, Ken Page,
Timothy Scott
Songs: "Jellicle Songs for Jellicle Cats"; "The Old Gumbie Cat"; "The Rum Tum
Tugger"; "Old Deuteronomy"; "The Jellicle Ball"; "Grizabella";
"Macavity"; "Mr. Mistoffelees"; "Memory"
New York run: Winter Garden, October 7, 1982; (still running 10/1/93)

At this writing, *Cats* is still running in London (where it opened May 11, 1981)
and in New York. Charged with incredible energy, flare, and imagination, the
feline fantasy has been staged in its Broadway version as even more of an
environmental experience than it was in its West End original. With the entire
Winter Garden auditorium transformed into an enormous junkyard, a theatergoer
is confronted by such sights as outsized gabagy object spilling into the audience,
a stage area without a proscenium arch, and a ceiling that has been lowered and
turned into a twinkling canopy suggesting both cats' eyes and stars.

Composer Andrew Lloyd Webber began setting music to T.S. Eliot's poems
in *Old Possum's Book of Practical Cats* in 1977. Later, he arranged the music for
concerts, and still later — now in collaboration with director Trevor Nunn — he
reworked the concept into a dramatic structure. In the song-and-dance
spectacle, which has only the barest thread of a story line and no spoken
dialogue, are such whimsically named characters as Jennyanydots, the Old
Gumbie Cat who sits all day and becomes active only at night, the never
satisfied Rum Tum Tugger, Bustopher Jones, the well-fed, elegant cat about
town, Mungojerrie and Rumpleteazer, those two-knockabout clowns and cat
burglars, the patriarchal Old Deuteronomy, Skimpleshanks the Railway Cat, and
the mysterious Mr. Mistoffelees. The musicals song hit, "Memory," is sung by
Grizabella (Betty Buckley), the faded Glamour Cat who, at the evening's end,
ascends to the cats' heaven known as the Heaviside Layer. On October 7, 1992,
Cats celebrated its tenth anniversary, with 4,177 performances as of that date,
making it the second longest running show in Broadway history (second only to
A Chorus Line). At this point cast changes run to two single spaced pages.
During the run, ticket prices have ascended from $40 to $65. The Broadway box
office gross by the 10th anniversary performances was $254 million, worldwide
(including London and New York) the gross was more than $1.4 billion. Four
touring companies continue on the road.
Geffen OC/Faber & Faber, London (1981).

Cats. "The Jellicle Ball" number. (Martha Swope)

ON YOUR TOES

Music: Richard Rodgers
Lyrics: Lorenz Hart
Book: Richard Rodgers, Lorenz Hart & George Abbott
Producers: Alfred de Liagre Jr., Roger L. Stevens, John Mauceri, Donald Seawell, Andre Pastoria
Director: George Abbott
Choreographers: George Balanchine, Donald Saddler, Peter Martins
Cast: Natalia Makarova, George S. Irving, Dina Merrill, George de la Peña, Christine Andreas, Lara Teeter, Betty Ann Grove, Peter Slutsker, Michael Vita
Songs: Same as original production
New York run: Virginia Theatre, March 6, 1983; 505 p.

(See page 94.)

MY ONE AND ONLY

Music: George Gershwin
Lyrics: Ira Gershwin
Book: Peter Stone, Timothy S. Meyer
Producers: Paramount Theatres (Dan Sherkow), Lester Allen, Francine LeFrak, Kenneth Greenblatt, Mark Schwartz
Director-choreographers: Thommie Walsh & Tommy Tune (Mike Nichols, Michael Bennett uncredited)
Cast: Twiggy, Tommy Tune, Charles "Honi" Coles, Bruce McGill, Denny Dillon, Roscoe Lee Browne
Songs: "I Can't Be Bothered Now"; "Blah, Blah, Blah"; "Boy Wanted"; "Soon"; "High Hat"; "Sweet and Low-Down"; "He Loves and She Loves"; " 'S Wonderful"; "Strike Up the Band"; "Nice Work If You Can Get It"; "My One and Only"; "Funny Face"; "Kickin' the Clouds Away" (lyric with B.G. DeSylva); "How Long Has This Been Going On?"
New York run: St. James Theatre, May 1, 1983; 767 p.

Within a week after the Broadway première of *Nine,* which he had directed, Tommy Tune was in rehearsal with Twiggy for what was originally announced as a revival of the Gershwins' 1927 musical *Funny Face.* By the time the show opened in New York, however, it had a completely new story, at least four directors, a score with only six of the original 12 songs (augmented by 11 other Gershwin standards), and it was now called *My One and Only.* Initially, the director and librettist were to have been Peter Sellars and Timothy Meyer, but after disagreements Sellars was replaced first by Mike Nichols then by Tune and Thommie Walsh, and Meyer by Peter Stone. The resulting book, still set in 1927, was an often anachronistic framework for the imaginatively staged song-and-dance numbers which found Tune playing a barnstorming aviator and Twiggy a champion swimmer who incongruously get involved with a bootlegging Harlem minister (Roscoe Lee Browne), an enigmatical tap-dancing philosopher (Charles "Honi" Coles), and a blackmailing Russian spy (Bruce McGill). Twiggy and Tune were succeeded on Broadway by Sandy Duncan and Don Correia. For the tour, Tune was co-starred with Miss Duncan.
Atlantic OC.

On Your Toes. George de la Peña and Natalia Makarova in the "Princess Zenobia" ballet. (Martha Swope)

My One and Only. Tommy Tune and Charles "Honi" Coles dancing to the title song. (Kenn Duncan)

LA CAGE AUX FOLLES

Music & lyrics: Jerry Herman
Book: Harvey Fierstein
Producer: Allan Carr
Director: Arthur Laurents
Choreographer: Scott Salmon
Cast: George Hearn, Gene Barry, Jay Garner, John Weiner, Elizabeth Parrish, Leslie Stevens, William Thomas Jr., Merle Louise
Songs: "A Little More Mascara"; "With You on My Arm"; "Song on the Sand"; "La Cage aux Folles"; "I Am What I Am"; "Masculinity"; "The Best of Times"
New York run: Palace Theatre, August 21, 1983, 1,761 p.

French author Jean Poiret's successful play and film about the relationship between the owner of a St. Tropez drag-queen nightclub and his star attraction provided Broadway with its first homosexual musical. In the story, the flamboyant Albin (George Hearn) — known on the stage as Zaza — and the more conservative Georges (Gene Barry) are middle-aged lovers who have been together for over 20 years. Their domestic peace is shattered, however, when Jean-Michel (John Weiner), Georges' son as a result of a youthful indiscretion, advises his father that he plans to wed the daughter of Edouard Dindon (Jay Garner), a local morals crusader. In order that Georges appear to his future in-laws as an upstanding citizen, he agrees that Albin must somehow be put back into the closet. Though hurt and defiant ("I Am What I Am"), Albin swallows his pride and aids the deception by dressing up as Georges' wife. After inadvertently revealing that he is what he is, Albin is not above a little blackmail to force Dindon to permit the marriage to take place.

Except for the homosexual angle, *La Cage aux Folles* (the name of Georges' nightclub) was in the tradition of the big, splashy Broadway book musical, complete with a glamorous chorus line (which even has two female dancers among the Cagelles). And though it was originally to have been put together by a different team of collaborators (when it was known as *The Queen of Basin Street*), the musical was a predestined smash by the time of its Boston tryout. The show marked Jerry Herman's tenth score (as well as his first hit since *Mame*) and playwright Harvey Fierstein's first experience as a librettist. George Hearn, who scored a notable hit as Albin, was succeeded by Walter Charles and Keene Curtis; Gene Barry was followed by Jamie Ross, Keith Michell, Van Johnson, Steeve Arlen, and Peter Marshall. The show's two road companies were headed by, respectively, Michell (replaced by Barry) and Charles, and by Marshall and Curtis. *La Cage aux Folles* was the first musical to charge $47.50 for orchestra seats.

Male actors appearing in drag have long been part of the Broadway musical scene. In the late 19th Century, Tony Hart made a specialty of performing women's roles in Harrigan and Hart shows, and other early female impersonators were Julian Eltinge (the most celebrated of all) and Bert Savoy (of the team of Savoy and Brennan). Later actors who donned feminine attire — usually as a transvestite sight gag — included Ole Olsen in *Hellzapoppin*, Bobby Clark in *Mexican Hayride, Sweethearts,* and *As the Girls Go,* Ray Bolger in *Where's Charley?,* Myron McCormick in *South Pacific,* Bert Lahr (as Queen Victoria) in *Two on the Aisle,* Jack Gilford in *A Funny Thing Happened on the Way to the Forum,* Robert Morse and Tony Roberts in *Sugar,* Mickey Rooney in *Sugar Babies,* and James Coco in the revival of *Little Me.* Actual homosexual — or at least effeminate — characters have been portrayed by Bobbie Watson in *Irene,* Danny Kaye in *Lady in the Dark,* Ray Bolger in *By Jupiter,* Joel Grey in *Cabaret,* Rene Auberjonois in *Coco,* Lee Roy Reams in *Applause,* Tommy Tune in *Seesaw,* and Michel Stuart and Sammy Williams in *A Chorus Line.*
RCA OC/ Samuel French (1987)*/ SF.

La Cage aux Folles. Les Cagelles. (Martha Swope)

La Cage aux Folles. The ''Masculinity'' number with Gene Barry and George Hearn. (Martha Swope)

Zorba. Anthony Quinn in the title role. (Martha Swope)

ZORBA

Music: John Kander
Lyrics: Fred Ebb
Book: Joseph Stein
Producers: Barry & Fran Weissler, Kenneth Greenblatt & John Pomerantz
Director: Michael Cacoyannis
Choreographer: Graciela Daniele
Cast: Anthony Quinn, Lila Kedrova, Robert Westenberg, Debbie Shapiro
Songs: Same as original production, plus "Mine Song" and "Woman"
New York run: Broadway Theatre, October 16, 1983; 362 p.

(See page 225.)

THE TAP DANCE KID

Music: Henry Krieger
Lyrics: Robert Lorick
Book: Charles Blackwell
Producers: Stanley White, Evelyn Barron, Harvey Klaris, Michel Stuart
Director: Vivian Matalon
Choreographer: Danny Daniels
Cast: Hinton Battle, Samuel E. Wright, Hattie Winston, Alfonso Ribeiro, Alan Weeks, Martine Allard, Jackie Lowe
Songs: "Dancing Is Everything"; "Fabulous Feet"; "Class Act"; "I Remember How It Was"; "Dance If It Makes You Happy"
New York run: Broadhurst Theatre, December 21, 1983; 669 p.

The methods by which ambitious young blacks have been able to box or sing their way out of the ghetto have been documented in such musicals as *Golden Boy* and *Dreamgirls,* but *The Tap Dance Kid* offered the unaccustomed situation of an upper middle-class family in which a successful lawyer (Samuel E. Wright) tries to stifle the dreams of his ten-year-old son Willie (Alfonso Ribeiro) to follow the profession of his Uncle Dipsey (Hinton Battle) and become a dancer. Featuring Battle's exciting footwork, the show surmounted a divided press to chalk up a surprisingly long Broadway run. The musical's origin was a television play (in which librettist Charles Blackwell played the father) that had been based on a novel, *Nobody's Family Is Going to Change,* by Louise Fitzhugh.
Polydor OC/ Samuel French (1988)*/ SF.

SUNDAY IN THE PARK WITH GEORGE

Music & lyrics: Stephen Sondheim
Book: James Lapine
Producers: Shubert Organization & Emanuel Azenberg
Director: James Lapine
Cast: Mandy Patinkin, Bernadette Peters, Charles Kimbrough, Barbara Bryne, Dana Ivey, William Parry, Robert Westenberg
Songs: "Sunday in the Park With George"; "Finishing the Hat"; "We Do Not Belong Together"; "Beautiful"; "Sunday"; "Children and Art"; "Move On"
New York run: Booth Theatre, May 2, 1984; 604 p.

After six productions in a row with director Harold Prince, Stephen Sondheim joined with director-librettist James Lapine for an especially challenging and personal work. *Sunday in the Park With George* reveals what the authors feel about art, the creative process, the artist's sacrifice of human emotions, and the need to avoid being influenced by what is currently trendy and faddish. To express these feelings, Sondheim and Lapine concentrated on the creation of one painting, Georges Seurat's "A Sunday Afternoon on the Island of La Grande Jatte."

In the first act, which takes place on the island in 1884, George (Mandy Patinkin) is busily painting the Parisians who are enjoying a day off strolling through a park on the Seine. We get to know the people and their relationships with one another, and in particular we get to know George and his relationship with Dot (Bernadette Peters), his model and mistress. The artist's preoccupation with his work, however, makes theirs a doomed romance, and the model, who is pregnant, accepts a baker's offer of marriage. The second act jumps to the present in New York, where the painter's great-grandson, a multi-media sculptor also named George, is at a creative impasse after completing his seventh "Chromolume." His confidence is restored, however, when he visits La Grande Jatte and is urged by the ghost of his great-grandmother to stop worrying about where he is going and what others think and "just keep moving on."

Sunday in the Park With George, which was first staged as a Playwrights Horizons workshop production in July 1983, was awarded the 1985 Pulitzer Prize for drama. During its run, Patinkin was spelled by Robert Westenberg and Harry Groener, and Miss Peters was succeeded by Betsy Joslyn and Maryann Plunkett.

RCA OC/ Dodd, Mead (1986).

Sunday in the Park With George. Mandy Patinkin and Bernadette Peters. (Martha Swope)

BIG RIVER

Music & lyrics: Roger Miller
Book: William Hauptman
Producers: Rocco Landesman, Heidi Landesman, Rick Steiner, M. Anthony Fisher, Dodger Productions
Director: Des McAnuff
Choreographer: Janet Watson
Cast: Rene Auberjonois, Reathal Bean, Susan Browning, Patti Cohenour, Gordon Connell, Bob Gunton, Daniel H. Jenkins, Ron Richardson
Songs: "Guv'ment"; "Muddy Water"; "River in the Rain"; "Waiting for the Light to Shine"; "Worlds Apart"; "You Ought to Be Here With Me"; "Leaving's Not the Only Way to Go"
New York run: Eugene O'Neill Theatre, April 25, 1985; 1,005 p.

Producers Rocco and Heidi Landesman came up with the idea of a musical version of Mark Twain's *Adventures of Huckleberry Finn* primarily because they were anxious to find the right property that would best introduce Broadway to the talents of country music songwriter Roger Miller. *Big River* was tried out at the American Repertory Theatre (ART) in Cambridge, Massachusetts, early in 1984, and then at the La Jolla Playhouse in California before those connected with the show felt that it was ready for New York. Set in 1849, with the action taking place both on the Mississippi River and in various locations along its banks (thanks to Heidi Landesman's atmospheric settings), the imaginative and faithfully conceived adaptation of the picaresque novel is concerned primarily with the relationship between Huck Finn and the runaway slave Jim (Daniel H. Jenkins and Ron Richardson) as they enjoy the untethered life traveling on a raft down the Mississippi from Hannibal, Missouri, to Hillsboro, Arkansas. In 1957, a previous musical based on Mark Twain's Mississippi River stories was offered Off Broadway under the title *Livin' the Life.*
MCA OC/ Grove Press (1986)/ R&H.

Big River. Ron Richardson and Daniel H. Jenkins. (Martha Swope)

SONG AND DANCE

Music: Andrew Lloyd Webber
Lyrics: Don Black, Richard Maltby Jr.
Adaptation: Richard Maltby Jr.
Producers: Cameron Mackintosh, Shubert Organization, FWM Producing Group
Director: Richard Maltby Jr.
Choreographer: Peter Martins
Cast: Bernadette Peters, Christopher d'Amboise, Gregg Burge, Charlotte d'Amboise, Cynthia Onrubia, Scott Wise
Songs: "Capped Teeth and Caesar Salad"; "So Much to Do in New York"; "Unexpected Song"; "Come Back With the Same Look in Your Eyes"; "Tell Me on a Sunday"
New York run: Royale Theatre, September 18, 1985; 474 p.

The "Dance" of the title originated in 1979 when Andrew Lloyd Webber composed a set of variations on Paganini's A-Minor Caprice that seemed perfect for a ballet; the "Song" originated a year later with a one-woman television show, *Tell Me on a Sunday,* consisting entirely of musical pieces. Two years after that both works were presented together in London as a full evening's entertainment. In New York, this unconventional package won praise for Bernadette Peters, whose task in Act I was to create, without dialogue, the character of a free-spirited English girl who has dalliances in America with four men. The second act offered a choreographic self-examination of one of the men (Christopher d'Amboise) and the two halves were joined when girl and boy were reunited. After a year on Broadway, Miss Peters was succeeded by Betty Buckley. RCA OC/ R&H.

THE MYSTERY OF EDWIN DROOD

Music, lyrics & book: Rupert Holmes
Producer: Joseph Papp for the New York Shakespeare Festival
Director: Wilford Leach
Choreographer: Graciela Daniele
Cast: George Rose, Cleo Laine, Betty Buckley, Howard McGillin, Patti Cohenour, Jana Schneider, John Herrera, Jerome Dempsey
Songs: "Moonfall"; "The Wages Of Sin"; "No Good Can Come from Bad"; "Ceylon"; "Perfect Strangers"; "Both Sides of the Coin"; "Off to the Races"; "Don't Quit While You're Ahead"
New York run: Imperial Theatre, December 2, 1985; 608 p.

The Mystery of Edwin Drood came to Broadway after being initially presented the previous summer in a series of free performances sponsored by the New York Shakespeare Festival at the Delacorte Theatre in Central Park. It was the first stage work of composer-lyricist-librettist Rupert Holmes, whose lifelong fascination with Charles Dickens' unfinished novel had been the catalyst for the project. Since there were no clues as to Drood's murderer or even if a murder had been committed, Holmes decided to let the audience provide the show's ending by voting how it turns out. The writer's second major decision was to offer the musical as if it were being performed by an acting company at London's Music Hall Royale in 1873, complete with such conventions as a Chairman (George Rose) to comment on the action and a woman (Betty Buckley) to play the part of Edwin Drood. During the run, Miss Buckley was replaced by Donna Murphy, and Cleo Laine (as the mysterious Princess Puffer) by Loretta Swit and Karen Morrow. On November 13, 1986, in an attempt to attract more theatre-goers, the musical's title was officially changed to *Drood.*
Polydor OC/ Doubleday (1986)/ TW.

271

SWEET CHARITY

Music: Cy Coleman
Lyrics: Dorothy Fields
Book: Neil Simon
Producers: Jerome Minskoff, James Nederlander, Arthur Rubin, Joseph Harris
Director-choreographer: Bob Fosse
Cast: Debbie Allen, Michael Rupert, Bebe Neuwirth, Allison Williams, Lee Wilkof, Mark Jacoby, Irving Allen Lee
Songs: Same as original production
New York run: Minskoff Theatre, April 27, 1986; 368 p.

(See page 216.)

Me and My Girl. Robert Lindsay and Maryann Plunkett dancing to the title song. (Alan Berliner)

ME AND MY GIRL

Music: Noel Gay
Lyrics: Douglas Furber, etc.
Book: L. Arthur Rose & Douglas Furber; revised by Stephen Fry
Producers: Richard Armitage, Terry Allen Kramer, James Nederlander, Stage
      Promotions Ltd.
Director: Mike Ockrent
Choreographer: Gillian Gregory
Cast: Robert Lindsay, Maryann Plunkett, George S. Irving, Jane Connell, Jane
      Summerhays, Nick Ullett, Timothy Jerome, Thomas Toner, Justine
      Johnston, Elizabeth Larner
Songs: "Thinking of No-One But Me"; "The Family Solicitor"; "Me and My Girl";
      "Hold My Hand" (music with Maurice Elwin; lyric: Harry Graham); "Once
      You Lose Your Heart" (lyric: Noel Gay); "The Lambeth Walk"; "The Sun
      Has Got His Hat On" (lyric: Frank Butler); "Take It on the Chin"; "Love
      Makes the World Go Round" (lyric: Gay); "Leaning on a Lamppost" (lyric:
      Gay)
New York run: Marquis Theatre, August 10, 1986; 1,412 p.

One of the most unlikely Broadway hits of 1986 was an almost fifty-year-old London musical comedy that, despite its near record-breaking run of 1,646 performances, had always been deemed too "English" to be considered for a New York showing before. Yet, followed by a successful West End reincarnation in 1985, *Me and My Girl* became an instant smash upon being offered as the premiere attraction at the newly built Marquis Theatre (located in the Marriott Marquis Hotel on Broadway between 45th and 46th Streets). Part of the reason had to do with the imaginative staging, Noel Gay's simple, catchy melodies, and the show's general spirit of eager-to-please innocent merriment. But most of the show's popularity surely was due to the protean talents of Robert Lindsay, the original star of the London revival who made his Broadway debut in the musical. (Lindsay was subsequently succeeded by Jim Dale and James Brennan.) The road company, which began touring in 1987, was initially headed by Tim Curry.

    It was producer Richard Armitage, the son of the composer (Gay's real name was Reginald Armitage), who first saw the potential in bringing back *Me and My Girl*. The younger Armitage devoted years to tracking down the original score and script, then signed playwright Stephen Fry to do the text revisions with an assist from director Mike Ockrent. The book was still about a pugnacious Cockney, Bill Snibson (Lindsay), who turns up as the long-lost heir to the Earldom of Hareford. Complications arise over Bill's devotion to his Lambeth sweetie, Sally Smith (Maryann Plunkett), and the efforts of the Hareford clan (led by George S. Irving and Jane Connell) to send her back where she belongs. But the bluebloods—who even join in the high-strutting, thumb-cocking dance known as "The Lambeth Walk"—eventually give their consent and Bill ends up with both his inheritance and his girl (who has been miraculously transformed, *Pygmalion* fashion, into an elegant lady).

    The character of Bill Snibson was originated in 1935 by the diminutive clown Lupino Lane in *Twenty to One,* a race-track yarn in which Bill tilts with the stuffy killjoys of the Anti-Gambling League. Lane became so attached to the part that two years later he had the show's librettists fashion a new musical for him about Bill's tilting with the stuffy members of the aristocracy. *Me and My Girl* was such a personal triumph that Lane toured in it extensively and brought it back to London in 1941, 1945, and 1949.

MCA OC/ Samuel French, London (1954)*/ SF.

Les Misérables. Colm Wilkinson, Michael Maguire and David Bryant manning the barricade. (Michael Le Poer Trench/Bob Marshak)

LES MISÉRABLES

Music: Claude-Michel Schönberg
Lyrics: Herbert Kretzmer
Conception: Alain Boublil & Claude-Michel Schönberg
Original French Text: Alain Boublil & Jean-Marc Natel
Adaptation: Trevor Nunn & John Caird
Producer: Cameron Mackintosh
Directors: Trevor Nunn & John Caird
Choreographer: Kate Flatt
Cast: Colm Wilkinson, Terrence Mann, Randy Graff, Michael Maguire, Leo Burmester, Frances Ruffelle, David Bryant, Judy Kuhn, Jennifer Butt, Braden Danner
Songs: "I Dreamed a Dream"; "Who Am I?"; "Castle on a Cloud"; "Master of the House"; "Red and Black"; "Do You Hear the People Sing?"; "In My Life"; "On My Own" (Lyric with Trevor Nunn & John Caird); "A Little Fall of Rain"; "Drink With Me"; "Bring Him Home"; "Empty Chairs at Empty Tables"
New York run: Broadway Theatre, March 12, 1987; (still running 10/1/93)

Something of a follow-up to the Royal Shakespeare Company's highly acclaimed non-musical dramatization of Charles Dickens' *Life and Adventures of Nicholas Nickleby*, *Les Misérables* was again directed by Trevor Nunn and John Caird, designed by John Napier, and lighted by David Hersey. (This time, however, it was produced by Cameron Mackintosh in partnership with the RSC.) Once more those responsible put together an epic saga dealing with the theme of social injustice and the plight of the downtrodden that had inspired the earlier massive 19th-century literary classic.

Originally conceived in 1979 by the French team of composer Claude-Michel Schönberg and lyricist Alain Boublil (with the collaboration of poet Jean-Marc Natel), the pop opera gives dramatic life to Victor Hugo's sprawling 1,200 page novel of suffering and salvation during a tumultuous period in French history. The story takes the valiant hero Jean Valjean from 1815 (after he has been paroled following 19 years on a chain gang for stealing a loaf of bread) to the illfated 1832 student uprising in Paris, when Valjean saves the life of Marius (David Bryant), the beloved of his adopted daughter Cosette (Judy Kuhn). Throughout the saga, Valjean is relentlessly hounded by the fanatic police inspector Javert (Terrence Mann) for breaking his parole, a pursuit that ends only when Javert, after chasing his quarry through the sewers of Paris, drowns himself in the Seine because he has violated his obsessive code of justice by letting Valjean escape.

With Herbert Kretzmer writing the English lyrics (and James Fenton credited for "additional material"), *Les Misérables* was successfully launched in London in 1985 at the RSC's Barbican Theatre, then brought to New York two years later by Mackintosh with the original lead, Colm Wilkinson, repeating his impressive performance as Valjean. (Wilkinson was subsequently replaced by Gary Morris, Timothy Shew, and William Solo.) Equally vital to the musical's appeal were Nunn and Caird's inventive, fluid staging and Napier's atmospheric sets—including an immense barricade for the uprising—that moved on a mammoth turntable. *Les Misérables* was the first musical in Broadway history to open at a top ticket price of $50.00. Prior to this production, the most successful musical of French origin (which also crossed the Atlantic via London) had been *Irma la Douce*. Geffen OC.

STARLIGHT EXPRESS

Music: Andrew Lloyd Webber
Lyricist: Richard Stilgoe
Producers: Martin Starger & Lord Grade
Director: Trevor Nunn
Choreographer: Arlene Phillips
Cast: Ken Ard, Jamie Beth Chandler, Steve Fowler, Jane Krakowski, Andrea McArdle, Greg Mowry, Reva Rice, Robert Torti
Songs: "Rolling Stock"; "Engine of Love"; "Pumping Iron"; "Make Up My Heart"; "Starlight Express"; "I Am the Starlight"; "Only You"; "One Rock and Roll Too Many"; "Light at the End of the Tunnel"
New York run: Gershwin Theatre, March 15, 1987; 761 p.

At a cost of well over $8 million—the highest in Broadway history—*Starlight Express* solidified the British invasion by joining *Cats, Me and My Girl,* and *Les Misérables* as one of the four biggest Main Stem attractions during the first half of 1987. Dubbed *Cats* on wheels, this hi-tech spectacle offered not only humanized railroad trains but put them on roller skates zooming on multilevel tracks around a glow-in-the-dark Erector-set panorama of the United States (created by John Napier), dominated by a gigantic steel suspension bridge that could turn, spin, dip and rise. The original idea for the fantasy began in 1973 when Andrew Lloyd Webber was asked to write a rock score for an animated television series based on the British equivalent of *The Little Engine That Could.* That never worked out but it started the composer thinking about a vaguely Cinderella-ish fable in which a battered steam engine named Rusty, encouraged by his father named Poppa, wins a race against a flashy diesel locomotive named Greaseball and a slick electric locomotive named Electra. First opening in London in 1984, the show itself became a flashy, slick hit (the original version offered skaters on ramps that encircled the theatre), then was reconceived for the American production requiring the renovation of the Gershwin Theatre (formerly the Uris) that alone cost $2.5 million.
MCA SC.

Starlight Express. The "Engine of Love" number with Greg Mowry, Reva Rice, Jane Krakowski, Lola Knox (understudy for Jamie Beth Chandler), and Andrea McArdle. (©Martha Swope)

ANYTHING GOES

Music & lyrics: Cole Porter
Book: Timothy Crouse & John Weidman based on original by P. G. Wodehouse
& Guy Bolton, Howard Lindsay & Russel Crouse
Producer: Lincoln Center Theatre (Gregory Mosher, Bernard Gersten)
Director: Jerry Zaks
Choreographer: Michael Smuin
Cast: Patti LuPone, Howard McGillin, Bill McCutcheon, Rex Everhart, Anne
Francine, Linda Hart, Anthony Heald, Kathleen Mahony-Bennett
Songs: Same as original production plus "No Cure Like Travel"; "Easy to Love";
"I Want to Row on the Crew"; "Friendship"; "It's De-Lovely"; "Goodbye,
Little Dream, Goodbye"
New York run: Vivian Beaumont Theatre, October 13, 1987; 804 p.

(See page 88.)

INTO THE WOODS

Music & lyrics: Stephen Sondheim
Book: James Lapine
Producers: Heidi Landesman, Rocco Landesman, Rick Steiner, M. Anthony
Fisher, Frederic Mayerson, Jujamcyn Theatres
Director: James Lapine
Cast: Bernadette Peters, Joanna Gleason, Chip Zien, Tom Aldredge, Robert
Westenberg, Barbara Bryne, Kim Crosby, Danielle Ferland, Merle Lou-
ise, Ben Wright, Joy Franz, Edmund Lyndeck, Kay McClelland, Lauren
Mitchell
Songs: "Into the Woods"; "Hello, Little Girl"; "I Know Things Now"; "Giants in
the Sky"; "Agony"; "It Takes Two"; "Stay With Me"; "Any Moment";
"Last Midnight"; "No More"; "No One Is Alone"; "Children Will Listen"
New York run: Martin Beck Theatre, November 5, 1987; 764 p.

First tried out at the Old Globe Theatre in San Diego in December 1986, *Into the
Woods* took a look at the darker—or grimmer—side of fairy tales in dealing with
the themes of communal responsibility, the importance of showing consideration
to others, and the values we pass on to our children. The story brings together
such familiar characters as Cinderella and her Prince, Jack the Giant Killer, Little
Red Ridinghood and the Wolf, Rapunzel, Snow White, and Sleeping Beauty, plus
two original characters, a Baker and his wife, and puts them in a plotty tale that
gets somewhat burdened down by the allegorical references. This was Stephen
Sondheim's second musical with librettist-director James Lapine, the first being
Sunday in the Park With George. It also involved the same costar (Bernadette Peters), set designer (Tony Straiges), costume designer (Patricia Zipprodt), lighting
designer (Richard Nelson), and music director (Paul Gemignani). During the run,
Miss Peters was followed by Phylicia Rashad, Betsy Joslyn, Nancy Dussault,
and Ellen Foley. In the summer of 1988, Dick Cavett took over the part of the Narrator for two months. The road company, which toured for 10 months, was headed by Cleo Laine (Witch), Mary Gordon Murray (Cinderella), and Charlotte Rae
(Jack's Mother).
RCA OC/ Theatre Comm. Group (1987)/ TW.

THE PHANTOM OF THE OPERA

Music: Andrew Lloyd Webber
Lyrics: Charles Hart, Richard Stilgoe
Book: Richard Stilgoe & Andrew Lloyd Webber
Producer: Cameron Mackintosh & The Really Useful Theatre Co.
Director: Harold Prince
Choreographer: Gillian Lynne
Cast: Michael Crawford, Sarah Brightman, Steve Barton, Judy Kaye, Cris Groenendaal, Nicholas Wyman, Leila Martin, David Romano, Elisa Heinsohn, George Lee Andrews
Songs: "Think of Me"; "Angel of Music"; "The Phantom of the Opera"; "The Music of the Night"; "Prima Donna"; "All I Ask of You"; "Masquerade"; "Wishing You Were Somehow Here Again"; "The Point of No Return
New York run: Majestic Theatre, January 26, 1988; (still running 10/1/93)

Turn-of-the-century French novelist Gaston Leroux wrote *Le Fantôme de l'Opéra* after visiting the subterranean depths of the Paris Opera House—including its man-made lake. Though not a success when published in 1911, the ghoulish tale of the mad, disfigured Phantom who lives in the bowels of the theatre and does away with those who would thwart the operatic career of his beloved Christine, became internationally celebrated in 1925 when it served as a movie vehicle for Lon Chaney. (Subsequent film versions were made in 1943 with Claude Rains, in 1962 with Herbert Lom, in 1989 with Robert Englund, and—for television—in 1982 with Maximilian Schell.)

In 1984 a stage adaptation, using excerpts from public-domain operas by Verdi, Gounod, and Offenbach, was written and directed by Ken Hill and produced by Joan Littlewood at an East London fringe theatre. Andrew Lloyd Webber thought it might be developed into a campy West End musical—something along the lines of *The Rocky Horror Show*—that he would co-produce with Cameron Mackintosh. After reading the Leroux novel, however, Lloyd Webber realized that far from being a penny dreadful, Leroux's work was a genuinely romantic and moving tale, and he decided to write the score himself. His lyricist and co-adapter was Richard Stilgoe and his director was Harold Prince. After a tryout of the first act at a summer festival at his home in Sydmonton (with Colm Wilkinson as the Phantom and Lloyd Webber's wife Sarah Brightman as Christine), the composer felt that there was need for a more romantic approach in the lyrics and, after first trying to enlist Alan Jay Lerner and then Tim Rice, he settled on the relatively inexperienced Charles Hart to augment Stilgoe's work.

The Phantom of the Opera opened in London in 1986 with Michael Crawford and Miss Brightman. It won a resoundingly affirmative reception for its cast, staging, and scenic effects, including a chandelier that descends from the auditorium ceiling and crashes on stage. At this writing, the musical is still running at Her Majesty's Theatre. Basically the same production was transferred to Broadway, with Crawford, Miss Brightman, and Steve Barton (as The Phantom's romantic rival) repeating their roles. A presold hit with an $18 million advance, the show made Andrew Lloyd Webber the first composer to have three musicals running simultaneously in London and New York. (The other two: *Cats,* and *Starlight Express.)*

So far during the Broadway run, Crawford has been succeeded by Timothy Nolen and Cris Groenendaal; Miss Brightman by Patti Cohenour and Rebecca Luker; Barton by Kevin Gray; and Judy Kaye by Marilyn Caskey. Two road companies opened in 1989: the first, in Los Angeles, had a cast headed by Crawford, Dale Kristien, Reece Holland, and Leigh Munro; the second, in Toronto, featured Colm Wilkinson, Rebecca Caine, Byron Nease, and Lyse Guerin.
Polydor OC/ Henry Holt (1987).

The Phantom of the Opera. Michael Crawford and Sarah Brightman. (Clive Barda)

CHESS

Music: Benny Andersson and Bjorn Ulvaeus
Lyrics: Tim Rice
Book: Richard Nelson; based on an idea by Tim Rice
Producer: Shubert Organization; 3 Knights Ltd.; Robert Fox Ltd.
Director: Trevor Nunn
Choreographer: Lynne Taylor-Corbett
Cast: Judy Kuhn, David Carroll, Philip Casnoff, Dennnis Parlato, Marcia Mitzman, Paul Harman, Harry Goz, Ann Crumb
Songs: "The Story of Chess"; "Quartet"; "Nobody's Side"; "Terrace Duet"; "Pity the Child"; "Heaven Help My Heart"; "Anthem"; "One Night in Bangkok"; "You and I"; "I Know Him So Well"; "Someone Else's Story"; "Endgame"
New York run: Imperial Theatre, April 28, 1988; 68 p.

There have been musicals about the cold war (e.g. *Leave It to Me!, Silk Stockings*), but *Chess* was the first to treat the conflict seriously, using an international chess match as a metaphor. Tim Rice first tried to interest his former partner, Andrew Lloyd Webber, in the project. Like the Lloyd Webber-Rice shows *Jesus Christ Superstar* and *Evita, Chess* originated as a successful record album before it became a stage production. The story concerns itself with a romantic triangle involving a Bobby Fischer type American chess champion, his Russian opponent who defects to the West, and the Hungarian born American "second" who transfers her affections from the American to the Russian without bringing happiness to anyone. As staged in London, the show was an elaborate high tech spectacle with minimal dialogue. Though a sellout for most of its three year run, it never quite made back its initial investment there. A revised version, in a more conventional dramatic form (and the added song "Someone Else's Story"), opened in New York, where the show lost $6 million. RCA OC

JEROME ROBBINS' BROADWAY

Music and lyrics: Miscellaneous writers
Producers: The Shubert Organization, Roger Berlind, Suntory Intl. Corp., Byron Goldman, Emanuel Azenberg
Director and Choreographer: Jerome Robbins
Cast: Jason Alexander, Charlotte d'Amboise, Susann Fletcher, Susan Kikuchi, Michael Kubala, Robert LaFosse, Jane Lanier, Joey McKneely, Luis Perez, Faith Prince, Debbie Shapiro, Scott Wise
Songs: "New York, New York" (Leonard Bernstein-Betty Comden, Adolph Green); "Charleston" (Morton Gould); "Comedy Tonight" (Stephen Sondheim); "West Side Story" dances (Berstein); "The Small House of Uncle Thomas" (Richard Rodgers-Oscar Hammerstein II); "You Gotta Have a Gimmick" (Styne-Sondheim); "I'm Flying" (Mark Charlap-Carolyn Leigh); "On a Sunday by the Sea" ballet (Styne); "Mr Monotony" (Irving Berlin); "Fiddler on the Roof" scenes (Jerry Bock-Sheldon Harnick)
New York run: Imperial Theatre, February 26, 1989; 633 p.

The stage equivalent of MGM's *That's Entertainment* series, *Jerome Robbins' Broadway* is a sampling of highlights from Robbins' 21-year career—from *On the Town* in 1944 to *Fiddler on the Roof* in 1964. Featured in this well-organized *déjà vu* revue (which cost $8.8 million and utilizes a cast of 62) are sequences from nine of the 15 productions for which Robbins' served as choreographer or director-choreographer, plus one number, "Comedy Tonight" from *A Funny Thing Happened on the Way to the Forum,* which he had been called in to stage during the show's tryour and for which he received no program credit. Another piece, Irving Berlin's "Mr. Monotony," makes its Broadway debut in this production since it had been cut out of both *Miss Liberty* and *Call Me Madam.* The show established a new top ticket price of $55, subsequenlty raised to $60. So far during the run, Jason Alexander has been succeeded by Terrence Mann, and Debbie Shapiro by Karen Mason.
RCA OC.

Grand Hotel. David Carroll and Liliane Montevecchi (Martha Swope)

GRAND HOTEL

Music and lyrics: Robert Wright and George Forrest; *Music and lyrics by Maury Yeston; **Lyrics revised by Maury Yeston

Book: Luther Davis; based on Vicki Baum's Grand Hotel

Producers: Martin Richards, Mary Lee Johnson, Sam Crothers, Sander Jacobs, Kenneth D. Greenblatt, Paramount Pictures, Jujamcyn Theatres, in association with Marvin A. Krauss

Director and Choreographer: Tommy Tune

Cast: John Wylie, Yvonne Marceau and Pierre Dulaline, Timothy Jerome, Jane Krakowski, Michael Jeter, Karen Akers, Liliane Montevecchi, David Carroll

Songs: "The Grand Parade"*; "As It Should Be"**; "Some Have, Some Have Not"**; "At the Grand Hotel"*; "Who Couldn't Dance With You"; "The Boston Merger"**; "Love Can't Happen"*; "I Waltz Alone"**; "Roses at the Station"**

New York run: Martin Beck Theatre; November 12, 1989; 1,018 p.

Instead of a linear story, Tommy Tune interwove the stories of the staff and guests of the Grand Hotel with a choreographer's vision and swirled them about for almost two intermissionless hours. The stories of the penniless Baron (David Carroll) turned cat burglar who fell in love with the aging ballerina (Liliane Montevecchi) instead of stealing her jewels as he had planned; the devoted dogsbody (Karen Akers) who loves the ballerina; the industrial magnate (Timothy Jerome) who wrestles with his conscience before surrendering to the big lie; the young out of work typist (Jane Krakowski) who dreams of becoming a success in Hollywood but has to sell herself first; and the accountant (Michael Jeter) who wants to live before his unnamed fatal illness carries him off were all fluidly unfolded through crosscutting scenes and dance, dance, dance on a dazzling Tony Walton set that placed the orchestra on a level above the hotel lobby.

During the run, the production moved to the Gershwin Theatre. David Carroll was replaced by John Schneider and later by Rex Smith; Liliane Montevecchi by Zina Bethune and later by Cyd Charisse (making her Broadway debut); Michael Jeter by Austin Pendelton; Jane Krakowski by Lynette Perry; Karen Akers by Valerie Cutko.

Vicki Baum's novel had been a play in Berlin, had had a successful run on Broadway (459 performances during the 1930-31 season) and had been a 1932 megastarred Hollywood film, with a cast headed by Greta Garbo, John and Lionel Barrymore, and Joan Crawford. In 1958 the team of Wright and Forrest, book writer Luther Davis and director Albert Marre presented *At the Grand* in California. (It opened in Los Angeles and closed in San Francisco.) "We'll Take a Glass Together" was from that earlier version. The cast was headed by Paul Muni and Joan Diener and lasted eight weeks.

RCA/OC

GYPSY

Music: Jule Styne
Lyrics: Stephen Sondheim
Book: Arthur Laurents
Producers: Barry and Fran Weissler
Director: Arthur Laurents
Choreography: Original production directed and choreographed by Jerome Robbins; Mr. Robbins' choreography reproduced by Bonnie Walker
Cast: Tyne Daley, Crista Moore, Tracy Venner, Robert Lambert, Jonathan Hadary, John Remme
Songs: Same as original production
New York run: St. James Theatre, November 16, 1989; 477 p.

(See page 182.)

CITY OF ANGELS

Music: Cy Coleman
Lyrics: David Zippel
Book: Larry Gelbart
Producers: Nick Vanoff, Roger Berlind, Jujamcyn Theaters, Suntory International Corp., The Shubert Organization
Director: Michael Blakemore
Choreographer: musical numbers staged by Walter Painter
Cast: James Naughton, Gregg Edelman, Randy Graff, Dee Hoty, Kay McClelland, Rene Auberjonois
Songs: "Double Talk"; "What You Don't Know About Women"; "The Buddy System"; "With Every Breath I Take"; "Ev'rybody's Gotta Be Somewhere"; "All Ya Have to Do Is Wait"; "You're Nothing Without Me"; "It Needs Work"; "You Can Always Count on Me"
New York run: Virginia Theatre, December 11, 1989; 878 p.

In *City of Angels*, a spoof of the hard boiled private eye movies of the '40s, Larry Gelbart (*A Funny Thing Happened on the Way to the Forum*) chronicled the troubles of Stein (Greg Edelman), a writer of detective fiction who is in Hollywood working to adapt his own novel about the detective Stone (James Naughton) into a screenplay. The story begins with Stone in hospital with a bullet wound in his shoulder commenting on how it happened. Shortly thereafter, the scene shifts as a man sitting at a typewriter appears on stage. The man is Stein and the story Stone is telling is the film Stein is writing. As he rewrites, the film is rewound and the actors move backwards and speak backwards. The film sequences are in black, white and gray, and the writer is in living color. Two casts are listed in the program, the Hollywood cast and the film cast. Each Hollywood actor has a counterpart in the film cast on stage, and the action shifts between the film and the real people of the story. Stein's personal life falls apart as his wife accuses him of selling out and she returns to New York. Eventually he realizes he *has* sold out, and he reclaims his values. Michael Blakemore's direction, aided by the Angel City 4, a scat singing Greek chorus, Robin Wagner's sets (grayish for the film sequences and creamy for the "live" scenes) and Florence Klotz's costumes (black, whtie and gray for the film and color for the "real" people) sorted everything out.

Mr. Coleman had been represented on Broadway in April 1989 by *Welcome to the Club* (book by A. E. Hochner and lyrics by A.E. Hochner and Cy Coleman). It lasted 12 performances.
CBS Records Inc./OC

ASPECTS OF LOVE

Music: Andrew Lloyd Webber
Lyrics: Don Black and Charles Hart
Book: Andrew Lloyd Webber; based on the novel by David Garnett
Producer: The Really Useful Theatre Company Inc.
Director: Trevor Nunn
Choreographer: Gillian Lynne
Cast: Ann Crumb, Michael Ball, Kevin Colson, Walter Charles, Kathleen Rowe McAllen, Deanna DuClos, Danielle DuClos
Songs: "Love Changes Everything"; "Seeing Is Believing"; "A Memory of Happy Moments"; "She'd Be Far Better Off With You"; "Other Pleasures"; "The First Man You Remember"; "Anything But Lonely"
New York run: Broadhurst Theatre, April 8, 1990; 377 p.

Andrew Lloyd Webber first mounted a "cabaret" production of *Aspects of Love* in 1983 at the annual music festival on his Sydmonton estate. The musical again involved him with his *The Phantom of the Opera* colleagues Charles Hart, Gillian Lynne, Maria Bjornson, and Andrew Bridges, and reunited him with director Trevor Nunn for the first time since *Starlight Express*.

Based on the novelized autobiography of David Garnett, a minor Bloomsbury figure and a nephew of Virginia Woolf, the prologue of this through-composed soap opera of musical beds covers a seventeen year period. It begins in 1964 with Alex recounting the story of his life ("Love Changes Everything"). Flashback to 1947 when, at 17, he fell in love with 25 year old Rose Vibert, the star of a touring acting company. He persuaded her to spend her forthcoming two week layoff period lying in with him at his Uncle George's unoccupied estate. George unexpectedly arrived (from an assignation in Paris with mistress Giulietta, who lives in Rome) and fell in love with Rose. In La Ronde fashion, Alex returns to the army, George continues his relationship with Giulietta, but eventually marries Rose (she also has a bit of a fling with Giulietta). George and Rose produce a daughter (who may or may not be the daughter of Alex), Jenny, who falls madly in love with Alex when he gets back to George and Rose some twelve years later. George dies, Alex falls in love with Giulietta. Perhaps to continue this madness.

Polydor/London OC

Aspects of Love. Ann Crumb and Michael Ball (Clive Barda)

ONCE ON THIS ISLAND

Music: Stephen Flaherty
Lyrics and book: Lynn Ahrens (based on *My Love, My Love* by Rosa Guy)
Producers: Shubert Organization, Capital Cities/ABC, Suntory International and James Walsh in association with Playwrights Horizons
Director and choreographer: Graciela Daniele
Cast: Jerry Dixon, Andrea Frierson, Sheila Gibbs, La Chanze, Kecia Lewis-Evans, Afi McClendon, Gerry McIntyre, Milton Craig Nealey, Nikki Rene, Eric Riley, Ellis E. Williams
Songs: "We Dance"; "One Small Girl"; "And the Gods Heard Her Prayer"; "Pray"; "Forever Yours"; "The Sad Tale of Beauxhommes"; "Mama Will Provide"; "Some Girls"; "Why We Tell the Story"
New York run: Booth Theater, October 18, 1990; 469 p.

Set in the French Antilles, the story of *Once on This Island* is a fable told to calm a young girl during a storm. It tells of the journey of Ti Moune (La Chanze), plucked from just such a storm by the gods and sheltered in a tree. She grows into a beautiful peasant girl who rescues Daniel (Jerry Dixon), the mulatto son of a wealthy landowner after he has been hurt in an automobile accident. Ti Moune makes a pact with the gods—her life for Daniel's— for she is convinced that the power of her love is so strong it can conquer death. Eventually he is healed, and even though he is grateful for her help, he rejects her love. The gods give her eternal life by turning her into a tree. The musical was first produced at Playwrights Horizons for 3 weeks in May 1990, then transferred in tact to the Booth Theatre in October.
RCA/OC.

Miss Saigon. Lea Salonga and Rian R. Baldomero. (Trench/Marcus)

MISS SAIGON

Music: Claude-Michel Schönberg
Lyrics: Richard Maltby, Jr. and Alain Boublil; adapted from original French lyrics by Alain Boublil; additional material by Richard Maltby, Jr.
Producer: Cameron Mackintosh
Director: Nicholas Hytner
Musical Staging: Bob Avian
Cast: Jonathan Pryce, Lea Salonga, Hinton Battle, Willy Falk, Barry K. Bernal, Liz Callaway, Kam Cheng
Songs: "The Heat Is On in Saigon"; "The Movie in My Mind"; "Why God, Why?"; "Sun and Moon"; "The Last Night of the World"; "The Morning of the Dragon"; "I'd Give My Life for You"; "What a Waste"; "The American Dream"
New York run: Broadway Theatre, April 11, 1991 (still running 10/1/93)

First there was difficulty finding a suitable Broadway house. *Les Misérables* moved to the Imperial to make the Broadway available, and while the Broadway is one of New York's larger houses, it is much smaller than London's Drury Lane (a significant fact when the production includes sets such as a life-size helicopter), where *Miss Saigon* opened September 20, 1989. Then in August 1990 Actors Equity ruled that Asian actors must have acting opportunities racism has denied them in the past, and that Jonathan Pryce (who had created the role in London) could not play the Eurasion pimp. Cameron Mackintosh threatened to cancel the production and to return the $25 million in advance ticket sales. (The advance later grew to about $37 million.) After petitioning by its members, Actors Equity reversed its decision saying it "had applied an honest and moral principle in an inappropriate manner." Later Equity challenged the casting of Lea Salonga in the title role, but lost in arbitration. Then the helicopter landed.

Claude-Michel Schönberg and Alain Boublil *(Les Misérables)* updated Belasco/Puccini's *Madama Butterfly* to a through-sung musical (only some of the songs are listed in the program). In a 1989 interview Mr. Schönberg and Mr. Boublil explained that seeing a news photograph of a Vietnamese woman giving up her child to an American G.I. during the fall of Saigon gave them the idea for a modern operatic story showing the clash of two cultures. There the similarity to Puccini ends. The tale begins with the fall of Saigon in 1975, then crosses time and place between 1975 and 1978 in Saigon, Bangkok, and the United States. Kim (Lea Salonga and at some performances Kam Cheng), a young Vietnamese woman from the country is forced to become a bar girl in Saigon. On her first meeting with Chris (Willy Falk), a Marine guard at the U.S. Embassy, they fall in love. Not knowing she is pregnant, Chris, evacuated by that famous helicopter, returns home and marries. A few years later he and his American wife come back to find Kim, who wants Chris to take their son back to the U.S. To make sure he does, she kills herself. Superimposed on this innocence is the Engineer (Jonathan Pryce), the pimp, the fixer, the sleazy epitome of naked greed who can survive under any circumstances.

During the run, Jonathan Pryce was replaced by Francis Ruivivar, then Herman Sebek. Lea Salonga was replaced by Leila Florentino.

With the opening of *Miss Saigon*, Cameron Mackintosh had four productions in New York — *Cats, Les Misérables* and *The Phantom of the Opera* being the other three. *Miss Saigon* was the first musical production to charge $100 for the mezzanine seats.

THE SECRET GARDEN

Music: Lucy Simon

Book and lyrics: Marsha Norman; based on the novel by Frances Hodgson Burnett

Producers: Heidi Landesman, Rick Steiner, Frederick H. Mayerson, Elizabeth Williams, Jujamcyn Theatres and Dodger Productions

Director: Susan H. Schulman

Choreographer: Michael Lichtefeld

Cast: John Babcock, Daisy Eagan, Alison Fraser, Rebecca Luker, John Cameron Mitchell, Mandy Patinkin, Barbara Rosenblat, Tom Toner, Robert Westenberg

Songs: "There's a Girl"; "The House Upon the Hill"; " I Heard Someone Crying"; "A Fine White Horse"; "Show Me the Key"; "Lily's Eyes"; "Round Shouldered Man"; "The Girl I Mean to Be"; "Come Spirit, Come Charm"; "How Could I Ever Know?"

New York run: St. James Theater, April 25, 1991; 706 p.

Inspired by the sentimental Frances Hodgson Burnett novel, *The Secret Garden* tells the story of a spoiled, lonely Mary Lennox (Daisy Eagan, but Kimberly Mahon on Tuesday evenings and Wednesday matinees), who, orphaned by a cholera epidemic in India, is sent to live at Misselthwaite Manor in Yorkshire with her uncle Archibald (Mandy Patinkin). Still in mourning for his wife, Lily (Rebecca Luker), who died 10 years earlier in childbirth, and grief stricken for his bedridden 10 year old son, Archibald suffuses the manor with gloom and mystery. Mary discovers a secret garden, formerly Lily's, and in revitalizing it she restores life to her sick cousin and her miserable uncle. Marsha Norman who had previously won the Pulitzer Prize for her play *'night Mother,* won a Tony for Best Book of a Musical. Daisy Eagan became the youngest actress ever to win a Tony.

Columbia OC.

The Secret Garden. Daisy Eagan, Rebecca Luker, Mandy Patinkin. (Bob Marshak)

The Will Rogers Follies. Keith Carradine and the ensemble.

THE WILL ROGERS FOLLIES

Music: Cy Coleman
Lyrics: Betty Comden and Adolph Green
Book: Peter Stone
Producers: Pierre Cossette, Martin Richards, Sam Crothers, James M. Nederlander, Stewart F. Lane, Max Weitzenhoffer in association with Japan Satellite Broadcasting, Inc.
Director and choreographer: Tommy Tune
Cast: Keith Carradine, Dee Hoty, Dick Latessa, Cady Huffman, Vince Bruce, Paul Ukena Jr., and the voice of Gregory Peck
Songs: "Will-a-Manina"; "Give a Man Enough Rope"; "My Unknown Someone"; "No Man Left for Me"; "Once in a While"; "Without You"; "Just a Couple Indian Boys"; "Never Met a Man I Didn't Like"
New York run: The Palace Theatre, May 1, 1991; 983 p.

Ziegfeld's *Follies* were revues with innumerable dancing girls on stairways they could ascend and descend, assorted acts, and headliners. *The Will Rogers Follies* has lots of dancing girls ascending and descending the stairway, the disembodied voice of Florenz Ziegfeld coming from the rafters, and a dog act. Rogers was one of the headliners of the *Follies,* but in Peter Stone's book Rogers (Keith Carradine) seems to have been the only one. Designed as a "this is my life" production, Rogers returns from heaven to put on—with Ziegfeld's guidance (the voice of Gregory Peck)—one more Follies. Periodically Ziegfeld's Favorite (Cady Huffman) traipses across the stage holding up cards to identify the scene. Tommy Tune's exhuberantly inventive dances recalled some of the flavor of the Ziegfeld productions. During the run Keith Carradine was succeeded by Mac Davis and Larry Gatlin, Dee Hoty by Nancy Ringham, and Cady Huffman by Marla Maples.
Columbia OC.

CRAZY FOR YOU

Music: George Gershwin
Lyrics: Ira Gershwin
Book: Ken Ludwig; co-conceived by Ken Ludwig and Mike Ockrent; inspired by material by Guy Bolton and John McGowan
Producer: Roger Horchow and Elizabeth Williams
Director: Mike Ockrent
Choreographer: Susan Stroman
Cast: Harry Groener, Jodi Benson, Beth Leavel, Bruce Adler, Jane Connell, John Hillner, Irene Pawk, Stephen Temperley, Amelia White, The Manhattan Rhythm Kings
Songs: "K-ra-zy for You"; "I Can't Be Bothered Now"; "Bidin' My Time"; "Things Are Looking Up"; "Could You Use Me"; "Shall We Dance?"; "Someone to Watch Over Me"; "Slap That Bass" (orchestration by Sid Ramin); "Embraceable You"; "Tonight's the Night (lyric by Ira Gershwin and Gus Kahn); "I Got Rhythm"; "The Real American Folk Song (Is a Rag)"; "What Causes That?"; "Naughty Baby" (lyric by Ira Gershwin and Desmond Carter); "Stiff Upper Lip"; "They Can't Take That Away from Me"; "But Not For Me"; "Nice Work If You Can Get It"
New York run: Shubert Theater, February 19, 1992 (still running 10/1/93)

For *Crazy For You* Ken Ludwig (author of *Lend Me a Tenor*) and Mike Ockrent (director of *Me and My Girl*) used five numbers and part of a sixth ("Bidin' My Time," "Could You Use Me?," "Embraceable You," "I Got Rhythm," "But Not For Me," and part of "Bronco Busters") from the 1930 score of *Girl Crazy*, and added a dozen more songs, of which two ("Tonight's the Night" and "What Causes That") were rediscovered in a warehouse in Seacaucus, New Jersey in 1982. In their version of boy-meets-girl, banker Bobby Child (Harry Groener), who would rather be in show business, is sent by his overbearing mother (Jane Connell) to foreclose a mortgage on a property in Deadrock, Arkansas. (Bobby also has an overbearing fiancée.) The property turns out to be a theatre. Bobby falls for the postmistress (Jodi Benson) who just happens to be the daughter of the man with the mortgage. Then boy loses girl, and for a while there are mistaken identities à la Marx Brothers. At the end they "put on a show" to save the theatre, and boy gets girl back.
Broadway Angel OC.

Crazy For You. Harry Groener and ensemble (Joan Marcus)

FIVE GUYS NAMED MOE

Music and lyrics: Miscellaneous writers
Book: Clarke Peters
Producer: Cameron Mackintosh
Director-Choreographer: Charles Augins
Cast: Jerry Dixon, Doug Eskew, Milton Craig Nealy, Kevin Ramsey, Jeffrey D. Sams, Glen Turner
Songs: "Early in the Morning" (Louis Jordan/Leo Hickman/Dallas Bartley); "Beware, Brother, Beware" (Morry Lasco/Dick Adams/Fleecie Moore); "I LIke 'em Fat Like That" (Claude Demetriou/Louis Jordan); "Push Ka Pi Shi Pie" (Joe Willoughby/Louis Jordan/Walt Merrick); "Ain't Nobody Here But Us Chickens" (Joan Whitney/Alex Kramer); "Choo, Choo, Ch'boogie" (Vaughn Horton/Denver Darling/Milton Gabler); "Is You Is or Is You Ain't My Baby?" (S. Austin/Louis Jordan)
New York run: Eugene O'Neill Theatre, April 8, 1992; 445 p.

Some of the songs associated with Louis Jordan (alto sax player, band singer, composer, and lyricist) are presented in a perfectly innocuous story of five guys named Moe who leap out of a jukebox to reveal to a sixth named Nomax how to repair his relationship with his friend Lorraine. Clarke Peters and Charles Augins also involve the audience in lending a helping hand, first by showering them (hundreds of leaflets are thrown from the stage and from the balcony) with the printed lyrics of "Push Ka Pi Shi Pie," so that everyone can teach Nomax the song, and later by having the actors lead a conga line out to the bar to buy refreshments after all that hard work. The story line gets lost in Act II, but the energy, charm and talent of all six guys appeals to audiences in what is a watered down version of a British Music Hall production.
Columbia OC.

Five Guys Named Moe. Jeffrey Sams, Kevin Ramsey, Doug Eskew, Milton Craig Nealy, Glenn Turner, Jerry Dixon (seated) (Joan Marcus)

289

GUYS AND DOLLS

Music and lyrics: Frank Loesser
Book: Jo Swerling and Abe Burrows
Producers: Dodger Productions, Roger Berlind, Jujamcyn Theaters/TV ASAHI, Kardana Productions and The John F. Kennedy Center for the Performing Arts
Director: Jerry Zaks
Choreogrpher: Christopher Chadman
Cast: Peter Gallagher, Nathan Lane, Josie de Guzman, Faith Prince, Walter Bobbie, John Carpenter, Steve Ryan, Ernie Sabella, J.K. Simmons, Herschel Sparber, Gary Chryst, Scott Wise
Songs: Same as the original production
New York run: Martin Beck Theatre, April 14, 1992 (still running 10/1/93)

(See page 148.)
RCA OC

Guys and Dolls. Peter Gallagher and Josie de Guzman (Martha Swope)

Guys and Dolls. Faith Prince and Nathan Lane as Miss Adelaide and Nathan Detroit (Martha Swope)

Guys and Dolls. "Sit Down You're Rockin' the Boat" (Martha Swope)

JELLY'S LAST JAM

Music: Jelly Roll Morton, musical adaptation and additional music composed by Luther Henderson

Lyrics: Susan Birkenhead

Book: George C. Wolfe

Producers: Margo Lion and Pamela Koslow in association with PolyGram Diversified Entertainment, 126 Second Avenue Corp./Hal Luftig, Roger Hess, Jujamcyn Theaters/TV Ashahi and Herb Alpert

Director: George C. Wolfe

Choreographer: Hope Clarke

Tap Choreography: Gregory Hines and Ted L. Levy

Cast: Gregory Hines, Keith David, Savion Glover, Stanley Wayne Mathis, Tonya Pinkins, Mary Bond Davis, Ann Duquesnay, Mamie Duncan-Gibbs, Stephanie Pope, Ruben Santiago-Hudson, Allison Williams

Songs: "Jelly's Jam"; "In My Day"; "The Creole Way" (music by Luther Henderson); "The Whole World's Waiting' to Sing Your Song"; "Lonely Boy Blues" (traditional); "Michigan Water"; "Something More"; "That's How You Jazz"; "The Chicago Stomp"; "Play the Music for Me"; "Lovin' Is a Lowdown Blues"; "Dr. Jazz" (music by King Oliver and Walter Melrose); "Good Ole New York"; "Too Late Daddy"; "That's the Way We Do Things in New Yawk"; "The Last Rites" (music by Henderson/Morton)

New York run: Virginia Theatre, April 26, 1992; 569 p.

Unlike other "and then he wrote" biographies of composers, *Jelly's Last Jam* not only explores the music, but also explores the man. In the opening scene Jelly Roll Morton (Gregory Hines) is at death facing the Chimney Man (Keith David), the "concierge of your soul," who accuses Morton of having denied his African heritage and of believing that he invented jazz. He forces Morton to re-examine his life and to possibly save his soul. In a series of flashbacks led by the Hunnies (Mamie Duncan-Gibbs, Stephanie Pope and Allison M. Williams), Jelly's life and sins are revealed. Gregory Hines' brilliant and likable performance softened some of the bragadoccio and cruelty of the man.

George C. Wolfe has said "we are all mutts here. We reinvent ourselves striving for some sort of purity." Ferdinand Joseph Le Menthe Morton, a middle class, light skinned Creole of color who disdained darker skinned blacks, reinvented himself to deny his race ("ain't no coon stock in this Creole"), but he absorbed all the culture and street sounds of New Orleans and expressed them in his own music. Keith David was replaced by Ben Vereen during the run, Gregory Hines by Brian Mitchell.

Mercury OC

Jelly's Last Jam. Keith David and Gregory Hines (Martha Swope)

FALSETTOS

Music and lyrics: William Finn
Book: William Finn and James Lapine
Producer: Barry and Fran Weissler
Director: James Lapine
Cast: Michael Rupert, Stephen Bogardus, Chip Zien, Barbara Walsh, Heather MacRae, Carrolee Carmello, Jonathan Kaplan, Andrew Harrison Leeds
Songs: "Four Jews in a Room Bitching"; "A Tight Knit Family"; "Love Is Blind"; "Thrill of First Love"; "I'm Breaking Down"; "March of the Falsettos"; "Making a Home"; "I Never Wanted to Love You"; "Everyone Hates His Parents"; "Unlikely Lovers"; "What Would I Do":
New York run: John Golden Theatre, April 29, 1992; 486 p.

William Finn's *Falsettos* was originally three separately produced one act musicals—*In Troussers* (1987), *The March of the Falsettos* (1981), and *Falsettoland* (1990). In 1991 the Hartford Stage combined the last two into one production.

Falsettos takes place from 1979 to 1981 and is a story of neurotic, bisexual Marvin (Michael Rupert), who leaves his wife Trina (Barbara Walsh) and son Josh (Jonathan Kaplan) to have a life with his friend Wizzer (Stephen Bogardus). Later, Trina marries Marvin's psychiatrist (Chip Zien). Wizzer leaves Marvin, then they reconcile. As Wizzer is dying of AIDS, Jason holds his bar mitzvah in Wizzer's hospital room. This basically simple tale of friends, lovers and family values is told with warmth, love, compassion, and without camp. Michael Rupert, Stephen Bogardus and Chip Zien created their roles in *The March of the Falsettos* and continued them in *Falsettoland.* Mandy Patinkin took over the role of Marvin during the run.

DRG Records recorded March of the *Falsettos* (with Alison Fraser as Trina) and *Falsettoland* (with Faith Prince as Trina). These two recordings are now combined into one package. With the exception of the addition of "I'm Breaking Down," the score is the same.
DRG.

Indexes

Show Index

Composer/Lyricist Index

Composer/Lyricist Index

Librettist Index

Librettist Index

Director Index

Abbott, George
Best Foot Forward, 114
Boys from Syracuse, The, 107
Call Me Madam, 147
Damn Yankees, 167
Fiorello!, 186
Funny Thing Happened on the Way to the
Forum, A, 198
High Button Shoes, 136
Jumbo, 93
Me and Juliet, 157
New Girl in Town, 173
On the Town, 126
On Your Toes, 94 & 264
Once Upon a Mattress, 181
Pajama Game, The, 161
Pal Joey, 112
Too Many Girls, 108
Tree Grows in Brooklyn, A, 152
Where's Charley?, 138
Wonderful Town, 155

Alexander, David
Pal Joey, 153

Alton, Robert
Pal Joey, 153

Anderson, John Murray
Dearest Enemy, 48
Greenwich Village Follies, 31
Jumbo, 93
Life Begins at 8:40, 87
New Faces of 1952, 154
Ziegfeld Follies, 85 & 93

Anthony, Joseph
Most Happy Fella, The, 170
110 in the Shade, 203

Ashman, Howard
Little Shop of Horrors, 262

Augins, Charles
Five Guys Named Moe, 289

Baker, Word
Fantasticks, The, 189
I'm Getting My Act Together and
Taking It on the Road, 252

Balanchine, George
Cabin in the Sky, 111

Bay, Howard
As the Girls Go, 139

Beal, John
New Faces of 1952, 154

Bennett, Michael
Chorus Line, A, 243
Dreamgirls, 261
Follies, 232
My One and Only, 264

Benrimo, J. H.
Blue Paradise, The, 21

Besoyan, Rick
Little Mary Sunshine, 186

Blakemore, Michael
City of Angels,282

Boleslawsky, Richard
Three Musketeers, The, 63

Breen, Robert
Porgy and Bess, 156

Brentano, Felix
Merry Widow, The, 120

Brook, Peter
House of Flowers, 165
Irma la Douce, 190

Brooks, Walter
Shuffle Along, 34

Burnside, R. H.
Watch Your Step, 20

Burrows, Abe
Can-Can, 156
How to Succeed in Business Without
Really Trying, 196
What Makes Sammy Run?, 206

Cacoyannis, Michael
Zorba, 268

Caird, John
Les Miserables, 275

Capalbo, Carmen
Threepenny Opera, The, 159

Carroll, Earl
Earl Carroll Vanities, 76

Carroll, Vinnette
Don't Bother Me, I Can't Cope, 235

Champion, Gower
Bye Bye Birdie, 188
Carnival, 195

Director Index

Choreographer Index

Adolphus, Theodore
Sweethearts, 134

Albertieri, Signor
Firefly, The, 18

Alfred, Julian
Poppy, 40
Vagabond King, The, 48

Alton, Robert
Anything Goes, 88
By Jupiter, 116
DuBarry Was a Lady, 109
Hooray For What!, 100
Leave It to Me!, 105
Life Begins at 8:40,87
Me and Juliet, 157
Pal Joey, 112 & 153
Panama Hattie, 111
Show Is On, The, 97
Too Many Girls, 108
Ziegfeld Follies, 85 & 93

Arenal, Julie
Hair, 224

Astaire, Fred
Sunny, 50

Augins, Charles
Five Guys Named Moe, 289

Avian, Bob
Chorus Line, A, 243
Miss Saigon, 285

Balanchine, George
Babes in Arms, 98
Boys from Syracuse, The, 107
Cabin in the Sky, 111
I Married an Angel, 102
Louisiana Purchase, 110
Merry Widow, The, 120
On Your Toes, 94 & 264
Song of Norway, 124
Where's Charley?, 138
Ziegfeld Follies, 93

Barclift, Nelson
This Is the Army, 117

Barstow, Richard
New Faces of 1952,154

Bennett, David
Andre Charlot's Revue of 1924,42
Rose-Marie, 43
Sunny, 50
Very Good Eddie, 23

Bennett, Michael
Chorus Line, A, 243
Company, 229
Dreamgirls, 261
Follies, 232
My One and Only, 264
Promises, Promises, 226

Berkeley, Busby
Connecticut Yankee, A, 58

Birch, Patricia
Candide, 239
Grease, 234
Little Night Music, A, 237
Pacific Overtures, 245
They're Playing Our Song, 252
You're a Good Man, Charlie Brown, 221

Breaux, Marc
Do Re Mi, 194

Broadbent, Aida
Red Mill, The, 128

Broome, John
Stop the World—I Want to Get Off, 199

Ceballos, Larry
Fifty Million Frenchmen, 69

Chadman, Christopher
Guys and Dolls, 290

Champion, Gower
Bye Bye Birdie, 188
Carnival, 195
42nd Street, 257
Happy Time, The, 222
Hello, Dolly!, 204
Lend an Ear, 139
Sugar, 235

Charmoli, Tony
Woman of the Year, 260

Clarke, Hope
Jelly's Last Jam

Cole, Jack
Funny Thing Happened on the Way to the Forum, A, 198
Jamaica, 176
Kismet, 158
Man of La Mancha, 215

Connolly, Bobby
Desert Song, The, 54

Choreographer Index

Original Major Cast Members Index

(Includes only major cast members of opening night Broadway performances.)

Original Major Cast Members Index

Original Major Cast Members Index

Original Major Cast Members Index

Original Major Cast Members Index

Deagon, Arthur
Rose-Marie, 43

Deane, Sydney
Florodora, 6

Deas, Lawrence
Shuffle Along, 34

DeCarlo, Yvonne
Follies, 232

Deems, Mickey
Little Me, 200

de Gruzman, Josie
Guys and Dolls, 290

DeKoven, Roger
Funny Girl, 207

de la Peña, George
On Your Toes, 264

de Lappe, Gemze
King and I, The, 151
Paint Your Wagon, 152

De Lavallade, Carmen
House of Flowers, 165

Delroy, Irene
Follow Thru, 67

de Luce, Virginia
New Faces of 1952,154

DeMarco, Antonio
Girl Crazy, 72

DeMarco, Renee
Girl Crazy, 72

Demarest, Frances
Blue Paradise, The 21
Madame Sherry, 17

Demarest, William
Earl Carroll Vanities, 76

Demas, Carole
Grease, 234

Dempsey, Jerome
Mystery of Edwin Drood, The, 271

Denham, George
Babes in Toyland, 8

Dennen, Barry
Jesus Christ Superstar, 233

Derr, Richard
Plain and Fancy, 166

Derricks, Cleavant
Dreamgirls, 261

Derwent, Clarence
Three Musketeers, The, 63

De Shields, Andre
Ain't Misbehavin', 251
Wiz, The, 241

Devine, Loretta
Dreamgirls, 261

Diamond, Jack
Kiss Me, Kate, 141

Dickey, Annamary
Allegro, 136

Dickson, Dorothy
Oh, Boy!, 24

Diener, Joan
Kismet, 158
Man of La Mancha, 215

Dillon, Denny
My One and Only, 264

DiLuca, Dino
House of Flowers, 165

Dingle, Charles
Miss Liberty, 144

Dittman, Dean
On the Twentieth Century, 249

Dix, Tommy
Best Foot Forward, 114

Dixon, Jerry
Five Guys Named Moe, 289
Once on This Island, 284

Dixon, Harland
Oh, Kay!, 53
Tree Grows in Brooklyn, A, 152

Dixon, Lee
Oklahoma!, 119

Dodge, Jerry
George M!, 223
Hello, Dolly!, 204

Dolores
Sally, 33

Donahue, Jack
Rosalie, 62
Sunny, 50

Donath, Ludwig
She Loves Me, 202

Donen, Stanley
Pal Joey, 112

Doner, Kitty
Sinbad, 29

Donlevy, Brian
Hit the Deck!, 56
Life Begins at 8:40, 87

336

Original Major Cast Members Index

Original Major Cast Members Index

Original Major Cast Members Index

Grey, Joel
Cabaret, 219
George M!, 223

Griffies, Ethel
Miss Liberty, 144

Griffith, Andy
Destry Rides Aqain, 180

Grimes, Tammy
42nd Street, 257
High Spirits, 208
Unsinkable Molly Brown, The, 191

Groenendaal, Cris
Phantom of the Opera, The, 278

Groener, Harry
Cats, 263
Crazy for You, 288
Oklahoma!, 255

Groody, Louise
Hit the Deck!, 56
No, No, Nanette, 47

Grossmith, Lawrence
Cat and the Fiddle, The, 77

Grout, James
Half a Sixpence, 211

Grove, Betty Ann
George M!, 223
On Yollr Toes. 264

Guittard, Laurence
Little Night Music, A, 237
Oklahoma!, 255

Gunton, Bob
Big River, 270
Evita, 254

Guyse, Sheila
Lost in the Stars, 144

Gwynne, Fred
Irma la Douce, 190

Haakon, Paul
At Home Abroad, 89
Hooray For What!, 100
Mexican Hayride, 122
Show Is On, The, 97

Hackett, Albert
Whoopee, 66

Hadary, Jonathan
Gypsy, 282

Haines, A. Larry
Promises, Promises, 226

Hale, Chester
Music Box Revue, 37

Hale, George
Cocoanuts, The, 51

Haley, Jack
Follow Thru, 67
Inside U.S.A., 137
Take a Chance, 82

Hall, Adelaide
Blackbirds of 1928, 63
Jamaica, 176

Hall, Bettina
Anything Goes, 88
Cat and the Fiddle, The, 77
Little Show, The, 67

Hall, Delores
Best Little Whorehouse in Texas, The, 250

Hall, Juanita
Flower Drum Song, 178
House of Flowers, 165
South Pacific, 143
St. Louis Woman, 129
Street Scene, 132

Hall, Natalie
Music in the Air, 81

Hall, Thurston
Fifty Million Frenchmen, 69

Halliday, Gordon
Shenandoah, 242

Halliday, Robert
Desert Song, The, 54
New Moon, The, 64
Tip-Toes, 52

Hallor, Edith
Leave It to Jane, 26

Hamilton, Caroline
Robin Hood, 5

Hamilton, Gloria
Lend an Ear, 139

Hamilton, Nancy
New Faces, 86

Hamilton, Thomas
As Thousands Cheer, 83

Hanan, Stephen
Cats, 263

Haney, Carol
Pajama Game, The, 161

Hanley, Ellen
Annie Get Your Gun, 130
Fiorello!, 186

Original Major Cast Members Index

344

Original Major Cast Members Index

Original Major Cast Members Index

Original Major Cast Members Index

Original Major Cast Members Index

Original Major Cast Members Index

Original Major Cast Members Index

Theatre Index

369

Theatre Index

Theatre Index

Online
Communities

Commerce, Community Action, and the Virtual University

Chris Werry and Miranda Mowbray, Editors

Hewlett-Packard Company

www.hp.com/hpbooks

Prentice Hall PTR
Upper Saddle River, NJ 07458
www.phptr.com

Library of Congress Cataloging-in-Publication Data available

Editorial/Production Supervision: *Faye Gemmellaro*
Acquisitions Editor: *Jill Pisoni*
Editorial Assistant: *Justin Somma*
Marketing Manager: *Dan DePasquale*
Manufacturing Manager: *Maura Zaldivar*
Cover Design Director: *Jerry Votta*
Cover Design: *Talar Agasyan*
Interior Design: *Gail Cocker-Bogusz*

Manager, Hewlett-Packard Retail Book Publishing: *Patricia Pekary*
Editor, Hewlett-Packard Professional Books: *Susan Wright*

Published by Prentice Hall PTR
Prentice-Hall, Inc.
Upper Saddle River, NJ 07458

The Free Universal Encyclopedia and Learning Resource
Copyright 1999 Richard Stallman
Verbatim copying and redistribution of this entire article are permitted in any
medium provided this notice is preserved.

Prentice Hall books are widely used by corporations and government agencies for
training, marketing, and resale.

The publisher offers discounts on this book when ordered in bulk quantities.
For more information, contact: Corporate Sales Department, Phone: 800-382-3419;
Fax: 201-236-7141; E-mail: corpsales@prenhall.com; or write: Prentice Hall PTR,
Corp. Sales Dept., One Lake Street, Upper Saddle River, NJ 07458.

Printed in the United States of America
10 9 8 7 6 5 4 3 2 1

ISBN 0-13-032382-9

Prentice-Hall International (UK) Limited, *London*
Prentice-Hall of Australia Pty. Limited, *Sydney*
Prentice-Hall Canada Inc., *Toronto*
Prentice-Hall Hispanoamericana, S.A., *Mexico*
Prentice-Hall of India Private Limited, *New Delhi*
Prentice-Hall of Japan, Inc., *Tokyo*
Pearson Education Asia P.T.E., Ltd.
Editora Prentice-Hall do Brasil, Ltda., *Rio de Janeiro*

To everyone in our online communities

Contents

Chapter 4   Computer Networks Linking Network Communities
by Robin B. Hamman 71

Chapter 5   Reducing Demographic Bias *by Miranda Mowbray* 97

Chapter 12 The Free Universal Encyclopedia and Learning Resource
by Richard Stallman 257

Chapter 16 The Rise and Persistence of the Technological Community
Ideal *by Randy Connolly* 317

Chapter 17 Online Community Action: Perils and Possibilities
by Luciano Paccagnella 365

Preface

This book will not tell you how to become an Internet millionaire. In our opinion, there are more interesting things that you can do with online communities than just use them for e-commerce.

Online communities are increasingly important in commerce, in education, and in the nonprofit sector. In this book, experts from these three areas write about the theory and practice of online communities. Issues discussed include the effects of commercial communities on the social interaction of community members; intellectual property implications of the commercial provision of educational online communities; alternative models for online community organization; and lessons drawn from contributors' experiences in the use of online communities for development work, in online activism, and in the Open Source movement. As part of their studies of the use of online communities, several authors also examine the practical implications of the metaphors and rhetorical strategies that are commonly used to talk about them.

Online communities are an international phenomenon, and this book has a truly international perspective. There are chapters by authors in New Zealand, the United States, France, Great Britain, Canada, Mexico, and Italy, and the chapter of interviews with staff of Oxfam GB mentions uses of the Internet in Mali, South Africa, Burkina Faso, Brazil, Nicaragua, Bosnia, and Albania, among other places. Much of the literature on online communities has tended to look only at the United States—or at best, only in the United States, Canada, Western Europe, and Australia. This book's chapters about the work of Oxfam and about Red Escolar in Mexico give evidence that some of the most interesting developments, both potentially and actually, are outside these regions. This book is itself the product of an online community. Almost all the communications between editors and contributors took place over the Internet. We (the editors) live in different continents, and would have had a hard task indeed to edit this book without the Internet.

At the end of William Mitchell's book *City of Bits* (1995), there is an image of a near-future in which "bitsphere planners and designers" shape the interfaces through which commerce, education, and community take place. He writes:

> For designers and planners, the task of the twenty-first century will be to build the bitsphere—a worldwide, electronically mediated environment in which networks are everywhere. . . . This unprecedented, hyperextended habitat will transcend national boundaries; the increasingly dense and widespread connectivity that it supplies will quickly create opportunities—the first in the history of humankind—for planning and designing truly worldwide communities (p. 167).

We think that this vision of the civic design of the bitsphere is praiseworthy, but that more groups should be involved than just the designers and planners that Mitchell mentions. In keeping with this, we considered it important that this book should include contributions by authors with different backgrounds. Janelle Brown is a journalist; Robin Hamman and Miranda Mowbray are employed by high-technology companies; Richard Stallman and Doug Schuler are long-standing Internet activists; Walter Aprile and Teresa Vazquez Mantecón work at the Latinamerican Institute for Educational Communication; other authors include academics in several different disciplines. We have not attempted to produce a book with a homogeneous tone, since we believe that the variety of styles and perspectives in different chapters is valuable, and that preserving this variety is in the spirit of online community.

Although we believe that the Internet has a great potential for social good, we are far from believing that this potential will necessarily be realized. Much of this book describes worrying trends in the way online communities are currently being used, and warnings about future developments. We have encouraged the contributors to include practical recommendations for the administrators and citizens of online communities that may help to counter, or at least defend against, these trends. Randy Connolly's fascinating historical chapter is more pessimistic: he argues that the online community ideal may be not only unrealizable, but actually counterproductive. He shows that the rhetoric with which earlier communication and transportation technologies were greeted in the United States is in some cases eerily reminiscent of the optimistic predictions made for the social effects of Internet technologies. But these earlier technologies, far from increasing social cohesion as was promised, arguably reduced it. So why should the Internet be different?

Part 1 of the book looks at commercial online communities—that is, communities on Internet sites that are run for a profit. Commercial online community sites are used by many millions of people. They have become an important part of how the Internet is experienced and are central to contemporary models of e-commerce. However, when we investigated the literature and visited conferences on online communities before working on this book, we found relatively little specifically written about the social effects of commercial online community. At academic conferences the papers were largely concerned with communities hosted by noncommercial organizations, while at business conferences most papers addressed technical considerations and business models for online communities, rather than their social aspects. The chapters in Part 1 attempt to bridge this gap, just as the book as a whole attempts to bridge the gap between the views of online communities in the commercial, educational, and non-profit sectors.

Part 2 is concerned with educational online communities. Distance education is an application for which in some ways online communities are particularly well suited. Technology that enables geographically dispersed pupils and teachers to communicate with each other, and to interact with pooled information sources, has clear potential in education. This part includes a description of a remarkable online community, Red Escolar, which assists the education of over one and a half *million* school students in Mexico. Red Escolar is not intended as a substitute for face-to-face education, but as a complement to it. The "courseware" industry in the United States has sometimes been bolder in its claims. Several of the chapters in Part 2 discuss problems arising with the courseware model of the Virtual University, and experiences with different models. (In some instances, the same organizations that specialize in developing commercial online communities have adapted their business models to the "education market," and are involved in developing resources for academic communities.) Some of the chapters in this part also examine what happens to the resources produced by academic communities when they are moved online. Tim Luke looks at some of the models of community that are emerging for online education, and at issues they raise concerning the ownership and organization of academic communities' resources. Also in Part 2, Richard Stallman, founder of the Free Software movement, calls for a project like the Free Software Foundation for online educational material.

Apart from supporting distance education, what else can you do with online communities that is more interesting than just using them for e-commerce? The final part of this book, Part 3, gives some examples. You can use online communities to assist community activism, or as support groups for personal change; Luciano Paccagnella writes about the potential benefits and dangers of these uses. You can use online communities to strengthen local democracy; Doug Schuler of CPSR writes about the vibrant local online community scene in Seattle. Or you can use online communities to help overcome poverty and suffering. This book includes two interviews with some people who are doing just that, staff of Oxfam GB, who describe candidly the lessons they learned about how to build online communities involving people in developing countries, and about how charitable organizations can best use online communities.

The Internet is yours. Whether it is used for good or for ill depends on you, the citizens of cyberspace. We hope that this book will inspire you to use online communities in new, surprising, and socially beneficial ways. If it does, tell us. We'd love to hear from you.

Chris Werry (cwerry@mail.sdsu.edu)
Miranda Mowbray (mjfm@hplb.hpl.hp.com)
July 2000

Contributors

Joanne Addison is Assistant Professor at the University of Colorado at Denver.

Walter Aprile is Telecommunications Director of the Red Escolar project at the Instituto Latinoamericano de la Comunicación Educativa.

Maria Bakardjieva is Assistant Professor in the Faculty of Communication and Culture at the University of Calgary.

Hillary Bays is a doctoral candidate at the Ecole des Hautes Etudes en Sciences Sociales in Paris. Her dissertation examines Internet Relay Chat from a conversational analytical point of view.

Janelle Brown is Technology Correspondent at *Salon* magazine. She has written a number of pioneering articles at *Salon* about corporate-sponsored online communities.

Norman Clark is Assistant Professor at Appalachian State University.

Randy Connolly is Instructor in Computer Science and Political Science at Mount Royal College in Calgary, Canada.

Andrew Feenberg is Professor of Philosophy at San Diego State University.

Julia Flynn is Head of Internet at Oxfam GB. Oxfam is an organization that works with others in 80 countries to overcome poverty and suffering.

Robin B. Hamman is founder of the digitalartisans.org local virtual community for new media artisans, and Communities Evangelist at Talkcast.

Timothy W. Luke is Professor of Political Science at Virginia Polytechnic Institute and State University. Luke is an authority on the virtual university and has published on this and other technology-related topics.

Teresa Vazquez Mantecón is National Coordinator of the Red Escolar project at the Instituto Latinoamericano de la Comunicación Educativa.

Miranda Mowbray (editor) is a Technical Contributor at Hewlett Packard Laboratories. She studies societal aspects of the Internet.

Cary Nelson is Professor of English and Criticism and Interpretive Theory at the University of Illinois, Urbana-Champaign.

Luciano Paccagnella researches the sociology of cyberspace at Milan University and is a long-time observer of social movements and activism on computer networks.

Geoffrey Sauer is Assistant Professor in the Technical Communications Department at the University of Washington.

Douglas Schuler is a member of the faculty at The Evergreen State College and one of the founders of the Seattle Community Network. He has been working with CPSR and other organizations all over the world on democratic technology projects for nearly 20 years.

Richard Stallman is founder of the Free Software Foundation and a major force behind the Open Source free software movement.

Chris Werry (editor) is Assistant Professor in the Rhetoric and Writing Studies department at San Diego State University.

Trademarks

Addison Wesley® is a registered trademark of Addison Wesley Longman, Inc. American Cybercast® is a registered service mark of Cyber Oasys Corp. AOL® is a registered trademark and registered service mark of America Online, Inc. American Psychologist® is a registered trademark of the American Psychological Association. Apple® and Macintosh® are registered trademarks of Apple Computer, Inc, and Apple® is a registered service mark of Apple Computer, Inc. AT&T® is a registered trademark and registered service mark of AT&T Corp. Banner® and SCT® are registered trademarks of Systems and Computer Technology Corporation, and SCT is a registered service mark of Systems and Computer Technology Corporation.

Bantam Books® is a registered trademark of Bantam Books, Inc. Barnes & Noble® is a registered service mark of Barnes & Noble Bookstores, Inc. Basic Books® is a registered trademark of Harper & Row Publishers, Inc. Borders® is a registered service mark of Borders Properties, Inc. Brill's Content® is a registered trademark of Brill Media Ventures, L.P. Business Week® and McGraw–Hill® are registered trademarks and registered service marks of McGraw–Hill, Inc.

Café Herpé® is a registered service mark of SmithKline Beecham Corporation. Cambridge University Press® is a registered trademark of the Chancellor, Masters, and Scholars of the University of Cambridge. Campus Pipeline^{TM,SM} is a trademark and service mark of Campus Pipeline, Inc., and My Pipeline^{SM} is a service mark of Campus Pipeline, Inc. Carnegie Mellon® is

istered trademarks of HarperCollins Publishers Inc. Harvard Business School® is a registered service mark of the President and Fellows of Harvard College, and Harvard University Press^{SM} is a service mark of the President and Fellows of Harvard College. Hewlett Packard® is a registered trademark and registered service mark of Hewlett-Packard Company. Homestead® is a registered trademark of KartoffelSoft, Inc.

IBM® is a registered trademark and registered service mark of International Business Machines Corporation. Ingram® is a registered service mark of Ingram Industries Inc. Intel® is a registered trademark of Intel Corporation. Internet Commerce Expo® is a registered service mark of International Data Group, Inc. Iridium® is a registered trademark and registered service mark of Iridium IP LLC. iVillage® is a registered service mark of iVillage Inc.

Java® and Sun® are registered trademarks of Sun Microsystems, Inc., and Java® is a registered service mark of Sun Microsystems, Inc. Johnson & Johnson® is a registered trademark of Johnson & Johnson. Junkbusters® is a registered service mark of Junkbusters Corporation.

Knopf® is a registered trademark of Alfred A. Knopf, Inc. Linux® is a registered trademark of Linus Torvalds.

MacMillan® is a registered trademark of MacMillan, Inc. Marlowe & Company® is a registered trademark of Avalon Publishing Group. Mary Poppins® is a registered trademark of Creative Characters, Inc. Mattel® is a registered trademark and registered service mark of Mattel, Inc. Media Metrix® is a registered service mark of Media Metrix, Inc. Microsoft® Windows® and PowerPoint® are registered trademarks of Microsoft Corporation, and Microsoft® is a registered service mark of Microsoft Corporation. Minitel® is a registered trademark of France Telecom. MIT® is a registered service mark of the Massachusetts Institute of Technology. Mrs. Fields ® Cookies® is a registered trademark of Mrs. Field's Development Corporation. MyBytes^{SM} is a service mark of CommonPlaces LLC. Netscape ® Navigator® is a registered trademark of Netscape Communications Corporation. MSNBC® is a registered trademark and registered service mark of MSNBC Cable L.C.C.

Nebraska Farmer® is a registered trademark of Farm Progress Companies, Inc. Nielsen® is a registered service mark of A. C. Nielsen Company.

Oxford University Press® is a trademark of the Chancellors, Masters and Scholars of the University of Oxford.

Paragon House® is a registered service mark of Paragon Book Reprint Corp. Penguin® is a registered trademark of Penguin Books Limited. Pittsburgh Post-Gazette® is a registered trademark of PG Publishing. Prentice-Hall® is a registered trademark of Prentice-Hall, Inc. Pretty Good Privacy® and PGP® are registered trademarks of Philip Zimmermann. Princeton University Press® is a registered trademark of the Trustees of Princeton University.

RAND® is a registered trademark and registered service mark of The RAND Corporation. RCA® is a registered trademark and registered service mark of General Electric Company. Reuters® is a registered trademark and registered service mark of Reuters Limited. Rocky Mountain News® is a registered trademark of the Denver Publishing Company. Rutgers® is a registered service mark of Rutgers, The State University.

Sage ® Publications® is a registered trademark of Sage Publications, Inc. Salon® is a registered service mark of Salon Internet, Inc. Scientific American® is a registered trademark of Scientific American, Inc. Sears® is a registered service mark and registered trademark of Sears, Roebuck and Co. Sesame Street® is a registered trademark of the Children's Television Workshop. Simon & Schuster® and Touchstone® are registered trademarks of Simon & Schuster, Inc. Shearwater® is a registered trademark of The Center for Resource Economics. SmartGirl® Internette® is a registered service mark of SmartGirl Internette, Inc. Stanford® is a registered trademark and registered service mark of The Board of Trustees of the Leland Stanford Junior University. Star Trek® is a registered trademark of Paramount Pictures Corporation.

Talk City® is a registered service mark of LiveWorld Productions, Inc. Telephony® is a registered trademark of Intertec Publishing Corporation. The American Prospect® is a registered trademark of The American Prospect, Inc. The Boston Globe® is a registered trademark of Globe Newspaper Company. The Chronicle of Higher Education® is a registered trademark of The Chronicle of Higher Education, Inc. The Economist® is a registered trademark of The Economist Newspaper Limited. The Spot® is a registered service mark of Scott C. Zakarin and GEM/F&C. The Times® is a registered trademark of Times Newspapers, Limited. WebCT™ is a trademark of Universal Learning Technology, Inc. The University of New Mexico® is a registered service mark of The University of New Mexico. The WELL® is a registered service mark of Whole Earth Lectronic Link, Inc. The World Bank® is a registered trademark of the International Bank for Reconstruction and Development. TheGlobe.com® is a registered service mark of TheGlobe.com, Inc. Thor® is a registered trademark of Thor Power Tool Company. Time Warner® is a registered trademark and registered service mark of Time Warner, Inc. Toyota® is a registered trademark and registered service mark of Toyota Jidosha Kabushiki Kaisha. Toys "R" Us® is a registered trademark and registered service mark of Geoffrey, Inc. Tripod® is a registered service mark of Tripod, Inc. Unext.com^SM is a service mark of Knowledge Universe, Inc.

Universitas 21® is a registered service mark of the University of Melbourne. University of Oregon® is a registered service mark of University of Oregon and the State of Oregon acting by OSSHE on behalf of the University of Oregon. University of Phoenix® is a registered service mark of The University of Phoenix, Inc. University of Washington® is a registered trademark and registered service mark of the University of Washington. UNIX® is a registered trademark of Unix System Laboratories, Inc. USA Today® is a registered trademark of Gannett Co., Inc.

Viagra® is a registered trademark of Pfizer Inc. Villanova® is a registered service mark of Villanova University in the State of Pennsylvania.

Western Governors University® is a registered service mark of Western Governors University. Westinghouse® is a registered trademark of Westinghouse Electric Corporation. WHA® is a registered service mark of the Board of Regents of the University of Wisconsin System. Wiley® is a registered trademark of John Wiley & Sons, Inc. WiReD® is a registered trademark of Advance Magazine Publishers, Inc. World Future Society® is a registered service mark of World Future Society. WWF® is a registered service mark of the World Wildlife Fund. WWJ® is a registered service mark of CBS Worldwide Inc.

Yahoo!® is a registered service mark of Yahoo!, Inc. Yale® is a registered trademark of Yale University.

ZDNET® is a registered service mark of ZD Inc.

Commercial
Online
Communities

This part of the book is about online communities run in order to make a profit. Chris Werry plots changes in the meanings given to the word "community" within e-commerce, and warns that not all commercial online communities live up to the promise of empowering members. Janelle Brown gives case studies of prominent commercial online communities, showing several business models that failed, and one that has been successful but raises questions. Hillary Bays and Miranda Mowbray find a connection between cookies (edible or otherwise), gift-giving, and online community, and discuss the implication of this connection for business plans involving commercial online communities. Robin Hamman's chapter reports a study of members of AOL, the world's largest commercial online community provider. He finds that rather than using online communities to meet strangers online, as the stereotype of Internet use might suggest, AOL members are using them principally to communicate with people who they know offline. Finally, Miranda Mowbray gives recommendations for administrators of commercial (and noncommercial) online communities interested in reducing demographic bias in their membership.

chapter

1

Imagined Electronic Community: Representations of Online Community in Business Texts

by Chris Werry, cwerry@mail.sdsu.edu

This chapter presents a history of how online community has been represented in business texts. It critically examines some of the arguments, narratives, and rhetorical strategies drawn on within business texts to represent online community. The chapter outlines some of the changes that occur between 1994 and 1999 with respect to how community is represented, and the role assigned it in business models. I suggest that one can identify three main ways of conceptualizing community during this period. Online community is first represented in business texts either as peripheral to commercial goals, or as a minor impediment to them. By 1995, online community has become a synonym for new strategies of interactive marketing, as dreams of online sales fade, and advertising and marketing become the primary means of making money on the Net. In 1997 and 1998, online community is depicted as central to models of commercial Internet development, as well as to the future of narrowcasting and mass customization in the wider world of marketing and advertising.

The chapter discusses two business texts, Canter and Siegel's *How to Make a Fortune on the Information Superhighway* (published in 1994), and Hagel and Armstrong's *Net Gain: Expanding Markets Through Virtual Communities* (published in 1997), to illustrate how representations of online community shift over time. The chapter discusses why these shifts occur, and provides a critique of some of the ways in which contemporary business models seek to commodify and privatize online community, regulate social interaction, and organize the resources and knowledges produced within communities. The chapter ends by discussing why academics may have an interest in helping construct alternative models of online community formation and resource organization in the context of moves to corporatize and commodify Higher Education. It is argued that this is particularly important given the connections that are emerging between corporate-sponsored online community development, and commercial online education.

Early Business Texts and "The Community That Isn't"

> It is important to understand that the Cyberspace community is not a community at all (Canter and Siegel 1994, p. 187).

Early business texts tend to have little to say about issues of culture or community on the Internet. Texts describing online commerce begin to emerge in 1993 and 1994 as the Internet is opened to commercial development. The focus of these early books and journals is on how to establish a presence on the Net; set up a Web site, virtual storefront, or online mall; get listed on a directory service; and access lists of email addresses (examples of early business texts include Cronin 1994, Ellsworth and Ellsworth 1994, and Resnick and Taylor 1994). The Web design that grows out of such business models tends to emphasize electronic product lists, online catalogues, order forms, and static mall-like architectures. There is little attention to issues of culture or community in the business models advanced (the only place in these texts where community is sometimes considered is in the occasional discussion of "Netiquette"). The general thrust is nicely summarized in the title of a section from one of the most popular books on Internet commerce, Ellsworth and Ellsworth's *The Internet Business Book*. It reads: "If you build it they will come" (Ellsworth and Ellsworth 1994, p. 68). Internet users are the anonymous "they" in this formulation, an undifferentiated mass, and Web commerce is primarily about setting up a shop in cyberspace to which "they" will naturally gravitate.

One of the first business texts to consider online community in any detail is, ironically, Canter and Siegel's book *How to Make a Fortune on the Information Superhighway*. The irony stems from the fact that it was Canter and Siegel who first came to symbolize for many Net users that their community was under threat by commercial development of the Internet. Canter and Siegel, immigration lawyers from Phoenix, became notorious for spamming advertisements for their services across USENET news in 1993 (dubbed "the Green Card incident," the controversy was widely reported in the popular press). Canter and Siegel's actions led to mass protests in cyberspace, and to the charge that cultural and community norms had been violated. Because of the enormous controversy they were involved in, Canter and Siegel's book displays a self-consciousness about questions of online community that is absent in previous business texts.

Canter and Siegel's account of the Internet and of doing business on it is organized around a very familiar trope, namely the Internet as frontier. Slotkin, a historian who has written extensively on the various uses of the idea of the "frontier" in historical and political discourse, argues that the frontier narrative continues to be a myth of great importance in contemporary America:

> The myth of the frontier is arguably the longest-lived of American myths, with origins in the colonial period and a powerful continuing presence in contemporary culture (Slotkin 1985, p. 15).

Although I would question Slotkin's positing of an uninterrupted line of descent in the use of frontier mythology, appropriations and reworkings of the idea of the frontier in writings about the Internet confirm its contemporary significance. The notion of the Internet as a new "frontier" in which "pioneers" explore and/or colonize the terrain has been pervasive since the earliest works about the Internet were published. For example, in an article entitled "Jack In, Young Pioneer," John Perry

Barlow, cofounder of the Electronic Freedom Foundation, wrote in 1994: "Today another frontier yawns before us, far more fog-obscured and inscrutable in its opportunities than the Yukon" (Barlow 1994). In an earlier article by Barlow, in the "Electronic Frontier" column of *Communications of the ACM*, each of the main groups on the Internet is consistently assigned a role based on frontier mythology. For example, Barlow writes: "Some of the locals . . . the UNIX cultists, sysops, netheads and byte drovers . . . are like the mountain men of the Fur Trade." However the early hackers are, by contrast, described as

> nomadic and tribal. They have an Indian sense of property and are about as agreeable to the notion of proprietary data as the Shoshones were to the idea that the Union Pacific owned the landscape of southern Wyoming (Barlow 1991).

Canter and Siegel use similar language in describing how to do business on the Internet. In a chapter entitled "What it Means to Be a Pioneer," they write:

> In Cyberspace, the homesteading race is on. Hoards of anxious trailblazers are prospecting for the best locations in Cyberspace. At the moment, everything seems up for grabs. We've staked our own claim. We've explained to you how to do the same (1984, p. 216).

The frontier narrative pervades Canter and Siegel's writings. It is central to their understanding of the Internet, the people who use it, and the nature of online commerce. It is used to distinguish between the two main populations that exist on the Internet, namely "natives" and "pioneers." "Natives" are those who have so far constituted the majority on the Net, and include researchers, students, those working in government institutions and other non-commercial areas. "Pioneers," on the other hand, are those in business who are advancing the process of commercial "exploration." Canter and Siegel's deployment of the frontier trope works to define exploration as the expansion of commercial development into the "undeveloped" lands of cyberspace.

In this scenario, much as with Frederick Jackson Turner's original frontier thesis,[1] the people who are already there exist largely at the margins of the narrative. (Canter and Siegel argue that the only real cultural contact necessary is that pioneers must "learn a few words of the language spoken here so you can converse with the natives" (Canter and Siegel 1994, p. 3). The native population exists primarily to be explored and mapped by commercial pioneers. Natives are equated with the frontier itself, subsumed into the "natural" environment, incorporated into a narrative of progress in which this environment is "developed." Canter and Siegel's text represents the Internet and the groups of people on it as part of nature, and both are seen as operating via certain immutable natural laws. Such "nostalgic progressivism" implies that what will be found on the Net is in a sense already there, and that what will emerge in the future is prefigured in an idealized past of commercial and colonial conquest. The ideological force of this representation, as with many previous uses of the frontier narrative in American history, is to legitimize a narrow set of interpretations of the landscape, who has the authority to own and shape it, and what its future will look like.

There are several aspects of Canter and Siegel's representation of the Internet community that are worth focusing on. First, the population of Internet users, when not merely a territory to be mapped, constitutes a potential threat to the operation of Internet commerce. Canter and Siegel state that,

> like the Old West with which analogies are often drawn, Cyberspace is going to take some taming before it is a completely fit place for people like you and me to spend time.

---

1. Frederick Jackson Turner's highly influential treatise, "The Significance of the Frontier in American History," written in 1893 (Edwards 1989), defined the roots of American identity as growing out of the experience of settling the West. According to Turner, the frontier was a geographical force that profoundly shaped the character and institutions of American life, as well as the nature of American democracy and individualism. As many critics have pointed out, Turner's thesis both naturalizes and backgrounds the colonization and depopulation of native peoples by conflating this with the development of the land by European settlers.

There is a small but extremely vocal group that will do almost anything to keep out the new settlers (1994, p. 187).

The many negative characteristics attributed to natives reinforce the idea that they cannot be left to control the Internet. They are described as incapable of self-government, as having the wrong attitude toward private property, as prone to committing criminal acts, and as consisting of significant numbers of "electronic sociopaths" (pp. 187–208). In a chapter entitled "Crimes in Cyberspace: Why the Net Needs You," Canter and Siegel describe the threat that groups of Internet users pose to online commercial practices, and how this population ought to be policed and disciplined in ways that safeguard business interests.

Second, Canter and Siegel's definition of the native population is constructed so as to deny the legitimacy of their claims for control or ownership of cyberspace. Canter and Siegel stress that unlike pioneers, whose work transforms the landscape in productive and worthwhile ways, natives produce nothing of value. Their resistance to commercial development is defined as aggression, and their attitude toward private property is deemed so backward that claims to ownership or control carry no weight. One of the most striking aspects of the rhetoric of *How to Make a Fortune on the Information Superhighway* is the way it reproduces some of the language and arguments used by Locke in the "property" sections of the *Second Treatise*. There Locke asserts that land belongs primarily to those who engage in productive labor to develop it. Indigenous people who resist European development can thus be defined in certain contexts as "aggressors." (This reading of the Second Treatise is discussed in Glausser. According to this interpretation of Locke's position, "people occupying (or claiming as property) land that they either cannot or will not develop may become aggressors against those who can and would develop that land" (Glausser 1990, p. 208). Canter and Siegel's text works similarly in defining opposition to commercial development as illegitimate hostility by a population with only limited claims to ownership and control of the "lands" they inhabit. Canter and Siegel argue that the deficiencies shown by natives stem from the fact that the Internet was for so long populated by academics and researchers, who made volunteerism and a "gift economy" the norm (p. 192).

However, one of the most distinctive aspects of Canter and Siegel's text is the way it is organized in consistent opposition to the notion that Cyberspace is characterized by authentic social or community relations. Canter and Siegel go to great pains to dismiss the idea that the "natives" who populate the Internet constitute any kind of community. They describe the Internet as "the community that isn't" (p. 187) and write:

> Some starry-eyed individuals who access the Net think of Cyberspace as a community, with rules, regulations and codes of behavior. Don't you believe it! There is no community (1994, p. 12).

Canter and Siegel argue that the Net consists solely of "individuals and inert messages" and that, just as owning a phone does not make one a member of "phonesville," communicating and interacting online does not make one part of an online community. Canter and Siegel's notion of the Internet, and of how commercial development is to proceed, is predicated on the notion that online community does not exist. In this way they can argue that no social or community relations exist that could be encroached upon by the spread of advertising and commercial activity. While *How to Make a Fortune on the Information Superhighway* is sometimes almost hysterical in its attitude to online community, it is nonetheless symptomatic of business texts produced at the time, in that it presents community as largely at odds with commercial development of the Internet. Online community is seen as at best irrelevant to models of Internet commerce, and at worst a potential impediment.

Community As Interactive Marketing

> The successful marketspace will invite consumers into a communal experience and let them meet people as well as buy products . . . it will make shopping a transaction involving not

just goods and services but also experience. It will not forsake community for commerce (Alburty 1995).

Less than two years after the publication of Canter and Siegel's book an explosion of interest in online community is identifiable. A variety of journals, magazines, and guides begin mentioning community in relation to online business strategies. "Making your online business a site that fosters community" is described by *Internet World* magazine as one of the "5 Keys to Successful Net Sales . . . Even though a store resides in cyberspace, it should build a community—a place where it feels good to shop" (Internet World 1995). A series of influential articles in the *Harvard Business Review* begin charting the dynamics of "marketspace," the term given to an emergent cyberspace in which commerce is central, and in which communication and social interaction between customers and vendors is important. According to an editorial in *The New York Times* written in 1995, to succeed in this new "marketspace" one needed business strategies that took community into consideration:

> The successful marketspace will invite consumers into a communal experience and let them meet people as well as buy products . . . it will make shopping a transaction involving not just goods and services but also experience. It will not forsake community for commerce (Alburty 1995).

There are several primary reasons why this sudden interest in online community emerges in 1995 and 1996. First, the Web mall model proved a disaster. The motto "if you build it they will come" became a grim joke, a slogan that would haunt early business texts (in a list of the top ten "ecommerce myths," a recent issue of *Computer User* magazine states: "Myth #2: If you build it they will come. The web is not a field of dreams. Unfortunately, the ecommerce pioneers found this out the hard way" (Kurkowski 2000, p. 1). Few people came to such sites, and fewer still bought anything. In a 1997 survey of Internet business models, *The Economist* argued that the Web malls that had sprung up in their thousands over the previous two years had been an "abject failure," adding that "the industry has defined electronic commerce too narrowly." A successful alternative model could be found, it was argued, in "the few businesses that are increasingly grouping themselves by theme, joining or creating consumer communities with shared interests" (Anderson 1997).

Second, as with traditional mass media, advertising became where money was made online. Or, as a number of industry commentators put it, the focus switched from talk of sales to talk of "capturing eyeballs." Marketing analysts discovered that while people might not yet buy very much online, they did make purchasing decisions based on what they read on the Net. It thus became important to bring people back to a site, and "community" became a kind of synonym for this imperative.

Third, from 1995 onward a significant amount of demographic information had been gathered, and a number of key market segments identified. "Community" became a polite way of talking about audience, consumer demographics, and market segmentation while seeming sensitive to Internet users, their culture, and community. (Numerous examples of this can be found in the sections of commercial Web sites where companies describe for advertisers how attractive their Web site users are. Since this information is usually public, available to site users as well as prospective advertisers, the word "community" functions to signal demographic desirability while appearing sensitive to the groups of people who frequent the site. Thus several of the best known online brokerage firms invite advertisers to "reach our community" of demographically desirable members. Or, as the E*TRADE Web site puts it, "Advertise with Us: Reach our community of tech-savvy investors.")

In practice, what this new-found interest in "community" often meant when translated into Web design was that commercial sites began to add chat rooms, bulletin boards, games, forms for people to enter personal information, and celebrity guests to host discussions. In 1995 and 1996 one can identify a movement away from the Internet mall design that dominates early business texts. There was instead an attempt to

build sites that enabled interactivity, allowing users to communicate with each other and with site sponsors, and encouraging people to revisit the site. Many commercial Web sites
began to graft interactivity and various forms of "community
ware" onto advertising and marketing strategies. A rather
strange hybrid of "community" and marketing imperatives is
often identifiable in Web design during this period. One of the
most striking examples of this can be seen in the Café Herpé
site. Sponsored by the pharmaceutical company SmithKline
Beecham, the Café Herpé site promotes itself as "the genital
herpes resource information spot for U.S. audiences." The site
is designed to simulate a café, complete with reading lounge,
espresso bar, terrace, and buffet. Café Herpé strives valiantly
to make genital herpes a topic of relaxed conversation and fun.
The site has games, a "gallery of romantic art," a guest book,
links to online support groups and Web sites, as well as information about genital herpes and SmithKline Beecham products. (SmithKline Beecham declined to grant us permission to
show an image of the site; however, it is located on the Web at
http://www.cafeherpe.com/.)

Café Herpé is paradigmatic of the first wave of Web sites to
make online community a central part of their business
model. In this model, "community" functions largely as a synonym for new strategies of interactive marketing, and signals a
shift in Net commerce from a focus on product sales to a focus
on advertising, promotion, and the collection of demographic
information.

Online Community and the Future of Internet Commerce

Community is one of the biggest buzzwords in the Internet
business, with nearly every site trying to incorporate some
kind of bulletin board or chat room (Brown 1999, "Must AOL
Pay 'Community Leaders'?").

In electronic markets . . . your creativity and ability to leverage the communal ethos of the marketspace dictate whether
you win or lose (Hagel and Armstrong 1997).

In contemporary business discourse online community is no longer seen as an impediment to online commerce. No longer is it thought of as just a useful add-on to Web sites, or as merely a synonym for strategies of interactive marketing. Instead, community is frequently described as central to the commercial development of the Internet, and to the imagined future of narrowcasting and mass customization in the wider world of marketing and advertising. In the last few years business texts with titles like "Expanding Markets Through Virtual Community," "Creating Compelling Commerce Sites Via Community," and "Hosting Web Communities: Building Relationships, Increasing Relationships and Maintaining a Competitive Edge" have become widespread. A paper delivered at the Internet Commerce Expo in March 1999 states:

> Many electronic commerce sites have fallen short of expectations because they failed to create compelling reasons for customers to change their buying behavior. The missing element: community. By using interactive discussions, businesses can infuse electronic commerce sites with community, thereby delivering value in addition to convenience, enhancing perceived trustworthiness, and creating online experiences conducive to shopping instead of simple browsing or buying. "Virtual communities" built around products can increase sales, reduce marketing and customer acquisition costs, foster brand loyalty, and provide cost-effective market research and focus groups . . . community is the fourth evolution of the Internet, and commerce sites that don't harness it will miss out (Wilson 1999).

Such claims about online community have been accompanied by heavy investment in commercial community software, by the sale of large Web-based community sites to major media corporations and Internet portals, and by high stock-market valuations for community sites such as GeoCities, iVillage, Talk City, and AOL. The new-found financial value of online community is perhaps best exemplified in the planned merger between AOL, the world's leading developer of commercial online community, and Time Warner, the world's largest traditional mass media company. (At the time this chapter was written the merger was still pending.)

One of the most influential business texts to theorize commercial community development is Hagel and Armstrong's *Net Gain: Expanding Markets Through Virtual Communities.* I will discuss some of the main arguments, metaphors, and narratives used by Hagel and Armstrong to represent online community, since their text has been important in shaping the way community is talked about in business discourse, has influenced corporate Web design, and, as I shall describe in the next section, has an interesting status in the context of recent charges made concerning the exploitation of online community members.

Hagel and Armstrong talk about online community in a way that differs significantly from Canter and Siegel. Hagel and Armstrong not only acknowledge the existence of community, but they consider in almost ethnographic detail various different aspects of online community and culture (in many respects their work can be read as a kind of corporate cultural studies). Hagel and Armstrong believe that commercial development of the Internet centers on organizing and exploiting the potential of online communities. They write:

> We suspect that the skills required to organize a community will be as important as any initial advantage a company might appear to have based on its assets . . . . The keys to becoming a successful organizer over time will be the abilities to aggregate members, retain them, and encourage them to make transactions (1997, pp. 128–129).

The text provides a description of how to design, build, and organize online communities. For example, it describes how to train "community architects" whose job it is to "acquire members, stimulate usage, and extract value from the community." Hagel and Armstrong describe how to identify community members who can be paid to manage subcommunities, and volunteers who can be encouraged to build parts of a site.

In contrast to Canter and Siegel, who represent the user environment as something to be controlled, dominated, and planned, a landscape to be reterritorialized and repopulated with people who engage in or are receptive to commercial development, Hagel and Armstrong do not consider online space as something one can design or organize the way one would a mall. Instead, they allow for a certain degree of autonomy, flexibility, and local control. Hagel and Armstrong's discussion of community is organized around metaphors of the organic and of the ecosystem. For example, at the center of their model is what they term an "organic management style" (p. 155). They argue that with online community a radically different approach to management must be followed in which a high degree of autonomy is ceded to members, and managers display "a gardener's touch" (p. 150). They write that "seeding, weeding and feeding are the best metaphors for online organization and evolution." The figure of a dynamic, partially "self-organizing" ecosystem is perhaps the most pervasive means of representing virtual communities, a result of the fact that member-generated content and interaction is of prime importance in models of commercial online community, and this cannot be controlled too directly. An organic management style involves such practices as "planting" conversations and provocative ideas, allowing a high degree of self-organization, and carefully balancing factors such as size, intimacy, continuity, and growth (pp. 151–156).

Unlike the position taken in Canter and Siegel's book, there is little sense of conflict either between the "native" population and commercial developers, or within "native" populations. The figure of the community as "self-organizing" ecosystem is used to promote the idea that community interaction is essentially conflict free. The community will naturally contain a mix of four types of people: "builders," "browsers," "users," and "buyers," and since these groups differ in value, one must try to encourage the correct ratio between them (pp. 59–61). The metaphor of community as ecosystem is used to promote the idea that if left to themselves, communities will evolve in ways that are rational, suit commercial development, do not require coercion, and will fit traditional patterns of ownership and control. For example, Hagel and Armstrong argue that virtual communities will "naturally" become run less by volunteer, noncommercial groups, and more by corporations and professionals. When it comes to ownership, there exist what they term "natural owners": businesses and groups that have related interests and are specifically suited to the task of building virtual community. Natural owners are those who "enter the arena with a strong advantage because of assets such as brand name, deep customer relationships, and in some cases, published content that they own" (Hagel and Armstrong 1997, p. 128). Thus they suggest that Johnson & Johnson, Toys "R" Us, health maintenance organizations, and other such groups would be naturally suited to constructing and managing a community devoted to parenting (p. 206).

A central argument made by Hagel and Armstrong is that the knowledge, content, and resources produced by online communities are extremely valuable commodities. They write that online communities

> aggregate an enormous collective expertise that could not possibly be matched by any individual expert, no matter how well trained or experienced. In many cases the value may not be so much in the experience and knowledge of any one individual but in the comparative experiences and perspectives of many individuals (p. 30).

Unlike Canter and Siegel, they believe that the "gift economy" and tradition of volunteerism on the Internet are assets. They assert that "in electronic markets . . . your creativity and ability to leverage the communal ethos of the marketspace dictate whether you win or lose." However they argue that up until now, such potential resources have been highly disorganized. They propose that community architects, developers, and archivists could organize, structure, and store community knowledges and resources so that they are searchable and accessible in ways that are profitable to the community, vendors, advertisers, and marketers.

Member-generated content is seen by Hagel and Armstrong as particularly valuable for several reasons:

- It attracts new members.
- The investments people make in their writings and relationships foster strong member loyalty. This inhibits what

the authors call "churning" (or, to use the terms commonly employed in business texts, it promotes "stickiness," raises "switching costs," and enables "lock-in").

■ It enables more subtle ways of interweaving marketing and advertising, media form and content, communication, and community formation than exist in traditional mass media.

■ It allows for sophisticated forms of customization, which in turn creates another barrier to people switching to a different virtual community.

■ It provides detailed and inexpensive demographic information on people's interests, habits, and buying practices, and reduces the costs for vendors to find potential customers (Hagel and Armstrong 1997, pp. 8–12).

In general, online community is seen as a means of intensifying and advancing existing trends in mass customization and narrowcasting. Thus in describing the evolutionary paths of online community development, they argue that the highest stage of development is the "infomediary," where there is perfect symmetry between user interests, profiles, and the interests of vendors (pp. 104–108). This is where the most sophisticated mass customization can exist, where transaction costs are negligible, geography is insignificant, intermediaries disappear, and consumers are fully informed and can maximize the value of their personal information. In short, this is the "frictionless capitalism" described by Bill Gates in *The Road Ahead* (Gates 1996). At this point, we stand at the threshold of the perfect market and the fully realized individual who is a "market segment of one." The interpenetration of community, communication, commerce, and marketing is so perfect that they are practically indistinguishable. Or, as Hagel and Armstrong put it, "at this point the community redefines the market by becoming it." In essence, virtual communities have the potential to enable the formation of a subject closer to the ideal, fully informed customer of traditional economic theory, and enable market efficiency to leave the realm of abstract theory and descend to Earth.

Interestingly, while online community is often described as helping decrease "friction" in market exchange (by enabling more efficient quality/price comparisons), it is also sometimes represented as a strategy designed precisely to produce friction, or "stickiness" (by giving customers some reason to frequent a company's Web site other than the commodity quality/price of the goods offered there), thus working to increase search costs, price dispersion, and margins and to lower price competition. On the role of online communities as friction-producers, see Smith 1999.

Hagel and Armstrong's representations of online community and strategies for developing it have been echoed in the business plans and press releases of many present-day corporate sponsored sites. Consider the case of Talk City. Talk City has become a pioneer in the field of commercial community development, has built a substantial network of sponsorship and cross-promotion deals, and builds customized online communities for Fortune 500 companies. For example, a number of Hagel and Armstrong's suggested strategies and arguments about the commercial value of online community are echoed in the following press release from Talk City:

> Thanks for coming to learn more about Talk City—the Internet's leading community site. We offer our advertisers and sponsors an integrated portfolio of effective and innovative online marketing opportunities that deliver what web marketers are looking for: real interactivity with your customers. Tighter, real-time relationships with your customers. And exceptional targeting. All at very affordable prices. We're pleased (and even a little bit flattered!) that some of the most influential brands in the world have chosen Talk City as their online community advertising destination. The list includes Procter & Gamble, Mattel, Columbia–TriStar, Intel, The Discover Card, Sears, Toyota, Microsoft, and many others. . . . As you're probably aware, community sites are one of the fastest-growing and most envied categories on the Internet today. Why? Because community sites deliver real customer loyalty and tremendous usage patterns. People who join community sites have decided to put down a stake in a cyberneighborhood, which means they'll come back and stay for long periods of time (Talk City 1999).

The kind of Web design that emerges out of such strategic use of community can be seen in the Talk City home page. (Talk City declined to grant us permission to show an image of the site; however, their homepage can be viewed at http:// www.talkcity.com.)

On the Talk City homepage, member-generated content is often tightly integrated into marketing and advertising strategies. For example, a selection of "Cool Home Pages" produced by members is regularly featured on the site, with a frequent focus on current or forthcoming television shows and films. Bulletin board topics are clearly influenced by demographic and marketing considerations, divided as they are into such categories as "Autos," "Business & Finance," "College," "Computing," etc. Interaction between members and the community organizers is heavily influenced by product testing and market research. For example, the "Speak Up Poll" that appears on the homepage invites people to "vote" on issues such as their marshmallow consumption. And the topics selected for chatline discussions are often a similar mix of promotion, advertising, and market research, as in the "Fashion Chat" sponsored by Sears in May 1999, which urged members to "tell us all about YOUR personal style this year."

Other corporate-sponsored community sites have attempted to leverage the value of member-generated content in more direct ways. For example, Keen, Infomarkets, and Experts Exchange[2] have set up sites in which they invite community members to assemble various resources and pieces of information (jokes, riddles, recipes, stock tips, etc.). Keen's home page says "Got **questions**? Talk to people with **answers**, live over the phone." And here is a statement from Experts Exchange:

> Experts Exchange has pioneered the IT knowledge sharing community marketplace since 1996, enabling its members to

---

2. http://www.keen.com, http://www.infomarkets.com, http://www.experts-exchange.com/info/about.htm

quickly find specific solutions to their specific questions. Through its community, Experts Exchange developed an open marketplace where experts compete and collaborate with each other in the process of answering questions.

At these sites, member-generated content is stored as text or audio messages (live advice is also sometimes available), and this is then sold as part of an online information market or auction. This enables such sites to make money from the valuable and extensive "collective expertise" that Hagel and Armstrong argue exists within online communities.

A Critique of Contemporary Internet Business Models

To those committed to the project of democratizing media, and to producing what one might loosely call an oppositional public sphere, the techniques of community formation discussed in *Expanding Markets Through Virtual Communities*, and the strategies embodied in many contemporary corporate-sponsored community sites are hardly encouraging. In this section I will discuss some of the ways in which contemporary business models seek to commodify community, to organize and regulate social interaction, and to control practices of online knowledge production.

Online community is frequently described in the popular press as a kind of "media from below." Yet in spite of the rhetoric of democracy, accessibility, participation, and utility surrounding virtual communities, real control by members is often very limited. Corporate-sponsored online communities are characterized by many of the same limited constructions of the "popular," the same forms of creative ventriloquism identifiable in mainstream media genres such as talk shows, "reality TV," and docudramas. The power of members is defined largely in terms of consumption rather than production or control of community resources. Much of the framework for conversation and interaction is constructed around the imperatives of advertising, sales, and market testing. Where member opinions are sought, it is frequently in the form of surveys and polls; a consumer model of power, politics, and participation is clearly preferred over a citizenship model that would require deliberative interaction. While members obviously use corporate-sponsored community sites in creative ways, it is important to note that real power tends to be in the hands of site owners. This is evident in the closings of a number of community sites. AOL has shut down big community areas without any warning on a number of occasions. And as Brown writes, when the community area of the Netscape Netcenter Web site was closed in April 1999, members were neither consulted nor given advance notice: "No warning— canceled, the hosts let go, the community members left to consider what, exactly, happened to their home" (Brown 1999, "Netscape to Community: You're Evicted"). Such acts of "weeding," to use Hagel and Armstrong's term, have begun to occur more often as community sites come under pressure to organize member content in ways that are commercially profitable, or to get rid of them. While it seems perfectly reasonable that commercial organizations that provide the financial backing for online communities also have the option to close them, it is worth noting that the amount of control by members is far more limited than the popular media and much of the promotional material produced by community developers would suggest.

The strategies described in Internet commerce texts, and implemented in corporate-sponsored community sites, can also be exploitative. Watchdog groups such as the Center for Media Education charge that community Web sites for children have been used to gather personal information and conduct market research without proper disclosure (Horowitz 1999). A more pervasive problem exists in the way that contemporary models of Internet commerce advocate exploiting the volunteerism and "gift economy" traditions that prevail on the Internet. (For a discussion of the genealogy of this tradition, see Barbrook 1998.)

As Hagel and Armstrong note, community members produce knowledges and resources that are commercially valuable. Furthermore, much of the work carried out on community sites has, for many years, been done by volunteers. However, the practice of using volunteers has come under scrutiny. For example, in 1999 the U.S. Labor Department opened an investigation of AOL's treatment of their volunteers. AOL was reported in April 1999 to employ 10,000 unpaid volunteers, as compared to 12,000 paid employees (Napoli 1999). AOL volunteers had been required to work specific shifts and file time cards, which, it was argued, may have been a violation of labor laws. As community became more central to Internet commerce, AOL volunteers were put under increasing pressure to engage in community-building activities that were profitable. It was in part due to this tendency that volunteers were initially moved to complain to the Labor Department about AOL. Zaret cites the comments of a former AOL employee, who says:

> When it gets to "We want to keep this fresh so people buy things," you're not doing this for fun anymore—you're doing this for the company. And when you're doing it for the company you're not a volunteer anymore. There is a place for volunteers online, but not in a for-profit company. That's getting real close to exploitation (Zaret 1999).

When the question of exploitation is raised, commercial community sites typically defend themselves by echoing Hagel and Armstrong's description of online community as "organic" and an "ecosystem." Consider for example these statements by spokespersons for iVillage and AOL in defense of their use of volunteers:

> iVillage.com community leaders are true volunteers and not employees. Our community leaders typify the organic, member-driven nature that drives Internet community development in general. . . . Volunteerism is one of the central attributes of the Internet. Our hope is that the Internet's participatory nature is not what's at issue here.

> AOL denies that the volunteers are that critical to developing the communities. According to AOL spokeswoman Ann Brackbill, the volunteers don't build the communities, they simply

emerge out of them. "It's less about whether [volunteerism] is critical or not critical, but is it organic to the Net and will it just happen. We think natural leaders who participate arise in both the online world or the offline world" (cited in Brown 1999, "Must AOL Pay 'Community Leaders'?").

Such representations of online community as an organism suggest that maintenance and growth are qualities inherent to the system, and happen automatically. This takes for granted the work done by community members. While the metaphors and narratives used to describe online community differ from Canter and Siegel's, they still picture the Internet population as part of the natural environment in a way that denies both the legitimacy of work done and the potential for claiming ownership rights.

Online community is frequently described as an alternative to traditional mass media, yet it is being rapidly integrated into existing networks of corporate commodification. In texts such as Hagel and Armstrong's, and in the press releases of community developers, online community is described primarily as a means of advancing existing techniques of market segmentation, mass customization, and narrowcasting. Online community is touted as a more sophisticated way of inscribing commercial imperatives into communication and interaction. Many of the same mass media genres that interweave marketing, advertising, media form, and content have been produced for online communities. Online equivalents to product placement, complementary copy, and advertorials abound, and companies such as Talk City have pioneered new genres such as "infochats" and "intermercials" (the CEO of Talk City states that their aim is to develop "Internet advertising [that] will draw upon the Net's unique real-time and social interactive qualities" (Talk City 1998). The Internet greatly extends the ways in which content, marketing, and sales can be integrated within publishing. For example, many online news sites collect a commission for books sold via the links in their news stories with booksellers such as Barnes & Noble. As Hansell (1997) notes, "Never before have publications had such a direct interest in sales directly tied to their news reports."[3] Similar tendencies have taken shape in online communities. Content that supports links to commercial sites and can generate sales commissions is exerting a gravitational force on community formation. For example, community members on GeoCities are encouraged to create content with links to company Web sites and are paid a commission on sales that result, or for traffic generated (Guernsey 1999). The development of corporate-sponsored community sites is becoming influenced at a number of different levels by such practices, which tend to skew community formation and the production of online resources in ways that are aligned with corporate interests, rather than wider public or community interests. This makes alternative forms of community formation within corporate-sponsored community sites difficult to achieve, and makes community knowledge production that responds to a variety of social interests and needs harder to attain.

Last, what is often downplayed in e-commerce texts and sites is the various ways that communities are organized, regulated, and policed. Commercial online communities are organized via systems of rewards, disincentives and punishment, and the normalization of particular modes of behavior. This can be seen explicitly in the rules that members must sign when joining, in the training volunteers are given, and in the policing functions volunteers and other workers are assigned. Control and regulation is also identifiable in less explicit areas, such as in how member content is categorized, links are organized, and search facilities ordered. While a certain degree of regulation and ordering is necessary in any online community, the degree of freedom and autonomy associated with life in cyberspace by the popular media is greatly exaggerated. The modes of organization within some commercial sites do not

---

3. Such interpenetration of content and marketing has resulted in several minor scandals, as for example when *The New York Times* revealed that lists of recommended books published by the online bookseller Amazon.com (with titles such as "What We're Reading" and "Destined for Greatness") were in fact bought by publishers. See Gardner 1999, pp. 1, 40.

encourage a fully open, participatory, democratic context for community formation.

Online Community and the University

The commercial exploitation of online community foregrounds the importance of both safe-guarding and expanding spaces for community formation that are not entirely dominated by the market; that are open, diverse, and democratic; and where member participation goes deeper than voting about marshmallows. It suggests the need to think about strategies for organizing existing online community resources in ways that keep them in the hands of the communities that produce them. And it makes clear the need for critical work by academics that deals with the complex specifics of discourses, practices, institutions, and economics that shape the Internet. Unfortunately, too much academic work ignores the most important forces shaping online culture, leaves large areas of debate uncontested, and doesn't really speak to groups actively involved in new media who could constitute potential allies. I would like to conclude by suggesting several possible strategic responses to the commercial development of online community. I believe that the way we talk about and organize community in models of electronic commerce opens up a number of challenges and opportunities for academics as teachers, knowledge producers, and "specific intellectuals."

In our teaching practices we might creatively appropriate a concept of Hagel and Armstrong's and try to produce our own "community architects." This would mean placing courses that deal with online information within an expanded project of critical practice, in which students are seen not just as technical problem solvers, but as critics who actively intervene in situations in which issues of value, power, and social organization are negotiated. Such classes should promote the idea that it is important that those designing and publishing content and tools for online communities think about the cultural, political and social implications of their work. Training of community architects should involve looking at how competing "discourses of community" and competing information architectures organize community space, activity, access, assembly, public use, control, and ownership. However, it should also involve consideration of how such knowledge can be made to work, politically and technologically. This would entail working on producing alternative models of community, alternative systems of "community ware," and alternative models for building, storing, indexing, sharing, and searching community resources.

Such a project might find support in several areas outside the university. Groups within the Free Software Foundation and the Open Source movement might constitute important allies. The Free Software Foundation and Open Source movement provide useful examples of alternative online community formation, and offer instructive models of distributed, collaborative, online community resource management. The similarities between the academy and the free software/open source movements have been noted by a number of writers. For example, Michael Jensen states that "we should remember that research and scholarship are fundamentally open-source enterprises" (Jensen 1999), and Richard Barbrook has written of the role that volunteerism and a "gift economy" play within both academic and free software/open source communities (Barbrook 1998). The next step might be to explore the possibility of constructing something like a "Free Courseware Foundation," or an open source movement for online academic resources. Richard Stallman's article in this book can be seen as an attempt to describe some principles and strategies that such a project might be guided by. Academics might also look to the example of community "freenets" such as the Seattle community network (described by Doug Schuler in his chapter in this book) and the Blacksburg Electronic village in Virginia. However, models for the organization of community knowledges online also exist within academia, as for example in the "Linguist" project (http://linguistlist.org/), which enables communication, coordinates activities, and acts as a repository for the large amounts of electronic text produced by members of the American linguistic community. And the

English server, a cooperatively run student site started at Carnegie Mellon University, which publishes humanities texts, journals, and other scholarly resources, has developed an extensive collection of community-building resources that are publicly available (http://eserver.org).

Finally, the uses of online community in contemporary models of Internet commerce suggest the need for constructing strategic alliances between academics and community groups as a way of keeping both sets of resources in the public domain. Contemporary models of electronic commerce seek to commodify social interaction and community knowledge production in ways that have certain parallels with processes identifiable in the university. The Higher Education sector in North America is increasingly shaped by corporatization, commercialization, and digitalization (Luke 1997, Noble 1998). Tim Luke describes the growing trend toward what he calls the "thin, for-profit, and/or skill competency versions of virtual universities being designed by corporate consultants and some state planners" (Luke 1997). Similarly, David Noble has argued that as teaching materials and knowledge production go online, the ability of the universities and corporations to automate, commodify, reproduce, and claim ownership rights over academic work expands.

An important aspect of the changes that are transforming Higher Education in North America centers on who will organize and control the resources produced within academic communities. Interestingly, many of the same organizations that specialize in developing commercial online communities have adapted their business models to the education market. In the United States, companies such as Campus Pipeline (described by Norman Clark in this book) provide commercial community sites targeted at the Higher Education sector. Furthermore, a number of universities have outsourced email, Web, and other online services to corporations that specialize in developing commercial online community (Blumenstyk 1999). And colleges looking to establish online instruction have sometimes partnered themselves with companies that specialize in online community development. For example, Berkeley has granted AOL, the world's largest online community developer, the worldwide rights to market, license, distribute, and promote a number of the University's online courses. Not surprisingly, the commercial "courseware" being sold to universities often has much in common with the "community ware" developed for commercial online communities.

If resistance by academics to such trends takes the form of claims that education and academics are somehow "special," exempt from conditions that so many others must work under, then we run the risk of being represented as backward, obstructionist, and selfish. Instead, opposition to the commercialization of teaching ought to proceed via commitment to an expanded project of public service. Polster's notion of "knowledge collectives," in which pools of intellectual capital are organized so that usage entails a concomitant requirement to share knowledge with the collective, is interesting, as is the idea of vesting with the public certain rights to the knowledge that academics produce (Polster 1998). Another component of such a project could be a commitment to constructing information technologies that democratize online community formation and knowledge production both inside and outside the university, and which seek means of bridging the resources produced by both groups.

There is also a place for certain strategic partnerships between academic groups and commercial organizations, as the history of the technical development of the Internet plainly shows. The various "parallel networks" described by Luke (this book) that exist between government, industry, and the university will likely play an important role in the future development of online community. Certainly, there are many connections, coalitions, and possibilities to be explored, and the particular strategies adopted by academics will need to be worked out across a range of different contexts. What is clear is that academics need to be more involved in the analysis and contestation over online community formations and resources. After all, the World Wide Web, along with many other Internet protocols, was created in large part by academics needing tools for collaboration and communication within dispersed disciplinary communities. It seems fitting that academics should continue to develop these technologies in ways that benefit a broader constituency of people.

Acknowledgments

An early version of this chapter was presented at the "Exploring Cyber Society" conference and appears in the conference proceedings, John Armitage and Joanne Roberts, eds., *Exploring Cyber Society: Social, Political, Economic and Cultural Issues, Vol. 2.* Proceedings of the Conference 5–7 July 1999, School of Social, Political and Economic Sciences, University of Northumbria at Newcastle, UK. ISBN 0 9536450 1 0. Thanks to the organizers of "Exploring Cyber Society."

An article based on the conference presentation was also published in First Monday (http://www.firstmonday.org), vol. 4, no. 9; this chapter appears here with the kind permission of First Monday.

References

Alburty, Steven, "It's a Buyer's Marketplace," *The New York Times*, March 20, 1995, p. A17.

Anderson, Benedict, *Imagined Communities: Reflections on the Origin and Spread of Nationalism*, p. 6. Rev. Ed., London: Verso, 1991.

Anderson, Christopher, "In Search of the Perfect Market: A Survey of Electronic Commerce," *The Economist,* May 10, 1997.

Armour, Stephanie, "Online Volunteers Question Fairness of Free Labor," *USA Today*, April 15, 1999, p. B1.

Barbrook, Richard, "The High Tech Gift Economy," *First Monday,* vol. 3, no. 12 (December 1998). On-line: http://www.firstmonday.org/issues/issue3_12/barbrook/index.html

Barlow, John Perry, "Coming Into the Country," Electronic Frontier column in *Communications of the ACM*, January 1991. Online: http://www.eff.org/pub/Publications/John_Perry_Barlow/HTML/complete_acm_columns.html#coming

———, "Jack In, Young Pioneer," *The Inside Passage*, August 11, 1994. Online: http://www.eff.org/pub/infrastructure/virtual_frontier_barlow_eff.article

Blumenstyk, Goldie, "Colleges Get Free Web Pages, But with a Catch: Advertising," *New York Times*, September 3, 1999.

Brown, Janelle, "There Goes the Neighborhood," *Salon*, January 19, 1999. Online: http://www.salon.com/21st/feature/1999/01/cov_19feature.html

———, "Netscape to Community: You're Evicted," *Salon*, April 6, 1999. Online: http://www.salon.com/tech/feature/1999/04/06/netcenter/index.html

———, "Must AOL Pay 'Community Leaders'?" *Salon*, April 16, 1999. Online: http://www.salonmagazine.com/tech/feature/1999/04/16/aol_community/index.html

———, "Cool-hunters Hit the Web Jungle," *Salon*, May 13, 1999. Online: http://www.salon.com/tech/feature/1999/05/13/smartgirl/index.html

Canter, Laurence, and Martha Siegel, *How to Make a FORTUNE on the Information Superhighway*. New York: HarperCollins, 1994.

Cronin, Mary, *Doing Business on the Internet*. New York: Van Nostrand Rheinhold, 1994.

Edwards, Everett, *The Early Writings of Frederick Jackson Turner*. Freeport, NY: Books for Libraries Press, 1969.

Ellsworth, Jill, and Matthew Ellsworth, *The Internet Business Book*. New York: Wiley, 1994.

Gardner, Elizabeth, "Cautionary Tale, Courtesy of Amazon: You Can't Tell a Book by Its Cover," *Internet World*, February 15, 1999, pp. 1, 40.

Gates, Bill, *The Road Ahead*, Penguin USA, 1996. Online: http://www.theroadahead.com

Glausser, Wayne, "Three Approaches to Locke and the Slave Trade," *Journal of the History of Ideas* 51, April/June 1990.

Gonyea, Wayne, and James C. Gonyea, *Selling on the Internet: How to Open an Electronic Storefront and Have Millions of Customers Come to You!* New York: McGraw-Hill, 1996.

Guernsey, Lisa, "Geocities Encourages Members to Make Their Web Pages Pay," *The New York Times*, March 18, 1999.

Hagel, John, and Arthur Armstrong, *Net Gain: Expanding Markets Through Virtual Communities*. Harvard Business School Press, 1997.

Hansell, Saul, "News-Ad Issues Arise in New Media," *The New York Times*, December 8, 1997, p. D12.

Holmes, David, ed., *Virtual Politics: Identity and Community in Cyberspace*. Sage Publications, 1997.

Horowitz, Bruce, "Critics Say Web Sites Take Advantage of Teen Girls," *USA Today*, May 17, 1999, pp. 1A–2A.

Internet World, "5 Keys to Successful Net Sales," *Internet World*, March 1995, p. 3.

Jensen, Michael, "Information Technology at a Crossroads: Open-Source Computer Programming," *The Chronicle of Higher Education*, October 29, 1999, p. A92.

Kurkowski, Cynthia Rose, "Myths of the New Economy," *Computer User*, March 2000, pp. 1, 7, 8. Online: http://www.computeruser.com/archives/cu/1903/index.html

Labaton, Stephen, "U.S. Urges New Rules to Guard Privacy of Children on Internet," *The New York Times*, April 22, 1999, p. A8.

Luke, Tim, "Discourse and Discipline in the Digital Domain: The Political Economy of the Virtual University." Paper presented at Virtual Technologies in Tertiary Education: A Vision for New Zealand. Wellington, New Zealand, October 11–12, 1997.

Napoli, Lisa, "America Online Is Facing Challenge Over Free Labor," *The New York Times*, April 14, 1999. Online: http://crab.rutgers.edu/~goertzel/aolvolunteers.htm

Noble, David, "Digital Diploma Mills: The Automation of Higher Education," *First Monday*, vol. 3, no. 1, 1998. Online: http://www.firstmonday.org/issues/issue3_1/noble/index.html

Polster, Claire, "Situation Critical? The Future of the Liberal University in the Era of the Global Knowledge Grab." Paper presented at the 14th World Congress of Sociology, July–August 1998, Montreal, Canada.

Rayport, J. F., and J. J. Sviokla, "Managing in the Marketspace," *Harvard Business Review*, November–December 1994.

———, "Exploiting the Virtual Value Chain," *Harvard Business Review*, November–December 1995.

Resnick, Rosalind, and Dave Taylor, *The Internet Business Guide: Riding the Information Super-highway to Profit*. Sams, 1994.

Slotkin, Richard, *The Fatal Environment*. New York: Atheneum, 1985.

Smith, Michael D., "Understanding Digital Markets: Review and Assessment," in Erik Brynjolfsson and Brian Kahin, eds, *Understanding the Digital Economy*. MIT Press, 1999.

Talk City, "Talk City, the Chat Network, Rolls Out New Advertising Medium for the Web," Press release, 1998. Online: http://www.liveworld.com/news/releases/rel-970813.html

———, Media Kit, May 1999. Online: http://www.talkcity.com/mediakit.welcome.html

Verity, John, and Robert Hof, "The Internet: How It Will Change the Way You Do Business," *Business Week*, November 14, 1994.

Wilson, David, "Creating Compelling Commerce Sites via Community." Paper delivered at the Internet Commerce Expo, Boston, March 1999.

Zaret, Elliot, ZDNET Tech News, April 15, 1999. Online: http://www.zdnet.com/zdnn/stories/news/0,4586,2242290,00.html

2 Three Case Studies
by Janelle Brown

The business model goes like this: Assemble a few million people or so. Give them home page tools, chat rooms, surveys, polls, or bulletin boards. Encourage them to make friends and return to your Web site often. And then sell, sell, sell—put ads on every square inch of their home pages and chat rooms, encourage them to buy CDs and software from your e-commerce partners, sell their email addresses or opinions to direct marketers. Make a million, have an IPO. Bingo!

The Web has proven a receptive home for communities from all walks of life; the very nature of the world's greatest communication medium encourages the formation of special interest groups, support groups, friendships. Mailing lists, home pages, chat rooms, bulletin boards: people like to congregate and socialize wherever like-minded individuals might alight.

And wherever people congregate, there is money to be made. The MBAs of the Web figured this out early, and have been trying to figure out how to monetize community ever since. Many of the biggest Web sites on the Net are "community" hubs—for every communications tool that exists, you'll find a company that is trying to turn it into a business model. For mailing lists (also referred to as listservers), you'll find eGroups and Topica—companies which help you set up a mailing list and then sell ads on the email messages that list members send. Companies like Deja.com are commercializing Usenet: their Web interfaces to these universal bulletin boards are easy to use, as long as you don't mind banner ads. And if there is one company that is offering free home pages and chat rooms, there must be a hundred: AOL, GeoCities, Xoom, TheGlobe.com, FortuneCity, Homestead, Tripod. The list goes on and on.

These companies serve a useful purpose: Net users have benefited immensely from the simplifying tools that these Web sites provide. If these tools didn't exist, online community would still be squarely in the hands of the technologically elite. And there is no doubt that these corporate-owned services have helped their users forge strong connections with new friends.

Yet there is a natural tension between community and corporate profits. Companies need to make money. And to become profitable, most dot-com startups need to build the largest, most monetized communities possible. Companies like GeoCities or Xoom or TheGlobe.com—all publicly traded companies—have stock market prices that are directly tied to the number of members they can boast and the number of ads they can serve to those members. Communities, on the other hand, tend to be strongest when they are small and tightly focused. As Laurent Massa, the CEO of home-page hub Xoom.com, bluntly puts it:

> If you think about community and affinity groups, there is a limiting factor down the road for this concept, because you are gathering a core of purists. . . . We're not in the business of building art colonies.

The smaller the community, the stronger the links will be between the individual members—yet there will be fewer opportunities to make money off them.

But what happens to community when it becomes commodified? To those who believe in pure, unadulterated community, it is easy to look across the Web and be appalled at the way communities are exploited by their corporate sponsors. These fragile networks of friendship are vulnerable to the machinations of the companies that have brought them together. Companies go bankrupt, and those bulletin boards suddenly disappear; corporations change their business tactics, and communities are suddenly revamped to fit the new market expectations.

No corporate-sponsored community comes without a price.

During the course of four years of reporting on online communities, I've seen hundreds of companies try to turn community into a profitable enterprise; and I've witnessed the struggles that have ensued. The case studies of GeoCities, SmartGirl Internette, and Electric Minds that follow—based on these years of interviews with community developers, members, and volunteers—reflect the fact that corporate-backed communities do not always have the best interest of their members at heart. Despite good intentions and executive rhetoric about "building networks," the company's bottom line usually gets top priority, to the detriment of the community's needs.

Case Study 1: GeoCities[1]

In 1994—those very first days of the Web—a marketing executive named David Bohnett had a brilliant idea. Everybody, it seemed, suddenly wanted a home page on the World Wide Web, but few had the proper tools, skill sets, and access to server space. More importantly, people wanted home pages that were in proximity to those of their friends. Bohnett's brainstorm: What if you offered free home pages to the Web population at large, built around the concept of "neighborhoods" where homesteaders shared common interests?

With a pocketful of venture capital and a big vision, GeoCities was born, and began its meteoric rise as the granddaddy of all online community sites. When the company went public, in August of 1998, its stock price doubled on its first day to a market valuation of $1 billion. Its IPO ushered in six months of red-hot community site IPOs (TheGlobe.com, a second-rate competitor to GeoCities, watched its stock price rise 606 percent

---

1.   http://www.geocities.com

on its opening day, before beginning a slow descent into single-digit prices). By early 1999, GeoCities was boasting 3.3 million members in what it said was the "largest and fastest growing community of personal Web sites on the Internet." As GeoCities CEO Tom Evans proudly put it in January 1999,

> Community is such a hot topic, everyone is claiming they have community on their site. It is the first and only reason for Geocities. That's the reason why people come to Geocities.

And certainly, in the early days of GeoCities, it was a vibrantly interesting community. The site's "neighborhoods" were built around quirky special-interest topics: Area 51, for example, was where alien and paranormal enthusiasts congregated to build their home pages. Gay and lesbian communities descended on an area called West Hollywood, after the famous nightlife district of Los Angeles. And although many other GeoCities users really didn't care where their home pages were located—they were only concerned with slapping a few pictures of their cat on a Web site—others participated in GeoCities' active Community Leader program, volunteering to lead chats, host bulletin boards, and promote other "neighborhood activities."

But by the summer of 1998, around the time of its IPO and the market boom that sent the stock prices of community companies soaring, GeoCities had begun to metamorphose.

The changes happened gradually, but they soon became overwhelming. The GeoCities business model was based on selling banner ads on the home pages of its members, monetizing the traffic that those pages attracted. The number of these banners steadily increased. Soon, the single static ad banner at the top of every GeoCities home page had turned into a pop-up window with rotating animated ads, which refreshed every time you clicked on a link within the Web site. Even more annoying was a ghostly GeoCities watermark that suddenly appeared on the bottom of every member's home page, obscuring the text on the page and causing browsers to crash because of its glitchy Javascript programming.

This corporate drive for revenue expanded into other parts of the site as well, as the money-burning GeoCities struggled to turn a profit. The entryway to each "neighborhood" was filled with banner ads, solicitations, and e-commerce links; it became easier to find a "GeoShop" hawking flowers or software than it was to find a directory of the home pages in your neighborhood. To make matters worse, the sweetly metaphorical "neighborhoods" were buried, reorganized into generic topical directories—arts and entertainment, finance, and so on—which would appeal to advertisers.

Community leaders were also disempowered. In January 1999, there were a daunting 3.3 million GeoCities members, but only 1600 community leaders. Although community leaders were supposed to patrol their neighborhood for "inappropriate" or unfinished pages and encourage newcomers to join the community, expecting these volunteers to be responsible for the activities of thousands of members was unrealistic. Bulletin boards and chat rooms became ghost towns. And community leaders weren't given support or training they needed to moderate their communities—training being an expense that GeoCities just wasn't willing to undertake.

> Community leaders used to pick the pages [to promote on neighborhood front doors], and have a real power which gave them a sense of ownership. They would set up all kinds of programs in their neighborhoods.

explains Amy Jo Kim, author of *Community Building on the Web*, who spent the large part of a year researching GeoCities.

> GeoCities took away their power, backed away from neighborhoods, were lax about the giving community leaders advance notice about new features, and stopped soliciting input about redesigns.

When the GeoCities watermark materialized across the network with no warning, many community leaders took this as the last straw and fled the service, building new homes at other free-home-page services. Some started anti-GeoCities Web rings and petitions. Competing services, like FortuneCity, claimed that they saw significant increases in new member-ships after GeoCities imposed the pop-up ads and watermarks.

As a bitter community leader, "Beth P.," explained after she fled the service in early 1999,

> Within the past year, GeoCities has become just like all the other big, heartless corporations. They no longer want to be "your home on the Web," they just want money from their advertisers.

She, along with a few of her community leader pals, dismantled her home page and moved it to competing service Angelfire.

Indeed, it seems that GeoCities was never truly a commu-nity to the vast majority of those 3.3 million members. Many visited once, started a home page, and never returned, their neglected Web site lying stagnant and half-finished for years. Others never used the bulletin boards, chat rooms, or special interest clubs. Those who did were happy to migrate to some other service the moment that GeoCities became too big, impersonal, or commercial for their tastes. As Kim puts it,

> [These members] want a place with as much [server] space as they possibly can get, with as few ads as possible. . . . It has nothing to do with community—it's like squatters in burned out buildings in London. It's completely opportunistic.

In other words, it was never GeoCities that was the commu-nity—although it served as a useful tool for bringing together a small number of active participants. Although GeoCities—and similar sites—may have sold themselves to investors by tout-ing their "dedicated community" and millions of members, only a small percentage of that number ever considered the service a community at all. For most, it was simply a place to play with pixels and post some pictures, until some other free-home-page service offered a better deal.

On January 25, 1999, the Web directory Yahoo! purchased GeoCities, in a stock deal valued at $3.5 billion. GeoCities cur-rently exists as a subcategory of the Yahoo! search engine. Although Yahoo! reinstated some of the previously popular

GeoCities features—bringing those 41 "neighborhoods" back to the fore—the bulletin boards and chat rooms have been dismantled. Instead, GeoCities members are rerouted to Yahoo!'s own chat rooms and deserted bulletin boards. The community leader program is nowhere to be found.

Are GeoCities executives devastated that the "community" they had built is now simply a site-building tool for the Web's biggest search engine? Hardly—they lined their pockets with millions of dollars. And despite the vocal protests of a few of GeoCities' most dedicated members, it seems that the vast majority of those millions of users don't particularly care that they no longer have neighborhood get-togethers or rollicking bulletin boards. "Community," in this example, was a term used both carelessly and opportunistically—a word bandied about to take advantage of market hype, but not an ideology that was taken seriously by either its developers or its members. The Web's biggest community was not a community at all.

Case Study 2: SmartGirl Internette[2]

As far as corporate Web sites go, SmartGirl Internette is relatively modest. The roughly designed pages are home to a community of teenage girls; thousands visit every day to read teen-penned reviews of games, books, magazines, and movies—many write their own, as well. They post sweetly sincere notes in the active bulletin boards, on topics ranging from vegetarianism to sex to the pain of parental divorce. They can ask advice of site "experts" like Arielle and Adam, who proffer thoughts on love, relationships, on "how guys think." The Web site's slogan is "smart girls decide for themselves."

But besides communicating with their peers, the girls who visit SmartGirl Internette are also invited to participate in dozens of weekly surveys, answering questions about everything from their taste in celebrities to what they would like to

---

2. http://www.smartgirl.com

see in advertisements to whether Hawaiian print shirts are "very hot with the people in my school." These surveys may seem unimportant, but in fact, they are both the backbone and the stealthy commercial underside of the site.

The woman behind SmartGirl is Isabel Wolcott, a trim blonde professional with degrees from Harvard and Columbia, who keeps the Web site going along with a staff of fourteen. The site began almost by accident; in 1996, as part of her master's degree in technology and education, Wolcott posted a survey on her Web site asking teenage girls what they wanted to see in computer games. When the survey drew a phenomenal response, she had a sudden brainstorm:

> I was doing market research as a consultant—leading focus groups and writing up analysis. I noticed, doing that, how much faster, easier and cheaper it was to do my online survey than these focus groups. . . . I've got this database coming to me from the girls filling out the survey; if you want to do a "find" all you have to do is type in the keyword and hit enter.

When Wolcott put two and two together, SmartGirl Internette was born—not just as a community for girls, but as a vehicle for collecting market research and trend reports on teenage tastes. The information that those girls so painstakingly offer to that invisible hand is collected and sold to corporations—teen magazines, clothing companies, advertising firms, anyone who might be interested in the fads, trends, and tastes of teenage girls. This, in the world of trend reporting, is valuable information. Every time a visitor to SmartGirl explains that beaded flip flops or Latin-tinged music is what turns her on this month, someone is assessing that information and using it to better create and market products that she will *have to have*.

The SmartGirl community is, in fact, a vehicle that helps companies turn kids into better consumers.

Of course, SmartGirl is also a terrific community for teenage girls; there is no doubt that Wolcott truly wants to create a meaningful place where girls can let it all out. She gushes with excitement when she speaks about how "cute" the girls on her

Web site are, and is earnest about the way the bulletin boards break down the walls that teenage girls erect:

> You have people who are coming from completely different sides of the coin who would never talk in real life; you've got the popular girl with lots of friends talking with the geeky girl who is lonely and depressed. They are giving each other advice. They are having conversations they would never have with the girls who sit next to them in math.

In fact, she even sees the surveys themselves as a similar kind of female empowerment.

> Their impulse of wanting to be heard by other girls is the same thing that makes them want to be heard by other companies; they won't hesitate to tell us how they feel about things. . . . The girls want companies to listen to what they think. Here's the one place in their lives where what they have to say really does matter; they love the fact that their opinion is getting showcased for the world to see.

She is also quick to point out that, because the market research supports the site, the girls aren't forced to view advertisements.

Do the girls truly understand that they are participating in what is essentially an ongoing focus group that helps corporate sponsors sell merchandise? On the bottom of survey pages, in very tiny type, SmartGirl explains that

> SmartGirl does research for companies that make things for girls. They pay us to tell them what teens want. When you fill out a survey, you're helping us make money, and you're helping companies learn how to make better products, services, and advertising for girls like you.

The odds are slim that the girls actually read this tiny disclaimer; it is more likely that they simply get excited when they see their first name and comments show up in the monthly newsletters that SmartGirl sends out to its teenage members (a different, more cursory newsletter than the detailed $10,000-a-year reports that clients receive).

This kind of data collection has infuriated media watchdog groups in the past, which accuse SmartGirl of exploiting the teens. Katharina Kopp, a senior policy analyst at the Center for Media Education, points out that

> A lot of teen sites have these so-called surveys or polls where they get information from kids; they package it as if it's empowering to girls to speak out and have someone listen. I think that's deceiving, because they aren't always clear about how the information is used.

Wolcott is unapologetic about the fact that her Web site gathers and sells information from teenage girls.

> Of course it is all about making money; nobody can deny that we're a for-profit business. But to me the best way to make money is to do the right thing for your audience.

And the right thing, in her opinion, is to give these teenage girls a forum to opine to each other, and to the world at large.

And, in fact, her community seems blissfully unconcerned about these issues, as thirteen-year-old girls are wont to be. Instead, they prattle on about cliques and sexual harassment, crushes and homework: glad, no doubt, to have finally have a place where they can do just that.

Case Study 3: Electric Minds[3]

It is very common for corporate communities to be effaced from the Net; this often happens abruptly, and to the horror of the people who have forged friendships in those forums. AOL chat rooms suddenly disappear, bulletin boards are shut down without warning, Web sites offer free home pages until they suddenly go bankrupt—communities constantly find themselves displaced by their corporate sponsor's financial woes.

---

3. http://www.minds.com

Netscape's ambitious Professional Connections bulletin boards were scrapped just a year after their launch, for example, after the company decided that community was not going to be a lucrative endeavor after all. The boards were abruptly removed from the site, with no warning whatsoever—not even the paid and volunteer discussion leaders had advance knowledge of the community's demise. Members were left scrambling to find email addresses and contact information for friends they had known only by their login names (or pseudonyms, in some cases). Only persistent and vocal protests convinced Netscape to revive the boards for 30 days, giving members enough time to connect and try to move their community elsewhere.

And many *do* move their communities elsewhere. The Spot, a campy online soap opera popular in the early days of the Web, had a fan base that gathered daily in the adjacent bulletin boards; this group regularly flew across the country to participate in "SpotFan gatherings" and discuss not only the shenanigans of their favorite soap opera characters, but their own lives. The Spot was yanked from the Web in 1997, when the company behind it, American Cybercast, went bankrupt. But instead of disappearing into the ether, The Spot's fans built their own bulletin boards elsewhere: SpotFans.com, hosted on a fan's personal Web page, where the same group continued to chat away for two years after the soap opera's demise.

Then there's the case of Electric Minds: a community that was built by one of the most respected names in online community, Howard Rheingold, and still managed to fail financially and displace its members.

Rheingold, the author of *Virtual Community*, envisioned Electric Minds as a free and open—but equally erudite—alternative to subscription-only communities like The WELL and Echo (established bulletin-board systems known for the literati that gathered within their walls). Electric Minds, which launched on the Web in 1996, was a bulletin board built around a core of daily, staff-penned content on provocative topics. Net personalities like Laura Lemay and Justin Hall offered columns discussing community, virtual reality, and technology; inside the discussion boards, some 70,000 registered users participated in thoughtful debate.

With nearly $2 million in their pocket; a plan to make money on advertising, books, television shows, and content syndication; and a staff of well-respected "digerati" versed in online networking, Electric Minds was an online community that should have survived.

It didn't.

Despite plaudits from *Time* magazine (which listed Electric Minds as one of the ten best Web sites in 1996), the company ran out of money merely eight months after it launched. Although Electric Minds' plans were ambitious, its audience of geeks who wanted to chat about high-concept and academic topics was simply too narrow to appeal to the advertisers the site needed to survive; of those 70,000 registrants, merely hundreds actually posted regularly. Revenues were elusive, the Internet market was soft, and Electric Minds' primary funder—the Japanese investment firm Softbank—eventually pulled its money out of the company. Just days from being shut down for good, Electric Minds was finally purchased by Durand Communications, a conferencing software and services company.

Durand executives promised not to disrupt the community; but they also suspended the editorial content and denied the community members the resources that they needed to keep going. Rheingold explains,

> The people who bought Electric Minds wanted the brand, the publicity, because they were aiming to sell their company. . . .
> There's an awful lot of window-dressing in the community business, on the bottom of the food chain; there are a lot of companies that throw in "community" and they just want to flip [their stock]. The community smells it and it doesn't cohere.

And, in fact, the community soon fell apart, unhappy with its new owners. As the Electric Minds staffers and hosts departed, community members were unable to assemble any kind of democracy or charter that would organize the remaining discussions. Members fled. Today, although the Electric Minds Web site still exists, it is a shell of its previous self; where hundreds posted before, mere dozens remain today. Most of the "digerati" are gone.

But the community, in part, lives on elsewhere. Many of the departing members ended up at Rheingold's next community, a nonprofit project called Brainstorms hosted on Rheingold's personal Web site. The lesson learned, says Rheingold, is that it is difficult to build any kind of business model on community alone, and, in turn, that communities are probably better off without those corporations in the first place. He explains,

> Community is almost orthogonal to funding. You need the box to stay up, the bills to be paid, to be able to pay online facilitators, you need to have some marketing to draw people to [the community], but that's it. The people, other than your paid hosts, are the people who create the community content.

> Can you make money with community? No, and you shouldn't try to make money at it. If community is not a multiplier of an already sound business model, forget it. If you sell widgets . . . then an online social network can enhance your ability to make money doing that. But people are not going to pay your company for what they can find elsewhere.

But *can* they find these kinds of communities elsewhere? Do these social networks need to rely on companies that will use them as market-research guinea pigs, try to sell them products, bombard them with advertising, and eventually dismantle their community if the business model doesn't fly? Certainly, the examples of Electric Minds and The Spot suggest that communities don't need their corporate sponsors to continue existing.

Looking at the examples of GeoCities, SmartGirl, Electric Minds, and other for-profit communities, you could come to the conclusion that the Web would be better off if community were left to nonprofit entities. Any company that builds a community at the core of its business is going to discover a natural tension between what best serves its members and what best serves its bottom line. The teenage girls at Smart-Girl should be able to discuss their favorite movies without having their opinions scrutinized by marketers; if given more community leaders and fewer pop-up ads, GeoCities members might actually be able to build a community; had the Electric Minds community been nonprofit from the start, its members wouldn't have been displaced so soon.

It's difficult to turn a profit in the community business; but it would also be short-sighted to dismiss the idea altogether. Web sites like these *have* served their purpose: bringing together like-minded individuals who might not otherwise have discovered each other. Sure, there are thousands of noncorporate communities online—IRC chat rooms, Usenet discussions, and bulletin-board systems abound—but they aren't always easy to find and navigate. Only a small number of technologically advanced Web users have the skills and tools required to build community areas on their own personal Web sites.

These community companies, despite their flaws, have introduced millions of Web users to the notion of online community; they have established networks, enlightened individuals, and stimulated new friendships. Disturbing as it may be to watch these struggling companies exploit their users on the quest for profits, at the end of the day a community is only the sum of its members. And if they are unhappy, those members can always move.

chapter

3 Cookies, Gift-Giving, and Online Communities

*by Hillary Bays, hdbays@ehess.fr,
and Miranda Mowbray,
mjfm@hplb.hpl.hp.com*

This chapter arose from a question: why are there so many connections between cookies and the Internet? We describe some of these connections. Cookies appear in contexts which have to do with giving and sharing. We explore the larger social context of cookies as food, as a gift for children, and as a symbol of sharing, and we also look at the relationship between women and giving. There turns out to be a connection between the Internet gift economy, the U.S. tradition of giving cookies as a present, and the future of online communities. We describe this connection and its implication for those designing and running online communities.

Cookies may summarize succinctly a very American ethic that is prevalent in the world of the Internet: a curious mixture of Christian values, individualism, endless/innumerable bounty, strict socialization, and a touch of the child in all of us.

Introduction: How This Research Came to Be

All of us involved in online communities in some way have come across the idea of Web cookies, and wondered where this term comes from and what significance it holds. First, they remind us of sweet biscuits and childhood, and yet now, in an electronic context, they can seem dangerous, invading, and annoying (Cléo 1999). These are the most obvious remarks, but surprises came up when we were working on other research, namely about politeness phenomena in Internet Relay Chat conversations (Bays 1999). On two separate occasions (and it wouldn't be surprising if this happens more often) cookies were discursive objects that were distributed around to the whole group as tokens of kindness and unity. Giving in chat seemed like a child's game of make-believe in which the child invites his/her friends to partake in a little tea party (with their little fingers raised as they "sip" from delicate cups). Discursive objects are a way of communicating emotions and friendliness in a limited medium with little scope for tone of voice, for example. We asked why cookies were the objects chosen on these occasions to represent an atmosphere of convivial sharing. The multiple meaning and complexity of the term associated with the gesture of giving became more and more apparent as we looked into further associations on the Internet and in real life. This led us to a deeper investigation of the use and meaning of cookies, whether in online communities or in the "real-life" communities that shape us and our online participation.

To begin with, it is difficult to arrive at a firm definition concerning the word *cookies* in the context of the Internet, for all we have is the result of the word in context and not a clear idea of the process of how the word was chosen. To draw semiotic conclusions about this word and reach an understanding of the term, we must first recognize that it is a sign, which is attributed a certain value in a certain context (as a programming term, in Internet culture, or in American society, for example). Like all signs, this one has no single definition or significance, and has the possibility to evolve over time or in a different context. As such, we are constantly recontextualizing and interpreting, verifying the meaning we have attributed to the sign or object in a particular occurrence.

The metaphor of cookies is pervasive in online communities, being used in a variety of contexts that are interrelated, but yet seem to lack cohesion. To come to a clear understanding of this term, it is necessary to review its different meanings in order to expose some of the underlying similarities between these examples and discuss their significance in the larger social context.

The Gift Economy in Online Communities

In their articles about the economics of Internet communities, Rishab Aiyer Ghosh (1998) and Richard Barbrook (1998) describe how online communities with member-contributed content operate as gift economies. Individual members donate content for other members to use free of charge. In return, each individual receives access to all the content made available by others. The amount an individual receives is much more than they could ever produce, so the gift economy works in the interest of the members. This economic model also facilitates the cooperative production of free high-quality software and other digital content. Ghosh and Barbrook note that the assumption that information will be shared for free is built into the technological design of the Internet.

We will show in this chapter that the metaphors about cookies (and related terminology) that were chosen by those who built and use the technology underlying online communities both reflect and constitute a gift culture.

Cookie Exchange

First, let us evoke an example of cookies as symbols in the gift economy. At Christmastime (another moment especially charged with the idea of gift giving) in some neighborhoods in the United States, women bake dozens of cookies and trade them with their friends so that each has a variety of home-baked cookies to offer to guests. This is something like a modern sewing bee, and it reduces the number of hours spent in the kitchen for these women, because each only bakes one type of cookie but then each ends up with a huge variety once all are traded. Here we can draw parallels to knowledge-rich online communities where individual members have their own areas of expertise, but the results are made available to the community to contribute to the general knowledge base. The scientific community has long depended on this type of open exchange to make time-saving breakthroughs via data sharing (Barbrook 1998). For example, the information produced by several independent laboratories can be compared and unified for further research. Prestige is consequently gained by sharing noteworthy information.

But this exchange is not limited to the pursuit of science or the exchange of weighty data as was intended in the early days of the Internet.

Online Recipe Collections

One of the first prolific uses of bulletin-board online communities was for the sharing of recipes. This may be because recipes suit the functioning of an electronic gift economy in which members contribute their own knowledge to the common capital, just as in some offline communities it is normal for friends and neighbors to share recipes freely with each other. The Yahoo! directory lists 702 recipe sites on the World Wide Web, nine of which are exclusively for cookie recipes. The CookieRecipe.com site has "Over 1,800 cookie recipes last time we checked," donated by visitors to the site. So, sharing cookie recipes represents part of an extensive open exchange of information found on the Internet.

Cookies As Food

Cookies are often thought of primarily as a kind of food, and many different descriptions and recipes of cookies circulate within online communities (as demonstrated by the abundance of online cookie recipes, although the chocolate chip is probably the quintessential cookie in our study). On the Internet there are also other food-related metaphors such as Java, which is associated with coffee (and drinking coffee late into the night or meeting friends for a coffee at a café or at someone's house). Similarly, the term Applets, small Java applications, seems to mean "small apples," and is now included by a process of folk etymology as an example of a food metaphor, as a recent semantic query on the LinguistList shows[1] (Bruendl 1998). Apple Computer, Inc., sells Macintosh personal computers, taking the word "Macintosh" from an edible variety of apple.

Food metaphors are familiar and unthreatening, thereby making this technical universe easier for the layman to understand and thus more user friendly. Food metaphors also imply a form of material sustenance that we derive from using computers and the Internet.

Symbolic Sustenance and Virtual Cookies

From our observations, giving things online often involves giving food or drink, different kinds of light sustenance. For example, in the Internet Relay Chat Bar channel (among other channels), people give each other cocktails or they pass out beers. Cookies are another form of sustenance. They are given as symbolic sustenance, fillers and snacks to hold us over with a smile until the real meal is served. Although they have no intrinsic nutritional value, there is still a social function to these gifts. In a few instances on some other chat channels, participants gave out discursively described cookies, each user expanding on the shape, ingredients, and flavors of the cookies.

The Virtual Cookies site (Cheryl&Co no date) enables Internet users to send pictures of cookies over the Internet to their family and friends. The site says, "Virtual Cookies are now the easiest way to say 'Happy Birthday,' 'Thank You,' or even just 'I'm thinking about you' to someone special!" The site is encouraging the use of virtual cookies as an online means of reinforcing ties within existing communities of friends and relations.

---

1.   The LinguistList reference also contains a summary of some metaphorical meanings of cookies.

Cookies As Discrete Units (Stereotypical/ Mythological Image)

Cookies are individual little gifts. They are small enough to be given as presents between meals without spoiling a child's appetite (although some American firms sell ENORMOUS cookies that are enough to spoil anyone's appetite). They are designed to be ready to be given and eaten at once whenever there is occasion for it, rather than being confined to meal-times. This makes them the perfect instant-gratification gift. They are integral units, so that in receiving a cookie we are getting individual treatment, not just part of a cake or a larger whole.

The individual nature of each cookie may also appeal to an American sensibility, as individualism is a strong part of Americans' cultural identity. There is the feeling that each cookie is potentially unique, although it may come from the same batter (there may be more chocolate chips in this one, or it may be slightly undercooked and chewy compared to the others . . .). Likewise, cookies are practical and neat: they are not messy and do not require cutting, plates, or forks, only napkins. The recipient of a cookie also never has to touch the food of another if he gets a cookie, and his piece never has the same close contact with the rest of the batch (like slices of a cake or pie) except in its conception. Finally, giving cookies does not involve the same effort as giving a whole cake, so the necessity to reciprocate in like manner does not become unbalanced, as the gift does not overextend the giver and oblige an expensive countergift.

Although today cookies are readily bought and sold in many different places from gas stations to convenience stores and supermarkets, and sold in bags, packets, and as individual snacks, a mythology of the cookie as a home-baked treat persists. Thus, the stereotypical home-baked representation, which we found in our interviews (described later) directed toward uncovering people's associations with cookies, overrides the reality of the market. So, even when buying baskets of cookies, they are rarely counted or quantified. In some cases, the treat even seems to be infinite. For example, in the idyllic house in "Leave it to Beaver" (an American TV sitcom from the 1950s) there is a never-ending supply of cookies in the cookie jar for when the kids get home from school.

Pursuing this idea, when we think of the stereotypical cookie and baking, one cannot estimate the percentage of the batch that a cookie contains, so one cannot estimate its particular, exact "price." Here the idealistic representation of the perfect cookie does not take into account quantification and market logic. Nor can we see that there is something missing when one cookie is taken from the cookie jar (whereas it is painfully obvious if someone steals a piece of a cake before the party).

It is only recently that we associate the term "cookies" with morsels of data. But, with these former definitions in mind, it can be understood that they are individual packets with various functions that can be subjectively manipulated. The origins of the word are lost in the folklorization of the terminology and its social significance.

Let us then look at how the term "cookies" is used on the Internet by dividing the examples into pertinent categories, which form a kind of continuum from the computer/Web cookie definition to the metaphoric/symbolic nature of cookie giving.

Cookies in Early Internet Terminology

We start with the computer-oriented definitions of the term "cookie." Several of these first arose in earlier days of the Internet (or even earlier), when the programming community was quite small.

Web Cookies

Web cookies are tokens that can let a Web server know that you are the same person who accessed the server the last time you accessed it, so that an extended interaction with the Web server is possible. The cookie is given from the server to your browser (if your browser has been programmed to accept it) when the Web page is accessed, and is given back to the server at the next visit. This is the most common reference to "cookies" on the Web. Web cookies are one technology that enables members of a Web-based online community to have a persistent identity within the community.

The name "cookie" is an unthreatening name for a token that can be used for purposes that some people find threatening. However, this name was not given in an attempt to make Web cookies sound friendly. The token is called a cookie because it is an instance of a "magic cookie."

Magic Cookies

"Magic cookie" is a common programming term for a handle given to a piece of information shared between cooperating programs. The entry for "magic cookie" in the *New Hacker's Dictionary* (Raymond 1996, 2000) defines it as "something passed between routines or programs that enables the receiver to perform some operation; a capability ticket or opaque identifier." So a magic cookie is, as part of the definition, something shared.

Similarly, the entries in the *New Hacker's Dictionary* and its online version, the Jargon file, are donated by hackers and edited by volunteers; they are the product of an online community.

Fortune Cookies

Early computer programmers also shared data in ways other than via a data-transfer protocol. The fortune cookie program was an early, and popular, UNIX utility. There was a shared fortune cookie file of quotes, jokes, epigrams, and pithy sayings. Anyone with access to the file server could type "fortune" and one of the fortunes would be chosen at random and printed on their screen. The fortune file was shared not only in its distribution, but also in its creation. Anyone could submit a fortune to add to the fortune file. The fortune file, therefore, was created by an online community, and was a resource for that community.

Incidentally, the name of this utility is a reference to the fortune cookies that are given at the end of a meal in Chinese restaurants in the United States. Inside the cookie is a strip of paper on which is printed an epigram or piece of advice. Fortune cookies are not paid for explicitly on the bill—their cost is absorbed in the price of the meal.

GNU emacs

Programmers also began to create software collaboratively and to share it without restrictions on use. Perhaps the most famous item of open source free software is the GNU emacs text-editing program which is available as part of the Linux operating system, or can be downloaded separately. When you download the files for GNU emacs, in addition to the text editor you get a cookie recipe.

This is not the only reference to cookies in GNU emacs: the documentation for the HTML-helper-mode in emacs uses the name "cookies" for HTML tags. HTML-helper-mode was programmed by Nelson Minar (1999), who says that he does not remember why he chose the term "cookie" but that it was probably derived from the "magic cookie" meaning.

Open source free software is produced as part of an online gift economy. Software like Linux and GNU emacs is produced by volunteers and made available to all for free. Open source free software programs are often developed within online communities of collaborating programmers.

The Cookie Virus

Some people feel that the terminology of Web cookies derives from a practical joke that has now taken on larger proportions. Computer viruses similarly developed into something alarming from early manifestations which were harmless to the computer and rather silly.

The Cookie Monster is a character on the American children's TV program "Sesame Street." It is a cuddly-looking monster that lives in a cookie jar. It shouts out I WANT COOKIE, GIVE ME COOKIE, I WANT COOKIE and continues to shout until you give it a cookie (which it devours immediately).

One of the early computer viruses was known as the Cookie Monster virus. This did not destroy data, but continually printed out I WANT COOKIE, GIVE ME COOKIE on the screen of the infected computer. If you typed in "cookie" (or, in some versions, "chocolate chip") it stopped (Bruendel 1998, Raymond 1996, 2000). It was reported in some very early online communities, in shared file systems for researchers, predating the Internet.

The Childlike Spirit in Cookie Terminology

The close-knit and relatively homogeneous group of programmers in the early stages of the development of the Internet created the environment in which UNIX fortune and magic cookies, HTML helper tags, and the Cookie Monster virus could be understood and thrive.

These examples suggest that there was a childlike spirit while integrating this word into computer science terminology. On his home page Ari Halberstadt, owner of the magiccookie.com domain, says that the word is a whimsical term for a number (or tag) used to identify something in a piece of code but with no intrinsic value. Indeed, in and of themselves, Web cookies are harmless pieces of data transferred from your computer to the Web page, leaving a trail of cookie crumbs, or information, as Hansel and Gretel did to help them find their way back out of the dark forest; see Dan Loehr's comments in Bruendl 1998.

There is nothing sinister about Web cookies per se, but Web cookies have acquired a negative reputation as a result of some uses that have been made of them. Some companies use Web cookies to keep track of users' behavior on the Web, and sell the information obtained for advertising and direct marketing purposes (Green et al. 2000, Roeder 1997). Junkbusters (1999) describes this problem and also gives a link to free cookie management software.

Cookies Are Meant to Be Shared

The next category of our discussion slides us into a more sociological approach to cookie metaphors on the Internet. Recalling the childlike expression and ambience of certain online practices, we see that cookies and their recipes are an important means of gift giving and sharing, like the online recipe catalogues or the recipe with emacs software.

Giving online in itself is often immaterial, like sending virtual flowers (or virtual cookies) or electronic postcards. It is often make-believe and replicates the social practices that we believe we should engage in. Thus, like children in a make-believe tea party, we demonstrate our kindly behavior toward our fellow man, even if (and perhaps especially because) it doesn't cost us any measurable amount of time, money, or effort. Indeed, it is a collection of these small actions that make up the social gift economy within online communities.

Clifford Stoll's Cookies

Another good example comes from an early Internet personality, Clifford Stoll. He first came to fame when his investigation of a 75-cent accounting discrepancy ended with his tracking down a German cracker who was stealing military information for the KGB over the Internet. Clifford Stoll's book about this experience, *The Cuckoo's Egg* (Stoll 1989), was the first best-seller on Internet security. He includes his cookie recipe on page 152, although it has little obvious relevance to the book's main narrative. A later book (Stoll 1995) quotes an online discussion about *The Cuckoo's Egg* that shows readers remembering the recipe as a particular feature of that book. Assuming the ambience of sharing and perhaps following the example of GNU emacs, Clifford Stoll found it pertinent (and perhaps generous) to include his cookie recipe in his book.

One of Clifford Stoll's objections to crackers who try to break into systems is that they cause systems administrators to lock up their sites, so that resources once freely available become more difficult to access for good purposes, and the sense of community is threatened. Sharing recipes like his (and other useful resources), on the other hand, is one way of fostering this sense of community.

Kindergarten

As we have seen, people are actively involved in sharing cookies. This behavior seems to be natural to us; it is something that we have been socialized to do early on.

The socialization process is widespread on the Internet as well. The poem "All I really need to know I learned in kindergarten" by the Unitarian minister Robert Fulghum (1988) is quoted on over a hundred Web sites and mentioned on many more. The poem talks of eating cookies in kindergarten and learning there to share with others. There are minor variations in the quoted versions, but all mention cookies and sharing. (The poem is also quoted on management training cassettes and is available in an audio-book edition in public libraries; it seems to be part of an American ethic.) Following the poem's logic, it appears that kindergarten provides a link between cookies and community values.

The Scouts monopolize the image of cookies and charity. There is an American tradition of Girl Scouts selling cookies once a year to raise money for their troops—it has been estimated that more than two million Girl Scouts in the United States take part in cookie sales (Montgomery 1998–1999). To support these good-deed-doers, people buy boxes of their cookies. They do this not necessarily because they want these types of cookies (although the chocolate mint cookies are definitely worth buying all year round) but principally because it supports the budget of the Scout troop, permitting youngsters to gain experience in survival skills, learn home economics, and help elderly people, etc. Good Scouts are the ones who sell the most cookies, and the troops are rewarded for this, too. By buying them the public is also performing an act of charity, and supporting the local community.

In-Group Politeness

Sharing information and gifts is a way of promoting positive social interactions. It is part of a complex process of socialization in which social relations are learned and conducted and which ensure a state of relative cohesion and cooperation in our interactions. In their theory of politeness as an interactional grammar, Brown and Levinson (1987), in their seminal work *Politeness*, also address the question of giving as a way of demonstrating politeness (calling it "Strategy 15"). They associate it with the notion of positive-politeness—this can be thought of as proactive politeness, and is a collection of interactional strategies used to maintain the consistent self-image claimed by one's interlocutor. Positive-politeness aims at demonstrating that the other is ratified, included, liked, or admired.

Gifts, then, in both material and immaterial form (e.g., advice, sympathy, human-relations), are concrete tokens of this affirmation. In giving, the giver is actually fulfilling some of the recipient's desires or needs (which in turn reinforces the assumption that the giver knows the recipient's wants sufficiently and wants to fulfill them). In addition, gifts serve to build bridges, common experiences, and common ground between the people interacting.

In a similar manner, since jokes are based on mutual shared background knowledge and values, jokes tend to reinforce those shared traits and demonstrate complicity. So, by sharing (i.e., giving) a joke, the agent is including the hearer into this realm.

Seen from this angle, a practical joke, like the Cookie Monster virus, could also be considered a gift, intended for a particular "in-group" audience. It is the equivalent of giving a surprise birthday party for a large-scale group of friends. The author of the joke designs it to be funny or effective for the person or people subjected to it (in the case of the Cookie Monster virus, a few other programmers and scientists). Since the author knows his audience, he attempts to fulfill certain of the recipients' wants, such as the desire to be recognized as an "in" member. If the joke is well targeted, only the intended receivers will find it funny, thus creating and reaffirming a greater bond between the author and his audience, despite the temporary annoyance that this virus originally provoked.

The Hau of Cookies

In his treaties on the gift-giving rituals of primitive peoples, Marcel Mauss (1950/1990) mentions the Maori belief in the *hau*, or spirit, of something given (that is, where each object is invested with a life and individuality). This hau is circulated as the gift and its intentions are exchanged between the multiple participants of the gift cycle. The hau is also used to generate the gift-giving cycle and manifests itself as a kind of positive magic force. For the Maori, it is the vital force, the wind that breathes life, and the source of growth and maturation when they give to the forest or other peoples. It is the force which, in turn, generates a reciprocal gift. So, even when this gift has been transferred to the next person, it still possesses something of the giver. "Hence, it follows that to make a gift of something to someone is to make a present of some part of one's self" (p. 12).

Claude Levi-Strauss adds that we can postulate that the hau is coextensive in generalized giving (Godbout 1992, p. 187). The hau does not represent a product of an economic value, but its use favors a link or a relation to community and well-being. In its circulation, the gift enriches the link and transforms the protagonists into those who share in a communitary cycle.

Cookies then could be thought of as having a hau, which could be that they are "good for you" (especially when eaten warm with cold milk, as Robert Fulghum advises). They supply some sort of spiritual and corporal nourishment. For example, in a study on politeness in Internet Relay Chat (Bays 1999), an Internet Relay Chat user gave two cookies to another participant to help him get over a headache, a condition which might have hindered the pleasant atmosphere of the group. Similarly, as Erma Bombeck observes (1983), the stereotypical mothers of TV sitcoms could heal even the most traumatic situations with cookies and milk.

Reciprocal giving of food is also related to festivities, conjuring the notions of hospitality, communion, and peace. People want to pass this on to their friends, family, and extended network of online friends. Gifts of cookies then replicate a gift of a feast, and as such, they serve as tiny drops of glue to forge community spirit among the millions of strangers online. Finally, the hau, completing its cycle, as gifts are exchanged from one person to the next, is returned to its place of origin.

Women and Giving

We now come to the most complex of our analytic findings: the special relationship between women and giving. Women give not only sustenance to their dependents, but they give life itself. Traditionally, they are given in marriage, they give of themselves making love, they give birth.

True, the early programmers of online communities were not generally women, so it is all the more curious that there are so many references to cookies on the Internet. These programmers may have associated the giving of cookies with memories they had of their home environment or of their grandmothers and mothers. As Godbout (1992) notes, women have long been symbols of giving: the three Graces in Greek mythology, who give gifts of learning and art, are female, and the name of the first woman, Pandora, is derived from the words for "all" and "gift."

Here also, we are struck by the double nature of the gift, as for the Web cookie.

Cookies and Mom

Many of the cookie recipes found on the Internet are called "grandma's favorite" or appear to be feminine-descendant heirlooms. This folklore is substantiated further by certain brand names like Mrs. Field's Cookies.

Additionally, one can order baskets of cookies online and send them, like flowers, to loved ones and friends. The marketing strategy of one such company for Mother's Day was to suggest that their customers "return the favor" for all the cookies Mom had baked for them as a child (Schmidt 1999). In the study of Internet Relay Chat interaction mentioned previously (Bays 1999), several instances of cookie giving were found in which female-presenting characters distributed imaginary cookies to the others in a chat room. In one case, a participant distributes homemade cookies that her own mother had sent her for Easter. There is a maternal quality in giving these cookies that serves to create a bond between the giver (mother) and the recipient (child).

Archetype of a Cookie Baker

For this research we asked some people to uncover the associations they make with baking cookies and cookie bakers. Our interviewees included both people with many years' experience of online communities, and people who had never accessed the Internet; and they included both North Americans and Europeans. The associations uncovered by these different groups of interviewees were similar, except that the Europeans saw cookies as being essentially American.

Here are extracts from three of the interviews, depicting three generations involved in cookie baking. The first interviewee mentions a stereotypical Mom.

> American, that's the first thing I think of. Mother and apple pie. Obesity—no, that's too strong, a rounded figure. Mom. She's the kind of person who wears an apron [laughs]. I never wear an apron, although it's impractical, I get my clothes dirty. I don't know people who bake cookies, they probably

did when their children were there. Good housewives, mothers, cooks—it's not just for their children though, it's "have a cookie" [gesture of offering a cookie]. For neighbors. It might be for a social event like tennis parties. People who volunteer to help out at fetes, mothers' unions, social circles.

The second interviewee associates cookies with her grandmother.

My grandmother making cookies because we came over. She was wearing an apron and she had oven gloves on after taking the cookies out of the oven. She was late 60s, I was 7 or 8. She's Irish. She's very chatty, bubbly, kind, a real grandmotherly type. Grandmothers are never nasty, annoyed, or bad.

The third describes his children involved in cookie baking.

My kids baking cookies, they're girls aged 5 and 6, they're very excited when they do cooking and not very helpful. Their Mummy is baking cookies and they've decided they want to help. There are bowls full of sticky cookie mixture, girls standing on stools wielding various tools dangerously, oblivious of everything else.

The composite image of the ideas of these and the other interviewees' ideas on cookies reveals a middle-aged or older, plumpish housewife who bakes cookies to share with her children or to give to a charity or church function. She also shares in the baking itself (in a teaching endeavor) with her children. In this way the mother is teaching her children the value of generosity with information (and patience). Our interviewees' testimonies show an archetype of a traditional woman, the rounded mother of abundance who gives graciously to her children, who does not deprive them of their wants (nor does she discipline them). She is the modern Ceres with the cornucopia.

In essence, the logic of a woman's role in giving is contradictory to capitalist/market logic. They do not give to receive or to earn in the cycle described by Mauss as the obligation to give, to receive, and to reciprocate. They break this chain and give freely to their children and to others with no thought of reciprocity (Godbout 1992). All of these forms of the circulation of goods and services between strangers function outside of the market and without borrowing or taking up the state-organized model of redistribution. This is part of what constitutes the investment that community members make in their community.

Learning from an Urban Legend

One feature of communities is that they develop shared wisdom and folklore. Urban legends are stories that are probably untrue but strike such a chord that their listeners spread them to others. Since online communities provide cheap and fast ways of spreading stories to many people, they form an efficient medium for urban legends.

Cookies in online communities are the subjects of some legends. In many of our inquiries about where cookie-related terminology came from, our correspondent said that he or she did not know, but then continued with, "It might be from . . ." or "I heard that it comes from . . ." These are prefaces for oral history and the making of urban legends, with hearsay information passed down from person to person. It then becomes transformed, taking on a metalanguage and significance of its own.

The Expensive Cookie Recipe

The story of the expensive cookie recipe is a famous online urban legend, propagated via email and bulletin boards. Jolley (1995) gives one version of the story, and a recipe. McMillen (1998) gives strong evidence that the story is not true, and another recipe.

In the story, a woman visiting a café with her daughter eats a cookie and asks for the cookie recipe. The waitress tells her that it will cost "two fifty" and she asks the waitress to add the price to the tab. She discovers later that the cost is

$250, not $2.50. She asks them to take back the recipe and reduce the bill,

> and they said they were sorry, but all the recipes were this expensive so not just everyone could duplicate any of their bakery recipes . . . the bill would stand.

As revenge, she decides to make sure that every cookie lover has a free copy of the $250 recipe.

> So, here it is, and please pass it to someone else or run a few copies. . . . I paid for it; now you can have it for free.

The story of the expensive cookie recipe also links this folklore to women. The woman, who was sharing a nice time with her daughter, decides that she will subvert the system of overpricing by giving away the recipe she has just been forced to buy, countering the market logic with the gift economy. This online legend becomes a parable to demonstrate what qualities are unacceptable (overpricing and hard-sell capitalism) or acceptable (giving, generosity) to members of the online community. It also demonstrates the action to take when confronted by the unacceptable force of aggressive capitalism online—that is, you can beat capitalism by sharing freely.

Conclusions and Business Implications

Cookie-giving becomes a unifying device, because we learn to share the resources that we have. All of the examples above seem to demonstrate that cookie-giving is a quality that every one of us Internet users should develop and nurture.

Implication for Online Community Business Strategies

The young American men who built early online communities experienced the sharing of ideas in the academic and scientific community. But they also experienced a gift economy in kindergarten and among their mothers, grandmothers, and women neighbors of the type who volunteer to help in the local community, and who bake cookies. The Internet builders associated cookies with gift-giving and sharing. So when they set up communities building open source free software, or built the World Wide Web to support the exchange of documents within academic communities, or set up shared file systems, they thought of cookies.

One of the fastest-growing demographic segments of Internet users in the past few years has been women over the age of 50. Surveys disagree to the exact numbers, but agree that this is a significant demographic segment. These women are enthusiastic about the Internet and spend more time online than younger Internet users. Their principal reason to use the Internet is to communicate with their family and friends (CNN 1998, DN Wire 1998, Georgia Tech Research Corporation 1998, Nielsen Media Research 1998, Opinion Research Corporation International 1999).

Anecdotal evidence suggests that the American women over 50 coming to the Internet tend to be religious, traditional, and family oriented—they are exactly the type of women identified in our interviews as the archetypal cookie-baker. It is not a coincidence that they feel at home in the Internet gift economy: it was partly inspired by them.

This has an implication for business strategies for those building and running online communities. The cookie-givers are not motivated by monetary profit; they give their cookies away. Companies that assume that in the future most transactions on the Internet will be in exchange for money will miss this important demographic group. It is certainly possible to make money from cookie-givers. Baking cookies requires cookie tins and chocolate chips, which the cookie-givers buy. But it has to be done with tact and understanding of the gift economy.

It is considered wrong by cookie-givers to charge $250 for the source code for your cookies, or to collect recipes that others give you for free and then sell them without adding any value yourself. There are examples of precisely this type of behavior on the Internet. Clashes between the volunteer philosophy and the business strategies of prominent Internet companies have already taken place. To cite two examples that are mentioned elsewhere in this book, AOL was investigated by the U.S. Labor Department after complaints by some of its online community volunteers (Zaret 1999, see also Werry's chapter in this book), and Yahoo! was forced to withdraw its claim to unlimited commercial use of the content of GeoCities home pages, after an organized protest by GeoCities homesteaders (Fiedler no date, see also Bakardjieva and Feenberg's chapter in this book).

Conclusion

The reason that there are so many connections between cookies and online community is that in the United States cookies are a symbol of giving and sharing. In the future, online communities are likely to be dominated demographically by people used to operating in gift economies. Commercial online communities run by companies that understand the gift-giving philosophy are likely to prosper.

Acknowledgments

An earlier version of this chapter was published in *First Monday* (http://www.firstmonday.org) vol. 4, no. 11; this chapter appears here with the kind permission of *First Monday*. Thanks to everyone who told us about cookies. Thanks also to the organizers of "Exploring Cyber Society."

References

Barbrook, Richard, "The Hi-Tech Gift Economy," *First Monday*, vol. 3, issue 12 (December 1998). Online: http://www.firstmonday.dk/issues/issue3_12/barbrook/index.html

Bays, Hillary, "The Gift Economy in Internet Relay Chat—Giving Immaterial and 'Material' Gifts," John Armitage and Joanne Roberts, eds., Exploring Cyber Society: Social, Political, Economic and Cultural Issues, Vol. 2. Proceedings of the Conference 5–7 July 1999, School of Social, Political and Economic Sciences, University of Northumbria at Newcastle, UK.

Bombeck, Erma, *Motherhood, the Second Oldest Profession*, New York: McGraw–Hill, 1983.

Brown, Penelope, and Stephen C. Levinson, *Politeness: Some Universals in Language Usage*. London: Cambridge University Press, 1987.

Bruendl, Monika, "Summary: 'cookies,' " *LinguistList,* vol. 9 no. 309, March 2, 1998. Online: http://www.linguistlist.org/issues/9/9-309.html#1

Cheryl&Co, Virtual Cookies Site, no date, http://www.virtual-cookie.com

Cléo, "Sabir Cyber: Cookies," Le Monde Interactive Insert, *Le Monde,* p. v (13 October 1999).

CNN, "Retirees Revel in Net," news report, June 28, 1998.

DN Wire, "Wired UK Families Spend More Time Logged on Than Eating," November 18, 1998. Online: http://www.pcpro.co.uk/jbilbo/news/98-10-18-17326.html

Fiedler, David, "Boycott the Content Robbers," no date. Online: http://www.dragonflames.com

Fulghum, Robert, *All I Really Need To Know I Learned in Kindergarten*. New York: Ivy Books, 1988.

Georgia Tech Research Corporation, GVU Center, "GVU's 10th WWW User Survey," October 1998. Online: http://www.gvu.gatech.edu/user_surveys/survey-1998-10

Ghosh, Rishab Aiyer, "Cooking Pot Markets: An Economic Model for the Trade in Free Goods and Services on the Internet," *First Monday*, vol. 3, no. 3 (March 1998). Online: http://www.firstmonday.dk/issues/issue3_3/ghosh/index.html

Godbout, Jacques, *L'esprit du don*. Paris: Editions de la Découverte, 1992.

Green, Heather, Norm Alster, Amy Borrus, and Catherine Yang, "Privacy: Outrage on the Web," *Business Week*, February 14, 2000. Online: http://www.businessweek.com/2000/00_07/b3668065.htm

Jolley, Jeff, "Urban Legends," AMS BBS posting, July 27, 1995. Online: http://www.mcs.drexel.edu/~gcmastra/mail/legends.txt

Junkbusters Corporation, "How Web Servers' Cookies Threaten Your Privacy," December 18, 1999. Online: http://www.junkbusters.com/ht/en/cookies.html

Mauss, Marcel, *The Gift*, W. D. Halls, trans. London: W. W. Norton, 1990. Original title *Essai sur le Don*, Paris: Presses Universitaires de France, 1950.

McMillen, John, "The Cookie Hoax," *Hoaxes & Viruses*, June 2, 1998. Online: http://bedfordonline.com/hoax/nmcookie.htm

Minar, Nelson, private email communication, August 1999.

Montgomery, Dana J., "Troop 1440, Wakefield, MA—Our Girl Scout Cookie Sale, 1999," 1998–1999. Online: http://cheesecakeandfriends.com/Troop1440/1999/cookies.htm

Nielsen Media Research/Commercenet, "Internet Demographics Survey," June 1998.

Opinion Research Corporation International, "Internet User Survey," 1999.

Raymond, Eric, ed., *The New Hacker's Dictionary*, 3d ed. Cambridge, MA: MIT University Press, 1996. Online version http://www.tuxedo.org/~esr/jargon/html/index.html, the online hacker Jargon File, version 4.2.0, 31 January 2000.

Roeder, Konrad, "All About the Internet Part 21—The Dark Side of Cookies," *All About the Internet*, vol. 1, no. 21, 1997. Online: http://shell.rmi.net/~kgr/internet/part21.html

Schmidt, Jimmy, "Pay Tribute to Mom with Fresh Cookies," *Detroit Free Press*, May 5, 1999. Online: http://www.freep.com/fun/food/qjimmy5.htm

Stoll, Clifford, *The Cuckoo's Egg*, New York: Doubleday, 1989.

Stoll, Clifford, *Silicon Snake Oil: Second Thoughts on the Information Highway*. New York: Doubleday, 1995.

Zaret, Elliot, "Volunteer Rebels Rock Web Community," MSNBC, April 15, 1999. Online: http://www.zdnet.com/zdnn/stories/news/0,4586.2242290,00.html

chapter

4

Computer Networks Linking Network Communities
by Robin B. Hamman

Many social scientists have written about the development of online communities. Online communities are communities which are formed in cyberspace, often consisting entirely of people who have never met each other offline. In the fourteen years I have spent online, I have been a member of dozens of online communities of this type and have met hundreds of users who use computer networks primarily to meet other users and to build new online relationships with them. However, the research presented here suggests that many America Online (AOL) users first obtain an AOL account to conduct research and to communicate with people from their preexisting network communities. This breaking down of the borders between online and offline communities stands in contrast to most existing notions of online communities and points to wider changes important to our understanding of the term "community."

In this chapter, I present the findings of research I've recently conducted on the users of the popular online service AOL. The primary purpose is to look at the motivations of AOL users and, more specifically, to see if social isolation or loneliness has played any part in their motivation to join and use the computer network. The second purpose is to investigate how AOL users are actually choosing to spend their time online. The final purpose is to investigate how spending time online effects users as individuals as well as their preexisting offline friendships, social networks, and communities. The findings suggest that many AOL users are motivated to join the online service to conduct research and to communicate via computer with people they already know offline rather than to meet new people online and to build new friendships with them. My findings also suggest that, when we use computer-mediated communication to communicate with members of our preexisting social networks, our time spent online may be beneficial to the solidarity of these groups. This contradicts a number of theorists and researchers who have written that computer-mediated communication can lead to the disintegration of preexisting communities, a finding which is most notably present in the recent HomeNet study.

Ambiguity in the Definition of "Community"

Within the social sciences, there is little agreement upon the definition of the term "community" other than that it is almost always used to describe a group of people. Poplin (1979) writes,

> From its inception as a discipline, sociology has been plagued by inconsistency and ambiguity in some of its basic terminology . . . the word community falls into this category. As an element in the sociological vocabulary, this term has been used in so many ways that it has been described as an omnibus word (p. 3).

Even the *Oxford Dictionary of Sociology* (Marshall 1994) states that

> the ambiguities of the term community make any wholly coherent sociological definition of communities, and hence the scope and limits for their empirical study, impossible to achieve (p. 75).

The term community is commonly used in a number of different ways in everyday life. This causes ambiguity and confusion when we then try to use the term in the social sciences. Some examples of the diverse uses of the term "community" outside the social science literature include:

- In advertising: "Use your **community**-based grocery store. We create jobs for local people."
- In the names of buildings: "Independence Village Retirement **Community**."
- To describe a city or its inhabitants: "Liverpudlians have a strong sense of pride in their **community**."
- When talking about minority groups such as the "Black **Community**" or "Gay **Community**."
- When describing a feeling of togetherness felt by a group of friends or work colleagues.
- When describing abstract groups who are distributed worldwide. For example, the "Academic **Community**" is made up of thousands of academics who communicate through newsletters, journals, and other forms of interpersonal contact both directly and indirectly.

While imprecise usage leads to misunderstandings when we attempt to use the term in social scientific texts, another important source of ambiguity is that the social construct which it describes is particularly dynamic. The term has also become value loaded due to the political nature of its usage in many texts. For example, Durkheim writes about the changes which occurred in the move from early rural agricultural societies, largely based upon kinship bonds and shared geography (mechanical solidarity), to modern urban industrial societies where communities are based upon common interest as well as shared geography (organic solidarity) but not necessarily upon kinship bonds. For Marx, the bonds found in modern communities are influenced to a significant extent by economic relations, and by the inequalities entailed in the capitalist mode of production. Specialized groups, according to Marx, are formed on the basis of class, which in itself is determined largely by the organization of relations of production, and by capital accumulation. For the New Left of the 1960s and 1970s, "community" was a way of organizing people who were interested in a specific cause. For example, the San Francisco gay community was formed to support a social movement aimed at gaining and formalizing the rights of homosexuals. For the May 1968 revolutionaries in France, community was seen as an alternative to capitalist consumerism (Barbrook 1995, pp. 91–114). Just about every social theorist and activist using the term community ties a political meaning and agenda to it.

The above is by no means an exhaustive listing of the uses of the term "community" over the past century. However, this limited set of examples does illustrate that there are many competing conceptualizations of the term depending upon who is using it, when they are doing so, and what their purpose is. The development of the written word, mechanization, increased stratification, suburbanization, and so forth have all led to changes within communities and the ways in which we conceptualize them. The term "community" has dozens if not hundreds of distinct definitions in the social sciences; consensus upon one sociological definition for the term has been impossible to reach. Because of this ambiguity, Freilich (1963) instructs us that

> since a requisite of science is specificity of terminology, we must conclude . . . that at this time "community" is a non-scientific term unless separately defined in every paper which uses it (p. 118).

For this reason, it is important to present a clear sociological definition of the term "community" here before proceeding.

"Community"

In what may be the best attempt yet to assess agreement among definitions of community, George Hillery, Jr., subjected 94 sociological definitions of the term "community" to qualitative and quantitative analysis (Hillery 1955, p. 111). He was able to identify 16 different defining concepts within this sample (p. 115). Hillery found only one concept that was common among these 94 definitions: they all deal with people (p. 117). Despite this, there are other areas where the majority of studies analyzed by Hillery are in agreement. Hillery states that "of the 94 definitions, 69 are in accord that social interaction, area, and a common tie or ties are commonly found in community life" (p. 118). Poplin (1979, p. 8) notes that in a more recent empirical study of 125 sociological definitions of the term community, the above defining aspects were still present in the majority of definitions despite some minor changes in the usage of the term over the years.

In the interests of brevity, and to avoid confusion, I have used Hillery's analysis of definitions of community to reach a single concise definition rather than to present dozens of different definitions here. The sociological term *community* should be understood here as meaning (1) a group of people (2) who share social interaction (3) and some common ties between themselves and the other members of the group (4) and who share an area for at least some of the time. (In some cases, this shared area may be occupied by every member of a community at one time. However, it seems more likely that members of the community will move in and out of this shared area, meeting most often in pairs or small groups.)

I choose to deny the term its historical politicization in favor of presenting a clear definition here. For the remainder of this chapter, it can be assumed that when I talk about community in the physical world, I am referring to something with all four aspects described above.

Later in this chapter, we will see that community has not disappeared over the years, as some social theorists have written, but has indeed changed. The work of Barry Wellman and others demonstrates that community is increasingly becoming privatized. Privatized communities take the shape of networks, and network communities are more likely to be based upon individuals rather than in neighborhoods. This shift toward private network communities and away from communities rooted in a specific, confined geographic area is due to the privatization of public spaces once important to the development of community. In the absence of public gathering places of the type which often facilitate the development of geographically based communities, the Internet becomes a practical, efficient, and valuable tool for interpersonal communication which is important to the continuance of private network communities based upon individuals.

The private network community of an individual may or may not be shared, in its entirety, with others. For example, my personal network community is made up of members of my own family, people I only know through email and other forms of online communication, people I have met on my travels, and people whom I have come to know at various universities and conferences I have attended. We are a group of people and I am the common tie between us, although in many cases the interests of members of my personal network community do overlap. Some people within my network community interact with each other directly, while others do so exclusively through me. Our online interaction takes place in a shared area, the electronically created space along the wires which connect our computers. Communication between us takes place mostly through electronic communications technologies such as the telephone and the Internet, although there are members of my network community whom I regularly meet face to face. This is my own private network community and there isn't anyone anywhere in the world who shares this same exact community with me, although there are some who share large sections of it.

The concept of private network communities, based upon the individual, is not inconsistent with the definition presented above. Network communities consist of a group of people. Members of the community share at least one common tie, even if it is only that they know an individual within the network community. They also interact with each other, although sometimes this is done indirectly through an intermediary. Within network communities, the area shared by community members may be offline and tangible, or it may be electronically created space such as those found between telephones or online. For many people who are part of network communities, face-to-face meetings are rare, so they spend time associating with each other and building community in electronically created spaces.

Changing Demographics of Computer Network Users

As the user base for online services and the Internet increases dramatically in number, it is also changing rapidly in its demographic makeup. Many of these new users are motivated to come online for different reasons than those who came online before them. Just a few years ago most users of computer networks were academics, hobbyists, "Netheads," and technophiles—the people the computer industry calls "early adopters." In contrast, many users today are people who aren't particularly interested in the technology but who have a job to do and who choose to use computer networks as a tool for doing it.

While computer networks remain entirely inaccessible to most sections of society, for some groups, and within some communities, access to an online service or the Internet is almost as commonplace as having a telephone. Computer-mediated communication is increasingly being used between members of such communities.

It has been suggested by some sections of the mass media, and by a small number of academics, that those using computer networks do so at a cost to their offline community life. They suggest that by using computer networks, users turn their backs upon friends, family, and colleagues within their local community in favor of communities found entirely online. Within the sample of AOL users who take part in the study presented here, I have not found this to be true. In fact, my findings suggest that users taking part in this study are motivated to use AOL by the need to do research for academic or business purposes and to communicate with others within their preexisting offline communities. None of the AOL users in my sample report having any interest, need, or desire to meet new people online, to build new online communities, or to take part in their own social experimentation online. While I agree that there are some who use computer networks such as AOL to meet new people and to build new communities online with those they have never met offline, the findings presented here suggest that the majority of respondents using computer networks do so in order to complete specific research or work-related tasks and to communicate with people they know. When they're done, they log off.

Existing Research on the Social Impact of Computer-Mediated Communication

The Internet and other computer networks are increasingly being used within industry, business, and in our personal lives. Computer networks allow us to more easily do many everyday tasks such as information gathering, researching, and communicating. Newspapers, educators, and computer corporations alike have pointed out that online education is in some cases giving geographically remote students access to courses taught by the very best experts in their field (Hamilton and Miller 1997, Spender 1995, p. 146).

There is no shortage of academic and theoretical critiques that cast a positive light on the Internet and other computer networks. In fact, most researchers who have undertaken empirical fieldwork in cyberspace note a number of possible benefits of participation on computer networks. For example, they write about the freedom of anonymous users to experiment with their multiple selves (Turkle 1996) and their gender (Stone 1995) and to gain political power they would not otherwise have obtained (Schmitz 1997).

Despite all the benefits of using computer networks, there are still those who feel that the use of computer networks is detrimental to both individuals and society. For example, it's hard to miss the frequent articles about the availability online of dangerous information, such as bomb-building instructions, or about the use of the Internet by child pornographers or Neo-Nazis. It is fair to characterize the Internet as a dangerous place, but only if we also admit that the library or the streets in front of our homes are at least equally dangerous, and probably more so. Computer networks do allow people to gain access to potentially dangerous information, but this information is also available in bookstores and libraries. Similarly, the chance of children meeting pedophiles online is no higher, and probably much lower, than it is offline. The point is that children probably shouldn't be left alone while they use AOL or the Internet, just as they shouldn't be left alone to watch late night television or allowed to play outside without supervision. Dangers exist everywhere, but there is nothing about computer networks which makes them inherently more dangerous than anywhere offline.

Within contemporary culture it is also sometimes suggested that users of computer networks are technologically minded nerds, many of whom have few or no friends. For example, a popular soft drink brand in the United Kingdom recently ran an advertising campaign suggesting that trendy people drink their beverage while pathetic nerds wear anoraks and use the Internet. Across the Atlantic, a store near Fort Myers, Florida, reports that a T-shirt reading "What part of http://www.getalife.com don't you understand?" is one of their best-selling designs. With such views remaining credible within mainstream culture, it's no surprise that the popular media went into a feeding frenzy when the authors of the recent HomeNet study, conducted at Carnegie Mellon University, concluded that Internet use could lead to increased self-reported levels of social isolation and depression. Later in this article we'll take an in-depth look at flaws in the HomeNet study, which raise serious questions about its validity.

Others have noted the existence of negative portrayals of computer network users as socially isolated nerds. Howard Rheingold (1998) writes that, in the late 1980s,

> the media myth about people who used computers to communicate was that we were pencil-necked nerds, totally lacking in social skills, whose online communications are robotic and unemotional.

This myth, as Rheingold calls it, has influenced the work of a number of social theorists and researchers.

Existing Research on the Negative Social Impact of Computer-Mediated Communication

Michael Heim sees a danger that reality will be gradually supplanted by computer simulations. (Heim cites lyrics by The Doors about going to the theatre to recall what rain felt like, in order to suggest the possibility of a future in which even the most basic sensations are mediated: see Heim 1993, p. 82.) Heim later claims (without proof) that

> Technology increasingly eliminates direct human interdependence. While our devices give us greater personal autonomy, at the same time they disrupt the familiar networks of direct association (p. 100).

In *Data Trash*, Kroker and Weinstein (1994) warn of the increased loneliness of the online community member when they write,

> The "virtual community" of electronic networking has such charismatic appeal today because, like a failing spacecraft, we are re-entering the burning atmosphere of the lonely (virtual) crowd. Not David Riesman's famous image of the "lonely crowd" written for America in the modern century, but now lonely telematic individuals huddled around terminal event-scenes (computer screens, TV sets, high-performance stereos) willing themselves to become members of a virtual community. A technologically generated community that has no existence other than as a perspectival simulacrum, and on behalf of the media-net functions as a violent, but always technically perfectible force-field (the "perfect sound," "more memory capacity") for hiding the loneliness within. The appeal of electronic networking operates in inverse proportion to the disconnectedness of people from each other, of the recombinant sign from the human species, and of the body digitized from the abandoned site of the organic body. Consequently, the ruling ideological formula of virtual culture: electronic mediation at the (recombinant) top; organic disconnection from below (p. 39).

While Heim, Kroker, and Weinstein write powerful warnings about the dangers of online communication, or as Kroker calls it our "will to virtuality," none of these have put their theories to test using empirical social scientific methodology.

The recent HomeNet study undertaken at Carnegie Mellon University in the United States has been widely reported in the media and echoes the dystopia of Heim, Kroker, and Weinstein. The results of the study even made the front page of the Sunday *New York Times* (October 25, 1998) with the headline, "Sad, Lonely World Discovered in Cyberspace." Several global news organizations, including AP, CNN, and the BBC, used similar headlines when reporting on the findings of the study.

According to the Carnegie Mellon researchers, the study "examines the social and psychological impact of the Internet on 169 people in 73 households during their first one to two years on-line." Their findings (Kraut et al. 1998) suggest that

> greater use of the Internet was associated with declines in participants' communication with family members in the household, declines in the size of their social circle, and increases in their depression and loneliness. These findings have implications for research, for public policy, and for the design of technology.

Despite these claims and the great media attention given to them, "the statistically significant changes the researchers report are quite small—like a 1 percent increase on the depression scale for people who spend an hour a week online" (Rosenburg 1998).

While the authors of this study should be applauded for undertaking such important and timely research, their research design is seriously flawed in a number of ways. These design flaws have caused a number of well-known authors to question the validity of the findings.

The HomeNet study is based upon data collected from a sample consisting of 256 members of 93 families drawn from four schools and several neighborhood groups in the Pittsburgh area. Respondents are members of families with no previous access to computer networks from their homes who were given free computer equipment, a second telephone line, Internet access, and training in exchange for taking part in the study. This free equipment and training, worth several thousand dollars, was probably their main motivation for going online and for taking part in the study. In contrast, most users of computer networks have certainly not been motivated to go online by the promise of free computer equipment and training. Because respondents taking part in the HomeNet study have an entirely different motivation for going online than most users of computer networks, the findings of the study certainly cannot be generalized outside of the population studied. Furthermore, it is possible that some participants in the HomeNet study may have been unduly influenced by the training that they received prior to the study. For example, it is possible that they were taught to use the Internet to access anonymous chat rooms at Yahoo or to visit entertainment Web sites instead of using their access to join in real online communities or to keep in touch with people they already knew from offline. If this is the case, it is very possible that this training caused them to use the Internet in ways that led them to feel more socially isolated. The HomeNet study ignores the different motivations for going online which are exhibited by the diverse population of Internet users, and fails to recognize that the gift of several thousand dollars worth of computer equipment, access, and training could have any number of unexpected and unpredictable consequences upon the ways in which respondents choose to use the Internet.

Another serious flaw of the HomeNet study is that its findings are based upon data collected during only a pretest questionnaire and a single subsequent questionnaire which was administered between the 12th and 24th month of the research. Considering that the HomeNet study is meant to be a longitudinal one, there should have been more questionnaire tests administered to assess the validity of findings. Outside factors which could have caused members of the sample population to report "changes in their social involvement and psychological well-being" between the 12th and 24th weeks of the study were not investigated. In his critique of the HomeNet study for *Salon* magazine, Rosenburg (1998) writes that

> the researchers only tested people twice . . . which doesn't provide a very wide set of data points to offset the impact of other factors (time of year, state of the economy, random personal crisis).

The researchers responsible for the HomeNet study could not possibly have controlled all outside variables, such as the local economy or weather, and further steps should have been taken to investigate the possibility that such outside factors may have led to the slight increase in respondents' self-reported levels of depression and social isolation. In fact, Rosenburg (1998) writes,

> the researchers have no idea whether their subjects got bummed out because of what they encountered on the Net, or simply because they wound up sitting in front of a computer monitor rather than working in their gardens or playing ball. Is the increase in "loneliness and depression" caused by the Internet itself or simply by computer use, regardless of whether the modem's on? The study can't say.

In any case, a 1 percent increase in loneliness and depression, as measured through the self-reports of participants, is not a very large change, especially when dealing with such a small sample of users.

Another possibility, not discussed in the study, is that using the Internet may simply have led members of the sample to become aware of already existing deficiencies in their offline relationships. Online communication can often lead to improved self-awareness, since people have been known to be very open and self-reflective while online (Hamman 1996). This new self-awareness could lead to reports of increased levels of depression, isolation, and loneliness among respondents. Similarly, having many friends online, but few offline, could lead to an awareness that something is missing from respondents' offline lives. Because the HomeNet study is flawed methodologically, it is impossible to conclude that there is a causal relationship between using the Internet and increased levels of depression and loneliness.

Another serious flaw of the HomeNet study is that it assumes that relationships conducted offline through face-to-face interaction are qualitatively better than relationships conducted online through computer-mediated communication. The study uses the existing (pre-test) level of communication within sample families as a benchmark, and assumes that increased levels of communication between these family members is always positive. This benchmark is inappropriate, since many people find much to be negative about when it comes to interfamily communication. Certainly for the unhappy spouse, the abused child, or the isolated individual, online communication may be more beneficial and positive than much of their offline communication.

In summary, the validity of the Carnegie Mellon study, which suggests that by using the Internet people may reduce their social involvement and see declines in their psychological well-being, may be challenged on a number of important grounds. The findings of the study are unreliable and cannot be generalized because they:

1. use a sample population consisting of people with little or no prior access to personal computers or the Internet and who have very different motivation for going online than most users do,

2. rely upon questionnaire data collected on only two occasions,

3. base their conclusions upon a small (1 percent) increase in self-reported levels of loneliness and isolation among respondents,

4. value too heavily, and assume the positivity of, offline communication (especially within families) in comparison to online communication.

Howard Rheingold (1998) concludes that, "Now that I have read the research report . . . I can't say that HomeNet offers anything resembling significant evidence that cyberspace is undermining civil society."

Another well-publicized study, this one by the Stanford Institute for the Quantitative Study of Society and published in February 2000, also suggests that use of the Internet causes social isolation. There are similar methodological weaknesses in this study, those being the use of self-reporting surveys and the assumption that non-computer-mediated communication is more desirable than computer-mediated communication. For a thoughtful and detailed response to the Stanford study, see Jakob Nielsen (2000).

The findings of my own research of AOL users stand in sharp contrast to the dystopian accounts of the collapse of community suggested by writers such as Heim, Kroker, and Weinstein, as well as the HomeNet and Stanford Institute studies. In this research, I have spent over 200 hours over a four-month period conducting participant observation on AOL. Data was also collected through the use of email questionnaires and online interviews. Ideally, those conducting social scientific research in cyberspace would conduct follow-up face-to-face or telephone interviews to verify some of the self-reported data online (Hine 1998). In my case, limited time and financial resources have made this impossible.

During this research, I spoke with approximately 100 AOL users. All respondents gave their informed consent in exchange for guarantees that steps were taken to protect their anonymity. I sought out members of AOL who were willing to disclose their feelings about community, online community, and friendship. I did this by spending time hanging out in chat rooms, reading posts to public message boards, seeking out people using the members directory and later contacting those people using private messages. These users were individually selected to come from a wide range of demographic backgrounds and to reflect various levels of experience using computer networks. This sampling method, frequently employed by ethnographers such as myself, does introduce researcher bias to the study. The introduction of such bias is generally viewed as acceptable by social scientists conducting exploratory research where little is known about the sample population, as is the case here. It is usually unwise to generalize the findings of research conducted in such a way, but the findings do offer a valuable and much needed starting point for later studies.

Changing Notions of Community

Barry Wellman, a researcher at the University of Toronto, was one of the first to note the current shift away from communities based upon geographic areas toward private network communities. Wellman, who writes from a predominately North American perspective, describes how today, rather than gathering with neighbors in public places such as street corners or cafes, people now communicate with their friends by telephone or email or in small groups in private homes (1995, p. 1).

Wellman calls this the domestication and privatization of community. Fordism has divided labor and laborers, and zoning restrictions have created a situation where many must travel long distances to work (p. 1). When we travel to work, many of us do so without travelling companions, and there is less chance of unplanned meetings since we spend so little time in public areas. Unused public areas often become privatized, and as the public space in which community members may freely associate disappears, community life has also increasingly become privatized. Wellman states that although transportation and communication technologies have allowed people to keep in touch with their distant friends and relations,

> these technologies are essentially privatising, with telephones and electronic mail usually being between two persons only and most automobiles carrying one or two persons on trips between private garages (Wellman 1995, p. 1).

Additionally, Wellman notes that the home of the average person, especially within the suburbs, is larger today than ever before. This makes the private home an ideal place to host small, invitation-only gatherings.

Wellman is not alone in noting the loss of public community spaces. Ray Oldenburg (1997) writes of the decline in publicly accessible places for informal association among community members. He calls these places "the great good place" because, in his view, such places are "the core settings of informal public life" (p. 16). The "great good place" exists as a third place in the lives of community members, following the first place (home) and the second place (work). According to Oldenburg, the existence of the great good place, or third place, is necessary for the good health and strength of communities. Without such third places, interaction between community members declines and the common ties shared by members of the community go largely unknown (pp. xxiii, 72).

Oldenburg notes that the number of third places within cities throughout the Western world have been in decline for quite some time and that this phenomenon is especially pronounced in the United States, where the population of suburbs is growing rapidly while the population of inner cities remains fairly constant or is even in decline. Suburb dwellers usually don't live within easy walking distance of places traditionally used as third places such as neighborhood shops, a local pub, or a coffee shop. Oldenburg (1997) writes that

> Houses alone do not a community make, and the typical subdivision proved hostile to the emergence of any structure or space utilisation beyond the uniform houses and streets that characterised it (p. 4).

Or, as Richard Goodwin complains, in the suburbs "there is virtually no place where neighbors can anticipate unplanned meetings—no pub or corner store or park" (Goodwin 1974). It has even been suggested that the automobile-centric, "secure" architecture of many large cities increasingly discourages free association among members of the community (Davis 1992).

Wellman also notes that fewer people are bothering to visit the few third places that are still available to them. He gives as an example the fact that Canadians went to the movies one fifth as often in 1987 as they did in 1952. Moreover, suburban shopping malls are not designed to promote social interaction:

> They encourage fast-turnover consumption and discourage leisurely discussion. Unlike the public space of previous centuries, these privately-owned, profit-oriented spaces sell goods primarily for private, domestic use (Wellman 1995, p. 1).

For Oldenburg and Goodwin, as community spaces disappear, the communities that once utilized them also go into decline. What Oldenburg, Goodwin, and many others have suggested is that there is a noticeable loss of community feeling within neighborhoods where the third place has become absent.

This does not, however, necessarily mean that community no longer exists. In his research of social networks, Wellman goes looking for the people who no longer inhabit third places, and finds that instead of disappearing completely, interaction among community members has shifted away from physical space into spaces created by new technologies. People now have to actively contact their friends and acquaintances if they wish to remain in touch, rather than visiting a public space and talking with anyone they know who passes by. In later paragraphs, Wellman explains the findings of his own research group when it studied the social ties of residents of the Borough of East York in Metropolitan Toronto (Wellman et al. 1988). People living in the same neighborhood made up only 18 percent of the active socially close ties of the people they studied. One quarter of the ties lived outside Metropolitan Toronto, and many lived a long journey away by car or plane.

> Hence, it is cars, phones, planes and electronic mail that sustains community, and not people walking to their neighbours' homes. For example, our research shows that people get more companionship and emotional support from friends and relatives who live elsewhere in Metro Toronto than they do from their neighbours (Wellman 1995, p. 1).

Wellman concludes that the idea of neighborhood community does not reflect current reality but is a nostalgic longing for the past. Indeed, it is a longing for a past that might never have been, because some research suggests that there also were many long-distance ties in preindustrial times (p. 1).

An earlier part of this chapter discussed several theoretical critiques about possible negative effects of computer-mediated communication upon community. The work of Wellman, on the other hand, stands juxtaposed to these critiques of computer-mediated communication. For him communities based primarily upon third places and neighborhoods are a thing of the past, if they ever existed at all. Communities continue to exist, but are supported through a number of technologies including the printed word, transportation, and new communications technologies. Computer-mediated communication is just one of the many technologies used by people within existing communities to communicate, and thus to maintain those community ties over distance.

In this study, I used individual respondents as the starting point of network communities rather than looking at the network communities themselves. Because of this, when I talk of network communities, I am speaking of the private network community of an individual.

The Findings

In the longer paper upon which this article is based, the ethnographic stories of a number of individuals are presented. Due to restrictions of the present format, however, it is only possible for me to comment more generally upon the findings of this research. Nearly all of the AOL users who have taken part in this study were initially motivated to obtain an AOL account by the need to conduct research online for academic or business purposes and to communicate with members of their preexisting network communities. Not a single respondent, out of a sample consisting of just over 100 users, reports being motivated to join AOL with the intention of building new friendships there.

Not only were respondents motivated to join AOL by the need to conduct research online or to communicate with members of their preexisting network communities, but these tasks continue to be their primary activities even after several months, or even years, online. As continuing users, only 10 percent report that they ever seek to build new friendships online using their AOL account, and this remains only a secondary motivation in their continued use of the service, after research and communication with members of their preexisting social networks.

Seventy-five percent of the respondents reported that their private social networks were healthy and that they felt positively about the number and strength of their interpersonal relationships. Nineteen percent of respondents agree with the statement that they "sometimes feel socially isolated," 5 percent report data in ways which make it impossible to determine whether they ever feel socially isolated or not, and 1 percent report that they "always feel socially isolated or alone." In reference to the 19 percent above, it is entirely natural for most people to feel socially isolated at one time or another in their lives, so this finding is not at all surprising or troubling.

Every single respondent in this study feels that using AOL has helped him or her to maintain preexisting offline relationships. In fact, I have found no evidence that using AOL harms offline social networks or that it leads to social isolation for certain users. If anything, computer-mediated communication through networks such as AOL or the Internet appears to help people stay a part of a network community despite barriers of distance and time. However, when a person decides to spend time online, whether for work or leisure, it cuts into the time available for other purposes. In the case of employees using the Internet, many businesses have recognized this and are limiting the amount of time employees can spend online. When people spend their leisure time online, it similarly cuts into the time available for other leisure activities offline. For 97 percent of the respondents to this study, online time reduces television viewing or reading. For them, each hour spent online during leisure time means one hour less spent watching television or reading. Much of this time spent online is used to send emails to members of users' preexisting network communities, to participate in online chats with these people, or to conduct research.

Conclusion

AOL users who have taken part in this study are not socially isolated individuals desperately seeking contact, as some would have us believe. They are not motivated by social isolation or loneliness, but by the ease with which they can access information online and keep in touch with their friends, colleagues and relatives from offline who increasingly have email accounts and Web pages themselves. For some of these people, distance is an issue, since they may find that members of their social circle have moved far away, but this needn't be the end of that social circle. Many who research cyberspace write about the ease with which barriers of distance are overcome by computer networks, and this is never more apparent than when members of a network community are able to communicate when they are located thousands of miles apart.

For the very few respondents who do report that they are socially isolated, most of them say that it is only some of the time that they feel this way. Being online gives them the hope of making new offline contacts and friendships that will continue into their offline lives. This is an entirely realistic hope: many members of online communities attend "flesh meets" where they get together with people they may or may not previously have known face to face. Some users even bond so strongly with other users online that they go into business together or get married offline (Case 1997, p. 2). In other words, even for the minority of respondents who do report that they sometimes feel socially isolated, using computer networks is a beneficial use of time.

For those who have access to computer networks such as AOL, computer-mediated communication can be an efficient way to communicate with members of their preexisting network communities. Although such communication can be used by those seeking new contacts and friendships online, it appears that such a use of computer networks is more rare than once thought.

Acknowledgments

This chapter is based on an article, "Computer Networks Linking Network Communities: Effects of AOL Use Upon Pre-existing Communities," which first appeared in *Exploring Cyber Society*, Conference Volume 1, edited and introduced by John Armitage and Joanne Roberts, Newcastle upon Tyne: University of Northumbria at Newcastle, 1999. A German translation of the article appears in *Virtuelle Gruppen—Charakteristika und Problemdimensionen* (*Virtual Groups: Characteristics and Problematic Dimensions*), edited by Udo Thiedeke and published by Westdeutscher Verlag GmbH, Opladen/Wiesbaden.

References

Barbrook, Richard, *Media Freedom: The Contradictions of Communications in the Age of Modernity.* London: Pluto, 1995. Online: http://www.hrc.wmin.ac.uk/ (follow links to "theory" section).

Baym, Nancy K., "The Emergence of On-line Community," Jones, S., ed., *Cybersociety 2.0: Revisiting Computer Mediated Communication and Community*, pp. 35–68. London: Sage Publications, 1998.

Boal, Iain A., "A Flow of Monsters: Luddism and Virtual Technologies," James Brook and Iain A. Boal, eds., *Resisting the Virtual Life: The Culture and Politics of Information*, pp. 3–17. San Francisco: City Lights Books, 1995.

Caldwell, Barrett S., and Lilas H. Taha, "Starving at the Banquet: Social Isolation in Electronic Communication Media," *Interpersonal Computing and Technology: An Electronic*

Journal for the 21st Century, 1, no. 1 (January 1993). Online: http://www.helsinki.fi./science/optek/1993/n1/caldwell.txt

Case, Steve, "Community Update from Steve Case" (email sent to AOL members), January 6, 1997, available on AOL at Keyword: "Community Update."

Davis, Mike, *City of Quartz: Excavating the Future in Los Angeles*, 1st Vintage ed. New York: Vintage Books, 1992.

Derlega, Valerian J., and Stephen T. Margulis, "Why Loneliness Occurs: The Interrelationship of Social-Psychological and Privacy Concepts," Letitia Anne Peplau and Daniel Perlman, eds. *Loneliness: A Sourcebook of Current Theory, Research and Therapy*, pp. 152–165. New York: John Wiley & Sons, 1982.

Fischer, Claude S., and Susan L. Phillips, "Who Is Alone? Social Characteristics of People with Small Networks," in Letitia Anne Peplau and Daniel Perlman, eds., *Loneliness: A Sourcebook of Current Theory, Research and Therapy*, pp. 21–39. New York: John Wiley & Sons, 1982.

Freilich, Morris, "Toward an Operational Definition of Community," *Rural Sociology*, vol. 28 (June 1963), pp. 117–127.

Garton, Laura, Caroline Haythornthwaite, and Barry Wellman, "Studying Online Social Networks," *Journal of Computer Mediated Communication,* vol. 3, no. 1 (June 1997). Online: http://jcmc/huj/ac/il/vol3/issue1/garton.html

Goodwin, Richard N., "The American Condition," *The New Yorker*, January 28, 1974, p. 38.

Hamilton, K., and S. Miller, "Internet U—No Ivy, No Walls, No Keg Parties," *Newsweek*, March 10, 1997, p. 12.

Hamman, Robin, *Cyborgasms: Cybersex Chat Amongst Multiple Selves and Cyborgs in the Narrow-Bandwidth Space of AOL Chat Rooms*. MA Thesis, University of Essex, England, Department of Sociology, 1996. Online: http://www.cybersoc.com

Heim, Michael, *The Metaphysics of Virtual Reality*. Oxford: Oxford University Press, 1993.

Hillery, George A., Jr., "Definitions of Community: Areas of Agreement," *Rural Sociology*, vol. 20 (June 1955), pp. 111–123.

Hine, Christine, "Virtual Ethnography?" Conference Paper: IRISS 1998, International Conference on Internet Research and Information for Social Scientists, Bristol, UK, March 25–27, 1998. Online: http://www.sosig.ac.uk/iriss/papers/paper16.htm

Kraut, R., M. Patterson, V. Lundmark, S. Kiesler, T. Mukophadhyay, and W. Scherlis, "Internet Paradox: A Social Technology That Reduces Social Involvement and Psychological Well-Being?" *American Psychologist*, vol. 53, no. 9 (1998), pp. 1017–1031. Online: http://www.homenet.andrew.cmu.edu/progress/HN.impact.10.htm

Kroker, Arthur, and Michael A. Weinstein, *Data Trash: The Theory of the Virtual Class*. New York: St. Martin's Press, 1994.

Marshall, Gordon, ed., *The Concise Oxford Dictionary of Sociology*. Oxford: Oxford University Press, 1994.

Nielsen, Jakob, "Does the Internet Make Us Lonely?," *Useit.com: Alertbox*, May 1, 2000. Online: http://www.useit.com/alertbox/20000220.html

Oldenburg, Ray, *The Great Good Place: Cafés, Coffee Shops, Community Centers, Beauty Parlors, General Stores, Bars, Hangouts and How They Get You Through the Day*, 2d ed. New York: Marlowe & Company, 1997.

Peplau, Letitia Anne, and Daniel Perlman, "Perspective on Loneliness," *Loneliness: A Sourcebook of Current Theory, Research and Therapy*, pp. 1–20. New York: John Wiley & Sons, 1982.

Poplin, Dennis E., *Communities: A Survey of Theories and Methods of Research*, 2d ed. New York: MacMillan Publishing Co., Inc., 1979.

Rheingold, Howard, *The Virtual Community: Surfing the Internet*. London: Minerva Publishing, 1993.

———, "Misunderstanding New Media," *Feed Magazine*, September 10, 1998. Online: http://www.feedmag.com/essay/es102lofi.html

Rosenburg, Scott, "Sad and Lonely in Cyberspace: Why the New Net Depression Study Is Something to Get Bummed

About," *Salon*, September 3, 1998. Online: http://www.salonmagazine.com/21st/rose/1998/09/03straight.html

Schmitz, Joseph, "Structural Relations, Electronic Media, and Social Change: The Public Electronic Network and the Homeless," Steven G. Jones, ed., *Virtual Culture: Identity and Communication in Cybersociety*. London: Sage Publications, 1997, pp. 80–101.

Schofield, Jack, "The New Seekers," *The Guardian* (London/Manchester), November 6, 1997, Online Supplement, pp. 2–3.

Slater, Philip E., *The Pursuit of Loneliness: America at the Breaking Point*. Boston: Beacon Press, 1970.

Spender, Dale, *Nattering on the Net: Women, Power and Cyberspace*. North Melbourne, Australia, 1995.

Stone, Rosanne Alluquere, "Sandy," *The War of Desire and Technology at the Close of the Mechanical Age*. Cambridge, MA: MIT Press, 1995.

Turkle, Sherry, "Virtuality and Its Discontents: Searching for Community in Cyberspace," *The American Prospect*, vol. 24 (Winter 1996), pp. 50–57. Online: http://www.prospect.org/archives/24/24turk.html

Wellman, Barry, "The Privatization of Community," Presented to the Conference on Urban Regions in a Global Context, University of Toronto, October 19–20, 1995.

Wellman, Barry, Peter J. Carrington, and Alan Hall, "Networks as Personal Communities," Barry Wellman and S. D. Berkowitz, eds., *Social Structures: A Network Approach*. Cambridge, MA: Cambridge University Press, 1988, pp. 130–185.

chapter

5

Reducing Demographic Bias
by Miranda Mowbray,
mjfm@hplb.hpl.hp.com

This chapter reports some significant differences between the behavior of traditional and nontraditional member groups in Little Italy MOO, an Italian-language online community. As a result of these findings and other data, I suggest some ways to reduce the demographic bias in online communities.

Introduction

The demographics of Internet access have undergone dramatic changes over the last few years. Although the idea of equal access is far from being realized, demographic trends have been away from the traditional Internet user (a U.S. male between the ages of 18 and 40, with Internet access from University or computer-related employment) and toward a much broader cross section of society. The nontraditional users now accessing the Internet include more women, more users connecting from home, more non-U.S. users, more over-50s, and users with more varied educational and cultural backgrounds.

However, the ability to access the Internet does not imply an ability to make use of it on an equal footing with traditional Internet users. Internet products and services are still largely designed and built by traditional Internet users. The content and structure as a whole are biased (often unconsciously) toward a narrow demographic section of those with Internet access. Some examples are given in one section of this chapter.

Market forces may reduce some of the biases against nontraditional user groups. There have been noticeable, and often successful, efforts by large e-commerce companies to entice female customers to their sites. But market forces cannot be relied upon to reduce bias against groups without large purchasing power, or bias in noncommercial applications. There is moreover a danger of self-perpetuating biases, in which the "Internet Market" is identified largely with traditional users, so that the Internet continues to be designed mainly for and by traditional users, alienating nontraditional users and possibly leading to wider disadvantages for these groups. As an analogy, there is some evidence that a self-perpetuating bias in the computer games market has contributed to the sex bias in employment in the UK and U.S. computing industry (Frenkel 1990).

There is a growing trend for online communities to be used as a means of delivering public services targeted at nontraditional as well as traditional members. So it is crucial that there should be an attempt to minimize biases against nontraditional user groups in such online communities. To do this, it is necessary to identify in what ways the needs and preferences of these user groups differ from those of traditional users. This chapter concentrates on two nontraditional user groups: female users and European users connecting from home.

First, I report a case study of differences between the behavior of traditional and nontraditional members of an Italian-language online community, Little Italy MOO. Some features of the community, in particular the ability to create complex objects, appeared to be significantly more attractive to nontraditional than to traditional members, whereas others appeared to be more attractive to traditional members. The nontraditional members spent significantly fewer hours in a given time period logged into Little Italy than the traditional members did, which suggests that this online community may have a bias disadvantaging nontraditional members.

The next section gives some examples from other sources of bias in Internet products and services that may deter some types of nontraditional user, including language, interface design, telephone bills, and privacy concerns. The final section gives suggestions, arising from the two previous sections, for possible ways to reduce demographic bias in online communities.

Case Study

Little Italy MOO is a five-year-old online community, run on a server at the University of Milan.[1] Most members are Italian. It is by far the largest Italian-language MUD/MOO/MUSH. MOO stands for Multiuser Object-Oriented space; a MOO allows real-time chat between geographically distributed members, but also a much richer set of interactions, including the creation by members of persistent software objects which all members can interact with. For further information on Little Italy (in Italian) see (Little Italy Staff 1996).

Data Collection

In order to select a representative sample of the members of Little Italy MOO I sampled those present at different times of the day and night until I had identified over 100 characters. This provided information on the times of day when the members controlling these characters connected. In this MOO members are allowed only one character each.

Data not included in the statistics

In this chapter I do not report the results for robots, guests, and wizards.

---

1. To access Little Italy MOO, telnet to kame.usr.dsi.unimi.it port 4444, and type connect guest.

Robots are characters that appear to be controlled by a person, but are actually controlled by a software program. There were two robots in the samples.

A guest character is not controlled by a single person, as other characters are, but is available to be used by anyone wanting to try out the MOO.

The wizards are a special group of characters with extended powers that administrate the MOO. On this MOO the wizards—or more precisely the people controlling the wizard characters—were all students at the University of Milan, which runs the server on which the MOO is hosted. Five wizards appeared in the samples. Their behavior is significantly different in several respects from that of the nonwizards: for example, they create many more rooms and room exits than the nonwizards, and they are likely to have been on the MOO for significantly more years than nonwizards.

I only sampled the MOO during the week, so my results do not hold for weekends. I suspect that some of the nighttime users may use the MOO during the day on Saturday and Sunday.

Data included in the statistics

I divided the members controlling the remaining characters into three groups: D (standing for members connected to the MOO only during the daytime), N (members connected only during the nighttime or evening), and B (members connected during both the daytime and the nighttime). These groups were size 49, 40, and 13 respectively.

I also looked at a different division of the members in the samples, according to the presenting gender. There are a large number of possible options for the gender of a character on this MOO (including a personalized gender option, under which you can choose any word or phrase you like to specify the gender of your character). However, the two most popular presenting genders are male and female. I looked at the three groups M, F, and O, where M consisted of the members with male presenting gender, F the members with female presenting gender, and O the members of presenting gender other than male and female. These groups were size 46, 27, and 29 respectively.

I also collected data according to real-life gender. In order to collect a sample of members of known gender, the character names of members connecting to the online community were recorded for a month. I then compared these names with photographs from meetings. Face-to-face reunions are common for this online community, and photographs from these meetings are typically published with a link from the community Web pages and a label listing character names. It was possible to identify 38 male and 18 female community members, totaling about one in four of the members connecting during the month. This method of gender identification is not immune to error or deception, but may be more reliable than asking members directly. I will refer to the group of 38 male community members as Photo-M and the group of 18 female community members as Photo-F.

In this chapter I compare behavior between the three groups D, B, N, the three groups M, F, O, and the two groups Photo-M, Photo-F. I first assume that any two members in the same group of D, B, N have behavior governed by an identical and independent distribution, and compare the behavior between these three groups. (What I do is look at the differences in the mean values of a given variable between these groups. If the difference between the mean values for two of these groups is so large that it is unlikely that these two groups have identical behavior distributions, I can say that the difference between the mean values for these groups is statistically significant.)

Then I drop this assumption and assume instead that any two members in the same group of M, F, O have behavior governed by an identical and independent distribution, and compare the behavior between these three groups. (The reason that I have to drop the first assumption when testing for differences between M, F, O is that group M intersects with each of groups D, B, N, and groups F, O also intersect with each of groups D, B, N. So, for example, if I assume that any two members in D have behavior governed by an identical and indepen-

'bution, then I am automatically assuming that some
of M and some members of F have an identical
_vior distribution.)

Finally I assume that any two members in the same group
of Photo-M, Photo-F have behavior governed by an identical
and independent distribution and compare the behavior of
these two groups. I do not make any comparisons between the
behavior of one of D, B, N and one of M, F, O, since such a
comparison would not be justified by my assumptions on distributions. I also do not make any comparison between the
behavior of one Photo-M, Photo-F and one of D, B, N, M, F, O,
since the sampling method for Photo-M and Photo-F was different from that for the other groups. Where one mean value is
described as significantly larger than another, this means that
at least 75 percent of the t distribution with the appropriate
number of degrees of freedom lies below the test statistic (see
Montgomery 1976).

The results for groups Photo-M and Photo-F were first
reported in "Reducing the Geek Bias in Online Communities:
Suggestions from a Case Study" (Mowbray 1999), and the
results for the other groups were first reported in "Differences
in the Use of a Cyber Community According to Habitual Time
of Connection and Presenting Gender" (Mowbray 1999).

Participation of Community Members

I informed the members of the online community of the case
study and its goals and gave them the option to have all or part
of their data excluded from the study. In fact no one took up
the option of having their data excluded from the statistical
part of the study, although some members thanked me for
offering it. The data forming the basis of the statistical results
reported in this chapter was obtained from publicly available
sources, mostly via commands available to all community
members. The nonstatistical information was collected via
interviews (and public sources) and is reported with the
explicit permission of the interviewees. I presented the results
back to the community before making them public outside the
community.

The active input from community members, which I sought in order to ensure their data was used only with their permission, also gave other advantages. Community members had some useful ideas on what results might be interesting and how to measure them, suggested some explanations for statistical phenomena that had puzzled me, and confirmed some of my hypotheses for other phenomena. Presenting the results back to the community was enjoyable, as well as being useful and a polite thing to do, and I would recommend it to other researchers.

I did have to take special care when presenting my findings not to reveal the identity of individual members who had given me information to other members of the community. Not only were other members of the community likely to be able to guess their identity from very small clues, they were also curious as to the identity of the members I quoted. This ties in with Maria Bakardieva and Andrew Feenberg's observation in their chapter in this book that there may be disagreements between members of the community about the level of privacy that there should be within the community. I would endorse their suggestion of involving the data subjects in a discussion about the way data should be handled.

Demographic Profiles for D, B, and N

The language of the MOO is Italian. In English-speaking MOOs it is common to have members from English-speaking countries in widely different time zones, so it would not be straightforward to determine in an English-speaking MOO whether a member was accessing the MOO during their daytime or their nighttime. Italian, on the other hand, is rare as a mother tongue outside Italy, which has the effect that almost all of the members of Little Italy are in Italy, and in particular in the same time zone.

A majority of the members in the samples either connected only during the day during office hours, or only during the evening and night. I interviewed members of groups D, B, N to give a picture of demographic profiles.

The day-only members, group D, are mostly University students. The University pays for their access. They are likely to be in the Computer Science, Science, Engineering, or Economics faculties, which generally have better computing facilities and larger groups of students involved with computers. Students attend University at a more advanced age in Italy than in some other countries, but they are likely to be in the age range 18–26.

The small number who connect both during the day and during the night, group B, typically have computer-related or academic employment, connecting from their office or University (or home, if they work at home) during the day and from home at night. They fit the typical profile of traditional users.

The community members in group N, who visit Little Italy only during the evening and nighttime, are nontraditional users of the Internet. They typically connect from home, are generally older than members in other groups, and are often in the creative professions. Their access is not free, nor is it cheap. Local telephone calls are expensive in most parts of Italy. Computer equipment costs more than in the United Kingdom or United States. So they have an economic incentive to use their time online productively. Members of Little Italy in group N tend to have jobs which involve computers directly (software programmers, research scientists, teachers) or jobs for which a home Internet link is an advantage as a means of contact and document transfer (artists, writers, musicians, Web-site designers, consultants).

The profile of members who connect during the day (either only during the day or during both the day and the night) is similar to that of traditional users of the Internet. Current Internet demographics worldwide are moving in the direction of those who connect to the MOO only during the night. Current worldwide trends are for more people connecting to the Internet from home, for more older (and younger) users, and for more users in jobs not directly connected with science and computing. This change in demographics has already happened to a noticeable extent in the United States and is likely to be repeated in the rest of the world. (For information on recent trends, see for example GVU's WWW User Survey [Georgia Tech Research Corporation 1998], or the Nua survey site, http://www.nua.net/surveys.) Differences in the way in which nighttime community members use Little Italy MOO may be an advance indicator of future directions for the use of online communities in general.

Presenting Gender versus Real Gender

Members of Little Italy MOO have a free choice as to presenting gender. It need not correspond to the member's real gender, and there does not appear to be a social stigma attached to cross-gendering, as there is in some other MOOs. (A cross-gendered character is a female-presenting character controlled by a man or a male-presenting character controlled by a woman. For early examples of cross-gendering in online environments, see Elizabeth Reid's fascinating Master's Thesis [1994].)

However, there is some evidence that cross-gendering is rare in this MOO, in contrast to some U.S. MOOs and MUDs where it is commonplace, especially male-to-female cross-gendering. According to Rheingold (1994), "Gender deception occurs often enough in MUDs that female-presenting characters usually are assumed to be lying until they can prove otherwise." The members of Little Italy whom I interviewed were of the opinion that cross-gendered characters did exist in the MOO, but in very small numbers, perhaps two or three among the hundreds of characters frequently present.

Not one of the 56 members in the groups Photo-M and Photo-F had a cross-gendered character. It is plausible that members with cross-gendered characters would be less likely to come to a meeting, and/or less likely to want to be photographed there. So it is probably unwise to rely too much on this evidence, but it does support the members' own opinion that cross-gendering is rare.

In this section I study the differences in behavior according to presenting gender, as well as real gender. I have two justifications for this. The first is that if it is true that cross-gendering is rare in this MOO, then significant differences in the behavior of male-presenting and female-presenting characters will be indicative of significant underlying differences in the behavior of community members of different genders. If I find that there are significant differences between Photo-M and Photo-F and the same significant differences also occur between M and F, this will be extra evidence that the differences really are gender based and not just an accident arising from my sampling methods for Photo-M and Photo-F. Significant differences in the use of online communities according to gender are particularly interesting in the light of the increasing use of the Internet by women. According to Reuters (2000), by December 1999 users of the Internet in the United States were 50:50 male and female—although female U.S. Internet users spent less time online than male U.S. Internet users—whereas Media Metrix (1999) report that in January 1996 only 18 percent of U.S. users of the Internet were female. This trend is expected to spread to other countries.

The second justification is that in applications in the design of online environments which adapt themselves to the member, the information which will be collectable will typically be the member's presenting gender. This means that for this application it is more useful to know how the member's likely use of the environment differs with presenting gender than with real gender.

Table 5.1 shows the distribution of presenting genders for each group. Members in group N are significantly less likely to be male-presenting than members in group B, and significantly more likely than members in group B or D to have a presenting gender other than male or female. There are no other statistically significant results in the differing distributions of presenting gender between D, N, and B. Members in the group Photo-M are significantly more likely than members in group Photo-F to have male-presenting gender, are significantly less likely to have female-presenting gender, and are significantly more likely to have a presenting gender other than male or female.

TABLE 5.1 Percentage of members with presenting gender male, female, other

GROUP	M	F	O
D	47	29	24
B	54	23	23
N	40	25	35
Photo-M	63	0	37
Photo-F	0	89	11

For the tables in the rest of the chapter, if I do not say explicitly that a comparison between the mean values for D, N, B or between the mean values for M, F, O in a table is statistically significant, it can be assumed that it is not.

Frequency and Longevity of Presence in the MOO

The number of samplings in which a member was detected during the time-based sampling process by which I obtained the groups D, B, N, M, F, O give an indication as to how frequently the member is present in the MOO. The results are shown in Table 5.2.

TABLE 5.2 Number of samplings in which a member was detected

GROUP	GROUP SIZE	MEAN NUMBER OF SAMPLINGS	SAMPLE VARIANCE OF NUMBER OF SAMPLINGS
D	49	3.04082	6.6233
B	13	12.2308	244.692
N	40	2.25	2.44872
M	46	4.95652	80.3092
F	27	2.62963	4.31909
O	29	3.41379	20.3227

It is statistically significant that group B has a larger mean number of samplings than D, D has a larger mean number of samplings than N, and B has a larger mean number of samplings than N. It is also statistically significant that M has a larger mean number of samplings than O, O has a larger mean number of samplings than F, and M has a larger mean number of samplings than F. The mean number of samplings is a measure of the frequency with which members in a particular group access the MOO.

The groups Photo-M and Photo-F were obtained by a different sampling process. However, an idea of the relative frequency of the presence of members of these two groups can be obtained by looking at the members of these groups that were also sampled during the sampling process. Eighteen members of Photo-M and 6 members of Photo-F are also members of one of D, B, N, M, F, or O, and hence were sampled at least once. The mean number of samplings in which members of Photo-M appeared was 1.92, with sample variance 19.51. This is significantly larger than the mean number of samplings in which members of Photo-F appeared, which was 0.67, with sample variance 2.12.

So on this evidence the members in nontraditional member groups (nighttime members, female-presenting members, and women) spend fewer hours per week on the MOO than their counterparts.

The number of days elapsed since a given character was created on the MOO is known as the MOO age of the character. The MOO age does not, in itself, indicate how much time a member has spent logged into the online community. For example, if someone became a member a year ago but did not log into the online community at all on any of the days after the one in which she became a member, her character's MOO age is one year. However, the combination of MOO age and the number of time-based samplings in which a member was present gives an indication of how much time that member has spent logged into the online community. Data on MOO age for the different groups is shown in Table 5.3.

TABLE 5.3 MOO age

Group	Group Size	Mean MOO age	Sample variance of MOO age
D	49	617.163	207207
B	13	688.538	153596
N	40	700.85	140832
M	46	684.326	185681
F	27	604.222	151708
O	29	670.103	179805
Photo-M	38	1059.42	104454
Photo-F	18	819.222	102633

It is statistically significant that group M has a greater mean MOO age than group F and Photo-M has a greater mean MOO age than Photo-F.

This may be because this online community is more satisfying for men, so women leave permanently after a shorter time. Alternatively, or in addition, it may be related to the observation by Little Italy members that women have joined the community in larger numbers in the recent past, reflecting the general increase in the proportion of Internet users who are female.

No group has a mean MOO age of under 600 days: the MOO is clearly succeeding in retaining the interest of its members a long time after they first connected. The mean MOO age for Photo-M and Photo-F is particularly high, reflecting the fact that members who come along to meetings are likely to be long-established members of the community.

The statistically significant differences between M and F, and between Photo-M and Photo-F, from Tables 5.2 and 5.3 suggest this online community is more attractive, or addictive, for men than for women.

Creative Powers

A member of the MOO may have two different kinds of creative powers, the ability to create objects and the ability to create actions. New members have neither of these powers, which are bestowed at the whim of the wizards. The longer a member has spent in the MOO, the more likely they are to be awarded these powers. Table 5.4 shows what percentages of the different groups have these creative powers.

TABLE 5.4 Percentages of members in different groups with creative powers

Group	Object Creation	Action Creation
D	51	14
B	43	36
N	63	25
M	57	30
F	44	7
O	59	21
Photo-M	84	45
Photo-F	61	22

The differences between B and D and between M and O in object-creation powers are not statistically significant; but all other comparisons in creative powers between D, B, N, between M, F, O, and between Photo-M and Photo-F are statistically significant.

The significantly lower frequency of connection for women than for men, and the significantly lower MOO age for women, together give a plausible explanation why a significantly lower proportion of women than men have the powers to create objects and actions. The same explanation holds for the significantly low proportion of female-presenting members that have creative powers.

Object Creation

The next two tables (5.5 and 5.6) are concerned with differences in object creation by those members of each group who are able to create objects.

A rough measure of the creativity of a member with object-creation powers is the amount of space in the database of the online community that is taken up by descriptions of objects owned by the member, divided by the amount of time that the member has spent in the MOO. This is only an approximate measure, because it does not take into account how imaginative these objects are.[2]

The measure reported in Table 5.5 is the number of bytes in the online community database taken up with descriptions of the member's objects, divided by (the number of samplings in which the member was present times the MOO age of the member's character).

TABLE 5.5 Object-creativity measure

Group	Group Size	Mean of Measure	Sample Variance
D	24	130.318	63,713.7
B	6	66.6067	3,408.28
N	25	279.998	344,300
M	26	127.218	38,728.2
F	12	317.908	680,509
O	17	200.273	85,661.5

---

2. Also, it is possible (although uncommon) for the creator of an object to change its ownership, so a member who owns very few objects might be a very creative and very generous person who changes the ownership of nearly all the objects he or she creates.

Note that the group sizes in this table are not the same as in previous tables, because only members with object-creation powers are considered.

It is statistically significant that N has the largest mean value of this measure among D, B, N, and B has the smallest mean value. So the nighttime members use their infrequent visits productively, as far as object creation is concerned, but the members who are present on the MOO both during the day and during the evening or night are the least productive of D, B, N. In fact the number of bytes taken up by the description of the objects created by a member in group B is significantly smaller than for a member in D or N, despite group B's having the most frequent visits to the MOO.

It is statistically significant that F and O have larger mean values of the object-creativity measure than M. The female-presenting members, like the nighttime members, make productive use of their shorter hours on the MOO.

It is not appropriate to use this measure for Photo-M or Photo-F, because some members of Photo-M and Photo-F did not appear during the time-based samplings. A different measure to indicate the creativity of the members of these groups that have the power to create objects is the total size in bytes of the descriptions of the member's objects, divided by the MOO age. This is only a rough measure, because it does not take into account the frequency of visits to the online community. The 16 members of Photo-F with the power to create objects have a significantly larger mean value of this measure (319.726, sample variance 150,107) than do the 24 members of Photo-M with the power to create objects (190.654, sample variance 15,442.4). This is despite the fact that members of Photo-F appeared in significantly fewer samplings than members of Photo-M, so it suggests that members of Photo-F with the power to create objects are more productive in the use of this power than are members of Photo-M with the same power.

One way to obtain a high value for the object-creativity measure would be to create a large number of simple objects, perhaps just by repeated use of basic object-creation commands. Another way would be to create particularly complex and detailed objects, since the number of bytes in an object description is larger for more complex objects. In order to determine which of these is the case for the groups with a high value of the object-creativity measure, I calculated the number of bytes used for members' objects, divided by the number of objects they possess. The results are reported in Table 5.6.

TABLE 5.6 Average size of owned object, in kilobytes

GROUP	GROUP SIZE	MEAN OF MEASURE	SAMPLE VARIANCE
D	24	6.5	109.359
B	6	5.52833	9.4655
N	25	7.3868	118.314
M	26	5.27038	70.3327
F	12	7.7725	106.168
O	17	8.44471	133.631
Photo-M	32	3.7214	27.3163
Photo-F	11	11.1052	250.713

A member who creates many complex, imaginative objects and few simple objects will have a high value of this measure. The mean value for N is significantly larger than for B, the mean value for M is significantly smaller than for O and for F, and the mean value for Photo-M is significantly smaller than for Photo-F.

Members of Little Italy MOO create objects for a variety of reasons. Some objects are functional, such as doors to rooms and objects that assist the member with finding his or her way around the MOO. Others are for personal adornment, such as clothes and jewelry, or ornaments for rooms in the MOO. Others are created as presents for other members. One interesting question is whether the members with the power to create objects are using this power principally for themselves, or also to benefit other members. This is difficult to measure, but a possible indication of the relative use by others of objects is the number of objects owned by the member's character and currently in the pocket of another character, divided by one fewer than the number of objects owned by the character (one fewer because the character object belongs to itself, and character objects cannot go in the pocket of another character). This is only an indication of relative generosity, not a precise measure of the proportion of the objects created by the member for others to use. For example, useful objects include rooms, furniture, and hot air balloons, which are all unlikely to be carried in a character's pocket. The results for this measure are shown in Table 5.7.

TABLE 5.7 Measure of sociability of object creation

GROUP	GROUP SIZE	MEAN OF MEASURE	SAMPLE VARIANCE
D	24	0.153333	0.0118319
B	6	0.156667	0.0225501
N	25	0.1872	0.024896
M	26	0.163462	0.0201275
F	12	0.208333	0.0175606
O	17	0.15	0.0178125
Photo-M	32	0.177069	0.0176637
Photo-F	11	0.1608	0.0145252

It is statistically significant that the mean value for N is larger than that for D, and the mean value for F is larger than that for O or M.

Two Examples

Here, for two characters on the MOO, are lists of the objects created by this character and in the pocket of a character other than the object's creator. They illustrate two reasons why a member might have a high value of the measure of sociability of object creation. I have translated the object names into English, keeping an idea of some idiosyncrasies of capitalization and spelling. For reasons of privacy I have replaced all names of characters by (—). As you can see, the first member creates personalized presents for her friends.

She employs the multimedia capacities of the MOO in an inventive, quirky way for social ends. The second member appears to have rather more limited reasons for the creation of objects, but is also using them as a means of social interaction.

First example: This member connects to the online community during the night. Fifteen other members have at least one of her objects in their character's pocket. Several of her objects use the multimedia capabilities of the Internet—one is a recording of her voice and some others have associated JPEG pictures. The names of her objects show that she creates personalized presents, often humorous or surreal, for other members.

Sugary Lollipop in the shape of a Jamjar

A generic Mexican poncho

(—)Essence

The second real Mary Poppins bag

Mp3 with (—)'s voice

MOOamp v.1.9

The Essential Kit for the Japanese style Mud Fight

Green and yellow parrotlet

(—)'s favorite (—)

The Big Viagra Pill

The real Pzichologist's notebooQQ

A comfortable "come on you reds" football shirt with blue and green stripes

Generic pajamas with black and white vertical stripes

Model no.4 Giuditta Giuditta

ICQ

Perugian Chocolate

Pillow for Calm Dreams

Little present just for (—)

Juniper bush

Second example: This member connects during the day. Seven other members have objects of his in their character's pocket: six of these members are female-presenting, the seventh's character has neutral gender and wears a dress.

All my love

All my love

My love

My love

All my love is for you

MY LOVE IS ONLY FOR YOU!

My LOVE FOR YOU!

(—)'s Engagement ring

Action Creation

Another way in which a member can be creative is to create not objects, but actions in the online community. The measure taken of the creativity of a member with action-creation powers was the number of publicly available actions created by the member, times 1000, divided by (number of samplings in which the member was present, times the MOO age in days). The number of female-presenting members with action-creation powers was too small to give a meaningful comparison with other groups. There was no statistically significant difference in the means of this value for groups D, B, N, or in the means for groups M, O. This measure was not appropriate for Photo-M, Photo-F, since some members of these groups were not present in any sampling; and in any case the number of members of Photo-F with action-creation powers was too small to give a meaningful comparison.

Blaster Use

Little Italy MOO contains a game in which players use a "blaster" to silence an annoying robot, Mario, that tells jokes and recites advertisements. The blaster can be purchased for virtual currency at a Little Italy shop. Scores in the game are visible on a scoreboard that anyone in the online community can read. The blaster can be used only when it is carried in the member's pocket.

The numbers of members in each group whose characters carried a blaster in their pocket were 12, 4, 7, 12, 5, 7, 13 and 6 in groups D, B, N, M, F, O, Photo-M, and Photo-F respectively. It is statistically significant that the proportion of group N that carried a blaster in their pocket is smaller than for groups D or B, and that the proportion of group F that carried a blaster in their pocket is smaller than for group M.

If the popularity or otherwise of this game is indicative of a more general result, this would suggest that arcade-style games, which occur on some other MOOs, may not be a significant attraction for nontraditional members.

(In Mowbray 1999, "Reducing the Geek Bias in Online Communities: Suggestions from a Case Study," the numbers reported for Photo-M and Photo-F with respect to the blaster are 18 and 6, but these are the numbers who possess a blaster at all, rather than the numbers who keep the blaster in their pocket. The proportion of the group Photo-M that possess a blaster is significantly larger than the proportion of Photo-F that possess a blaster.)

Common Features of Nontraditional Groups

In all four cases in which a traditional user group (D, B, M, Photo-M) is compared with a nontraditional user group (N, F, Photo-F), the nontraditional group has a significantly higher measure of object creativity. In three out of the four cases the objects owned by members of the nontraditional group with object-creation powers are significantly more complex than those owned by members of the traditional group with these powers. In the remaining case (N vs. D) there is no significant difference in the complexity of objects owned. In three out of the four cases the nontraditional group is less likely to play the blaster game. In the remaining case (Photo-M vs. Photo-F) there is no significant difference between the groups in the likelihood of having a blaster in their pocket (although the members in the nontraditional group are significantly less likely to possess a blaster at all). So there appears to be a consistent difference in the features of the online community which appeal to traditional and to nontraditional groups.

In none of the four cases does the traditional group have a significantly smaller MOO age. In all four cases the nontraditional group has a significantly smaller value of frequency measure, which estimates how many hours in a given time period a member spends in Little Italy. This suggests that nontraditional members may be deterred from making full use of the online community once they have accessed it.

Qualitative Description of Group Behavior

In this section I interpret the statistically significant data reported above, to give an outline of the different ways in which different demographic groups use the online community.

Group B. This is the group of nonwizards who connect both during the day and during the night. They are present in the online community more often than any other group (in fact, they are also present more often than the wizards, even though being present in the online community is part of a wizard's job). They have a smaller value of the object-creativity measure than nighttime members and daytime members and are more likely to have action-creation powers. The behavior of this group suggests a use of the online community influenced by multiuser games. The group is small relative to the daytime members or the nighttime members.

Group N. The members who access the online community only during the evening and nighttime spend the smallest number of hours in the online community per week of the groups B, D, N, probably because they pay for their access time. They are the least likely of these groups to have a blaster. They are more likely than these groups to have presenting gender other than male or female.

Object creation appears to be particularly attractive for these members. They are the most likely to have object-creation powers and they use these powers prolifically; they have the largest value for the measure of object creativity. However, they do not have a measure of action creativity significantly different from those for members in groups B, D, which suggests that they are specifically interested in creating objects, not actions. Their objects are significantly more complex than those created by group B, and significantly more likely to end up in the pockets of other members' characters than those created by group D.

The fact that they are the group of B, D, N most likely to have object-creation powers is impressive. In order to obtain the power to create objects it is necessary to persuade a wizard to give you this power. The wizards rarely access the MOO during the evening and night. Members of group N are less frequently present in the MOO than the members of groups B, D, and do not have significantly larger MOO ages than members of these groups. So members of group N will have had noticeably less opportunity to communicate with the wizards. The fact that a large proportion of this group has object-creation powers may be due to their being particularly keen on having these powers. It may also be that they are more persuasive than members of groups B, D, reflecting their greater maturity and the fact that many have jobs requiring persuasive powers.

Group D. For the measures reported, group D does not have a mean value significantly larger than those for both N and B, nor a mean value significantly smaller than both of these. However, it is instructive to compare the daytime members (who are mostly University students) directly with the nighttime members (who are mostly home PC users) in the light of demographic changes in Internet use.

The daytime members are less likely than nighttime members to have a presenting gender other than male or female. This may be connected with opinion given in interviews with members of this community that there was more flirtation on Little Italy MOO during the daytime, or it may be further evidence of the nighttime members' creative thinking. The daytime members are more likely to have a blaster than the nighttime members, suggesting a more playful use of the online community. They are present more often, probably because most of them do not have to pay for access. They are less likely to have creative powers, either for object creation or for action creation.

The daytime members who have the power to create objects are less productive in their creation than nighttime members, and less likely to give their objects to other members. This suggests that the nighttime members' drive to create objects may be partly a result of desire to use MOO objects to enhance their social interaction with other members.

Group O. This is the group of members with presenting gender other than male or female. For the measures reported, the mean value for group O is neither significantly larger than both the mean values for groups F and M, nor significantly smaller than both. This is what would be expected if the differences in behavior between groups F and M were largely a reflection of differences between MOO use by women and men. Indeed, for every measure reported in this chapter, if the mean value for Photo-M is significantly larger than the mean value for Photo-F, then mean value for M is significantly larger than the mean value for F, and if the mean value for Photo-M is significantly smaller than the mean value for Photo-F, then mean value for M is significantly smaller than the mean value for F.

Groups F and Photo-F. Since group O has behavior somewhere between that of groups M and F, and groups F and Photo-F have similar behavior in comparison with groups M and Photo-M, I will compare groups F, Photo-F directly with groups M, Photo-M.

Members of groups F, Photo-F are less frequently present in the MOO than members of groups M, Photo-M. They also have smaller MOO ages. They are less likely to have creative powers, either for creating objects or for creating actions. The fact that they spend less time on the MOO may be a contributory factor. On the other hand, the members of groups F and Photo-F who do have the power to create objects are significantly more productive than the members of groups M, Photo-M with this power. The objects that they create are significantly more complex. The objects created by members of group F are significantly more likely to be used for social ends than those created by members of group M. (There is no significant difference between Photo-M and Photo-F in this regard.)

Members of group F are significantly less likely than members of group M to have a blaster in their pocket. There is no significant difference between Photo-M and Photo-F in this regard.

These results suggest that there may be an untapped desire among women members of the online community to create complex objects. They are less likely to have the power to create objects, but those who have this power are particularly productive with their limited time.

Examples of Internet Bias

Although in February 2000, 46 percent of the global Internet population were not native English speakers (Global Reach 2000), and this proportion is increasing, the language of the Internet is still predominantly English, and most sites support only one language.

In much of Europe local telephone calls are not free, indeed are expensive, and are paid by the minute. This may discourage European home users (and home users in other parts of the world where local calls are expensive) from participating in online communities, which require more time online than other Internet applications. Computer hardware and software usually costs more outside the United States, and cheap public access points are rarer. (The problem of cost of access and use is even more of an issue in developing countries.)

Some Internet application designers appear not to have thought through the types of users they might attract. For example, some Web sites with content of general interest ask users for their U.S. Zip Code.

Many Internet sites have an interface design which appeals to technically oriented users, who like using the latest technology, but not to nontraditional users. Nontraditional users consistently prefer sites which are simple and quick to use, as opposed to sites with complex navigational structure, or with unnecessary moving images, or which take a long time to access (Nielsen 1996). Home users in particular are likely to have slow modems, and have to dial in, so are especially sensitive to download times.

The Internet has been marketed principally as an information tool. This may attract men, who tend to have a communication style based on information exchange, more than women, whose communication style tends to be based on social empathy (Tannen 1990). Online communities are well placed to support a social use of the Internet, if they decide to do so.

In the 10th GVU survey (Georgia Tech Research Corporation 1998), female users, users aged over 50, and users with less than a year of experience all cited privacy as the most important issue facing the Internet. (Traditional users were more concerned about speed/bandwidth.) The principal financial model for commercial online communities is that they are funded by the sale of personal data collected from the members. If the data subjects cannot object to the use of their data for direct marketing, this may alienate nontraditional users. It is also illegal in some countries. The European Directive on Data Privacy requires that data subjects can object to their data being processed for the purpose of direct marketing (European Communities 1995).

Conclusion: Suggestions for Reducing Demographic Bias in Online Communities

Here are some suggestions of ways to reduce bias against non-traditional members in an online community.

Suggestions from the Case Study

■ Since nontraditional users appear to enjoy creating objects, promote applications in the online community harnessing the members' creativity in object creation.

■ Give limited object-creation powers to all members, rather than requiring members to be promoted before they can create objects.

■ Develop tools that reduce the time needed for members to create complex objects.

■ Focus on social communication and creativity in the online community, rather than directing members toward attaining set goals or increasing personal scores.

■ Do not rely on arcade-style games to attract members.

Suggestions from the Examples of Internet Bias

■ Consider supporting languages other than English.

■ If you run a public-service online community, consider sponsoring cheap public access points.

■ Decide which demographic groups you are targeting. Consult members of these groups on the design. In online communities it is possible to track which groups use which applications and services; with members' permission, collect this data and use it to identify possible biases.

- Design interfaces for simplicity and ease of use, rather than to show off advanced technology. Avoid long download times.
- Make your online community a place for social communication, rather than just information exchange.
- Respect the privacy of community members.

Acknowledgments

This chapter is essentially a combination of two conference papers (Mowbray 1999, "Differences in the Use of a Cyber Community According to Habitual Time of Connection and Presenting Gender," and Mowbray 1999, "Reducing the Geek Bias in Online Communities: Suggestions from a Case Study") and is published here with the kind permission of the organizers of Ethicomp 1999 and Exploring Cyber Society 1999. Thanks to them.

Thanks to the Georgia Tech Research Corporation and the GVU Center for the GVU 10th survey results.

And an especially big thank you to the citizens of Little Italy (including Veronica, Yoko Tomonaga, Joker, XS, Paolo Marchiori, and Alessandro Pengue) for their help and friendliness.

References

European Communities, Directive 95/46/EC, *Official Journal of the EC*, 23, L.281, 31 (November 23, 1995). Unofficial text online at http://www2.echo.lu/legal/en/dataprot/directiv/directiv.html

Frenkel, Karen A., "Women & Computing," *Communications of the ACM*, vol. 33, no. 11 (November 1990), 34–46.

Georgia Tech Research Corporation, GVU Center, "GVU's 10th WWW User Survey," October 1998. Online: http://www.gvu.gatech.edu/user_surveys/survey-1998-10

Global Reach, "Global Internet Statistics (by Language)," February 2000. Online: http://www.euromktg.com/globstats

Little Italy Staff, "Little Italy MOO Info Page," September 1996. Online: http://kame.usr.dsi.unimi.it/home/li/info.html

Media Metrix Editorial Staff, "Media Metrix Chronicles the 'History' of the Internet," Media Metrix press release, New York, March 18, 1999. Online: http://www.mediametrix.com/Press/Room/Press_Releases/03_18_99.html

Montgomery, Douglas C., *Design and Analysis of Experiments*, 2d ed. New York: John Wiley & Sons, 1976.

Mowbray, Miranda, "Differences in the Use of a Cyber Community According to Habitual Time of Connection and Presenting Gender," John Armitage and Joanne Roberts, eds., *Exploring Cyber Society: Social, Political, Economic and Cultural Issues*, vol. 2. Proceedings of the Conference 5th–7th July 1999, School of Social, Political and Economic Sciences, University of Northumbria at Newcastle, UK. ISBN 0 9536450 1 0.

———, "Reducing the Geek Bias in Online Communities: Suggestions from a Case Study," in Proc. 4th ETHICOMP International Conference on the Social and Ethical Impacts of Information and Communication Technologies, LUISS Guido Carli University, Rome, October 6–8, 1999, ISBN 88-900396-0-4.

Neilsen, Jacob, "Top Ten Mistakes in Web Design," *Alertbox*, May 1996. Online: http://www.useit.com/alertbox/9605.html

Reid, Elizabeth, *Cultural Formation in Text-Based Virtual Realities*. Melbourne: Department of English, University of Melbourne, Australia, MA Thesis, 1994.

Reuters, "Web Gender Gap Narrows As More Women Go Online—Survey," Press release, January 20, 2000. Online: http://www.foxnews.com/vtech/0120/t_rt_0120_71.sml

Rheingold, Howard, *The Virtual Community*. London: Secker & Warburg, 1994. Online: http://www.rheingold.com/vc/book/5.html

Tannen, Deborah, *You Just Don't Understand*. New York: William Morrow and Company, 1990.

Educational Online Communities

his part of the book is about educational online communities. Norman Clark, Tim Luke, and Joanne Addison describe their experiences of different models of online educational communities operating in three U.S. universities (Appalachian State University, Virginia Tech, and the University of Colorado at Denver). Maria Bakardjieva and Andrew Feenberg talk about the subtle gradations between private and public that exist in online communities, and the implications of this for researchers. Geoff Sauer gives some historical context to changes in the intellectual property status of academic material online, and describes the English Server, an online community run by and for academic researchers. Walter Aprile and Teresa Vazquez Mantecón's chapter is about Red Escolar, an educational online community serving one and a half *million* school students in Mexico, which operates successfully using remarkably few resources. Finally, Richard Stallman, the founder of the free software movement, calls for a similar movement for educational material. Cary Nelson's afterword to this part of the book warns of the potential for negative change from the use of online communities in education.

6 Education, Communication, and Consumption: Piping in the Academic Community
by Norman Clark,
clarkne@appstate.edu

Picture a typical college student on a typical day. She wakes up, late as usual, and rushes out of the room past her notebook computer, which is made by the same company as those on all the other students' desks, since they're all required to buy this brand as freshmen. Running down the hall, she passes the soft drink vending machines, wishing not for the first time that her campus had an exclusive contract with Pepsi instead of Coca-Cola. As she crosses campus to get to her first class, she passes the Do-It-Yourself Depot Stadium, the MassiveCommunicationIndustry FieldHouse, and the Mega-BookWarehouse Bookstore. Unfortunately, she is so late today that she doesn't have time to stop at the McDonald's restaurant for breakfast. Arriving just seconds before the start of class, she barely notices the plaque on the wall that celebrates the sponsorship of this classroom by the law firm of Consu, Memo, and Restuff. Her professor begins speaking just as she sits down (a bit out of breath): "Today's class is brought to you by ShopTillYouFlop.com, your one-stop online shopping community. Join today for a uniquely satisfying experience. You'll find a link to ShopTillYouFlop.com on our class Web page."

The last scene of our imaginary journey seemed, I hope, a bit out of place. But the rest of the trip no doubt sounded completely plausible, especially if you have ever been on a U.S. college campus. The commercialization of U.S. college campuses has been going on for years, typically starting with athletic programs. Today, corporate connections can be found at the bookstore, the stadium, the cafeteria—in fact, almost anywhere you look. At least until recently, colleges have kept some areas free from advertising, including their online services. But not for long. Many schools are now contracting their Web sites and email services to outside commercial companies. And with these contracts come the increasingly ubiquitous banner ads and email advertising.

One of the first schools to do this was Appalachian State University, where I teach. ASU is located in the mountains of Western North Carolina and enrolls over 12,000 students. The college currently has a contract with one of the largest campus portal companies, Campus Pipeline™. As a faculty member, I'm concerned about the impact of this move on the academic community in which I live and work. As a rhetorical critic, I tend to look very carefully at the words people use to persuade others. So, in this chapter, I examine Campus Pipeline's persuasive efforts to get its portal accepted. In these efforts we find more than just a debate about putting more advertising on campuses; what's at stake here is the very definition of the academic community in an age of increasing commercialization and digitization.

I'll begin by providing some background information, showing how the rise of campus portals is linked to students' rising technological expectations and schools' shrinking budgets. After detailing what Campus Pipeline has done at ASU, I will discuss the four key words that continually emerge during the discussion over commercializing campus online services. Finally, I will conclude with some thoughts on the impact of commercialization on the academic community as it moves into an increasingly online world.

Laying the Pipe: The Rise of Campus Portals

Walk through a computer lab on almost any college campus, and chances are very good that many of the students you see will be browsing the Web. Chances are also very good that (depending on the time of day and year) most of the computers will be in use. Every year, the students entering college are more technologically literate than the students of the year before. With this increasing literacy come increasing demands for more technology on campus, and for more data to be available online.

Appalachian State University is no exception. In the fall of 1999, Appalachian's freshman class participated in several assessment tests to measure their computer literacy. These tests revealed several important attitudes about technology, as well as the general skill level of incoming students. Not too surprisingly, the general attitude toward technology was that it was essential for education. Almost every student surveyed believed that owning a computer "provides an academic advantage" (Swing 1999). Most of the students said that they have had "wide access to computing, entertainment, and communication technologies," more than half already had a personal email account, and over 70 percent had brought a computer to campus. These computers were not obsolete cast-offs, either: half were less than three months old; 75 percent were less than a year old. Clearly, students come to this college with the expectation that computing technology is critical to success.

Some interesting discrepancies were found when students reported their experiences with computers. Almost 90 percent had searched the Web for information, nearly 80 percent sent email to a friend or relative at least once a week, and 57 percent had participated at least weekly in a chat room. These data showed that incoming students were familiar with using computers for basic communication tasks; however, few had used them for more academic purposes. Nearly 90 percent had never sent an email to a teacher or produced a graded Web page. Close to half of the students had not used a spreadsheet, database, or desktop publishing program during the year before college. When students were tested on their ability to use email, 70 percent successfully sent a message. But only half knew that "@appstate.edu" was a domain name, and only 40 percent could attach a file. Students could conduct basic Web searches, but 60 percent believed that "the federal government required Web sites to identify the authors, dates created, and host institutions" (Swing 1999).

The conclusion that ASU reached from this data was that freshman were "capable of using computers for basic tasks and casual communications but not prepared for greater demands of collegiate academic computing" (Swing 1999). But another conclusion that could be drawn is that incoming students are increasingly expecting their education to be technologically enhanced. As more students get used to searching for information online, they expect the University to make information available 24/7 also. Unfortunately, all of this requires more and more resources at a time when budgets are getting increasingly tight. To give students what they want, universities are forced to hire more HTML coders, database programmers, network technicians, lab assistants, and other support personnel. Time and money have to be spent on instructing both faculty and students. And of course, the technology has to be kept up-to-date—which means buying new computers. Imagine trying to get the money necessary to do this from a state legislature that is still dealing with the aftermath of serious flooding in the eastern half of the state.

Campus Portals to the Rescue?

This world of increasing demands and shrinking dollars has led to the creation of a new type of Internet company: the campus portal. Companies such as Campus Pipeline, MyBytes, Jenzabar, and others are approaching colleges and universities, offering to set up an all-encompassing Web system. These campus portals allow students to check their email and schedules, register for classes, jump to class Web pages, and get campus announcements specific to their interests and activities, all in one place. Of course, the service does not come without a cost. With Campus Pipeline, for example, a University has two options. They can pay a licensing fee based on the size of the school, ranging from $72,000 for schools with up to 4,000 students, to $541,000 for schools with over 35,000 students (Feemster 1999). Or, they can get the software for free if they choose the "sponsorship" plan. With this option, Campus Pipeline sets up the portal at no charge to the University, but places advertising banners on the Web pages and sends e-commerce offers to students' email accounts. Not too surprisingly, all of the more than 400 schools that have signed up with Campus Pipeline so far have opted for the "sponsorship" plan.

The net result of the sponsorship plan is that University administrators get a free campus Web site, students get Web access to their email accounts—accounts that they already have, provided by ASU at no charge to the students, independent of Campus Pipeline—and to academic information peppered with sponsors' logos and animated advertisements, and Campus Pipeline gets a share of the profit every time a student clicks on a banner ad or buys a book online. Students also have the option of filling out a survey that collects demographic and lifestyle information. This data is then used to send them microtargeted advertising. For example, an automobile manufacturer can come to Campus Pipeline and have them send an email describing a "new special financing plan" to all senior students studying a subject at ASU that is likely to lead them on to well-paying jobs.

Campus Pipeline has emerged as the campus portal company to beat for one primary reason: corporate alliances. The most critical alliance was with Systems and Computer Technology Corporation (SCT), which is the largest provider of administrative software to college campuses. Campus Pipeline and SCT developers worked together to ensure a seamless connection between campus databases and the Web interface that students would see. Campus Pipeline has also formed partnerships with several other systems integrating companies that create connections between archaic University databases and new telephone or online registration systems. Part of the deal that Campus Pipeline struck with these companies is that they cannot recommend a competitor's Web platform. With this near-lock on schools across the nation, it's not surprising that Campus Pipeline's CEO, Chad Muir, thinks they have a chance to become "the fifth largest portal on the Web" (Feemster 1999).

Campus Pipeline at ASU

Appalachian State University had the distinction of being the first school to pour their students down the pipe. At the beginning of the Fall 1999 semester, over 2,500 incoming students (both freshman and transfers) were given IDs and passwords to login to Campus Pipeline, which they would use for email and to access campus information. By the summer of 2000, Campus Pipeline was "available and encouraged for use by ALL students at Appalachian" (Campus Pipeline 2000, "Welcome to Campus Pipeline!"). Faculty as well were being encouraged to try out the system. This was the largest rollout of the new campus portal. Other universities, including Villanova, the University of Memphis, and the University of Oregon, planned to first test the system on a small group of students. Like all of the other schools, ASU opted for the sponsorship plan, since it would have cost $204,000 to have an advertisement-free portal (Blumenstyk 1999).

At ASU, the Campus Pipeline Web platform consists of five primary pages: My Pipeline^{SM}, School Services, Campus Life, Web Life, and the email interface. The My Pipeline page (Figure 6–1) is the first one that students (and faculty) see after they login.

This page features campus announcements, which up to this point are rarely used by the University. This summer, at ASU, the primary announcement has been a promotion sponsored by Campus Pipeline. Also on this page are links to campus resources, which are actually existing Web pages created by ASU and accessible from ASU's regular Web site (which is still up and running). News headlines, links to other sections of the portal, and a few basic research tools round out the initial page.

When students go to the School Services page (Figure 6–2), the first thing they see are the courses in which they are currently enrolled. Clicking on these links is supposed to take them to their course Web page, but ASU currently has that feature disabled, since we use different software (WebCT) for most course Web pages. Instead, there is a link to available course Web pages. Faculty visiting this page, from any computer with Internet access, can view course lists, initiate secure course-specific chat sessions with classes, link to syllabi and other class documentation, and utilize system-generated class-specific email distribution lists. Starting in the fall of 2000, ASU

FIGURE 6–1 My Pipeline: The home page for Campus Pipeline at ASU

faculty will be able to complete these administrative tasks and more, such as register students for classes, process grades, post current course information to interactive message boards, or review transcripts. But as of the summer of 2000, those services were still unavailable. This was because ASU had not yet purchased another product needed to make these features accessible: SCT's Web for Faculty software. Clicking on the link to "schedule a meeting with other faculty members" actually takes you to Evite.com, an entirely different advertising-supported service not at all connected with ASU.

The Campus Life section (Figure 6–3) primarily provides links to already existing ASU information. For example, the "student organizations" link takes you to an online directory of campus clubs. In the fall, student leaders are expected to have authorization to maintain information about their student groups in this area, and the "Off Campus" link page is supposed to have information about local restaurants, shopping, etc.

FIGURE 6–2 School Services: Accessing your records online (some day)

However, as of the summer of 2000, these features were still "coming soon!" Finally, students can also create their own Web page at no charge. However, setting up a Web page requires them to register with Homestead, yet another advertising-supported partner that actually hosts the Web sites.

"The best of college living online" (Figure 6–4) is what students are told they will find on the Web Life page. Here the advertisements hit them full force, and here is where the vast majority of offsite links are found. Basically, nothing on this page has anything to do with ASU, and many of the links on this page connect to a commercial service. The fifth primary page of the Campus Pipeline portal is the Web-based email

FIGURE 6-3 Campus Life: What's happening at ASU

interface, which opens up a separate window. This interface is basically the same as any other online email interface, including the ubiquitous advertisement in the upper right corner.

Corporate connections to college campuses are not new. From advertisements on scoreboards, to collegewide contracts for a particular brand of computer or soft drink, the corporate presence in U.S. higher education has been seen as a mixed blessing. On the one hand, it allows colleges to provide students with services the school cannot afford otherwise. But on the other hand, critics claim that it cheapens education by sending the message that everything can be bought—including the institution, the students, and even learning. As Thomas Ehrlich (1999) put it in his letter to *The Chronicle of Higher Education*:

> Selling a college curriculum to the highest bidder subverts the very purpose of a college education. Placing advertisements on web pages that contain academic materials needed in a

FIGURE 6–4 Web Life: AKA the Mall

college course compromises those materials. To some students, the materials could become secondary to the information in the advertisements (p. A76).

In the discussion surrounding Campus Pipeline, you will find more than just a simple debate over whether or not colleges should accept advertising on their Web sites. It's far more serious than that. In fact, what you will find is an attempt to work out what exactly colleges are supposed to be. In the rest of this chapter, I will go through a careful analysis of Campus Pipeline's attempts to sell their portal despite these criticisms. What we will learn from this analysis is how the very concept of academic community is being reshaped in this age of increasing commercialization.

Deconstructing the Pipe: Critical Analysis

Social theorists know that in public debates more goes on than just jockeying for position. While the argument rages, certain key words come up time after time. McGee (1980) calls these terms "ideographs," which are sloganlike terms that signify collective commitment. An example of an ideograph in American society would be freedom: nearly everyone would agree that freedom is a good thing, but if pressed to define it, very few would be able to do so. Ideographs are powerful words or phrases that are persuasive because of their very lack of definite meaning. As nearly empty signifiers, they can be filled with a variety of meanings, and in public debates this is exactly what happens. The different groups involved struggle to get their definitions of key words accepted by various audiences. By looking at how these key words get redefined, we can also see the shift in a society's view of the world.

Campus Pipeline has to reach out to several different audiences. Obviously, they have to sell their service to campus administrators. They have to persuade corporate partners such as SCT and outside investors to join forces with them (and not their competitors). To pay their salaries, they have to convince advertisers to make use of their portal. When they are interviewed by the media, their target audience includes the general public. Finally, they have to provide students with reasons to keep returning to the site. In their messages to these various audiences, four key concepts come up over and over, and as they are repeated get redefined: education, communication, community, and consumption.

Education

Not too surprisingly, Campus Pipeline does not talk in specific details about education. They no doubt realize that educators don't wish to be told how to do their job. But it is also not too surprising that they do feature the word prominently in their communication to schools. In fact, their mission statement is: "We will revolutionize education by connecting the collegiate community" (Campus Pipeline 2000, "Who We Are"). They claim to be the builders of "the first Web platform for higher education" (Campus Pipeline 2000, "Who We Are"). When I accessed their site in April of 2000, they stated that this Web platform "creates one-to-one relationships between institutions of higher education by **building the online campus experience.**"

If you're confused by the last statement, you're not alone. Who are they supposedly building relationships *between*: different colleges? And what exactly is the "online campus experience?" When I accessed the site again in June of 2000, they had moved this marketing hype to the home page of the site and simplified the wording on the "What We Do" page to make the connection to community more explicit: "The Campus Pipeline creates comprehensive online communities for colleges and universities" (Campus Pipeline 2000, "What We Do"). Certainly, they are not the *first* Web platform. Their mission statement directly connects education to community, but, as we will see, there's not much substance to this connection, or to the claim that they are revolutionizing education. Joanne Hugi, the director of the University of Oregon's computing center, summed up Campus Pipeline's claims with a nice bit of understatement: "They might be overdoing the marketing a little bit" (Feemster 1999). The only thing approaching a revolutionary change to education is the direct, one-stop, continual access for students to administrative functions such as checking their schedule, fees, etc. Campus Pipeline calls this "must-use functionality":

> Students will turn to it not because they like it or because it provides interesting content, but because it is an essential part of registering for classes and communicating with professors, of doing business with the university (Feemster 1999).

Of course, all of these services can be provided online by the University without Campus Pipeline's help—and already are in some places. The only real revolution here is that the services are paid for through advertising, and not student fees.

The claim that they are revolutionizing education is also a bit premature. None of the interactive functions for faculty that I've read about, such as the ability to automatically email students in a class or send them a reading list as soon as they register for the course, are available yet. The only student interactive functions currently operating are ones that they can already access from ASU's old Web site. I've heard that the new release of the software that will be running in Fall 2000 adds some more of these promised functions, but nothing revolutionary. In fact, the primary benefit of Campus Pipeline to education as far as I can see it is to reduce the number of times I have to login to secure campus services. Before, I might have had to login to three different secure sites to perform different functions. Now, after logging into Campus Pipeline, those different functions can be accessed without having to login again. Easier, yes; revolutionary, no.

Communication

Campus Pipeline's goal is to be an essential part of student-to-professor communication. But what they mean by communication is not improved listening skills, better interpersonal interactions, or more sophisticated critical thinking. Their focus is on the tools for communication: specifically, email (and to a lesser extent, chat rooms).

This is where the marketing hype reaches an all-time high. Their Web site promises easy-to-use chat rooms, automatically generated class lists, online office hours, and other tools that I have yet to see at ASU. In a letter to the *editor of The Chronicle of Higher Education*, CEO Chad Muir gets carried away by his company's marketing vision and claims that "Campus Pipeline has developed a distinctive new way for teachers to communicate with students in which time, distance, and cost have been radically diminished as barriers to learning" (Muir 1999). Unfortunately, they have done no such thing: their "distinctive new way" of communicating is simply email, which by no stretch of the imagination did they develop.

It is not surprising that much of the talk about communication is hyperbole. At a time when investors are pouring money into any new Internet company that seems to have a possibility of success, it makes sense to focus a lot of energy on marketing. But so far, the talk about communication has not yet translated into much action. Students in my classes at ASU who are using the Campus Pipeline system continually complain about the slow speed of the email interface. During both the Spring and Summer of 2000 sessions, students who had Campus Pipeline email accounts often did not receive mail sent to the class mailing list. Chat rooms are nonexistent. However, students who take the time to fill out the demographic and lifestyle survey do receive plenty of e-commerce advertisements in their email accounts.

Community

As I noted earlier, Campus Pipeline's "What We Do" page states that their platform "creates comprehensive online communities for colleges and universities" (2000). A sensible person might ask, "How?" Their answer is as follows:

> The Campus Pipeline Web platform links existing campus systems to new tools and Web applications allowing schools to leverage current investments in technology and bring all current and future Web applications together in one place. The result is a secure campus Intranet incorporating the latest educational and communication tools that enhances teaching and learning and enlivens community life (Campus Pipeline 2000, "What We Do").

After wading through all the high-tech talk, the message that you get from this statement is a slightly modified, *Field of Dreams*-esque "If we build it, they'll come." The basic assumption behind Campus Pipeline, and many other online "community" builders, is that a sense of community can be established by simply providing access to information and a Web interface to email.

However, communities are developed by forming relationships not with information, but with other people. If students are to feel a sense of commitment to the campus, they have to build relationships with other people. Before they can build relationships, they have to be persuaded somehow to either value or else overlook the differences between them and the other person. In other words, someone has to create ties to bind people together. It is much easier to create a sense of commitment and community if you can communicate. Of course, students can already communicate in a variety of ways with their professors and each other. What Campus Pipeline has promised is improved communication. But so far, the only improvement has been Web access to email. The other promised tools have yet to materialize. The lack of effort and development in this area leads me to question their commitment to community.

If all Campus Pipeline does is provide students with 24-hour, online access to their course schedules, email boxes, and shopping sites, it will not create an online community. In fact, two things that are present on the portal actually might detract from it. First, the initial page that students see is My Pipeline (Figure 6–1), which is a highly personalized and customizable portal page. By customizing each page for each student, Campus Pipeline is actually ensuring that students will have less and less in common to discuss. Second, as Muir himself noted, the Internet works to diminish barriers of time and space. This is made obvious on the Web Life page (Figure 6–4), where students are provided with hundreds of links to off-campus booksellers, clothing retailers, music stores, and much more. By providing students with access to merchants around the world, and then placing no local links in the Off Campus section, Campus Pipeline potentially decreases students' sense of commitment to the local community.

When you carefully read the statements that Campus Pipeline makes to other audiences besides universities, including investors and potential partners, it becomes clear that they do not see students primarily as members of the academic community. Instead, they are a locked-in audience, or an elusive but valuable demographic group. Remember the phrase "must-use functionality?" Eventually at ASU, students will have to use the portal if they want instant and easy access to academic-related information. When they speak to potential investors, Campus Pipeline representatives like to talk a lot about the "stickiness" of their site, and that they will have "eyeballs coming into the site on a regular basis" (Spirrison 1999). In another moment of marketing frenzy, Muir claimed that Campus Pipeline will "redefine portal loyalty" (Feemster 1999). But this is perhaps the least far-fetched of his claims. What keeps many investors away from other portals such as Yahoo! or Excite is that it takes a lot of effort to build up customer loyalty so that they continue to use only one portal. But with Campus Pipeline, portal loyalty is built-in, since students do not have a choice. Many investors see this as a tremendous economic advantage. Fredric Harmon, the head of Oak General (one of Campus Pipeline's partners), noted that without this must-use functionality, and forced loyalty, "the cost of creating that community of users and replicating that recurring traffic pattern would be enormous" (Spirrison 1999).

The second way that the student community is defined by Campus Pipeline is as the elusive but valuable demographic. College students are part of the most highly sought-after age group, since (for the most part) they are making all of their own purchasing decisions for the first time, and tend to spend a large portion of their income on products (as opposed to a mortgage, for example). Their brand loyalty has not yet been established, they have a potential for large future earnings, they are fashion trendsetters in some sectors, and they are relatively willing to experiment with new products. But for a long time, advertisers have found them difficult to reach. With Campus Pipeline's promise of a locked-in audience, many are seeing college portals as a golden opportunity. As one writer put it:

> The Internet habits of college students have rekindled marketers' hopes of establishing relationships with this notoriously elusive demographic. Because students are likely to move at least once a year, list their phone in a roommate's name, and be far too busy to watch television or read local newspapers, marketers are hoping students will frequent a few

well-established addresses on the net. And so the gold rush for college portals is on (Feemster 1999).

Time and time again, the relationships that Campus Pipeline talks about creating are between students and advertisers. Most of the time, the academic community is essentially defined as a target demographic. Sometimes, the connection is jarringly blunt: one author reported that Campus Pipeline is in a competition with other college portal companies "to build a community within the University, with an audience for advertisers" (Duval 1999).

In short, Campus Pipeline promises investors a locked-in audience that has to be loyal to the portal—an image of students that some might find a bit hard to swallow, and definitely at odds with the traditional image of an academic community. The "revolutionary" aspect of Campus Pipeline is this: they have found a way to convince people in academia, who are traditionally somewhat reluctant to commercialize, to *actively participate* in the transformation of their community into a consuming audience.

Consumption

Given the way that community gets redefined as a target demographic, it is not surprising that consumption gets the most attention. And in this case, the attention is far from symbolic. While Campus Pipeline talks a lot about improving community, communication, and education, their portal actually does little to foster any of these goals. Few in the academic community wish to talk about consumption. However, Campus Pipeline does not hesitate to point out that this is a unique opportunity to reach the college market when they address other audiences, such as potential investors and advertisers.

In reading statements from various schools that were signing on with Campus Pipeline, I was amazed at how infrequently anyone mentioned the advertisements and email marketing. At the University of Memphis, Campus Pipeline was called an "enterprise information portal" (Stoever 1999)—a marvelously vague phrase, one whose meaning I find hard to ascertain. Northwestern State University quoted Chad Muir, who praised them for "demonstrating national technology leadership in introducing their Campus community to the convenience of online campus services" (Northwestern State University Alumni Association 1999). The page that introduces ASU students to Campus Pipeline calls it a "personalized Web interface that is integrated with Web services and products available through the Appalachian Web pages" (Campus Pipeline 2000, "Welcome to Campus Pipeline!"). All of these schools in their public relations releases talk about how they're using technology to make students' lives easier. But none of them say a word about the advertisements and targeted email messages. The ASU welcome page mentions the survey that students are asked to fill out the first time they login, and says that it is optional, but says nothing about how Campus Pipeline uses that information.

And use it they do. The effort to persuade students to consume permeates the site. Obviously, advertisers are scattered on every page. Even the supposed "campus announcement" on the My Pipeline page (Figure 6–1) is an advertisement. The Web Life page (Figure 6–4) promises "the best of college living," which apparently means shopping. Nearly every link on this page, and its subsections, takes students to a Web site were they can spend money. And while many of the other promised services and features of Campus Pipeline's portal have yet to come online, the advertisements and e-commerce links have been functional since day one.

The primary response to the overwhelming emphasis on consumption seems to be, "Get used to it." Jeff Williams, the director of information technology services at ASU, pointed out that students see advertising online all the time, so the partnership between Campus Pipeline and ASU is just "exposing them to a few more" (Blumenstyk 1999). When asked whether colleges should be adopting an advertising model for their information services, he noted that "some people will say that it's not ethical to advertise. Given our druthers, we'd rather not ourselves. But it's a pretty attractive model. We'll live with it" (Guernsey 1999). The most obvious example of the unthinking acceptance of the invasion of advertising into all areas of life came from a principal of a high school that had signed on with ZapMe (which provides computers to schools for free, in exchange for the continual display of banner ads): "I don't see anything wrong with these partnerships with businesses. Advertising is a part of life, and kids need to be able to live with it" (Salkowski 1999).

Draining the Pipe: Conclusions

When we take a close look at Campus Pipeline's persuasive efforts, and at the actual portal they have created for ASU, it becomes clear that even though there is a lot of talk about community, there is little actual effort. Of the four key terms that drive this issue, the only one that receives any real attention is consumption. Campus Pipeline clearly avoids education, and actually most educators would prefer things to stay this way. But beyond providing an email interface, the campus portal does nothing to improve communication yet. The promised automated messages and chat rooms have not yet arrived, and even when they do, I seriously doubt that more interaction with computer programs will do much to improve a sense of community on campus. Campus Pipeline clearly understands that community is a word that matters to universities, and mentions it often when speaking to administrators. But looking at their messages to other audiences, and the actual content that they have put on the campus portal, makes it clear that they see the academic community as nothing more than a captive audience.

I imagine if Campus Pipeline's CEO Chad Muir were with me right now, he would say "So what?" In fact, here is his response to Thomas Ehrlich's essay critical of Internet advertising on college Web pages that was printed in *The Chronicle of Higher Education*:

> Perhaps we would all wish for billboardless highways and commercial-free television, and many of us might be cynical about the corporate sponsorship of professorships, hospital wings, and public television. But perhaps we should spend

more energy and goodwill to make the best out of potential partnerships between the for-profit and non-profit sectors for the benefit of all (Muir 1999).

My response to his comment would be that thus far at ASU I have seen a lot of work put into benefiting advertisers, and by extension Campus Pipeline, but not much benefit to the academic community. All of the services currently available on Campus Pipeline I could get before without advertising. Perhaps as more advanced services are added, I might be convinced to login and try to ignore the banner ads.

But I doubt it. Because I am troubled by the increasing emphasis on consumption in education. Advertising is becoming more and more pervasive on campuses, and is in danger of becoming intimately tied to instruction. When email from a professor comes with an advertisement attached, how much easier does it make it for students to connect consumption with education, to see knowledge as just one more thing that can be bought? But in my opinion, education is not something to be consumed. You cannot build a viable academic community if its members are only interested in coming to campus for a few years to "get" a degree. Education should be about conversion, an ongoing process in which students learn to value the give and take of ideas. By engaging others in debate and discussion, students become less self-centered and more aware of the impact of their ideas on others, and vice versa. This is how academic communities are formed, and nothing I have seen so far on Campus Pipeline leads me to believe it will help in this process.

I am also concerned about another potential result of a close connection between education and consumption. The more we view education as something to be consumed, the more we focus in on pleasing the consumers. Do we really want education to be subject to the rapidly changing whims of taste so common to a consumer culture? Shouldn't education transcend these forces, and be judged by how well it transforms students into valued members of society, and not by how well it appeals at any given moment to a rapidly changing consumer? As Lury notes, consumption in our society has become "increasingly specialized, with individualized and hybrid consumption patterns. Consumers are more volatile; their preferences change more often and are more unpredictable" (1996, p. 94). By linking the academic community to consumption, we risk fragmenting it even further.

Finally, I'm concerned about the difference between having and being. According to Lury, "modern Euro-American societies are characterized by the strongly rooted belief that *to have is to be*" (1996, p. 7). To a large extent, people see their identity as connected to what they possess. In fact, we even see our identity as something we possess. But I believe that it is better if we view possessions as things we can use to express ourselves, rather than things that determine ourselves. I agree with Pope John Paul II, who stated that "it is not wrong to want to live better; what is wrong is a style of life presumed to be better when directed towards 'having' rather than 'being' " (John Paul II 1991). What students ought to gain from the academic community, whether virtual or real, is a more mature sense of identity, and an ability to distinguish between artificially created needs and higher forms of satisfying genuine needs. The disturbing question I am left with is, can we do this if everywhere they turn, students are confronted not by the more essential issues of life, but by advertisements for cologne or running shoes?

This chapter was brought to you by Hewlett Packard and Prentice Hall. However, simply possessing it will not make you a better person. Thinking about it and discussing it with other people might.

References

Blumenstyk, G., "Colleges Get Free Web Pages, But with a Catch: Advertising," *The Chronicle of Higher Education*, vol. 46, no. 2 (September 3, 1999), p. A45.

Campus Pipeline, "Welcome to Campus Pipeline!" 2000. Online: http://www.appstate.edu/www_docs/cp/

————, "Who We Are," 2000. Online: http://www.campuspipe-line.com/whoweare/home.html

————, "What We Do," 2000. Online: http://www.campuspipe-line.com/whatwedo/home.html

Duval, M., "Net Start-ups Take New Course: Information Portal Companies Compete to Become Teacher's Pet," *Interactive Week*, vol. 6, no. 26, pp. 25–26, 1999.

Ehrlich, T., "Keep Internet Advertising Out of the Curriculum." *The Chronicle of Higher Education,* vol. 46, no. 5 (September 24, 1999), p. A76.

Feemster, Ron, "Selling Eyeballs," *University Business*, September 1999. Online: http://www.universitybusiness.com/9909/eyeball.html

Guernsey, G., "Welcome to College. Now Meet Our Sponsor," *The New York Times on the Web*, 1999. Online: http://www.nytimes.com/library/tech/99/08/biztech/articles/17college.html

John Paul II, "Centesimus Annus," para 36, in *Origins*. Washington: CNS Documentary Service, vol. 21, no. 1, 1991. Online: http://listserv.american.edu/catholic/church/papal/jp.ii/jp2hundr.txt

Lury, C., *Consumer Culture*. New Brunswick: Rutgers University Press, 1996.

McGee, M., "The 'Ideograph': A Link between Rhetoric and Ideology," *Quarterly Journal of Speech*, vol. 66, 1980, pp. 1–16.

Muir, C., Letter to the editor, *The Chronicle of Higher Education,* vol. 46, no. 11 (1999), p. B13.

Northwestern State University Alumni Association, "NSU Takes Lead in Campus Technology," 1999. Online: http://www.northwesternalumni.com/news.htm

Salkowski, Joe, "Have a Coke and a Diploma: Companies Offer Schools High-Tech Goodies for Ad Space," *StarNet Dispatches*, July 21, 1999. Online: http://www.dispatches.azstar-net.com/features/1999/0721-932538251.htm

Spirrison, J., "Campus Pipeline Adds $25M to Curriculum," *Private Equity Week,* vol. 6, no. 34, 1999, p. 3.

Stoever, Margie, "Pilot Program Explores the Possibility of Web Home Bases," *Technology,* Spring 1999. http://www.memphis.edu/is/technology/spr99/pipeline.htm

Swing, R., "Appalachian State University Freshman Computing Skills and Experiences," 1999. Online: http://www.appstate.edu/www_docs/depart/irp/assessment/Compute99.html

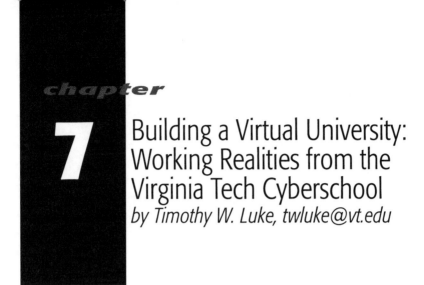

chapter

7 Building a Virtual University: Working Realities from the Virginia Tech Cyberschool
by Timothy W. Luke, twluke@vt.edu

This chapter looks back at the project of building a virtual university around online communities—with their many perils and prospects—amid broader shifts in the global economy. It focuses on one particular North American university: Virginia Polytechnic Institute and State University, or Virginia Tech. From this experience it suggests, first, why many existing offline university practices prevent change, and, second, how some online functionalities lead more easily to change. Yet, in considering how universities might change, it also worries about what changes, and defined by whom in the larger society?

Most importantly, however, it sees virtual universities as an ongoing reinvention of existing university institutions. This organizational innovation can enable universities to create new learning communities and learned discourses, rather than permitting corporate substitutes for present-day universities to fabricate alternatives in a misguided effort to commodify the higher learning that universities have always produced, but that should never be sold as packaged training.

Basic Foundations

Virginia Tech began constructing virtual versions of itself in 1993 with the launch of the Faculty Development Initiative.

An experiment in the implementation of distributed computing, which was launched by the Provost's Office and the Vice President for Information Systems, the Faculty Development Initiative put a new Apple desktop computer, a suite of applications, and nearly a week's worth of hands-on training into the hands of Arts and Sciences faculty with the hope that they would quit using an old, expensive mainframe computing system and start playing around with these new personal computers in their teaching, research, and service. Without this first piece of almost accidental history, much less would be occurring on this particular campus, because this decision got computers out of the control of those who everyone once knew should have them—engineers, computer scientists, physicists—and into the possession of those who many still think do not need them—philosophers, political scientists, poets. Once those who supposedly did not need or allegedly could not use personal computers got hold of them, many new communities—both online and offline—were more easily "imagined" (Anderson 1991), and everything began to change rapidly, fundamentally, and unpredictably.

At the same time, a small group of faculty in the College of Arts and Sciences was charged by the new Dean, Robert C. Bates, to think about how to use computers to break the paradigm by which students get credits according to the number of hours they spend in the lecture hall, in response to rising enrollments and decreasing funds. Led by Associate Dean Lucinda Roy, this committee advanced a proposal to construct a virtual college in November 1994 (Luke 1994) around a series of online courses: the Virginia Tech Cyberschool. Because of the presence of the off-campus online local community, the Blacksburg Electronic Village, based in a local community physically near to the campus, many students and faculty had the Internet access and technical skills to put this initial vision into practice during summer 1995 with the first Virginia Tech Cyberschool courses. At this juncture, a major Sloan Foundation grant also allowed another team to develop new computer-enhanced introductory biology courses in the

ACCESS project, and a larger mix of totally online courses was offered at a distance over the Net in summer 1996.

Running parallel to these successes, the university self-study of 1996–1998 aimed its energies at reimagining Virginia Tech around its high-technology strengths, including the enhancement of the university's online teaching capabilities. Totally online MA programs in physical education and political science went up on the Web in 1996–1997 and 1997–1998, and Virginia Tech Online—a full-service virtual campus site—was activated in support of the online courses during 1997–1998. Finally, all graduate theses and dissertations were required to be archived as digital documents in 1997, and all entering students were required to have a computer during the Fall 1998 semester.

The Cyberschool Idea

The key issue for Cyberschool, which the founding faculty anticipated in 1994, has been the value of instruction in virtual teaching environments. Does online teaching enhance and enrich the education the university now provides? For the most part, our students tend to agree that it does, both as an on-campus complement for face-to-face instruction and an off-campus virtualization of on-campus educational activities, because online technologies create a new kind of community. Students consistently indicate that Cyberschool classes increase their interactions with each other and faculty, give them more convenient access to learning opportunities, and enhance their opportunities to work with course materials in newer, more informative ways.

By 1996, then, the exponents of Cyberschool-style classes could say Cyberschool had fulfilled most of its original design agendas. As the 1994 Cyberschool plan proposed,

> The Cyberschool must be designed as an experiment to change (but not increase) faculty workloads, enhance (but not decrease) student interactions, equalize (and not short-

change) the resources, prestige, and value of all disciplines, balance (and not overemphasize) the transmittal of certain vital skills, concentrate (and not scatter) the investment of institutional resources, and strengthen (and not reduce) the value of all academic services. Technologies do not have one or two good and bad promises locked within them, awaiting their right use or wrong misuse. They have multiple potentials that are structured by the existing social relations guiding their control and application. We can construct the Cyberschool's virtual spaces and classrooms so that they help actualize a truly valuable (and innovative) new type of higher education (Luke 1994).

There have been many rewards in creating Cyberschool-style classes. Most students were enthusiastic about these innovations, and many measures of their learning showed considerable gains. Nonetheless, it also proved to be a punishing way to work for faculty. Instruction modules take time to develop, and most online course interactions with students are much more intense, time consuming, and demanding than regular face-to-face teaching. Keeping machines, software packages, network links as well as course Web sites, listservers or chat rooms up and running was an exhausting ordeal on top of simply "teaching" the class once all of the IT components do, in fact, work online. The instructor for virtual classes becomes, all too often, the functional equivalent of a computer help desk, a network troubleshooter, an online cop, an information service provider, and a software consultant as well as remaining "the teacher."

So the professor was by default "the Web master" with roles, statuses, and powers that needed to be implemented gracefully for success. These demanding new work obligations also caused frictions inside many units, because so few departments materially support or financially reward these creative new initiatives. Of course, success also brought additional expectations, as faculty colleagues and administrators made demands upon the pioneers to do demonstrations, speak their mind about the pluses and minuses of Cyberschooling work, or consult with the next wave of innovators as they launched Cyberschool-like classes.

Many of the changes in workload brought by Cyberschool were, at bottom, net individual add-ons as well as basic departmental increases. Cyberschool faculty did new kinds of work, but also more of it. Resources were provided temporarily through infusions of one-time grants and other funds, but the university has not made changes in the basic structures of faculty rewards. Similarly, it has not altered an academic culture that still balances, for instance, the prestige and resource needs of humanities programs as against those of the sciences, business or engineering. While the College of Arts and Sciences responded positively, the university is still moving more slowly to rethink the rewards (in tenure and promotion, as well as in salary and the like) for this new kind of teaching-centered, research-and-development work at the heart of many Cyberschool innovations.

The combined faculty challenges—measured in terms of workloads and rewards—have led to cases of "burnout." Most who helped initiate the Cyberschool project have moved on to other interests. They feel that they cannot afford the costs that their participation incurs against professional research projects or their tenure and promotion reviews. Early Cyberschool pioneers often expressed a sense of exhaustion as they struggled to achieve excellence on both new and traditional scales of teaching, research and service. Cyberschool was an initiative originating with Virginia Tech's faculty.[1] Even so, most of Cyberschool's efforts focused on the classroom. No school, however, is merely a collection of classrooms for faculty teaching. Every school also needs an extensive administrative infrastructure to support its activities. Yet, unless the online community of each class could be supported by online community infrastructure at the university level, Cyberschool could not move forward.

---

1. Most importantly, Len Hatfield in English, Valerie and Gary Hardcastle in Philosophy, Mary Beth Oliver in Communications, John Husser in Music, Karen Swenson in English, Patsy Lavender in Theater Arts, Lucinda Roy in English, Bailey Van Hook in Art History, Scott Patterson in Communication, Richard Winett in Psychology, Bill Claus in Biology, Tim Luke in Political Science, and Art Buikema in Biology.

From 1994 to 1999, Cyberschool also ran on a "demonstration project" basis.[2] Yet, it was time by 1999 to move beyond the "demonstration project" stage so that online education at Virginia Tech did not lose momentum entirely.

Pushing Cyberschool Up to the University Level

In 1994, the Cyberschool faculty proposed that Virginia Tech construct a set of virtual environments for online education that could provide:

a) a set of basic orientation, enrollment, credit-acquisition, syllabus, and fee-payment information about all cyberschool instructional sessions;

b) a system of secure access and use rules to insure that students are who they represent themselves to be, are fee-paying legitimate users of the system, and are guaranteed confidentiality in their interactions with the Cyberschool, which also would protect their right to use online copyrighted material in the Cyberschool, under the "fair use" exemption to copyright restrictions;

c) a series of multiuser domains, structured as online chat sessions or time-delayed bulletin-board structures, that can be assigned to an instructor, a student or groups of instructors and students in order to work through prearranged courses of instruction;

d) a linkage to second-source educational packages switched from Virginia Tech libraries, other Virginia Tech cyberschool

2. In times of very tight budgets, Dean Robert C. Bates in Arts and Sciences was able to support Cyberschool with some college funds and the time of his staff, especially Associate Dean Lucinda H. Roy. Terry Wildman in CEUT has provided seed money for developing online courses, John Moore and Tom Head with their Faculty Development Initiative support staff have helped immensely, and the Departments of English, Communications, Biology, Art and Art History, Music, and Political Science also have contributed to the Cyberschool initiative.

systems, or off-campus sources of video/audio/textual educational information; and,

e) a means of collaborating with off-campus corporate, university and government offices to test new networking, software, hardware, multimedia technologies and services that might improve the Virginia Tech cyberschool campus (Luke 1994).

Cyberschool faculty made these proposals, because their biggest needs were logistical or administrative. Virginia Tech had many distance and learning courses, but lacked a friction-free means of publishing distance learning course details through an online catalogue, updating an online timetable, managing the mechanics of online class enrollments, administering the demands of online student grading or major/minor/core requirements fulfillment, or, perhaps most importantly paying for class credits and other student fees online. Initially, Virginia Tech Online provided some of these services, and by 1998 it was helping a great deal in the management of online education at Virginia Tech. Still, something more comprehensive was plainly needed. Most of Virginia Tech's online classes were undergraduate classes. No single program of study was put entirely online until 1997; most of the online courses were core curricular offerings. No course was designed outside of the normal time/credit/work rules of conventional contact teaching. Finally, Cyberschool was regarded as a College of Arts and Sciences project, which limited its spread in the professional schools and more applied fields.

In many ways, the virtual university is an uneasy amalgam of post-Fordist flexible work organizations and digital network technologies (Jameson 1991). When combined together by academics and policy makers, they can provide a new model for flatter, leaner, more responsive work organizations coupled with the innovations made possible by computer-mediated communications over the Internet. Despite such alluring prospects, however, none of the changes made possible by these developments comes to pass without determined groups of people reordering how any university actually works now. One of the first articulations for virtualizing an existing university, then, is its creation of new special administrative units like Virginia Tech's Institute for Distance and Distributed Learning (IDDL).

Virginia Tech's IDDL

The Cyberschool faculty and the Dean of Arts and Sciences provided the real push needed during 1994–1998 to get the university focused on online learning and its new institutional requirements. By 1996–1997, Cyberschool coordinated about fifteen online classes, and collaborated with the Vice President of Information Systems to construct Virginia Tech Online as Virginia Tech's portal to distance and distributed education courses. The College of Arts and Sciences covered Virginia Tech Online's administrative costs and also paid buy-outs for faculty to teach online in 1997–1998. This year spent as a focused pilot project demonstrated the demand for more online instruction, which brought the Provost's Office, Educational Technologies, and the College of Arts and Sciences together to build the IDDL organization. The IDDL was organized by the Provost's Office, but much of its personnel and resources come from the Vice President for Information Systems, Extension and Outreach, and the College of Arts and Sciences. With a teaching and research faculty executive director as well as an administrative and professional faculty director, the IDDL was assigned the task of bringing more Virginia Tech classes and programs to the Web in addition to the Commonwealth's large ATM network, or Network.Virginia.

The semester in which the IDDL was launched, there were 17 distance and learning courses in Virginia Tech, with under 1,000 enrollments. Most of these courses originated in the College of Arts and Sciences from Cyberschool, but the IDDL gradually promoted more diversity and depth in the course offerings. In Summer 1999 there were 35 distance learning classes with 1,155 enrollments; in Fall 1999, 73 distance learning classes with 2,218 enrollments, and Spring 2000 saw 88 distance learning courses with 3,001 enrollments. While it is not a huge number, 6,374 enrollments in distance learning classes in 1999–2000 represented a 24 percent increase over

1998–1999. At the same time, the number of courses offered rose from 135 to 214, a 60 percent increase.

Much of this increase came from IDDL efforts to support distance learning in the colleges and departments of the university. Of the university's nearly 1,500 faculty, 136 were involved in 1999–2000 as instructors in distance and distributed learning. The IDDL gave fifteen faculty summer stipends for courses in Summer 1999, and fourteen more course development fellowships were given out in 2000. An online IDDL newsletter was started to publicize distance learning achievements and developments, and the IDDL touted the merits of online teaching for faculty to their deans, directors, and department heads. New personnel were hired to manage marketing, assessment, and new course development, which also demonstrated the university's resolve to take new teaching techniques seriously.

Building Online Communities for Education

While financial challenges are difficult, they often are easier to tackle than the entrenched routines of face-to-face interaction embedded by everyday administrative practice. Virginia Tech was teaching courses over the Web in 1995, but it still has not updated all of its administrative and information systems to reflect the Internet. The contradictions made obvious by doing coursework online, but registering for class with paper forms, paying with a paper check, getting paper documentation of registration, and checking on records with paper archives all brought the university to a major upgrade of its administrative and information services in the mid-1990s. Existing administration and information service systems from the 1970s tended to pull data into peculiar pockets of power and privilege from which it neither circulated widely nor linked easily with other information sets.

The infiltration of Net-centered thinking in the classroom as well as the desire for an enterprise-level integration system moved Virginia Tech to contract with the technology company

SCT. This partnership adapted SCT's Banner software to Virginia Tech's workings to make it better able to support network-based teaching and administration at this university. Nonetheless, the IDDL still has had to lobby hard to convince the Bursar's, Registrar's, and Treasurer's Offices to accept credit cards from distance learners for tuition and fee payment, dedicate specific index numbers for online classes, break courses with three hours' teaching a week into smaller units for distance learning students, and allow flexible scheduling for online classes. All of these provisions are necessary for Virginia Tech to succeed at distance learning, but each one of them transgresses existing practices that favor students on campus over students taking distance learning courses. The architecture of the Banner system has been modified to deal with these needs, but it would have been much more difficult to make such policy innovations without this ongoing enterprise reintegration project growing alongside, albeit separate and apart from, the IDDL.

Instead of starting with a clean sheet of paper to build a corporate-oriented, thin, for-profit, skill-competency-based virtual university, like the University of Phoenix or Western Governors University, Virginia Tech is renovating the public-supported, thick, not-for-profit, and degree-granting structures of the traditional university, injecting bits of market response while remaining committed to liberal education. After offering their first classes in 1995, Cyberschool faculty have continuously worked as change agents, pushing the university to adopt many new reforms, ranging from mandatory individual computer ownership for students, new technology support fees, student peer learning and teaching, and mandatory electronic thesis and dissertation submissions to online student registration, electronic records access, digital university press publications at a digital discourse center, alumni-centered life-long learning initiatives, and redefined faculty reward systems. At the end of the day, these reforms have been directed at restructuring the university's research, teaching, and extension services to be more responsive to changing demands off campus and new needs on campus.

Virtual universities, then, can advance radical changes that are far greater and much more diverse than simply deploying computer multimedia to teach workplace skills, because they build new online communities. Many visions of the virtual university do little to move past a limited set of changes in content delivery, while a few, including the Virginia Tech, push to make these technology-driven changes much more creative.

First, a virtual university can be in many ways an entirely new form of learning community. Anyone who operates extensively through computer-mediated communications notices this fact every working day. Email interactions are displacing telephone conversations, face-to-face meetings, and personal exchanges in ways that are carried in written texts. While this traffic often is also fleeting, underdeveloped, and exhausting, it has textual, hypertextual, or multimedia qualities unknown outside of computer networks. Written words carry more and more instructional activity, while most basic information resources once printed in catalogues, mailed out as brochures, accumulated in libraries, or posted on bulletin boards now are pulled down from Web sites. Physical location, synchronously shared times, and group meetings are becoming less vital to learning than network connectivity. So access to education is quickened and broadened. In addition to everyone who would be traditionally on campus, one finds nontraditional students, clients abroad, not-for-credit students, and residential students temporarily located elsewhere, all commingling together at virtual university sites in new kinds of communal interactions.

Second, new discursive possibilities are developing within, and as integral parts of, a virtual university, as online technologies begin to do much more than simply electrify print documents. The Web, CD-ROMs, hard-drive software, and floppy disks all represent new communicative media whose functionalities sustain fresh modes of discourse with their own conventions, formations, and practices as well as unconventionalities, misformations, and malpractices. In-house administrative discussions and external research communications on the World

Wide Web, or using software such as PDF, Eudora or Word, are generating technoscientific forms of dialogue with hypertextual and multimedia elements. These lead to a profusion of new linguistic conventions and rhetorical strategies. Research is being conducted, written up, peer reviewed, published professionally, and then permanently archived, all entirely online. This experience suggests that research, reflection, and reasoning about knowledge in almost every discipline should confront these new communicative possibilities in tertiary education.

Third, a virtual university develops new disciplinary coalitions and social networks. The pervasiveness of changes brought on by computer-mediated communication is remaking the disciplinary divisions and canonical conceptualizations embedded in the deep structures of the university's essentially industrial, nationalist, and scientific organization. Globalization and marketization are reshaping economies and societies, and forms of knowledge about them also are evolving in ways that no longer mesh as accurately with the existing organizational outlines of academic disciplines. Networks of knowledge production, consumption, circulation, and accumulation often nest now in professional consultancies, for-profit enterprises, and state agencies. Therefore, a market-based sense of knowledge consumption, and a quick-and-dirty approach to knowledge production, are reshaping what some disciplines do research on, when they do it, why they do it, and how it gets done. Virtual universities often import insights or experts from these parallel networks of investigation off campus as well as begin to rebuild traditional on-campus faculties to emulate these new modes of research.

The virtual university is technologically feasible at this juncture. Yet, there are many obdurate material practices and cultural values impeding its development. On one level, if the model is that all distance learning students access the university from a home computer, then there are tremendous infrastructure requirements whose costs and complexities have not been fully grasped by most supporters of the virtual university. Barely 50 percent of all households in the United States have a personal computer with Internet connectivity, and most connections move up and down their link at baud rates of 28,800 to 56,600. More political jurisdictions in the world, following trails blazed by the Commonwealth of Virginia and the city-state of Singapore in 1995–1996, are building widely available ATM networks; fast-speed Internet 2 networks are spreading, and wireless technologies can address some of these problems. Nonetheless, like most traditional media, the Internet creates its own inequality (Schiller 1996). Connectivity is geographically patchy, unequally enjoyed, and technically immature. Even then, these new telecom systems can fail, like the Iridium telematic satellite network, whose high basic rates and limited equipment choices militated against communicative ease, ready connection, and cheap Web surfing.

On a second level, there is a real gap between, on the one hand, the predicted level of network use puffed up by hardware producers, telco operators, and cybertouts, and, on the other hand, the actual numbers of users that show up at the virtual university's digital doorsteps. Most people use their PCs primarily for email, and sex sites or shopping outlets are where in 2000 many Web surfers still end up. After three years of intense public relations on campus, our Cyberschool enrollments in Summer 1997 barely hit 350, or an average class size of about 10 students. Off-campus interest is quite intense, but total IDDL enrollments for its courses during Spring 2000 barely exceeded 3,000. So face-to-face connections at our university's home and extended campus outreach sites still anchor Virginia Tech's enrollments. Much of this is due undoubtedly to access costs, bandwidth limitations, and hardware shortages, but institutional barriers, cultural inertia, and professional prejudices also cannot be discounted as sources of serious resistance to virtualized instruction.

For academics, the key question raised by virtual universities essentially is "job control." The University of Phoenix and Western Governors University claim that efficiencies can arise from their model of online university instruction conducted through multimedia packages. This claim obscures a knotted tangle of job-control questions, by bundling them up with technological innovations. Such a model can abridge many prerogatives now exercised by professors in face-to-face classroom teaching. These online alternatives mostly presume that professors are simply dispensing information in their traditional lectures and seminars, and therefore their information-dispensing efforts should be enhanced, extended, or even extinguished by technological surrogates.

Such technological interventions can rob professors of their authority, and cheapen the educational experience. Nonetheless, some officers of EduCause (the large professional organization that promotes online learning in the United States) assert that many course syllabi will be designed and constructed by technical designers, panels of experts, or outside consultants and then sold as mass-media products online or in boxes by publishers. Lectures, in turn, would be automated with such multimedia replacements. Testing might be contracted out to assessment businesses, and student advising, tutorial discussions, or independent studies could be conducted by paraprofessional workers without Ph.D.s.

This image of the future rarely is favored by academics; instead, it is the fancy of corporations, like Microsoft or Intel, lobbying groups like EduCause, and the digerati, like Nicholas Negroponte or Bill Gates. These simplistic narratives claim technological imperatives, economic necessity, or unserved markets make change inevitable in the role of professors as researchers, teachers, and service providers. Such allegedly inexorable forces of change are, in fact, lobbying campaigns by hardware manufacturers, software publishers, telecommunications vendors, and educational consultants.

At this time online education at Virginia Tech still works in the opposite register: small-scale, handicraft production for local use, not global exchange. Often one instructor is mapping his or her existing courses over to a Web site, generating computer-animated overheads, or organizing multimedia demonstrations to enliven traditional contact-style teaching and/or to experiment with asynchronous learning interactions. The material still mostly is a "home-made" production for "on-campus" circulation through "in-house" means of student consumption or "on-site" centers of knowledge accumulation. The IDDL's biggest project is a joint master's degree in Information Technology being created by Computer Science, Electrical Engineering, and the School of Business. While the enterprise is larger, it too follows these handicraft models. Therefore, existing pedagogical practices in the university, academic department, and professional discipline still provide the structure in which the distance learning takes place, by providing virtual flexibility and multimedia enhancements within established programs of study.

Despite the rhetoric of accessibility, democracy, flexibility, participation, or utility associated with cybernetic technologies, most networks today are, in fact, formations whose characteristic qualities in actual practice are inaccessibility, nondemocracy, inflexibility, nonparticipation, or disutility. Many Web domains are not readily accessible, and those that are accessible often remain nearly worthless. There are at least two billion pages on the Web, but the best search engines capture only about 300 or so million of them. No one voted to empower Microsoft, Intel, IBM, or Netscape to serve as our virtual world projectors, online terrain generators, or telematic community organizers, but they act as if we did by glibly reimagining our essentially choiceless purchases in monopolistic markets as freely cast votes. Inequality and powerlessness are not disappearing in the digital domain; they simply have shifted their shapes and substances as human beings virtualize their cultures, economies, and societies in networked environments.

Conclusions

On one level, the project of distance learning in the knowledge business is the latest promised land in many corporate market-building strategies. There are 3,600 colleges and universities, for example, in the United States alone, and the equivalent of over 12 million full-time students (counting part-time students as fractions of a full-time student) are enrolled in their courses of instruction. If every department, all libraries, each dormitory, every student center, all classrooms, each faculty office, not to mention administrative and support personnel, got a personal computer and/or Web appliance installed at a level of concentration approaching one per student and faculty user, then millions of new product units could be sold, installed, and serviced. Being rational entrepreneurs, all of the world's computer builders, software packagers, and network installers are exerting tremendous pressure on colleges and universities to open their campuses to computerization so that these markets can be made, serviced, or conquered.

On a second level, however, the project of online teaching meets stiff resistance on campus. Few faculty see the merits of computerized teaching, not all students are computer literate, and most administrators are unable to find funds to pay for all of the computers and network connectivity that the private sector wants to sell them. There are a few on-campus agents of change who ally themselves with new economic modernizers off campus to transform education through computerization and networking. They are aided, in part, by digital capitalists, who want to build new markets on campus for their hardware, software and netware; in part, by the digital mass media, which want to popularize wired cultures and informational communities; and in part by digitizing content providers in the entertainment and publishing industries who want to reconfigure or repackage their products for computer-mediated on- and offline delivery systems.

The sale of computer-mediated communication and multimedia to teachers, however, is not where the virtual university starts and stops. Increasingly, as the Virginia Tech Cyberschool illustrates, when these technologies are introduced into the practices of university administration, they create new online communities whose members can force very closed, hierarchical, and bureaucratic institutional structures to become slightly more open, egalitarian, and consensual sites of collective decision making. Online information sources, self-paced online application forms, and user-oriented online records management can take access to information out of the hands of special administrative personnel and hand it over to the faculty and students who actually are using it to coproduce educational services. Universities can retain their older, closed bureaucratic structure, but online enterprise reintegration applications usually restructure them as looser, flatter and more responsive entities by deploying computer-mediated communication technology. A virtual university, then, does not necessarily represent business as usual plus some computer multimedia. Instead, it often marks the onset of far more fundamental organizational changes, which give many on campus the opportunity to rethink and rebuild what they are doing.

Seven years after the launch of the Faculty Development Initiative, Virginia Tech has hundreds of fully online classes up and running, scores of faculty participating in this extensive rethinking of university's affairs, and thousands of students trained and equipped to deal after graduation with the digital cultures of work, leisure, and public life that are burgeoning off campus. Almost all of this change came from within the faculty ranks, but it has been assisted significantly at every turn by the leadership from the Vice President of Information Systems and a small dedicated cadre of technical specialists in the Office of Educational Technologies.

The scope and depth of these moves toward a virtual university show that the ideas advanced by the original pioneers at Virginia Tech have broken out of the skunkworks box they occupied in 1993 or 1994. Indeed, the concept of a "virtual university" complements, questions or even challenges the ways the "material university" works at Virginia Tech in many fundamental ways. This collision of values and practices obviously influences the on-going reinvention of institutions at play in the virtual university. Like Lucinda Roy, many believe Virginia Tech made it through the first phase, but deeper cultural contradictions require us "to assess what we've learned and start anew with some new approaches" (Young 1998).

To understand the significance of using computers to teach college and university courses, and begin making a new start, as our experience at Virginia Tech shows, one ought not to fixate upon the machines themselves. The shopworn laments about boxes and wires trapping autonomous personal development in a telematic tangle of electronic alienation misses what is happening: these online communities are developing out of foundational changes in the tools and practices of intellectual discourse. The acts and artifacts used to diffuse collective understandings among specific social groups are changing profoundly: print discourses, face-to-face classes, and paper documents are being displaced by digital discourses, online classes, and electronic documents. Because they are so flexible, the former will not entirely disappear, but neither can they be counted upon to continue uncontested. The latter will never fully be perfected, but neither can they be expected to remain oddities.

Many misread this shift as a classic confrontation of humans with machines, but it is, in fact, a conflict between two different technocultures—one older and tied to mechanism, print, and corporal embodiment, another newer and wired into electronics, codes, and telepresences (Deibert 1997). Building the facilities of a virtual university is one piece of this new technoculture, just as the founding of medieval universities was connected with yet another technoculture tied to the scriptorium, lecture hall, and auditor. While they can throw much light upon each other, the workings of new university technocultures do not exhaust the full range of structural change occurring with informationalization in the global economy and society.

Without being as apocalyptic about this shift as Birkerts (1994) is, the process of digitalization itself does bring a fundamental transformation in many fixed forms of being, especially those tied to communication, discourse, and memory. With the proliferation of computer-mediated networks,

> the primary human relations—to space, time, nature, and to other people—have been subjected to a warping pressure that is something new under the sun. . . . We have created the technology that not only enables us to change our basic nature, but that is making such change all but inevitable (Birkerts 1994, p. 15).

This change brings about a move from printed matter to digital bits to accumulate, circulate, and manipulate stores of knowledge. There are, as Turkle (1996, p. 17) claims, different "interface values" embedded in each particular medium, and those embodied in print lead to a special measured, linear, introspective type of consciousness that has anchored our understandings of higher education for several centuries.

Inasmuch as digital communications with their own digital debates, documents, and disciplines, supplant libraries of print, and the print libraries are not digitized, a remarkable erasure of experience from the predigital age can indeed occur. Again, Birkerts (1994) asserts:

> our entire collective subjective history—the soul of our societal body—is encoded in print . . . if a person turns from print—finding it too slow, too hard, irrelevant to the excitements of the present—then what happens to that person's sense of culture and continuity? (p. 20).

Shrewdly enough, Birkerts recognizes that his worries and warnings are in the form of complex, knotty questions and there is no effective way of pulling single strands out at a time for easy analysis. Instead, we may be left with a sense of both profound loss and immeasurable gain as the popularity of digital modes of communication builds and spreads.

Without succumbing to Birkerts' fears that everything changes unalterably, and mostly for the worse, when it is run through electronic circuitries, we should realize in the same moment that everything will not remain the same in online communities, only now in silicon instead of on paper. Instead of "the death of distance" (Cairncross 1997), the Internet is causing the creation of community. What is new and different in digital communities should be uncovered as they are being created so that we can address the impact they have upon the culture of universities. No educational technology exists simply as such with its own immanent dynamics separate and apart from the declared and implied uses for it (Bowles and Gintis 1976). As Lyotard (1984) points out, some of these uses are unintended and unanticipated, but they will emerge from human use. Online learning, then, represents a cluster of much more performative technical applications that are invested with special importance and power—this is not just another way for delivering content.

Technology is not, as many believe, "just technology." It also is culture, economics, and politics, and, when combined with education, becomes even more culturally unstable, economically demanding, and politically threatening. On one side, many exponents of technologically enhanced teaching see it as leading to new forms of communication, intellectual conventions, and scientific practices. On the other side, many opponents regard any efforts taken toward effecting such change as malformations, unconventionalities, and malpractices. There is merit in both positions that deserves a hearing.

These conflicts are crucial, because they shape the discussion that is taking place. Like many other groups elsewhere, the Cyberschool faculty at Virginia Tech operated as an advocacy organization, issue group, or social movement to analyze and popularize the use of computer-mediated communication in university instruction. This point is important, because despite what the digital futurists claim, technology does nothing on its own. Technically driven change is neither automatic nor easy, and every apparent technological innovation either is hobbled by significant antitechnological resistance or advanced by supportive allies. Unfortunately, the myths that most people share about technological inexorability make it difficult to think outside of the box when it comes to most new technology (Luke 1989).

These remarks here summarize my experience and understanding gained in working seven years with Cyberschool and three years with the IDDL at Virginia Tech. They have outlined our attempts, first, to change this one specific university; second, to assess what we have learned at Virginia Tech; and third, to provide some new approaches in a broader national context to learning in online communities.

References

Anderson, B., *Imagined Communities*, rev. ed. London: Verso, 1991.

Birkerts, S., *The Gutenberg Elegies: The Fate of Reading in an Electronic Age*. New York: Fawcett, 1994.

Bowles, S. and H. Gintis, *Schooling in Capitalist America: Educational Reform and the Contradictions of Economic Life*. New York: Harper Colophon, 1976.

Brockman, J., *Digerati: Encounters with the Cyber Elite*. San Francisco: Hardwired, 1996.

Cairncross, F., *The Death of Distance: How the Communications Revolution Will Change Our Lives*. Boston: Harvard Business School Press, 1997.

Deibert, R. J., *Parchment, Printing, and Hypermedia: Communication in World Order Transformation*. New York: Columbia University Press, 1997.

Jameson, F., *Postmodernism, or the Cultural Logic of Late Capitalism*. Durham: Duke University Press, 1991.

Luke, T. W., "Going Beyond the Conventions of Credit-for-Contact," 1994. Online: http://www.cyber.vt.edu/docs/papers.html

Luke, T. W., *Screens of Power: Ideology, Domination, and Resistance in Informational Society*. Urban: University of Illinois Press, 1989.

Lyotard, J.-F., *The Postmodern Condition: A Report on Knowledge*. Minneapolis: University of Minnesota Press, 1984.

Reich, R., *The Work of Nations: Preparing Ourselves for 21st Century Capitalism*. New York: Knopf, 1991.

Schiller, H., *Information Inequality: The Deepening Social Crisis in America*. New York: Routledge, 1996.

Turkle, S., *Life on the Screen: Identity in the Age of the Internet*. New York: Touchstone, 1997.

Young, J., "Skeptical Academics See Perils in Information Technology," *The Chronicle of Higher Education*, vol. 44, no. 35 (May 8, 1998), pp. A29–30.

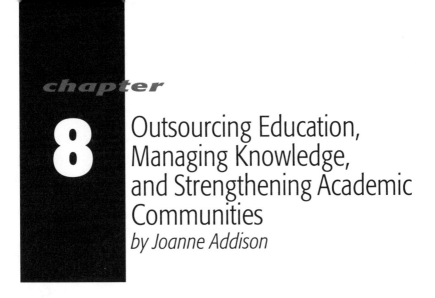

chapter

8

Outsourcing Education, Managing Knowledge, and Strengthening Academic Communities
by Joanne Addison

n 1999, the American Association of University Professors (AAUP), an organization many U.S. universities defer to on policy matters, adopted a policy concerning the rights and responsibilities of faculty in relation to distance education. The main force of the report is summarized below:

> As with all other curricular matters, the faculty should have primary responsibility for determining the policies and practices of the institution in regard to distance education. The rules governing distance education and its technologies should be approved by vote of the faculty concerned or of a representative faculty body, officially adopted by the appropriate authority, and published and distributed to all concerned (American Association of University Professors 1999, "Statement on Distance Education").

In the section labeled "Technical Considerations," the report states:

> The institution is responsible for the technological delivery of the course. Faculty members who teach through distance education technologies are responsible for making certain that they have sufficient technical skills to present their subject matter and related material effectively, and, when necessary, should have access to and consult with technical support personnel. The teacher, nevertheless, has the final responsibility for the content and presentation of the course.

A later report (American Association of University Professors 1999, "Suggestions and Guidelines: Sample Language for Institutional Policies and Contract Language on Distance Education") clarifies what the AAUP intends when stating that "the institution is responsible for the technological delivery":

> This means that the institution shall ensure that the necessary technology and equipment is identified and in place, that the institution shall provide appropriate training for faculty members, and that the institution shall ensure that faculty members have access to adequate technical support personnel.

It is interesting that while the AAUP's "Statement on Distance Education" insists on the rights and responsibilities of faculty members when it comes to curricular matters related to distance education, the technological delivery of courses is left up to the institution. In other words, the instructional content of the course is left to the faculty but the instructional design and delivery of the course is left to the institution. While the language of these statements may be broad enough in principle to include faculty governance over matters related to technological design and delivery, nowhere is it specifically stated that faculty members should be part of the research, development and design process of the technological delivery of their courses. Similarly, in the AAUP's "Suggestions and Guidelines," the section labeled "Workload" does not list the research, design and development of educational technology, or the significant modification of existing educational technology, as a scholarly or pedagogical activity for which faculty should be compensated. Also not addressed is the growing trend in the United States toward outsourcing instructional technology and the ways that the counterproductive division between developing educational content and delivering educational content furthers the commercialization of academic activities.

Policy positions such as that promoted by the AAUP, intentionally or not, encourage a schism between the development of educational content and the delivery of educational content, with some potentially dangerous results. Increasingly, universities are claiming the rights to the educational material developed by their faculty and outsourcing the technological delivery of this content to private companies. As David Noble (1998) points out, universities are working to commercialize instruction in such a way that instructional activities are developed as discrete, reproducible items, which "are then converted into marketable commodities by means of copyrights and licenses to distribute copyrighted instructional products."[1] Dividing content from delivery allows universities to make a profit from educational content while private companies make a profit from instructional delivery systems, thus commodifying the instructional process "as educators are transformed into mere producers of marketable instructional commodities which they may or may not themselves 'deliver'" (Noble 1998).

By neither insisting on instructional design as part of the rights and responsibilities of faculty, nor addressing the relationship between faculty and those companies to whom their universities outsource instructional technology, the AAUP missed an opportunity to address some of the most important factors influencing the direction of U.S. distance education in particular and universities in general. Instead, the AAUP (and many others) positions technology, and the corporations controlling it, as somehow transparent instead of as one of the most important forces vying for control of higher education today.

In 1993 Paul LeBlanc predicted:

> American corporations are spending huge sums on electronic communications systems and are adopting technologies such as electronic mail, hypermedia, and computer conferencing at a furious pace. Like it or not, corporate needs and practices exert a powerful influence on curricula in both secondary and higher education, and corporate America's widespread adoption of the computer as a commu-

---

1.　This move to demand copyright to faculty material related to distance education seems to be in direct conflict with legal precedent in this area except in a few gray areas. See the AAUP's "Statement on Copyright" and "Suggestions and Guidelines," linked from http://www.aaup.org/spcintro.htm.

nications tool will have a significant impact on the English classroom (p. 124).

Currently, this impact is seen most clearly through the development of distance education. It can be expensive to establish and maintain a distance education program. As a result, many public colleges and universities have turned to private companies as they outsource the necessary educational technology, technology staff, and even educational content. Thus, the current growth in distance education as an economic market is largely fueled and controlled by software makers, hardware companies, telecommunications companies, and others outside of educational institutions.

As the Internet becomes the primary means through which educational technology is developed and delivered, policy positions such as that forwarded by the AAUP obscure the Internet's role in the privatization and commodification of academic activities. Esther Dyson, in her article on intellectual value (1995), argues:

> Contrary to the notion that the Net will be a disintermediated world, much of the payment that ostensibly goes for content will go to the middlemen and trusted intermediaries who add value—everything from guarantees of authenticity to software support, selection, filtering, interpretation, and analysis. The redistributor's goal is to be the most convenient source of content and to put its own attitude or personality around the content; the underlying content is unlikely to be exclusive, since the content provider wants to maximize its distribution (either for revenues—however small per item—or for advertising breadth).

In relation to distance education, the middlemen who provide software support, selection, filtering, interpretation and analysis are often private software and telecommunications companies whose job it is to provide convenient packages for pedagogical content and who want to maximize their distribution in order to make a profit. These middlemen, such as eCollege, Unext.com, and many others, are quickly and with relative ease taking on the role of knowledge manager for academic communities.

Where once professors working with students were primarily responsible for the way that educational resources were created, mediated, organized, disseminated, etc., many new and established companies have begun to involve themselves in this process due to the growth potential of the educational technology market. Through their technology these companies are starting to influence the way that information is stored, presented, and modified.

They are aided by universities who are demanding that their faculty give them the copyright to their course material, thus further inhibiting the free exchange of knowledge. When the academic knowledge that any good course contains is securely stored in the electronic bowels of some company, that knowledge may or may not continue to be shared freely within the academic community. Further, these companies determine the way that this knowledge will be mediated, organized, and disseminated—and they are not interested in finding the best or most progressive way of doing so, but rather the most economical. Without the free exchange of knowledge that academic progress is rooted in, and the time-consuming work of professors on the best and most progressive ways of mediating, organizing and disseminating knowledge, academic progress in general becomes constrained. This is a loss to professors, students, and society as a whole. For example, here is promotional material from eCollege's Web site:

> eCollege.com is a provider of technology and services that enable colleges and universities to offer an online environment for distance and on-campus learning. Our software and services allow colleges and universities to outsource the creation, launch, management and support of an online education platform. Our technology and services consist of online campuses, courses, course supplements and support services, including design, development, management and hosting services, as well as ongoing administration, faculty and student support. We can create and deliver a complete online campus, including training of faculty and administration, typically in 60 business days. Our technology enables our customers to

reach a large number of additional students who wish to take online courses at convenient times and locations. Our customers can also use our technology to supplement their on-campus courses with an online learning environment (http://www.ecollege.com/company/about/).

In the educational community eCollege envisions, the company provides everything necessary and presents it to faculty and students for consumption. The process is quick and economical—an online campus can be created in only 60 days. In other words, in only 60 days eCollege can provide universities with the tools they need to turn instructional activities into commodities that can be sold for a profit on the open market. Made invisible are the labor-intensive nature of education and the far-reaching requirements of commodity production:

> Speed-up, routinization of work, greater work discipline and managerial supervision, reduced autonomy, job insecurity, employer appropriation of the fruits of their labor, and, above all the insistent managerial pressures to reduce labor costs in order to turn a profit (Noble 1999).

For example, the experiences of many members of my English Department in working with eCollege have shown that in order to speed up and routinize our work, we are allowed to develop a specific course only once, and all people who teach that course online are expected to use the same course material semester to semester in order to reduce development costs, even when it is not in the best educational interests of the students. The faculty are supervised and monitored not only by their department but also by the company (especially when it comes to trying to revise course material) and they lack job security, as most who teach online courses are non-tenure-track, part-time employees. The university appropriates faculty work primarily by requiring faculty to turn the copyrights for course material over to the university. And the additional cost of these courses—approximately $100—is passed directly on to the students. While some or all of this may be against AAUP rules, the rules don't seem to be stopping the spread of such activities.

This increasingly common model stands in stark contrast to one of the most successful and proven models of distance education, The Open University, located in London. Open University boasts an enrollment of over 200,000 students and customers. Courses with high expectations are designed by teams of expert faculty who put significant time and effort into developing and revising challenging educational material. Videotapes and textbooks are of the highest quality, and an emphasis is placed on interaction among instructors and students. As Nelson and Watt (1999) point out: "The courses are tremendously time-consuming [for students] and expensive to prepare. The aim is education, not profit or mere convenience" (p. 115). Not only is The Open University the largest in the United Kingdom, it is also ranked as one of the best teaching universities and supports a faculty whose research has gained international recognition. The Open University claims: "We have created a vibrant academic community dedicated to the advancement and sharing of knowledge around the globe" (http://www.open.edu/about_usou.html). It is this commitment to the academic community and sharing of knowledge that differentiates The Open University from other distance education programs, and which fosters its success.

While there are many concerns about the quality of educational material presented when profit is placed above education, the issue of copyright has lead to the greatest outcry among many faculty. A common model for outsourcing distance education is that faculty are asked to sign away the rights to distance education courses they develop, primarily so that the institution can sell that material to other students at their own and other institutions. Sometimes faculty receive a part of the profit from such sales, often they do not. This assembly-line model of education, many institutions reason (and are counseled by the private companies to whom the university has outsourced its distance education), allows them to cut down on development costs, as the course will need to be developed only once, and to make a profit where none existed before. Such policies have led to faculty working to protect their intellectual property rights. For example, the professors at Denver's Metropolitan State College recently filed a lawsuit in relation to distance education against their administrators. Among the reasons listed for the lawsuit are violations of intellectual property rights, assembly-line education as part-timers teach courses developed by only a few professors, use of course material after its content or approach has become outdated, and a lack of fair compensation for the sale of these courses to other educational organizations (Scanlon 2000).

The conflict over intellectual copyright is usually portrayed as a matter of ownership and fair compensation. But, contrary to a recent *New York Times* article that the wide distribution of a single distance education course can make newly minted millionaires out of professors who retain ownership of their material,[2] there is relatively little new money to be had. Whence, then, does this conflict arise? As David Noble states,

> For faculty and their organizations it is a struggle not only over proprietary control of course materials per se but also over their academic role, their autonomy and integrity, their future employment, and the future of quality education (Noble 1998).

More specifically, the conflict is often less about ownership and money and more about who has the power and authority to manage knowledge in the academic arena. For hundreds of years, faculty have played a central role in managing academic knowledge, but distance education, via Internet technologies, may be changing this. The influence of corporate money in U.S. education has been present for many years, especially in the sciences, but corporate influence via the outsourcing of distance education is beginning to have much more widespread effects.

All of this is not to suggest that the role of faculty within higher education and society as a whole should not change to meet current social and economic needs. In fact, the role of faculty must change if they are going to actively participate in

---

2. While it may be possible for a few high-profile professors at division-one research institutions to make a significant amount of money through distance education, the vast majority of academics will not directly benefit from this source of revenue.

early faculty software developers and confirms "an early notion that how a tool gets built, and who is building that tool, will have important implications for how that tool looks and works" (p. 7). In other words, those who control this process have the power to determine who will use the resulting technology and how it will be used. In this book LeBlanc predicted:

> As faculty see and use hypertext/hypermedia applications, and as those authoring programs become even easier to use, there should be an increase in faculty-based software development (p. 110).

Further, LeBlanc quotes Helen Schwartz, who believed that faculty would soon be able to obtain software programs with built-in authoring systems that could be significantly modified (p. 111). This certainly hasn't happened when it comes to distance education, or to hybrid courses, primarily because faculty still aren't given the time, recognition, or compensation necessary for developing tools that best fit the needs of their students. Too many universities have decided not to invest in the efforts of their faculty to develop educational technology. Instead, many have invested in private companies with little interest or motivation in understanding the discipline-specific needs of professors and students or in developing software programs with built-in authoring systems that can be significantly modified.

In fact, the most recent trend among companies that produce distance education technology is specifically *not* to provide faculty with built-in authoring systems that can easily and significantly be modified. To create a product so pliable would most likely erode a company's market share in an increasingly competitive sector. Instead, the trend is to make educational technology so easy to use that it becomes transparent. When a company's advertising exclaims "No HTML Required" they have reached a level of use that makes the workings of the software unseen and unknown by its users. But what is unseen and unknown is also usually unchangeable. This places control in the hands of the private companies and should lead to alarm, not relief, on the part of educators. Overall, current trends in distance education are leading to a purely consumption-based model of education on the part of both teachers and students—reinstating the "banking model" of education that was first articulated by Paolo Friere and actively worked against by many educators. In light of this situation, LeBlanc's 1993 call to action still stands:

> If we wish to take a proactive role in the shaping of electronic literacy, software design should be as mainstream an activity for composition professionals as teaching a writing class, conducting a research study, or writing an article. Otherwise, we risk leaving the new electronic literacy in the hands of "IBM, Disney, and the U.S. Air Force," as Lunsford warns, and relinquishing our proper role as central players in shaping the writing spaces of the future (p. 10).

But just how can academics take a proactive role in the shaping of electronic literacy via distance education at a time when many companies are aggressively courting universities, and universities face both a lack of funds for technological development and increasing legislative pressure to establish distance education programs? This becomes complicated when considering the findings by a number of people that there is no direct correlation between the amount of time and money invested in instructional technology and improved performance (Malhotra 1998). Thus, the question becomes not just how can academics take a pro-active role in the shaping of electronic literacy, but how can they do so in a way that leads to improved performance—that is, better teaching and research? One answer is to reestablish the prominence of the role of an academic community in a democratic society as it relates to educational technology.

Academic Communities and the Future of Distance Education

First and foremost, the vast majority of colleges and universities need to remind themselves of who and what they are—

nonprofit organizations made up of academic communities, who have as one of their primary goals working toward furthering knowledge in the arts and sciences for society. As Peter Likins, the president of the University of Arizona, points out, "A for-profit's mission is to create as much value for its stockholders as possible, within the constraints of society. The non-profits' mission is to create as much value for society as possible, within the constraints of its money" (Jensen 1999). This can be difficult to remember at a time when many public universities are underfunded and state legislatures are pushing for more self-sufficiency on the part of higher education. But this distinction is a crucial guide for outlining the role that faculty should play in the development of educational technology in particular and public life in general.

Faculty must become their own best advocates in the fight to maintain public access to their knowledge. Instead of allowing access to their work to be bought and sold by private companies, they should work to develop instructional delivery systems. These delivery systems may or may not be developed in conjunction with private companies, but they should represent best practices in instructional delivery uninhibited by a profit motive that constrains the free flow of academic knowledge. In short, as Michael Jensen (1999) situates the issue,

> We need to decide what kind of relationship academe should have with the tools that underpin its knowledge bases—that of a huge corporate customer that goes to private industry for software, or of a supporter and underwriter of open and free software tools that serve our needs.

Following Jensen's lead within academic publishing, faculty should lobby their administrators for the time and money needed to develop open source programming for educational technology that can be shared widely and freely. Universities—especially public universities—should not become dependent on the educational technology of companies that do not share their nonprofit mission. This dependency hinders self-help, mutual aid, and community development, as users cannot freely share proprietary software with others in their community, are limited in terms of building support and maintenance systems, and cannot modify software to fit their specific needs (Sclove 1995). Further, professors and students are not given the opportunity to use software development as a means of advancing local and national educational communities through the types of innovation that occur when professors and students work together toward real solutions.

> Free software both encourages learning and experimentation and in turn benefits from it. Free software is widespread in educational institutions, since access to the source code makes free software an ideal tool for teaching; indeed much free software began as learning exercises (Yee 1997).

This ultimately hinders the companies these students will eventually work for, as they lack experience in creative problem solving and working with users.

If academic communities across the country come together to develop the educational software they need and share it freely, the many people involved can develop a solution that is flexible enough to be frequently adapted and improved. This democratic approach mirrors that which faculty already engage in as they research and publish their work so that it can be further developed by others. More specifically, universities need to hire and support faculty who have expertise in a specific academic discipline and are capable of furthering the mission of their discipline and university via the development of open source programming for specific academic purposes. As Bezroukov (1999) claims, "The creation of a program is similar to the creation of applied theory"—a designation with which many academics are familiar. In supporting this type of academic, universities further their mission by employing faculty who fully understand how to integrate technology within specific disciplines, can contribute to the academic and technological knowledge of other academics by sharing both their theoretical and applied work freely in the pursuit of academic and technological progress for society as a whole, can work closely with students who develop both content knowledge and technical knowledge, and can collaborate with corporations to improve the educational experiences of the students who will eventually work for those corporations without sacrificing their education to corporate profits.

If universities decide to empower academic communities through furthering open source programming for educational technology, instead of subsidizing corporate profits, they can foster collaboration across varied academic contexts. Diverse participation, from impoverished urban community colleges to flagship research universities, increases the possibility for innovative change, allows for a range of social, political and economic issues to be addressed, and allows for constructive sharing of ideas across different contexts (Yee 1997). In doing so, universities can accomplish their main obligation to our democracy—to provide access to the best education and research for students in particular and our society in general.

References

American Association of University Professors, "Statement on Distance Education," *Academe,* May/June 1999. Online: http://www.aaup.org/spcdistn.htm

————, "Statement on Copyright," *Academe*, May/June 1999. Online: http://www.aaup.org/spccopyr.htm

————, "Suggestions and Guidelines: Sample Language for Institutional Policies and Contract Language on Distance Education," *Academe*, December 1999. Online: http://www.aaup.org/deguide.htm

Bezroukov, Nikolai, "Open Source Software Development As a Special Type of Academic Research (Critique of Vulgar Raymondism)," *First Monday,* vol. 4, no. 10, October 1999. Online: http://www.firstmonday.dk/issues/issue4_10/bezroukov/index.html

Dyson, Esther, "Intellectual Value," *WiReD,* issue 3.07, July 1995. Online: http://www.wired.com/wired/archive/3.07/dyson.html

Hagel, John, and Arthur Armstrong, *Net Gain: Expanding Markets Through Virtual Communities*. Boston: Harvard Business School Press, 1997.

International Data Corporation, "Number of Remote Students Growing by 33% Annually to Reach 2.2 Million in 2002," Online Report, February 9, 1999. Online: http://www.idc.com/ Data/Consumer/content/CSB020999PR.htm

Jensen, Michael, "Information Technology at a Crossroads: Open-Source Computer Programming," *The Chronicle of Higher Education*, October 29, 1999. Online: http:// www2.ncsu.edu:8010/ncsu/chass/communication/ciss/tltr/ readings/chronicle10-29-99.html

LeBlanc, Paul, *Writing Teachers, Writing Software: Creating Our Place in the Electronic Age*. NCTE, Illinois, 1993.

Malhotra, Yogesh, "Knowledge Management for the New World of Business," 1998. Online: http://www.brint.com/km/ whatis.htm

McCormack, John, *Newsweek*, April 24, 2000. Online: http:// www.newsweek.com/nw-srv/printed/us/so/a18729- 2000apr16.htm

National Center for Education Statistics, U.S. Department of Education, *Distance Education at Post-secondary Education Institutions: 1997–98*, NCES 2000-013.

Nelson, Cary, and Stephen Watt, *Academic Keywords: A Devil's Dictionary for Higher Education*. New York: Routledge, 1999.

Noble, David, "Digital Diploma Mills, Part II: The Coming Battle Over Online Instruction," Online Essay, March 1998. Online: http://communication.ucsd.edu/DL/ddm2.html

———, "Digital Diploma Mills, Part IV: Rehearsal for the Revolution," Online Essay, November 1999. Online: http://communication.ucsd.edu/DL/ddm4.html

Scanlon, Bill, "Metro State, Profs Lock Horns over Rights to Online Courses," *Denver Rocky Mountain News*, April 22, 2000, p. 22A+.

Sclove, Richard, *Democracy and Technology*. New York: Guilford Press, 1995.

University of Texas, "Distance Education: A Primer," No date. Online: http://www.utexas.edu/cc/cit/de/deprimer/master.html

Yee, Danny, "Development, Ethical Trading and Free Software," *First Monday,* vol. 2, no. 12, December 1997. Online: http://www.firstmonday.org/issues/issue4_12/yee/index.html

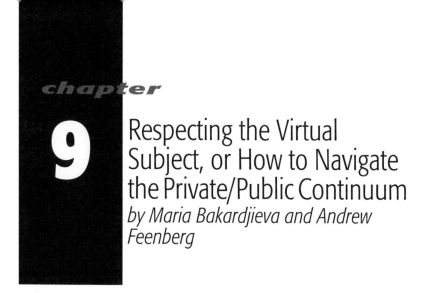

chapter

9

Respecting the Virtual Subject, or How to Navigate the Private/Public Continuum
by Maria Bakardjieva and Andrew Feenberg

Our interest in learning how to navigate the private/public continuum in cyberspace was motivated by the demands of our research on online communities. We were engaged in studying how ethical principles are established and sustained in these groups. To pursue this project we signed on to several such groups to take a preliminary look at their activities and the human relationships they sustained. We soon were ready with a grant proposal to pursue our project, but to our surprise the granting agency questioned the legitimacy of intruding on the private discussions of online communities for the purpose of studying them. We had assumed that research on open online groups posed no special ethical problems, but reviewers of our proposal challenged this assumption. We learned that from a rather unproblematic enterprise, research on online groups had recently become the focus of contentious ethical debates. Some researchers seemed to have contracted a case of moral panic over privacy and intrusion (Cavanagh 1999). We were caught in the middle.

Early studies of online communities had treated the Net as a public space in which everything was available to download and analyze, but this attitude had given way to a widely shared ethical anxiety over the rights of human subjects. And once ethical questions were posed, the problems appeared insuperable. Social life in cyberspace defies the existing formalities of research ethics: "What constitutes informed consent in an observational or survey study on-line where there is no actual signature on a form?" worried a participant in the MediaMOO

Symposium, "The Ethics of Research in Virtual Communities," organized on January 20, 1997. We were soon to discover that a whole range of conceptual dilemmas lurked behind such seemingly formalistic concerns. We encountered these dilemmas in the context of a research project, but their significance goes far beyond this particular area of practice and ultimately bears upon the very possibility of online social life.

Indeed, the debate over online research ethics can serve as a guide for finding one's bearings on the broader question of privacy in cyberspace. Some of the central dichotomies and paradoxes of this problem are mapped out in a special issue of the *Information Society Journal,* "The Ethics of Fair Practices for Collecting Social Science Data in Cyberspace" (Thomas 1996). There, researchers representing different disciplines and methodological orientations reflect collectively on their own dealings with "virtual" human subjects.

For these researchers the foremost factor determining ethical access in cyberspace is whether the group under study operates in the public domain or in a private space. Contributors such as Herring (in Thomas 1996, pp. 159, 165–166) argue that any group whose interactions take place in the public domain can be observed by researchers without participants' consent—indeed, without even an explicit announcement of the presence of a researcher in the group. Accordingly, Herring and other pioneer researchers of MUDs acted behind the scenes in some of their early studies of online behavior (Allen 1996, Reid 1996). They treated statements posted in public bulletin boards or rooms in MUDs as public data.

However, the status of online forums with regard to publicness/privacy is ambiguous. The question "Is technical accessibility equal to publicness?" has been raised repeatedly. One side of the debate is represented by the following comment: "Some spaces are simply public by their brute empirical nature—anybody can get to them—Coyote" (Malcolm Parks in the 1997 MediaMOO symposium.[1]) Opponents have insisted

---

1. This statement is not necessarily representative of Parks' own approach, as it becomes clear throughout the discussion.

that this is not always the opinion of the actual participants in online communities and that researchers should take seriously the "perceived privacy" (King 1996) of forums as experienced by these participants. But if participants' opinions are respected and their forums defined as private, it follows that they should be asked for their permission to be observed in all circumstances.

Thus we found ourselves facing the daunting task of determining the publicness or privacy of the online community we wanted to study. But is there an "objective" standpoint or a commonly accepted criterion on the basis of which such a decision can be made? Robson and Robson (1999), for example, present a continuum of levels of privacy in real and online settings. Spanning the range between Web sites/billboards, at the most public end of the continuum, to private chat, email and telephone conversations, at the most private end, this continuum still leaves online communities represented by open mailing lists and computer conferences in the intermediate gray area. And this was precisely our chosen object of study. As our thinking on the subject progressed, we came to realize that this gray area represents the heart of the novelty and the main source of the excitement generated by computer networks in their capacity as social environments. The ethical dilemmas arising in this gray zone, however, cannot be easily resolved.

Online groups are a peculiar social form escaping clear definition. Some have called them, perhaps accurately, but not very helpfully, "publicly private" and "privately public" (Wascul and Douglass 1996). They resemble what Goffman (1963) called "accessible engagements." According to Goffman, these are get-togethers carried out in situations containing bystanders. In such settings, Goffman observes, special social arrangements regulate communication. "Properly conducted members of the community" will recognize communication barriers allowing for a "conventional situational closure" even in the absence of actual "physical closure." Thus we easily recognize and honor the communication barrier existing between ourselves and a group of people engaged in a conversation in the public park or café. However, no social conventions have been established yet to regulate the communication boundaries of online gatherings. What is more, online communities often welcome anyone who wishes to join. Indeed, one of the few shared beliefs people have about cyberspace is that it is essentially a place for communicating freely with others, most often strangers. Unlike Goffman's only apparently accessible engagements, many online engagements are truly accessible to outsiders. This ethos raises questions about the argument that researchers should respect online participants' right to privacy. What sense does it make to ask for special permission to join an online community as a researcher when it is open to everyone to join as a participant? If people go online in order to be heard, why should they be concerned about privacy?

It should be noted that this situation is qualitatively different from those arising in the widely discussed and quite entangled cases of violation of individual privacy and surveillance in electronic environments. Illegally accessing individuals' electronic medical records or monitoring employees' electronic mail exploits the materiality of the traces unintentionally left by subjects' activities in computerized settings. The subjects' underlying (often incorrect) assumption in these activities is that they are acting in the private realm. In the case of online discussion groups or communities, the very motive of the activity is to break out of the private realm, although we will see that this motive is complicated and qualified in important respects. To understand this difference in actors' intention, the ways in which people experience the private/public spectrum online must be examined more closely.

The Private/Public Spectrum

One of us had been engaged in an ethnographic study of the experience of online communities before we set out to study the more specialized topic of the ethical basis of these communities. We turned to the observations made in that study hoping to discover how subjects themselves perceive and navigate the public/private continuum that poses so many ethical challenges to researchers/observers. The data from the study revealed that people do not construct a clear dichotomy between the public and the private in their everyday experience of the online groups to which they belong. Rather, they make subtle distinctions between various degrees of privacy and adjust their behavior accordingly. The boundaries between the private world, in which the individual feels in control of personal information, and public spaces online, are constantly shifting. As a matter of fact, the Internet, with its ease of social association, appeared to be employed as a medium for the socialization (or publication) of private experience. From personal Web sites exposing intimate details of private life to broad undifferentiated audiences, to participation in more or less selective virtual groups, the Internet emerged as a flexible medium for articulating the private and the public. In practice, then, it does not always make sense to categorize a particular online space (or activity within that space) as private or public.

How significant is this blurring of boundaries for the ethics of online research? The answer depends on the degree to which participants in online communities are themselves active in blurring the boundaries, rather than simply passive and unwitting victims of the technology. Thus, before we return to the ethical questions, we will discuss some examples from the ethnographic study in order to demonstrate that blurring the boundaries was not an unintended consequence of the online experience, but an intentionally sought prerequisite or even the objective of the participants' activities.

Most of the people interviewed for the study remembered feeling unease when they first used the Internet. This was because they were not sure exactly what information about themselves would be made available to others. The very prospect of putting one's words, name and/or email address before a large unidentifiable number of strangers felt "creepy." After a while, users developed mechanisms for controlling the personal information that was available in different online situations. These mechanisms could be quite complex and subtle. One way of using the technology to protect privacy was to have an "anonymous" email address, sometimes even in a different country, and also a "home" email address. The "anonymous" email address was used to communicate with certain types of people, including others hiding behind pseudonyms, whereas the more revealing address was used to communicate with people for whom the user did not feel the need to cloak his or her identity.

One of the interviewees described the gradual progress of an online relationship that started out with a high degree of anonymity. At first, she described her interlocutor as "that guy that I also thought was a Pole." They exchanged messages in a newsgroup on serious political subjects; she posted her messages using an email account in Italy. They continued the political discussion by email for months, and then started asking questions about each other as human beings—for example, "What kind of wine do you like?"

She says of this transition, "I started joking." It does appear that joking is a common strategy used to suggest a change to the public/private boundaries of an online relationship. The advantage of starting out with a joke may be that the suggestion can be turned down without anyone losing face.

Their exchange of emails continued for about a year until she asked him if she could call him on the telephone to hear his voice. She felt shy about this because "I knew nothing about his private life" and she did not want to intrude. Once again, it is clear that a boundary was being crossed, this time with an addition of a new communication medium.

More phone conversations followed, these became regular, and they started having long Internet chats, and also continued to communicate by email. They exchanged pictures. Changes in their use of communication media during this period corresponded to a gradual increase of intimacy. He sent her a marriage proposal by email in the form of a joke. Their correspondence grew more and more romantic, and finally, a year and a half after they first exchanged messages, they met at an airport, "and that was it."

One lesson from this heartwarming story is that it is not possible to categorize the use of email by the two people involved as either "public" or "private." At the beginning their conversations were only on "public" topics, at the end their email conversation was intimate, and in between there were minute gradations between the two levels of privacy. Their gradual movement toward the more private end of the spectrum was skillfully negotiated between the two of them at each step of the way.

From this example, we conclude that not only is it impossible to classify an online communication medium as public or private per se, it is even impossible to classify its use by a fixed pair of people as public or private. In fact, this example shows that even at a fixed point in the developing relationship between a fixed pair of people over a fixed medium, there can be subtle agreements that locate the level of privacy somewhere between completely public and completely private.

The account of a second interviewee shows that similar changes in the level of privacy can take place not only between individuals, but also for a whole group. This example also shows that collective life online involves two-way movements between the private and the public. Changes need not necessarily be in the direction of increasing intimacy.

The second interviewee was a reader of an open online forum with a large number of participants. The forum was public in the sense that anyone was allowed to join either to read or to contribute. She was intimidated by the size of the forum and did not contribute to it. However, in the course of reading the forum she identified some active contributors who had similar interests and attitudes to her own, and wrote to them by email. One of the women she contacted set up a "semiprivate" group of about 17 people who had found each other via the forum, and this group exchanged carbon-copied emails with each other. The members of the semiprivate group exchanged very personal messages, revealing themselves deeply. The interviewee became an active participant in this group.

There was considerable interest in the group, and as a result there was a suggestion to transform the group into an open mailing list, which anyone would be allowed to join. The group discussed this, and some members were uncomfortable with the idea, fearing that opening up to the public might adversely affect the quality of the exchanges, particularly the depth of sharing of experiences and emotions. She was unsure whether she would continue posting to an open list, because "I am a very, very private person." The consensus of the group, however, was that they should offer what they had to other people, and also allow the inflow of new information and ideas. The transformation took place. Thus, interestingly, the members chose to open up their comfortable intimate space to public scrutiny and participation.

After some time reading the open list the interviewee was satisfied that her online group had preserved its supportive atmosphere and sense of common interest. At this point she became an active contributor to the publicly accessible list. Through the support of her online community she had been empowered to break out of the confines of her strictly private space and to participate on the public stage.

This example tells the story not just of one individual, but of a group. It reveals negotiations by group members concerning the level of privacy of an online community, from public (in the sense of open access), to private via one-to-one emails, to semiprivate, and back to public.

Of course, communities that meet face-to-face also change their agreed privacy levels. However, online communications media allow individuals and groups to control what is revealed about them to a degree difficult to attain in face-to-face situations. As a result of this control, online communities can experiment with extremely subtle gradations in the level of privacy. The second interviewee commented on this when she talked about her reaction to personal biographies exchanged between members of the open list. She said that she found it fascinating to read what other members chose to reveal about themselves, and also thought about what she wanted to convey about herself "in this unique online environment where I can't be seen, I can't be heard."

Given the subtleties in the level of privacy expected online, and its variation according to medium, according to the group or individual involved, and over time, how is the online researcher to decide which uses of data collected from online communications are ethical? One answer is to involve the research subjects in this decision. This is exactly what we tried to do by posting a call for participation in our project to the mailing list we were interested in studying. This list involved victims of a devastating chronic illness, and their exchanges were often quite personal. And yet they were taking place in a publicly accessible online forum. How did the group resolve this contradiction for itself? How did members view their meeting place? As we will show in the next section, the response we received from group members was far from straightforward. Instead of pointing a way out of our dilemma, it revealed another public/private spectrum—one constituted by the different perceptions of privacy within the online group itself.

How Private Is the Group?

The question regarding the degree of privacy within the group we chose to study was far from settled before we arrived on the scene. In fact, our invitation to the group to participate in our study spurred a lively discussion, which brought out a whole range of privacy perceptions held by different group members. Some participants admitted that they felt "funny" when they read our letter to the list. They found it hard to agree to allow deeply personal feelings shared with the group to become part of a study, to be quoted in publications and other unknown places. Such participants invested a lot of themselves in the list. They saw it as a secure place, as a much-needed safety net because they trusted the community as it was. The prospect of having an outsider lurking for purposes other than those shared by the group filled them with unease and suspicion. The very idea of a study, as one member put it, "seems to cut away at the roots of our connection as a group—the spontaneity, the warmth, the illusion of privacy." Some even warned that they might need to back-channel people, that is, retreat to private email, in order to avoid the stranger's gaze.

Our appearance made group members ask themselves and each other questions about the status with regard to publicness versus privacy of their group communication. In this process they revealed assumptions that were often at odds with the actual state of affairs. It turned out many were unsure whether their real names appeared in the list archives on the Web. Many didn't know who could access these archives. Some even thought that the list moderator, a woman whom everybody adored, had to "O.K." people before they could join the list, which was not the case.

Prompted by this discussion, the moderator issued the following advice to list members:

> So keep in mind that anything you put on the Internet is pretty much available to anyone. . . . The only sure way to protect something is to not give it out. But then this also limits what one is able to do and how one is able to interact with others. So each of us needs to decide where we want to draw the line between open interaction and privacy/security.

Along with the members whom our study invitation had upset, there were other people in the list who had drawn that line quite differently. These participants understood the risk they were taking with regard to privacy by discussing personal matters on the Internet. Some even spoke of the "horror" they had needed to overcome in order to start participating in the list. However, the attraction of open interaction with numerous previously unknown people, the solidarity, the support, the wisdom gleaned from the online community had proven a strong enough motivation. Such members spoke about adopting a "publish and be damned" attitude despite their misgivings. This category of participants didn't mind our presence on the list. They saw our study as an expansion of the open interaction that they were there for. One list member wrote to us: "I don't mind at all for the world to see my underwear, pink, white or whatever. There is nothing here to be ashamed of and hopefully, it may help someone else."

Was this an invitation to us, or to any other outsider for that matter, to use the list material for our own purposes? We believe it was not. Despite the fact that the majority of the participants in this online community had appeared to have sacrificed their privacy consciously for the sake of open exchange with others, they still would not agree that what they created online could be appropriated for any purpose whatsoever. If they had willingly become involved in a "gift economy," as Barbrook (1999) has suggested, they felt moral ownership over their online product and were far from indifferent to how it might be used. In the next section, we suggest that respect for the intent with which online communities have generated content emerges as a fundamental ethical principle of social life online.

Privacy or Nonalienation?

We contend that resolving the public/private dilemma in online communities is not possible in terms of the existing ethical standards relating to publicness and privacy. The question about the degree of privacy of online communities can be answered only subjectively and even the group members themselves, as the experience from our studies has shown, would find it hard to agree upon a shared definition. The key to reconciling the "empirical" openness of online communities, which gives the appearance of publicness, with the expectation of privacy by their members lies in reformulating the problem in terms of the concept of alienation.

Participation in online communities can be a source of anxiety for members and observers alike, as it involves a complex dialectic of objectification and alienation. Objectification refers to producing material and symbolic traces of one's conscious life. We objectify ourselves in the products of our action that are observable, interpretable and usable by other people. Objectification in this sense is akin to self-realization, voice, and creativity. The Internet has opened up a rich variety of new forms of objectification from personal Web pages to online communities.

Alienation implies the appropriation of the products of somebody's action for purposes never intended or foreseen by the actor herself, drawing these products into a system of relations over which the producer has no knowledge or control. Henri Lefebvre, in his "Critique of Everyday Life" (1947) put forward the question as to whether all objectification involves an alienation. Whatever the general answer to this question, it is certainly true that by virtue of objectifying themselves in a variety of new forms, Internet users have made themselves vulnerable to new unforeseen forms of alienation. This is unfortunate as it undermines the spirit of what has been called the online "gift economy," based on the free exchange of participants' "products." Alienation cuts at the roots of the spontaneous informational and interactional gift giving that has made the Internet such an exciting arena. If left unchecked, alienation threatens to destroy the very possibility of social life online.

We believe that alienation, not privacy, is the actual core of the ethical problems of online community research and all other practices that draw on material created in the context of online community life. While practically everybody is allowed and often welcome to join these communities (which undermines the claim to privacy), most participants would agree that the person who joins is not authorized to exploit or sell the product of the group communication. The person who so "harvests" (Sharf 1999) online content would normally be expected by the group to ask for permission, preferably before the content has been produced, thus granting participants' the right to control their own product. This "nonalienation principle" should be the basis of emergent social conventions in cyberspace. It would apply to researchers as to anyone else.

A comment by one of the members of the group that we studied illustrates the difference between privacy and nonalienation. In the process of negotiating access to the group this woman categorically refused to allow us to save, analyze and quote her comments in the mailing list. She made a very clear distinction between two approaches to studying the list—one that she would accept without reservations, and another that was unacceptable. She was ready to let us observe the list and accumulate impressions of its life and then ask list members pointed questions on the basis of what we had seen. Then those answers, she thought, could be anonymously quoted. What she was reacting against was the possibility of estranging the product of her personal objectification meant for one purpose and context and putting it in use for another unrelated purpose beyond her control. Analyzing and quoting answers to researchers' questions would be different from analyzing and quoting postings to the list in that answers were formulated to serve the purposes of the study. In her letter to us, the woman explained that she desperately needed the security of the list and the possibility that her comments would be quoted compromised this security: "Read all you'd like. I simply don't want to be quoted," she insisted.

This last remark is particularly revealing. It demonstrates clearly that not privacy, but alienation is the central concern for this list member. She was posting her thoughts and feelings on the Internet for others to read and respond to. By doing that she was stepping out of her closed and controllable private world and was exposing herself to others' scrutiny. At the same time, she wanted to be able to trust that those she was opening herself up to would respect her intention in doing so. This trust would be violated if her words ended up in a study. Even the fact that we were asking for permission— that is, striving to establish nonalienation—was not sufficient for her.

The determination to avoid alienation could be recognized also in the reaction of the moderator whose mailing list we wished to study. At one point in our negotiation for access to the list we suggested using past postings from the archive in order not to disturb the ongoing communication of the group. We saw this option as a way to obtain an actual sample of naturally occurring discourse for our study while sparing the group possible damage from our observations. To this suggestion, the list moderator responded:

The main issue is that when the folks sent the messages which are in the archives, they did not know that their comments might be used for something/some other purpose. I think it is important for folks to know this up front when they decide what they will post. I try to provide the folks on the list with some security and confidentiality, and to respect what they have written, so these issues are important to me.

What might the nonalienation principle imply for people other than researchers? For example, how might it apply to a case such as this one: a company collects and sells information about members of a community in return for giving the community online facilities. Are members of the group alienated by this arrangement? If not, what feature of this case exempts it from the principle? It is reasonable to argue that there is no problem for members who consent, but then should members who do not consent still have access to the facilities?

When Is Alienation Justified?

Should the justifiable expectation and sometimes explicit demand for nonalienation be translated into a strict norm binding researchers to seek informed consent when they want to use community-generated materials? This would certainly impede some types of research that appear socially useful and do no harm to subjects beyond the alienation they imply. That harm is more easily mitigated (by anonymity for example) than violations of basic rights or health. Perhaps this is why our review of the literature on the ethics of online community research did not turn up publications that make a convincing argument for the need for informed consent under all circumstances. All authors recognized the fact that certain research goals and methodologies are legitimate under particular circumstances even if incompatible with informed consent. In many other areas of practice, such as journalism, law, management and commerce, these subtleties, unfortunately, have rarely been a matter of reflection. That is why we will briefly look at the debates in virtual community research as an exemplary area where important ethical questions have been raised.

Herring (in Thomas 1996, pp. 165–166) has brought to the fore the intricate connection between research ethics and research objectives and methodology. Different types of research imply differences in the relationships between researcher and subjects and, consequently, in research ethics.

- Naturalistic research—you (the researcher) want to disturb the "natural order" of the research object as little as possible, ideally not at all.
- Participatory research—you want subjects to consciously reflect on the research questions and contribute to your research.
- Consensual/"Understanding" research—your aim is to reconstruct the subject's own view of the world.
- Critical research—you put subjects' performance to a test/judgment under certain principles (of equity, fairness, ideological distortion, etc.).

Naturalistic and critical research are hard or impossible to reconcile with seeking informed consent, yet they can be fully legitimate under certain circumstances. Exposure of male domination in electronic discussions is an example of a research result that could not have been achieved if informed consent in the strict sense had to be received from the group members under study. Explaining to potential subjects the goals of the research and asking for their informed consent would have either changed their behavior or met with rejection. Herring has presented a convincing argument along these lines.

On the other hand, it should be noted that participatory and consensual research seem to have gained unprecedented new opportunities in the online environment. First of all, the electronic medium offers a level field for the encounter between subject and researcher. Not only the former, but also the latter, has been "virtualized." In optimistic accounts, this means that the notorious white lab coat does not grant authority to the researcher while pressing the subject into submission. The opposite might be true, as subjects remain protected by the relative anonymity of their email addresses or avatar names, while the researcher exposes herself in all relevant detail when communicating with them.

Furthermore, the permanently open two-way communication channel between subjects and researchers makes possible a dialogue between them. This dialogue need not be restricted in time and situation and driven by the research agenda as in the case of face-to-face interviewing. Subjects retain the opportunity to talk back at any time, thus sharing with the researcher the ability to initiate interaction and, potentially, to influence the direction of the study. In a reversal of the usual situation, the researcher and the research itself become objects for the subject to manipulate and appropriate.

In other words, doing research online presents us with new ways to involve the virtual subject as collaborator in our project. Furthermore, we would argue, this circumstance suggests new possibilities for elaborating new ethical approaches that elegantly combine research objectives and methods with subjects' right to nonalienation. Where permission can be received from the group without distorting the research, then researchers should engage in a discussion with the group about the best ways to ensure confidentiality, security, etc. No one best solution can be prescribed, as different groups will be supported by different technical configurations that will inevitably raise different issues, not to mention the different ideas subjects may have about what it means to secure confidentiality.

It would be naïve to suggest that these conclusions can be applied as-is to other areas such as politics, commerce, etc. Interests quite different from the quest for knowledge are involved in such practices, and exploitation of subjects is often an inevitable part of the game. Yet, we suggest that nonalienation and the involvement of subjects as partners and contributors is at least a relevant consideration for actors in these fields too. Failure to involve subjects in decision making concerning the use of their online products can have undesired consequences for commercial and political players. In mid-1999 the management of Yahoo! experienced the wrath of users whom it had failed to consult. Yahoo! included in its Terms of Service a clause stipulating that by posting material in public areas of the Yahoo! servers, users grant the company "the royalty-free, perpetual, irrevocable, nonexclusive and fully sublicensable right and license to use, reproduce, modify, adapt, publish, translate, create derivative works from, distribute, perform and display such content (in whole or part) worldwide and/or to incorporate it in other works in any form, media or technology now known or later developed" (see Junnarkar 1999). Outraged Web-site builders rallied through various Internet forums and put pressure on Yahoo! to reconsider its policy. The controversy ended with a compromise on both sides, demonstrating that the medium allows "subjects" to talk back and act when their personal investment in Internet content is treated with disrespect.

Nonalienation As a Norm

Many online communities are active in online public spaces that anyone can peek in on at any time. This was true of the community we studied, although its members seemed only dimly aware of their exposure. No doubt it was this openness to inspection which earlier researchers interpreted as an invitation to observation and analysis without concern for subjects' consent. Yet the very fact that members of online communities such as the one we studied are only vaguely aware of the public nature of their exchanges suggests the need for caution. Their trust may be misplaced, but nevertheless it is not good for researchers to violate it without a compelling rationale.

There are other ethical and, in some cases, legal models on which we can draw for insight into this new situation. Similar issues arise in photography, where lawsuits have cleared up some of the ambiguities. Photographers have been documenting street life for a century, and their efforts have played a recognized role in public discourse. Pictures of war and of the poor and oppressed have had an important impact on politics, legislation and public policy. Using the argument of freedom of expression and public interest, photographers have defended their right to publish anything that appears in public. Yet individuals have prevailed in lawsuits aimed at protecting their image from exploitation by photographers. They have won compensation for the sale of their image or reparation for harm from being exposed to ridicule or retaliation. Increasingly magazines and newspapers have demanded that photographers obtain signed releases from anyone who can be recognized in a picture, especially if they might reasonably complain about their portrayal or the associations evoked by it. The line is still somewhat fuzzy, but it is clear now that individuals do retain a certain right over their image even when they are photographed in a public space.

Nevertheless, the ethical issue in online research differs from these cases in one important respect. The subjects of street photography are not involved in the reproduction of their image for publication. The means of publication, cameras, are brought to the situation by the witness. In the case of the Internet, the subjects themselves construct the public transcript of their own actions. The exploitation of that transcript requires no special technical intervention on the part of the exploiter. This suggests that courts will be unlikely to grant as much legal control over their online image to individuals as they have granted to photographic subjects.

Should researchers be influenced by this difference? Certainly there is an important distinction between violating ethical and legal norms. A newspaper may quote online comments without fear of legal consequence, where researchers might feel held to a higher standard of respect for their subjects. This is a reasonable distinction. Yet, as noted above, certain kinds of research would be impossible without exploiting the naive self-publication of online participants. It would be absurd to deny researchers the right to study important public issues such as educational achievement or gender inequality routinely discussed by journalists on the basis of public evidence available to all. On the other hand, the very possibility of research depends on the good will of the populations studied. To needlessly alienate them by exploiting their online activities, where consent might have been negotiated, is not only disrespectful but also destructive of the research enterprise.

Systematic alienation could lead to loss of trust and retreat to the private realm on the part of virtual community participants, thus disrupting the very practice of online community as we know it. We therefore conclude that the right of nonalienation of online communities should be respected wherever possible, and on the basis of our experience we believe that to be easier than is sometimes supposed.

In summary, our recommendations for researchers who seek to respect the principle of nonalienation are:

- Where it is possible without distorting the research, involve the community in the planning and design of the study through a preliminary engagement with the group. Draw on group members' input to formulate research objectives meaningful to subjects.

- If approval and funding for the study can go ahead only once there is a fixed plan, do the preliminary engagement before applying for approval and funding.

- Engage in a discussion with the community about the way data should be handled.

- Keep communication channels with the community members open during the study.

References

Allen, Christina, "What's Wrong with the Golden Rule? Conundrums of Conducting Ethical Research in Cyberspace," *The Information Society Journal*, vol. 12, no. 2 (1996), pp. 175–189.

Barbrook, Richard, "The High-Tech Gift Economy," in John Armitage and Joanne Roberts, eds., *Exploring Cyber Society: Social, Political, Economic and Cultural Issues*, vol. 2. Proceedings of the Conference 5th–7th July 1999, School of Social, Political and Economic Sciences, University of Northumbria at Newcastle, UK.

Cavanagh, Allison, "Behaviour in Public: Ethics in Online Ethnography," *Cybersociology*, no. 6 (1999): Research Methodology Online. Online: www.cybersociology.com

Goffman, Erving, *Behavior in Public Places: Notes on the Social Organization of Gatherings*, p. 154. New York: The Free Press, 1963.

Junnarkar, Sandeep, "How Much Content Do Community Sites 'Own'?" CNET News.com, June 28, 1999. Online: http://news.cnet.com/category/0-1005-200-344193.html

King, Storm, A., "Researching Internet Communities: Proposed Ethical Guidelines for the Reporting of Results," *The Information Society Journal*, vol. 12, no. 2 (1996), pp. 119–129.

Lefebvre, Henri, *Critique of Everyday Life, Vol. 1: Introduction*. London, New York: Verso, 1947.

Reid, Elizabeth, "Informed Consent in the Study of Online Communities: A Reflection on the Effects of Computer-Mediated Social Research," *The Information Society Journal*, vol. 12, no. 2 (1996), pp. 169–175.

Robson, Kate, and Mark Robson, "Your Place or Mine? Ethics, the Researcher and the Internet," in John Armitage and Joanne Roberts, eds., *Exploring Cyber Society: Social, Political, Economic and Cultural Issues*, vol. 2. Proceedings of the Conference 5–7 July 1999, School of Social, Political and Economic Sciences, University of Northumbria at Newcastle, UK.

Sharf, Barbara, "Beyond Netiquette: The Ethics of Doing Naturalistic Discourse Research on the Internet," in Steven Jones, ed., *Doing Internet Research: Critical Issues and Methods for Examining the Net*, pp. 243–256. London, New Delhi: Sage, 1996.

Thomas, Jim, section editor, "The Ethics of Fair Practices for Collecting Social Science Data in Cyberspace," special issue of *The Information Society Journal*, vol. 12, no. 2 (1996).

Wascul, Dennis, and Mark Douglass, "Considering the Electronic Participant: Some Polemical Observations on the Ethics of On-line Research." *The Information Society Journal*, vol. 12, no. 2 (1996), p. 131.

10 Community, Courseware, and Intellectual Property Law
by Geoffrey Sauer

> The major change to befall universities over the last two decades has been the identification of the campus as a significant site of capital accumulation, which has resulted in the systematic conversion of intellectual activity into intellectual capital and, hence, intellectual property. —David F. Noble, 1998

> There's a revolution brewing on college campuses these days. Its goal is to make higher education more accessible . . . and more profitable too. —WebCT (an online courseware vendor and publisher), unnumbered page distributed with press release, 1999

Jean-François Lyotard's prediction in *The Postmodern Condition* (Lyotard 1984) that market segmentation would encourage both a proliferation of fields and commodification of knowledges has proven correct. Intellectual property rights for publishers have been expanded. Public policy and venture capital funding have encouraged the growth of "information industry" jobs in the United States. Media industries have grown in their cultural influence, and the corporations that run them have found it useful to reorganize to produce diverse markets for information. Knowledge distribution has become increasingly motivated by the logic of commodity trading and market demand. And while it seems clear that academic knowledges will be a rich growth market in the coming decade, this change is not simply egalitarian progress toward accessible scholarship, but also (or instead?) the rationalization of contemporary knowledge as a commodity. It is important to study how this is happening, as academics struggle to clarify how to engage new media technologies in our teaching and research, and as the resources produced within academic communities acquire an increasingly important online component.

This present state of publishing certainly isn't always fully understood by either advocates or antagonists of online publishing. Some writers equate the Internet with commodification—either as a symbol of contemporary problems (as in Noble 1998), or a utopian alternative to current hegemonies (as in Negroponte 1995). But the numerous parallels between the views of corporate interests and university administrators have undeniably led to a redistribution of resources away from stolid academic disciplines toward fields such as business and the sciences—which have adapted more readily to the commodity model (see Berube 1998 and Nelson 1997 for discussion of this). This chapter will examine changes in intellectual property rights over the past few decades in order to examine their implications for teaching and for the organization and control of academic resources online. It will then look at new Internet technologies becoming incorporated into classroom practice. Last, it will propose alternative strategies that might be useful to scholarly communities.

Changes in the Duration of Copyright in the United States

In order to analyze these cultural changes of the past few decades, it is helpful first to look at material changes in intellectual property that enable recent reforms. Since the mid-1960s the entertainment industry in the United States has won significant legislative victories to increase the value of their intellectual properties. The enormous strength of commercial publishing interests can be seen in a pattern of extensions to copyright law; the U.S. Congress enacted a succession of laws that extend the duration of copyright—preventing works from moving automatically into the public domain. The total duration of copyright has been extended potentially as long as 150 years, if the author lives to the age of 80, as can be seen in Table 10.1.

Although it's not usually obvious to those who don't follow intellectual property law, these changes actually affect teachers' and writers' relations with their work. For example, in addition to the duration changes above, Congress has also changed the definitions of intellectual property in 17 U.S. Code 101. This change of definitions creates differences between the interests of university administrations (which have won some new property rights to faculty work) and those of instructors—who have not won any increases in salary, royalties or participation in distribution of their works.

Many writings about new media issues take up utopian narratives from the early 1990s about the Internet which assume that new media are an opposite to print—as if "publishing" had somehow been a fixed or stable institution since the fifteenth century. The impulse to vilify "dot-commodification" may lead to the opinion that the rise of commerce-driven new media provides a simple explanation of the commercialization of academic work. In particular, it may suggest that the expectation by courseware companies that the copyright of academic works distributed over their systems should belong to the University, or to the courseware companies themselves, rather than to the authors of the works (or to the public), is a phenomenon that has not been prefigured in other forms of publishing. The equation of print publishing with *Gutenberg*, as if the contemporary publishing industry somehow resembled fifteenth-century incunabula, recurs alarmingly often. From Table 10.1 it becomes clear that new media have become popular only in the later stages of a change within the organization of property by media industries, and that the attitude of courseware companies toward copyright is not the *cause* but rather a *symptom* of the emergent order.

TABLE 10.1 Increase of Duration of Copyright

YEAR	LAW	MAXIMUM DURATION OF COPYRIGHT
1962	Pub. L. 87-668	59 years
1965	Pub. L. 89-142	61 years
1967	Pub. L. 90-141	62 years
1968	Pub. L. 90-416	63 years
1969	Pub. L. 91-147	64 years
1970	Pub. L. 91-555	65 years
1971	Pub. L. 92-170	66 years
1972	Pub. L. 92-566	68 years
1974	Pub. L. 93-573	70 years
1976	Pub. L. 94-553	75 years (or 50 past author's death)
1998	Pub. L.105-298	95 years (or 70 past author's death)

The 1976 Copyright Act

When copyright protection was first extended to creative works in Great Britain in 1710, that protection could be held for only a few years. After the term expired, works would enter into the common weal, becoming a part of the culture, and would no longer be private property.

While the rhetoric of the early laws was to encourage creative genius by allowing authors to benefit from their works, it has been well documented elsewhere that the original eighteenth-century lobby for copyright consisted of publishers (see, for instance, Darnton 1979). Individual authors did benefit from being able to sell creative works to publishers (who would then hold exclusive rights to publish), but few individuals owned their own publishing firms, and publishers rapidly developed standard contracts which paid authors as little as possible. (Today, publishers routinely offer authors as little as

7 percent of net sales—which means retail sales minus the cost of desk copies, remaindered volumes, etc.)

Following the 1976 Copyright Act, property rights in the United States are today given by default to the employer, unless a particular contract that grants the individual creator some rights to his or her work is negotiated *before the work is begun*. This is the reason for the complex term lengths in the final two rows of Table 10.1. The default term (95 years in the final row) applies if the work is owned by a corporate entity, and only if the work were owned by an individual does the second term (life + 70 years) apply—rare indeed for published books, since publishing contracts today as a matter of course transfer ownership entirely to the publisher.

This change has had many effects on creative work. Eminent authors, musicians and actors today require professional agents to negotiate their share of rights to creative works—all of which would otherwise be presumed simply to be corporate (publisher, media distributor or film studio) property. This produces a sort of "class" dichotomy between those who can afford to engage in current practices, and those who either don't have the celebrity to negotiate, or those who don't question current practice.

This has not often become noticed in academic work. Non-profit university presses pay quite little for publishing contracts, and even commercial publishers seldom pay well for academic productions—so it is seldom indeed that academic authors require agents to negotiate on their behalf. Textbook contracts have a reputation for being lucrative, but the stories about this circulate mostly around notable successes, such as the University of Tennessee's English department, which is said to fund its graduate programs with revenues from its share of the *Harcourt Brace Handbook*. But those stories are from sales successes and are hardly representative of academic writing.

Changes in copyright law which favor employers and creators with lawyers and agents affect academic and commercial employees today because organizations have tended to market their newly found rights to intellectual properties much more fully than before, with a general desire to obtain commercial value from many forms of knowledge. For example, many research universities today have "Technology Transfer" offices, whose task is to represent the university's share of commercially valuable intellectual properties.

These changes may affect academics in the future in an additional way. Academics provide copies of varied types of course material to the University as part of employment. Colleges may claim that such syllabi, handouts, annotated bibliographies and even audio or video recordings of lectures are the property of the employer.

Copyright is legal protection for expression; it does not protect ideas, and by statute applies only to forms recorded in some permanent medium. As a result, copyright has rarely been considered to apply to lectures and in-class discussions—and even property law has generally been considered irrelevant to these, since they tend not to be recorded. (The preservation of lectures in students' notes has led to a few legal arguments, since student notes are often notoriously creative works in their own right, rather than simple transcription.)

But when a university administration makes a contract with a corporate Web provider to run course Web sites, the Web courseware host is acting as an authorized agent of the university. If faculty members voluntarily (or as a matter of policy, as is beginning to be seen at some colleges) place course materials onto a Web server run by or for the university, it could be argued that this constitutes transfer of ownership of the materials from the instructor to his or her employer, and that this transfer of materials constitutes a contractual transfer of distribution rights (which the university might then market or redistribute at its discretion). Although this may be a tempting way of raising funds to assist hard-up faculties, it may have lead to the types of unfortunate side-effects described in (for example) Norman Clark's chapter in this book.

Few academics understand that such a transfer need not be in the form of a signed contract. Indeed, college administrations are not necessarily conniving to seize properties that were traditionally seen to belong to the faculty—administrators may only discover their rights to such properties five or ten years from now. Or they may sign contracts with commercial Web courseware providers that (unintentionally) transfer intellectual property rights to the commercial courseware provider (as is done routinely in book-publishing contracts). But the increases of intellectual property rights in the United States in recent decades have coincided with an increasing recognition of the value of intellectual property, and academic knowledges are a ripe prospective territory for expanded commodification (given that a four-year U.S. university tuition can exceed $100,000 per student). The fact that classroom knowledges, and various other less formalized resources produced within academic communities, have not circulated as commodities in the past cannot be thought to be an adequate protection against this happening in the future. Contract law has a tremendous bias toward the presumption that contracts are entered into by equal partners, capable of negotiating for their own interests and cognizant of the implications of their contract. But the current strength of publishing corporations (as seen in recent intellectual property law) and the relative naïveté shown by academics casts that presumption into doubt here. David Noble, a sociologist who has received much attention for his public stands against course Web sites, cites very effectively (Noble 1998) the moment in Kurt Vonnegut's *Player Piano* (1952) when the ace machinist Rudy Hertz is flattered by the automation engineers who tell him his genius will be immortalized. They buy him a beer. They capture his skills on tape. Then they fire him.

Of course, although some teachers might be improved by being immortalized on tape, it is as impossible to completely capture a good teacher on tape as it is to train a Player Piano to be a sensitive accompanist. What is missing from a recording is the teacher's and students' interaction, with two-way or multiway communication in which all interlocutors respond flexibly, adjusting their utterances (and sometimes changing their beliefs) in response to the social and conversational dynamics. In short, it is the aspect of communication that is enabled on the Internet by what is referred to as "community" communication tools. The simpleminded translation of print publishing models to Internet publishing models, ignoring "community" interaction and communication, was a resounding flop in some highly visible cases, and now it has become almost obligatory for any ambitious media site to give its readers the possibility of dynamic multiway communication among themselves. An interesting development (described by Janelle Brown and Chris Werry in this book) is the attempted commodification of these communication methods as well, continuing the long-term trend in publishing already identified in this chapter. However, as much as media companies might want to "tape" the social skills of human experts in community communication, and despite technical advances in Internet bots and interactive and personalized systems, so far teaching and learning in online communities still work best when most of the interacting personas are directly ventriloquized by human beings. Administrators who manage to record all the available course material would be wise not to fire the teaching staff quite yet.

The Thor Power Tool Case, 1979

These changes do not necessary imply Manichean dichotomies of innocent, virtuous authors versus scheming, devious publishing executives or university administrators. The present state of intellectual property law has evolved over decades. In this section we study this evolution, in order to discern potential positions for academic workers in the future.

Although many influences in U.S. publishing history could exemplify changes in the past few decades, the clearest may be the Supreme Court's 1979 *Thor Power Tool* decision (*Thor Power Tool Co. v. Commissioner*, 439 U.S. 522, 1979). The *Thor* decision ruled that a hardware manufacturer's parts, stored over a five to ten-year period for distribution to retail stores, should be taxable property in one year *at the retail value of the parts.*

An unforeseen effect was that books stored by publishers in warehouses after large runs (for long-term future sales) would also be taxed much more highly than before, so that whatever backlist a publisher has at the end of each fiscal year becomes a financial liability. This is important, because offset lithography makes printing books less expensive when done once, in large volume, rather than via multiple print runs of small quantities for each year's sales. Publishers of specialized and abstruse works with small audiences—such as academic and lesser-known literary texts—had (before this decision) simply printed a large number of copies of such books and amortized their cost over five or ten years of sales. The *Thor* decision made this course untenable, as such publishers had to pay far greater tax on backlists. As a result, many publishers today prefer to publish marketable books they believe can be sold within a single fiscal year.

This has offered material advantages to books which could become events, complete with public relations campaigns and marketing which seek to demonstrate their relevance and timeliness. Popular authors such as Stephen King and Harry Potter author J. K. Rowling today write on a schedule of one book per year, and the cyclic nature of the writing suits a marketing apparatus designed to maintain the visibility and recognizability of "event" authors. Even in academic writings (where this celebrity is less common), the "event" theory of publishing has encouraged market segmentation and differentiation in order to create "hot" new subdisciplines and disciplinary "star systems," whose greatest authors' new works receive "must-read" status. Meanwhile, older and more measured works with smaller (if constant) reading audiences have quietly gone out of print.

Among the longer-term results of this has been that four large book distribution corporations have come to dominate publishing in the United States. These firms, such as Ingram and Publisher's Group West, warehouse books for their member publishers and have a strong inventory computer network in place, with connections to bookstore franchises across the country, so stores can automatically order from centralized distributors. American readers have seen how these networks have made possible a hegemony of heavily computerized retail franchises with strong connections to the distributors: Barnes & Noble, Borders, and Amazon.com are all examples of this. These bookstores have databases designed to keep track of inventory, to reorder popular works automatically from distributors, and to keep track of what books go out of print and what new offerings should be added to catalogues and shelves.

On the one hand, such a system may seem efficient. It is certainly true that the total number of works available has increased. However, much interesting work is also being lost because it does not fit into the new economics of publishing, especially "esoteric" works and books published by small presses. As local bookstores are replaced by these franchises, many traditional relationships between academics and bookstore management have decreased, and in many ways the influence of those of us in the humanities in book sales seems to be the weakest it has been this century. The response of some groups of authors traditionally published by small presses, including many academics in sciences as well as in the humanities, has been to despair of the print publishing world and to flee to the Internet. For example, the most prestigious physics journals are now almost without exception online publications. Some of the "democratic" aura of Internet publishing today derives from online publication's freedom from the economic realities which structure publishers' calendars.

Imbalance of Powers: Corporate, Government, and Consumer

Many colleagues over recent years have argued to me that these extensions of property do benefit authors. Following a Reagan-era "trickle-down" theory, these colleagues argue that greater revenues for publishers will generate a better position for faculty. And it could even be true. Certainly the "star systems" in publishing which have emerged post-1979 have worked to the advantage of the few academics who become famous within their disciplines (and, following market segmentation and differentiation, now even subdisciplines). Authors whose work fits the "event" paradigm of book publishing—and who therefore sell sufficient copies to hire agents to negotiate—may benefit from their celebrity.

But the increased costs which computerized databases, publicity, marketing and rapid obsolescence have added to books have had visible costs for all of us who read and teach. The increases in the cost of "leisure" reading have already had noticeable effects for communities of readers in everyday life. Quality paperbacks in the United States begin in the $15 range, and hardcover books range upward from $20—this builds popular support around less-expensive "bestseller" books, and further decreases the base of support for academic knowledges. In this world, the futures for leisure reading in the humanities seem more difficult to imagine, particularly as young readers seem to find early focus of their reading interests economically rewarding, thus decreasing the sort of breadth more common earlier this century.

Historians have written at length about the dangers of allowing the price of written works to escalate, creating elite knowledges with narrow bases of support in culture. I have written elsewhere to draw parallels to the eighteenth-century print history of the French Bourbon monarchy, as have historians such as Robert Darnton. Darnton's work on Swiss book smuggling as part of the business and economics of the Enlightenment argues that economic and material exigencies can have dramatic impact on the value of knowledges within cultural contexts. I have a personal friend who works as a manager in my neighborhood Barnes & Noble, who has told me that his store wants to limit its stock of university press books, because they are comparatively difficult to find, to order, and to negotiate profit margins comparable to those found from presses which distribute via the four large distribution companies.

Alienated Labor—Even within the Star System

Walter Benjamin (1968), Roland Barthes (1968/1989), and Michel Foucault (1979) have written about the principles that a culture uses to organize written works. Because the complexities of comparing the many details of works make this practically impossible, social institutions are developed to assist us. The author-function, one instance of this, is the creation of a myth around particular authors, which can be used to connect their works to one another, in order to think of single books as belonging to a progression of books by the same author.

As we look to the possibility that academic knowledges will be more thoroughly commodified in the future, we should beware the possibility that the author-function that will organize scholarship will be organized around employers (Harvard University courses online!) or publishers (WebCT or eCollege courses online!) rather than in terms of individual instructors, whose diminution may not benefit all of us. Michael Milken, the ex-junk-bond king, has invested heavily in companies offering online education technology, which suggests that academic commodities may be marketed as any other media or information commodities. And the argument of Alan Gilbert (the chair of Universitas 21, an international association of research-based universities), in a statement to *The Chronicle of Higher Education* that U.S. universities are not good brand names overseas (Maslen 2000), suggests that neither individual faculty nor parent universities constitute the author-function most likely to be used to organize these commodities.

The workplace realities of creative labor will be influenced by the ways in which the author-function works in emerging media. Recently even the beneficiaries of the corporate "star system" have expressed dissatisfaction with the current balance of power between artists and corporations in intellectual property. In May 2000, singer-songwriter Don Henley received popular attention for his assertion that the copyright act favored the Recording Industry Association over recording artists. And a similar argument was made in June 2000 by singer

Courtney Love, who studied a hypothetical but very autobiographical-sounding recording contract in an article for *Salon* magazine titled "Courtney Love Does the Math." The article found that a sample recording contract generated $45,000 for musicians from a one-year album project, while providing the record company $6.6 million. She concludes with a desire for some alternative to the current music industry:

> I want to work with people who believe in music and art and passion. And I'm just the tip of the iceberg. I'm leaving the major label system and there are hundreds of artists who are going to follow me. There's an unbelievable opportunity for new companies that dare to get it right (*Salon* 2000, p. 363).

Music celebrities by definition have already-written identities within the popular music star system. If Web courseware is to become a part of our work process, it may be important to examine how author identities will be acknowledged within academic online publishing—for example, how credit for online publishing will be reflected in tenure review.

A common joke in English departments is that English faculty fight so fiercely because the stakes are so small. In fact, I believe the stakes are large. The inequities which affect even media celebrities will have comparable effects upon us (the more so for the remarkably small pay we receive for our writings), and the same property laws which are becoming known for their anti-author bias in other media will begin to affect us as well, as new markets emerge for circulating the scholarly knowledges that emerge out of academic communities.

Commercial Publishing Influence in Web Courseware

One of the fastest-growing applications for online academic publication in the United States is that of online courseware. This is in part because commercial e-commerce interests have begun to copy the catalog-commodity software engines currently available to wholesale and retail distributors, attempting to transform these to distribute academic commodities. The negotiations currently under way for the most part are not visible to faculty (with the exception of the numerous one- and two-page advertisements in *The Chronicle of Higher Education*—the most widely read publication about higher education in North America—and the sponsorships of National Public Radio).

But the peril of this new system can be seen when reading the brochures circulated by courseware vendors to college and university administrators. For example, the company RealEducation (which recently became WebCT) has for two years distributed to administrators a marketing packet that contains a document (WebCT 1999, "RealEducation Raises $15 Million to Build Online Campuses for Colleges, Universities & Corporations") which asks the following:

> Why would anyone want to go to class on-campus when they can go to www.realeducation.com and get an entire degree from a growing list of the best institutions of higher learning in the country via our reliable, easy-to-use, yet sophisticated Internet education system? (p. 3)

Why, indeed. There are clues that this question is one asked of college administrators, rather than students or faculty. Included in the brochure is a photograph of a middle-class housewife in classically styled clothes, her young daughter on her lap, sitting at her kitchen table with orange juice, her notes, and a laptop computer. This offers some insight into one vision planned to intrigue school administrators: expanding student populations to nontraditional students.

Another WebCT brochure (WebCT 1999, "Take a Shortcut to Putting Your College or University Online") suggests that its company's courseware system would provide virtual replacements for many of the cost centers that dominate university budgets. The brochure suggests expanding university access without the costs of investment in real estate or a physical plant:

> Build a new kind of campus, not new buildings. Imagine a university without walls, without limits. [WebCT] customizes

your online campus and classrooms to fit the look and feel of your institution. And both will mirror your traditional campus in every way; with all the services, all the interaction, and all the vibrancy of the educational experience your traditional students enjoy (p. 2).

Later, the same brochure suggests that WebCT's online facilities might replace numerous existing cost centers:

Your online campus will include: Course Catalog, Academic Calendar, Inquiry/Application Forms, Registration Information, Degree Requirements, Add/Drop Policies, Admissions, Financial Aid & Bursar's Office, Administrative Services, Student Services & Faculty Directory, Academic Advising, Career Counseling, Bookstore, Student Union (p. 4).

The plan here is to substitute electronic replicas of some of the more expensive services (non-revenue-generating departments are known as "cost centers" in corporate jargon) provided by traditional academic institutions to their students.

Each course is consistent in look, functions and features; so it's uncomplicated for faculty developing the courses and the students who use them (p. 6).

Last (and perhaps least), the brochure talks about working with the faculty who will actually create the course content.

Education instructional designers and course developers consult one-on-one with faculty to help convert their course materials into compelling and effective Internet presentations (p. 3).

Perhaps not surprisingly, when U.S. courseware vendors discuss online education in materials intended for faculty, a very different tone is registered, one in which "community" tends to be the central motif. For example, *The Chronicle of Higher Education* is crammed to the brim with advertising from online education companies, almost all of which stresses the extent to which their systems will enhance community life in universities, make academic community resources easier to use, and connect academics with the wider communities outside their gates. One of Campus Pipeline's advertising slogans in issues of *The Chronicle of Higher Education* in 1999–2000 (for example, on p. A53 of the September 3, 1999 edition) was "A community dedicated to meeting individual needs. A business streamlined for maximum efficiency. And a campus that never closes." Furthermore, Campus Pipeline (discussed in more detail by Norman Clark in this book) announces in its mission statement that "We will revolutionize education by connecting the collegiate community," and asserts that its software "revolutionizes the way higher education builds relationships with its students, faculty, staff and alumni." In this context, "community" perhaps functions as a way of reassuring educators that courseware vendors are sensitive to the social and communicative aspects of teaching, and that courseware does not involve an automation of education resembling Vonnegut's *Player Piano*.

Student Dissatisfaction with Traditional Teaching

As bizarre as some commercial courseware seems to professional scholars, such systems may not appear as abhorrent to undergraduates. Market segmentation and the focused disciplinary nature of contemporary research produces scholars often disenchanted with undergraduate teaching—which appears less and less connected to prestigious work.

The alienation many academics have from representing their work to nonexperts may well be a symptom of the current publishing era. But the "online community" model of teaching may appear to students as an *improvement* over the traditional lecture hall or the adjunct classrooms that have become such a part of the research university core curriculum. What is necessary (if we wish to preserve traditional teaching from commodity courseware) is a form of accessibility in our teaching which contemporary publishing does not seem to support.

Courseware Advantages

The first step would be to consider whether online technologies might offer a form of accessibility currently missing from teaching practice. In the introduction it was suggested that there are advantages to these media for teaching. There is nothing to say that course Web sites are inherently exploitative. I don't want to fall prey to the technological-determinist fallacy that assumes that certain "democratic" relationships inhere within technologies, but course Web sites can and do offer specific and understandable advantages to classroom teaching when students have adequate Internet access. I myself have found a number of these, having used course Web sites every term since 1995.

The traditional paper-based syllabus is a powerful tool for structuring a course. But I have always found that my expectations from before the term begins should be reconsidered in the face of what actually appeals to students in the classroom. Some works seem to merit more in-depth study than I could predict ahead of time, and others prove less relevant than expected. When I teach with a course Web site syllabus, the students always know where to look for upcoming assignments, but we have a certain freedom to change upcoming assignments (as long as everyone uses the system to see any changes).

But in these marketing brochures written to college and university administrators, it is interesting to note that students, faculty and the classroom features available in the Web courseware are the seventh (and last) item in the list. And for this reason, received ideas about online courseware deserve careful study—few of us can trust publishers', administrators' or even our own first impulses regarding these technologies.

Alternatives: The English Server

There are, of course, some alternatives to corporate commercialization of scholarly knowledges. Other chapters in this book will speak about several of these, but effort should be given to explore alternatives to current commercial plans in this area—before they become a *fait accompli.*

Protection within Disciplines

It may be possible to protect academics' positions by action from academic disciplinary communities, at the national and international level. In his 1998 article from *First Monday*, David F. Noble engages an argument from the point of view of academic disciplines, against distance education as an institution. By equating distance education programs with "diploma mills" and by citing academic organizations' policy documents from the 1970s condemning institutions which may resemble new online distance education programs from even prestigious universities, Noble attempts to undermine university administrators' claims that distance education equals (or improves) traditional teaching methods.

As described above, and in contrast to David Noble's view, the Internet is seen by some as a place to escape commercial and economic pressures, including the imbalance of intellectual property rights. The Internet may have been first constructed as a territory where strict hierarchical relationships between writers and publishers (or academics and faculty administration, or software developers and corporate managers) did not apply. The subsequent investment that writers, software developers, and community correspondents began to make in Internet writing may be seen to be a direct result of that benign neglect. The neglect was unintended by management and is being "reformed" today with a greater corporate presence. The extraordinary success of the Internet may enable the preservation of such relative autonomy, but it is likely that many "do-it-yourself" sites will not be able to continue without more formal institutional support. In the case of academia, perhaps as faculty realize their vested interest in creating independent online distributors of scholarly knowledges, communities of academics will be able to produce for themselves more scholar-friendly alternatives to the commercial courseware.

Independent Course Materials

Examples of this sort of practice can already be found in the work of many young academics. For example, in the United States there are the online sites of the *Voice of the Shuttle* at the University of California-Santa Barbara, the *Eighteenth-Century Web* at Rutgers, the *Poststructural Theory* Web site at Southern Illinois (Carbondale) and the *English Server*, formerly at Carnegie Mellon and now at the University of Washington. This chapter will conclude by examining the last of these, the English Server (http://eserver.org/, Figure 10–1), which has published electronic works since 1990 and in 2000 has created an electronic course Web site system.

The English Server is an academic cooperative that has published humanities texts to more than forty million readers, today serving between two and four million works per month. It currently distributes almost thirty thousand works in total, including literary classics and new writing, representing a wide range of topics in the arts and humanities.

It is run as an academic cooperative, sharing most writings with the public, but some only among particular communities of its members. One becomes an English Server "member" only by participating in the process of publishing works, either by writing, editing, or formatting submissions for online publication. The site hopes to demonstrate the potential that collaborative uses of communications technologies holds for the arts and humanities—the need for "public intellectuals"—while at the same time providing useful and otherwise unavailable facilities for collaboration in new subdisciplines and interdisciplinary areas. It may mitigate some of the drawbacks of the academic "star system." For example, jointly authored papers, including those from authors in different disciplines, are facilitated by the English Server, whereas (in the humanities at least) joint authoring is often problematic within U.S. academic systems of tenure and review.

The English Server provides a means of linking members' work to disciplinary groups and organizations that recognize such contributions—via lists and conference lines, for exam-

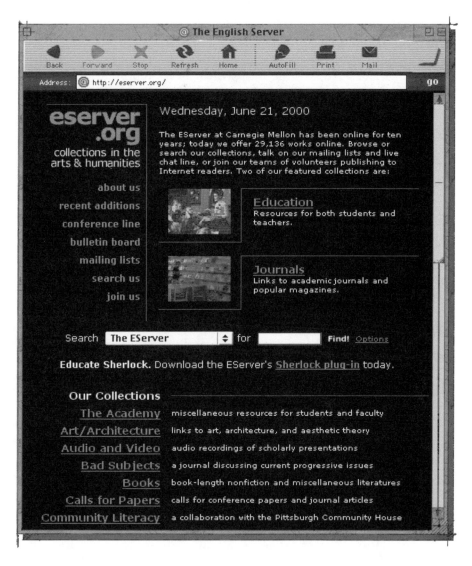

FIGURE 10–1 The English Server

ple. Furthermore, the English Server enables readers to contribute individually or cooperatively to its holdings. Unlike many other online humanities collections, readers may submit their own work for consideration by colleagues editing other English Server collections. Because it is not a commercial enterprise, authors can be permitted to retain ownership and control of their work, rather than signing away copyright in exchange for an economic opportunity for publishers who must pay for typesetting, printing, marketing and staff to organize every stage of publication. Because the English Server is a member-run collective managed according to principles derived from hacker co-op sites, it is not nearly as bureaucratic as comparable corporate or official university Web sites, which results in greatly larger collections and increased efficiency in the publication process.

The English Server does not charge its readers for access to texts, and although contributions are always welcome, the site is provided due to volunteer labor by our writers, editors and administrative board. English Server equipment is maintained by grants, donations, and a small annual budget from the Carnegie Mellon English Department. The Department benefits in turn from the publicity generated by the site, which receives sought-after Internet "hits" from its association with the collections of popular reading available to academic communities worldwide (and therefore attracts undergraduate and graduate students to the Department's programs). Moreover, the English Department can circulate its official brochure and internal policy manuals on the system, without any need for professional administrators paid for from the department budget. In this case, the policy and brochure distribution rides on the back of the distribution of academic content, in comparison to the vision in the WebCT brochure quoted earlier, which reads as if the electronic distribution of academic content were a minor (although pleasant) side-effect of the digitization of university administration systems.

Several members of the English Server's administrative board (including myself) worked in 1998 to develop a simple courseware server for the English Department at Carnegie Mellon. Taking that initial work as a model, and working with longtime English Server members such as Seattle-based professional relational-database designer Ellen Meserow and Pittsburgh-based Web designer Alice Crawford, the site released in the summer of 2000 a prototype of a Web courseware system. This system will be opened to all English Server members in time for the Fall 2000 term.

Returning to the discussion of copyright law, if a faculty member sends his or her academic work to an online community without using the servers of the university where he or she is employed, this does not constitute a contractual "submission" of work-for-hire to an employer under U.S. law. (The relevant law is 17 U.S. Code 101.) As a result, the faculty member can retain the copyright to work on the English Server, or similar online communities, whereas work put online via a courseware system based at the faculty member's university becomes the property of the university. If academics can maintain systems that allow copyright to be kept by the author, this may encourage independent thinking. A gift economy among academics (as opposed to an economy in which each university tries to hang on to its own exclusive intellectual property) may be more helpful to accessibility of scholarly knowledges and may improve the teaching of undergraduates.

Because the English Server adopted the new Internet technologies as they emerged (FTP in 1990, Gopher in 1991, World Wide Web in 1993, Java and dynamic HTML in 1997, etc.), the system was of necessity in contact with both its constituencies: hackers and academics. Academics who work daily with Internet protocols and hardware have strong incentives to keep in contact with communities of experts who specialize in these technologies. This may be particularly useful for those academics modeling themselves on Antonio Gramsci's ideal of the "organic intellectual"—a scholar honestly serving a particular constituency. With the increasing importance of Internet technologies in practically every sphere of life, an organic intellectual who has ongoing contacts with experts on the technical details of the Internet is likely to be more useful to the community that he or she serves.

Cultural studies has skirted the edges of disciplinary positionality while retaining the freedom to negotiate its interests strategically; the English Server has engaged a very similar practice, preserving its academic position while enjoying the relative autonomy made possible by the novelty of its position.

It is hardly revolutionary: it merely spans a gap in conventional publishing. Since it publishes some works with commercial value together with other works which do not fit into contemporary commercial publishers' interests, it is, of necessity, an imperfect compromise. But I would argue that this sort of position offers a certain liberation from the naïve individualism of technophile utopias, while at the same time questioning current corporate publishing norms.

Conclusion: Public Intellectualism

David Noble's assertions (Noble 1998) about the dangers of adopting commercial courseware can act as a wake-up call, but they lead him to a defensive strategy. Rather than engaging with university administrations by offering public and visible alternatives to the emerging commodification of knowledge, Noble withdraws into privacy, keeping his courses offline and limiting their audiences to those he can see in his classroom. One might question how powerful this alternative to corporate commodification might be in persuading university administrators and new faculty to follow his lead.

The practical response I would recommend takes a different course than Noble's. Following Richard Stallman, who argues that open source software is more than merely a marginal alternative to corporate commodification but rather a moral imperative, I would argue that the moral imperative for faculty is a form of public intellectualism that will allow us to broaden support for our interests.

The third option I can see, continuing on our present course, hardly needs much discussion. Continuing upon our present course may well result in a continued diminution in the importance of humanities disciplines, in the United States and elsewhere, and in a consequent impoverishment of the wider culture.

References

Barthes, Roland, "The Death of the Author," 1968, in Philip Rice and Patricia Waugh, eds., *Modern Literary Theory: A Reader*, New York: Edward Arnold, 1989.

Benjamin, Walter, "Unpacking My Library: A Talk about Book Collecting," in *Illuminations: Essays and Reflections*, Hannah Arendt, ed., Harry Zohn, trans. New York: Schocken Books, 1968, pp. 59–67.

Berube, Michael, *The Employment of English: Theory, Jobs and the Future of Literary Studies*. New York: NYU Press, 1998.

Darnton, Robert, *The Business of Enlightenment: A Publishing History of the Encyclopédie 1775–1800*. Cambridge: Harvard University Press, 1979.

Eldred v. Reno, filed in D.C. District Court against Janet Reno in her official capacity, challenging the constitutionality of the 1998 Copyright Term Extension Act. Filed 1/11/99.

Foucault, Michel, "What Is an Author?" in *Textual Strategies: Perspectives in Post-Structuralist Criticism*, Josué V. Harari, ed. Ithaca: Cornell University, 1979, pp. 141–160.

Love, Courtney, "Courtney Love Does the Math," *Salon* (June 14, 2000). Online: http://www.salon.com/tech/feature/2000/06/14/love/

Lyotard, Jean-François, *The Postmodern Condition: A Report on Knowledge*. Minneapolis: University of Minnesota Press, 1984.

Maslen, Geoffrey, "Rupert Murdoch Joins with 18 Universities in Distance-Education Venture," *The Chronicle of Higher Education*, Wednesday, May 17, 2000. Online: http://chronicle.com/free/2000/05/2000051701u.htm

Masley, Ed, "Playing on Discord," *Pittsburgh Post-Gazette* (May 31, 2000), p. D1.

Negroponte, Nicholas, *Being Digital*. New York: Alfred A. Knopf, 1995.

Nelson, Cary, *Manifesto of a Tenured Radical*. New York: NYU Press, 1997.

Noble, David F., "Digital Diploma Mills: The Automation of Higher Education," *First Monday,* vol. 3, no. 1. Online: http://www.firstmonday.dk/issues/issue3_1/noble/index.html

Vonnegut, Kurt, *Player Piano*. New York: Scribner's, 1952.

WebCT, "Marketing Support for RealEducation Partners." Marketing brochure, 1999.

WebCT, "RealEducation Raises $15 Million to Build Online Campuses for Colleges, Universities & Corporations." Press release, January 12, 1999.

WebCT, "Take a Shortcut to Putting Your College or University Online." Marketing brochure, 1999.

chapter

11 The Red Escolar Project Considered As an Online Community

by Walter Aprile, walter@raingod.com, and Teresa Vazquez Mantecón, tvazquez@ilce.edu.mx

This chapter describes one particular educational online community serving over one and a half million students, the Red Escolar project in the Mexican state school system. This project is intended to complement, rather than substitute for, traditional teaching methods. The chapter describes the current status and future plans of Red Escolar, and points to some aspects that can be improved as well as to aspects that work as well as planned.

A Brief Description of Red Escolar

The Red Escolar project is a technology outreach effort aimed at improving the quality of the teacher and student experience in the Mexican state school system. Red Escolar (which means "school net" or "school network") currently includes 3,000 schools, for an approximate total of 1,500,000 students and 2,000 teachers all over Mexico. The project was started in 1997 by ILCE (Instituto Latinoamericano de la Comunicación Educativa), a publicly funded international institution that has four decades of experience in distance learning.

Our activity extends as well outside the geographical borders of Mexico: a small but growing number of schools in other countries have enrolled. In particular, some U.S. schools that serve a Mexican-American student population are attracted by the availability of teaching material in Spanish.

We operate by equipping the schools with the *aula de medios*, a basic multimedia and Internet room consisting of several PCs (at least one for forty students: students, working in couples, enjoy at least three hours per week of access), a printer, a modem, and a local network.

Three hours are not a lot of time, but enough for the purposes of the project, which are, as we will show, *supplementing traditional education, not supplanting it*.

Another very important piece of equipment that we install in every school is the Edusat system, consisting of a dish antenna, a receiver, a decoder, a VCR, and a TV set. Mexico owns one digital broadcast satellite with ten channels (Satmex 1) dedicated solely to broadcasting educational TV. ILCE produces content for four channels 24 hours a day and seven days a week, DGTVE (Direccion General de Televisión Educativa) handles four more, while the remaining two are dedicated respectively to retransmitting in real time all of the Discovery Kids Channel and Jugando con Clase (a Brazilian education channel).

One teacher in every school is trained to maintain the equipment and resolve small problems; for bigger difficulties, we provide on-site assistance. The Red Escolar project employs 50 people in Mexico City (where most content production happens); on the other hand, each State has a staff of at least two, dedicated to the diffusion and running of the Red Escolar project on a local basis. Red Escolar is thus a fairly *light* project, both at the school level (it does not take over the school) and as an organization.

Integration with Face-to-Face Education

Our project is not a substitute for face-to-face education; rather the intended aim is to augment and enhance the student and teacher experience in the school. Red Escolar provides stand-alone content (like CD-ROMs and digital library material) and communication-centered projects, together with suggestions on how to integrate both into classwork.

Most of our modules are meant to last for some weeks, the idea being that the teacher in the field will decide to use Red Escolar in teaching a particular section of his course. Some projects, like *Como ves*, are permanent.

Red Escolar operates mainly in two modes: Proyecto Colaborativo (collaboration project) and Circulo de Aprenti-zaje (learning circle).

Collaboration Projects

Collaboration projects are one of the main modes of operation of the project; they allow a large number of schools, students, and professors to take part in discovery and research activities. They are Web based, with participants typically numbering in the thousands. Collaboration projects center on a well-defined theme (for instance, the Monarch butterfly, or volcanoes, or Protected Natural Areas in Mexico). The main feature is collaboration (in the form of discussion, results sharing, and document writing) between teams in different schools.

Some collaboration projects have a tightly paced development, comprising from four to eight "phases," each one lasting one week. In these projects the participants are supposed to perform the same activities or research the same topics at the same time. This type of project is particularly appropriate for schools and professors that are newcomers to Red Escolar, since it provides a maximum of handholding and eases the transition into the new activity.

Other projects like *Como ves* last one school year: the professor may use only part of the materials, or work through the whole course at his own pace.

Many collaboration projects employ weekly Edusat programs to provide yet another form of interaction: the broadcasts touch upon common problems and occasionally present an expert.

Learning Circles

Learning circles are another type of interaction within the Red Escolar project. They comprise six to nine schools that choose to work for six weeks on a common theme. Heavy use is made of a mailing list (currently hosted at ILCE) in order to produce a final document.

Learning circles allow the Red Escolar participants to choose the themes of discussion. Every circle has a moderator; while at the beginning the moderator was an employee of ILCE, currently most moderators are professors in the field.

The Digital Library

The Red Escolar Digital Library (Biblioteca Digital) is being developed in collaboration with the Universidad Nacional Autónoma de México. It contains already several hundred electronic texts. Some of them have been produced by Red Escolar students and professors, while others are works of literature and science published by the Fondo de Cultura Economomica.

All these texts are indexed and searchable. Along with them, we index for our users certain other external document bases, such as *Cervantes Virtual*.

Teacher Training

Initial teacher training is largely face-to-face, while subsequent courses are imparted via the Internet and Edusat satellite broadcasts. While initial face-to-face training concentrates on the use and application of the Red Escolar media room, subsequent courses touch on basic computer skills, lesson planning, and tasks like moderating mailing lists.

Means of Interaction within Red Escolar

In order to understand the nature of the Red Escolar online community, we will now examine in some detail the means whereby the Red Escolar community interacts.

Email

Email can be considered the *killer application* of the Internet. This was probably truer in the past, before the growing importance of the World Wide Web; all the same, it remains true that email is a low-bandwidth, symmetric, asynchronous communication tool of great importance.

Our teachers and students delight in the possibility of communicating at their own pace with colleagues all over the country. Let us not forget that Mexico is a big country where travel is slow or expensive.

Currently, we do not provide our users with email accounts: instead, we rely on the Internet provider (be it local or nationwide). This is proving to be a bad choice, both because of poor customer service and because usually Internet service providers give only one mailbox per Internet account, which is clearly not enough.

We have an ongoing project (discussed later on) to provide one mailbox per user on our servers. This is going to be a large-scale effort, since we expect a massive growth in the user base: design and management of email systems with tens of thousands of users are not trivial, if only because of the congestion and help-desk issues.

Forums

All of our collaboration projects have at least one associated Web-based forum. On some projects we have more than one active forum at the time. The discussion in the forum is led by a moderator, who is usually the same person who designed the collaboration project. The forum does not wander freely; discussion is usually focused on a particular theme. Moderation is *post hoc*—moderators are given a Web form that allows them to erase messages at will.

To make more visible a change of subject (and rein in stragglers who may ignore moderation notices), forums are usually "frozen" once per week or per fortnight. This means that the Red Escolar staff saves the current messages, write-protects them, and presents to the user a fresh "new" forum. Saved messages are kept on line for reference.

At the end of a project it is customary to review the whole forum (which can have collected anywhere between 100 and 2,000 postings) and distill it into a somewhat more accessible digest called a Memoria de Proyecto (project memory).

The current forum system does not scale well, because it is based on invoking CGI programs by the Web server and updating various flat files in the server file system. We currently plan to move the forums under the old but extremely practical Network News system, which has the vast advantage of being distributable and easily accommodating growth. The move will not be without pain for the users that will have to learn a new interface; luckily current News clients (like the ones integrated into Netscape Navigator and Microsoft's Internet Explorer) are quite user friendly. The difficulties will probably be on the conceptual side, that is to say in easing the user transition from a central, Web-centric forum system to a distributed hierarchical newsgroup architecture such as Network News. In Network News postings propagate (quite slowly) through the Net and reside on servers close to the user. The system also allows for the creation of local interest groups.

Mailing Lists

The learning circles make heavy use of mailing lists (currently there are about 300 of them). Mailing lists are very easy to set up and close down, and they can be managed by an outside moderator. Also, being an email application, they are very easy on bandwidth and do not require a high-quality connection: a message can be several hours late and nothing bad happens. At least for now the mailing lists are hosted on one of our central servers, a high-capacity Sun computer system.

In the future, we will probably decentralize the mailing lists, encouraging State Technology Centers to maintain their own locally managed mailing lists.

Chat

We do not make very heavy use of real-time chats, mostly because they imply a synchronous communication model, which does not fit in very well with the way in which Red Escolar integrates itself with face-to-face class work. Nonetheless certain projects, particularly *Cuéntame*, have made use of Microsoft Comic Chat in the past.

Difficulties with the program, mostly concerning its instability, have prompted us to move to a vastly better solution, namely the LambdaMOO server system, a generic, object-oriented server that can be used both as a very flexible chat system and as a simulation tool. We are happy to report that the users did not experience major difficulties in transitioning to LambdaMOO, which they access through a generic MUD client.

Probably in the future we will get around the need for a stand-alone MUD client (with its attendant installation and configuration difficulties) by providing a Java client applet, embedded in the project Web pages.

Magazine, Phone Calls, Visits

It should not be forgotten that Red Escolar also employs "traditional" means of interaction:

- We publish a quarterly magazine for teachers, used for proposing new ways of teaching and reporting on projects.
- Low-tech as it may sound, we answer phone calls—in fact a whole office within Red Escolar provides phone assistance for computer-related problems, and frequently our pedagogy experts front calls from teachers in the field.
- Lastly, we occasionally visit schools, both to get a better understanding of the environment where Red Escolar operates and to motivate the Mexico City personnel. These face-to-face encounters also help to reinforce the community ties within Red Escolar.

Joining Red Escolar

Schools hear about the Red Escolar project in the media or at teachers' meetings. Enrollment in the project usually takes some months, since it entails establishing the mutual commitment of ILCE and the candidate school, preparing the media room, equipping it and training the local "media room steward," a professor who knows the basic operation of PC systems.

Requisites

The school is asked to provide a protected environment for the Red Escolar hardware. This usually boils down to a room with barred windows and an adequate power connection. Additional requirements exist for the installation of the Edusat dish antenna.

The local Parents' Association usually commits to equipping the classroom *una tantum* and providing monthly consumables (paper, toner, diskettes, and phone charges).

We estimate consumables to cost approximately $200 U.S. per month: offloading this cost onto the students' families (for a typical fee of 20 cents per student per month) both relieves the school and gives a sense of ownership to the families. We have observed that a sense of ownership soon turns into equipment stewardship, an important concern in marginal areas.

Notice that the Red Escolar equipment initiative addresses public schools and, except for the consumables, comes at no cost for the school and the students' families.

Getting In

Once the school has completed the enrollment project, it gets a Red Escolar ID, which allows tracking of project participation and eases the task of identifying the school in problem reports. Along with the hardware comes a collection of educational CDs and videotapes.

Schools are encouraged to participate in the Internet-based activities; however, the vagaries of Internet connectivity often force the schools to fall back on the locally available CDs, tapes and Edusat broadcasts.

The Red Escolar Community Environment

The Red Escolar community environment is inhabited basically by three kinds of people: the users in the field, the moderators who work at ILCE in Mexico City, and the administrators (basically technical staff). The community interacts in various ways: broadcast, one-to-one, and in groups. Interaction also employs a variety of methods, low and high-tech.

What Is a Red Escolar User?

From a naive point of view, a Red Escolar user is either a student or a professor. On the other hand, in our model the students work in couples (and at times in groups of three) on the same machine. The school as a whole has a Red Escolar ID, but the single person within the school has not. Students and professors may acquire a personal identity by getting an email address by means outside Red Escolar (such as freenets or services akin to Hotmail), but not all do so.

Use of the Red Escolar ID is not authenticated, and since most Internet service providers use dynamic IP number assignment, we cannot do domain or subnet-based authentication.

So, in the standard setup, we have one or a few email addresses for the whole school—and currently no means of enforcing individual (or, for the matter, school) identity within the Red Escolar system. Currently we believe the user's declaration of identity when he signs his contribution to the mailing list or the forum. So far our trust has very rarely been abused.

On the other hand, we are conscious of the weakness of this model. We are going to provide within the current year free email accounts to all that request them (as a way of allowing individual and private communication). The new model, based on the Linux operating system, allows for authentication of the individual school connection (using DynDNS software) and of the single user within the school.

Current technology could allow us to establish an identity system where one user of Red Escolar corresponds to exactly one individual person in real life: it still remains to be seen whether such stricture is actually useful or productive in an education environment. At the very least, a space for anonymity should be provided—for example, for the public discussion of sensitive issues.

This somewhat fuzzy plural identity, combined with the fact that the student group works under teacher supervision, explains why certain discussion forums that touch upon "sensitive" issues, like women's rights or democracy, seem to elicit mostly stereotypical answers; the group mind, as it were, will not stray far from the "acceptable" path. As Nuria de Alva, one of the Red Escolar staff, puts it, "The student internalizes the *must-be.*"

Authority

Authority exerts itself in Red Escolar in many ways: two of the most visible are the publishing decisions on our main Web site, and the moderator's actions in the forums. Regarding the first, our objective is to enable the professor in the field (and his pupils) to independently publish the materials they produce. On the forums, we would like to make moderation easier and to make forum creation, archiving, and deletion more efficient.

Three steps toward the delegation of Web publishing authority

To reach this empowerment goal, we have planned three steps: currently we are at Step 2.

Step 1: publish everything. The Red Escolar project encourages decentralization: we publish large quantities of material produced by the participant schools, and encourage World Wide Web publishing efforts.

In the past, we used to publish everything that was sent to us, even material which would not be considered an example of good Web design. The reason for our laxness was that, for the professors in the field, to be published is in itself a reward. This allowed us to fortify the project and build enthusiasm.

Step 2: quality counts. Currently we are not publishing all user-generated material: Web pages go through a graphic design and usability review, Word files are carefully turned into Web pages and all information is checked for accuracy and copyright issues.

All these activities take up a lot of resources, which explains why we are rejecting material that does not have good academic quality or comes in an inconvenient format. For example, PowerPoint presentations may look very impressive on screen but require an inordinate amount of work to be turned into usable Web pages.

Step 3: local publishing and filtering. As professors in the field become more and more technology savvy, we would like to see a move toward more "local" publishing. In other words, we hope that schools will build and operate their own Web servers under their responsibility.

In fact, we consider our collaboration projects as *training wheels* that will eventually push the teacher to publish directly his own training material. To accomplish that, we already provide a minimal HTML editing and Web publishing course.

Forum Moderation

As observed before, the moderators act *post hoc.* Their actions have two main aims:

- Deleting messages deemed inappropriate either because they contain disruptive content or because they were meant for another forum, and
- Steering the discussion, keeping it on the subject.

Users of any kind of forum system are familiar with the phenomenon of topic drift, in which discussion threads wander very far from the starting subject and from the subjects specified in the forum charter. This is not a problem for social forums and for situations where the readers enjoy good bandwidth and are highly computer literate, but for the Red Escolar context it is disastrous, since messages take a significant amount of time to download.

A typical forum sees several hundred new messages per week. A forum subject usually lasts from two to three weeks, and the moderator must review every message as soon as possible. We estimate that message reviewing and editing ties up half of the workday. Upon request from the moderator, the Red Escolar staff freezes the forum, preventing further contribution and commentary to the existent message set. Frozen forums are kept available for on-line reading.

Naturally moderators moderate at their own pace and may differ in their definition of "on topic." To make the forums into more useful resources, we are going to introduce more stringent moderation policy. This is analogous to the second of the three steps introduced above, because it fosters contribution quality. Our third step for the forums will be to enable the school community and groups of school to create their own, autonomously moderated, discussion spaces.

The User's Point of View

Users take part enthusiastically, and we think that the bottleneck in user participation is equipment availability.

The Administrator's Point of View

From the system administrator's viewpoint, the current forum system means a minimal load for the server (the combined traffic of all the forums remains below one message per minute), but a lot of administration work. Since we are using a simplistic piece of software for our forums, setup, freezing, archiving, and in general manipulating the message base is getting increasingly complex. Our current forum software (Matt Wright's WWWBoard) is not built upon a database and actually does not maintain a consistent index of messages: its only concern is with the HTML presentation.

Our proposed replacement is a Network News implementation that might be called a mini-USENET. Particularly at the school level it depends critically upon the adoption of Linux as a server operating system.

Designing for Growth

Linux evangelists declare without qualms that their objective is to take over the world. More modestly, we would like to reach every public primary and secondary school in Mexico. This would imply enrolling several tens of thousands of schools in the Red Escolar project. The funding and organizational problems are obvious; perhaps less obvious is the system architecture problem.

Currently Red Escolar depends critically on a single WWW site, physically residing in Mexico City on the ILCE premises. While the current server is holding up well to traffic and will foreseeably keep doing so for at least another two years, we would like to decentralize our architecture for two reasons:

■ empowerment of state technology centers
■ robustness

Our requirement for a robust architecture that promotes technological developments at the state level is well met by a design developed by Arturo Espinosa, Jose Chacón, and Miguel Ibarra, of the Universidad Nacional Autonoma de Mexico, during a placement with us. This design, well described and documented at http://redescolar.linux.org.mx/, is based on a tree structure with regional servers (usually at the state level) and local server (at the school level). The servers run Web server and proxy caching software, a Network News server, a mail server and DNS. All services are redundant, and the structure allows for easy growth up to millions of users.

This design is based on some fairly traditional concepts derived from USENET; in fact it might be called a mini-USENET. Particularly at the school level it depends critically on the adoption of Linux as a server operating system.

Linux on the School Server

Linux, due to its Open Source nature, fits the bill for a server operating system for the Red Escolar project. We can (and in fact the aforementioned group of researchers did) develop our own custom distribution so that it supports both our current architecture and the new tree design. Its robustness and its fitness for remote administration (even via a telephone line) will allow us to offer the schools a Linux server as an administration-free black box of services.

The server will run a Dynamic DNS server that registers the school name with a regional server as soon as an IP connection is obtained. The school administration will be able to give a local mailbox to every student and professor in the school. Miguel Ibarra developed both the DynDNS server and a simplified application for creating and destroying accounts in batches.

Easy availability of a local World Wide Web server will stimulate the publication of local material, while the presence of a Network News server will facilitate the creation and management of local and regional newsgroups (in Network News parlance, forums with a subject and a charter).

Lessons Learned

The Red Escolar project is still operating at the time of writing; that is why we would prefer to speak of "lessons learned" rather than conclusions. The main point we have learned is that it is possible to do distance education despite scarcity of means, if the project is supported by a committed and voluntary user base. Red Escolar is the people in the schools, and their desire to teach and learn better.

Second, we have learned that certain technological choices (in our case distributing multimedia CDs) can unintentionally lock a project into a certain technological context (in our case Microsoft Windows software).

Third, when designing on the scale of Red Escolar, hardware and software obsolescence must be taken into account; luckily some new technologies may breathe new life into old metal.

Last, even though outsourcing the communication infrastructure (in our case to various Internet providers) is economically attractive, the resulting lack of control may reduce efficiency and lead to high support costs.

We believe that the Red Escolar project can be used as a blueprint for technology outreach and distance education initiatives in developing countries. It is our, and ILCE's, mandate to assist such initiatives.

12 The Free Universal Encyclopedia and Learning Resource
by Richard Stallman

The World Wide Web has the potential to develop into a universal encyclopedia covering all areas of knowledge, and a complete library of instructional courses. This outcome could happen without any special effort, if no one interferes. But corporations are mobilizing now to direct the future down a different track—one in which they control and restrict access to learning materials, so as to extract money from people who want to learn.

To ensure that the Web develops toward the best and most natural outcome, where it becomes a free encyclopedia, we must make a conscious effort to prevent deliberate sequestration of the encyclopedic and educational information on the Net. We cannot stop business from restricting the information it makes available; what we can do is provide an alternative. We need to launch a movement to develop a universal free encyclopedia, much as the Free Software movement gave us the free software operating system GNU/Linux. The free encyclopedia will provide an alternative to the restricted ones that media corporations will write.

The rest of this article aims to lay out what the free encyclopedia needs to do, what sort of freedoms it needs to give the public, and how we can get started on developing it.

An Encyclopedia Located Everywhere

In the past, encyclopedias have been written under the direction of a single organization, which made all decisions about the content, and have been published in a centralized fashion. It would not make sense to develop and publish the free encyclopedia in those ways—they fit poorly with the nature of the World Wide Web and with the resources available for writing the encyclopedia.

The free encyclopedia will not be published in any one place. It will consist of all Web pages that cover suitable topics, and have been made suitably available. These pages will be developed in a decentralized manner by thousands of contributors, each independently writing articles and posting them on various Web servers. No one organization will be in charge, because such centralization would be incompatible with decentralized progress.

Who Will Write the Encyclopedia?

In principle, anyone is welcome to write articles for the encyclopedia. But as we reach out for people to help, the most promising places to look are among teachers and students. Teachers generally like to teach, and writing an article a year for the encyclopedia would be an enjoyable change from their classroom duties. For students, a major school paper could become an encyclopedia article, if done especially well.

Small Steps Will Do the Job

When a project is exciting, it is easy to imagine a big contribution that you would like to make, bite off more than you can chew, and ultimately give up with nothing to show for it.

So it is important to welcome and encourage smaller contributions. Writing a textbook for a whole semester's material is a big job, and only a small fraction of teachers will contribute that much. But writing about a topic small enough for one meeting of a class is a contribution that many can afford to make. Enough of these small contributions can cover the whole range of knowledge.

Take the Long View

The encyclopedia is a big job, and it won't be finished in a year. If it takes twenty years to complete the free encyclopedia, that will be but an instant in the history of literature and civilization.

In projects like this, progress is slow for the first few years; then it accelerates as the work that has been done attracts more and more people to join in. Eventually there is an avalanche of progress. So we should not feel discouraged when the first few years do not bring us close to completion. It makes sense to choose the first steps to illustrate what can be done, and to spread interest in the long-term goal, so as to inspire others to join in.

This means that the pioneers' job, in the early years, is above all to be steadfast. We must be on guard against downgrading to a less useful, less idealistic goal, just because of the magnitude of the task. Instead of measuring our early steps against the size of the whole job, we should think of them as examples, and have confidence that they will inspire a growing number of contributors to join and finish the job.

Evangelize

Since we hope that teachers and students at many colleges around the world will join in writing contributions to the free encyclopedia, let's not leave this to chance. There are already scattered examples of what can be done. Let's present these examples systematically to the academic community, show the vision of the free universal encyclopedia, and invite others to join in writing it.

What Should the Free Encyclopedia Contain?

The free encyclopedia should aim eventually to include one or more articles for any topic you would expect to find in another encyclopedia. In addition, since there is no practical limit to the amount of encyclopedic material that can be on the Web, this encyclopedia should eventually also cover the more advanced and specialized topics you might expect to find in specialized encyclopedias, such as an "Encyclopedia of Physics," "Encyclopedia of Medicine," "Encyclopedia of Gardening," or "Encyclopedia of Cooking." It could go even further; for example, bird watchers might eventually contribute an article on each species of bird, along with pictures and recordings of its calls.

However, only some kinds of information belong in an encyclopedia. For example, scholarly papers, detailed statistical databases, news reports, fiction and art, extensive bibliographies, and catalogs of merchandise, useful as they are, are outside the scope of an encyclopedia. (Some of the articles might usefully contain links to such works.)

Courses in the learning resource are a generalization to hypertext of the textbooks used for teaching a subject to yourself or to a class. The learning resource should eventually include courses for all academic subjects, from mathematics to art history, and practical subjects such as gardening as well, to the extent this makes sense. (Some practical subjects, such as massage or instrumental ensemble playing, may not be possible to study from a "book" without a human teacher—these are arguably less useful to include.) It should cover these subjects at all the levels that are useful, which might in some cases range from first grade to graduate school.

A useful encyclopedia article will address a specific topic at a particular level, and each author will contribute mainly by focusing on an area that he or she knows very well. But we should keep in the back of our minds, while doing this, the vision of a free encyclopedia that is universal in scope—so that we can firmly reject any attempt to put artificial limits on either the scope or the free status of the encyclopedia.

Criteria Pages Must Meet

To ensure this encyclopedia is indeed a free and universal encyclopedia, we must set criteria of freeness for encyclopedia articles and courses to meet.

Conventional non-free encyclopedias published by companies such as Microsoft will surely be made available on the Web, sooner or later—but you will probably have to pay to read an article, and you surely won't be allowed to redistribute them. If we are content with knowledge as a commodity, accessible only through a computerized bureaucracy, we can simply let companies provide it.

But if we want to keep human knowledge open and freely available to humanity, we have to do the work to make it available that way. We have to write a free encyclopedia—so we must first determine the proper interpretation of "free" for an encyclopedia on the Internet. We must decide what criteria of freedom a free encyclopedia and a free learning resource should meet.

Permit Universal Access

The free encyclopedia should be open to public access by everyone who can gain access to the Web. Those who seek to gain control over educational materials, so they can profit by restricting access to them, will push us to "compromise" by agreeing to restrict access in exchange for their participation. We must stand firm, and reject any deal that is inconsistent with the ultimate goal. We are in no hurry, and there is no sense in getting to the wrong place a few years sooner.

Permit Mirror Sites

When information is available on the Web only at one site, its availability is vulnerable. A local problem—a computer crash, an earthquake or flood, a budget cut, a change in policy of the school administration—could cut off access for everyone forever. To guard against loss of the encyclopedia's material, we should make sure that every piece of the encyclopedia is available from many sites on the Internet, and that new copies can be put up if some disappear.

There is no need to set up an organization or a bureaucracy to do this, because Internet users like to set up "mirror sites" which hold duplicate copies of interesting Web pages. What we must do in advance is ensure that this is legally permitted.

Therefore, each encyclopedia article and each course should explicitly grant irrevocable permission for anyone to make verbatim copies available on mirror sites. This permission should be one of the basic stated principles of the free encyclopedia.

Some day there may be systematic efforts to ensure that each article and course is replicated in many copies—perhaps at least once on each of the six inhabited continents. This would be a natural extension of the mission of archiving that libraries undertake today. But it would be premature to make formal plans for this now. It is sufficient for now to resolve to make sure people have permission to do this mirroring when they get around to it.

Permit Translation into Other Languages

People will have a use for encyclopedia material on each topic in every human language. But the primary language of the Internet—as of the world of commerce and science today—is English. Most likely, encyclopedia contributions in English will run ahead of other languages, and the encyclopedia will approach completeness in English first.

Trying to fight this tendency would be self-defeating. The easier way to make the encyclopedia available in all languages is by encouraging one person to translate what another has written. In this way, each article can be translated into many languages.

But if this requires explicit permission, it will be too difficult. Therefore, we must adopt a basic rule that anyone is permitted to publish an accurate translation of any article or course, with proper attribution. Each article and each course should carry a statement giving permission for translations.

To ensure accuracy of translation, the author of the original should reserve the right to insist on corrections in a translation. A translator should perhaps have to give the original author a reasonable amount of time to do this, perhaps three months, before publishing the translation in the first place. After that, the translator should continue to make corrections at the author's request, whenever the author asks for them.

In time, as the number of people involved in encyclopedia activity increases, contributors may form Translation Accuracy Societies for various languages, which undertake to ensure the accuracy of translations into those languages. An author could then designate a Translation Accuracy Society to check and correct a certain translation of a certain work. It may be wise to keep the Translation Accuracy Societies separate from the actual translators, so that each translation will be checked by someone other than the translator.

Permit Quotation with Attribution

Each encyclopedia article or course should permit anyone to quote arbitrary portions in another encyclopedia article or course, provided proper attribution is given. This will make it possible to build on the work others have done, without the need to completely replace it.

Different authors may—if they care—set different rules for what constitutes proper attribution to them; that is O.K. As long as the rules set for a particular work are not unreasonable or impractical, they will cause no problem.

Permit Modified Versions of Courses

Courses must evolve, and the original authors won't keep working on them forever. And teachers will want to adapt course materials to their own curriculum plans and teaching methods. Since courses will typically be large (like a textbook today), it would be unacceptably wasteful to tell teachers, "Write your own from scratch, if you want to change this."

Therefore, modifying an existing course must be permitted; each course should carry a statement giving permission to publish a modified version.

It makes sense to require modified versions to carry proper attribution giving credit to the authors of the previous version, and to be labeled clearly as modified, so that there is no confusion about whose views they present.

Permit Modified Versions of Pictures and Videos, for Courses

Pictures and videos, both drawn and photographic, will play an important role in many courses. Modifying these pictures and videos will be pedagogically useful. For example, you could crop a picture to focus attention on a certain feature, or circle or label particular features. Using false color can help make certain aspects easier to see. Image enhancement is also possible.

Beyond that, an altered version of a picture could illustrate a different but related idea. You could start with a diagram useful for one theorem in geometry, and add to it, to produce a diagram that is relevant to another theorem.

Permission to modify pictures and videos is particularly important because the alternative, to make your own picture or video from scratch, is often very hard. It is not terribly hard to write your own text, to convey certain facts from your own angle, but doing the same thing with a picture is not feasible.

Of course, modified versions of pictures and videos should be labeled as modified, to prevent misattribution of their contents, and should give credit properly to the original.

Only Free Software in the Encyclopedia

Articles, and especially courses, will often include software—for example, to display a simulation of a chemical reaction, or teach you how often to stir a sauce so it won't burn. To ensure that the encyclopedia is indeed free, all software included in articles and courses should meet the criteria of free software (http://www.gnu.org/philosophy/free-sw.html) and open source software (http://www.opensource.org).

No Central Control

People often suggest that "quality control" is essential for an encyclopedia, and ask what sort of "governing board" will decide which articles to accept as part of the free encyclopedia. The answer is, "No one." We cannot afford to let anyone have such control.

If the free encyclopedia is a success, it will become so ubiquitous and important that we dare not allow any organization to decide what counts as part of it. This organization would have too much power; people would seek to politicize or corrupt it, and could easily succeed.

The only solution to that problem is not to have any such organization, and reject the idea of centralized quality control. Instead, we should let everyone decide. If a Web page is about a suitable topic, and meets the criteria for an article, then we can consider it an article. If a page meets the criteria for a course, then we can consider it a course.

But what if some pages are erroneous, or even deceptive? We cannot assume this won't happen. But the corrective is for other articles to point out the error. Instead of having "quality control" by one privileged organization, we will have review by various groups, which will earn respect by their own policies and actions. In a world where no one is infallible, this is the best we can do.

Encourage Peer Review and Endorsements

There will be no single organization in charge of what to include in the encyclopedia or the learning resource, no one that can be lobbied to exclude "creation science" or holocaust denial (or, by the same token, lobbied to exclude evolution or the history of Nazi death camps). Where there is controversy, multiple views will be represented. So it will be useful for readers to be able to see who endorses or has reviewed a given article's version of the subject.

In fields such as science, engineering, and history, there are formal standards of peer review. We should encourage authors of articles and courses to seek peer review, both through existing formal scholarly mechanisms, and through the informal mechanism of asking respected names in the field for permission to cite their endorsement in the article or course.

A peer-review endorsement applies to one version of a work, not to modified versions. Therefore, when a course has peer-review endorsements, it should require anyone who publishes a modified version of the course to remove the endorsements. (The author of the modified version would be free to seek new endorsements for that version.)

No Catalogue, Yet

When the encyclopedia is well populated, catalogues will be very important. But we should not try to address the issue of cataloguing now, because it is premature. What we need this year and for the coming years is to write articles. Once we have them, once we have a large number of volunteers producing a large number of articles, that will be the time to catalogue them. At that time, enough people will be interested in the encyclopedia to provide the manpower to do the work.

Since no one organization will be in charge of the encyclopedia, there cannot be one authoritative catalogue. Instead, anyone will be free to make a catalogue, just as anyone is free to provide peer review. Cataloguers will gain respect according to their decisions.

Encyclopedia pages will surely be listed in ordinary Web search sites, and perhaps those are the only catalogues that will be needed. But true catalogues should permit redistribution, translation, and modification—that is, the criteria for courses should apply to catalogues as well. To start off, we will use http://www.gnu.org/encyclopedia for this.

What can usefully be done from the beginning is to report new encyclopedia articles to a particular site, which can record their names as raw material for real catalogues, whenever people start to write them.

Making Links to Other Pages

The last and most important rule for pages in the encyclopedia is the exclusionary rule:

> If a page on the Web covers subject matter that ought to be in the encyclopedia or the course library, but its license is too restricted to qualify, we must not make links to it from encyclopedia articles or from courses.

This rule will make sure we respect our own rules, in the same way that the exclusionary rule for evidence is supposed to make police respect their own rules: by not allowing us to treat work which fails to meet the criteria as if it did meet them.

The idea of the World Wide Web is that links tie various separate pages into a larger whole. So when encyclopedia articles or courses link to a certain page, those links effectively make the page part of the encyclopedia. To claim otherwise would be self-deception. If we are to take seriously the criteria set forth above, or any criteria whatsoever, we have to base our actions on them, by not incorporating a page into our network of pages if it doesn't fit the criteria.

When a topic ought to be covered in the encyclopedia or with a course, but it isn't, we must make sure we don't forget that we have a gap. The exclusionary rule will remind us. Each time we think of making a link to the unacceptable page, and we stop because of the exclusionary rule, that will remind us that someone ought to write another page about the same topic—one that is free enough to be part of the encyclopedia. Eventually, one of us will do the job.

On the other hand, many Web pages cover material that wouldn't normally be included in an encyclopedia—for example, scholarly papers, detailed statistical databases, news reports, fiction and art, extensive bibliographies, and catalogs of merchandise. Such pages, regardless of whether they are free enough to be in the encyclopedia, are outside its scope. They do not represent gaps in the encyclopedia. So there is no need to apply the encyclopedia criteria in making links to such pages.

To produce a complete encyclopedia that satisfies the principles of freedom stated here will take a long time, but we will get it done eventually—as long as we remember the goal. The greatest danger is that we will lose sight of the goal and settle for less. The exclusionary rule will make sure we keep going all the way.

Uphold the Freedom to Contribute

As education moves online and is increasingly commercialized, teachers are in danger of losing even the right to make their work freely available to the public. Some universities have tried to claim ownership over online materials produced by teachers, to turn it into commercial "courseware" with restricted use. Meanwhile, other universities have outsourced their online services to corporations, some of which claim to own all materials posted on the university Web sites.

It will be up to professors to resist this tendency. But there is more than one way to do so. The most obvious basis for objection is to say, "I own this work, and I, not the university, have the right to sell it to a company if I wish." But that places the faculty on the same selfish moral level as the university, so that neither side has a moral advantage in the argument.

If, on the other hand, professors say, "I want to be able to make my work fully available to the public without restriction," they occupy the commanding moral position, which a university can oppose only by setting itself against the public, against learning, and against scholarship.

Resisting the selling of the university will not be easy. Professors had better make use of any advantage they can find—especially moral advantages.

Two other points that will help are that (1) a few prestigious universities will probably gobble up most of the commercial business, so other universities would be deluding themselves to think they can really get a great deal of funds from selling themselves, and (2) business is likely to drive even the elite universities out of the most lucrative parts of the field.

Spread the Word

When you post a potential encyclopedia article or a course, you can reference this plan if you wish, to help spread the word and inspire others to help.

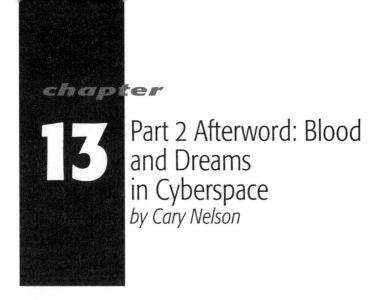

13 Part 2 Afterword: Blood and Dreams in Cyberspace
by Cary Nelson

It is easy enough to give the Burn Web site at the University of California at San Diego (burn.ucsd.edu) a political designation. It is a leftwing Web site in every respect. It is less easy to characterize the mix of discontinuous and tightly knit communities the site has brought together. For the Colombian Left—caught between a repressive military, the U.S. Congress, the reach of global capitalism, and a vicious drug culture—the site has been a means to communicate with a wider public not always much inclined to hear an unofficial point of view. For students and faculty at UC San Diego and across the world the site is a way not only to participate in world affairs but also a historical archive. The site is simultaneously a venue for activism and an object of ongoing study. Burn's subdirectories range from entries for contemporary political groups to historical exhibitions. There is a powerful exhibit of photographs and drawings about the 1945 bombings of Hiroshima and Nagasaki, a site devoted to the anti-Nazi collage artist John Heartfield, and a collection of posters from the student rebellion in Paris in May 1968. There is also an exhibit of posters from the 1936–1939 Spanish Civil War. It was the Spanish Civil War exhibit that first drew me to the Burn site in 1999. I left the site without discovering anything else about it. That day I was surfing the past, not the present.

More contemporary Burn sites include Scott Sady's Web site (http://burn.ucsd.edu/~ssady/) about the "people, politics, land, and culture of Chiapas, Mexico," illustrated with stunning color photographs, and the "Mid-Atlantic Infoshop," billed as "your guide to anarchy on the web" (http://burn.ucsd.edu/~mai). The site for the FARC-EP (*Las Fuerzas Armadas Revolucionarias de Colombia Ejercito del Pueblo*) is but one link up from the UCSD Food Co-op's site. A bulletin board provides for long-running debates about contemporary social and political issues.

People use the Burn Web site to disseminate information and to receive it. Others study the site itself as a model of plural modes of communication in the new millennium. Intelligence agencies are interested not only in what is on the site but in who uses it. For some time the site provided the only way to counteract false stories printed in newspapers. Getting the word out can segue into a matter of life and death. For others Burn is an occasional curiosity. For some the site is a threat to their profits. The site is at once a direct form of political action and an object of disinterested analysis. It is used by faculty and students, used in conjunction with classes, and used by spies and capitalists and revolutionaries. Its university location provides a degree of protection and independence for some of its users.

In June 2000 all this activity came to a halt. The site had run afoul of some of UCSD's corporate and political partners and allies, some of the same folks who profit from investments in Colombia's cultural and political struggles. In any event, following contacts and conversations about which we are not likely to find out a great deal, a UCSD administrator contacted the head of the Communication Department and directed that Burn be shut down. Instead of taking a firm stand on academic freedom, the department head regrettably complied. I met with UCSD faculty members Susan Davis and Dan Schiller two days later, and they reported that UCSD had already received 650 emails protesting the decision. Meanwhile a UCSD student organization—the Groundwork Collective—put up a mirror of the Burn site almost immediately.

Faced with a major protest, the Communication faculty did what faculty are destined to do. They met and proposed forming a committee. There was, after all, much to decide and adjudicate before deciding whether or not to accept responsibility for the site again. Who should have the right to post messages on a university-sponsored site? What aims are acceptable and not acceptable for Burn projects? Should academics be *virtually* assisting revolutionaries? Should people outside the university community be free to decide what to post on a university site? Should all political points of view be equally represented? Shouldn't the department decide in advance how the site could and could not be used? These were, after all, subjects that faculty members were supposed to know. Surely they could master the hydra-headed network in the hallway, classify its discourses and uses and audiences.

Burn may be a virtual community, and some of its participants no doubt want their co-users of cyberspace dead, but a community of sorts it is nonetheless. The virtual conflicts among the community of Burn site visitors are grounded in material struggles. Burn is mirrored in, plugged into, knee deep in, blood and money, dreams and wishes, avarice and utopia. On any dimension its future is, moreover, utterly unpredictable. To know how Burn will be used tomorrow, to know what ends it will serve, to know who will visit the site, to know what actions and impressions and alliances or disputes will coalesce in part out of its data streams is simply impossible. The faculty committee has not a snowball's chance in hell of putting out the fire.

The Burn example demonstrates that the Internet already is a scene of cultural and political struggle. As some of this book's contributors astutely point out, the Internet is not *inherently* anything. Once a Tower of Babel, it is now partly a department store. Those who seek to privilege one of its myriad identities may find others determined to subvert such projects. Certainly people who charge a fee for access to posted information will find others mirroring that information and offering it for free. I find it hard to find that displeasing. The sooner the better. When I dialed up the *Boston Globe* Web site last year and had to pay $3 for each article I read (at nighttime rates), I longed for an online Boston Tea Party. Would the participants be thieves or freedom fighters? And that example is only minor commerce. What about the day when the National Security State has its secrets broadcast on the Web? Would those responsible be saboteurs or saints?

As the contributors repeatedly point out in their essays, the Internet has tremendous potential to facilitate more frequent interaction among the members of existing communities. It can help those communities expand their membership and offer a space for more fully participatory discussion and decision making. It is already proving a unique environment for political organizing, since no previous technology enabled large numbers of geographically dispersed people to stay in regular simultaneous contact with one another. Existing organizations are already changing as a result, among them the organizations representing academic disciplines. This follows the pattern of a more democratic use of this technology, but demonstrates again that democratic uses come into being only when groups intervene to create opportunities.

On the other hand, much about the World Wide Web—at every level—is taking undemocratic shape. Prices for basic computers have fallen significantly. In 1981 the University of Illinois purchased me an IBM PC and dot matrix printer for over $10,000. Such a primitive machine—no hard drive, only 64K memory—could not be found today. But even a $500 computer today exceeds the purchasing power of the world's poor. To obtain fast Web access and download time I pay $12 a month to the University and $42 a month to AT&T for cable modem service. On days when it works, it works well, though software and hardware incompatibilities prevent me from using some software. My university connection lets me search a number of databases for free, something a private person could not do. Meanwhile, $648 a year for email and Web access is not exactly cheap. In the Illinois city where I live there is a project afoot to construct a health information network for the poor, but most members of the target audience will have neither computers nor fast Internet access in their homes.

Distance education, on the other hand, as several of these chapters demonstrate, is even more undemocratic. With the tuition for Duke University's online MBA approaching $90,000 and the tuition for Stanford University's online engineering MA heading toward $60,000, the poor are not clamoring to sign up. Online discussions for all these courses are password controlled and accessible only to paying customers. For-profit Internet ventures, as this book shows clearly, now dominate the Web.

These essays also show how all the differential power relations among U.S. campus disciplines are not merely replicated but actually intensified in distance education. Significant sums of money may be available for Web-based course development in fields like business and engineering, with humanities course development being done either on a volunteer basis or for a symbolic honorarium. Per-course salaries for part-time faculty have typically been barely 10 percent–20 percent of salaries for full-time faculty. Salaries for those teaching Web-based courses often drop still more, often by half or more.

Distance education instructors often become unpaid course administrators as well. The same software that lets instructors manage online discussion groups, administer online exams, and put up online class notes or lectures also makes it possible for instructors to monitor and approve course participation, report grades, and track student payments and degree progress. Tasks previously handled by the department office or the central administration thus get passed on to the instructor hand-in-hand with a pay cut.

That is not to say the experience of teaching an online course is necessarily bad. An online discussion among motivated students can be genuinely rewarding. An international enrollment in a distance education course can offer intellectual challenges not available from a face-to-face class of local residents. Instructors I have interviewed often repeat the same story: "The experience was terrific; I'm glad I did it, but I'll never do it again. It took over my life; I could not protect my personal time. I was online with the students every day and every night. And I was paid virtually nothing for this virtual course that became the equivalent of a full-time job. Plus I hated being turned into a low-level administrator."

It is not surprising that Tim Luke's chapter in this book reports repeated burnout throughout the online teaching community. The parallels with support services for Web-based commercial enterprises off campus are striking. While some firms are making significant profits designing corporate Web sites, low-status, low-paid (or unpaid) Web design is often the rule at the bottom of the industry. There are unpaid Web workers both on and off campus, the only difference being that unpaid Web workers on campus are kept in place with pseudo-religious ideologies of service.

Where the essays in this book can help is first in alerting us to these issues and then in encouraging us to learn from other people's experiences. The stories of exploitation and exhaustion detailed here should serve as fair warning to employees on and off campus that dreams cannot substitute for good labor practices and adequate funding. The essays here should urge us all to resist personal sacrifice designed to increase someone else's profit.

As the profit-making motive penetrates U.S. campus life ever more thoroughly—a trend I detail in *Academic Keywords: A Devil's Dictionary for Higher Education* (Routledge, 1999)—while for-profit enterprises multiply on the Web, the need for employee organization and self-protection becomes increasingly clear. Worldwide, across all segments of the economy, cyberspace workers should unionize. The need for contractually negotiated wages and working conditions is stronger here than in any other industry except among migrant labor in agriculture.

The miraculous Internet is successfully democratizing unpaid labor, installing it in every segment of the economy. Meanwhile the Web has also made the products of intellectual labor uniquely transferable and manipulable. Twenty years ago a book, a magazine article, an architectural design, a photograph, an illustration, a musical composition, a course plan, a lecture, a proposal, might be revised and negotiated, but once produced in some final form it often had a high degree of stability. With computerized production and distribution it's not just a question of who owns the right to profit from such

products but of who controls the rights to revise and recon-
ceive them. The Internet course you design today may well be
revised or reorganized tomorrow with aims you find deplor-
able or worse. The book you read tomorrow may not be the
book you write today. The products of your labor can be
remade to serve quite different social and political ends. Perhaps because of the leisure afforded me by my university salary, I find the potential for product manipulation and redesign
more disturbing than the control over profits.

Power in the new Foucaultian millennium, we are increasingly realizing, is going to be more invasive and transformative
than ever before. It is not just a matter of the right to privacy,
a right that is rapidly disappearing, but of the right to create
and control what others see and hear. In most countries other
than the United States, authors do have the right by law to
control the uses of their written work, at least as far as being
able to object to uses likely to harm their reputation. However
in the United States—and by extension, much of the Internet—this is not the case. Throughout history the meaning of
messages has always been outside any message maker's control, just as the means of distribution have often been decidedly controlled. But the material manifestation of a message
has often been highly controllable. Assuming that readers
could see it at all, what they saw has often been what you
made. No longer. Every object and every communication in
cyberspace can be decomposed and remade. Some argue that
this is in fact liberating, in that already existing cultural
objects can be more easily and more creatively appropriated.
This power when exercised from below perhaps has great
potential for the democratization of cultural activity; this can
be seen most obviously in "scratch" culture and rap. However,
when it enables a more fine-grained and pervasive form of control, its implications are disturbing. Worst of all, perhaps, is
the possibility that your remade work *would* be partially recognizable. For your transformed work to be unrecognizable
might be a relief.

The whole meaning of individual agency changes under
these conditions. Human identity loses more than its numeri-
cal identifiers; it cedes major elements of its ground, its foun-

dations. Life and its legacy enter demonstrably different emergent conditions in cyberspace. For much that we do on earth is now mutable. For every freedom in cyberspace a dystopic alternative is thus in the making, on the way, or already here. Web resistance—properly resistance on the Web and resistance to its controlling interests, not resistance to the Web—is increasingly necessary.

Every utopian prophet of cyberspace needs a cold shower. There is, as these essays amply demonstrate, real potential for progressive community on the Web. But we need fair warning about the equivalent potential for negative change growing out of other uses of the new technology. If this book helps sound that warning, it will have done its job.

Alternative Online Communities

This part of the book is about online communities run for nonprofit motives, as an alternative motive to the more common ones of commercial and educational purposes; and also about whether online communities should be seen as an alternative to face-to-face communities. Douglas Schuler talks about the use of online communities to strengthen local democracy, with examples from Seattle. Staff of Oxfam GB describe uses of online communities in international development and disaster relief, with examples from a very wide range of countries. Randy Connolly's chapter considers the dangers of "virtual" community as an alternative to face-to-face community, and shows that some of the hopes invested in online communities have a long history, considerably predating the Internet. Finally, Luciano Paccagnella's discussion of the sociology of online communities argues that they should not be considered as separate from the everyday world. His chapter considers, among other things, the potential and the limitations of online communities for personal change and for activism.

chapter

14

What Kind of Platform for Change? Democracy, Community Work, and the Internet

by Douglas Schuler,
dschuler@evergreen.edu

A t a recent conference in Germany the question of the Internet as a "platform for change" received top billing. While the rapidly expanding worldwide communication and information network may very well become a platform for change, it is far from obvious what the nature of the change will be. Different people say different things. Over the past few years the chorus of cyberpundits (or digerati) have told us that in the future things will be really great, really exciting, really cool. We also learn that the Net will be "immensely democratic" and, incidentally, there will be no need for government support, or, for that matter, government at all.

These views are dangerously simplistic, for they ignore (unbelievably) the most powerful social—including economic—forces of our times—namely the large, multinational corporations. Certainly there is potential for wider democratic participation using the new medium. For the first time in human history, the possibility exists to establish a communication network that spans the globe, is affordable and is open to all people and points of view: in short, a democratic communication infrastructure. Unfortunately, the communication infrastructure of the future may turn out to be almost entirely broadcast where the few (mostly governments and large corporations) will act as gatekeepers for the many; where elites can speak and the rest can only listen. Six years ago, fewer than 2 percent of Web sites were commercial; now over 90 percent are for financial gain. The future network will likely focus on selling things and entertainment, those features which can bring in the most revenue—sex, violence, special effects—and devote little attention to services that educate, inspire, or help bring communities together. Unfortunately these services aren't profitable—at least in the short run.

Responsive government, at least in theory, is the best ally that communities have in shaping an information and communication infrastructure that effectively meets human needs. This realization, however, may come too late. Government (in the United States at least) has already ceded nearly all of the leadership role it once had. In the next few years the large telecommunications and media corporations are likely to control nearly all aspects of the Internet and the technologies that arise from it. Unfortunately a proactive government approach is unlikely to develop in the absence of a strong, unified voice from citizens, activist organizations, nonprofits, libraries, and other groups, and this effort is unlikely to coalesce with the necessary strength and speed.

Humankind is faced with a multitude of critical decisions, and communication technology will undoubtedly play a major role in these decisions in the years to come. The world is faced with a growing, gaping chasm between rich and poor (and computers and communication technology exacerbates this problem); environmental challenges are legion and profound; and new technologies may actually be the enablers for entire new classes of potential catastrophes (Joy 2000). Because of the massive resources that corporations can bring to bear, new communication technology will probably be used to reinforce and bolster existing patterns of ownership and control—merely reiterating the historical pattern we've seen within the United States with other media, such as radio and television. On the other hand, the possibility, though remote, that new communication technology *could* be used to reorient the fulcrum of control by promoting a more democratic and inclusive dialogue does exist. New communication technology *could* provide forums for voices that have long been ignored—voices of women, the poor, minorities, disabled people. And it *could* be used to enable communities to have a deeper involvement in their own health, education, and civic decisions. Moreover, the new communication technology *could* help relieve strains on government by unleashing the creativity and civic problem-solving capabilities of people and communities. To understand how we might begin to actually realize some of these possibilities, let us look more closely at what we mean by democracy.

Elements of Democracy

Democracy is not a commodity like shampoo or patio furniture. One doesn't buy it at a shopping mall or discover it nicely wrapped under a Christmas tree, a gift from the government or the technology gods. It is more like a perspective, a way of seeing things and thinking about things in a public way, and a lens for addressing social concerns. It is less like a noun and more like a verb.

Democracy is notoriously difficult to define; even among scholars there is no agreement on an exact definition. Nearly everybody, however, agrees on certain elements. One of these attributes is inclusivity. This means that everybody can participate and, in theory, that those with more money than others should not be able to purchase more influence with their money either directly or indirectly. (For example, weapon makers shouldn't determine foreign policy; prison-guard unions shouldn't develop "three strikes you're out" laws, computer and media conglomerates shouldn't define proper use of public airwaves, and software billionaires shouldn't determine whether or not a city needs a new football stadium.) This means that society needs to closely examine the ways in which people participate in public decision making (at community meetings, for example) and help ensure that those ways don't favor the privileged. Second, there must be ways that citizens can place their concerns on the public agenda. If the public agenda is monopolized and manipulated by corporations, politicians, or the media, for example, democracy is seriously imperiled. Third, democracy requires a deliberative public process. This point contains three critical ideas: deliberative—adequate time must be allotted for hearing and considering multiple points of view; public—the discussion takes place in the daylight where it can be observed by all; and process—the procedures through which concerns are brought up, discussed, and acted upon are clear and widely known. Fourth, there needs to be equality at the decision stage. At some point in the process, the measure under consideration is accepted or rejected by a vote, in which all those who are entitled to vote have equal influence. Finally, representation is usually part of a modern democracy because of the impracticality of involving extremely large numbers of people in a legislative process. Incidentally, in a democracy, this approach can be changed—by the will of the people—into a system that is more "direct" or, even, into one that is less direct. The existence of the Internet does little to obviate the need for representation. Imagine the complexity, confusion, and chaos if every citizen of a large country—or even a small city—were expected to propose, consider, discuss, and vote on legislation. We'd certainly get a lot more email!

A system of government without active participation from the people is not a democracy no matter how enlightened or benign the de facto guardians may be. If democracy is not championed and exercised by the people, it atrophies like a muscle that is never stressed. Moreover, citizen participation must be encouraged—not merely tolerated—by the government. Democratic participation in the United States and in many other developed countries (Castells 1997), according to most indicators, has been steadily declining for several decades, and many observers feel that this is at least partially due to the concentration of media ownership in private hands.

Democracy must be a partnership between the governed and the governors—a partnership with blurred and negotiated lines of responsibility, but a partnership nonetheless. Although many in government roles have not given this matter sufficient thought, all of these observations have important and immediate implications for proactive government involvement in the development and management of new democratic digital networked systems.

Democracy and the Internet

Technological utopians and cyberlibertarian pundits often ascribe near-magical qualities to the Internet. George Gilder, for example (1997), thinks that the Internet is "inherently" democratic (although any government intervention would diminish this magical quality). On the other hand Gilder believes that television is inherently undemocratic and there is nothing (especially government action!) that could possibly be done about that. Fantasies aside, even a cursory glance reveals that the Internet is far from democratic, given the attributes of democracy discussed in the last section. Unfortunately, the situation seems to be deteriorating. While Internet usage is still wildly accelerating, and email is still the most frequently used Internet application, much of the use of the Internet is passive—surfing the Web has many of the same connotations of compulsive purposelessness that channel surfing on television has. Moreover, almost all new users still arrive from the upper economic brackets. The use of the Internet among those in the bottom economic fifth in the United States has hardly budged in the last decade. (I would be very surprised if this didn't pertain to nearly all countries.) People in this quintile do not generally have computers at home—and if they do, the computers are more likely to be obsolete—nor have they received the specialized training or free access that business people and university attendees have historically enjoyed. Outside of the United States and other wealthy developed countries this trend is even more amplified. While approximately half of the world's population has never made a telephone call (Sykes 2000), U.S. use of the Internet accounts for about half of the world's usage while an additional 25 percent will be found in (mostly western) Europe. Only 1 in 10,000 in India, Bangladesh, or Pakistan—where a modem can cost more than a cow[1]—have Internet access. Nearly 80 percent of all Web pages are in English while China, with approximately 25 percent of the world's population, can read and understand approximately

---

1. See http://www.bytesforall.org/1st/bg.htm

0.6 percent of the Web pages. (The statistics quoted in this paragraph were given in Boyd-Barrett 2000.)

Currently there are few examples of democratic processes on the Internet. People typically equate and confuse open and undirected discussion with "democracy." Henry Robert took nearly 40 years to devise his "rules of order" which enable people in face-to-face meetings to raise issues, discuss and debate alternatives, and make decisions collectively in an open, orderly manner. This system, in everyday use by associative bodies both small and great all over the world, by no means guarantees that the decisions will be the best, or that everybody will be happy with the outcome. The process only guarantees that there will be an opportunity for each person present to participate on an even footing.

It is also important to realize that there is nothing inherently democratic about Internet technology; both radio or television could have been shaped into media that were more strongly democratic, yet this potential was largely ignored and swept aside as economic and legal policies that favored private use were enacted. (Vocal chords may be the communication technology that comes closest to being equalizing. History has since produced policies, economic and otherwise, that have raised some voices to higher platforms, while advanced communication technologies have produced media that enable some voices to travel even farther . . . .) And, finally, it must be pointed out that the American taxpayer who paid for the initial Internet was never consulted on possible directions; all of the major decisions involving the development, deployment, or use of the Internet have been done in the almost total absence of public participation. In fact, it almost appears that many of these decisions were made with uncharacteristic speed so as to avoid public input that might in fact raise uncomfortable questions about social uses or public ownership.

Democratic Communication Technology in Seattle

Currently in the United States there is an astonishing number of grassroots projects in the area of democratic communication technology. Not only are these projects evidence of an overdue renewal of interest in democracy, but they suggest that now is the time for a concerted effort to weave these projects—heretofore disconnected—into a tapestry of compelling community strength and creativity.

In this section I focus on projects in a single city in order to show the richness and popularity of this new type of activism. Seattle may have more of these projects than many other cities, but similar projects are being organized all over the United States and the world. (The U.S. Department of Commerce TIIAP awards[2] showcase the diversity and creativity of these projects in the United States.) The Seattle projects can track their origins from many sources, including city government, grassroots activism, academia, and libraries, and many are the result of new collaborations and coalitions. (Although I have listed the projects below according to certain categories, this is not a rigid or exhaustive way to describe them. Also many of them fall under two or more categories.)

University Collaboration. There is apparently a renewed interest within academia in community collaboration on mutually beneficial projects. The "Civic Capital" project[3] at the University of Washington is a good example. I've described some of the many important opportunities that I see for increased academia/community collaboration in other essays (Schuler 1996, Schuler 1997).

Community Activism. A number of community activism projects in Seattle use communication technology. Community activist Anthony Williams launched Project Compute to establish access to computer equipment, network services, and training programs in a low-income neighborhood community center. Roy Sahali, Michael Grant, and others have worked to build a coalition of similar projects, while Madeline Lewis, Lorraine Pozzi, and other activists have organized the Homeless

---

2. http://www.ntia.doc.gov/otiahome/tiiap/
3. http://www.gspa.washington.edu/Trust/tighome.html

Women's Network[4] that is "dedicated to empowering women and youth to overcome the limitations of homelessness and poverty." Recently a new effort called N*Power, headed by Joan Fanning, has been launched to bring networked computer technology to nonprofits and social service agencies. And ONE/ NW (Online networking for the environment/northwest) is exploring new ways for environmental groups to work together.

Free Public Networks. Loosely based on the "Free-Net" model, which was itself loosely based on the public library model, the Seattle Community Network (SCN) is the best example of a free public computer network in Seattle.[5] Offering free email, mail lists, Web siting, and other Internet services to anybody (currently over 18,000 registered users) and computer training and support to community organizations, SCN, working in conjunction with the Seattle Public Library, is striving to remove barriers to communication technology. SCN, unlike most community networks, has developed a strong set of principles (see sidebar) that are intended to institutionalize the democratic objectives upon which it was founded.

Government Programs. Although the government needs to be more proactive in this area, it has not been totally inactive. The city government in Seattle, for example, is pushing in several directions. The Seattle Public Library provides public access terminals in all its branch libraries. The city also runs PAN[6] (the "Public Access Network") which provides extensive information on city agencies and city issues. People with the PAN project also work with community groups to help them develop in-house expertise and an electronic presence. (PAN, amid some controversy, recently dropped its "chat" capability.) The use of electronic media has received more attention from the city recently, largely due to former City Council

---

4.   http://www.speakeasy.org/hwm, http://www.speakeasy.org/hwm/
      hwm_mission.html

5.   http://www.scn.org

6.   http://www.pan.ci.seattle.wa.us/

Seattle Community Network Principles

The Seattle Community Network (SCN) is a free public-access computer network for exchanging and accessing information. Beyond that, however, it is a service conceived for community empowerment. Our principles are a series of commitments to help guide the ongoing development and management of the system for both the organizers and participating individuals and organizations.

Commitment to Access

Access to the SCN will be free to all

We will provide access to all groups of people, particularly those without ready access to information technology.

We will provide access to people with diverse needs. This may include special-purpose interfaces.

We will make the SCN accessible from public places.

Commitment to Service

The SCN will offer reliable and responsive service.

We will provide information that is timely and useful to the community.

We will provide access to databases and other services.

Commitment to Democracy

The SCN will promote participation in government and public dialogue.

The community will be actively involved in the ongoing development of the SCN.

We will place high value in freedom of speech and expression and in the free exchange of ideas.

We will make every effort to ensure privacy of the system users.

We will support democratic use of electronic technology.

Commitment to the World Community

In addition to serving the local community, we will become part of the regional, national, and international community.

We will build a system that can be a model for other communities.

Commitment to the Future

We will continue to evolve and improve the SCN.

We will explore the use of innovative applications such as electronic town-halls for community governance, or electronic encyclopedias for enhanced access to information.

We will work with information providers and with groups involved in similar projects using other media.

We will solicit feedback on the technology as it is used, and make it as accessible and humane as possible.

member Tina Podlodowski, who has been promoting the idea of "technology literacy" within the city. It now also appears that several other City Council members will weigh in on these issues.

Community Research. One of the most intriguing possibilities that the medium offers is community research, in which community members develop and implement research projects that they themselves have deemed relevant to their lives. The Sustainable Seattle project[7] developed a set of indicators (including participation in the arts, wild salmon population, voting rates, and many others) that provide useful data regarding Seattle's "sustainability" over time. The project has launched electronic "forums" on SCN and has also put a lot of information available on SCN to help Seattlites (as well as people in other locations—"Sustainable Penang" in Malaysia, for example) get involved with similar projects. In early 2000 the City of Seattle Department of Information Technology and the Citizens Telecommunications and Technology Advisory Board (below) launched the "Information Technology Indicators for a Healthy Community" project. This innovative project, patterned somewhat on the Sustainable Seattle project, aims to uncover what effects—both negative and positive—communication and information technology is having on the city of Seattle.[8]

Independent media. The Web currently is a natural haven for independent media both as an adjunct to existing print media and as the sole publishing medium. *Amp Magazine, Real Change, Steelhead, Washington Free Press,*[9] and other Seattle-based periodicals are currently using the Web in this way. Also, in late 1999, the strong reaction to the WTO helped provide the impetus for a new Independent Media Center. The

---

7. http://www.scn.org/ip/sustainable/
8. http://www.cityofseattle.net/tech/indicator_main.htm
9. http://www.wrldpwr.com/amp, http://www.speakeasy.org/realchange, http://www.speakeasy.org/steelhead, http://www.speakeasy.org/wfp

Independent Media Center, though very new, is also helping to raise the idea of democratic technology to higher visibility.

Public Advisory Boards. The city of Seattle established a Citizen's Telecommunications and Technology Advisory Board (CTTAB)[10] in 1996 to help advise the city on a wide range of communications technology issues, including public access television, the city government channel, citizen access to city government and to other electronic services, and citizen "technology literacy" in general. Although this board is relatively new and the results are not in, the advisory collaboration seems to be working out well. This type of "advisory partnership" is a step in the right direction, but it is not without challenges. The power asymmetry between citizens who are volunteering their time and of the city staff members and corporate lobbyists who are paid to do this work is a structural feature of this arrangement. Also care must be taken to ensure that the people on the board are "citizens" in a public sense and not just representatives of corporations.

Internet Cafés and Other Public Technology Centers. The Speakeasy Café[11] is probably the most successful Internet café in Seattle. Offering an informal atmosphere with food, drink, inexpensive Internet access, poetry readings, and art exhibits, the Speakeasy is a good example of how technology can be integrated with other community functions. There are several other Internet cafés in Seattle and several projects in community centers. There are also several community computer centers set up in subsidized housing as part of the Neighborhood Network program of the U.S. Department of Housing and Urban Development.[12] At a national level, the Community Technology Centers Network (CTCNet) has been a strong force for organizing these centers into a coalition.

Other public access media. There are also other types of access programs such as public access television (Channel 29). Radio

10. http://www.pan.ci.seattle.wa.us/seattle/cttab
11. http://www.speakeasy.org
12. http://www.hud.gov

station KSER in Lynnwood, north of Seattle, offers a wide range of community programming. And last but not least, realizing that the telephone may be the easiest and most commonly used two-way communication technology, the Community Voice Mail program[13] helps set up programs in cities all over the United States to provide homeless and phoneless clients with free voice mail.

Conferences and Symposia. Public discussion forums on the uses of information and communication technology that are not cheering sessions for new technology sponsored by computer companies and other economically motivated institutions are also important. In May 2000, for example, Computer Professionals for Social Responsibility convened an international symposium entitled "Shaping the Network Society: The Future of the Public Sphere in Cyberspace" (CPSR 2000) in which artists, activists, government officials, researchers, students, journalists, and citizens got together to discuss their plans and projects for democratic technology. The most important outcome may have been the realization that there is a strong interest worldwide in this work and that individuals are not alone. On the last day of the conference, a group of attendees crafted the "Seattle Statement" (CPSR 2000), laying out six working hypotheses which, they hope, will form a conceptual platform for research and activism related to democratic technology.

Community Networks

The Seattle Community Network (mentioned above) is just one instance of a larger movement to develop community-oriented computer systems. This section describes the general philosophy behind community networks and how they relate to community work and democratic participation.

Community computer networks, now numbering over 400 worldwide, represent one of the most authentically democratic and community-oriented approaches to communication

---

13. http://www.scn.org/ip/cti/home.html

in existence. At a very general level, a community network is a big electronic Bulletin Board System that provides "one-stop shopping" for information and communication about community-related meetings, projects, events, issues, and organizations. Community networks are free to use, and free public-access terminals are part of the community network vision. In addition to providing a convenient repository for information these networks offer new participatory opportunities for community dialogue. These dialogues can be used to explore community concerns, debate issues, build support networks, or to discuss cats, dogs, children, parents, sports, computers, or any topic that people care to talk about.

Roles of Government and Community

It is the case, particularly in Western Europe, that government can provide an effective impetus for alleviating social hardships. Now there is increasing evidence that the conditions under which this is true (namely competent and responsive government, adequate resources, and popular support) may not be holding: governments around the world are retreating from many of their previously shouldered social responsibilities. While this trend may be not be as inexorable and inevitable as it is sometimes portrayed, it seems prudent to briefly consider the proper roles of government and the citizenry.

It is obvious that even under the benign eye of the hypothetically most concerned and custodial government there are many tasks and enterprises that people and social groups will instigate and carry out on their own. The ability of the citizenry to address social challenges could be referred to as community work or community problem-solving competence.

Community work is any activity that helps strengthen any of a community's core values. When U.S. Navy veteran and antiwar activist Country Joe McDonald (with the help of many others) made the names, ranks, and other information of all of Alameda County's military casualties available electronically on Berkeley's "Community Memory" (Farrington and Pine 1992) bulletin-board system, he was doing community work. When people tutor neighborhood kids, testify to city council on the need for safe streets, publish an alternative newspaper, help paint a day-care center, organize a rent strike, start a farmer's market or neighborhood garden, they're all doing community work.

With some provisos regarding the specific principles and practices, it is clear that the stronger the community problem-solving competence the less need there would be for government intervention. This does not imply that government competence and community competence sum to a constant, where a decline in one means an increase in the other. On the contrary, some societies will be strong in both, while others, sadly, will be deficient in both. In fact, increasing the effectiveness of community work is important even if government competence is high. (And increasing community competence may even lead to increased government competence.) In any case, a strengthened community competence is necessary—not just to compensate for diminished government involvement but to guide the future of government involvement. In other words, the community should play a substantial part in any change in the role of government, even if this means flaunting conventional wisdom of the digerati. Finally it is important to point out that increasing community competence (through supporting community networks, for example) is a critical role of democratic governments, regardless of whether the government is reducing its role in promoting social welfare.

Actions for the Future

Clearly communication is at the heart of any democratic revitalization, and communication in the modern age necessarily implies communication technology. We therefore need to devise and implement projects that integrate democracy and communication technology. Disconnected projects are insufficient, however, as they are likely to remain marginalized and unnoticed. A tapestry of democratic technology projects that is part of a broad social movement is required. Only if large numbers of people are involved in the movement is there any realistic hope for increased democratization. And only if there is a heightened awareness and a sense of necessity and opportunity could any major change and reorientation occur.

The answer to the issue of democracy and cyberspace is not to cling blindly to simplistic technocratic or libertarian platitudes. While the Internet as "platform for change" may ultimately be dominated by a handful of corporate interests (as is the rest of the media), there are scores of opportunities for communities that want to develop communication systems that are open, equitable, and useful. Communities need to develop these systems and at the same time fight for policies that strengthen public media and diminish the stranglehold of corporate media giants.

The future begins today. We begin with a vision of the future—of democracy and of community and of increased human actualization—but also with the reality of the present, which includes people, programs, institutions, policies, and technology. Therefore, of necessity, our work involves new collaborations and coalitions. Community groups must find common cause with many groups, including academia, labor, environmental groups, political parties, government, and, where appropriate, business. It will be helpful to look at what people are doing in Seattle and in other places, but these are only the first steps.

The future is not preordained, and we know that the shape that a technology ultimately assumes depends on many factors. For that reason, activists for democratic technology must work together if there is any hope of developing democratic space in cyberspace. It won't be easy. For as American antislavery activist Frederick Douglass stated, "Without struggle, there is no progress." I urge you all to enter that struggle. This may be our best and last chance.

References

Agre, Philip, and Douglas Schuler, *Reinventing Technology, Rediscovering Community: Critical Explorations of Computing As a Social Practice*. Norwood, NJ: Ablex Publishing Co, 1997.

Boyd-Barrett, Oliver, plenary presentation at "Shaping the Network Society: The Future of the Public Sphere in Cyberspace," Seattle, May 20, 2000.

Castells, Manuel, *The Power of Identity*, Volume II of *The Information Age: Economy, Society, and Culture*. Malden, MA: Blackwell Publishers, 1997.

Cisler, Steve, ed., *Ties That Bind: Converging Communities*. Cupertino, CA: Apple Computer Corp. Library, 1995.

CPSR, "Shaping the Network Society: The Future of the Public Sphere in Cyberspace," 2000. Online: http://www.scn.org/cpsr/diac-00/program.html

———, "The Seattle Statement," 2000. Online: http://www.scn.org/cpsr/diac-00/seattle-statement.html

Farrington, Carl, and Evelyn Pine, "Community Memory: A Case Study in Community Communication," 1992, in Phil Agre and Doug Schuler, *Reinventing Technology, Rediscovering Community: Critical Explorations of Computing As a Social Practice*. Norwood, NJ: Ablex Publishing Co, 1997.

Gallagher, Art, Jr., and Harland Padfield, eds., *The Dying Community*. Albuquerque, NM: University of New Mexico Press, 1980.

Gilder, George, presentation at the Camden Conference on "Shaping American Communities," October 24, 1997, Camden, ME.

Joy, Bill, "Why the Future Doesn't Need Us," *WiReD* 8.04 (April 2000). Online: http://www.wired.com/wired/archive/8.04/joy_pr.html

Levin, H., "The Struggle for Community Can Create Community," in Art Gallagher, Jr., and Harland Padfield, eds., *The*

Dying Community. Albuquerque, NM: University of New Mexico Press, 1980.

Robert, Henry M., *Robert's Rules of Order, Revised*. New York: William Morrow and Co., 1971. 1915 version online: http://www.constitution.org/rror/rror–00.htm

Sandvig, C., "Welcome To 1927: The Creation of Property Rights and Internet Domain Name Policy in Historical Perspective," in Proceedings of *DIAC-2000, Shaping the Network Society: The Future of the Public Sphere in Cyberspace*. Palo Alto, CA: Computer Professionals for Social Responsibility, 2000.

Schuler, Douglas, *New Community Networks: Wired for Change*. Reading, MA: Addison-Wesley, 1996.

———, "Community Computer Networks: An Opportunity for Collaboration among Democratic Technology Practitioners and Researchers," in Proceedings of *Technology and Democracy: Comparative Perspectives*. Oslo, Norway: Centre for Technology and Culture (TMV), 1997. Online: http://www.scn.org/ip/commnet/oslo-1997.text

Sirianni, Carmen, Lewis Friedland, and Douglas Schuler, "The New Citizenship and the Civic Practices Network (CPN)," in Steve Cisler, ed., *Ties That Bind: Converging Communities*. Cupertino, CA: Apple Computer Corp. Library, 1995.

Sykes, Lisa, "Hanging on for the Phone," *Info 21*, February 9, 2000. Online: http://www.undp.org/info21/bg/phone.htm

15 Oxfam GB Interviews: Experience and Thoughts about Online Communities
edited by Julia Flynn,
jflynn@oxfam.org.uk

O xfam GB is an organization working with others in 80 countries to overcome poverty and suffering through the most effective, appropriate, and enduring solutions. In this interview, which took place in January 2000, Oxfam GB staff discuss lessons they have learnt from using online communities as a tool for development work and disaster relief.

The chapter is in two parts. The first half is about using Internet technology as a way to bring voices from developing countries in the Southern Hemisphere to a meeting of the Commonwealth Heads of Government and also about a project setting up links between schools and communities in the United Kingdom and in West Africa.

The second half is an edited version of a group interview with Oxfam staff who have experience in using online communities for communication within Oxfam. They talk about successes, failures, and issues, concentrating on Oxfam's pioneering use of intranet and Internet, with particular reference to the experience in the Managua office. They end with some suggestions for other nongovernmental organizations (NGOs).

The interview brief asked the interviewees to talk about the problems that they had encountered. The focus on the lessons learnt should not blind the reader to the successes, however. Oxfam's use of the Internet shows that although this technology has its limitations, it really can be used as a tool to help change the world for the better.

—Miranda Mowbray

Building Blocks for Bringing About a True Exchange of Ideas between North/South Communities

Miranda: Can you tell me about your involvement with online communities?

Rona Alexander (*Oxfam's Internet Manager 1996–1998, and currently Program Manager for On the Line, Oxfam's joint Millennium project*): I have two examples of trying to create communities online. The first was event focused, around the Commonwealth Heads of Government meeting (CHOGM) in Edinburgh in 1997, just after the UK election, and the second is through the On the Line project which aims to bring together communities crossed by the Greenwich Meridian Line.

The CHOGM Meeting Web Site

Rona: The CHOGM was the first major foreign showcase of the new Labor Government, so I knew that it would get a lot of attention in the UK. Also there was a big push within the Commonwealth to open up this meeting to the NGO community and to civil society, so there was some funding available to promote this. We had a stand at the big NGO Forum that was running alongside the main CHOGM meeting. When the heads of government came to our stand, we were able to show them the Web site we had set up. Dignitaries, including Prince Charles, and high-ranking officials attached to CHOGM also came to the stand.

We had done a lot of work on Oxfam-related themes for the Web site, but had also really tried to work with other partners to get their content on the site. The number one lesson was how difficult it can be to work with others. The Internet is supposed to make things easy, and it might be easier now, but at that stage most of the other NGOs had not developed their Web presence. This meant they could not provide information in a way that we could use quickly, so we had to do a huge amount of processing.

Miranda: What was on the stand that was specific to the Internet?

Rona: There was a discussion site where people from the South had put up in-depth opinion pieces, and then came online to answer people's questions about them. Those involved included a community activist from India and an Oxfam representative from Southern Africa who had worked on the land mines campaign. People could log in their questions at the stand or from anywhere else in the world.

Miranda: Do you think the personal contact online made a difference that you could not achieve through posters?

Rona: Yes, you couldn't speak to our representative from Southern Africa through a poster. You couldn't directly ask her a question, get an answer directly back, then bounce that off somebody else's answer that maybe contradicted or added a bit to what she said.

Miranda: Can you describe what happened online?

Rona: There was a big debate about land mines during the conference. There was input from a range of people involved: our representative in South Africa, who had played a big part in the Southern Africa campaign against land mines; Graça Machel[1], who spoke about armed conflict and land mines in Southern Africa; people from the Working Group against Land Mines and officials from the Canadian Government who had been taking a lead on land mines. When the Canadian delegation came to the stand we interviewed them online and asked them: We've got so far with the land mine campaign, what should we be doing now? They replied: We've had big successes over land mines, what about Small Arms? So we were moving the agenda on.[2]

---

1. Graça Machel is one of the world's foremost advocates of children's rights. Her seminal work is "Impact of Armed Conflict on Children," published by UN in 1996. She has worked closely with many UN organizations. She is the widow of the first president of Mozambique. Ms. Machel is currently married to Nelson Mandela.

2. A comprehensive ban on antipersonnel land mines was signed by over 100 countries in December 1997. The campaign to ban land mines involved hundreds of NGOs, as well as several governments (notably Canada). Oxfam is currently campaigning on the use of Small Arms, as part of an international network on this issue.

Another thing we did was totally publicity led; Prince Charles was coming round, so we set up a live chat between him and our Southern Africa representative, who was in an Internet Café, in South Africa, with a film crew present.

For the other live Web chat[3] we had someone from Swaziland, as well as our representative in South Africa, people from Scotland, and someone from India who was at the CHOGM meeting involved and people could come online and ask questions. In retrospect, that took a huge amount of effort to set up for very small participation. The things we were discussing were not what most people who go to chat rooms want to talk about. Members of the public would come in and say "This is really boring." Those involved were mainly people who had been alerted beforehand, plus visiting members of the public whom we persuaded to add questions. Thus it was a self-defining audience. The live Web chat was mainly used by people at the conference; although they were from other places all over the world they were actually physically in the room together! They were typing in answers to each other when they could have waved at each other across the room.

What We Learned

Rona: What we learned was that there was a lot of potential, but although the Web is instant, it takes a lot longer than you think to get a community going and talking. Up to the end we spent a disproportionate amount of time processing basic content rather than developing the community. The site was not live early enough to encourage people to use its features.

We made a critical mistake with people in Latin America who wanted to contribute to the debate around bananas—a big issue at the conference was about limits on Caribbean

---

3. Oxfam worked with One World Online (now OneWorld.net) and others on the Web initiatives at Edinburgh. One World.net is a community of over 450 Web sites devoted to human rights and sustainable development, http://www.oneworld.net.

bananas in the EU.[4] We had planned live interviews with some banana growers, but it was difficult for them to access the site because of the way our domain name was set up. We ended up emailing them questions, they emailed back, and their answers were put onto the Web. What we were doing was unpicking the technology, which was an interesting lesson.

We still constantly get caught out making it difficult for people in the South to do things through the Web. A big part of me says forget the Web, just do the basic communicating through an email group. If you were really trialing equality within a global community, that would be where you would invest the time.

Miranda: Can you summarize what you learned?

Rona: The numbers that you get involved in an initiative can be relatively small for a lot of effort, even though there's millions of people out there using the World Wide Web. Preparatory work in building up the community before the event could be a way of getting other voices in. A big event can be a good focus for a Web initiative, as these draw in a lot of press attention. Traditionally at big UN Summits like Beijing[5] Oxfam would bring lots of key people to the NGO lobbying forum, set up workshops and briefings; huge amounts of investment. There must be an alternative to that, and a way of affecting and influencing the agenda using email and Internet. We need to get the Southern voices into big high-profile events.

---

4. The U.S. has been trying to get the EU to liberalize its banana import regime since its introduction in 1993. It is feared that further liberalization would seriously affect the livelihoods of the Windward Island banana growers who depend on their preferential access to the EU market. In September 1997, the EU accepted the WTO decision that its banana import and licensing system contravened WTO rules. At the time of writing of this chapter (June 2000) the U.S. and EU have yet to resolve the dispute.

5. The United Nations Fourth World Conference on Women, in Beijing in 1995.

On the Line

Miranda: Can you tell us about online communities and the On the Line project?

Rona: On the Line, which aims to link up the countries crossed by the Greenwich Meridian Line, is a joint project[6] for the Millennium with two overall objectives—raising interest in the South, and trying to counterbalance the view that students in many British schools may have about Africa which they get from the news and from wildlife documentaries. Through the project we want people to discover there are people just like us in these other places, doing some things just like us, some things quite different.

Miranda: Do you think that having online communities from the North and South will help this?

Rona: This is a big part of the overall objective. First to get people interested in the idea, then to give them the ways of making a direct link with similar people or communities elsewhere. We put a lot into developing school links, and this coincided with a huge growth of access to email and Internet in UK schools. The next issue is how they communicate with the African schools and what access they have in the South.

It's a two-year project, and in the first year the West African schools accessed the Web site very little. This was depressing. We knew it was because they often don't even have functioning phone lines. This year our staff there are working hard to get the partner schools some access to the Internet. One approach has been to liaise with universities and institutions in these countries which are already online and with the facilities and training, to buy some time online; then we bus in the school kids once a month, and they can look at the Web site, latch onto topics, and send their emails.

---

6. The On the Line site is at http://www.ontheline.org.uk. The Greenwich Meridian Line passes through Togo, Ghana, Burkina Faso, Mali, Algeria, Spain, France, and the United Kingdom. On the Line is a partnership of Channel 4, WWF-UK, and Oxfam GB.

We hope that over the next year of the project the linked schools will themselves begin to come up with appropriate solutions. It's already happening—there are a number of schools in London linked with schools in Ghana, and in the middle of the year 2000 they are going to go over with computer equipment and set up their partner schools, which do have phones and basic things. For some who don't, it won't ever happen and we've got to work out how you keep them in contact.

Miranda: What else is there apart from school links?

Rona: There are community links. On the Line is a real partnership project working with a lot of European NGOs, as well as with NGOs in the West African countries. Channel 4 has been involved, and also the Guides. Christian Aid is one partner doing community links; they are linking a women's café in Wales with a community café in Mali—they're exchanging news, recipes, whatever. There are organic horticulturists in Mali linked with others in Scotland. We are now trying to link the after-school study center at Blackburn Rovers with a football school in Mali, so they can talk.

Examples of good things coming from school links are beginning to emerge: we found that Ghanaian teachers were achieving better results in numeracy while UK teachers were achieving better results in English language; now the teachers are swapping ideas for good practice.

Not all of this is happening on the Internet, some of it is just by plain post, but where we've got the Internet connections it's great. For instance, a group of kids in Cumbria have got a sustainable development link, and their schools have bought a flock of sheep that they're keeping at an agricultural college, and the Burkinabè schools have bought a flock of goats, and every month they exchange what's happening and put information on the Web.

We are unsure how things will be carried on and sustained at the end of this project. We're going to spend a lot of the next six months looking for ongoing support. But I would say, even in a project running over two years, you do get a chance to promote real dialogue between people, and a sense of community.

A Good Way to Create a Community

Rona: It helped a lot that Channel 4 was involved. People could see something that related to the project that they were involved in on TV. Some of the programs were even shown on West African television. That can make people feel part of something bigger, and it encourages them to carry on with the dialogue.

Miranda: Is it helpful having small initiatives under the same umbrella project?

Rona: Yes, and also the fact that it is a partnership project. I think there's a lot of potential for using the freedom of the Web technology. Rather than channeling people down one way, we are saying, "Get in touch with each other, develop your own project, if it's on this theme we'd love to hear about it."

Miranda: What role does the Web site have for the whole of the On the Line project?

Rona: There are resources for teachers to use in the class-room. There's also the space to exchange ideas and informa-tion—the kids' noticeboard and the teachers' noticeboard are getting quite heavily used now. Anyone can put up anything, although the noticeboards are moderated. They can put up their poems, their millennium wishes, or ask questions. The teachers' noticeboard tends to be more concrete: "This is what we've worked on with On the Line in my class." It was slow to start, but now the project's running there's more and more going up. Among the issues we have faced are the language dif-ferences. A small part of the site is translated into French, but language is certainly an issue for us.

Miranda: What have you learned about online communi-ties from the On the Line project?

Rona: A good way to create a community is to focus on a central theme and invite people to make their own thing of it. You need to give them lots of feedback about what they are doing, and consciously put people in touch with each other.

Learning from One Office and Applying It to Other Situations

Staff contributing to this interview were all involved with online communications between Oxfam House in the United Kingdom and offices in the Latin American/Caribbean region[7] and beyond. Though they had different roles and were geographically dispersed, staff describe how they were interconnected, via the Internet. The interview took place in Oxfam House in the United Kingdom.

Miranda: How did Oxfam's use of the Internet in the Latin America/Caribbean region get going?

Francisco Alvárez *(Information Management Researcher, working for the Latin America/Caribbean program and also in the Information Systems Team in Oxford)*: The first Web page in Oxfam was for the Information Systems Team (IST) in the International Division. It was a technical page to share software, manuals, and some useful tips to do with email, backups. When I went to Managua, one of the first things that we tried to test was the connection to this IST page. We managed to set up a connection with the Web administrator, and he gave us authorization to go into the Web page. That was a miracle for us; we realized the power of the Internet for sharing information and documents online. Then we started to play, and set up the intranet in the Managua office.

The Managua Office

Francisco: At the beginning it was just a test. Although staff in the office were not negative about what we were doing, there was certainly anxiety, caution, and resistance to a new technology. We learned that we couldn't introduce change and new things immediately. We started by testing

---

7.   Oxfam's Latin America/Caribbean region covers program activities in countries in the Andean region, Brazil, Central America, and the Caribbean.

the Internet in Managua to let people get familiar with it, to know how to work it.

The communications officer based in Managua played an important role in implementing new technology. The communication infrastructure there is awful, the phone lines are really bad, so we tested using a radio modem instead. It was a successful experiment that showed we could discuss and transmit data really fast. Then a private bank came with another tower with a radio modem, and our signal was broken. We lost all contact between the office and the Internet Service Provider and had to change back to the traditional system, the telephone line.

When I came back to Oxfam House, we started to develop the Latin American program site. And after that other regions developed sites—Asia, Africa—and it mushroomed.

Miranda: What did happen in the Managua office?

Becky Buell (*Regional Representative for Oxfam in Central America/Mexico from 1992 to 1998 based in Managua, now Head of Regional Policy in Oxfam House*): I started in 1992, when there were two computers in the office. Then in 1996 we were networked and we started with shared files and the electronic filing system. The next debate was around the Internet, and who would have access to it. The managers imagined everyone surfing the Net all day long. I've learned since that there's a sort of blip at first of people being online a lot, but that doesn't normally continue.

Then there was the intranet; at first this was between the techies, between the team in the United Kingdom and the technical staff in Managua. I thought "great for them," but I didn't see the application to us as a team, to management, program, administration, to anyone except the technical people. I didn't see it as a priority. We were in an office with two adjoining rooms, we already had a shared file directory, why do we need Web pages? I still question whether the investment in creating a specific team-based intranet is a necessary way to share information and knowledge.

Francisco: When we started it, the aim was to save costs, because communication between headquarters and regional offices is quite expensive in terms of sending a large volume of documents, manuals, books, etc.

Experiences in Other Offices

Steve Ainsworth (*Program Administrator for Latin America/Caribbean from 1997 to 1999 based in Oxford, who has had secondments in Brazil, Kosovo, and Macedonia*): In my first days on the Latin America desk in Oxford, things were already set up for sharing information via the shared filing system. We benefited greatly from that, it was part of the culture which Francisco and others were instrumental in taking forward—although some of our hardware was not up to scratch, which could add complications.

Suddenly I was sent over to the Recife office in Brazil. It had a network of 14 Pentium PCs, functioning efficiently, but maybe not using shared information as well as we do in Oxford. They had Internet access on only one machine. While I was there we arranged for the whole of the network to have Internet access and intranet access. We eventually got it so that every member of staff had access to the Internet and intranet on their PCs.

They didn't need the intranet, in the sense that they could carry on their work without it, but in Recife locally recruited staff didn't have any real concept of the wider Oxfam and its work. So they were actively encouraged to use the intranet for general information, for more information about Oxfam in general, to keep up to date with different campaigns like the Education Now campaign.[8]

Becky: They were linked into the Corporate Intranet site in Oxford. It was different in Central America because the

---

8. Oxfam is campaigning for a free basic education for all by 2015. Currently 125 million children worldwide are denied the right to an education. For information on this, on other campaigns, and on Oxfam in general, see http://www.oxfam.org.uk.

communications officer in Managua was designing our own, in-house, Central America Intranet site.

Some Issues: Language and Content

Steve: There are benefits in having your own site—you obviously have to look at costs and benefits—for instance in the Recife office they were trying to contact the other luso-phone countries. They wanted some information on details of the Mozambique program, which was on the Corporate intra-net site held here in Oxfam House. But if the Mozambique office had their own site which could be accessed directly, there would be a lot more information, probably in Portu-guese, that could be accessed by the Brazil office. Whereas with the centralized model you get: "Yes, that's a wonderful report on the state of rural education in Mozambique, but it's in Portuguese so we're not putting it onto the intranet site." If they've got their own one, people in Brazil, people in Angola, can access it directly. It's about sharing information across the programs.

Miranda: With the technology in place can you let people do things on their own without central control and report back to you?

Becky: There are issues about that. In Central America content was put on the Internet site that was not consistent with a policy line in the organization. So how you determine what sort of material goes on, who has access, all these issues need to be addressed.

A Cultural Shift

Becky: The technological shift has been massive. And that entails a total cultural shift in terms of the way you work and the way you relate to information. And that is going to take time. But what is it, this desired community that is brought together through intranet and Internet? These are tools for information sharing that we use better in some places than others, but is this a community?

Miranda: Don't you agree that you already have communities that use the Internet partly as a way of communicating with each other?

Becky: If you call Oxfam a community, then we have tools that bring us together as an organizational unit, email being the main one. The intranet here in Oxfam House is becoming a tool, but we haven't gotten to grips with how to make it more than this.

For example, Oxfam's in the process of refocusing its global program around five broad program areas. We've set up virtual teams that are international and cross-organizational, but we're having a huge problem figuring out how to use the intranet to create community or to bring these geographically dispersed groups together.

Two things occur to me. In order to use the intranet as a tool to create a group identity you need initial human contact or the joining together of the group on a very personal level to get it going. It's very hard to get it going just electronically. Also ways of communication are becoming much more fluid, fast, and varied, but people's ability to engage with them is quite limited. There have been very few visits to the new intranet site set up for the five program areas. I don't think this is about design, it's more basic, about figuring out what the intranet is useful for and what it's not useful for.

Steve: It is a cultural shift, which is still happening; with email we're there, people use it to a different extent, but everyone uses it. But it's not the same with intranet, given my experience in Oxford; people phone up saying: "Have you got this report, have you got those details?" You say, "Well, look on the intranet, it's there." It's not that people don't know how to use it or don't know what's there, it's just not automatically in their minds.

John Wood (*Senior Web Editor and part of the team responsible for developing the Corporate Intranet in 1998*): The organization has had email for over five years now and the Corporate intranet has only been in about a year and a half. And it is growing. The greater use of intranet in the Latin American region seems to be something to do with the early trials of the intranet which our Corporate intranet is based on. The other regions are now just starting.

Giulietta Bianchini (*Area Administrator for Oxfam's program in Latin America/Caribbean, based in Oxfam House, with secondments in Nicaragua and Albania*): Back to your original question, about how did it start. I think it began in the Latin America/Caribbean desk in Oxford. I arrived in 1991, and we had about two or three stand-alone computers. The new area director began about the same time, from an organization which was very advanced in electronic networking, and the first question was, "Why haven't we got a network?" so he invested in computers. There were about 14 of us at the time and we began a small network, which we started with shared folders and directories in 1992.

Becky: The effect is striking. You used to walk into the Latin America desk and there were ten offices, all of them stacked to about waist high with documents. Now you go into people's offices and you see a bookshelf and a filing cabinet.

Giulietta: When I went to Managua one of the first things I had to do was set up a shared electronic filing system based on the system we were using on the Desk in Oxford. It was very easy to set up, but difficult to encourage people to use it.

Francisco: There are problems with the electronic filing system, not just in Managua, but in other offices, in Lima and Santo Domingo. People prefer to save their own document on their own PC drive, rather than in the shared electronic filing system. Sometimes it is due to lack of training but sometimes it is habit and discipline.

The Managua Web Site: A Key Resource

Miranda: What about the Internet?

Becky: In Central America and Mexico the communications officer set up a site for Oxfam, where we posted general information about Oxfam in the region, and as a focus initially for our policy work. It had key policy papers and messages, press releases, translations. And then what happened around Hurricane Mitch was really significant.[9]

Francisco: Yes, the page became one of the most important sites, not just for Oxfam but also for external organizations. Both CNN and the World Bank linked to the page, and they also called the office to get more information.

Becky: The site became a key resource on what was happening on the ground with Hurricane Mitch, with links into all the regional newspapers, what Oxfam was saying about the situation, links into all the other Oxfams' Web sites. It was an amazing tool.

Right after Hurricane Mitch, I was in Bosnia. We were out in Drvar, which is in the western part of Bosnia, in the middle of nowhere.[10] We were meeting with program staff and local leaders, and we had to meet with the local UNHCR official. He was Honduran and his family had been affected by Mitch. He said, "I don't know what's going on," and we linked him up to the site there. It was linking someone in Western Bosnia right into what was going on within his community. It was amazing. For Oxfam, as a global organization, to be able to keep a global view. No matter where you are you can find out what's going on somewhere else.

John: The site also had a regional view, because it was more tailored to the regional media and to regional agendas than we were able to do on the Corporate Internet site. Not just in terms of language but also the focus and direction of the information.

---

9. Hurricane Mitch, a hurricane with sustained wind speeds of 180 mph, struck Central America in October 1998. Oxfam worked through local counterparts to provide water-sanitation, food, and health care in the immediate aftermath, followed by reconstruction of housing. Oxfam's program reached hundreds of thousands of people, mainly in Nicaragua and Honduras.

10. Oxfam managed a return program in Drvar in 1999, helping people who had left their homes as a result of conflict in Bosnia to return there.

Steve: It was a defining moment because the quality of the information on Hurricane Mitch was so useful, both for the general public and for other people within Oxfam. I was in Brazil at the time and our communications officer was seconded over to work on Hurricane Mitch. She got a lot of her information from the site—and she needed as much information as possible to be able to make the switch from being in Brazil to Central America.

Julia Flynn (*Internet Manager since 1998 and project manager developing the Corporate intranet in 1998*): What part did the Internet site play in furthering relationships with local organizations with which we were working?

Becky: The Internet site in Managua was used a lot, particularly around debt and structural adjustment, where we were working with a network on those issues. The site was one of the first ones in Central America—this was before NGOs got into having their own sites—and partners could put their papers on it. Later we supported them in setting up their own sites.

For example, CRIES (CRIES is the Spanish acronym for the Regional Research Center on Economic Policy) would post their documents on our site in relation to debt or adjustment. Then we supported them—with a grant, plus some technical support—in setting up their own.[11] And as CRIES is part of a global network, this skills transfer, and the resourcing to do it, was very important.

Some Advice for NGOs

Miranda: Do you have suggestions for other NGOs as to ways they could use the Internet?

Giulietta: I was in Albania this year, setting up the emergency office there, an office that had gone from three staff to 80 within two weeks.[12] I arrived at the same time as an IT person and we set up a network for over 20 computers. The first

---

11. The Web site of CRIES is http://apc.nicarao.org.ni/cries.htm
12. Over 800,000 refugees fled from Kosovo to Albania and Macedonia in April 1999. By May, Oxfam's program covered particular needs, especially water, for around 200,000 people in Albania.

thing I did was ensure that we had a shared directory. It was a very positive first step. We didn't have the intranet, but just having a directory and then meeting with key staff who could share it with their teams, training them on it, immediately gave us an outlet for all the information that was pouring in. We had lots of situation reports every day, updates on the situation in Albania: these were immediately filed in a set place in the directory; people knew they could go there and get background information, and it did draw us together.

Steve: That information came to Oxfam House and went on the intranet site. So not only was it available in your little network, but it was available to a wider audience as well.

Becky: Giulietta's role was a key one for cultural change within the organization because she was the first point of contact for any new staff member. The person who you first meet, who says, "This is what you need to know, and this is where you go for information," can establish the information culture.

Julia: So key advice for an NGO moving in for the first time is to set up a network of computers with a key person who has a role in developing the basic systems and inducting incoming people. Where possible use existing systems, and improve and build on what's there already. What about the role of the manager in this?

Becky: The key for management is to give sufficient scope for creativity. Give creative people scope to try things out, and put a little bit of money in too because that's part of the cultural change. Get a few things going and see what happens. Some, like the radio modem, might not work out, but some, like the Web site, become incredibly powerful.

Giulietta: Looking at another area: just before I left Albania we introduced the intranet, but just on a couple of PCs. There were queues of people waiting to go onto those two PCs. A manager needs to trust his or her staff enough to give them access to information, to be able to browse and find out for themselves. As Becky said earlier, there's a surge at the beginning, because you're interested and it's new, but in the end it settles down.

Francisco: It's difficult to answer your question about giving advice to others, because I don't think there are exact recipes to apply to an organization. But it is always good to learn from failures and mistakes.

So far we have been talking about information but not about knowledge. Knowledge is getting more and more important in trying to overcome poverty. The World Bank has developed a good Internet site, intranet site, and extranet. They are in the forefront because their approach is around knowledge management. I think that NGOs, both Northern and Southern, have to try to share more knowledge rather than data and information. We are facing email overload—every day, people complain about receiving too much email. How do we turn all this into useful knowledge? That's the main challenge for NGOs using the Internet. Sharing knowledge.

Miranda: Thank you.

16 The Rise and Persistence of the Technological Community Ideal
by Randy Connolly

Of our conceptions of the past we make a future. —Thomas Hobbes (1640)

Communities are to be distinguished, not by their falsity/genuineness, but by the style in which they are imagined. — Benedict Anderson (1991)

In the past several years online communities have generated a great deal of interest in both the popular and academic press. One of the more common themes in this literature is that of a sickly social world in need of the communal cure available in online communities. According to their adherents, online communities are "about giving individuals a taste of democracy, helping them create new kinds of communities, and reconnecting them with the institutions that shape their daily lives" (Katz 1997). They "may help counter the economy's tendency to break apart traditional bonds, to force people to move away from their families and communities in order to find work or living space" (Miller 1996); they "could bring conviviality and understanding into our lives and might help revitalize the public sphere" (Rheingold 1993, p. 14). Statements such as this one have become commonplace: "In this dog-eat-dog world, in which life has become so fragmented, isolated, and rootless for so many of us, the electronic frontier has offered a home of sorts" (Burstein and Kline 1993, p. 115). Taken in this light, online communities are thus potentially political instruments, because they seem to offer a solution to a set of social and political problems, namely rootlessness, lack of community, loneliness, isolation, the lack of public spaces, and an inability to contribute to public policy discussion.

Perhaps the best way to begin evaluating these claims about the political potential of online communities is to recognize that several other technologies over the past 150 years have also been praised using the same highly charged moral language. Boat canals, trains, telegrams, telephones, automobiles, and radios were each initially seen in their time as a way to rebuild a lost sense of community in the United States. This chapter will argue that the political hopes invested in online communities, like those invested in the technologies just mentioned, are best understood as a continuation of one of the oldest political traditions in the United States: that of Jeffersonian Republicanism. Generally considered to have been buried by a victorious individual-rights liberalism in the nineteenth and twentieth centuries, the hopes and ideals of Jeffersonian Republicanism have periodically reemerged into common political discourse attached to the rugged coattails of revolutionary technologies. This chapter will argue that this Jeffersonian Republican heritage is a key reason why many people believe that online communities can recreate lost community virtues and at the same time preserve or even enlarge individual freedom and choice. By recognizing this political heritage we can better evaluate the claims being made about the political potential of the new communities developing in today's cyberspace.

To bring this political heritage to light, this chapter will begin by describing some of the previous periods of technological enthusiasm in the United States. It will recount the political hopes that were attached to canals, trains, telegraphs, telephones, automobiles and the radio. The chapter will then focus on the Jeffersonian Republican political heritage at the root of these technological enthusiasms. With this backdrop brought to light, we will be able to see the political hope being invested in online community for what it is: just the latest chapter in a continuing hope that a technology can ameliorate the political problems of a large and geographically dispersed republican democracy. The sad irony of this hope is that each of these technologies has facilitated and encouraged the very phenomenon that is at the root of these political problems: geographically dispersed communities. But to see this we must first chart the rise and persistence of the technological community ideal.

Previous Technological Enthusiasms

Canals

Online community is not the first technology to be greeted as a potential cure for the ills of society. In fact, if we could transport ourselves back to Rome, New York, on July 4, 1817, we would have been able to hear an enthusiasm for a cutting-edge technology that would not be out of place in a current issue of *WiReD* or *The Futurist*. The event was a ceremony marking the beginning of work on the Erie Canal (Sheriff 1996). The hope was that this canal, and the many others that soon followed, would benefit the nation by easing the passage of trade (Harrison 1987, Larson 1987, R. Shaw 1990). Due to constitutional concerns, however, these canals were not federally funded; funds had to be raised by the individual states or by private investors. Canals thus needed promoters. Despite their potential economic benefits, canals were often promoted as a potential public good due to their ability to bring people together. Shaw quotes New York Representative Thomas R. Gold arguing in 1817 that by improved roads and canals the disparate people of the American Republic can "be cemented and preserved in a lasting bond of union" (p. 27). Shaw also quotes a typical prediction that the Erie Canal "will unite the two most populous and powerful sections of the nation and form one of the strongest safeguards of the union" (p. 202). Governor De Witt Clinton emphasized in 1817 that the Canal and other canals in the future would turn the nation into

> one vast I[s]land, susceptible of circumnavigation to the extent of many thousand of miles. . . . To be instrumental in producing so much good, by increasing the stock of human happiness—by establishing the perpetuity of free govern-

ment—and by extending the empire of improvement, of knowledge, of refinement and of religion, is an ambition worthy of a free people (Sheriff 1996, p. 51).

In other words, canals were evidence that "it was not necessary to choose between material progress and a godly society" (Sheriff 1996, p. 62). Canals, by bringing people together, were seen as a instrument of democratic governance. It was claimed that in a nation growing geographically and commercially, transportation technology could reunite and reinvigorate community and public spiritedness. "We are . . . rapidly, [I] was about to say fearfully, growing," warned future vice-president John C. Calhoun. For Calhoun, this is

> our pride and danger, our weakness and our strength . . . we are under the most imperious obligation to bind the Republic together with a perfect system of roads and canals. Let us conquer space (Wiebe 1984, p. 137).

To abet this conquest, American state governments undertook a canal-building frenzy. But canals were not destined to be the Cortéz of North American space. That honor would fall to the railway.

The Railway

In the 1820s, visionary entrepreneurs laid down tracks for carrying horse-drawn carriages. While they were swifter and smoother than carriages on America's crude roads, the promise of tracks was only felt with the importation of the steam engine locomotive from England. On May 30, 1830, Peter Cooper tested his new steam locomotive, the Tom Thumb, on the carriage tracks of the Baltimore & Ohio Company. By 1831, more practical engines had been built for the Mohawk and Hudson Railroad in New York and then scores of others throughout Pennsylvania and New England. While these early locomotives often suffered dangerous breakdowns—in 1838 alone, 496 people died of boiler explosions—Americans were rapt in their praise for the new technology. Leo Marx

(1964) quotes one American, George Perkins Marsh, enthusing in 1847:

> Just as we are prepared to go forward in building the frame of our national enterprise, a new power presents itself! . . . The spirit of the republic grasps it, . . . hails the agency of steam (p. 205).

Indeed Americans did hail the agency of steam—that is, the steam puffing out of locomotives as they crossed and crisscrossed the continent-sized republic. As Leo Marx notes, Americans "gasped and panted and cried" for railways. Michael Chevalier claimed that America "has a perfect passion for railroads; he loves them . . . as a lover loves his mistress" (Marx 1964, p. 208). "The people are Railroad mad," complained a jealous telegraph stock promoter in 1849 (Thompson 1947, p. 203).

Why this passion for railroads? Certainly locomotives with their "terrible energy" (Hawthorne 1967) were amazing machines. They were the first qualitative leap in land transportation since the adoption of the horse. The locomotive sucked in air noisily, ravenously consumed fire and trees, and belched noise and smoke, all within a mighty iron frame that was inexorable in its movement—"a fate, an *Atropos*, that never turns aside," Thoreau (1962) complained, not without wonder. It indeed was a sublime machine. (For an excellent examination of America's fascination with the sublime in technology, see Nye 1994.) Yet while a number of Englishmen wondered "Is there no nook of English Ground secure / From rash assault?" from the railways (Wordsworth 1969), Americans tended to embrace the machine due to their belief in its moral benefits. In particular, railways were praised, as were the canals, as instruments of unity, as a way to bring dispersed Americans together in a community of interests. Ward (1986) quotes one enthusiast, Kimball Minon, claiming in 1847 that railways are "bands of iron binding us together, a family of states" (p. 21), and another enthusiast arguing that "Railroads throughout the world . . . have brought the great family of mankind into newer and more genial communion" (pp. 19–

20). In an 1847 speech celebrating the opening of a new railway line in New Hampshire, Daniel Webster, past and future secretary of state, praised the railroad for its power to unify the nation into a "great mass of the community" and thereby "equalize the condition of man" (Marx 1964, p. 210). A Tennessee editor in 1847 argued that "these railroads are the iron bands that will bind the various sections of this country together by a community of interest" (Ward 1986, p. 25). Promoters for the railways often rhetorically linked the railways to moral and political themes. Lecturers declaimed on "The Moral Influence of Steam" (Nye 1994, p. 57) and promoters urged ministers "to take an early opportunity to deliver a discourse before your congregation on the moral effect of railroads on our wide extended country" (Smith 1981). One key moral effect was, of course, how the railway would unite the citizens of the United States by facilitating communication and person-to-person contact. Ward (1986) quotes one railway proponent who declared in 1851 that "iron rails will become another electric wire through which any persons upon a line of railway in the most remote part of the country can touch every section of the Union" (p. 30), and another who promised in 1847 that:

> Railroads tend to elevate, to extend and increase knowledge as well as business, and in *our* country especially, they will unite us more closely as a people, and bind us together as a common brotherhood (p. 47).

The Telegraph

Similar hopes were attached to the great communications technologies of the nineteenth century: the telegraph and the telephone. As railroads were beginning to crisscross the nation, Samuel F. Morse patented his telegraph in 1837. Despite the rapid appreciation that Americans and their governments formed for canals and the contemporaneous railroad, Samuel Morse had a difficult time in the first decade after his patent in attracting government or business interest. Morse was convinced that the telegraph could be an instrument for general good; he fruitlessly tried to convince Congress in 1837 and 1838 to create and run a telegraphic postal system. Finally, in 1843, Morse convinced Congress to authorize a $30,000 payment to construct a line between Washington and Baltimore (Thompson 1947).

The arguments Morse made to Congress in those years were prophetic—and already a bit nostalgic. In testimony before Congress in 1837, Morse, pointing to the benefits to government and business brought by the railroad and canals, argued that "the greater the speed with which intelligence can be transmitted from point to point, the greater is the benefit derived to the whole community" (Blondheim 1995). The following year, again before Congress, Morse predicted that through the agency of the telegraph,

> it would not be long ere the whole surface of this country would be channeled for those nerves which are to diffuse, with the speed of thought, a knowledge of all that is occurring throughout the land; making, in fact, *one neighborhood of the whole country* (Thompson 1947, emphasis added).

Some commentators (see, e.g., Lebow 1995) have seen Morse's justification as a strikingly original prefiguration of today's "global village" idea.

Finally, after five years of struggle and poverty, Morse was able to convince Congress to pay for a trial telegraph line from Washington to Baltimore. After several successful tests, Morse sent the famous message "What hath God wrought?" on the public opening of the line in 1844. The public in Baltimore and Washington "flocked to see the latest wonder of the age. Hundreds begged and pleaded to be allowed merely to look at the instrument" (Thompson 1947, p. 25). Nonetheless, it still took several years before the telegraph received wider public acclaim. Until the middle years of the 1850s, the principal users of the early telegraph lines were brokers and bookies. But by the mid-1850s, the telegraph had entered in a more substantial way into the American public consciousness. In Britain, "the public, though intrigued, appeared largely indifferent to the values of the new invention" (Kieve 1973, p. 26), but in America the telegraph's implications "were the subject of extended, often euphoric, and often pessimistic debate" (Carey 1989, p. 202). The extension of telegraph lines from city to city was invariably greeted with acclaim and wonder. "One of the greatest events ever," claimed the *Cincinnati Daily Commercial* in August 6, 1847 (Czitrom 1982, p. 7). In January 15 of the previous year the *Philadelphia North American* hailed the telegraph that

> leaves, in our country, no elsewhere—it is all *here*: it makes the pulse at the extremity beat—throb for throb and in the instant—with that at the heart. . . . In short, it will make the whole land one being (Czitrom 1982, p. 12).

This was already becoming a common theme. The telegraph promised that the city and its periphery would be brought together due to its ability to improve communication. Again and again, the claim was made that instantaneous communication could only increase cooperation and humanity among people. The selection of quotations below provides an idea of the way that railroads were consistently thought about in terms of advancement of social and community ties:

> Yes, this electric chain from East to West
> More than mere metal, more than mammon can,
> Binds us together—kinsmen, in the best,
> As most affectionate and frankest bond;
> Brethren as one; and looking far beyond
> The world in an Electric Union blest!
> —Martin F. Typper, 1875 (Carey 1989, p. 208).

> The electric telegraph is the nervous system of this nation and of modern society by no figure of speech, by no distant analogy. Its wires spread like nerves over the surface of the land, interlinking distant parts, and making possible a perpetually higher cooperation among men, and higher social forms than have hereto existed. —1855 (Thompson 1947, p. 253).

> How potent a power, then, is the telegraph destined to become in the civilization of the world! This binds together by a vital cord all the nations of the earth. It is impossible that old prejudices and hostilities should longer exist, while such an

instrument has been created for an exchange of thought between all the nations of the earth. —1858 (Carey 1989, pp. 208–209).

Nearly all our vast and wide-spread populations are bound together, not merely by political institutions but by a Telegraph and Lightning-like affinity of intelligence and sympathy, that renders us emphatically "ONE PEOPLE" everywhere. —1852 (Czitrom 1982, p. 12).

The announcement on August 5, 1858 from Cyrus W. Field that the Atlantic cable connecting Old World and New was laid and working poured fuel on this fire of technological enthusiasm. Henry M. Field (1866) describes how the news "everywhere produced the greatest excitement. In some places all business was suspended; men rushed into the streets, and flocked to the offices where the news was received" (p. 219). The president telegraphed Cyrus Field with these words: "I trust it may prove instrumental in promoting peace and friendship between the kindred nations" (p. 221). A similar message was telegraphed to Queen Victoria on August 16, 1858:

May the Atlantic Telegraph, under the blessing of Heaven, prove to be a bond of perpetual peace and friendship between the kindred nations, and an instrument destined by Divine Providence to diffuse religion, civilization, liberty, and law throughout the world (p. 230).

Interestingly, the English reaction to the achievement was much more subdued (Kieve 1973, p. 109; Czitrom 1982, p. 232). But in America, editors, preachers, and poets loudly celebrated the occasion. One typical offering, quoted by Field (1866, p. 235), emphasized both peaceful nature and the hegemonic power of the event:

Speed, speed the cable; let it run
A loving girdle round the earth,
Till all the nations 'neath the sun
Shall be as brothers of one hearth.
As brothers pledging, hand in hand,

One freedom for the world abroad,
One commerce over every land,
One language and one God.

Yet despite these hopes, the telegraph did not long maintain these aspirations. The frequently litigious struggle between dozens of upstart telegraphic companies (Congress refused to purchase Morse's patent rights) and the emergence of a monopolistic Western Union by 1866 alienated many citizens. While public acclaim and hope flew with disappointment away from the telegraph, it was, however, soon to land at a new technological home, that of the telephone.

The Telephone

On the morning of February 14, 1876, Alexander Graham Bell's father-in-law Gardiner Hubbard filed on Bell's behalf a patent application for a speaking telephone system. Just a few hours later, at the same patent office, Elisha Gray also filed a patent caveat for a very similar telephone system. Those few hours of priority would give Bell legal claim to the telephone and would be the foundation for the development of what was once the world's largest corporation, AT&T. (For this and the following, see Brooks 1975, Fischer 1992.) After exhibiting the telephone at a New York church in 1877, Bell, Hubbard and the father of one of Bell's students incorporated the Bell Telephone Company and began to market their invention. By the early 1880s they had about 60,000 subscribers scattered around the country and a court-imposed monopoly on telephone services. They initially marketed their device as a replacement for the telegraph for business users. In fact, it wasn't until the 1920s that AT&T began to emphasize the social and residential uses of the telephone (Fischer 1992, p. 75). Yet despite the decision to focus their marketing on business users, Bell's vision was not unlike that of Morse. In an 1878 letter to a group of British investors, Bell wrote:

> The simple and inexpensive nature of the Telephone . . . renders it possible to connect every man's house, office or manufactuary with a Central Station so as to give him the benefit of

direct telephonic communication with his neighbors at a cost not greater than that incurred for gas or water. . . . I believe that in the future wires will unite the head offices of Telephone Companies in different cities and a man in one part of the country may communicate by word of mouth with another at a distant place. I am aware that such ideas may appear to you Utopian (de Sola Pool 1977).

It is interesting to note that this vision of a networked neighborly world might appeal to American sensibilities, but it did not appeal to British ones: Bell failed to garner British investment. The general opinion in British opinion tended to be that the telephone was simply a luxury for the rich. *The Times* newspaper argued:

When all is said and done the telephone is not an affair of the million. It is a convenience for the well-to-do and a trade appliance for the persons who can very well afford to pay for it. . . . An overwhelming majority of the population do not use it and are not likely to use it all, except perhaps to the extent of an occasional message from a public station (Perry 1997).

Yet even in America, Bell initially had a difficult time developing the telephone system. To sell telephones, Bell had to market the machine aggressively. A typical early advertisement stated "the telephone can put the user in instant communication with the grocer, butcher, baker" as well as people from an additional 176 other occupations (Aronson 1977). Other advertisements emphasized its ability to connect business people together in a more intimate way than the telegraph. While the high cost of lines made the telephone initially something only the wealthy could afford, it was only with the adoption of the telephone by the less wealthy for social uses that AT&T's fortune was secured. And this adoption was accompanied by the rhetoric of technologically abetted community.

As the telephone system grew in the 1880s and 1890s, editors, writers and marketers began to consider what the telephonic future would be. One of the most common themes was that the telephone would enable a more dispersed yet more accessible community life. *Scientific American* (1880) predicted "nothing less than a new organization of society—a state of things in which every individual, however secluded, will have at call every other individual in the country." Another writer, quoted by Marvin (1988, p. 66), argued that the telephone was introducing an "epoch of neighborship without propinquity." Bell itself claimed that it was turning America into "a nation of neighbors" (Fischer 1992, p. 24). AT&T's advertisements stressed the national purpose of the telephone. One advertisement linked the telephone to the earlier rhetoric of the telegraph and railway:

> They have facilitated communication and intervisiting, bringing us closer together, giving us a better understanding and promoting more intimate relations. . . . At first, the telephone was the voice of the community. As the population increased and its interests grew more varied, the larger task of the telephone was to connect the communities and keep all the people in touch, regardless of local conditions or distance (quoted in Fischer 1992, p. 163).

Other advertisements claimed that "You need your telephone to keep in touch with the rest of the world as well as your neighbors" (quoted in Fischer 1992, p. 165).

From this ability to create geographically dispersed neighbors, it was frequently deduced that a more civilized and united world was an inevitability:

> Any device that enlarges one's environment and makes the rest of the world one's neighbors is an efficient mechanical missionary of civilization and helps to save the world from insularity where barbarism hides (Marvin 1988, p. 192).

> Some day we will build up a world telephone system making necessary to all peoples the use of a common language, or common understanding of languages, which will join all the people of the earth into one brotherhood (de Sola Pool 1983, p. 89).

However, the majority of commentators who saw the telephone as a force of moral good, focused on its ability to make "the continent a community." It was hoped that the telephone would ameliorate or even solve the peculiar American city–country and community–individual antinomies. The telephone, just like those other technologies, would allow geographically dispersed individuals to get their social life virtually, through the technology. *Cosmopolitan* magazine ran a story in 1893 predicting that by 1993 the telephone would allow families to live on scattered homesteads, conduct their work and socializing from home via telephone, and meet together only on rare ceremonial occasions (Fischer 1992, p. 224). The telephone was seen as a way to integrate rural dwellers into the national community. According to Ithiel de Sola Pool (1983), one prognosticator claimed that it "destroys the barrier between city and country. Henceforth the country is but a vast suburb" (p. 54), and *Telephony* magazine ran many articles at the turn of the century about how the telephone "transformed farm life from a desperate struggle with loneliness and hardship into a tolerable career" (p. 49). Others saw the telephone as the means towards creating spontaneous sociability in new geographically dispersed communities of the early twentieth century (Keller 1977).

The Automobile

The automobile attracted similarly extravagant praise in its initial period of adoption. *World's Work* in 1903 saw it as greatly enhancing the quality of life:

> Every friend within 3000 square miles can be visited, any place of worship or lectures or concert attended and business appointment kept. . . . It is a revolution in daily life. With an automobile one lives three times as much in the same span of years, and one's life therefore becomes to that extent wider and more interesting (Flink 1970, p. 102).

Roads, Hulber Earle argued in 1905, "socialize the countryside . . . with the help of the automobile, turning the country into one big village" (Ling 1990). And Hayden Eames, general manager of Studebaker, claimed that the automobile "develops a sense of community in agricultural districts which was utterly impossible with the former methods of transportation" (Flink 1970, p. 111).

Progressive political reformers of the 1910s and 1920s looked to the automobile as a solution to an opposite problem: how to transport people out of the morally suspect, crowded cities to the morally pure countryside. McShane (1994) quotes one auto enthusiast who argued that "decent-minded folk" would be able to "live in a cottage colony, rather than a swarming tenement district filled with saloons and brothels." This vision was given institutional approval by the late 1920s in the writings of the new shapers of American space: urban planners. For instance, the vision of the Regional Planning Association of America in the 1920s was an America of hilly wildernesses joined by "motorways," with the valleys filled with the human overflow of metropolises (Hall 1988, p. 154). The National Conference of City Planners in 1924 had a similar dream. Learning from the crowded mistakes of the East, they proudly declared that in the West, the horizontal city was the way of the future (Hall 1988, p. 276).

Master architect Frank Lloyd Wright had a similar, if more provocatively worded, vision. From the late 1920s through to the 1950s, Wright proclaimed upon Broadacre City, his vision of an America in which each family lives on its own acre (Wright 1945). For Wright, the congestion of the American city was destroying the most important feature of the nation: individual freedom. Individuality, for Wright, is "the fundamental integrity of the man," and thus "the most valuable asset of the human race." This "integrity is the essential core of a democracy," and thus democracy is the "gospel of individuality." This individuality or democracy can not exist in the crowded city: it requires massive decentralization and dispersal across the vast American landscape. In this democracy, the central ideal is "reintegrated decentralization . . . [with] many free units developing strength as they . . . grow together in a spacious freedom." The phone and the automobile were essential to his vision. These technologies are "allowing a freedom and freshness of light from within that no civilization has yet attained." By creating a dispersed urban landscape, these technologies are being "brought to the service of the citizen as an individual." Wright's new homesteader can farm his own acre and yet drive to nearby factories or offices. He writes: "No longer the farmer envying the urban dweller his mechanical improvements while the latter in turn covets the farmer's green pastures." In contrast, these new homesteaders will live "free individual lives that enrich the communal life."[1]

The Radio

Radio, or wireless telegraphy as it was initially called, was also greeted with the now familiar language of social togetherness. On October 4, 1899, Marconi successfully used his wireless telegraph to report on the international yacht races off Sandy Hook, New Jersey (Lewis 1991). Within days, Marconi was featured on front pages across the nation. The wonder of wireless—the fact that it needed no wires—made it ripe for the rhetoric of the technological sublime. *The New York Times* saw a future in which "wireless telegraphy would make a father in the old New England farm and his son in Seattle . . . neighbors" (Douglas 1987, p. 24). Nikola Tesla declared in 1904 (Marvin 1988, p. 192) that radio would be "very efficient in enlightening the masses, particularly in still uncivilized countries and less accessible regions, and that it will add materially to general safety, comfort and convenience, and maintenance of peaceful relations." Ann Douglas (1987, pp. 25–27) sums up the popular response to early wireless as a belief that "wireless might be the truly democratic, decentralized communication technology people have yearned for, a device each individual would control and use whenever he or she wanted" and yet "wireless would restore a sense of community in an increasingly anticommunal world."

By the time of the *Titanic* disaster and the entry of America into World War One, the radio experience was being radically altered from the two-way, send-and-receive of wireless

---

1.   Pages 26, 46, 25, 34, 41, 66–67, 69.

telegraphy to the one-way, receive-only experience of radio. Nonetheless, the early period of receive-only radio had a period of technological euphoria no different from the previous technologies surveyed in this chapter. This era began in the fall of 1920 when KDKA in Pittsburgh, WWJ in Detroit, and WHA in Wisconsin began regular programmed broadcasting. By the following year there were a handful of other stations, but by 1922, there were 670. By March of 1922, the Department of Commerce was issuing over 70 radio broadcasting licenses a month. The sale of radio receivers had ballooned from $60 million in 1922 to $358 million in 1924 (Barnouw 1966). Radio fever had arrived. One not atypical commentator in the *Literary Digest* (1922, "Is Radio Only a Passing Fad?") described it as a "craze," and *The New York Times* observed in March 1922 that it was the most popular pastime in America. Herbert Hoover, then Secretary of Commerce, noted that the "tidal wave of interest in the subject" was "one of the most astonishing things that [has] come under my observation of American life" (Douglas 1987, p. 303). And not surprisingly, the enthusiasm for the new technology engendered the usual musings about the future social and moral consequences of this technology.

A constant theme was that radio was revolutionizing the world's thoughts and habits (Outlook 1922). "With almost stunning suddenness the radio has become a power boundless in possibilities for good or evil . . . [It] will prove to be the most potent unifying influence that had appeared since the railway and the telegraph were invented" declared the author of "Radio—The New Social Force" (Outlook 1924). "Radio broadcasting is both the most marvelous mystery and the greatest potentiality that has ever been harvested to man's use," pronounced Hudson Maxim (1924) in *The Nation*. The inaugural issue of *Radio Broadcast* prophesied that "government will be a living thing to its citizens instead of an abstract and unseen force," and as a result "at last we may have convenants literally arrived at" (Barnouw 1966, pp. 102–103). By allowing potentially all the country to hear the same debates and culture, radio would allow Americans to "feel together, think together, live together" (Kaempffert 1924, p. 772).

Just as for canals, railroads, automobiles, telegraphs, and telephones, radio was given these political capabilities due to its ability to integrate the "pure" but geographically isolated rural areas with the crowds and culture of the cities. *Nebraska Farmer* looked forward to the fulfillment of the radio's promise

> to bring actually to the home of the farmer or the city man, faster than by any other means, the news of the day, the markets for farm products, and the entertainments of the highest order from distant cities (*Literary Digest* 1922, "Radio and the Farm Boy").

Similarly, *Farm Mechanics* enthused that radio telephony was quickly revolutionizing social life for farmers, who now had a way to access high-class entertainment and education without travelling to the city (*Literary Digest* 1922, "Radio and Farm Life").

The author of "Will Radio Send Us 'Back to the Farm'?" (*Literary Digest* 1924) argued that in order to persuade more people to live in rural areas, it was necessary to make those areas more attractive through increased social intercourse. But unfortunately, increases in population density in such areas, while increasing the possibilities for social interaction, would have the effect of urbanizing the rural areas. This problem had been partially alleviated by the automobile, telephone, and a good postal service, but it was radio that finally made the ideal of rural isolation with social intercourse possible. Kaempffert (1921, p. 771) exclaimed,

> If these little towns and villages so remote from one another, so nationally related and yet physically so unrelated, could be made to acquire a sense of intimacy, if they could be brought into direct contact with one another!

With radio, according to *The Nation* (1923), "Every man may build his own Utopia!"

Why These Hopes?

Our own utopia is, however, still far off in the distance. Perhaps computer-mediated communication will finally bring it closer . . . or perhaps it is just the latest installment of a long-running story of hope and disappointment. In this review of previous technological enthusiasms, we saw a common set of themes voiced: technology as instrument of social cohesion, technology as integrator of rural and urban life, technology as device of individual freedom, and technology as rejuvenator of community life. Why this continuity of themes over almost one hundred and ninety years? Why do the same political hopes continue to be invested in certain types of technology?

The approach taken in this chapter is that a given technology is imagined and used in ways that are shaped by the moral and political horizon of a particular society. To understand why a particular technology is imagined in such a manner, we need to bring to light this context. Since there has been a great deal of similarity in how certain revolutionary technologies have been imagined, we must look further back to the American prehistory of these technological enthusiasms. The "American" in the previous sentence was intentional. While other countries have experienced periods of enthusiasm for the technologies mentioned earlier, it was principally in the United States that the tropes of freedom and community were consistently attached. Wolfgang Sachs (1992), in his chronicle of German enthusiasm over the automobile, shows that much of the initial reaction to the automobile was integrated into German nationalistic rhetoric. The automobile was praised as a symbol of German economic might, whereas in the United States the automobile was praised using the language of freedom and community. As David E. Nye (1994, p. 282) has commented:

> Europeans neither invented nor embraced the vertical city of the skyscraper. Europeans banned or restricted electric signs, and rightly saw the landscape of Times Square as peculiarly American. Europeans did not see atomic explosions as tourist sites. Europeans seldom journeyed to see rockets go into

space, but Americans went by the millions. There is a persistent American attraction to the technological sublime.

The search then for the moral sources of the hope in online communities must be solidly rooted in the American experience, because it is in the United States that such an ideal has found its most characteristic manifestations. Certainly, the desire for freedom and community may transcend the United States. It may also be a European, perhaps even a universal hope. But the particular way this desire has been articulated in the United States is unique. The American experience, exemplified in its two founding metaphors, the city on a hill and the log cabin in the wilderness, has uniquely shaped the way in which its citizens imagine the relationship between technology and the human world.

Jeffersonian Republicanism

What then is this American past? The rhetoric of American technological enthusiasm is deeply rooted in the political language of the Revolutionary and Constitutional era. In particular, the rhetorical shape, as well as the substantive moral content, of the technologically enabled community ideal grew directly out of Jeffersonian Republicanism, which was the dominant ideology in America between the 1790s and the 1820s. This ideology was a transitional moral language that attempted to harmonize the older civic republican language of the American Revolution with the emerging vocabulary of rights-based liberalism. The latter—rights-based liberalism—is quite familiar to us today. This is the language of freedom and choice that is the bedrock of almost all current American reasoning and pronouncements upon the social, economic, and political realms. But the former—that of civic republicanism—is less known, and for that reason will require some elaboration. By first fleshing out our understanding of civic republicanism, and then showing how the Jeffersonian Republican world view grew out of civic republicanism, my broad claim will, I hope, seem less outlandish. We will find that the rhetoric and hopes of the technological enthusiasts examined in the first part of this chapter were adopted from the rhetoric and hopes of the key political agents and political thinkers of the revolutionary to post-Constitutional era in the United States.

Recent scholarship in American revolutionary history from the past three decades has stressed the civic republicanism of almost all the Revolutionary leaders. (The classic texts are Bailyn 1967, Pocock 1975, Wood 1969.) Civic republican-oriented thinkers argued that the way to create a just and healthy political system was for individuals to regain their liberty by displaying civic virtue through action oriented toward the public good. This definition needs to be unpacked, as it contains three key terms whose meaning is different today than it was in the eighteenth century: namely, liberty, civic virtue, and the public good. The word whose meaning has changed the most over time is undoubtedly that of liberty. In the above definition, it might strike us as strange that liberty can come from virtuous actions on behalf of the common good. Is not liberty the right and ability to do what we please? Certainly not for Americans of the revolutionary struggle. The most important and dominant meaning of liberty of that time was liberty as political liberty, meaning "the liberty of the group to have local control" (Appleby 1984). The settlements of the American colonies were characterized by strong local or community focus. Not surprisingly, then, Americans of the period typically saw liberty as *public* liberty, as local self-government, not as individual freedom from constraint. As one eighteenth-century commentator, John Zubly, noted in 1775, "Liberty does not consist in living without all restraint" (Wood 1969, p. 23). Another, Ambrose Serle, declared in 1776 that to be free from coercion "is a privilege which no man has a right to enjoy" (Shain 1994, p. 170).

The other key term in the language of American republicanism—only liberty was invoked more often (Wood 1969, pp. 53–55)—was the public good. In a well-ordered society, according to a pastor quoted by Shain (1994, p. 27), "each individual gives up all private interest that is not consistent with the general good." John Adams claimed in 1776 that

> There must be a positive passion for the public good, the pub-
> lic interest, honour, power, and glory, established in the minds
> of the people or there can be no republican government, nor
> any real liberty (Sandel 1996, p. 126).

The people are a homogenous body, it was often claimed, with only one interest. This common interest was not the aggregate of each particular interest but a separate, single, common good. Public good was thus a translation of the vernacular ideal of community into the language of civic republicanism. With this emphasis on a homogenous and organic public good, republicanism was also Janus-faced. It looked forward to a day in which all parts of the political and social community are harmoniously integrated—an ideal that Winthrop, Bradford and the other Puritan fathers would have found congenial (Wood 1969, pp. 59–60)—by *returning* or *regenerating* America *back* to its former virtue.

These eighteenth-century republican writers did not believe that an individual's concern for the common good is automatic. Private interests have a powerful attraction. As Alexis de Tocqueville (1969, sec. 1, chap. 18) noted in 1840, "In democratic communities, each citizen is habitually engaged in the contemplation of a very insignificant person: namely, himself." The only remedy to this natural tendency to value private over public needs, these writers believed, is to foster an appropriate character. Virtue was widely praised as a shorthand concept for the type of character that resists private interests in favor of public, communal needs. John Adams in 1776 insisted that "Public virtue cannot exist in a nation without private, and public virtue is the only foundation of Republics" (McCoy 1980, p. 69). A decade later the belief in private virtue as the foundation upon which the public good rests was still taken for granted. "To suppose that any form of government will secure liberty or happens without any virtue in the people, is a chimerical ideal," James Madison declared (Kloppenberg 1987).

The kind of virtue required of the natural leaders of society was different than that of the common folk of society. The virtue of this natural aristocracy was to be simplicity, frugality, and political participation with an eye to the public good. For the common people, the chief virtue should be deference. But the rhetoric of revolutionary republicanism mobilized not only the elite but also the common citizen. A deferential, politically meek general public presupposed by every republican theorist from Aristotle to Montesquieu simply failed to appear (Pocock 1975, p. 516). In other words, the deference of the virtuous commoners to their natural leaders did not materialize after the Revolution was won. Republican rhetoric had spawned democratic equality, not virtuous civic republicans—or so it seemed to the natural leaders amongst the gentry. "This Revolution . . . has introduced so much anarchy that it will take half a century to eradicate the licentiousness of the people," David Ramsay complained in 1783 (Wood 1969, p. 403). America was "sliding down into the mire of a democracy which pollutes the morals of citizens before it swallows up their liberties," thundered Fischer Ames (Wood 1991, pp. 230–231). Their concern was that the various state constitutions created from 1776 to 1786 had given too much control to the people. The perception of a politically impotent Continental Congress hamstrung by the democratic excess in the state legislatures—"The legislative department is everywhere extending the sphere of its activity, and drawing all power into its impetuous vortex" (Madison 1996, "The Federalist No. 48")—as well as the violence of the Shays' Rebellion (1786-7) prompted a reform effort that culminated in the Philadelphia Constitutional Convention of 1787.

Governor Randolph, at the opening of the Convention, declared that "our chief danger . . . arises from the democratic parts of our constitutions" (McDonald 1979). This concern over the democratic excesses of the Articles of Confederation seems to have united many of the delegates at the convention. James Madison, for instance, worried that "symptoms of a leveling spirit" had become all too apparent in the new country (McCoy 1980, p. 129). While there was much laborious debate and wrangling over the Constitution between the participants of the Constitutional Convention of 1787, it was only the heated prelude to a national debate about the merits of their handiwork. There was a new outpouring of political debate about the relative merits of the constitutional proposal, the most enduring of which is the collection of essays known as *The Federalist* by James Madison, Alexander Hamilton and John Jay. The political turbulence of the 1780s seems to have marked the end of the belief that virtue is sufficient for a political order. As Pocock (1975, p. 512) points out, the decline in the belief that the people possessed public virtue led to "an increasing recognition of the importance, and the legitimacy, in human affairs of the faction pursuing a collective but particular interest." Madison's tenth essay in *The Federalist* (Madison 1996) is perhaps the most famous statement of this worry.

> Complaints are everywhere heard from our most considerate and virtuous citizens, . . . that our governments are too unstable, that the public good is disregarded in the conflicts of rival parties, and that measures are often decided, not according to the rules of justice and the rights of the minor party, but by the superior force of an interested and overbearing majority.

Faction is defined as

> a number of citizens, whether amounting to a majority or minority of the whole, who are united and actuated by some common impulse of passion, or of interests adverse to the rights of other citizens, or to the permanent aggregate interests of the community.

Notice the distinction Madison makes between rights of the citizen and that of the public good or "aggregate interests of the community," each of which is, in other parts of *The Federalist* (for example, nos. 45 and 51), declared to be the goal of government. This valuation of community interests over individual interests is in keeping with civic republicanism. But note how the public good is defined: as the aggregate interests of all individuals in the community. In general, republican thought imagined the public good as some separate entity, as an irreducibly social good. In contemporary language, Madison is extolling methodological individualism (Taylor 1995), that is, the belief that collectivities are best described and understood as collections of individuals. While Madison's essay still contains a residue of republican commitment to the general good, this good is now understood as the sum of individuals' interests. Madison's essay indicates that individualistic notions had become much more salient by the late 1780s and early 1790s. This individualism is also responsible for faction. It is, Madison declares, the result of the differing interests of individuals combined with the liberty to pursue and express those interests. But eliminating these interests or liberty would be a cure "worse than the disease." Instead we should try to control the bad effects of faction by rendering majority factions "unable to concert and carry into effect schemes of oppression" (Madison 1996b, p. 45). Pure democracies are unable to prevent this; a republican government, however, can prevent factious interests detrimental to the public weal because it has legislative delegates "whose wisdom may best discern the true interests of their country" (p. 46).

Having established the primacy of republican institutions for handling factions, the remaining question in Madison's essay is what type of republic will be "more favorable to the election of proper guardians of the public weal." While small and large republics have drawbacks, all-in-all in large republics it is

> less probable that a majority of the whole will have a common motive to invade the rights of other citizens; or if such a common motive exists, it will be more difficult for all who feel it to discover their own strength, and to act in unison with each other" (p. 47).

Madison's promotion of large republics flew in the face of what was accepted wisdom. Montesquieu, whose "authority exceeded even that of Locke" for Americans of the eighteenth century (Rahe 1994), argued in *The Spirit of the Laws* (Montesquieu 1900) that Republics could not be constituted on an extended territory: "It is natural for a republic to have only a small territory; otherwise it cannot long subsist. . . . In an extensive republic the public good is sacrificed to a thousand private views." Many of the opponents to the Constitution, collectively referred to as the Antifederalists, echoed Montesquieu in their critique of the Constitution. They seized upon the size issue because they were sure that a large republic could not possibly have a unitary general good. One such critic asserted that "It is impossible for one code of laws to suit Georgia and Massachusetts" (Wood 1969, p. 500). The Antifederalists argued that by accepting the large federal Republic defined in the Constitution, Americans were giving up on the belief that the general good should be the focus of public action.

Madison's (and the Constitution's) view of society offered, in contrast, a new and different interpretation of republicanism. Interests could no longer be controlled by classically inspired virtue, feudal deference, or by local communal norms. Separate and competing sovereignty was the only way to protect the geographically dispersed republic against what republicanism had created: too many private interests and its result, factionalism. But the institutional arguments of the Constitution, and their support in *The Federalist*, had legitimated and consolidated a liberal understanding of society. Rather than a politics of the public good, the constitution supported a politics of individual interests.

Despite the Constitution's eventual ratification, worries about the direction of development of the new Republic persisted. These worries eventually led to the formation of one of America's first political parties: the Republican-Democratic Party of Thomas Jefferson, and then James Madison. I will use the term Jeffersonian Republicanism to refer to a general set of beliefs, assumptions and policies held by those associated with the Republican-Democratic party and its primary leaders, Jefferson and Madison.

The Republican-Democratic party emerged in the 1790s in opposition to the policies of Hamilton as secretary of the treasury. In particular, it was Hamilton's ambitious *Report on Manufacturers* that galvanized opposition to Hamilton's system and precipitated the end of his friendship with Madison and Jefferson, and the beginning of party politics in America. The *Report* begins by stating some of the common explanations for why America does not need manufacturing: that agriculture is the most productive form of human activity, that government should not be involved in industry, and the smallness of America's population (Hamilton 1966, pp. 230–235). Hamilton does acknowledge that agriculture "has intrinsically a strong claim to pre-eminence over every other kind of industry" (p. 236). However, it does not have the only claim. Manufacturing, Hamilton argues, like agriculture, inculcates industrious virtue as well as, if not more than, agriculture (pp. 241–242). In fact, without the population growth in cities that manufacturing encourages, America will soon have too much agriculture for domestic *and* foreign consumption: the economy *and* morals will hence inevitably decline. "Whence it follows" argued Hamilton, "that it is the interest of a community with a view to eventual and permanent economy, to encourage the growth of manufacturers." Hamilton proposed that a public funded debt (via the National Bank) could be used to provide "pecuniary bounties"—stimulating by rewards—to domestic manufacturers (pp. 286, 298–301, 336–340).

Not long after the *Report on Manufacturers*, Madison, Jefferson and others began to voice their opposition. Hamilton, it was claimed, was out to "overwhelm and destroy . . . every free and valuable principle of our government." The Bank and the proposed manufacturing subsidies would create "monied interests" that would introduce "all the weakness, vices and deformities of the decayed and expiring constitution of Britain" (Banning 1978). They have "given rise to scenes of speculation calculated to aggrandize the few and the wealthy, by oppressing the great body of people, to transfer the best resources of the country forever into the hands of speculators . . ." (Elkins and McKitrick 1993). Drew McCoy (1980, p. 7) has convincingly argued that Hamilton's *Report on Manufacturers* challenged his opponents' system of political economy. The concept of political economy refers to the belief held by many of the republican revolutionaries that the economic order should encourage the development of a virtuous citizenry. Madison, Jefferson, and many other Americans of the time believed that the proper political economy for a republic is an economy of small-scale farms operated by independent farmers or yeomen. This was not at all a new way of thinking in America. Benjamin Franklin, for instance, believed that America's boundless frontier would allow America to maintain itself as an agrarian nation, thus ensuring the survival of the virtue necessary for republican government (McCoy 1980, pp. 60–64). And George Mason, urging against Virginia's Port Bill of 1784 (which would have restricted all foreign trade to five coastal towns), asked:

> If virtue is the vital principle of a republic, and it cannot long exist, without frugality, probity and strictness of morals, will the manners of populous commercial cities be favorable to the principles of our free government? Or will not the vice, the depravity of morals, the luxury, venality, and corruption, which invariably prevail in great commercial cities, be utterly subversive of them? (Sandel 1996, p. 126).

More famously, Thomas Jefferson in query nineteen in his 1782 *Notes on the State of Virginia* (Jefferson 1944) claimed that a society of independent landowning farmers is intrinsically more virtuous than any other. "Those who labor in the earth are the chosen people of God, if ever He had a chosen people, whose breasts He has made His peculiar deposit for substantial and genuine virtue." Why? Because the freehold farmer is independent in that he depends only on his own efforts. Any other type of dependence "begets subservience and venality, suffocates the germ of virtue, and prepares fit tools for the designs of ambition." In fact, corruption in a state is "the proportion which the aggregate of the other classes of citizens bears in any State to that of its husbandmen, is the proportion of its unsound to its healthy parts." America can avoid this improper proportion due to the blessings of its size.

> While we have land to labor then, let us never wish to see our citizens occupied at a workbench . . . let our workshops remain in Europe. It is better to carry provisions and materials to workmen there, than bring them to the provisions and materials and with them their manners and principles. The

loss by the transportation of commodities across the Atlantic will be made up in happiness and permanence of government.

Madison also argued, in a *National Gazette* article in 1792 (Madison 1906), that the "life of the husbandman" was that which maximized "health, virtue, intelligence, and competency in the greatest number of citizens." Madison added that "'Tis not the country that peoples either the Bridewells or the Bedlams. These mansions of wretchedness are tenanted from the distresses and vice of overgrown cities." In contrast, independent farmers "are the best basis of public liberty, and the strongest bulwark of public safety."

It is worth stressing that both of Jefferson and Madison's paeans to the virtue of the agricultural life are in the context of a criticism of manufacturing. Jefferson, Madison and other like-minded republicans were apprehensive about Hamilton's proposals on manufacturing because they feared what large-scale manufacturing would do to the nation. It would concentrate people in the cities where they would no longer be independent citizens and producers but part of the urban mob. Jefferson wrote:

> The mobs of great cities add just so much to the support of pure government, as sores do to the strength of the human body. It is the manners and spirit of a people which preserve a republic in vigor. A degeneracy in these is a canker which soon eats to the heart of its laws and constitution (Jefferson 1944).

While Jefferson was eventually able to reconcile himself with manufacturing, he did remain suspicious of cities. As he admitted in a letter to Benjamin Rush in 1800 (White and White 1962), "I view great cities as pestilential to the morals, the health and liberties of man." How then could the great plague of urbanization be avoided? For Jefferson, Madison, and others, republican governance would surely collapse if America went the way of England, in which the majority of the people are crowded together into cities. The solution lay in the very thing that worried critics of the Constitution: the vast size of the new country. Because America has "an immensity of land courting the industry of the husbandman," the vast majority of its inhabitants will be freehold farmers, Jefferson asserted (Jefferson 1944). The life of a husbandman generates independence; as such, these people will have "substantial and genuine virtue." This equality of ownership and workmanship in the land gives America the "spirit of a people which preserves a republic."

Since America had the frontier and its boundless lands to the West, America could safely accommodate growing commercialism due to a simultaneous expansion of agriculture in the new lands to the west. Jefferson's hope for the republic's future, repeated in 1817, "is built as much on the enlargement of the resources of life going hand in hand with the enlargement of territory" (Jefferson 1899a). As Pocock recognized (1975, p. 540), "So long as the settlement of new land was possible, the partnership between agrarian virtue and commercial industry could be maintained and could perpetuate the illusion that the American 'new man' had reentered Eden."

Despite the frontier, however, worries emerged in the 1810s and 1820s. Jefferson fretted over the possibility that manufacturing and its unvirtuous citizens would in fact overtake the agrarian way of life. Jefferson wrote that as "avarice and corruption advance on us from the north and the east, the principles of free government are to retire to the agricultural States of the south and west, as their last asylum and bulwark" (Jefferson 1899b). As well, the economic and foreign policies of Jefferson and then Madison as Presidents (1801–1808, 1809–1816) were committed to fostering an agricultural economic life that would also foster the republican personality. Jefferson's Louisiana Purchase of 1802, for instance, was justified as a way to maintain the frontier land necessary to preserve the agricultural nature of the American republic and to guarantee the Mississippi as transportation route to bring these agricultural products to market (McCoy 1980, pp. 196–203).

Jeffersonian Republicanism was an innovative, but ultimately unstable, political theory. Due to its civic republican heritage, it was wedded to the belief that individual virtue was still important for the political community. But since its adherents believed that only the agrarian way of life could create that virtue, a rather dubious set of conclusions about community were generated. The syllogism went as follows: the agrarian way of life necessitated distance between individuals, since a farmer needs a certain amount of land in order to be economically viable. In fact, it is in the farmer's economic interest to increase the size of his holdings, thus potentially widening the distance between himself and his neighbors. And if only this agrarian independence can generate the virtue necessary for community, therefore republican democratic political community can only be successfully created by geographically dispersed individuals. But can community be created by widening the distance between individuals?

The extraordinary enthusiasm that greeted boat canals, trains, telephones, telegrams, automobiles, radios, and the Internet, but not the gas light, the phonograph, the battleship, or the microwave, lies in the fact that the former technologies potentially tie geographically dispersed people back together. The extraordinary enthusiasm of Americans, but not the British, the Germans, or the French, for these technologies is due to the fact that geographic dispersal is not a political problem for these nations in the way it was and is for the United States. Due to the frontier experience, the methodological individualism of the Constitution, and the rhetoric of Jeffersonian Republican ideology, Americans have continually sought a range of one's own; that is, they have sought to geographically distance themselves from one another. But the community promised never materialized. The hope for these space-defeating technologies was that they would tie people back together, and create a community of geographically isolated individuals. Yet despite these technologies, in the nineteenth century, "a powerful ambiguity became the heart of a cultural agenda: the achievement of personal liberation without material selfishness, solitude without fragmentation, integrity without desperate loneliness" (Watts 1994).

Conclusion

Joseph Lockard has observed, in regard to contemporary computerized online communities, that what "the software
addresses is *desire* for community rather than the difficult-to-
achieve, sweated-over reality of community" (Lockard 1997,
emphasis added). Indeed, this can not be stressed enough. All
of the technologically enabled communities visualized by
enthusiasts for the various technologies mentioned earlier
should be seen as expressions of a desire for vibrant community life. That such expressions date back to the 1820s is
indicative that the desire for a revitalized community is not a
recent phenomenon. The persistence of this desire could be
explained in one of two ways. First, it could mean that rich,
interpersonal, face-to-face communities in which political and
social issues are debated within a geographically constrained
public sphere characterized by social solidarity have been
missing from American life for quite a long time. Indeed,
Derek L. Phillip's *Looking Backward* (1993) makes precisely
this argument.

The second explanation—and the one I prefer—for the
persistence of this hope is that the dominance of moral republicanism from the 1760s to the 1810s inculcated a set of
expectations about the nature of social and political life. As we
saw earlier, the set of moral ideas collectively called republicanism emphasized that individuals need to exhibit certain
types of civic virtues, principally the ability to act toward the
common good instead of for private gain, in order to support
political liberty and democratic institutions. The ideal of political liberty within civic republicanism was that of citizens with
virtue deliberating amongst themselves about how their community should be run. The Constitution of 1787, however, was
an expression of the constitutional framers' doubt about the
virtue of the majority of citizens. The democratically elected
state legislatures of the 1780s seemed, to the dismay of the
framers, to be run by factional interests pursuing their private

and particular interests. Believing that there was no civic virtue among the general populace, the participants of the Constitutional Convention crafted a series of institutional devices that would make republican governance less dependent on the virtue of the people.

But by concentrating at the federal level and not institutionalizing a local public sphere, the constitutional settlement of 1789 had left unsatisfied the desire for a public space contained within republican ideals. In fact, "this political space is precisely what the framers did not want to create. They had little interest in providing a public space for a demos" (Matthews 1987). As the economy began industrializing and urbanizing in the nineteenth century, the desire continued for a social glue to replace the missing civic virtue and the dialogic public realm. Gordon Wood (1991, pp. 327–337) has recounted how in the 1820s Americans struggled to find a new social glue. Voluntary associations, evangelical Christianity, and the pursuit of profit were different candidates for this force for social cohesion. The opening of the Erie Canal in 1817, the first steam locomotive tests in 1830, and the success of Morse's telegraph in 1844 were greeted by the press, social commentators, and the general populace with language that clearly suggested that technology might be the social glue required by an urbanizing and industrializing continent-sized republic. And as the community-based public space retreated further and further, the idea that community and its public space could be recreated via technology continued as a beacon of hope within a steadily individualizing America.

Certainly the desire for community and its discursive public space is not a crazy one. This desire can be found in many other contexts. For instance, community development corporations and community cooperatives are trying to reestablish the link between economic activity and community life (Ross and Usher 1986). The New Urbanism movement within urban planning is similarly attempting to reshape the "sprawl of automobile suburbia into communities that make sense" (Scully 1994). And within political science, communitarian theorists are endeavoring to reorient our self-understanding away from the individualist ethos of Kantian liberalism and, instead, toward an understanding of the self that recognizes the importance of history, language, and geography in constituting an individual's identity. (See, for example, Beiner 1995, Sandel 1982, Taylor 1985, and Walzer 1990.)

Today's online communities could thus be seen as yet another attempt by individuals to break out of the loneliness and anomie of contemporary American life. Many of the proponents of computer-mediated community point to how online communities might help reorient the focus of our culture away from private satisfaction and toward our fellow humans. The diversity of the Internet is also seen as a harbinger of this new ethos. But its other attributes—"Free, Egalitarian. Decentralized. Ad hoc. Open and peer-to-peer. Experimental. Autonomous. Anarchic" (Burstein and Kline 1993, p. 104) —mitigate against this new dawn of collective sociability and cooperation.

The online community has two key problems that reduce the possibility of this new dawn's ever rising. The first is economic. Since online communities tend to be defined by a single special interest, they lend themselves to commodification or capture by business interests. Special-interest online communities are a dream come true for marketers. The members of many of these communities tend to be economically homogeneous with an abiding interest in some single thing or issue. A business selling something related to that thing or issue can quickly and cheaply advertise its wares or services within that community. (Indeed, some USENET groups have been destroyed by "spammers"—individuals or companies that post or email advertisements en masse.) There are voices that claim, in contrast, that online communities can act as a localizing force against global capitalism, that since individuals can be their own publishers on the World Wide Web, the mass media's relentless centralization can be reversed, or because it is so decentralized no one can own the Net. But the example of radio is instructive. The early wireless enthusiasts were certain that radio would remain a communications technology for private citizens. They never believed that giant corporations would soon monopolize radio broadcasting—after all, how could the radio spectrum, the air itself, be privatized? As radio became easier to use—due to investment in research by RCA and other corporations—and with the provision of high-quality content, radio became a passive, receive-only medium controlled by large business interests.

The Internet could follow this same path. Surfing the World Wide Web has become increasingly popular. One reason is that the Web is relatively easy to use (my preschool son can use it). Although the creation of a basic Web page does not require much skill, large commercial Web sites are adopting increasingly sophisticated technology to attract users. The creation of Web sites with leading-edge technology requires a large amount of effort and resources: time spent learning increasingly complicated authoring tools, programming on the server-side to create dynamic database-driven pages, and funding to meet the high cost of providing attractive and efficient graphics, sound, video and special-effect content. As time progresses, it seems that only companies with plenty of capital will be able to provide this. Competition among these well-capitalized providers will further push the technological boundaries, making it even more difficult for less-financed players to compete. This is precisely what happened with radio. Stations that were sponsored by a corporation or that accepted advertising had the capital to produce high-quality radio broadcasts. Listeners were drawn to the stations with these high-quality shows. To compete, other stations had to also accept advertising, merge with others, or fold. Within just a few years, commercial pressure had almost completely wiped out the vast radio community.

But the second and most significant problem with the technological community ideal—from the canals to the computer—is that it is about withdrawal. The technology community is a withdrawal toward a closed and small circle of the like-minded. How, one might ask, can this be the case? Is not the Internet diversely populated? Yes, it is, but so is the U.S. interstate highway system. By driving in your car you can potentially encounter people of different races, creeds, and sexual orientation. With a car it is possible to drive from one's middle-class white suburb to a bondage club in a black ghetto. It is possible; it's just not very likely. So, too, with online communities. As Robin Hamman's research in this book has shown, many users of AOL join the service not to create new friendships or communities, but to communicate with people they already know offline. And while some computer-mediated communities do in fact have a relatively diverse culture (the WELL seemed to be an example), there is a certain amount of demographic homogeneity in cyberspace: Internet users are generally middle-class and highly educated, and around half are North American (Global Reach 2000, SIQSS 2000). (See, for example, Nua, http://www.nua.ie, for recent demographic surveys.)

Within that general populace, communities tend to be defined by a special interest—the *Star Trek* online community, the poodle fanciers online community, the lesbians of Nebraska online community, and so on. As one cynic noted, bulletin-board-based communities "encourage participation in fragmented, mostly silent, microgroups who are primarily engaged in dialogues of self-congratulation" (Hermosillo 1996). Indeed the fact that they are communities of interest, not geography, is typically a highly praised attribute of online communities. "Common interests rather than proximity will bind these communities together" (Cairncross 1997). The society of the future will thus "be composed of less heterogeneous communities, linked more by common interests than by common location" (Keyworth no date). Computers will

> play an important role knitting together . . . the diverse communities of tomorrow, facilitating the creation of "electronic neighborhoods" bound together not by geography but by shared interests (Dyson et al. 1994).

The hoped-for communities created by canals, trains, and automobiles ultimately resulted in suburbanization. Individuals used the technology to withdraw into enclaves populated by those of similar race and economic status. The hope had been that the technology would allow geographically dispersed individuals to communicate with each other, either face to face with the assistance of transportation technology, or indirectly, using telegraphs, telephones, radios and the Internet.

People could have refuge from the larger population within a pastoral or suburban home, yet still be able to transport themselves to, or communicate with, centralized spaces for work, culture, and politics. But rather than rejuvenate community, the ideal almost fatally wounded it. By emphasizing how the technology can also expand the realm of individual action and control, adherents of the technological community ideal undermined its potential communal uses. This is particularly clear in the literature on online communities, in which the twin themes of individual freedom and community are often intertwined. Again and again we read that the computer "has the potential to liberate the individual as well as . . . [the] potential for new forms of human interdependence and expression" (Provenzo 1986), or as Jennings writes:

> Now for the first time in history, a possible answer to the utopian dilemma is emerging. By applying new technology and adopting a new perspective, we may at last be able to achieve a way of life that is *personal yet communal*, secure yet flexible, practical yet spiritually rewarding (1982, emphasis added).

The focus on individualism in the literature on online communities has led some to the conclusion that there is indeed a "libertarian ethos that reigns throughout most of cyberspace" (*The Economist* 1995). Even if some prognosticators eschew the libertarian label, most still tend to focus on a future in which individual freedom and control is very much increased in online communities. "The Net gives awesome power to individuals," says Esther Dyson (1997), and according to David Whittle's *Cyberspace: The Human Dimension* (1997) the Net "offers us something that the traditional media does not—an opportunity to focus on individual excellence (Quality) as the fundamental unifying principle of cyberspace."

The technological community does not require commitment from its members. An individual can access it only when he or she wants to; if bored with it, or if it becomes distasteful, or upsetting, one can simply turn it off or disconnect from the community. One has the liberty to say what one pleases (at least in those communities with no censorship), without the risk of any physical ostracism. Online community adherents often praise its lack of history and geography. For instance, Elizabeth Reid (1996) says that

> the encouragement of what can only be called friendship between people of disparate cultural backgrounds helps to destroy any sense of intolerance that each may have for the other's culture and to foster a sense of cross-cultural community.

Yet successful real-life communities partake in the memory of shared group experiences within a bounded space. Being free of history and geography may be liberating at times for the oppressed, but such a freedom cannot be the foundation for a social world of extended cooperation. Such cooperation seems to require a willingness to accept risk by dint of the participants' shared history and geography, offline or online. By having this shared experience, it is more likely that one has had the same experiential conditioning and hence roughly similar characteristics and beliefs. But the attraction of the technological community ideal is that this type of shared, shaping experience will be voluntary due to the technology. This is the paradox of the technological community ideal. It is a community ruled by the norms of absolute autonomy of ideas, privacy, and the maximization of individualism. Technological communities offer conviviality and communication, but only on the individual's terms. In the virtual community, I can "talk" to others only when I want to. As one online participant recalls, online communities are "a way for me to have a relatively friendly and often interesting social life that I can basically handle in an hour or hour and a half a day." The Net "is a very convenient community" (quoted in Moore, 1995).

One of the grandfathers of the Internet, J. C. R. Licklider, prophesized back in 1968 (Licklider and Taylor 1968) that

> life will be happier for the on-line individual because the people with whom one interacts most strongly will be selected more by commonality of interests and goals than by accidents of proximity.

But if anything can be concluded from the long history of the technological community, it is that withdrawing from "the accidents of proximity" does not make us happier. The hope of the technological community is to recreate the pleasures of lost community life, yet the technologies that have been embraced have damaged real communities by making geographic dispersal easier. But the power of the ideal has not weakened over time. Currently, the new technological community being hailed in the computer press is that of networks within the household. Now it is evidently possible for family members to finally communicate with one another—not over the dinner table or within the living room, but via the technological marvels of email and networked file sharing. Truly an appalling vision, but the logical last stop in the long history of the technological community ideal: that of individuals turning their back on each other, withdrawing from real-world proximity and replacing it with technologically mediated proximity, all in the hope that this technologically enabled withdrawal would create pseudocommunities to replace the real-world communities left behind. To adapt a quote from de Tocqueville (1969, sec. 2, chap. 2), not only does life in the technological community "make every man forget his ancestors, but it hides his descendants and separates his contemporaries from him; it throws him back forever upon himself alone and threatens in the end to confine him entirely within the solitude of his own heart."

Despite de Tocqueville's pessimism, the technologies discussed in this chapter did not necessarily force an individualizing outcome. Telephone usage could have continued to be oriented around the party line, radios could have continued to be a two-way, broadcast-and-receive instrument. But by focusing on how the technology "liberates" individuals from the messy real-life proximity of others, the technological community idealists encouraged adopters of the technology to use it in an individualizing way. Once the goal of maximizing the freedom of the individual is dropped, it is possible to imagine several ways of using the Internet that might enhance real-life community. Activists and researchers in the community networking movement have endeavored to achieve this aim by creating networking infrastructure that serves local geographic communities (Schwartz 1998). For instance, Alan and Michelle Shaw's experience with neighborhood-focused computer networks in Boston and Newark used publicly available terminals that accessed bulletin boards, discussion groups, and real-time chat to "support and augment the social infrastructure that is at the core of the cohesiveness in tight-knit communities" (Shaw and Shaw 1999, p. 322).

However, the successful examples of neighborhood networking initiatives tend to be in already close-knit local communities (for example, Tardieu 1999); those in larger communities without strong self-identity seem less successful (for instance, Docter and Dutton 1998). While the effort to reorient the use of computer networks toward local geographic communities is laudable and desirable, the history of radio, the automobile, and the other technologies discussed in this chapter indicates that it is difficult to collectively reimagine a technology's use. Part of the popularity of these technologies was due to their being promoted and imagined as a way to strengthen community by increasing the freedom of the individual. Perhaps the only way to prevent computer networks from contributing to the breakup of community is to strenuously reimagine a different type of technologically enhanced community. Rather than imagining a community in which public virtue and individual freedom are maximized, we need to reimagine an online community in which geographic community norms of commitment and responsibility are the focus, not individual freedom. Only then might we rescue our real-life communities from the social isolation to which the technological community ideal has, unfortunately, contributed.

References

Anderson, Benedict, *Imagined Communities: Reflections on the Origin and Spread of Nationalism*, rev. ed., p. 6. London: Verso, 1991.

Appleby, Joyce, *Capitalism and a New Social Order: The Republican Vision of the 1790s*, pp. 16–18. New York: New York University Press, 1984.

Aronson, Sidney H., "Bell's Electrical Toy: What's the Use? The Sociology of Early Telephone Usage," *The Social Impact of the Telephone*, Ithiel de Sola Pool, ed. Cambridge: The MIT Press, 1977, p. 26.

Bailyn, Bernard, *The Ideological Origins of the American Revolution*. Cambridge: Belknap Press, 1967.

Banning, Lance, *The Jeffersonian Persuasion: Evolution of a Party Ideology*, pp. 168–169. Ithaca, NY: Cornell University Press, 1978.

Barnouw, Eric, *A Tower in Babel: A History of Broadcasting in the United States*, vol. 1. Oxford: Oxford University Press, 1966.

Beiner, Roland, *What's the Matter with Liberalism?* Chicago: University of Chicago Press, 1995.

Bender, Thomas, *Toward an Urban Vision: Ideas and Institutions in Nineteenth-Century America*, p. 3. Lexington: The University of Kentucky Press, 1975.

Blondheim, Menahem, "When Bad Things Happen to Good Technology: Three Phases in the Diffusion and Perception of American Telegraphy," *Technology, Pessimism, and Postmodernism*. Yaron Ezrahi, Everett Mendelsohn, and Howard P. Segal, eds. Amherst: University of Massachusetts Press, 1995, p. 77.

Brooks, John, *Telephone: The First Hundred Years*. New York: Harper & Row, 1975.

Burstein, Daniel, and David Kline, *Road Warriors: Dreams and Nightmares along the Information Highway*. Middlesex: Penguin Books, 1993.

Cairncross, Frances, *The Death of Distance: How the Communications Revolution Will Change Our Lives*, p. xii. Boston: Harvard Business School Press, 1997.

Carey, James, "Technology and Ideology: The Case of the Telegraph," *Communication As Culture: Essays on Media and Society*. Boston: Unwin Hyman, 1989.

Czitrom, Daniel J., *Media and the American Mind*. Chapel Hill: University of North Carolina Press, 1982.

de Sola Pool, Ithiel, ed., *The Telephone's First Century—and Beyond*. Cambridge: The MIT Press, 1977.

———, *Forecasting the Telephone: A Retrospective Technology Assessment*. Norwood, NJ: Ablex Publishing Corporation, 1983.

de Tocqueville, Alexis, *Democracy in America,* vol. II, George Lawrence, trans. New York: Anchor Press, 1969.

Docter, Sharon and William H. Dutton, "The First Amendment Online: Santa Monica's Public Electronic Network," *Cyberdemocracy: Technology, Cities and Civic Networks*, Roza Tsagarousianou, Damian Tambini, and Cathy Bryan, eds. London: Routledge, 1998.

Douglas, Ann, *Inventing American Broadcasting 1899–1922*. Baltimore: The Johns Hopkins University Press, 1987.

Dyson, Esther, *Release 2.0: A Design for Living in the Digital Age*, p. 6. New York: Broadway Books, 1997.

Dyson, Esther, George Gilder, George Keyworth, and Alvin Toffler, "Cyberspace and the American Dream: A Magna Carta for the Knowledge Age," August 22, 1994. Online document at Progress and Freedom Foundation Web site: http://www.pff.org/position.html

The Economist, "Right Turn in Cyberspace," *The Economist,* 334, August 26, 1995, p. 67.

Elkins, Stanley, and Eric McKitrick, *The Age of Federalism: The Early American Republic, 1788–1800*, p. 283. New York: Oxford University Press, 1993.

Field, Henry M., *History of the Atlantic Telegraph*. Freeport, NY: Books for Libraries Press, 1866 (reprint 1972).

Fischer, Claude, *America Calling: A Social History of the Telephone*. Berkeley: University of California Press, 1992.

Flink, James J., *America Adopts the Automobile, 1895–1910*. Cambridge: The MIT Press, 1970.

Foster, Mark S., *From Street to Superhighway: American City Planners and Urban Transportation, 1900–1940*, p. 170. Philadelphia: Temple University Press, 1981.

Global Reach, "Global Internet Statistics (by Language)," February 2000. Online: http://www.glreach.com/globstats

Hall, Peter, *Cities of Tomorrow: An Intellectual History of Urban Planning and Design in the Twentieth Century.* Oxford: Basil Blackwell, 1988.

Hamilton, Alexander, *The Papers of Alexander Hamilton, Volume X*, Harold C. Synett, ed. New York: Columbia University Press, 1966.

Harrison, Joseph H., "Sic et Non: Thomas Jefferson and Internal Improvement," *Journal of the Early Republic*, vol. 7 (Winter 1987).

Hawthorne, Nathaniel, *The House of Seven Gables,* p. 161. Seymore L. Gross, ed. New York: W.W. Norton & Company, 1967.

Hermosillo, Carmen, "Pandora's Vox: On Community in Cyberspace," *High Noon on the Electronic Frontier*, Peter Ludlow, ed. Cambridge: The MIT Press, 1996, p. 440.

Hobbes, Thomas, *The Elements of Law Natural and Politic*, 4, para 7, 1640.

Jefferson, Thomas, letter to M. Barre de Marbois, June 14, 1817, in *The Writings of Thomas Jefferson, Volume X*, Paul Leicester Ford, ed. New York: G. P. Putnam's Sons, 1899.

———, letter to Henry Middleton, January 8, 1813, in *The Writings of Thomas Jefferson*, Paul Leicester Ford, ed. New York: G. P. Putnam's Sons, 1899.

———, "Notes on the State of Virginia," in *The Life and Selected Writings of Thomas Jefferson*, pp. 280–281, Adrienne Koch and William Peden, ed. New York: Random House, 1944.

Jennings, Lane, "Utopia: We Can Get There From Here—By Computer," *Communications and the Future*, Howard F. Didsbury, ed. Bethesda: World Future Society, 1982, p. 48.

Katz, Jon, "The Digital Citizen," *WiReD*, 5 (December 1997), p. 274.

Keller, Suzanne, "The Telephone in New (and Old) Communities," *The Social Impact of the Telephone*. Ithiel de Sola Pool, ed. Cambridge: The MIT Press, 1977.

Keyworth, George, "People and Society in Cyberspace," Online document at Progress and Freedom Foundation Web site: http://www.pff.org/tsot-1.html.

Kieve, Jeffrey, *The Electric Telegraph: A Social and Economic History*. London: David & Charles, 1973.

Kloppenberg, James T., "The Virtues of Liberalism: Christianity, Republicanism, and Ethics in Early American Political Discourse," *Journal of American History*, vol. 74, no. 1 (June 1987), p. 27.

Larson, John Lauritz, "'Bind the Republic Together': The National Union and the Struggle for a System of Internal Improvements," *Journal of American History*, vol. 74, no. 2 (September 1987), pp. 363–387.

Lebow, Irwin, *Information Highways and Byways: From the Telegram to the 21st Century*, p. 11. New York: IEEE Press, 1995.

Lewis, Tom, *Empire of the Air: The Men Who Made Radio*, p. 37. New York: HarperCollins, 1991.

Lichty, Lawrence W., and Malachi C. Topping, eds., "History of Broadcasting and KDKA Radio," *American Broadcasting: A Source Book on the History of Radio and Television*. New York: Hasting House Publishers, 1975.

Licklider, J. C. R., and Robert Taylor, "The Computer as a Communication Device," *Science and Technology; For the Technical Men in Management,* 76 (April 1968), p. 40.

Ling, Peter J., *America and the Automobile: Technology, Reform and Social Change*, p. 42. Manchester: Manchester University Press, 1990.

Literary Digest, "Is Radio Only a Passing Fad?" *Literary Digest* 73, June 1922.

———, "Radio and the Farm Boy," *Literary Digest,* 73, June 1922, p. 25.

―――, "Radio and Farm Life," *Literary Digest* 73, September 23, 1922.

―――, "Will Radio Send Us 'Back to the Farm'?" *Literary Digest* 78, January 12, 1924.

Lockard, Joseph, "Progressive Politics, Electronic Individualism, and the Myth of the Virtual Community," in *Internet Culture*, David Porter, ed. New York: Routledge, 1997, p. 224.

Madison, James, "Republican Distribution of Citizens," *National Gazette*, March 5, 1792, in *Writings of Madison, Volume VI*, Gaillard Hunt, ed. New York: G. P. Putnam's Sons, 1906, pp. 96–99.

―――, "The Federalist No. 48," *The Federalist or The New Constitution*, William R. Brock, ed. London: Everyman's Library, 1996.

―――, "The Federalist No. 10," *The Federalist or The New Constitution*, William R. Brock, ed. London: Everyman's Library, 1996, pp. 44–47.

Marvin, Carolyn, *When Old Technologies Were New: Thinking about Electric Communication in the Late Nineteenth Century*. Oxford: Oxford University Press, 1988.

Marx, Leo, *The Machine in the Garden*. Oxford: Oxford University Press, 1964.

Matthews, Richard K., "Liberalism, Civic Humanism, and the American Political Tradition: Understanding Genesis," *Journal of Politics* 49 (1987), p. 1151.

Maxim, Hudson, "Radio—The Fulcrum," *The Nation* 119, July 23, 1924, p. 91.

McCoy, Drew, *The Elusive Republic: Political Economy in Jeffersonian America*. Chapel Hill: University of North Carolina Press, 1980.

McDonald, Forrest, *E Pluribus Unum: The Formation of the American Republic 1776–1790*, 2d ed., p. 276. Indianapolis: Liberty Press, 1979.

McShane, Clay, *Down the Asphalt Path: The Automobile and the American City*, p. 124. New York: Columbia University Press, 1994.

Miller, Stephen E., *Civilizing Cyberspace: Policy, Power, and the Information Superhighway*, pp. 213–214. New York: Addison Wesley Publishing Company, 1996.

Montesquieu, Charles, *The Spirit of the Laws, Volume 1*, p. 120 (1.8.16), Thomas Nugent, trans. New York: Colonial Press, 1900.

Moore, Dinty W., *The Emperor's Virtual Clothes: The Naked Truth about Internet Culture*, pp. 89–90. Chapel Hill, NC: Algonquin Books of Chapel Hill, 1995.

The Nation, "Radio As Revolutionist," *The Nation,* 114, March 29, 1923, p. 362.

Nye, David E., *American Technological Sublime*. Cambridge: The MIT Press, 1994.

Outlook, "Radio's Magic Wand," *Outlook* 131, May 3, 1922.

————, "Radio—The New Social Force," *Outlook* 136, March 19, 1924, pp. 465–466.

Perry, Charles R., "The British Experience 1876–1912: The Impact of the Telephone During the Years of Delay," *The Social Impact of the Telephone*, Ithiel de Sola Pool, ed. Cambridge: The MIT Press, 1977, p. 75.

Phillip, Derek L., *Looking Backward: A Critical Appraisal of Communitarian Thought*. Princeton: Princeton University Press, 1993.

Pocock, J. G. A., *The Machiavellian Moment: Florentine Political Thought and the Atlantic Republican Tradition*. Princeton: Princeton University Press, 1975.

Provenzo, Eugene F., Jr., *Beyond the Gutenberg Galaxy*, p. 5. New York: Teacher College Press, 1986.

Rahe, Paul A., *Republics Ancient and Modern, Volume III: Inventions of Prudence: Constituting the American Regime*, p. 41. Chapel Hill: The University of North Carolina Press, 1994.

Reid, Elizabeth, "Communication and Community on IRC," *High Noon on the Electronic Frontier*, Peter Ludlow, ed. Cambridge: The MIT Press, 1996, p. 407.

Rheingold, Howard, *Virtual Communities,* p. 14. New York: HarperCollins, 1993.

Ross, David P., and Peter J. Usher, *From the Roots Up: Economic Development As if Community Mattered.* Toronto: James Lorimer & Company, 1986.

Sachs, Wolfgang, *For Love of the Automobile: Looking Back into the History of Our Desires*, Don Reneau, trans. Berkeley: University of California Press, 1992.

Sandel, Michael, *Liberalism and the Limits of Justice.* Cambridge: Cambridge University Press, 1982.

————, *Democracy's Discontent.* Cambridge: Harvard University Press, 1996.

Schwartz, Ed, "An Internet Resource for Neighbourhoods," *Cyberdemocracy: Technology, Cities and Civic Networks*, Roza Tsagarousianou, Damian Tambini, and Cathy Bryan, eds. London: Routledge, 1998.

Scully, Vincent, "The Architecture of Community," *The New Urbanism: Toward an Architecture of Community.* New York: McGraw-Hill, 1994, p. 221.

Shain, Barry Alan, *The Myth of American Individualism: The Protestant Origins of American Political Thought.* Princeton, NJ: Princeton University Press, 1994.

Shaw, Alan, and Michelle Shaw, "Social Empowerment through Community Networks," *High Technology and Low-Income Communities*, Donald A. Schon, Bish Sanyal, and William J. Michell, eds. Cambridge: The MIT Press, 1999.

Shaw, Ronald E., *Canals for a Nation: The Canal Era in the United States 1790–1860.* Lexington: The University Press of Kentucky, 1990.

Sheriff, Carol, *The Artificial River: The Erie Canal and the Paradox of Progress, 1817–1862.* New York: Hill and Wang, 1996.

SIQSS (Stanford Institute for the Quantitative Study of Society), "Study of the Social Consequences of the Internet," February 16, 2000. Summary available online: http://www.stanford.edu/group/siqss/Press_Release/press_detail.html

Smith, Page, *The Nation Comes of Age*. New York: McGraw-Hill Book Company, 1981.

Tardieu, Bruno, "Computer As Community Memory: How People in Very Poor Neighborhoods Made a Computer Their Own," *High Technology and Low-Income Communities*, Donald A. Schon, Bish Sanyal, and William J. Michell, eds. Cambridge: The MIT Press, 1999.

Taylor, Charles, "Atomism," *Philosophy and the Human Sciences*. Cambridge: Cambridge University Press, 1985.

———, "Irreducibly Social Goods," *Philosophical Arguments*. Cambridge: Harvard University Press, 1995.

Thompson, Robert Luther, *Wiring a Continent: The History of the Telegraph Industry in the United States 1832–1866*. Princeton: Princeton University Press, 1947.

Thoreau, Henry D., *Walden*, Joseph Woodkrath, ed. New York: Bantam Books, 1962, p. 193.

Walzer, Michael, "The Communitarian Critique of Liberalism," *Political Theory*, 18 (February 1990), pp. 6–23.

Ward, James A., *Railroads and the Character of America, 1820–1887*. Knoxville: University of Tennessee Press, 1986.

Watts, Steven, "Masks, Morals, and the Market: American Literature and Early Capitalist Culture, 1790–1820," *New Perspectives on the Early Republic*, Ralph D. Gray and Michael A. Morrison, eds., p. 187. Urbana: University of Illinois Press, 1994.

White, Morton and Lucia White, *The Intellectual Versus the City*, p. 17. Cambridge: Harvard University Press, 1962.

Whittle, David B., *Cyberspace: The Human Dimension*, p. 187. New York: W. H. Freeman and Company, 1997.

Wiebe, Robert, *The Opening of American Society: From the Adoption of the Constitution to the Eve of Disunion*. New York: Knopf, 1984.

Wood, Gordon, *The Creation of the American Republic, 1776–1787*. Chapel Hill: University of North Carolina Press, 1969.

———, *The Radicalism of the American Revolution*. New York: Vintage Books, 1991.

Wordsworth, William, "On the Projected Kendall and Windermere Railroad," *Wordsworth's Poetical Writings*, p. 224, lines 1–2, Thomas Hutchenson, ed. Oxford: Oxford University Press, 1969.

Wright, Frank Lloyd, *When Democracy Builds*, rev. ed., Chicago: The University of Chicago Press, 1945.

17 Online Community Action: Perils and Possibilities
by Luciano Paccagnella,
luciano.paccagnella@unimi.it

Even those people who never use computers have begun to be influenced by social changes induced by the Internet. Commercial online communities, for example, are more and more often responsible for the good fortune of the shares that compose the new economy. Perhaps the theory of chaos will soon show, not only that the wingbeat of a butterfly in China can trigger a hurricane in Miami, but also that the bad mood of a MOO user in Taiwan can cause a financial earthquake on Wall Street. Things happening on the Net affect us all, even those of us who say that we hate computers and technology.

This chapter tries to highlight the contrasting and ambiguous aspects that are inherent to the online social phenomena. In the first section of its first part, it examines the concept of "online community." In recent years several books have been written on this topic, most of which are designed either to magnify the joys of online communities or, alternatively, to demonstrate that online communities do not even exist. I will point out, however, that these debates often conceal the lack of appropriate terms for describing the new online social phenomena. "Online community" is a temporary term that we use to refer to some aggregations of persons who gather on the Net for educational, commercial, or political reasons. Rather than struggling with conventional definitions, therefore, I will point out both the potential and the limitations of online communities and of online community action.

The second section concentrates on problematic aspects of communities, both on and offline. I try not to consider the world of computer networks as though it were separate from the everyday world. In the third section, through reference to the social-network approach, I will show some of the numerous links that exist between the online world and offline world. These links allow, for example, the use of cyberspace as a field of experimentation for innovative practices or for creative attitudes, which I expand on in the section "To Change the World, Begin with Yourself."

When these experiments take place collectively, we can sometimes speak of community action born on the network. In the second part of this chapter, I look more specifically at the activities of alternative online communities and digital activism. I suggest that their power comes not just from the mere access to information and communication, but from their potential to influence the symbolic codes that organize information and make sense of it. I propose some examples of community action that could be considered as a "symbolic challenge" to the dominant social models—for example, the world of hackers, or the GNU project, or the conflict over cryptography. In the final section, as well as speaking of benefits of collective action on the Net, I emphasize the limitations of this action, which sometimes becomes totalitarian and demagogical, reproducing online the fragmentation and the balkanization of contemporary society as a whole.

In summary, this chapter always keeps in mind that the world of computer networks is linked to the everyday world. It starts by looking at trends in contemporary communities in general and how these are reflected in online communities, and goes on to look at the potential for influence in the other direction, from online communities back to the wider society. This influence may occur indirectly through the use of alternative online communities as a vehicle for personal experimentation, or directly through online collective action. I indicate both some of its benefits and some of its dangers.

What Are We Talking About?

The concept of "community" begins its modern fortune with the work of Ferdinand Tönnies, who at the end of the 19th century interpreted the changes taking place at that time in terms of the dichotomy between *Gemeinshaft*, Community, and *Gesellshaft*, Society (Tönnies 1957/1887). The term, which entered from that time into the standard vocabulary of the social sciences, has been discussed, argued over, and redefined in countless studies. Perhaps precisely because of this, it is now a term of uncertain meaning, used to describe groups of people ranging from local neighborhoods to entire countries. A community can be described in the most general sense as a web of social relations held together by circumstances that may vary widely. There are unintentional communities, whose components may be chosen by fortuitous circumstance (as happens, at least in part, in the case of local neighborhood communities or groups of people who were in the same class at school). There are also intentional communities to which one can deliberately decide to belong, based on shared interests.

It is very difficult, and probably unnecessary by now, to arrive at a precise and commonly accepted definition of this term. However, the concept of community remains important as one of the endpoints of a continuum: that of groups of people held together by direct personal relationships, strong common values, feelings of solidarity, and reciprocal recognition. At the other extreme, normally, are groups based on contingent or temporary interests, on professionalism, on the interests of the individual and on rationality. These are obviously "ideal types"—that is, abstract concepts not found in reality; the ideal community does not exist. Instead there exist communities that may come closer to or not so close to the ideal.

In the course of the 20th century the idea of community was taken up again in several different ways, often bathed in a glow of romantic nostalgia for a happy past overturned by industrial transformation. Among the various successively emerging ideas of community are those tying it to the new communications technologies: from McLuhan's "global village" (1964), to the transformations of the sense of geographic place indicated by Meyrowitz (1985), up to the "virtual communities" popularized by Rheingold (1993).

In fact, community and communication are concepts that are often tied together. These words have common etymological roots: both are derived from the Latin word *communis* (common), which in turn may be derived from *com-* (together) and *munis* (obligation), or else—and here the interpretations disagree—from *com-* and *unus* (one). Communication may be seen as a crucial dynamic part of the fundamental process for the structure that we call a community. However, communication by itself does not necessarily create a community.

In the definition of "virtual community" given by Howard Rheingold, the communicative aspect plays a very important role:

> Virtual communities are social aggregations that emerge from the Net when enough people carry on those public discussions long enough, with sufficient human feeling, to form webs of personal relationships in cyberspace (Rheingold 1993, p. 5).

This general definition, widely used by the mass media, has been repeatedly brought up in academic debates that center on "proving" or "disproving" the existence of online community. It is a definition that has at times been described as converging with the notion of culture found in contemporary cultural theory, in that it no longer considers community as a product of a common physical space, but as the result of a collection of social relations and quality of interaction (Watson 1997). On other occasions the same definition has been accused of technological determinism (Jones 1998), especially in the light of a certain preconceived optimism expressed by Rheingold in other parts of his book (for example where he appears to affirm that communities inevitably arise in all cases in which people have technologies for computer-mediated communication at their disposal). On yet other occasions this definition has been simply considered to be too vague and imprecise (Jones 1997, Wilbur 1997).

It is the social transformation of computer networks, from instruments for calculation to environments for communication, that has led to the idea that "online communities" can exist. In particular, the metaphor of cyberspace as a space has led these networks to be considered as meeting places, virtual and convivial town squares or *agorà*. Places, that is, that reproduce in the network the spaces in which communities traditionally developed—the public spaces, or "third places" (Oldenburg 1989) essential to people's lives, in addition to the places in which they live and in which they work.

The association between communication technologies, "imaginary" spaces and the development of community has also led to a reinterpretation of the idea of virtual community, and its application to a wider context. According to this alternative concept the first virtual communities, based on scientific and literary texts, arose as far back as the mid-17th century (Stone 1991). It has been argued that a community between distant people can also form itself around a work of imagination, such as a romantic novel, that is capable of bringing together its readers on the basis of shared emotional responses. A modern example could be that of the community of fans of particular television series: the members of these communities share some common values and a system of symbols. The capacity to interpret these symbols distinguishes members of the community from outsiders.

Nevertheless, these examples reveal the difficulty in tracing a clean border between where community ends and a social aggregation of another type begins. Can the fans of *Star Trek* really consider themselves to be a community?

Several scholars (Kollock 1998, Kozinets 1998, McLaughlin et al. 1997) have sought to discover the characteristics that define an online community. They find that community is enhanced by consistent and stable *personae* (usually with names or pseudonyms that do not change frequently), interpersonal relationships conducted on several levels (public discussions, private email, contact by telephone, snailmail, or face to face), a shared language, development of a system of norms and roles, and the performance of rituals of varying degrees of complexity that mark out the borders of the community. These strictly social characteristics are capable of boosting the sense of community well beyond the level of technological advancement of the most sophisticated graphical "virtual worlds" currently in existence (Kollock 1998). Membership of a community is a social experience, only in part linked to the technical possibilities afforded by the means of communication that are used.

The Problematic Community

Whatever definition we choose, the notion of online community undoubtedly contains wide differences from Tönnies' 19th-century concept of *Gemeinschaft*. Unfortunately we are dealing with a term that, as soon it was born, suffered the effects of media hype. It appears that the press and television are required to say "online communities" or "virtual communities" when they refer to any group of people communicating via the Internet.

Critical reflection on the abuse of the term *community*, on the other hand, had already arisen in the early days of the mass media. In the 1940s the American sociologist Robert Merton (Beniger 1997) analyzed the way in which the presenter of a radio program managed to raise from listeners as much as 39 million dollars for war bonds during a single day of transmission, making use of their feelings of solidarity and patriotism. According to Robert Merton the key was to be found in the perception of sincerity that the presenter gave to her listeners, and in their consequent willingness to let themselves be convinced that they were part of a single "family," a single *community*.

Beniger takes up and develops further the notion of "pseudo-community" in order to analyze the vertiginous development of the practices of "personalized" mass communication made possible by digital technologies. These practices simulate a genuine and personal interest toward individual recipients, with the aim of influencing their behavior (for example, to influence their political vote, or their shopping habits, or to mobilize them into taking part in collective action on particular issues). According to Beniger, pseudo-communities grew up in parallel with the technological infrastructures capable of bringing flexible and personalizable communications channels into the home: digital telephony, cable television, computerized mail sorting. A banal example is the junk-mail letters that appear to have been written especially for us by someone to whom, inexplicably, we matter a great deal; letters that announce unexpected winnings or an offer that can't be turned down, made more convincing by the fact that our name appears here and there within the text. Of course these are just simple applications of office automation made possible by the combined use of word processing, databases, and mail automation systems.

In the era of data transmission we are witnesses to a phenomenal development of techniques that can induce the birth of pseudo-communities in the sense suggested by Beniger. For example, all the major commercial Web sites use a technology that allows them to keep track of which pages have been read and of the movements of individual visitors.[1] In this way the managers of the sites declare that they can offer a personalized service, made to measure for each user, giving the users the certainty that they are being given the consideration they deserve. If you are interested in cooking, and declare this when asked to fill in a form listing your interests, or follow a

---

1. This technology uses "cookies," small text files kept on the user's hard disk, which can be used to store information about the user's activities. Although the popular Web browsers offer an option which informs the user when a cookie is created, and gives the user the ability to reject it, and users can examine their cookie file to see what cookies they have, the default setting for these browsers is that the creation of cookies takes place without the user being directly informed. The ways in which cookies are used are still being contested by associations for civil and consumer rights, which consider certain uses—for example, the correlation of personal information about a user gathered from different sites—to be violations of privacy.

series of Web links on the essential ingredients for a Cantonese rice dish, or search for Chinese recipe sites using a search engine, the system will adjust the interface it offers you according to this information. For example, it may display an advertisement for a chain of restaurants specializing in Chinese food and accepting a particular credit card, which will pay the managers of the site a fee according to the number of visitors to which the use of this card is suggested.

This is not a hypothetical example. GeoCities,[2] an American company now owned by Yahoo!, was one of the first to introduce expressly commercial aims into the development of online communities (or pseudo-communities? Who can tell?). The example of GeoCities has come to be emulated today by many other commercial organizations, and bookshops have been selling books with titles such as "Net Gain: Expanding Markets Through Virtual Communities" (Hagel and Armstrong 1997). To react to these phenomena with the indignation of one who sees the market as a debasement of community is simplistic, useless, and naïve: the same strategies, for example, are used also by public institutions, through the establishment of "civic forums" which in reality are often nothing but showcases for self-promotion by the local administrations that finance them. Educational online communities, despite an apparent spontaneity and randomness in their meetings and discussions, often have a very precise strategy regarding what it is permissible to discuss. Even communities of digital activists, as will be shown in more detail later, at times promote superficial or demagogic ideas. But in all this there is nothing surprising. The goal of businesses is to sell, that of public administrators is to obtain legitimization from the citizens, that of schools and universities is to teach their courses, and that of political leaders is to mobilize the masses on the issues that they most care about.

The fact that people are scandalized about these things, or resort to terms like pseudo-community, indicates one of the main problems that the idea of community has inherited from

---

2. http://www.geocities.com

its first use by Tönnies, and that is its moral implication. Describing a group of people as a community usually indicates a value judgment, generally positive, with respect to which "pseudo-community" indicates a less positive judgement. This uninformed moral use of the term is derived from an idealized and romantic vision of rural preindustrial communities (Komito 1998). It does not appear to matter much that, according to ethnographers and historians, the life of the "community-dwelling" 19th-century peasant farmer was not at all pleasant. This is a problem that also comes forward again today in connection with the "communitarian" proposals of those who point to the local community as the solution to the pains, contradictions and dilemmas of complex societies. On a closer examination, some of the problems of contemporary societies appear to be caused precisely by the reawakening of feelings of community (real or presumed), expressed for example in the form of ethnic claims. In these cases community reveals itself as a reactionary and sectarian force which appears in identity politics, in deep barriers between insiders and outsiders, in localization and in fragmentation.

When communities become exclusively "communities based on shared interests," as is often implied in the definition of online communities, these problems are considerably increased (Fernback 1997). Communities based on voluntary aggregations of similar persons sometimes encounter the difficulties people have of understanding those different from themselves and of discussing their own idiosyncrasies, exactly in the age in which the contact between different cultures and traditions is the greatest it has ever been. The result may go in the direction of a reduced social and cultural richness, in the reinforcement of existing positions, in opposition rather than comparison, and in the recourse to ties with those who do not challenge our certainties. The discourse conducted inside the most cohesive and exclusive communities (whether online or offline) always involves a particular *ethos* (Gurak 1997): members believe and affirm only that which is consistent with the values of the community. Subjects of conversation are therefore not debated but rather "cultivated" (Lievrouw 1998), sheltered from any possible confutation. The numerous neo-

Nazi bulletin boards and Web sites are examples of this, even though in this particular case it has been noted that computer networks allow a smaller degree of protection from external influence than that afforded by traditional extremist groups (Zickmund 1997). Another less extreme example could be the insults exchanged by Greek and Turkish readers of the newsgroup soc.culture.europe, which probably did nothing to soften attitudes on either side. Online communities run the risk of becoming like inner-city ghettoes or suburban gated communities that bring together and enclose groups of similar people, excluding those who are dissimilar, thus threatening the existence of more broadly based local communities. Andrew Shapiro (1999) writes that "online associations tend to splinter into narrower and narrower factions" and warns that this may "undermine the strength and cohesion of local communities, many of which are already woefully weak."

From this point of view the dangers presented by online communities, which are typical phenomena of computer networks, should be no more than particularly visible and marked instances of problems and contradictions specific to complex societies. The risk of "cyber-balkanization" (Jones 1998, Van Alstyne and Brynjolfsson 1996) of online communities comes not from the technology in itself, but from the processes that accompany large-scale changes in the society in which we live, in our concepts of time and space, and in the forms and aspects of that which we call "home" and consider familiar.

When all is said and done, the use of the concept of community to describe the new forms of social groupings that are born on computer networks (but also outside these) presents numerous problems which are not always the object of explicit consideration. It is worth noting in any case the historical age of the term: Tönnies employed the community/society dichotomy more than a century ago to describe the changes he was witnessing that were taking shape through the process of industrialization. Now that this process of change has definitively ended in industrialized countries, we are witnessing a new change of paradigm, and to describe this a new lexicon is necessary. It is not surprising, therefore, that the term community seems to be so inadequate in the transformations that are taking place. We are witnessing a problem typical of times of social change: the phenomena specific to complex societies cannot be translated into the terms of the vocabulary for industrial sociology; on the other hand, we do not (yet) have other terms with which to name these phenomena. Not only is there no adequate name for the new "communities" (online and offline), but there is also—for example—no adequate name for the new "identities" and the new forms of community action. Confronted with these difficulties, we must accept for the time being the limitations of our language, explicitly recognizing that they are limitations, and thus press toward the definitive eclipse of the old paradigm and a "creative self-destruction" of the old terms (Melucci 1996).

The addition of the adjective "online" to the noun "community" is itself therefore only a temporary rhetorical device, useful for describing phenomena that are not covered by the sociological categories at our disposal. To dwell too much on the correctness or incorrectness of the term, on the fact that "online communities" do or do not exist, may obscure the fundamental issue: not only are "communities" changing, but the whole of society. We lack adequate terms to describe the new forms of society in general.

Networks of People

Leaving aside, therefore, the arguments about the terms used to describe these phenomena, let us try to understand better *how* communities and community activities are formed online. A little bit of theory may help here.

Social network analysis is a research methodology (Wasserman and Faust 1994) and a theoretical approach with very wide applications. That which it interprets as a network is the world of increasing global interdependencies between individuals and between organizations, in which disorder and flexibility tend to substitute order and hierarchy. At the level of individuals the significance of networks is accompanied, for example, by the concept of multiple identities, while at the level of large organizations of production it refers to models of flexible specialization, or of just-in-time production. The reference to a network, or rather a network of networks, allows moreover the analysis of complex systems: a network can be composed from other networks. The network of an individual's interpersonal relationships can be decomposed into distinct subnetworks according to function, formality, and intensity. Even the Internet itself, as is well known, is nothing but a network of networks. This metaphor has also been used, in a more general sense, to construct one of the many new representations of current society, the "network society" of Castells (1996).

Network analysis applies itself particularly well to the physical networks of connections between computers and to the networks of social relationships developed through these. The keys to the network approach are its antipathy to reductionism and to individual psychology; the emphasis is on relations *between* subjects, rather than their individual properties or characteristics.

The proponents of network analysis also deal in new terms with the problems given by changes in community. According to these scholars community is neither destined to disappear (as Tönnies' sociology would suggest) nor to resist the changes because it is "inherent in the social nature of human beings" (as utopian communitarians sometimes appear to believe). In complex societies community will neither be "lost" nor "saved" but rather "freed" into multiple networks, no one of which has the monopoly on solidarity and no one of which exhausts an individual's sense of belonging. These conclusions have been reached through carefully designed empirical studies (Wellman 1979, Wellman et al. 1988) which anticipate by a few years the observations of the development of interpersonal relationships on the Internet.

It is within this perspective that the theory of the "strength of weak ties" was developed (Granovetter 1973, 1982). This theory is very useful for the interpretation of the importance of the networks of acquaintances developed and cultivated online. According to Granovetter, "weak ties" make up the sparse networks that provide the means of communication between themselves and networks of "strong ties." While strong ties are between people with deep emotional bonds (the nuclear family, close relations and close friends) and have an importance that is immediately evident, the networks of weak ties carry out functions that are often undervalued. At the micro level, a person with few weak ties is excluded from information and opportunities not associated with his or her own group; at the macro level, a society with few weak ties is a fragmented, incoherent one in which ideas travel slowly. Weak ties can therefore be considered to be the basis for the cognitive flexibility that is fundamental in current society. Historically, the most important generator of weak ties is the division of labor, which according to traditional sociology was the source of alienation but at the same time was the essential process for the exposure of the individual to different points of view (Granovetter 1982).

Given the high emotional investment required by strong ties, their number tends to be relatively stable in varying conditions. On the other hand, the pool of weak ties that the individual can draw on can widen itself enormously with the use of communication methods like the Internet. The theory of the strength of weak ties has therefore been applied to the relationships developed online (Garton et al. 1999, Pickering and King 1995, Wellman and Gulia 1999). Computer networks have indeed an immense potential precisely because of their offer of weak ties, or, in other words, fields of available contacts (Lea and Spears 1995).

This permits us to understand better why people find the organization of community action online so easy and intuitive: the networks function as a catalyst. Through word of mouth, acquaintances, friends of friends, colleagues and even perfect strangers, elements that are in some way similar (individuals, organizations, ideas) are attracted to each other and organize themselves, crystallizing into unpredictable forms, like a chemical reaction.

Through communication networks the ties that make up the community of reference for an individual are multiplied. The prediction of the "global village" has come true: not in the sense that all the world has become a single village, but in the more modest and concrete sense that the "village" of reference of each one of us can include people dispersed throughout the planet (Wellman and Gulia 1999).

The analysis of social networks helps moreover to dispel a very common misunderstanding about online social relationships. Often the discussions of online social relationships consider, explicitly or implicitly, the relationships mediated by the network as alternative to traditional relationships. In reality, more often than not interpersonal relationships are integrated through contacts that occur through several different media. Cyberspace is sometimes considered to be a world apart and obstinately separated from "real life." Network analysis talks instead of "multiplex relationships" in order to indicate the complex quality of contemporary social ties, confirmed by studies that show the integration of computer-mediated communication with other communication methods. These studies (Parks and Floyd 1996, Hamman in this book) show that online relationships and offline relationships are intercommunicating systems: in general, people who meet each other and become friends through the network often end up meeting each other face to face as well. They often also keep in contact via traditional means of communication such as the mail or the telephone (Parks and Floyd 1996). The transformation into face-to-face relationships occurs not only for generic friendships, but also in more restricted and specialized environments such as self-help groups (King and Moreggi 1998) and sexual relationships (Shaw 1997). The educational online communities that arise within campus universities, or the mobilization of online support for political activism (for example, the Zapatista social net activism in Mexico, see Ronfeldt et al. 1998) are excellent examples of how online and offline relationships can be integrated.

In short, the conception of computer networks as pools of weak ties and as vehicles for cross-connections between groups sustained by strong ties offers a vision opposed to that which, with an eye to the risks connected with online communities, has been called "cyber-balkanization." This term indicates one of the limitations of communities based on specific shared interests, a limitation which brings the members of these communities to interact with people similar to themselves and to avoid contact with people who are different. Considering the networks as pools of weak ties suggests the possibility that an opposite phenomenon also exists: the drawing together and contact between groups which normally do not encounter each other (or even actively avoid each other.) While there are not yet consistent data to support this hypothesis, it is possible to cite at least one case in which a computer network seems to have functioned just in this way: the famous Public Electronic Network (PEN) of Santa Monica in the metropolitan area of Los Angeles (O'Sullivan 1995, Schmitz 1997, Wittig and Schmits 1996). The Shwashlock project (Shwashlock is an abbreviation of *showers, washers, lockers*: this was a project for the provision of essential services for homeless people), promoted within PEN from and by homeless people, genuinely appears to have helped to produce dialogue and reciprocal acquaintance between "mainstream" citizens and groups of people suffering discrimination, including homeless people (Schmitz 1997). In this case the computer-assisted means of communication, reducing the difficulties of the first encounter, made available another opportunity for contact between diverse groups of people who under normal circumstances would have been irremediably cut off from each other and kept apart by everyday life.

The network approach to the study of computer-mediated communication has the great advantage of saving itself from one-dimensional and simplistic perspectives, avoiding both those of the apocalyptic pessimists (according to whom no "real" social relationships mediated by the technology are possible) and those of the techno-utopians (according to whom the networks necessarily bring happiness, well-being, or democracy). Both of these positions are, in the words of network analysts, equally "Manichean, presentist, unscholarly and parochial" (Wellman and Gulia 1999, p. 167). The idea of cyberspace as a "separate reality" is becoming less and less adequate as a representation of the everyday life of millions of individuals for whom the computer and modem (and the technologies that will replace them in the near future) are by now just the latest instruments for making acquaintances and for accessing the world, wonderful and banal at the same time.

To Change the World, Begin with Yourself

Computer networks therefore do not construct a "virtual" world. This use of the adjective "virtual" often ends up in creating misunderstandings about experiences which, from the point of view of those who live through them, are no less real than any other experiences. The technical limitations imposed by the bandwidth of the network are partly overcome by everyday practices in the use of the medium. People construct the reality in which they live, and this construction, which occurs on the Net just as in any other space of interaction, is brought along day by day in ways that are not always predictable or foreseen. Online communities, rather than segregating their members in an exclusive world of computer mediated communication, propose new stimuli and new contacts (and sometimes new problems) which can be cultivated either online or via more familiar modes of communication.

Surfing the Internet, one can observe a paradoxical phenomenon: the widespread presence of places, situations, and discussions with erotic themes. The largest amateur computer network of past years was Fidonet, which for a long time represented the principal structure for communication between modem owners in the era before widespread access to the Internet from home. Fidonet was founded in the United States by an openly gay man, Tom Jennings, who was looking for places free from prejudice in which to interact with others (whether gay or not). In addition to being gay he describes himself as a punk, a hacker, and an anarchist: a decidedly nonmainstream individual. The majority of the tens of thousands of users of Fidonet worldwide do not know the history of its founder. In France the "messaggeries roses" made the fortune of Minitel, and leaving aside the content that is simply pornography, the Internet currently teems with sites and mailing lists concerned with movements for sexual liberation and experimentation.

To give a specific example, the Internet can represent the first opportunity to "come out" in a protected environment. There are sites and bulletin boards in which a non-heterosexual adolescent can gradually learn to live with his true sexual orientation without hiding it from himself and from others. In many cases coming out online, confronting the judgments and reactions of other people, prepares the subject for the same operation in the more delicate world offline.

The paradox should be obvious: the Internet, even with its limited bandwidth, attracts even those who should be the most interested in physical contact with very high bandwidth—that is, those looking for a new way of understanding their own bodies. This is a scenario that is very different from the one described in certain journalistic portrayals, of the computer network populated by the ghosts of people locked up in their own rooms, shy of physical contact and ready to abandon their bodies in favor of an ethereal identity which can only be affirmed online. Observations of this kind, together with the themes discussed so far, should help to make it clear how computer-mediated communication certainly does not *necessarily* imply the rejection of the physical world, or a flight from everyday reality. Rather, cyberspace can represent in certain cases a terrain for safe experimentation, with limited risks and consequences.

Of course, as often happens, the erotic and sexual sphere is a good indicator of more general dynamics. In particular, the Internet can function as a protected environment for experimentation in the acceptance of many types of "differences" and stigmas. People with physical disabilities can turn these into reasons for pride through interaction in self-help groups and through self-knowledge developed online. In these cases the fact of being able to interact with people in similar circumstances, which earlier in this chapter gave rise to a warning of the risk of cyber-balkanization, recovers its positive aspect:

the discovery that they are not alone in their "difference," and that it is something that can be talked about, both online and offline. This discovery often constitutes the first step toward forms of organized community action.

From an even more general perspective, computer networks can create a protected environment for experimentation by anyone, queer and straight, young and old, individuals and organized groups. On this subject, several scholars (Bruckman 1992, Turkle 1995) suggest applying to the Internet the concept of *moratorium* developed by the psychoanalyst Erik Erikson. In his original formulation, the moratorium indicates particular situations (for example, games) circumscribed in a limited period of time (for example, schooldays) in which people can allow themselves to experiment with new things without undergoing social consequences that are too heavy. According to Erikson, the moratorium provides an indispensable experience for the formation of adult personalities. The Internet could be seen as a new moratorium, available at all ages, which can serve as an experimental breeding ground for social innovation. Many new fashions and cultural novelties, in fact, appear to be spread in the first place via the Internet, and spread to other sectors of society as well in a second phase. These fashions have a large number of places devoted to them on computer networks, where pioneers and amateurs can meet: think of body art, satellite dish and cellular phone mania, or the independent music scene.

But the idea of the Internet as a moratorium also has its negative aspects. This is especially the case for young people, where the enlargement of possibilities and symbolic representations (of which computer networks themselves provide very good examples) sometimes ends up as a substitute for the physical aspects of experience, indefinitely prolonging a condition of irresponsibility. Melucci (1996) highlights the disappearance of rites of passage that in traditional societies used to provide a clear and irreversible mark of the transition to the adult state, often through the experience of physical pain and the confrontation with our mortal nature. The enormous amplification of the power of symbols offers the individual new places for play and experimentation, but at the same time reduces his responsibility to make choices ("I can try both this and that") and his awareness that many of his choices are in reality irreversible ("If I don't like it I can always turn back"). Despite the fact that our social world is increasingly built out of information, even we, people of the digital era, have bodies destined to be subjected to the insults of time and the elements. Time spent on computer networks could make us less keenly aware of the physicality of nature, of its force, and at times of its violence, until the moment when nature will definitively manifest itself through dramatic events (for example, through illness or death). We have more and more possibilities for experimenting with our lives, but we are also less and less able to accept those natural unavoidable events for which we cannot make a choice. Death, for example, used to be a moment embedded in a social framework that offered relief to the person who was dying and to his family and friends. Now it is usually a technical moment spent in a hospitalized environment, hidden from the eyes of the community.

The relationship between online experiences and everyday life is in my opinion one of the most fascinating and complicated subjects. The ambiguous and contradictory character of cyberspace manifests itself once again in its analogies with traditional rites of passage. If the suspended experience of the moratorium appears to contrast itself with the irreversibility of rites of passage, it is necessary to note that these rites themselves traditionally make provision for a phase of suspension or separation. During this phase the individual removes himself from the usual social order and prepares himself to return with a different role. Indeed, the rite of passage in traditional societies achieves its function through the three phases of the "separation," the "transition" or "threshold," and the "incorporation." The moment of the "threshold," the *limen*, is the temporary and magical moment on the borders between sacred and profane, in which the individual undergoing the rite can step out of the clothes that marked his previous social role and put on his new clothes. The experience of the *limen* survives even in societies that have lost the importance of rites of passage. Today *liminal* and *liminoid* phenomena (Turner 1982) are to be found in certain moments in games, in cultural productions such as theatrical performances, in carnivals. (Liminoid phenomena, as opposed to liminal phenomena, are typical of complex societies, idiosyncratic and tied to the individual rather than to the community.)

Online interaction can then be placed among these "liminoid" moments in everyday contemporary social experience (Allen 1996, Tomas 1991, Turkle 1995), on condition that certain other conditions are met. The online world is a candidate for threshold experiences because of its distinctive social conditions, not principally because of any of its intrinsic technical characteristics. These conditions can be summarized in three points (Allen 1996). First, there is the possibility of anonymous or pseudonymous interaction, or at least the possibility of interposing filters that mask some characteristics of personal identity, according to the wishes of the masked subject. Second, there is the possibility of a very clean demarcation of the subject's online participation, such that it is possible to keep it hidden from those who are physically close. This can be the case, for example, for those who use the Internet for relaxation, amusement, or social entertainment during working hours and via a monitor intended for work use or for study; the window in which the interaction takes place (in which the subject is reading or writing electronic mail, participating in a MUD, etc.) can be easily hidden among the other windows with "legitimate" activities. This contributes to the maintenance of an aura of involuntary secrecy, or at least of separation of online activities. Last, the subject has the ability to change the terms of his own participation, changing features of his online persona or, if need be, starting again with a completely new persona.

These are the conditions that, if present, can make online interaction into a liminoid experience in online communities (whether commercial, educational, or alternative), bringing it close in certain aspects to those of traditional rites of passage. There is, however, a substantial difference in that online interaction does not have precise limits in time, but rather can be indefinitely prolonged or have the timing of its beginning and end decided by the individual.

On the other hand it is profoundly misleading to try to classify computer-mediated communication too rigidly without taking account of the context in which it takes place. The conditions that favor a "liminoid" and creative experience, indeed, are completely absent from those contexts that provide for the forceful use of computer communications to carry out precise work tasks, in which the users are not allowed the cultural and technical possibilities to creatively manage their own use of the network tools. (I am thinking of many of the current applications of teleworking, the restricted access in some campus universities, and the intrusiveness of sponsors in commercial online communities.) In such cases, computer-mediated communication presents itself as something completely different from a liminoid experience, does not produce innovations, and often dies suffocated by its own limitations.

The New Riches: Information or Codes?

I have outlined a general theoretical framework for understanding the processes that go on when people get together online. We can now take a look, more specifically, at some of the activities of alternative online communities and digital activism. As an overarching principle, these groups often support the ideas that "information wants to be free" and "information is power." I do believe that these are important and reasonable ideas, but I also want to point out how they are often interpreted uncritically, leading to an oversimplified view of how the information society works.

We speak of the "information" society because information plays a fundamental role in the processes that reproduce the social system. This point of view, however, ignores the risk of a quantitative and naïve vision of information that is often implicit in everyday discussions. Indeed information is spoken of as though it were a form of riches, like money or material goods. The "nouveaux riches" would therefore be those who possess a great deal of information, using it as the key to access the mechanisms of social privilege and thus well-being.

But on a closer look, the mere access to information or the mere production of information does not appear to grant, in themselves, particularly important privileges. Currently every citizen of the western world possesses or has access to more information than that which he or she can reasonably use in the course of his or her life. The problem is, on the contrary, that of *information overload*, which leaves us "saturated" (Gergen 1991) with data, relationships, and commitments.

Even among the poorest social strata and even among prisoners—who are institutionally deprived of every social privilege—the television provides a constant flow of information. (Even the nonwestern world seems to be destined to follow this tendency: according to *WiReD* 6.06, p. 81, only 2 percent of the citizens of the People's Republic of China have hot water in their homes, but nine out of ten possess a television set. The recent strong interest by companies such as Microsoft in opening new markets for technology seems likely to push even more in this direction.) And television, the electrical domestic appliance *par excellence* in the information age, is at the point of representing a "negative" choice, in the sense that it is normally present in all houses and that it is increasingly the case that someone who decides *not* to have a television does so not because of economic barriers, but as the result of an alternative model of cultural consumption.

Analogous considerations can be applied for the access to computer networks. Undoubtedly the Internet today furnishes a very important information tool, an assistant for research, a vehicle for entertainment, a medium for social and political participation, or an opportunity for the user to make reasoned choices about his or her practices of consumption. Undoubtedly the possibility of access to the Internet today, which can translate into different social opportunities, is unequally distributed. It favors the upper-middle social strata at the local level, and the richer nations at the global level (even though the most rapid growth in the spread of the Internet is now recorded in developing countries). Nevertheless, to think that the widening of access to the Internet would assure *ipso facto* a guarantee of equal distribution of resources would be a gross simplification. Power and hegemony will still survive: it is worth noting that information on the Internet is still predominantly in English, even though an increasing proportion of people with Internet access do not speak English as a first language, and many do not speak it at all; in Italy it is normal for courses in Internet skills to include basic English as well.

Universal access to the Internet will be guaranteed in rich countries *in any case* in the near future, not only thanks to suitable social politics, but also (and perhaps especially) thanks to the logic of commercial and administrative opportunities. If cyberspace is destined to be the new marketplace that has been spoken about for so long, the consumers must be able to access it.

Although they have found it a struggle, even public administrators are adjusting their work to the possibilities offered by computer networks. In some cases it is already possible to request certificates, file tax returns, or carry out certain other types of paperwork online, saving time and money for both the officials and the users. (Italy, for example, already has laws on digital signatures that make it possible to file tax returns online for certain subjects.) For the future it is possible to see the image of a citizen–consumer–user who carries out a good part of his or her daily errands online. This citizen will pay taxes, fines, and bills, manage bank accounts, choose and buy goods and services, all through a domestic or portable terminal connected to the Internet. Individual access to the Internet and its information will become then not a privilege, but a necessary requirement for the smooth functioning both of the administrative apparatus of the state, and of the system of production.

It is therefore appropriate to be doubtful of over-simple readings and over-easy recipes for success, such as those that see in civic networks the solution to the problems of political participation and in multimedia equipment the solution to the problems of schools.

A more sophisticated version of this naïve view of information is one that involves communication processes and at times presents itself as a full-blown ideology: the preconceived idea that every problem can be resolved, every inequality can be ironed out, through a calm and candid communication between the different sides. Some of the most widespread texts on online communities (Rheingold 1993, Schuler 1996) appear at times to imply an ideology of this type, described effectively by Breton (1992) as "the utopia of communication" and by Lievrouw (1998) as "the UNESCO fallacy." (This last name refers to the illusion that the possibility of bringing together representatives of all nations around a table would automatically resolve the world's problems.)

What is at stake, however, is quite different from the simple possession of a personal computer and an Internet connection, just as it is quite different from the simple and general right to information or communication (keeping distinct two terms that are certainly not synonymous). What is at stake is rather the production and control of *symbolic codes* that organize information and make sense of it. For this reason the conflict that is inherent in the nature of the current social system, and was not inherent in the industrial society of the nineteenth century, is not about the appropriation of material resources, but rather about the development of alternative codes, or challenging codes (Melucci 1996).

In fact in the information society power moves from the control of material resources toward control of codes. This is a movement that renders power less visible but at the same time more pervasive. But what are the codes? The codes are those symbolic systems that precede information and permit us to recognize it and make sense of it. It is through control of the codes, for example, that one defines the entirely conventional borders between sickness and health, normal and abnormal, natural and artificial. Even the definition of the border between life and death is nowadays no longer a matter of common sense and human sensibility: it is instead given by the legal language (a particular type of code) that regulates, for example, organ transplants. The meaning of life (undoubtedly the basic question of human history) is thus delegated to lawyers and medical scientists and at the same time it is at least partially taken away from public debate and awareness.

The codes transmitted through the media impose values, cognitive models, and models of behavior that go well beyond the specific content of radio or television programs. (This is shown, for example, in the numerous studies of the social effects of mass media, especially over the long term. See, for example, the "Spiral of silence" model in Noelle-Neumann 1984 or "Cultivation theory" in Gerbner and Gross 1979.) The hegemonic systems (such as Microsoft Windows) form and inform the mental habits and even the bodies of millions of users (consider carpal tunnel syndrome, or the increase in problems of the back, joints and vision connected with workplace posture and ergonomics). Other examples could be added, but clearly in these cases individuals have access to *enormous* quantities of information, and sometimes contribute to the production of this information, but tend to be excluded from the logic that informs it. Some see the spaces for autonomy to be increasingly constricted by an invisible and omnipresent power (Foucault 1995), but it is also possible to discover the contradictions and weaknesses of the new forms of control.

The same processes that guarantee ever-increasing access to the circuits of information require individuals to become nodes of complex symbolic networks *themselves*. As members of the information society, increasing resources for individual autonomy are made available to us so as to permit us to be, for example, flexible and specialized in our work. At the same time these resources have to be controlled in order to guarantee the integration of the system. This vast and fundamental contradiction between resources for autonomy and the potential for control is a *systemic* contradiction: it does not depend on contingent aspects of the current system of social production and reproduction, but on its intrinsic characteristics.

This is a fundamental contradiction, via which it is also possible to read many of the contrasting and ambiguous aspects inherent in computer networks. Indeed the opposing potentials for liberty and social control, for censorship and resistance, have correctly been stressed (Mehta and Darier, 1998; Shade 1996).

Hacking the System

Computer networks evolve in ways that are difficult to predict: although they are generally planned with the direct or indirect aim of reproducing the social system, they always conserve ample possibilities for nonorthodox use. A historical example, other than the frequently cited one of the Internet (transformed, at least according to common myth, from a military tool into an anarchic organism), and of the telephone itself (which was originally marketed as a business tool, with stern warnings about the importance of not using it for "frivolous" purposes, and even discriminatory pricing to discourage its social use), is given by the French Minitel network. It was originally designed to facilitate bank transactions and value-added financial services, and to allow users to look up telephone numbers, but it had an enormous success thanks to chat lines and the "messaggeries roses" (Feenberg 1992, Lemos 1996).

The history of Minitel is in fact just one of the many examples of the "appropriation" of technology (Baym 1995) and of available communications resources in an unforeseen way. Other examples of this type demonstrate the glimmers of autonomy and identification offered by technologies that at first sight would appear to embody a total and Orwellian control over their users. The world of information and computer networks, on the other hand, has played right from the beginning to a culture that has made the creative appropriation of technology its trademark: the hacker culture.

The term "hacker," often used in common and journalistic parlance simply as a synonym for an abusive intruder in others' computer systems, in reality indicates something much more complex. In a work dedicated exclusively to bringing together the various definitions of the exclusive hacker lexicon (Raymond 1996, p. 189) this term is defined as follows:

> :hacker: /n./ [originally, someone who makes furniture with an axe] 1. A person who enjoys exploring the details of programmable systems and how to stretch their capabilities, as opposed to most users, who prefer to learn only the minimum

necessary. 2. One who programs enthusiastically (even obsessively) or who enjoys programming rather than just theorizing about programming. 3. A person capable of appreciating {hack value}. 4. A person who is good at programming quickly. 5. An expert at a particular program, or one who frequently does work using it or in it; as in "a Unix hacker". (Definitions 1 through 5 are correlated, and people who fit them congregate.) 6. An expert or enthusiast of any kind. One might be an astronomy hacker, for example. 7. One who enjoys the intellectual challenge of creatively overcoming or circumventing limitations. 8. [deprecated] A malicious meddler who tries to discover sensitive information by poking around. Hence "password hacker", "network hacker". The correct term for this sense is {cracker}.

The most general definition, the seventh, makes no reference at all to computer programming, indicating simply an attitude of curiosity and intellectual challenge when confronted with limitations (which are, however, understood to be usually the limitations posed by particular technological artifacts). It is this ethos that characterizes hackers worldwide: an open and curious mental attitude, which cannot be satisfied with standard solutions. There are hardware hackers and software hackers, hackers of model railways (Levy 1984), but also hackers of smart cards, of locks, or of musical products. (In each of these cases these subjects have been widely discussed in meetings of organized groups of hackers in recent years in the United States, Holland, Germany and Italy.) The element of illegality, if any, that is found in such practices is not an end in itself, but is subordinate to the experience of encountering and overcoming a limitation: a closed door, a possibility that is denied. This limitation is often experienced in full awareness that it is an artificial construction that can be deconstructed or moved elsewhere. This critical attitude toward technology is that which in this era can make the difference between an untroubled use of the different tools available and their unwitting transformation into instruments of control over the user.

The symbolic challenges carried forward by hackers and alternative online communities include computer networks and self-managed Internet servers, as in the case of the Italian collective "Isole nella rete," www.ecn.org. Another set of examples of symbolic challenges is given by the operating systems and alternative free software developed cooperatively, such as the operating system Linux (www.linux.org), which has become known as the principal rival to Windows, the operating system produced by the colossus Microsoft. A third set of examples is the concrete exposures of the false confidence in computer networks, such as the public demonstrations of intrusion into banking systems by the German group the "Chaos Computer Club" (www.ccc.de). A last example is the ethic of information as a good to be freely shared, as demonstrated in the GNU project, which anticipates a virtuous circle of free circulation of its products (www.gnu.org). Interpreted as an exquisitely postmodern phenomenon (Mayer and Thomas 1990), the hacker attitude makes visible the power hidden behind the code-producing monopolies. Hackers thus take on one of the most important responsibilities that is required today to ensure the freedom of individuals.

In so doing, the hackers reveal an extremely vulnerable society. There is a rhetoric, widely used by the mass media, of the terrorist hacker, the computer genius able to pass freely and with impunity among enormous masses of public or private data, altering or canceling them as he pleases with disastrous consequences at every level of society. This rhetoric is very far away from the real practices of hackers and from what is recounted by the various ethnographies and studies carried out inside the world of hackers (Taylor 1999). Nevertheless, the analysis of this type of talk itself highlights the fears and insecurities of the information society (Halbert 1997). The bravura of the hackers lies in their global comprehension of thousands of unseen technologies that are directly or indirectly in our everyday life. In such a scenario the contradiction between individual autonomy and social control arises once more.

Right at this moment there are thousands of adolescents who, having learned the rudiments of computer science at school, have gone on to obtain by themselves a considerable mastery of information systems. Each one of these young people is potentially capable of accessing, modifying, or destroying a large number of systems connected to the Internet which are managed by people who in contrast have confined themselves to learning about the "orthodox" uses of technology. This is not an unfounded assertion; it is demonstrated by the proliferation of simple actions of damage to Web sites (the most visible part of the Internet) with content that has a high symbolic value. Even the denial-of-service attacks on Yahoo! and other important e-commerce sites that were talked about in all the newspapers in February 2000 required only relatively simple technical competence and were within the reach of thousands of people, independently of whoever was actually responsible for those attacks.

The techniques of information warfare (Schwartau 1996), which are mostly yet to be developed, put in the hands of single individuals (including those who do not feel themselves to be bound by the "hacker ethic") enable maximum visibility with minimum effort. This opens new scenarios not just in the conflict between nations, but also and especially in internal conflicts, in transnational problems, and in topics involving the most excluded and radical voices. There are several examples of this (still simple) political use of hacking and information warfare techniques: for instance, the "netstrike" that temporarily blocked some Mexican government's sites achieved in September 1998 by Zapatista groups worldwide, or the threat that was made by some computer experts that they would attack important Indonesian financial systems if the referendum in which East Timor voted for independence did not go ahead.

Radical movements and alternative communities have learned to hack their way into the information society. They use their own media (free radios, newsletters, local television programs and Web sites) as "tactical weapons" and use computer networks to gain public visibility. Computer networks thus provide the possibility of hearing voices outside the mainstream.

The Perils and Possibilities of Online Community Action

Online communities are very good at supporting community action. They can be democratic, egalitarian, and friendly to the voiceless. But they can also be sectarian, demagogic, arrogant, and can disseminate incorrect information.

More often than not, alternative communities contain both of these aspects. Take, for example, the Linux community: I believe that this is one of the best achievements of online cooperation so far. Linux and, more generally, free software are challenging the industrial economic model at its roots, showing that "opening up" is better than "closing down." Members of the Linux community are usually computer enthusiasts, willing to share their knowledge with others. But, unfortunately, not all of them seem to be fully aware of the deep implications of free software. There are even people who think that the word "free" simply refers to the fact that Linux costs no money. (This misunderstanding is more frequent with non-English speakers, who don't grasp the multiple meanings of this word. In Italy, for example, "free software" is often translated as "programmi gratuiti"—software that is free of charge—rather than "programmi liberi," software that is free from restrictions on modification and distribution.)

Worse still, some of the Linux activists behave like digital totalitarians; for them, Linux is not just a great free operating system. Instead, it is the *only* operating system allowed. As in any totalitarian ideology, they build their own enemy (usually, Microsoft Windows) and split the world into Good and Evil. Nothing good can come from Evil ("Windows is not usable: it crashes every five minutes") and nothing evil can come from Good ("Linux does not crash: if it does, it is my fault, not the fault of Linux"). While it should be obvious that such a perspective is a childish oversimplification of the software market, one has only to browse the relevant newsgroups to see how widespread it is.

Another very interesting area in which to study the joys, pains, and oddities of online community action is the conflict over cryptography (in which the alternative *codes* proposed in opposition to the dominant ones are, literally, codes). For several years there has been a very visible political struggle between law enforcement agencies, on the one hand, and a variegated collection of civil rights associations and economic lobbies, on the other. This conflict has been particularly visible in the United States since 1993, when the two sides confronted each other over their respective proposals for cryptographic systems: the Clipper Chip and PGP (Pretty Good Privacy). More precisely, the confrontation was over the proposal of a "weak" cryptography standard, invented and supported by governmental agencies, as opposed to a "strong" cryptography standard, independently developed and in the public domain. In technical terms "weak" refers to the possibility that in case of weak cryptography the police or security forces would be able to decrypt the communication—if this was necessary and they had been awarded a license to decrypt it by the judiciary—even if they did not have the decryption key. Therefore with weak cryptography the police would be able to decrypt the message without the collaboration of the sender or receiver of the message.

The analysis of this conflict (Gurak 1997) has revealed a number of interesting issues, including the numerous pieces of inaccurate information that circulated about the Clipper Chip and its supporters. It has also uncovered the complexity of the conflict and of the sides involved. These cannot be reduced to the industrial-age dichotomy between exploiters and exploited (or right/left), but have multiple allegiances cutting across these categories. Indeed, in the conflict over cryptography there were alliances between traditionally right wing and traditionally left wing forces both at the institutional level and at the grassroots level.

The conflict over cryptographic codes is not just about the possibility of stopping others from reading one's own personal mail. Public-key cryptography, in fact, is the foundation stone of digital signature technology. (Public-key cryptography is one of the most important developments in cryptographic science. In contrast to traditional cryptography, in public-key cryptography the key for encoding a message, the "private" key, is different from the key for decoding it, the "public" key. This has several important implications, including for example the possibility for someone to confirm their identity by encoding something with their private key, which only they know, to produce a proof of identity which can be checked by anyone using the associated public key, which is made public.) Digital signatures will be a fundamental factor in the development of Internet social and economic activity in the near future. A digital signature allows legal standing to be given to online commercial transactions and contracts. It even allows the development of genuine "digital money" (Dorn 1997) that is anonymous and potentially outside the control of national fiscal systems. Clearly these are topics of exceptional significance, which are tied closely in several ways to the processes of globalization and the increasing difficulties encountered by typical modern/industrial institutions such as the nation state.

Alternative online communities also have an important role in specific areas such as that of cryptography. The network structure of interaction, the widening of the field of available contacts, and the public confrontation between geographically dispersed groups of people united by a common interest have played a fundamental role in the transformation of cryptography from an esoteric knowledge to a public issue. Not only this: they have also allowed, for the first time in history, the development of open cryptographic standards that are verified and tested collectively and in public.

It should not be forgotten that it is natural to consider PGP as a product of the Internet, rather than just as a creation of its original author. PGP is the software that introduced cryptography to millions of users and caused the FBI to raise in public the problem of the threat of strong cryptography to national security. Phil Zimmerman did indeed put together the first versions of the software using public algorithms that were already known. However, PGP earned its high reputation for trustworthiness (an essential quality for the success of cryptographic software) thanks to the spontaneous formation of numerous communities of experts scattered throughout different continents, who discussed the characteristics of PGP and weighed up its possible weaknesses, in public, over the Internet. Indeed, once PGP had become a de facto standard, it was able to count on these communities for the improvements which were introduced in subsequent versions, which make it today an extremely dynamic product that is able to keep up to date with evolutions in hardware and cryptographic techniques.

There is another connection between PGP, the Internet, and alternative communities. In order to demonstrate that your public key really is yours, in PGP you get people who know you to sign your public key. If someone with whom you have not communicated before wants to be sure that a PGP message apparently from you really is from you, they need to find a chain of people starting with someone they trust and ending with you, each of whom has signed the PGP public key of the person next in the chain. One way to provide such a chain is via a hierarchy, so that the first person in the chain might be a representative of a national government, for example. But since the Internet widens the field of available contacts, it is quite likely that two PGP users who have used the Internet for a long time and who have shared interests will be able to find a chain of Internet acquaintances linking them to each other, without resorting to the chains of trust provided by traditional hierarchies.

We are talking about a virtuous circle of social cooperation distributed on a planetary scale. (Many aspects of PGP communities are similar to those of the communities that support the development of the Linux operating system and other "open source" or, even better, "free software" products.) Online community action, within alternative online communities, makes this possible. In spite of the risks and contradictions that I have discussed above, in this case online communities show themselves to be therefore not only tools for widening everyday personal experience, but also a strong vehicle for social change.

This chapter has moved from the sociological concept of community, to a model for the interpretation of online and offline relationships. I have then used the theoretical tools presented in the first part of the chapter to describe some of the joys and pains of online community action. Collective action developed on computer networks seems to be quite similar to the new social movements that have emerged in society during the last three decades: they usually induce strong feelings of solidarity in their members, but this is not always enough for us to accept them as desirable phenomena. Online community action, too, may turn toward intolerance and fanaticism. Fortunately, the Internet today presents plenty of examples of genuine alternative online communities, where people learn to act cooperatively online as well as offline. My hope is that in the near future they will prove their effectiveness as models for action.

References

Allen, Christina, "What's Wrong with the Golden Rule? Conundrums of Conducting Ethical Research in Cyberspace," *The Information Society Journal*, vol. 12, no. 2 (1996), pp. 175–189.

Baym, Nancy K., "The Emergence of Community in Computer-Mediated Communication," in Steven G. Jones, ed., *Cybersociety: Computer-Mediated Communication and Community*. Thousand Oaks: Sage, 1995.

Beniger, James R., "Personalization of Mass Media and the Growth of Pseudo-Community," *Communication Research*, vol. 14, no. 3 (June 1997), pp. 357–371.

Breton, Philippe, *L'Utopie de la communication: Le mythe du "village planétaire."* Paris: Éditions La Découverte, 1992.

Bruckman, Amy, "Identity Workshop: Emergent Social and Psychological Phenomena in Text-Based Virtual Reality," MIT Media Laboratory Dissertation, 1992. Online: ftp://ftp.cc.gatech.edu/pub/people/asb/papers/identity-workshop.rtf

Castells, Manuel, *The Information Age: Economy, Society and Culture. Volume I: The Rise of the Network Society.* Oxford: Blackwell Publishers, 1996.

Dorn, James, ed., *The Future of Money in the Information Age.* Washington: The Cato Institute, 1997.

Feenberg, Andrew, "From Information to Communication: The French Experience with Videotex," in Martin Lea, ed., *Contexts of Computer-Mediated Communication,* pp. 168–187. New York: Harvester Wheatsheaf, 1992.

Fernback, Jan, "The Individual within the Collective: Virtual Ideology and the Realization of Collective Principles," in Steven G. Jones, ed., *Virtual Culture: Identity and Communication in Cybersociety.* London: Sage, 1997.

Foucault, Michel, *Discipline and Punish: The Birth of the Prison,* Alan Sheridan, trans. New York: Vintage Books, 1995.

Garton, Laura, Caroline Haythornthwaite, and Barry Wellman, "Studying Online Social Networks," in Steven Jones, ed., *Doing Internet Research: Critical Issues and Methods for Examining the Net.* Thousand Oaks: Sage, 1999.

Gerbner, George, and Larry Gross, "Living with Television: The Violence Profile," *Journal of Communication*, vol. 26, no. 2 (1979), pp. 173–199.

Gergen, Kenneth J., *The Saturated Self: Dilemmas of Identity in Contemporary Life*. New York: Basic Books, 1991.

Granovetter, Mark, "The Strength of Weak Ties," *American Journal of Sociology*, vol. 78, no. 6 (1973), pp. 1360–1380.

———, "The Strength of Weak Ties: A Network Theory Revisited," in Peter V. Marsden and Nan Lin, eds., *Social Structure and Network Analysis*. Beverly Hills: Sage, 1982.

Gurak, Laura J., *Persuasion and Privacy in Cyberspace: The Online Protests over Lotus Marketplace and the Clipper Chip*. New Haven: Yale University Press, 1997.

Hagel, John, and Arthur G. Armstrong, *Net Gain: Expanding Markets Through Virtual Communities*. Cambridge: Harvard Business School Press, 1997.

Halbert, Deborah, "Discourses of Danger and the Computer Hacker," *The Information Society*, vol. 13, no. 4 (1997), pp. 361–374.

Jones, Steven G., "The Internet and its Social Landscape," in Steven G. Jones, ed., *Virtual Culture: Identity and Communication in Cybersociety*. London: Sage, 1997.

Jones, Quentin, "Virtual Communities, Virtual Settlements & Cyber-Archaeology: A Theoretical Outline," *Journal of Computer-Mediated Communication*, vol. 3, issue 3 (1998). Online: http://www.ascusc.org/jcmc/vol3/issue3/jones.html

King, Storm A., and Danielle Moreggi, "Internet Therapy and Self Help Groups—The Pros and Cons," in Jayne Gackenbach, ed., *Psychology and the Internet: Intrapersonal, Interpersonal and Transpersonal Implications*, pp. 77–109. San Diego, CA: Academic Press, 1998. Online: http://www.concentric.net/~Astorm/Chapter5/support.html

Kollock, Peter, "Design Principles for Online Communities," *PC Update*, vol. 15, no. 5 (1998), pp. 58–60. Online: http://www.sscnet.ucla.edu/soc/faculty/kollock/papers/design.htm

Komito, Lee, "The Net As a Foraging Society: Flexible Communities," *The Information Society*, vol. 14, no. 2 (April–June 1998).

Kozinets, Robert, "On Netnography: Initial Reflections on Consumer Research Investigations of Cyberculture," in J. Alba and W. Hutchinson, eds., *Advances in Consumer Research*, vol. 25. Provo: Association for Consumer Research, 1998.

Lea, Martin, and Russel Spears, "Love at First Byte? Building Personal Relationships over Computer Networks," in J. Wood and S. Duck, eds., *Under-Studied Relationships: Off the Beaten Track*. Thousand Oaks: Sage, 1995.

Lemos, André, "The Labyrinth of Minitel," in Rob Shields, ed., *Cultures of Internet: Virtual Spaces, Real Histories, Living Bodies*, pp. 33–48. London: Sage, 1996.

Levy, Steven, *Hackers: Heroes of the Computer Revolution*. Garden City, NY: Anchor Press/Doubleday, 1984.

Lievrouw, Leah A., "Our Own Devices: Heterotopic Communication, Discourse and Culture in the Information Society," *The Information Society*, vol. 14, no. 2 (April–June 1998). Late working copy available online at http://www.slis.indiana.edu/TIS/abstracts/ab14-2/lievrouw.html

McLaughlin, Margaret, Kerry Osborne, and Nicole Ellison, "Virtual Community in a Telepresence Environment," in Steven G. Jones, ed., *Virtual Culture: Identity and Communication in Cybersociety*. London: Sage, 1997.

McLuhan, Marshall, *Understanding Media: The Extensions of Man*. New York: McGraw–Hill, 1964.

Mehta, Michael and Eric Darier, "Virtual Control and Disciplining on the Internet: Electronic Governmentality in the New Wired World," *The Information Society*, vol. 14, no. 2 (April–June 1998), pp. 107–116.

Melucci, Alberto, *Challenging Codes: Collective Action in the Information Age*. Cambridge: Cambridge University Press, 1996.

Meyer, Gordon, and Jim Thomas, "The Baudy World of the Byte Bandit: A Postmodernist Interpretation of the Computer Underground," in F. Schmalleger, ed., *Computers in Criminal Justice*. Bristol, Ind.: Wyndham Hall, 1990. Online: http://sun.soci.niu.edu/~gmeyer/baudy.html

Meyrowitz, Joshua, *No Sense of Place: The Impact of Electronic Media on Social Behavior*. New York: Oxford University Press, 1985.

Noelle-Neumann, Elizabeth, *The Spiral of Silence: Public Opinion—Our Social Skin*. Chicago: University of Chicago Press, 1984.

Oldenburg, Ray, *The Great Good Place: Cafes, Coffee Shops, Community Centers, Beauty Parlors, General Stores, Bars, Hangouts and How They Get You Through the Day*. New York: Paragon House, 1989.

O'Sullivan, Patrick B., "Computer Networks and Political Participation: Santa Monica's Teledemocracy Project," *Journal of Applied Communication Research*, vol. 23 (1995), pp. 93–107.

Parks, Malcolm R., and Kory Floyd, "Making Friends in Cyberspace," *Journal of Computer-Mediated Communication*, vol. 1, no. 4 (1996). Online: http://www.ascusc.org/jcmc/vol1/issue4/parks.html

Pickering, Jeanne M., and John Leslie King, "Hardwiring Weak Ties: Interorganizational Computer-Mediated Communication, Occupational Communities, and Organizational Change," *Organizational Science*, vol. 6, no. 4 (1995), pp. 479–485.

Raymond, Eric, ed., *The New Hacker's Dictionary*, 3d ed. Cambridge, MA: MIT University Press, 1996. Online version http://www.tuxedo.org/~esr/jargon/html/index.html, the on-line hacker Jargon File, version 4.2.0, January 31, 2000.

Rheingold, Howard, *The Virtual Community: Homesteading on the Electronic Frontier.* Reading, MA: Addison-Wesley, 1993.

Ronfeldt, David F., John Arquilla, Graham E. Fuller, Melissa Fuller, *The Zapatista Social Netwar in Mexico.* Santa Monica: RAND Corporation, 1998. Online: http://www.rand.org/publications/MR/MR994/

Schmitz, Joseph, "Structural Relations, Electronic Media, and Social Change: The PEN Public Electronic Network and the Homeless," in Steven G. Jones, ed., *Virtual Culture: Identity and Communication in Cybersociety.* London: Sage, 1997.

Schuler, Doug, *New Community Networks: Wired for Change.* New York: ACM Press, 1996.

Schwartau, Winn, ed., *Information Warfare.* New York: Thunder's Mouth Press, 1996. Online: http://www.infowar.com

Shade, Leslie Regan, "Is There Free Speech on the Net? Censorship in the Global Information Infrastructure," in Rob Shields, ed., *Cultures of Internet. Virtual Spaces, Real Histories, Living Bodies.* London: Sage, 1996.

Shapiro, Andrew, "The Net That Binds: Using Cyberspace to Create Real Communities," *The Nation*, June 21, 1999. Online: http://www.thenation.com/issue/990621/0621shapiro.shtml

Shaw, David, "Gay Men and Computer Communication: A Discourse of Sex and Identity in Cyberspace," in Steven G. Jones, ed., *Virtual Culture: Identity and Communication in Cyber-society.* London: Sage, 1997.

Stone, Allucquere Rosanne, "Will the Real Body Please Stand Up? Boundary Stories about Virtual Cultures," in M. Benedikt, ed., *Cyberspace: First Steps.* Cambridge, MA: MIT Press, 1991.

Taylor, Paul, *Hackers: Crime in the Digital Sublime.* London: Routledge, 1999.

Tomas, David, "Old Rituals for New Space: Rites de Passage and William Gibson's Cultural Model of Cyberspace," in Michael Benedikt, ed., *Cyberspace: First Steps.* Cambridge, MA: MIT Press, 1991.

Tönnies, Ferdinand, *Community and Society: Gemeinschaft und Gesellschaft*, Charles P. Loomis, trans. New York: Harper & Row, 1957/1887.

Turkle, Sherry, *Life on the Screen: Identity in the Age of the Internet.* New York: Simon & Schuster, 1995.

Turner, Victor, *From Ritual to Theatre: The Human Serious-ness of Play.* New York: PAJ, 1982.

Van Alstyne, Marshall V., and Erik Brynjolfsson, "Electronic Communities: Global Village or Cyberbalkans?" Presented at the International Conference on Information Systems, 15–18 December 1996. Online: http://web.mit.edu/marshall/ www.papers/CyberBalkans.pdf

Wasserman, Stanley, and Katherine Faust, *Social Network Analysis: Methods and Applications.* Cambridge: Cambridge University Press, 1994.

Watson, Nissim, "Why We Argue About Virtual Community: A Case Study of the Phish.Net Fan Community," in Steven G. Jones, ed., *Virtual Culture: Identity and Communication in Cybersociety*, pp. 102–133. London: Sage, 1997.

Wellman, Barry, "The Community Question: The Intimate Networks of East Yonkers," *American Journal of Sociology*, 84 (1979), pp. 1201–1231.

Wellman, Barry, Peter J. Carrington, and Alan Hall, "Networks as Personal Communities," in Barry Wellman and S. D.

Berkowitz, eds., *Social Structures: A Network Approach*. Cambridge, MA: Cambridge University Press, 1988, pp. 130–185.

Wellman, Barry, and Milena Gulia, "Net Surfers Don't Ride Alone: Virtual Communities as Communities," Peter Kollock and Marc Smith, eds., *Communities in Cyberspace*, pp. 167–194. New York: Routledge, 1999. Semi-final version online: http://www.acm.org/ccp/references/wellman/wellman.html

Wilbur, Shawn P., "An Archaeology of Cyberspaces: Virtuality, Community, Identity," in David Porter, ed., *Internet Culture*, pp. 5–22. New York: Routledge, 1997.

Wittig, Michele A., and Joseph Schmitz, "Electronic Grassroots Organizing," *Journal of Social Issues*, vol. 51, no. 1, (1996), pp. 53–69.

Zickmund, Susan, "Approaching the Radical Other: The Discursive Culture of Cyberhate," in Steven G. Jones, ed., *Virtual Culture: Identity and Communication in Cybersociety*. London: Sage, 1997, pp. 185–205.

Index